THE SENSE OF THE SEVENTIES

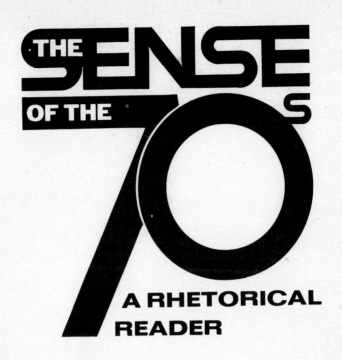

THE SENSE OF THE 70s

A RHETORICAL READER

Edited by

PAUL J. DOLAN
State University of New York at Stony Brook

EDWARD QUINN
City College of the City University of New York

New York   OXFORD UNIVERSITY PRESS   1978

Ten years later, and still magnificent

Deirdre, Colin, David, Jennifer
Peter, John, Paul II
Jonny and Julie

Library of Congress Cataloging in Publication Data
Main entry under title:

The Sense of the seventies.

1. College readers. I. Dolan, Paul J.
II. Quinn, Edward G.
PE1122.S39   808'.0427   77-24473
ISBN 0-19-502-309-9

CONTENTS

RHETORICAL TABLE OF CONTENTS

DESCRIPTION

ARGUMENTATION

NARRATION

PREFACE

This is a book of readings from the seventies designed to do two things. The first is to set you to thinking again about the shape and substance of a strange decade. The second is to give you models for putting your thoughts into forms that can reach and move others.

Since this is a book designed to help beginning writers, our emphasis has been on good writing. Earthy, personal and direct the writer of the seventies represents a new presence on the American scene. For one thing he is likely to be a she. (One thing the age has not developed and sorely needs is a new pronoun.) For another he/she has demonstrated that writing can be authoritative while remaining individual and human. The dirtiest word of the decade was "cover-up." The term describes not only a political crime but dishonest use of the language, and the writers collected here, regardless of their political persuasion, are united in their detestation of what was to become known as the "language of Watergate."

It was exciting for us to work with the material which we gathered and painful to leave out so much good writing. The excitement, we hope, remains in the texts, in the stunning honesty with which men and women have come to write about themselves and their world.

We are aware of the writers we have not been able to include and of the topics not finally represented in these pages; so we welcome your changes and additions. We wanted to create a collage, a collection of contemporary texts which would give some sense of this decade of American life, the decade of America's Bicentennial.

The seventies may well be christened The Paradoxical Decade, a time when America—and the rest of the world along with it—seemed to be going in two directions at once. On the one hand it was a time of retreat to a past that was safer, more secure. Nostalgia covered the land like a maternal blanket. It is as though we had become conscious of time and were engaged in some desperate effort to hold it back. On the other hand we were propelled into the future by the discovery of a new frontier—the frontier within.

For writers the new discovery meant a new challenge and a new opportunity to do what good writers have always done: to tell the truth, especially about the self. Revealing the truth, telling what it was really like for participant and spectator, making the private and hidden in myself and in my society open and public, that is an essential thread running through the selections and through the decade. For better or worse, everything from now on was going to be out in the open.

The final definition of the sense of the seventies will require a collaboration of more than two. In the meantime we invite you, the students who have come of age in this decade and will shape the next, to consider how some fellow citizens of your world have articulated their experience of these years. There were some things that were totally new. Watergate was first a place to move to and then a symbol the nation tried to flee. That great exposure colored the whole decade and continues to occupy our prime time. Race and sex and violence and religion are not new concerns, but they were redefined in extraordinary ways in these years. The very personal question, "How far do you go?" was applied in this decade to the limits of life itself.

There was an incredible variety of life in these years, but there were some core experiences which touched us all. We have selected some of the memorable statements of those core experiences. The writers provide models of how to describe individual experience so that others can share it, so that others can understand. Some day you may want to do the same. We hope this is the place from which you begin.

ACKNOWLEDGMENTS

The editors would like to thank the Hicksville Public Library and the Jericho Public Library. We could not have done it without them.

We would also like to thank Professor Andrea Lunsford for her careful analysis of the reading levels in the book.

THE SENSE OF THE 70s

Golden lads and girls all must,
As chimney sweepers, come to dust.

Shakespeare, *Cymbeline*

For many, the lines from *Cymbeline* summarize the tumultuous transition America has undergone in the last ten years. The spirit of the late sixties—the bright aspirations, the rich possibilities, the self-delusion, the antic style of that time—appears indeed to have come to dust. The golden lads and girls who roamed through San Francisco in 1967 distributing flowers while proclaiming love as an alternative to war have receded into history. A modern version of the medieval children's crusade, they seem to symbolize the futility of idealism on the one hand and the dangers of it on the other. (The distance from flower child to Manson murderer looks to have been a terrifyingly brief one in retrospect.) But the retrospective view offers its own distortion, and we should think twice before arriving at simple moral judgments about the sixties.

In any event, we know that for better or for worse sometime around the turn of the decade Something Happened. (The phrase itself echoes the title of Joseph Heller's novel of the seventies just as his *Catch 22* captured all the rebellious spirit of the sixties.) What caused it? Was it an economic, political, social, or personal phenomenon? Was it a consequence of a series of events ranging from Vietnam to Watergate, or was it a mood that emerged from the depths of the national psyche for no apparent reason other than to obey an elementary law of physics: every action begets a reaction?

Its causes remain hidden, but not its consequences. What happened in the 1970s is that Americans—chiefly young Americans—turned away from the great political and social issues that they had addressed in the sixties. And in turning away, they turned inward, focusing less on the society and more on the self. The result is the phenomenon, characterized by Tom

Wolfe in his piece, "The Me Decade." Others have characterized it as "The New Narcissism," an age of self-love. Jim Hougan, defiantly proclaiming his "Decadence," suggests that this movement away from political and social issues is rooted in a sense of futility about the future of American life. Against Hougan's pessimism stands the surging optimism of Jack Newfield and Jeff Greenfield's belief in the "imminent emergence of a 'new populism' "—a coalition of the ethnic and racial minorities with the working class and youth of the country. Less optimistic is Joseph N. Bell, who indicts the contemporary students for their "silence" but concludes with the interesting speculation that perhaps the moment of silence is a moment of transition. Perhaps the closing years of the 1970s will see a renewal of interest in political and social issues. In that case, one may come to see the "Me Decade" as a period of preparation, the process of discovering the self as a prelude to the realization of the self in the world.

SILENCE ON CAMPUS

JOSEPH N. BELL

A former student stopped by my office the other day. I remembered her instantly. Every teacher has a small collection of students, arranged carefully in a trophy case, to be brought down and examined in low periods. I've had maybe a dozen in eight years of teaching, and Susan was one.

She came to the Irvine campus of the University of California as a transfer student in 1970—a white, upper-middle-class product of southern California, blonde, pretty, athletic—and unhappy. She was tearing at her own roots, reluctantly, but she knew it was inevitable. It was a painful process that she tried to put on paper, not very successfully.

From those agonized writings of hers, I learned that her parents were politically and socially conservative, and that Susan—thoughtful but not belligerent—had gone off to the Santa Barbara campus of the University of California in the late 1960s. There she found herself increasingly disturbed at American activities in Vietnam and at Washington's lack of response to the public mood of disenchantment with them. Because activism was not her style, Susan was pulled between the strong need to declare herself and dismay at what seemed to her the excesses of some of her fellow students.

Then the United States invaded Cambodia, and American campuses erupted in protest. Susan saw policemen swarm into her campus community and drag students from their rooms and beat them up outside. Outraged and sickened, she joined the demonstrators, was picked up in a police dragnet, and spent two nights in jail before being released without any charges preferred against her.

She transferred to my campus the following fall, and as a student in my writing class tried to articulate the changes that were taking place in her, to put them in perspective without breaking completely from her roots. To some of the people in her hometown, this concerned young woman had been radi-

calized by university left-wingers when she graduated a year
later.

I didn't see Susan again until a few weeks ago. After working
for several years, she had returned to her old campus for a
graduate degree, earning her room and board as a counselor
in a freshman dormitory. She was depressed over what she had
seen and heard. She had been asked—and had agreed—to help
organize a student movement against a law that would effectively disenfranchise students by preventing them from regis-
tering to vote at their university home. Susan felt deeply about
this: she had once worked very hard to extend the vote to
eighteen-year-olds. For university students, those efforts would
be thwarted by the new law.

Petitions in hand, Susan worked her way through the dormitories. "It was awful," she said. "There wasn't the slightest interest among those students in what was being taken from
them. They weren't aware, and they didn't want to listen to
me. I came away defeated. I just couldn't believe the change
that has taken place in college students in the last few years."

I have found it hard to believe, too—particularly because the
change has been so abrupt and pervasive. I teach nonfiction
writing, and I tend to give students a lot of latitude in subject
matter. Three-fourths of the essays I read five years ago dealt
with some form of social change. Now they bear such titles as
"How Students Can Invest in the Stock Market" or "How I
Became a Christian."

A lot of Americans—most of them, I suspect—are relieved at
the quiet that has fallen over our college campuses after the
chaos of the Vietnam war years. I am not. The passive students
today alarm me far more than the activists of a few years ago
ever did. They are, I'm sure, the inevitable result of two things:
public hostility toward the universities during the hyperactiv-
ist years and private disenchantment—not always rational—
among young people over their inability to dent the system.

There is little question that many colleges today are being
punished for the campus upheavals that took place during the
war years. Public officials who always feared and suspected freewheeling intellectual give-and-take have used citizen revulsion
at student excesses (a relatively small part of campus activism)

as a club to beat down university budgets and anesthetize the troublemaking potential of students and faculty alike.

When Richard Nixon became President, the federal government spent $262 million annually to help support 51,400 graduate students in our universities; when he left office, federal support had shrunk to $33 million for 6,600 graduate students. At the same time, inflation was putting college out of reach for a growing segment of our society. During the same period at the University of California, I have watched faculty salaries go down relative to other top universities, research projects with considerable potential for public benefit aborted, and faculty-student ratios climb, as a result of a state administration that has denigrated its own fine university whenever possible. Moreover, this decrease in university funds and support has accompanied a wave of postactivist students who seem to reflect these public attitudes.

Last year, a high-school civics teacher wrote to a Los Angeles newspaper: "The majority of young people with whom I come in contact was never enthralled by politics. Now, they seem to be sinking even deeper into an apolitical torpor. Watergate taught them not to care. I see the silent majority growing in my classroom every school day. It is a frightening development."

Other evidence is all around. When the University of California at San Diego opened a new school recently that stressed "professional and pre-professional training," it was immediately oversubscribed—in a period of generally declining admissions elsewhere. This response, the provost explained, was due to "a new breed of student who is thinking more about jobs, money, and the future." A study by the Rockefeller Youth Task Force found that "the challenge of traditional cultural values has shifted to non-college youth," and the task force director, Daniel Yankelovich, added: "In a brief five-year period, the gap between the campus and the country has begun to close, but a new gap between working youth who have not gone to college and the country's social institutions is now opening up."

If this means that healthy challenges to pernicious national policies have moved from the campus to the young working class, it may also mean that the challenges will be more effective. But if it means that the young have simply detached themselves from social activism and criticism, we are in trouble.

I pondered these questions the other night on my way home from a talk I had given to a group of social-science classes at a local high school. My oldest daughter had been a student in this high school when John Kennedy was murdered. She had sat numbly in a classroom for a few minutes, then walked out of school and several miles to the ocean, where she sat on the beach alone until darkness drove her home. She had been expelled for this agonized act, and I vividly remember my own anger and outrage when I took her case before the school authorities.

Speaking in that same school a little more than a decade later, it came as a shock to me that many of the young people in my audience were no more inspired by John Kennedy than by Grover Cleveland or Millard Fillmore. A few minutes into my talk, I realized we weren't even on the same planet. I was assuming certain social awarenesses and interests they obviously didn't have, so I tried to penetrate the glaze over their eyes with more and more outrageous statements, hoping for some kind of response. *Anything* at all.

When nothing came back, I began asking them questions. And, slowly, I began to see that I was dealing with students who had happily accepted the social and political changes won by the activists of the 1960s, and totally discarded the commitment that produced the changes. At last I asked these students if they would be enough outraged to demonstrate if we started massive bombing of Vietnam again tomorrow. Nothing. In desperation, I said: "For God's sake, what *would* outrage you?" After a pause, a girl in the front row wearing a cheerleader uniform raised her hand and said tentatively, "Well, I'd be pretty mad if they bombed this *school.*"

I recognize that this is one upper-middle-class high school in a conservative area of California and that generalizing from such an experience is dangerous. But from this same background came young people who marched in Mississippi and unseated a President of the United States in New Hampshire, who demanded and got long overdue educational reforms, who broke down outmoded social castes and attitudes. True, they also disrupted classes, undermined useful social values and tra-

ditions, loved the sounds of their own voices, and frequently
substituted rhetoric for reason and self-indulgent impulse for
effective action. They were noisy and abrasive, and when it was
all over, I was relieved. For a while.

But now I contemplate the reaction—and I wonder about
our future. Now I'm told to honk if I love Jesus. I hear students dismiss Watergate as "the way it's always been, so why
hassle it?" I see them single-mindedly pursuing grades and
worrying about jobs with secure retirement plans. I even see
a resurgence of those pillars of the American social caste system, fraternities and sororities.

When I express dismay about these changes, I catch it from
all sides. My own children—formed ideologically by the Kennedy years—tell me I'm a crashing idealist as far as young people are concerned, that I should never have imputed all those
selfless motives to the activists of the Sixties. By way of cor-
roboration, they point out that the demonstrations stopped almost immediately after the military draft was suspended. The
point is well taken, and I've not heard any students of that period deny it when faced with this fact.

But it is also true that the threshold of social and political
awareness—for whatever reason—was extraordinarily high, was
acted on, and produced results that in my view were mostly
progressive and badly needed. Student activism had a direct
effect on our slow withdrawal from Vietnam, on the eighteen-
year-old vote, on progress in the black and other minority communities, on women's rights, and on the critical examination
of religious, ethical, and institutional values that were out of
step with the world in which we lived. Admittedly, there were
dangerous and distressing side effects, but too often the threat
of these side effects was allowed to obscure the progress initiated by the students of the Sixties.

Some of my old activist student friends are still around and
in touch. One is working as an organizer for a trade union,
fighting that monolith from within, while he writes and tries
to publish impassioned exposés of the perfidy and greed of the
automobile industry. Another is writing poetry in a secluded
southern California canyon and repairing automobiles for a
living. A young woman who worked for Robert Kennedy and
saw him killed is struggling through law school so she can join
the young attorneys who are fighting our system on behalf of

the powerless. A determined young man is trying to finish graduate school so he can teach, bedding down in various offices around the campus because inflation and rising university fees have made it impossible for him to afford a room. These people are oddly anachronistic on campus today, artifacts of a time and place that seem light years away.

Meanwhile, as noted by Professor Martin Marty, the nation continues to discourage social activists like them. "The people," writes Professor Marty, "have tended to turn from those who disturbed the peace with manifestos, experiments, or searching questions. Where people now rise above apathy at all, they seem to want only to be soothed. Today's prophets are invited to dinner, where they offer the sweets."

The good citizens who are relieved at this state of affairs might ponder the possibility that a group like the Symbionese Liberation Army arises, not from a society of young people working actively to correct social injustice, but from a society where injustice is ignored. Without responsible activism to contain them, revolutionaries can turn into dangerous, demented, and frustrated people, toting machine guns and a death wish.

At the other extreme are those students writing about the stock market, joining frats and sororities, sweating grades, and honking for Christ. Most of them are pleasant and terribly earnest. Maybe, I tell myself, this is just the transition generation, which will soothe public attitudes toward our universities. Maybe a new and idealist group of young people will follow them, and shake up their elders all over again. Maybe that excitement, or at least some of it, will return.

From Harper's Magazine, 1976.

QUESTIONS

(1) What are the reasons the author gives for the lack of political and social interest on the part of today's students?

(2) The author illustrates his discussion with two anecdotes—the story of Susan and the reaction of the high school class. Do the two illustrations effectively dramatize the difference between the sixties and the seventies? How would you describe that difference?

(3) As a member of the group—today's college students—described in this article, do you feel that your attitudes have been accurately described? If not, how would you answer the charges that the article makes?

(4) Do you agree that the "challenges to pernicious national policies have moved from the campus to the working class"? In your experience are friends and acquaintances who have not gone to college more conscious of social and political issues?

DECADENCE

JIM HOUGAN

It's amazingly simple. Things fall apart. There's nothing you can do. Let a smile be your umbrella.

It seems inevitable that a writer who describes the impending, *unavoidable* collapse of his culture will raise the upper lips and nostrils of some liberal critics and readers. Felonious nouns—"doomsayer" and "pessimist"—will be applied to him, and his book will enter the world in the brands and bandages of negative verbiage. But such judgments assume too much.

In particular, those who accuse the "doomsayer" of pessimism assume that all men and women share their affection for, and have an equal stake in, the moribund society. That's a mad assumption, and it would be best to correct it in advance.

It is the thesis of *Decadence* that, for some few hundred years, we've been living within an evolving *regime of culture,* an industrial Order whose internal pressures have—despite its expanding sphere of influence—increased to nearly stellar intensities. In the United States, we live within a machine-of-nation, a cultural Gizmo whose functioning is absolutely dependent upon an ever-increasing number of strategic resources,

both "natural" and not. As Harvard's resident Brainiac, B. F.
Skinner, realizes, we can no longer afford the "variables" of
freedom-'n-dignity. Nor any other variables, for that matter:
if each part of the whole does not function perfectly and predictably, the system will not function at all.

All this is a way of saying that we've reached the end of the
Industrial Age. Those who view Progress as a fate worth capi-
talizing—an inevitability or biological *right*—expect the "postindustrial age" to emerge as a meld of the Renaissance and the
New Deal. There is nothing rational about this faith in Progress, however, and those who look forward to a "greening" of
America will (along with everyone else) live to see the culture
pruned. There's nothing that anyone can do about this, either
collectively or solo. The same centrifugal forces that drive so
many of us to the edges of the culture—to wand-waving gurus,
glitter-rock, and gold—reduce all social movements to a wasting narcissism. Indeed, we're beyond the help of movements.
Marx is, as always, dead, and "the masses" are only the Wad.

That History recycles cultures more often than revolutions
do is obvious, ironic and (in the present case) *okay*. Those who
would tinker with the culture, adjusting its socioeconomic
knobs, labor under the delusion that a society which is industrial can also be humane and responsive. In fact, reform is
meaningless when it's not impossible. The rationalization of
labor and the state, begun in the seventeenth century by well-
intentioned men whose names are now highways, has delivered
us into a misery-dependent world. For the most part, we live in
boxes owned by banks, labor senselessly, eat synthetically, ball
methodically, compulsively, or desperately, and read for entertainment. For the rest . . . well, the rest do without. Suffering,
as much as oil, is the juice of industrialization.

So *Decadence* is not . . . pessimistic. . . . To diagnose the
society as Incurable, its malaise terminal, is something of a relief. That we can prescribe no regimen—except to act as witnesses and to indulge in those existential entertainments which
are still available—may be futilitarian, but that in itself is no
crime. Nero correctly understood that beauty, music and irony
can co-exist with disintegration, that the inevitable can be accompanied on the violin.

We have, then, arrived in a rush at history's watershed only
to find that the dam is about to burst. That rupture will be

catastrophic but—have you ever seen a dam burst? All sorts of things are freed.

. . . .

. . . It becomes necessary, therefore, to turn the world into a stage, to create an *existential theater*—a Forum, in fact. And because blood and pain are reliably à la mode, the Forum depends upon these for its subject matter. Death and injury offer the last opportunity for sustained sensation, recognition, and sympathy. And these, whether viewed as "news" or "drama," emerge as a steady diet. Fire, famine, hurricane, quake, assassination, riot, war, rape—we keep abreast of the country and the times.

Like pro football and the Indianapolis 500, politics becomes more popular as its practice becomes more brutal. The events of the Sixties—brought to us with the inevitable commercial interruptions—restored history to politics, a *de facto* de-Ike-ification. No effort was required to absorb the implications and impact of a man floating in space; a peasant village set afire with Zippos; young women heaved through the plate-glass windows of the Loop; black kids chewed by dogs in Alabama; the spectacle of a million people massing; or an *espontáneo* execution on Dallas TV.

These proved to be the lowest common denominators of a decade so full that most remember it as an Age. Their force and flamboyance empurpled the times, compelling each of us to reenter history, *to live inside it,* play a role, follow the plot. The present bloated with a stipulated importance as the historic sensibility transformed the world into a gestalt of symbols, settings, and props. *Nothing* was exempt from the infestation of Meaning. Fucking, dishwashing, lettuce, trees, hair, grapes, soul food, hems, Volkswagens—each act and thing underwent a mythic inflation. Nothing was so insignificant that one could pass it by without a sort of knowing look, a wink in the mind's eye. All things belonged to some *class* of things, each act participated in a *trend;* and so both acts and things demanded to be taken seriously. They were Statements. They spoke to the dead. There was no such thing as a "private" life.

History moved through us like cocaine. It was impossible not to be "political." The Kennedys, those Evel Knievels of populism, always promised to self-destruct before our eyes—threatened, in effect, to make us a part of history, if only as witnesses. And, just as one anticipates the unlikely possibility of a no-hitter whenever one goes to the ballpark, so one could not attend a Kennedy rally, or watch a speech, without secretly wondering whether this. might. not. be. THE. NIGHT. That possibility informed the banal occasion with an immediacy, an expectation of shock that had theretofore existed only in Vincent Price films. And the Kennedys' misfortunes—the magnetic north of their charisma—proved transferable. Any politician worth his salt might explode. And several did, heating up the scene.

Even our metaphors bespoke our entry into a cerebral Astro-dome, a Forum of gladiatorial expectations. Party hacks spoke glibly and at excruciating length of "the man in the Arena," comparing Vietnam with a "goal-line stand," and pointing to Agnew as "the man on deck." Nixon "called the signals" in Asia, delivering a yuletide "one-two punch" against Hanoi and Haiphong, while liberals "sat on the sidelines" awaiting their "turn at bat." And so on, *ad nauseam:* the world as spectator sport.

By the time the Seventies arrived, our excitement was tinged with the impatience of fans at an extra-inning ball game. Theoretically, the show could go on forever. More likely, however, it would end at any moment and, afterward, there would be fighting in the parking lots and traffic jams on the way home. The best place to be was next to an exit, bags packed, and ready to go.

From Decadence, 1975.

QUESTIONS

(1) Look at the opening paragraph of the essay. Its four simple sentences chart a progression in which one sentence appears to follow logically from the other. To what extent do the four sentences summarize the main idea of the essay? What effect is created by using popular expressions in each of the four expressions?

(2) In the essay the author coins new words (Brainiac, de-Ike-ification) and employs famous names to convey certain ideas (Marx, Nero, Evel Knievel). What are the advantages and disadvantages of such features?

(3) The author offers a description of our society as "Incurable, its malaise terminal." How does he support his argument? Are his details convincing? Does he appear to be too flippant and therefore not really serious?

(4) The essay attempts to offer a slightly different meaning of the word "decadence" from that which is found in the dictionary. Look the word up in the dictionary and compare it to the meaning that the author appears to be giving it. Write an analysis of "decadence" in the light of the original meaning and the meaning given in the essay.

THE NEW POPULISM

JACK NEWFIELD AND JEFF GREENFIELD

The American myth is dying. Things are not getting better. Instead, history seems deranged. We have lost our way.

The Kennedys and King, Evers and Malcolm X are murdered in public, while our sons march off to war, and we watch them burn Ben Tre in our living rooms. Pentagon documents reveal our leaders were liars; our sons come back with track marks on their arms, and throw their Purple Hearts over the White House Wall.

"Things fall apart/the center cannot hold" is true of products and neighborhoods and our moral universe. Our cars can kill; cans of soup are lethal; the telephone breaks down. So does the city's electricity. So do the links between parents and children. The neighborhood of a lifetime imprisons its elderly in their apartments after sunset. And their predators are themselves imprisoned by the heroin in their blood. There is desolation in Eastern Kentucky, where men in their forties look for work that is not there and die of black lung. In Brownsville, Sutter Avenue looks like a moonscape. A geography is drawn in blood: Birmingham, My Lai, Attica, Dallas, Kent State, the Ia Drang Valley.

These are differing evils. But if there is a unified sense of discontent, some impulse to which most Americans would assent, it is that we have lost the power to alter our society because those with power are exempt from accountability. This sensibility—which strikes to the core of America's foundations—has poisoned the wellsprings of trust. "The rich get richer and the poor get poorer." So 62 percent of white America tell the Harris Poll. "The medium is a false message." So the Vice-President tells the American people. A quarter of the American people abandoned their trust in our goverment between 1964 and 1970; by the start of this decade, two-thirds of us believed we had lost our national sense of direction; half of us thought we were on the verge of a national breakdown. If a presidential aspirant preaches war, and you vote for the man who promises peace, you have been duped; for the peacemaker has all along been plotting war—and lies to win your assent to that war. So the Pentagon papers tell us.

Nor is it just the government we have come to doubt. By one measure—a Harris Poll in September of 1971—*every major institution in America* was distrusted by a majority of Americans. The press, business, the courts, Congress, the media, the presidency—*none* of them commanded the respect of the citizenry.

And thus millions of citizens have come to believe that the men and institutions who hold power in this country do not mean what they say: that the Constitution, or a hosptial bill, or the label on a can of food, or a *Time* magazine story, or a union pension plan, all falter between the word and the deed. The institutions that govern us—from the presidency to a corporation to a university, a bank, a foundation—do not deserve the legitimacy that is supposed to come with authority. They endure not because they fulfill their purposes, but because they possess power.

This belief is not unique to any single group of Americans. It cuts across divisions of race, sex, class, age, and region. We are infested with the proposition that the rules of the game are not fair; that the fight is fixed; that the key to success in America is power, and that the key to power is the hidden angle, the fix, money.

The core of this manifesto lies in this perception: there are people, classes, and institutions that today possess an illegitimate amount of wealth and power; they use that power for their own benefit and for the common loss. This power, which is at root economic, corrupts the political process and insulates itself from effective challenge.

The fight against this concentration of privilege—open and covert, legal and illegal—is, we believe, the most important political question of this decade. Its goal is a more equitable distribution of wealth and power; its enemy is the entire arrangement of privileges, exemptions, and free rides that has narrowed the opportunity of most Americans to control their own destiny. This fight for fairness is political; it can be won only by organizing a new political majority in America.

There exists a 200-year-old native tradition behind this goal of fairness and equality. It is a tradition that stretches back to Jefferson and Tom Paine, to Andrew Jackson, the muckrakers, George Norris, and Robert La Follette; it runs through the early organizers of the CIO and the political battles of Estes Kefauver; and it comes down to us today in the campaigns and ideas of Martin Luther King, Robert Kennedy, and Ralph Nader. It is called populism. We believe that a new populism, stripped of the paranoia and racism that afflicted it in the past, can redress some of the key grievances that have stunted the lives of millions of us. It is a *political* movement with a *political* goal. It is *not* a cultural prescription or a revolutionary nostrum. Far from being a Utopian dream, the new populism rests on a new majority that is, we believe, both a necessary and an attainable coalition. It is also the most important work we have.

Three essential beliefs govern this manifesto, and we state them bluntly at the outset.

1. WEALTH AND POWER ARE UNEQUALLY AND UNFAIRLY
    DISTRIBUTED IN AMERICA TODAY

After a generation of predominantly liberal, predominantly reformist national governments, the concentration of wealth has *increased*. In 1949, the richest 1 percent of the population owned 21 percent of the wealth. Today, the richest 1 percent own almost 40 percent of our national wealth. Income distribution has not changed for a generation: the bottom fifth of American families gets 6 percent of the national income; the top fifth gets 40 percent.

This wealth is shielded by private corporate governments, which are themselves protected by the political process their wealth helps shape.* These are the corporate enterprises that pervade our society: General Motors and First National City Bank, the National Broadcasting Company and Columbia University, the American Medical Association and the AFL-CIO, Getty Oil and AT&T. These institutions are often at odds with each other; they often favor different aspirants to national power and prefer different national priorities. But each holds basic, sometimes life and death, power over the millions of individuals whose lives they touch; each of them maintains this power no matter who is elected to public office; and each believes, first and foremost, in self-perpetuation and aggrandizement—regardless of what that means for public policy.

These epicenters of power do not win every battle with the public: auto safety laws are sometimes passed, utility rate increases are occasionally denied. But as a general proposition, these groups possess the power to govern themselves and to affect the whole society, and this power is beyond the reach of public or individual redress. No individual who works for a living can avoid taxes; Atlantic Richfield Oil Company paid no taxes for four years although it earned $465 million during that period. No homeowner could hurl his garbage into the street because it hurt his family budget to buy a trash can; the U.S. Steel Corporation has turned Gary, Indiana and countless other communities into open sewers. If a motorist is caught speeding and offers money to the traffic cop, he is guilty of bribery; if doctors are caught participating in the padding of Medicare bills and the AMA spends thousands to stop Congress from legislating reform, it is engaging in public-

* So that we have Henry Jackson, whose servility to the biggest aerospace company in his state has won him the title of "Senator from Boeing"; and Russell Long, who inherited his role as protector of the oil industry when Robert Kerr died and Lyndon Johnson left the Senate; and Congressman Jamie Whitten, who is the spokesman for the big corporate farmers. And so on.

service advertising.* This imbalance of power is not the result of a conspiracy: such institutions are simply using the power they have to preserve their privileged status in the American hierarchy.

As city planner Charles Abrams first suggested, our economic system is best described as welfare for the rich and free enterprise for the poor. There are $4 billion in federal subsidies every year for big corporate farmers; there are depletion allowances and import quotas to enrich the oil industry; there are expense-account dodges, untaxed foreign bank accounts, and special exemptions for the income from stocks and bonds—all for the rich. Both big business and big labor organizations can hire lobbyists, raise money for political campaigns, and lend out their employees to candidates while keeping them on tax-deductible salaries. The biggest defense contractors—General Dynamics, Lockheed, Boeing—have been virtually subsidized by the Pentagon, as have elitist "think-tanks" such as the RAND Corporation.† And the tax system is itself a major subsidy to the wealthy.

Meanwhile, the billions of dollars spent as a result of the reform legislation of the Truman, Kennedy, and Johnson years—on such items as urban renewal, Medicare, the $60 billion highway construction program, the War on Poverty, and aid to education—have made little difference for the forgotten families living on less than $10,000 a year. Administrators profited from these programs, politicians and consultants profited, construction firms profited, but the poor and the nonaffluent did not.

And it is not just blacks or Chicanos or Indians who are victimized by our double-standard economy. Nor is it only those on the poverty level. The majority of Americans are victimized.

* A view certainly held officially. Despite intensive political lobbying by the AMA, the IRS continues to recognize the organization's tax-exempt status for most of its revenues; yet, the Sierra Club had its exemption challenged ostensibly for just such activities.
† As a result of congressional action in 1971, "virtually" and "Pentagon" are no longer necessary modifiers in the case of Lockheed. Now, direct subsidization is the rule. And, in announcing his import surtax in August, 1971, Mr. Nixon specifically exempted Lockheed from its application—another form of subsidy.

White factory workers in Birmingham and Flint still lead frustrated, dead-end lives: the average worker's income is $1,000 less than the Department of Labor says he needs to take care of a family of four, and more often than not his wife also works at a dull, unrewarding job that is nonetheless essential if the family is to make ends meet. The waitress in Cleveland still can't pay her mother's hospital bills, and the law still says her income makes her ineligible for public health care. Old people living on Social Security still have to shoplift cans of tunafish so they can eat. And in New York City, the gross income of 60 percent of white families is less than $9,400 a year—less, in other words, than a moderate standard of living. So much for the affluent society.

In his famous 1962 commencement address at Yale, President Kennedy argued that the crucial problems of the economy were no longer political or distributive, but had become managerial and technical. We argue the exact opposite.

2. THE KEY TO BUILDING ANY NEW MAJORITY IN AMERICAN POLITICS IS A COALITION OF SELF-INTEREST BETWEEN BLACKS AND LOW- AND MODERATE-INCOME WHITES; THE REAL DIVISION IN THIS COUNTRY IS NOT BETWEEN GENERATIONS OR BETWEEN RACES, BUT BETWEEN THE RICH WHO HAVE POWER AND THOSE BLACKS AND WHITES WHO HAVE NEITHER POWER NOR PROPERTY

Until recently, such an alliance seemed impossible, in part because middle-class liberals have persistently defined public issues primarily in terms of race rather than class. "White racism," the Kerner Commission said, was the core of the problem. The OEO bureaucrats did not start any legal-services storefronts in the white sections of Youngstown or South Boston. There were no Model City grants to rebuild the decaying white neighborhoods of Utica or Jersey City. Affluent liberals, living safely behind suburban fences, refused to recognize street crime as an injustice against the old and the poor still trapped in the cities. Middle-class reformers sent their own children to "smart" private schools, and then supported plans that forced white ethnics to bus their children to predominantly black schools where education was inferior. By promising and not delivering to the blacks, and by ignoring the blue-collar worker, the liberals in power during the 1960s managed to anger and polarize both halves of the other America.

But blacks and millions of white workingmen who earn between $5,000 and $10,000 a year do have common problems and share common interests. To get them to recognize this and to act requires that these mutual needs become clearly defined and that programs to meet these needs be offered—*all in terms that benefit both groups.* Despite all the ethnic and racial divisions, blue-collar workers were progressive during the 1930s and 1940s. There is no reason why they can't be again.

We have already noted some of the issues that can unite them. As for the programs, a unifying populist platform might include: stricter industrial safety laws; a 90 percent tax on inheritance and estates—and tax reforms to help the workingman; free medical care for everyone; public ownership of utilities; limits on land ownership by individuals and corporations; new antitrust laws to go after industrial concentration as well as monopoly; expanded Social Security benefits, including a decent income base for those who cannot work; cable television franchises for civic groups; free and equal access to television for all politicians; strict controls on the profits of banks; and an end to corporate power and control of both the market and the regulatory agencies.

The prospect for this new coalition appears uncertain today. Working-class whites and blacks are separate armed camps in Cicero, Illinois; school buses are bombed in Pontiac, Michigan, in an effort to halt racial busing. In 1968, New York watched as teachers—mostly Jewish—battled parents' groups—mostly black and Puerto Rican—for control of the city's schools. In public universities, on civil-service job lists, in housing, blacks and working-class whites collide, in large part because they are forced to compete against each other for what are, but need not be, inadequate resources. The result is distrust and hostility.

We do not argue that these disputes can be eradicated; racial and cultural hostilities are a fact of life. But we do argue that this competition is in part a consequence of economic concentration—concentration that leaves whites and blacks competing over too sarce public resources. We believe that a redistribution of wealth and power would diminish this combat that turns potential class allies into racial antagonists. If white and black communications workers find wages and promotions inadequate, whom should they blame? Each other? Or the conglomerate International Telephone and Telegraph that turned a profit of $350 million in 1970, and paid its board chairman, Harold Geneen, an annual compensation of $766,000? (Which is more than most Americans earn in a lifetime.) If white and black families are forced to compete against each other for decent housing at a fair price, whom should they blame? Each other? Or banks and insurance companies that finance a glut of new office buildings and luxury apartments and allow realty interests to make a profit out of slum housing?

Blacks and almost-poor whites do not have to love, or even like, each other to forge an alliance of self-interest. The Irish cop on the low end of the middle-income scale living in Brooklyn's Bay Ridge need not embrace the black family in Harlem or the Italian-American homeowner in Corona to know his kids are stuck with the same bad schools, dirty streets, and dangerous parks. The white miner in West Virginia and the Mexican-American migrant worker in Texas share a more important bond than friendship: because they and their families cannot get decent medical care, they will die younger, suffer more disease, and lose more children at birth. In short, the coalition we are describing is based on hard, practical politics. In 1932, Jewish trade unionists and southern segregationists did not love each other, but together they gave ballast to FDR's New Deal. Certainly the jobless youth in Watts and the steelworker laid off his job in Gary have more in common than antilabor millionaires like Senators James Buckley and William Brock III have in common with those blue-collar workers who voted for them.

In 1968, Robert Kennedy, an earthy enemy of war, hunger, and crime, won the votes of both blacks and ethnic whites who had been tempted to follow George Wallace. The organizing work of Saul Alinsky, Ralph Nader, and Msgr. Geno Baroni also indicates the existing potential for this alliance. So do the decisive electoral victories achieved in 1970 by Senators Hart, Proxmire, and Kennedy, by Governor Gilligan, and by Representatives Dellums and Abzug, and the 1971 election of independent populist Henry Howell as Virginia's Lieutenant Governor.

Once cemented, this pact between the have-nots could transform American politics. With the added weight of the burgeoning consumer, environmental, and women's movements, and the millions of new voters between eighteen and twenty-one, an effective political coalition could take power.

3. CONCEPTUALLY AND HISTORICALLY, THE NEW POPULISM DIFFERS FROM BOTH THE NEW FRONTIER AND THE NEW LEFT; IT IS A SYNTHESIS OF MANY RADICAL AND SOME CONSERVATIVE IDEAS

The new populism differs from the New Frontier in several distinctive and significant ways. First, it is a *movement*, a broad popular upsurge like the labor movement of the 1930s or today's antiwar movement; it is not a faction yoked to one political party or one charismatic personality. The new populists movement sees winning elections as only half the job because so much power is still locked beyond the reach of the democratic process. It mistrusts the technocrats from the RAND Corporation and the Harvard Business School. It is decentralist and participatory, believing change is generated from below. And, like most of the original populists, it is anti-imperialist in foreign policy.

At the same time, it understands that the New Left in its Weatherman, Panther, and Yippie incarnations has become antidemocratic, terroristic, dogmatic, stoned on rhetoric, and badly disconnected from everyday reality.

The new populism also recognizes that conservatives have been perceptive about such things as the menace of violent street crime, the failure of the welfare system, and the limits human nature places on the abilities of centralized government. Conservatives have been right, too, in sensing the country has lost contact with those human values the ethnic workingman prizes most: family, hard work, pride, loyalty, endurance.

Our basic argument in this manifesto is neither new nor novel. If it seems new, that is because over the last twenty years liberalism lost its vision and its memory, its élan and its program.

For a generation we have watched liberals gain more power and display less liberalism. It began in the early 1950s as liberal politicians and intellectuals dropped everything else to prove their anticommunism. Later in the decade, exhaustion and boredom set in, and political issues were subordinated to sociological concerns with affluence, organization men, suburbia, and mass culture. "The end of ideology" became an intellectual cliché.

During the Kennedy years, an eerie infatuation with management techniques and budgeting expertise—exemplified by Robert McNamara—became the new fashion. Increasingly divorced from a concern with programs, liberals turned these technocratic means into ends, ultimately chaining us by default to a set of distorted policies. So we became mired in a war begun by the anticommunists and the technocrats, and, since 1965, all our energies have of necessity been aimed at ending that war.

But now it is time to return again to the first questions of politics: who holds power—and by what right?

From *A Populist Manifesto*, 1972.

QUESTIONS

(1) The authors assert "The American myth is dying." To which myth do they refer? Is it, in your view, really dying?

(2) Look at the "three beliefs" that form the basis of the essay. Are they equally based upon observations of the way things really are? Which of the three is the most valid? Which the least valid?

(3) In the concluding section the authors write "For a generation we have watched liberals gain more power and display less liberalism." How do they support this assertion? Does it appear to be correct to you? Support your answers with examples.

(4) The authors call their essay a "manifesto." Look this word up in the dictionary and prepare a series of topics about which one might write a manifesto.

(5) In the last three paragraphs of the essay the authors attempt a summary of the political history of America in the past twenty-five years. To what degree is that summary accurate and to what extent inaccurate?

THE ME DECADE AND THE THIRD GREAT AWAKENING

TOM WOLFE

ME AND MY HEMORRHOIDS

The trainer said, "Take your finger off the repress button." Everybody was supposed to let go, let all the vile stuff come up and gush out. They even provided vomit bags, like the ones on a 747, in case you literally let it *gush out!* Then the trainer told everybody to think of "the one thing you would most like to eliminate from your life." And so what does our girl blurt over the microphone?

"Hemorrhoids!"

Just so!

That was how she ended up in her present state . . . stretched out on the wall-to-wall carpet of a banquet hall in the Ambassador Hotel in Los Angeles with her eyes closed and her face pressed into the stubble of the carpet, which is a thick commercial weave and feels like clothes-brush bristles against her face and smells a bit *high* from cleaning solvent. That was how she ended up lying here concentrating on her hemorrhoids.

Eyes shut! deep in her own space! her hemorrhoids! the grisly peanut—

Many others are stretched out on the carpet all around her, some 249 other souls, in fact. They're all strewn across the floor of the banquet hall with their eyes closed, just as she is. But, Christ, the others are concentrating on things that sound serious and deep when you talk about them. And how they had talked about them! They had all marched right up to the microphone and "shared," as the trainer called it. What did they want to eliminate from their lives? Why, they took their fingers right off the old repress button and told the whole room. My husband! my wife! my homosexuality! my inability to communicate, my self-hatred, self-destructiveness, craven fears, puling weaknesses, primordial horrors, premature ejaculation, impotence, frigidity, rigidity, subservience, laziness, alcoholism, major vices, minor vices, grim habits, twisted psyches, tortured souls—and then it had been her turn, and she had said, "Hemorrhoids."

You can imagine what that sounded like. That broke the place up. The trainer looked like a cocky little bastard up there on the podium, with his deep tan, white tennis shirt, and peach-colored sweater, a dynamite color combination, all very casual and spontaneous—after about two hours of trying on different outfits in front of a mirror, *that* kind of casual and spontaneous, if her guess was right. And yet she found him attractive. *Commanding* was the word. He probably wondered if she was playing the wiseacre, with her "hemorrhoids," but he rolled with it. Maybe she *was* being playful. Just looking at him made her feel mischievous. In any event, *hemorrhoids* was what had bubbled up into her brain.

Then the trainer had told them to stack their folding chairs in the back of the banquet hall and lie down on the floor and close their eyes and get deep into their own spaces and concentrate on that one item they wanted to get rid of most—and really feel it and let the feeling gush out.

So now she's lying here concentrating on her hemorrhoids. The strange thing is . . . it's no joke after all! She begins to feel her hemorrhoids in all their morbid presence. She can actually *feel* them. The sieges always began with her having the sensation that a peanut was caught in her anal sphincter. That meant a section of swollen varicose vein had pushed its way out of her intestines and was actually coming out of her bottom. It was as hard as a peanut and felt bigger

and grislier than a peanut. Well—for God's sake!—in her daily
life, even at work, *especially* at work, and she works for a
movie distributor, her whole picture of herself was of her . . .
seductive physical presence. She was not the most successful
businesswoman in Los Angeles, but she was certainly successful enough, and quite in addition to that, she was . . . *the
main sexual presence in the office.* When she walked into the
office each morning, everyone, women as well as men, checked
her out. She *knew* that. She could feel her sexual presence go
through the place like an invisible chemical, like a hormone,
a scent, a universal solvent.

The most beautiful moments came when she was in her
office or in a conference room or at Mr. Chow's taking a meeting—nobody "had" meetings any more, they "took" them—
with two or three men, men she never met before or barely
knew. The overt subject was, inevitably, eternally, "the deal."
She always said there should be only one credit line up on the
screen for any movie: "Deal by . . ." But the meeting would
also have a subplot. The overt plot would be "The Deal."
The subplot would be "The Men Get Turned On by Me."
Pretty soon, even though the conversation had not strayed
overtly from "the deal," the men would be swaying in unison
like dune grass at the beach. And she was the wind, of course.
And then one of the men would say something and smile and
at the same time reach over and touch her . . . on top of the
hand or on the side of the arm . . . as if it meant nothing
. . . as if it were just a gesture for emphasis . . . *but, in fact,
a man is usually deathly afraid of reaching out and touching a
woman he doesn't know* . . . and she knew it meant she had
hypnotized him sexually . . .

Well—for God's sake!—at just that sublime moment, likely
as not, the goddamn peanut would be popping out of her tail!
As she smiled sublimely at her conquest, she also had to sit in
her chair lopsided, with one cheek of her buttocks higher
than the other, as if she were about to crepitate, because it
hurt to sit squarely on the peanut. If for any reason she had
to stand up at that point and walk, she would have to walk
as if her hip joints were rusted out, as if she were sixty-five
years old, because a normal stride pressed the peanut, and the
pain would start up, and the bleeding, too, very likely. Of if
she couldn't get up and had to sit there for a while and keep

her smile and her hot hormonal squinted eyes pinned on the men before her, the peanut would start itching or burning, and she would start double-tracking, as if her mind were a tape deck with two channels going at once. In one she's the sexual princess, the Circe, taking a meeting and clouding men's minds . . . and in the other she's a poor bitch who wants nothing more in this world than to go down the corridor to the ladies' room and get some Kleenex and some Vaseline and push the peanut back up into her intestines with her finger.

And even if she's able to get away and do that, she will spend the rest of that day and the next, and the next, with a *deep worry* in the back of her brain, the sort of worry that always stays on the edge of your consciousness, no matter how hard you think of something else. She will be wondering at all times what the next bowel movement will be like, how solid and compact the bolus will be, trying to think back and remember if she's had any milk, cream, chocolate, or any other binding substance in the last twenty-four hours, or any nuts or fibrous vegetables like broccoli. Is she really *in for it* this time—

The Sexual Princess! On the outside she has on her fireproof grin and her Fiorio scarf, as if to say she lives in a world of Sevilles and 450sl's and dinner last night at Dominick's, a movie business restaurant on Beverly Boulevard that's so exclusive, Dominick keeps his neon sign (*Dominick's*) turned off at night to make the wimps think it's closed, but *she* (Hi, Dominick!) can get a table—while inside her it's all the battle between the bolus and the peanut—

—and is it too late to leave the office and go get some mineral oil and let some of that vile glop roll down her gullet or get a refill on the softener tablets or eat some prunes or drink some coffee or do something else to avoid one of those horrible hard-clay boluses that will come grinding out of her, crushing the peanut and starting not only the bleeding but . . . *the pain!* . . . a horrible humiliating pain that feels like she's getting a paper cut in her anus, like the pain you feel when the edge of a piece of bond paper slices your finger, plus a horrible hellish purple bloody varicose pressure, but lasting not for an instant, like a paper cut, but for an eternity, prolonged until the tears are rolling down her face as she sits in the cubicle, and she

wants to cry out, to scream until it's over, to make the screams
of fear, fury, and humiliation obliterate the pain. But someone would hear! No doubt they'd come bursting right into the
ladies' room to save her! and feed and water their morbid
curiosities! And what could she possibly say? And so she had
simply held that feeling in all these years, with her eyes on fire
and her entire pelvic saddle a great purple tub of pain. She
had repressed the whole squalid horror of it—*the searing peanut*—until now. The trainer had said, "Take your finger off
the repress button!" Let it gush up and pour out!

And now, as she lies here on the floor of the banquet hall
of the Ambassador Hotel with 249 other souls, she knows exactly what he meant. She can feel it *all,* all of the pain, and on
top of the pain all the humiliation, and for the first time in
her life she has permission from the Management, from herself
and everyone around her, to let the feeling gush forth. So she
starts moaning.

"Ooooooooooooooooooooooooohhhhhhhhhhhhhhhhhh!"

And when she starts moaning, the most incredible and exhilarating thing begins to happen. A wave of moans spreads
through the people lying around her, as if her energy were
radiating out like a radar pulse.

"Oooooooooooooooooooooooohhhhhhhhh!"

So she lets her moan rise into a keening sound.

"Ooooooooooooooooooooohhhhhhhhhhheeeeeeeeeeeeeeeeeeee-
eeeeeeee!"

And when she begins to keen, the souls near her begin keening, even while the moans are still spreading to the prostrate
folks farther from her, on the edges of the room.

"Eeeeeeeeeeeeeeoooooooohhhhhhhhhheeeeeeeeeeeeeeeooooo-
oooh!"

So she lets her keening sound rise up into a real scream.

"Eeeeeeeeeeeeeeeeeeaiaiaiaiaiaiaiaiaiaiaiaiaiaiaiai!"

And this rolls out in a wave, too, first through those near
her, and then toward the far edges.

"Aiaiaiaiaiaiaiaiaiaiaiaiaieeeeeeeeeeeeeeeeeeeeeohhhhhhhhheeeee-
aiaiai!"

And so she turns it all the way up, into a scream such as she
has never allowed herself in her entire life.

"AiaiaiaiaiaiaiaiaaaAAAAAAAAAAAAAAAARRRRRRR-
GGGGGGHHHHHH!"

And her full scream spreads from soul to soul, over the top of the keens and fading moans—

"AAAAAAARRRRRGGGGHHHaiaiaiaiaieeeeeeeeeeoooo-oohhh eeeeee aiaiaiaiaaaaAAAAAAAAAARRRRRRRGGGG-GHHHHHHHHHHHH!"

—until at last the entire room is consumed in her scream, as if there are no longer 250 separate souls but one noösphere of souls united in some incorporeal way by her scream—

"AAAAAAAAARRRRRRRGGGGGGGGHHHHHHHH!"

—which is not simply *her* scream any longer . . . but the world's! Each soul is concentrated on its own burning item—my husband! my wife! my homosexuality! my inability to communicate, my self-hatred, self-destruction, craven fears, puling weaknesses, primordial horrors, premature ejaculation, impotence, frigidity, rigidity, subservience, laziness, alcoholism, major vices, minor vices, grim habits, twisted psyches, tortured souls—and yet each unique item has been raised to a cosmic level and united with every other until there is but one piercing moment of release and liberation at last!—a whole world of anguish set free by—

My hemorrhoids.

"Me and My Hemorrhoids Star at the Ambassador" . . . during a three-day Erhard Seminars Training (est) course in the banquet hall. The truly odd part, however, is yet to come. In her experience lies the explanation of certain grand puzzles of the 1970s, a period that will come to be known as the Me Decade.

THE HOLY ROLL

In 1972 a farsighted caricaturist did a drawing of Teddy Kennedy, entitled "President Kennedy campaigning for reelection in 1980 . . . courting the so-called Awakened vote." The picture shows Kennedy ostentatiously wearing not only a crucifix but also (if one looks just above the cross) a pendant of the Bleeding Heart of Jesus. The crucifix is the symbol of Christianity in general, but the Bleeding Heart is the symbol of some of Christianity's most ecstatic, non-rational, holy-rolling cults. I should point out that the artist's prediction lacked certain refinements. For one thing, Kennedy may be campaigning to be President in 1980, but he is not terribly likely to be the incumbent. For another, the odd spectacle of politicians using ecstatic, non-rational, holy-rolling religion in Presidential campaigning was to appear first not in 1980 but in 1976.

The two most popular new figures in the 1976 campaign, Jimmy Carter and Jerry Brown, are men who rose up from state politics . . . absolutely aglow with mystical religious streaks. Carter turned out to be an evangelical Baptist who had recently been "born again" and "saved," who had "accepted Jesus Christ as my personal Savior"—i.e., he was of the Missionary lectern-pounding Amen ten-finger C-major chord Sister-Martha-at-the-Yamaha-keyboard loblolly piney-woods Baptist faith in which the members of the congregation stand up and "give witness" and "share it, Brother" and "share it, Sister" and "praise God!" during the service.* Jerry Brown turned out to be the Zen Jesuit, a former Jesuit seminarian who went about like a hairshirt Catholic monk, but one who happened to believe also in the Gautama Buddha, and who got off koans in an offhand but confident manner, even on political issues, as to how it is not the right answer that matters but the right question, and so forth.

Newspaper columnists and news-magazine writers continually referred to the two men's "enigmatic appeal." Which is to say, they couldn't explain it. Nevertheless, they tried. They theorized that the war in Vietnam, Watergate, the FBI and CIA scandals, had left the electorate shell-shocked and disillusioned and that in their despair the citizens were groping no longer for specific remedies but for sheer faith, something, anything (even holy rolling), to believe in. This was in keeping with the current fashion of interpreting all new political phe-

---

* Carter is not, however, a member of the most down-home and ecstatic of the Baptist sects, which is a back-country branch known as the Primitive Baptist Church. In the Primitive Baptist churches men and women sit on different sides of the room, no musical instruments are allowed, and there is a good deal of foot-washing and other rituals drawn from passages in the Bible. The Progressive Primitives, another group, differ from the Primitives chiefly in that they allow a piano or organ in the church. The Missionary Baptists, Carter's branch, are a step up socially (not necessarily divinely) but would not be a safe bet for an ambitious member of an in-town country club. The In-town Baptists, found in communities of 25,000 or more, are too respectable, socially, to be called ecstatic and succeed in being almost as tame as the Episcopalians, Presbyterians, and Methodists.

nomena in terms of recent disasters, frustration, protest, the
decline of civilization . . . the Grim Slide. But when *The
York Times* and CBS employed a polling organization to try
to find out just what great gusher of "frustration" and "protest" Carter had hit, the results were baffling. A Harvard
political scientist, William Schneider, concluded for the Los
Angeles *Times* that "the Carter protest" was a new kind of protest, "a protest of good feelings." That was a new kind, sure
enough: a protest that wasn't a protest.

In fact, both Carter and Brown had stumbled upon a fabu-
lous terrain for which there are no words in current political
language. A couple of politicians had finally wandered into
the Me Decade.

HIM?—THE NEW MAN?

The saga of the Me Decade begins with one of those facts that
are so big and so obvious (like the Big Dipper) no one ever
comments on them any more. Namely: the thirty-year boom.
Wartime spending in the United States in the 1940s touched
off a boom that has continued for more than thirty years. It
has pumped money into every class level of the population on
a scale without parallel in any country in history. True, nothing has solved the plight of those at the very bottom, the
chronically unemployed of the slums. Nevertheless, in the city
of Compton, California, it is possible for a family of four at
the very lowest class level, which is known in America today
as "on welfare," to draw an income of $8,000 a year entirely
from public sources. This is more than most British newspaper columnists and Italian factory foremen make, even allowing for differences in living costs. In America truck drivers,
mechanics, factory workers, policemen, firemen, and garbage-
men make so much money—$15,000 to $20,000 (or more) per
year is not uncommon—that the word "proletarian" can no
longer be used in this country with a straight face. So one now
says "lower middle class." One can't even call workingmen
"blue collar" any longer. They all have on collars like Joe Namath's or Johnny Bench's or Walt Frazier's. They all have on
$35 superstar Qiana sport shirts with elephant collars and

1940s Airbrush Wallpaper Flowers Buncha Grapes & Seashell designs all over them.

Well, my God, the old utopian socialists of the nineteenth century—such as Saint-Simon, Owen, Fourier, and Marx—*lived* for the day of the liberated workingman. They foresaw a day when industrialism (Saint-Simon coined the word) would give the common man the things he needed in order to realize his potential as a human being: surplus (discretionary) income, political freedom, free time (leisure), and freedom from grinding drudgery. Some of them, notably Owen and Fourier, thought all this might come to pass first in the United States. So they set up communes here: Owen's New Harmony commune in Indiana and thirty-four Fourier-style "phalanx" settlements—socialist communes, because the new freedom was supposed to be possible only under socialism. The old boys never dreamed that it would come to pass instead as the result of a Go-Getter Bourgeois business boom such as began in the U.S. in the 1940s. Nor would they have liked it if they had seen it. For one thing, the *homo novus,* the new man, the liberated man, the first common man in the history of the world with the much-dreamed-of combination of money, freedom, and free time—this American workingman—didn't *look* right. The Joe Namath–Johnny Bench–Walt Frazier superstar Qiana wallpaper sports shirts, for a start.

He didn't look right . . . and he wouldn't . . . *do right!* I can remember what brave plans visionary architects at Yale and Harvard still had for *the common man* in the early 1950s. (They actually used the term "the common man.") They had brought the utopian socialist dream forward into the twentieth century. They had things figured out for the workingman down to truly minute details, such as lamp switches. The new liberated workingman would live as the Cultivated Ascetic. He would be modeled on the B.A.-degree Greenwich Village bohemian of the late 1940s—dark wool Hudson Bay shirts, tweed jackets, flannel trousers, briarwood pipes, good books, sandals and simplicity—except that he would live in a Worker Housing project. All Yale and Harvard architects worshipped Bauhaus principles and had the Bauhaus vision of Worker Housing. The Bauhaus movement absolutely hypnotized American architects, once its leaders, such as Walter Gropius and Ludwig Mies van der Rohe, came to the United States from Germany in the 1930s. Worker Housing in America would have pure beige rooms, stripped, freed, purged of all moldings, cornices, and overhangs—which Gropius regarded as symbolic "crowns" and therefore loathsome. Worker Housing would be liberated from all wallpaper, "drapes," Wilton rugs with flowers on them, lamps with fringed shades and bases that looked like vases or Greek columns. It would be cleansed of all doilies, knickknacks, mantelpieces, headboards, and radiator covers. Radiator coils would be left bare as honest, abstract sculptural objects.

But somehow the workers, incurable slobs that they were, avoided Worker Housing, better known as "the projects," as if it had a smell. They were heading out instead to the suburbs—the *suburbs!*—to places like Islip, Long Island, and the San Fernando Valley of Los Angeles—and buying houses with clapboard siding and pitched roofs and shingles and gaslight-style front-porch lamps and mailboxes set up on top of lengths of stiffened chain that seemed to defy gravity, and all sorts of other unbelievably cute or antiquey touches, and they loaded these houses with "drapes" such as baffled all description and wall-to-wall carpet you could lose a shoe in, and they put barbecue pits and fish ponds with concrete cherubs urinating into them on the lawn out back, and they parked twenty-five-foot-long cars out front and Evinrude cruisers up on tow trailers in the carport just beyond the breezeway.*

By the 1960s the common man was also getting quite interested in this business of "realizing his potential as a human being." But once again he crossed everybody up! Once more he took his money and ran—determined to do-it-himself!

. . . .

* Ignored or else held in contempt by working people, Bauhaus design eventually triumphed as a symbol of wealth and privilege, attuned chiefly to the tastes of businessmen's wives. For example, Mies's most famous piece of furniture design, the Barcelona chair, now sells for $1,680 and is available only through one's decorator. The high price is due in no small part to the chair's Worker Housing Honest Materials: stainless steel and leather. No chromed iron is allowed, and customers are refused if they want to have the chair upholstered in material of their own choice. Only leather is allowed, and only six shades of that: Seagram's Building Lobby Palomino, Monsanto Chemical Company Lobby Antelope, Arco Towers Pecan, Trans-America Building Ebony, Bank of America Building Walnut, and Architectural Digest Mink.

HOW YOU DO IT, MY BOYS!

In September of 1969, in London, on the King's Road, in a restaurant called Alexander's, I happened to have dinner with a group of people that included a young American named Jim Haynes and an Australian named Germaine Greer. Neither name meant anything to me at the time, although I never forgot Germaine Greer. She was a thin, hard-looking woman with a tremendous curly electric hairdo and the most outrageous Naugahyde mouth I had ever heard on a woman. (I was shocked.) After a while she got bored and set fire to her hair with a match. Two waiters ran over and began beating the flames out with napkins. This made a noise like pigeons taking off in the park. Germaine Greer sat there with a sublime smile on her face, as if to say: "How you do it, my boys!"

Jim Haynes and Germaine Greer had just published the first issue of a newspaper that All London was talking about. It was called *Suck*. It was founded shortly after *Screw* in New York and was one of the progenitors of a line of sex newspapers that today are so numerous that in Los Angeles it is not uncommon to see fifteen coin-operated newspaper racks in a row on the sidewalk. One will be for the Los Angeles *Times,* a second for the *Herald Examiner,* and the other thirteen for the sex papers. *Suck* was full of pictures of gaping thighs, moist lips, stiffened giblets, glistening nodules, dirty stories, dirty poems, essays on sexual freedom, and a gossip column detailing the sexual habits of people whose names I assumed were fictitious. Then I came to an item that said, "Anyone who wants group sex in New York and likes fat girls, contact L—— R——," except that it gave her full name. She was a friend of mine.

Even while Germaine Greer's hair blazed away, the young American, Jim Haynes, went on with a discourse about the aims of *Suck*. To put it in a few words, the aim was sexual liberation and, through sexual liberation, the liberation of the spirit of man. If you were listening to this speech and had read *Suck,* or even if you hadn't, you were likely to be watching Jim Haynes's face for the beginnings of a campy grin, a smirk, a wink, a roll of the eyeballs—something to indicate that he was just having his little joke. But it soon became clear that

he was one of those people who exist on a plane quite . . .
Beyond Irony. Whatever it had been for him once, sex had
now become a religion, and he had developed a theology in
which the orgasm had become a form of spiritual ecstasy.

The same curious journey—from sexology to theology—has
become a feature of *swinging* in the United States. At the
Sandstone sex farm in the Santa Monica Mountains in Los
Angeles people of all class levels gather for weekends in the
nude. They copulate in the living room, on the lawn, out by
the pool, on the tennis courts, with the same open, free, liberated spirit as dogs in the park or baboons in a tree. In conversation, however, the atmosphere is quite different. The air
becomes humid with solemnity. Close your eyes, and you think
you're at a nineteenth-century Wesleyan summer encampment
and tent-meeting lecture series. It's the soul that gets a work-
out here, brethren. And yet this is not a hypocritical coverup.
It is merely an example of how people in even the most secular
manifestation of the Me decade—free-lance spread-'em ziggy-
zig rutting—are likely to go through the usual stages . . .
Let's talk about Me . . . Let's find the Real Me . . . Let's
get rid of all the hypocrisies and impedimenta and false mod-
esties that obsure the Real Me . . . Ah! at the apex of my
soul is a spark of the Divine . . . which I perceive in the pure
moment of ecstasy (which your textbooks call "the orgasm,"
but which I know to be heaven) . . .

This notion even has a pedigree. Many sects, such as the
Left-handed Shakti and the Gnostic onanists, have construed
the orgasm to be the *kairos,* the magic moment, the divine ecstasy. There is evidence that the early Mormons and the
Oneida movement did likewise. In fact, the notion of some
sort of divine ecstasy runs throughout the religious history of
the past twenty-five hundred years. As Max Weber and Joa-
chim Wach have illustrated in detail, every major modern religion, as well as countless long-gone minor ones, has originated not with a theology or a set of values or a social goal or
even a vague hope of a life hereafter. They have all originated,
instead, with a small circle of people who have shared some
overwhelming ecstasy or seizure, a "vision," a "trance," an hal-
lucination; in short, an actual neurological event, a dramatic
change in metabolism, something that has seemed to light up

the entire central nervous system. The Mohammedan movement (Islam) originated in hallucinations, apparently the result of fasting, meditation, and isolation in the darkness of caves, which can induce sensory deprivation. Some of the same practices were common with many types of Buddhists. The early Hindus and Zoroastrians seem to have been animated by an hallucinogenic drug known as *soma* in India and *haoma* in Persia. The origins of Christianity are replete with "visions." The early Christians used wine for ecstatic purposes, to the point where the Apostle Paul (whose conversion on the road to Damascus began with a "vision") complained that it was degenerating into sheer drunkenness at the services. These great draughts of wine survive in minute quantities in the ritual of Communion. The Bacchic orders, the Sufi, Voodooists, Shakers, and many others used feasts (the bacchanals), ecstatic dancing ("the whriling dervishes"), and other forms of frenzy to achieve the *kairos* . . . the *moment* . . . here and now! . . . the *feeling!* . . . In every case, the believers took the feeling of ecstasy to be the sensation of the light of God flooding into their souls. They felt like vessels of the Divine, of the All-in-One. Only *afterward* did they try to interpret the experience in the form of theologies, earthly reforms, moral codes, liturgies.

Nor have these been merely the strange practices of the Orient and the Middle East. Every major religious wave that has developed in America has started out the same way: with a flood of *ecstatic experiences.* The First Great Awakening, as it is known to historians, came in the 1740s and was led by preachers of the "New Light," such as Jonathan Edwards, Gilbert Tennent, and George Whitefield. They and their followers were known as "enthusiasts" and "come-outers," terms of derision that referred to the frenzied, holy-rolling, pentecostal shout tempo of their services and to their visions, trances, shrieks, and agonies, which are preserved in great Rabelaisian detail in the writings of their detractors.

The Second Great Awakening came in the period from 1825 to 1850 and took the form of a still-wilder hoedown camp-meeting revivalism, of ceremonies in which people barked, bayed, fell down in fits and swoons, rolled on the ground, talked in tongues, and even added a touch of orgy. The Second Awakening originated in western New York State, where so many evangelical movements caught fire it became known as "the Burned-over District." Many new sects, such as Oneida and the Shakers, were involved. But so were older ones, such as the evangelical Baptists. The fervor spread throughout the American frontier (and elsewhere) before the Civil War. The most famous sect of the Second Great Awakening was the Mormon movement, founded by a twenty-five-year-old, Joseph Smith, and a small group of youthful comrades. This bunch was regarded as wilder, crazier, more obscene, more of a threat, than the entire lot of hippie communes of the 1960s put together. Smith was shot to death by a lynch mob in Carthage, Illinois, in 1844, which was why the Mormons, now with Brigham Young at the helm, emigrated to Utah. A sect, incidentally, is a religion with no political power. Once the Mormons settled, built, and ruled Utah, Mormonism became a *religion* soon enough . . . and eventually wound down to the slow, firm beat of respectability . . .

We are now—in the Me Decade—seeing the upward roll (and not yet the crest, by any means) of the third great religious wave in American history, one that historians will very likely term the Third Great Awakening. Like the others it has begun in a flood of *ecstasy*, achieved through LSD and other psychedelics, orgy, dancing (the New Sufi and the Hare Krishna), meditation, and psychic frenzy (the marathon encounter). This third wave has built up from more diverse and exotic sources than the first two, from therapeutic movements as well as overtly religious movements, from hippies and students of "psi phenomena" and Flying Saucerites as well as from charismatic Christians. But other than that, what will historians say about it?

The historian Perry Miller credited the First Great Awakening with helping to pave the way for the American Revolution through its assault on the colonies' religious establishment and, thereby, on British colonial authority generally. The sociologist Thomas F. O'Dea credited the Second Great Awakening with creating the atmosphere of Christian asceticism (known as "bleak" on the East Coast) that swept through the Midwest and the West during the nineteenth century and helped make it possible to build communities in the face of

great hardship. And the Third Great Awakening? Journalists—historians have not yet tackled the subject—have shown a
morbid tendency to regard the various movements in this
wave as "fascist." The hippie movement was often attacked
as "fascist" in the late 1960s. Over the past year a barrage of
articles has attacked the est movement and the "Moonies"
(followers of the Rev. Sun Myung Moon) along the same lines.

Frankly, this tells us nothing except that journalists bring
the same conventional Grim Slide concepts to every subject.
The word "fascism" derives from the old Roman symbol of
power and authority, the *fasces,* a bundle of sticks bound together by thongs (with an ax head protruding from one end).
One by one the sticks would be easy to break. Bound together
they are indestructible. Fascist ideology called for binding all
classes, all levels, all elements of an entire nation together into
a single organization with a single will.

The various movements of the current religious wave attempt very nearly the opposite. They begin with . . . "Let's
talk about Me." They begin with the most delicious look inward; with considerable narcissism, in short. When the believers bind together into religions, it is always with a sense of
splitting off from the rest of society. We, the enlightened (lit
by the sparks at the apexes of our souls), hereby separate ourselves from the lost souls around us. Like all religions before
them, they proselytize—but always promising the opposite of
nationalism: a City of Light that is above it all. There is no
ecumenical spirit within this Third Great Awakening. If anything, there is a spirit of schism. The contempt the various
gurus and seers have for one another is breathtaking. One has
only to ask, say, Oscar Ichazo of Arica about Carlos Castaneda
or Werner Erhard of est to learn that Castaneda is a fake and
Erhard is a shallow sloganeer. It's exhilarating!—to watch the
faithful split off from one another to seek ever more perfect
and refined crucibles in which to fan the Divine spark . . .
and to *talk about Me.*

Whatever the Third Great Awakening amounts to, for better or for worse, will have to do with this unprecedented post-
World War II American luxury: the luxury enjoyed by so
many millions of middling folk, of dwelling upon the self. At
first glance, Shirley Polykoff's slogan—"If I've only one life, let

me live it as a blonde!"—seems like merely another example of
a superficial and irritating rhetorical trope (*antanaclasis**)
that now happens to be fashionable among advertising copy
writers. But in fact the notion of "If I've only one life to live"
challenges one of those assumptions of society that are so deep-
rooted and ancient they have no name—they are simply lived
by. In this case: man's age-old belief in serial immortality.

   The husband and wife who sacrifice their own ambitions
and their material assets in order to provide a "better future"
for their children . . . the soldier who risks his life, or perhaps consciously sacrifices it, in battle . . . the man who de-
votes his life to some struggle for "his people" that cannot possibly be won in his lifetime . . . people (or most of them)
who buy life insurance or leave wills . . . are people who
conceive of themselves, however unconsciously, as part of a
great biological stream. Just as something of their ancestors
lives on in them, so will something of them live on in their
children . . . or in their people, their race, their community—for childless people, too, conduct their lives and try to
arrange their postmortem affairs with concern for how the
great stream is going to flow on. Most people, historically, have
not lived their lives as if thinking, "I have only one life to
live." Instead, they have lived as if they are living their ancestors' lives and their offsprings' lives and perhaps their neighbors' lives as well. They have seen themselves as inseparable
from the great tide of chromosomes of which they are created
and which they pass on. The mere fact that you were only going to be here a short time and would be dead soon enough
did not give you the license to try to climb out of the stream
and change the natural order of things. The Chinese, in an-
cestor worship, have literally worshipped the great tide itself,
and not any god or gods. For anyone to renounce the notion

* This figure of speech consists of repeating a word (or words with the
same root) in such a way that the second usage has a different meaning
from the first. "This is WINS, 1010 on your dial—New York wants to
know, and we *know* it" (1. know = "find out"; 2. know = "realize" or
"have the knowledge") . . . "We're American Airlines, *doing* what we *do*
best" (1. doing = "performing"; 2. what we do = "our job") . . . "If you
think refrigerators cost *too much*, maybe you're looking at *too much*
refrigerator (1. cost; 2. size of complexity). The smart money *is* on Admiral
(Admiral's italics)" . . . There is also an example of the *pun* in the
WINS slogan and of *epanadiplosis* in the Admiral slogan (the ABBA pattern of *refrigerator* . . . *too much/too much refrigerator*).

of serial immortality, in the West or the East, has been to defy what seems like a law of nature. Hence the wicked feeling—the excitement!—of "If I've only one life, let me live it as a ————!" Fill in the blank, if you dare.

And now many dare it! In *Democracy in America* de Tocqueville (the inevitable and ubiquitous de Tocqueville) saw the American sense of equality itself as disrupting the stream, which he called "time's pattern": "Not only does democracy make each man forget his ancestors, it hides his descendants from him, and divides him from his contemporaries; it continually turns him back into himself, and threatens, at last, to enclose him entirely in the solitude of his own heart." A grim prospect to the good Alexis de T.—but what did he know about . . . *Let's talk about Me!*

De Tocqueville's idea of modern man lost "in the solitude of his own heart" has been brought forward into our time in such terminology as *alienation* (Marx), *anomie* (Durkheim), the *mass man* (Ortega y Gasset), and *the lonely crowd* (Riesman). The picture is always of a creature uprooted by industrialism, packed together in cities with people he doesn't know, helpless against massive economic and political shifts— in short, a creature like Charlie Chaplin in *Modern Times,* a helpless, bewildered, and dispirited slave of the machinery. This victim of modern times has always been a most appealing figure to intellectuals, artists, and architects. The poor devil so obviously needs *us* to be his Engineers of the Soul, to use a term popular in the Soviet Union in the 1920s. We will pygmalionize this sad lump of clay into a *homo novus,* a New Man, with a new philosophy, a new aesthetics, not to mention new Bauhaus housing and furniture.

But once the dreary little bastards started getting money in the 1940s, they did an astonishing thing—they took their money and ran! They did something only aristocrats (and intellectuals and artists) were supposed to do—they discovered and started doting on *Me!* They've created the greatest age of individualism in American history! All rules are broken! The prophets are out of business! Where the Third Great Awakening will lead—who can presume to say? One only knows that the great religious waves have a momentum all their own. Neither arguments nor policies nor acts of the legislature have been any match for them in the past. And this one has the

mightiest, holiest roll of all, the beat that goes . . . *Me* . . .
Me . . . *Me* . . . *Me* . . .

From Mauve Gloves & Madmen, Clutter & Vine, 1976.

QUESTIONS

(1) The author begins his essay not with a general statement of his main idea but with an example of it. What are the advantages and disadvantages of approaching the subject in this manner?

(2) On page 31, the author continues to give examples of his main idea—this time from the world of politics—without stating his thesis explicitly. What is the effect of postponing his definition and of citing two prominent political leaders as examples of his thesis?

(3) On page 32, the author offers as background a sociological analysis of the "thirty-year boom" and its effect on the lifestyle of working class Americans. Again he has not defined his subject yet he maintains his reader's interest by the accuracy and wit of his descriptions. Is the author, at this point, functioning only as an entertainer or is there a point to his apparent digression?

(4) On page 34, Wolfe's theme comes into focus and the earlier sections of the essay begin to assume their appropriate place in the overall presentation. Which sentence most completely summarizes the main theme?

(5) On pages 39–41, the author attempts to show the connection between the search for "Me" and the revival of interest in mystical and evangelical religion. According to the author what is the connection?

(6) On pages 35–36, the "Me" phenomenon is connected to the sexual liberation in the sense of sex as "a religion . . . a theology in which the orgasm had become a form of spiritual ecstacy." Is the description valid or does it appear to be exaggerated? Wolfe is sometimes described as a caricaturist of American life. What are the virtues and vices of caricature?

(7) Despite a light tone the author concludes with a very serious point about "serial immortality." Read that section again carefully in preparation for an essay assignment on the following topic:

"If I've only one life, let me live it as a ———."

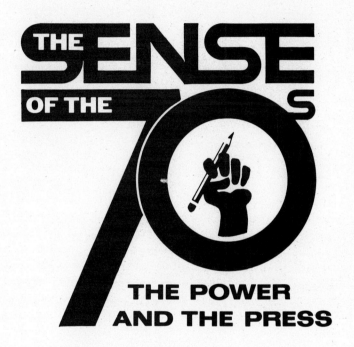

THE SENSE OF THE 70s

OF THE

70s

THE POWER
AND THE PRESS

In the seventies America relearned a lesson that it periodically forgets—that power, whether within the private or the public sphere, must always be subject to public inquiry. Without that constant monitoring process, a free society can all too easily lose its freedom.

Traditionally the agent of that inquiry has been a free press. Freedom of the press is, as a consequence, a vital element in the preservation of freedom. At no time was this truth more evident than in June 1972 when a group of men were arrested for breaking into the headquarters of the Democratic National Committee at the Watergate Hotel. The ensuing events—events that proved to be among the most dramatic and tumultuous in the history of American government—were the result, in no small way, of the activities of investigative reporters. Chief among these were Bob Woodward and Carl Bernstein, two young reporters for *The Washington Post*. Reprinted here is an editorial run by *The Post* when the news first broke. It is a fine example of the press engaged in its inquiring function and, incidentally, a remarkably prophetic statement, even to the point of emphasis on the self-destructing tape.

But, of course, the tape in this case did not self-destruct and the consequence was the destruction of Richard Nixon. Given below is an excerpt from one particularly significant conversation between President Nixon and his special counsel, John Dean. Dean's job was to keep the lid on Watergate, a task that had already become impossible by the time of this tape, March 1973.

The drama of Watergate proved to be as fascinating as any play America had ever seen, a fact that elicits the thoughtful and insightful commentary of America's best known play-

wright, Arthur Miller. Miller approaches the dialogues on the
tapes as a drama of character—the character of Richard Nixon.
He perceives the dialogues and the action that they record as
an abortive tragedy that finally must be seen as farce.

One consequence of the Watergate affair was a renewal of
prestige for the profession of journalism. Journalists had been
attacked, spied upon and downgraded during the Nixon administration. His downfall brought about a corresponding rise
in their reputations—to the point, as Tom Bethell suggests in
"The Myth of an Adversary Press," that there may be a danger of the pendulum having swung too far. Bethell fears that
the media have become a powerful and unofficial branch of
government. Whether or not his analysis is correct the danger
to freedom implicit in that possibility is one that we must all
be aware of.

EDITORIAL

THE WASHINGTON POST

Washington, D.C., June 21, 1972

As always, should you or any of your force be caught or killed, the Secretary will disavow any knowledge of your actions. This tape will self-destruct in five seconds . . . good luck . . .

From the CBS-TV show, *Mission Impossible*

As an example of life imitating art—of a sort—we have not for some time seen anything like the Watergate caper now unfolding in weird and scarcely believable detail, right down to the taped locks, the rubber gloves, the tear gas pens, the array of electronic equipment, and the crisp new hundred dollar bills in the hands of the five men who stole into Democratic Party headquarters the other night under cover of darkness and something less than impenetrable aliases. *Mission Impossible* it wasn't; experts in these matters all agree that the job was bungled at almost every step of the way. *Mission Incredible* it certainly is, both in terms of execution and, more important, in terms of the motives that could conceivably have prompted so crude an escapade by such a motley crew of former Central Intelligence Agency operatives and Miami-based, anti-Castro activists.

Mr. Ronald L. Ziegler, the White House spokesman, has already dismissed it as a "third-rate burglary attempt" and warned that "certain elements may try to stretch this beyond what it is." The implication of that last statement is that he knows what it is and if so, we wish he would tell us, because frankly it doesn't shape up as your ordinary, garden variety burglary—however "third-rate" its execution. An attempt to implant electronic surveillances in the headquarters of a major political party strikes us as something much more resembling what the Democratic National Chairman, Mr. Lawrence O'Brien, has called an "act of political espionage." And that, for all its comic, melodramatic aspects, is not quite so easy to dismiss.

In fact, without wishing to stretch things one bit beyond the demonstrable facts, there are certain elements here which could raise questions in even the least suspicious or skeptical minds. This is, for example, an election year, and while it is possible to suppose that this deed was done by a foreign government or even some extra-terrestrial interests, the finger naturally points, in a time of intense and developing political combat, to the Democrats' principal and natural antagonist; that is to say, it points to somebody associated with or at least sympathetic to—we may as well be blunt about it—the Republicans.

We do not so allege; we merely note that this is what some people are going to be saying, or thinking, and that their speculations, dark as they may sound, are going to be encouraged by word of various connection between several of the suspects and one part or another of the Republican power structure. For example, Mr. James W. McCord, one of the five men arrested, has worked on security problems both for the Republican National Committee and the Committee for the Re-Election of the President. Two of the group had in their personal effects the address of a Mr. Howard E. Hunt, another former CIA agent, who serves as a consultant to White House consultant Charles W. Colson. Other more tenuous links have been developed between the arrested suspects and elements of the Republican Party.

Mr. John Mitchell, the former Attorney General who is heading the committee for Mr. Nixon's re-election, has stoutly denied any knowledge of the affair as has the Chairman of the Republican National Committee, Senator Dole, as well as Mr. Ziegler. So life has imitated art up to a point; the "force" has been "caught"; "the Secretary" has "disavowed any knowledge" of its actions. What remains now to be seen—what is, in short, the crucial question in a time of waning confidence in the processes of government—is whether a Republican administration can bring itself to use every means at its command to prosecute perpetrators of the Watergate raid. From the sound of it, there would seem to be an abundance of evi-

dence in the captured equipment and freshly-minted currency.
It ought not to be left to the Democrats to dig into *Mission Incredible* by pressing a civil suit. In short, this particular tape
ought not to be allowed to self-destruct.

From *The Washington Post,* 1972.

QUESTIONS

(1) What is the connection the editorial wishes to draw between *Mission Impossible* and *Mission Incredible?*

(2) Why is the editorial so tenuous in indicating where "the
finger of suspicion" naturally points?

(3) What is the main point of the concluding paragraph?

(4) Why is the allusion to a self-destructing tape particularly
prophetic in this editorial?

MEETING: THE PRESIDENT, DEAN AND HALDEMAN, OVAL OFFICE, MARCH 21, 1973. (10:12-11:55 AM)

THE PRESIDENTIAL TRANSCRIPTS

P: Well, sit down, sit down.
  D: Good morning.
  P: Well what is the Dean summary of the day about?
  D: John caught me on the way out and asked me about
why Gray was holding back on information, if that was under
instructions from us. And it was and it wasn't. It was instructions proposed by the Attorney General, consistent with your
press conference statement that no further raw data was to be
turned over to the full committee. And that was the extent of

it. And then Gray, himself, who reached the conclusion that no more information should be turned over, that he had turned over enough. So this again is Pat Gray making decisions on his own on how to handle his hearings. He has been totally (unintelligible) to take any guidance, any instruction. We don't know what he is going to do. He is not going to talk about it. He won't review it, and I don't think he does it to harm you in any way, sir.

P: No, he is just quite stubborn and also he isn't very smart. You know—

D: He is bullheaded.

P: He is smart in his own way but he's got that typical (expletive deleted) this is right and I am going to do it.

D: That's why he thinks he is going to be confirmed. He is being his own man. He is being forthright and honest. He feels he has turned over too much and so it is conscious decision that he is harming the Bureau by doing this and so he is not going to.

P: We have to get the boys off the line that this is because the White House told him to do this and everything. And also, as I told Ehrlichman, I don't see why our little boys can't make something out of the fact that (expletive deleted) this is the only responsible position that could possibly be made. The FBI cannot turn over raw files. Has anybody made that point? I have tried to several times.

D: Sam Ervin has made that point himself. In fact, in reading the transcript of Gray's hearings, Ervin tried to hold Gray back from doing what he was doing at the time he did it. I thought it was very unwise. I don't think that anyone is criticizing your position on it.

P: Let's make a point that raw files, I mean that point should be made that we are standing for the rights of innocent individuals. The American Civil Liberties Union is against it. We are against it. Hoover had the tradition, and it will continue to be the tradition. All files are confidential. See if we can't get someone inspired to put that out. Let them see what is in one.

D: (expletive deleted) You—

P: Any further word on Sullivan? Is he still—

D: Yes, he is going to be over to see me today, this morning someplace, sometime.

P: As soon as you get that, I will be available to talk to you this afternoon. I will be busy until about one o'clock. Anytime you are through I would like to see what it is he has. We've got something but I would like to see what it is.

D: The reason that I thought we ought to talk this morning is because in our conversations, I have the impression that you don't know everything I know and it makes it very difficult for you to make judgments that only you can make on some of these things and I thought that—

P: In other words, I have to know why you feel that we shouldn't unravel something?

D: Let me give you my overall first.

P: In other words, your judgment as to where it stands, and where we will go.

D: I think that there is no doubt about the seriousness of the problem we've got. We have a cancer within, close to the Presidency, that is growing. It is growing daily. It's compounded, growing geometrically now, because it compounds itself. That will be clear if I, you know, explain some of the details of why it is. Basically, it is because (1) we are being blackmailed; (2) people are going to start perjuring themselves very quickly that have not had to perjure themselves to protect other people in the line. And there is no assurance—

P: That that won't bust?

D: That that won't bust. So let me give you the sort of basic facts, talking first about the Watergate; and then about Segretti; and then about some of the peripheral items that have come up. First of all on the Watergate: how did it all start, where did it start? O.K! It started with an instruction to me from Bob Haldeman to see if we couldn't set up a perfectly legitimate campaign intelligence operation over at the Re-Election Committee. Not being in this business, I turned to somebody who had been in this business, Jack Caulfield. I don't remember whether you remember Jack or not. He was your original bodyguard before they had the candidate protection, an old city policeman.

P: Yes, I know him.

D: Jack worked for John and then was transferred to my office. I said Jack come up with a plan that, you know—a normal infiltration, buying information from secretaries and all that sort of thing. He did, he put together a plan. It was kicked around. I went to Ehrlichman with it. I went to Mitchell with it, and the consensus was that Caulfield was not the man to do this. In retrospect, that might have been a bad call because he is an incredibly cautious person and wouldn't have put the situation where it is today. After rejecting that, they said we still need something so I was told to look around for someone who could go over to 1701 and do this. That is when I came up with Gordon Liddy. They needed a lawyer. Gordon had an intelligence background from his FBI service. I was aware of the fact that he had done some extremely sensitive things for the White House while he had been at the White House and he had apparently done them well. Going out into Ellsberg's doctor's office—

P: Oh, yeah.

D: And things like this. He worked with leaks. He tracked these things down. So the report that I got from Krogh was that he was a hell of a good man and not only that a good lawyer and could set up a proper operation. So we talked to Liddy. He was interested in doing it. I took Liddy over to meet Mitchell. Mitchell thought highly of him because Mitchell was partly involved in his coming to the White House to work for Krogh. Liddy had been at Treasury before that. Then Liddy was told to put together his plan, you know, how he would run an intelligence operation. This was after he was hired over there at the Committee. Magruder called me in January and said I would like to have you come over and see Liddy's plan.

P: January of '72?

D: January of '72.

D: "You come over to Mitchell's office and sit in a meeting where Liddy is going to lay his plan out." I said I don't really know if I am the man, but if you want me there I will be happy to. So I came over and Liddy laid out a million dollar plan that was the most incredible thing I have ever laid my eyes on: all in codes, and involved black bag operations, kidnapping, providing prostitutes to weaken the opposition, bugging, mugging teams. It was just an incredible thing.

P: Tell me this: Did Mitchell go along—?

D: No, no, not at all, Mitchell just sat there puffing and laughing. I could tell from—after Liddy left the office I said that is the most incredible thing I have ever seen. He said I agree. And so Liddy was told to go back to the drawingboard and come up with something realistic. So there was a second meeting. They asked me to come over to that. I came into the tail end of the meeting. I wasn't there for the first part. I don't know how long the meeting lasted. At this point, they were discussing again bugging, kidnapping and the like. At this point I said right in front of everybody, very clearly, I said, "These are not the sort of things (1) that are ever to be discussed in the office of the Attorney General of the United States—that was where he still was—and I am personally incensed." And I am trying to get Mitchell off the hook. He is a nice person and doesn't like to have to say no when he is talking with people he is going to have to work with.

P: That's right.

D: So I let it be known. I said "You all pack that stuff up and get it the hell out of here. You just can't talk this way in this office and you should re-examine your whole thinking."

P: Who all was present?

D: It was Magruder, Mitchell, Liddy and myself. I came back right after the meeting and told Bob, "Bob, we have a growing disaster on our hands if they are thinking this way," and I said, "The White House has got to stay out of this and I, frankly, am not going to be involved in it." He said, "I agree John." I thought at that point that the thing was turned off. That is the last I heard of it and I thought it was turned off because it was an absurd proposal.

P: Yeah.

D: Liddy—I did have dealings with him afterwards and we never talked about it. Now that would be hard to believe for some people, but we never did. That is the fact of the matter.

P: Well, you were talking with him about other things.

D: We had so many other things.

P: He had some legal problems too. But you were his advisor, and I understand you had conversations about the campaign laws, etc. Haldeman told me that you were handling all of that for us. Go ahead.

D: Now. So Liddy went back after that and was over at 1701, the Committee, and this is where I come into having put the pieces together after the fact as to what I can put together about what happened. Liddy sat over there and tried to come up with another plan that he could sell. (1) They were talking to him, telling him that he was putting too much money in it. I don't think they were discounting the illegal points. Jeb is not a lawyer. He did not know whether this is the way the game was played and what it was all about. They came up, apparently, with another plan, but they couldn't get it approved by anybody over there. So Liddy and Hunt apparently came to see Chuck Colson, and Chuck Colson picked up the telephone and called Magruder and said, "You all either fish or cut bait. This is absurd to have these guys over there and not using them. If you are not going to use them, I may use them." Things of this nature.

P: When was this?

D: This was apparently in February of '72.

P: Did Colson know what they were talking about?

D: I can only assume, because of his close relationship with Hunt, that he had a damn good idea what they were talking about, a damn good idea. He would probably deny it today and probably get away with denying it. But I still—unless Hunt blows on him—

P: But then Hunt isn't enough. It takes two doesn't it?

D: Probably. Probably. But Liddy was there also and if Liddy were to blow—

P: Then you have a problem—I was saying as to the criminal liability in the White House.

. . . .

P: Well, the erosion is inevitably going to come here, apart from anything and all the people saying well the Watergate isn't a major issue. It isn't. But it will be. It's bound to. (Unintelligible) has to go out. Delaying is the great danger to the White House area. We don't, I say that the White House can't do it. Right?

D: Yes, Sir.

From The Transcript of the White House Tapes, 1974.

QUESTIONS

(1) What two reasons does John Dean give for his belief that there is a "cancer within, close to the Presidency that is growing"?

(2) In Dean's account which officials are most responsible for the Watergate break-in?

(3) Look carefully at the questions and comments of the President. What do his comments suggest about the extent of his involvement in (1) the original break-in (2) the cover-up?

(4) According to Dean what are the most critical decisions made in the period prior to the break-in?

(5) What is meant by the reference to "Ellsberg's doctor's office"?

(6) Among other things the tapes offer striking examples of the difference between spoken and written language. Note the incomplete phrases, thoughts left unexpressed. What feature of conversation offers an advantage over writing? What feature a disadvantage?

(7) What characteristics of Dean's speaking style make it clear that he is a subordinate reporting to his boss?

THE LIMITED HANG-OUT

ARTHUR MILLER

Let us begin with a few meaningless statements. The President is the chief law-enforcement officer of the United States. He also represents what is best in the American people, if not in his every action then certainly in his aims. These assertions were violated by Lyndon Johnson, John Kennedy, Dwight Eisenhower, and Franklin Roosevelt, not once but many times in each case. Johnson fabricated the Tonkin Gulf hysteria. Kennedy set the country on the rails into Vietnam even as he espoused humanistic idealism. Eisenhower lacked the stomach

to scuttle Nixon despite his distaste, if not contempt, for Nixon's unprincipled behavior. Roosevelt tried to pack the Supreme Court when it opposed him, and stood by watching the
destruction of the Spanish Republic by Fascism because he
feared the outrage of the Catholic hierarchy if he supported
a sister democracy. And so on and on.

When necessity dictates, our laws are as bendable as licorice
to our Presidents, and if their private conversations had been
taped an awful lot of history would be different now.

Yet Nixon stands alone, for he alone is without a touch of
grace. It is gracelessness which gives his mendacity its shine of
putrescence, a want of that magnanimity and joy in being
alive that animated his predecessors. Reading the Presidential
transcripts, one is confronted with the decay of a language, of
a legal system; in these pages what was possibly the world's
best hope is reduced to a vaudeville, a laugh riot. We are in
the presence of three gangsters who moralize and a swarming
legion of their closely shaved underlings.

Let us, as the saying goes, be clear about it—more than forty
appointed cohorts of Richard Nixon are already either in jail,
under indictment, or on the threshold of jail for crimes which,
as these transcripts demonstrate, the President tried by might
and main to keep from being discovered. The chief law-enforcement officer could not find it in his heart to demand the
resignation of even one of them for betraying the public trust.
Those whom public clamor forced to depart were given sad
Presidential farewells and called "fine public servants."

This, to me, is the unexpectedly clear news in these transcripts—that, had he had the least civic, not to say moral, instinct, Richard Nixon could have been spared his agony. Had
he known how to be forthright, and, on discovering that the
direction of the Watergate burglary came, in part, from his
own official family, stood up and leveled with the public, he
would have exalted his partisans and confounded his enemies,
and, with a tremendous electoral victory in the offing, he
would have held an undisputed national leadership. Nor is
this as naive as it appears; it seems believable that he need not
have literally given the order to burgle Ellsberg's psychiatrist,
was surprised by it, in fact. If, as also seems likely, he gave the
nod to an intelligence operation against the Democrats at
some previous meeting, it would not have been the first such

strategy in political history, and he could have assumed the
responsibility for that while disclaiming the illegal means for
carrying it out. The nut of it all is that, even on the basis of
self-survival, he marched instinctively down the crooked path.

So we are back with Plutarch, for whom character is fate,
and in these transcripts Richard Nixon's character is our history. But to ask why he could not come forward and do his
duty as the chief law-enforcement officer is to ask who and
what Nixon is, and there is no one we can ask that question.
All one can really affirm is that these transcripts show certain
attributes which now are evidentiary. Like a good play these
dialogues spring from conflict surrounding a paradox: his
power as President depends on moral repute, at bottom; therefore, one would expect him to go after any of his associates
who compromised him. Instead, something entirely different
happens. He sits down with Haldeman and Ehrlichman and
proceeds to concoct a double strategy: first, to convince the
public that he was totally ignorant of the crimes, which is an
intelligent decision, and, second, to make it appear that he is
launching an outraged investigation of the facts in order to
reveal them, when actually he is using his discoveries to keep
his associates' infractions concealed. The latter objective is
impossible and therefore stupid, and in short order he finds
himself in possession of guilty knowledge, knowledge an honest man would have handed over to the requisite authorities.
So the crux is always who and what he is. Another man need
not have been swept away by events.

In the face of the sheer number of his appointees and their
underlings who turn out to be unprincipled beyond the point
of criminality, the issue is no longer whether he literally gave
the orders for the burglary and the other crimes. The subordi-
nates of another kind of man would have known that such
despicable acts were intolerable to their patron and leader
imply by their sense of his nature. That more than forty—thus
far—are incriminated or in jail speaks of a consistency of their
understanding of what this President was and what he stood
for. Many of his staff members he barely knew personally, yet
all of them obviously had caught the scent of that decay of
standards emanating from the center, and they knew what
was allowed and what was expected of them. The transcripts

provide the evidence of the leader's nature, specifically his
near-delusionary notion that because he was "the President"
he could not be doing what it was clear enough he was, in fact,
doing.

At one point he and Haldeman and Ehrlichman are discussing the question of getting Mitchell to take the entire rap,
thus drawing the lightning, but they suddenly remember John
Dean's earlier warning that the two high assistants might well
be indictable themselves.

> Nixon: We did not cover up, though, that's what decides, that's
> what's [sic] decides . . . Dean's case is the question. And I do not
> consider him guilty . . . Because if he—if that's the case, then half
> the staff is guilty.
> Ehrlichman: That's it. He's guilty of really no more except in
> degree.
> Nixon: That's right. Then [sic] others.
> Ehrlichman: Then [sic] a lot of . . .
> Nixon: And frankly then [sic] I have been since a week ago, two
> weeks ago.

And a moment later, Ehrlichman returns to the bad smell:

> But what's been bothering me is . . .
> Nixon: That with knowledge, we're still not doing anything.

So he knew that he was, at a minimum, reaching for the
forbidden fruit—obstruction of justice—since he was in possession of knowledge of a crime which he was not revealing to
any authority. One has to ask why he did not stop right there.
Is it possible that in the tapes he withheld (as of this writing)
there was evidence that his surprise at the burglary was
feigned? that, in short, he knew all along that he was protecting himself from prosecution? At this point there is no evidence of this, so we must wonder at other reasons for his so
jeopardizing his very position, and we are back again with his
character, his ideas and feelings.

There is a persistent note of plaintiveness when Nixon compares Watergate with the Democrats' crimes, attributing the
press's outcry to liberal hypocrisy. The Democratic party is
primarily corrupt, a bunch of fakers spouting humane slogans
while underneath the big city machines like Daley's steal elections, as Kennedy's victory was stolen from him in Chicago.
Welfare, gimme-politics, perpetuate the Democratic constitu-

ency. The Kennedys especially are immoral, unfaithful to family, and ruthless in pursuit of power. Worse yet, they are the real professionals who *know* how to rule with every dirty trick in the book. A sort of embittered ideology helps lower Nixon into the pit.

For the Republicans, in contrast, are naive and really amateurs at politics because they are basically decent, hardworking people. This conviction of living in the light is vital if one is to understand the monstrous distortions of ethical ideas in these transcripts. Nixon *is* decency. In fact, he is America; at one point after Dean has turned state's evidence against them, Haldeman even says, "He's not un-American and anti-Nixon." These men stand in a direct line from the Puritans of the first Plymouth Colony who could swindle and kill Indians secure in the knowledge that their cause was holy. Nixon seems to see himself as an outsider, even now, in politics. Underneath he is too good for it. When Dean, before his betrayal, tries to smuggle reality into the Oval Office—by warning that people are not going to believe that "Chapin acted on his own to put his old friend Segretti to be a Dick Tuck on somebody else's campaign. They would have to paint it into something more sinister . . . part of a general [White House] plan"—Nixon observes with a certain mixture of condemnation and plain envy, "Shows you what a master Dick Tuck is."

This ideology, like all ideologies, is a pearl formed around an irritating grain of sand, which, for Nixon, is something he calls the Establishment, meaning Eastern Old Money. "The basic thing," he says, "is the Establishment. The Establishment is dying and so they've got to show that . . . it is just wrong [the Watergate] just because of this." So there is a certain virtue in defending now what the mere duty he swore to uphold requires he root out. In a diabolical sense he seems to see himself clinging to a truth which, only for the moment, appears nearly criminal. But the *real* untruth, the real immorality shows up in his mind very quickly—it is Kennedy, and he is wondering if they can't put out some dirt on Chappaquiddick through an investigator they had working up there. But like every other such counterattack this one falls apart because it could lead back to Kalmbach's paying his investigator with campaign funds, an illegal usage. So the minuet starts up and

stops time after time, a thrust blunted by the realization that
it can only throw light upon what must be kept in the dark.
Yet their conviction of innocent and righteous intentions
stands undisturbed by their knowledge of their own vulnerability.

And it helps to explain, this innocence and righteousness,
why they so failed to appraise reality, in particular that they
were *continuing* to act in obstruction of justice by concealing
what they knew, and what they knew they knew, and what
they told one another they knew. It is not dissimilar to Johnson's persistence in Vietnam despite every evidence that the
war was unjust and barbarous, for Good People do not commit crimes, and there is simply no way around that.

Yet from time to time Nixon senses that he is floating inside
his own psyche. "If we could get a feel," he says, "I just have
a horrible feeling that we may react. . . ."

> HALDEMAN: Yes. That we are way overdramatizing.
> NIXON: That's my view. That's what I don't want to do either.
> [A moment later] Am I right that we have got to do something to
> restore the credibility of the Presidency?

And on the verge of reality the ideology looms, and they
scuttle back into the hole—Haldeman saying, "Of course you
know the credibility gap in the old [Democratic] days." So
there they are, comfortably right again, the only problem being how to prove it to the simpletons outside.

Again, like any good play, the transcripts reflect a single
situation or paradox appearing in a variety of disguises that
gradually peel away the extraneous until the central issue is
naked. In earlier pages they are merely worried about bad
publicity, then it is the criminal indictment of one or another
of the secondary cadres of the Administration, until finally the
heart of darkness is endangered, Haldeman and Ehrlichman
and thus Nixon himself. In other words, the mistake called
Watergate, an incident they originally view as uncharacteristic
of them, a caper, a worm that fell on their shoulders, turns out
to be one of the worms inside them that crawled out.

So the aspects of Nixon which success had once obscured
now become painfully parodistic in his disaster. He almost becomes a pathetically moving figure as he lifts his old slogans
out of his bag. He knows now that former loyalists are testify-

ing secretly to the grand jury, so he erects the facade of his own "investigation," which is nothing but an attempt to find out what they are testifying to, the better to prepare himself for the next explosion; he reverts time and again to recalling his inquisitorial aptitude in the Hiss case, which made him a national figure. But now he is on the other end of the stick, and, after a string of calculations designed to cripple the Ervin Committee, he declaims, "I mean, after all, it is my job and I don't want the Presidency tarnished, but also I am a law-enforcement man," even as he is trying to lay the whole thing off on Mitchell, the very symbol of hard-line law enforcement, the former Attorney General himself.

Things degenerate into farce at times, as when he knows the Ervin Committee and the Grand Jury are obviously out of his control and on the way to eating him up and he speaks of making a "command decision." It is a sheer unconscious dullness of a magnitude worthy of Ring Lardner's baseball heroes. There are scenes, indeed, which no playwright would risk for fear of seeming too mawkishly partisan.

For example, the idea comes to Nixon repeatedly that he must act with candor, simply, persuasively. Now, since John Dean has been up to his neck in the details of the various attempts to first discover and then hide the truth, should Dean be permitted by the President to appear before a grand jury, eminently qualified as he is as the knower of facts? The President proceeds to spitball a public announcement before Ehrlichman's and Ziegler's sharp judgmental minds:

NIXON: Mr. Dean certainly wants the opportunity to defend himself against these charges. He would welcome the opportunity and what we have to do is to work out a procedure which will allow him to do so consistent with his unique position of being a top member of the President's staff but also the Counsel. There is a lawyer, Counsel . . . [it starts breaking down] not lawyer, Counsel—but the responsibility of the Counsel for confidentiality.
ZIEGLER: Could you apply that to the grand jury?
EHRLICHMAN: Absolutely. The grand jury is one of those occasions where a man in his situation can defend himself.
NIXON: Yes. The grand jury. Actually, if called, we are not going to refuse for anybody called before the grand jury to go, are we, John?
EHRLICHMAN: Well, if called, he will be cooperative, consistent with his responsibilities as Counsel. How do we say that?
EHRLICHMAN: He will cooperate.

NIXON: He will fully cooperate.
EHRLICHMAN: Better check that with Dean. I know he's got cer-
tain misgivings on this.
ZIEGLER: He did this morning.
NIXON: Yeah. Well, then, don't say that.

Refusing himself his tragedy, Nixon ends in farce. After another of many attempts at appearing "forthcoming" and being
thwarted yet again by all the culpability in the house, he suddenly exclaims, "What the hell does one disclose that isn't
going to blow something?" Thus speaketh the first law-
enforcement officer of the United States. Excepting that this
government is being morally gutted on every page, it is to
laugh. And the humor of their own absurdity is not always
lost on the crew, although it is understandably laced with
pain. They debate whether John Mitchell might be sent into
the Ervin Committee, but in an executive session barred to the
public and TV and under ground rules soft enough to tie up
the Old Constitutionalist in crippling legalisms.

NIXON: Do you think we want to go this route now? Let it hang
out so to speak?
DEAN: Well, it isn't really that . . .
HALDEMAN: It's a limited hang-out.
DEAN: It is a limited hang-out. It's not an absolute hang-out.
NIXON: But some of the questions look big hanging out publicly
or privately. [Still, he presses the possibility.] If it opens doors, it
opens doors . . .

As usual it is Haldeman who is left to interpolate the consequences.

John says he is sorry he sent those burglars in there—and that
helps a lot.
NIXON: That's right.
EHRLICHMAN: You are very welcome, sir.

(Laughter), the script reads then, and along with everything
else it adds to the puzzle of why Nixon ordered his office
bugged in the first place, and especially why he did not turn
off the machine once the magnitude of Watergate was clear to
him. After all, no one but he and the technicians in the secret
service knew the spools were turning.

As a nonsubscriber to the school of psychohistory—having
myself served as the screen upon which Norman Mailer, no
less, projected the lesions of his own psyche, to which he gave

my name—I would disclaim the slightest inside knowledge, if
that be necessary, and rest simply on the public importance of
this question itself. Watergate aside, it is a very odd thing for
a man to bug himself. Perhaps the enormity of it is better felt
if one realizes that in a preelectronic age a live stenographer
would have had to sit concealed in Nixon's office as he exchanged affections with a Haldeman, whom he admired and
whose fierce loyalty moved him deeply. At a minimum, does it
not speak a certain contempt even for those he loved to have
subjected his relationship with them to such recorded scrutiny? Can he ever have forgotten that the record was being
made as he laughed with friends, heard their personal troubles
and perhaps embarrassing secrets? What manner of man can
so split himself? How could he have made this jibe with any
notion of honor? And again, why didn't he turn the damned
thing off once he saw where Watergate was leading him? It
seems to me that the very heart of his perplexing nature is in
this question. Is it conceivable for an Eisenhower, a Truman,
a Kennedy, a Roosevelt to have done this? It doesn't seem so,
and the reason is interesting—these men, different as they
were, possessed a certain spontaneity which could not have
borne the weight of knowing they were speaking into a microphone from morning to night, and spontaneity is a form
of grace that Nixon lacks.

One can imagine two purposes for Nixon taping his own
life. A secret record would help in case he needed it to confound political enemies who might distort what he told them.
But this has a paranoid implication. It means that he must
have felt himself utterly alone, surrounded by enemies. Sec-
ondly, the transcripts show him as wishing to go down in history as the great peacemaker, and his public speeches demonstrate that he relies heavily on his peacemaking role to justify
the highest place in history. The pre-Watergate rationale can
very possibly have been a desire to monumentalize himself, an
emotion by no means unprecedented in leaders. But to offer
one's every relationship to this monument is to live, in effect,
as though one were already dead. In the act of being permanently taped he becomes his own subject, his own feminine,
while at the same time he controls or masters whoever is sitting obliviously before him. He partakes secretly of that god-

head which remembers everything and thereby holds control. Taping his life is the conception of a man desperate for reassurance as to his power, and it was to that power that Nixon offered up himself and his associates, friend and foe alike, day after day.

The transcripts make it easier to understand why he should so doubt his innate potency, his authority. Ehrlichman and Haldeman interrupt him at will as though he were an equal or less, cutting across his statements so frequently that I am sure a count would show he has more broken speeches by far than anyone in those pages. He is almost never addressed as "Mr. President," or even as "sir," except by Henry Petersen, whose sense of protocol and respect, like—remarkably enough —John Mitchell's, stands in glaring contrast to the locker-room familiarity of his two chief lieutenants. He can hardly ever assert a policy idea without ending with, "Am I right?" or, "You think so?" It is not accidental that both Ehrlichman and Haldeman, like Colson, were so emphatically rough and, in some reports, brutal characters. They were his devils and he their god, but a god because the Good inhabits him while they partake of it but are his mortal side and must sometimes reach into the unclean.

To turn off the tapes, then, when an elementary sense of survival would seem to dictate their interruption, would be to make an admission which, if it were made, would threaten his very psychic existence and bring on the great dread against which his character was formed—namely, that he is perhaps fraudulent, perhaps a fundamentally fearing man, perhaps not really enlisted in the cause of righteousness but merely in his own aggrandizement of power, and power for the purpose not of creativity and good but of filling the void where spontaneity and love should be. Nixon will not admit his share of evil in himself, and so the tapes must go on turning, for the moment he presses that STOP button he ends the godly illusion and must face his human self. He can record his own open awareness that he and his two bravos are quite possibly committing crime in the sun-filled, pristine White House itself, but as long as the tapes turn, a part of him is intrepidly recording the bald facts, as God does, and thereby bringing the day of judgment closer, the very judgment he has abhorred and dearly wants. For the hope of being justified at the very,

very end is a fierce hope, as is the fear of being destroyed for the sins whose revelation and admission will alone crown an evaded, agonized life with meaning. The man aspires to the heroic. No one, not even his worst enemies, can deny his strength, his resiliency. But it is not the strength of the confronter, as is evidenced by his inability to level with John Mitchell, whom he privately wants to throw to the wolves but face to face cannot blame. It is rather the perverse strength of the private hero testing his presumptions about himself against God, storming an entrance into his wished-for nature which never seems to embrace him but is always an arm's length away. Were he alive to a real authority in him, a true weight of his own existing, such a testing would never occur to him. There are leaders who take power because they have found themselves, and there are leaders who take power in search of themselves. A score of times in those pages Nixon refers to "the President" as though he were the President's emissary, a *Doppelgänger*. Excepting in official documents did Roosevelt, Eisenhower, Kennedy, even Truman, so refer to himself? Surely not in private conversation with their closest friends. But to stop those tapes would mean the end of innocence, and in a most cruelly ironic way, an act of true forthrightness.

If such was his drama, he forged the sword that cut him down. It was a heroic struggle except that it lacked the ultimate courage of self-judgment and the reward of insight. Bereft of the latter, he is unjust to himself and shows the world his worst while his best he buries under his pride and the losing hope that a resurrected public cynicism will rescue his repute. For it is not enough now, the old ideology that the Democrats are even more corrupt. The President is not a Democrat or Republican here, he is as close as we get to God.

And if his struggle was indeed to imprint his best presumptions upon history, and it betrayed him, it is a marvel that it took place now, when America has discovered the rocky terrain where her innocence is no more, where God is simply what happens, and what has happened, and if you like being called good you have to do good, if only because other nations are no longer powerlessly inert but looking on with X-ray eyes, and you no longer prevail for the yellow in your silky hair. The most uptight leader we have had, adamantly resisting the

age, has backhandedly announced the theme of its essential
drama in his struggle—to achieve authenticity without paying
authenticity's price—and in his fall. The hang-out—it is a
marvel, is unlimited; at long last, after much travail, Richard
Nixon is one of us.

From Harper's Magazine, 1974.

QUESTIONS

(1) Arthur Miller suggests that the transcripts of the Watergate tapes read like the dialogue of a play that "spring[s] from
conflict surrounding a paradox." What is that paradox?

(2) Miller further develops his analogy to a play when he
writes "like any good play, the transcripts reflect a . . . paradox . . . that gradually peel[s] away . . . until the central
issue is naked." How does Miller proceed to describe the "central issue?"

(3) Again, using the play metaphor, Miller argues that the fall
of Richard Nixon is more a *farce* than a *tragedy*. What is the
basis for this observation?

(4) Miller is fascinated by the fact that Nixon continued to
tape himself even after the Watergate issue represented a clear
threat to him. What explanation does he offer for Nixon's self-
incriminating act?

(5) What does Miller mean by his frequent references to Nixon's desire to be God?

(6) Miller's concluding paragraph speaks of the struggle "to
achieve authenticity without paying authenticity's price."
What is the connection between that theme and his analysis of
the character of Richard Nixon?

THE MYTH OF AN ADVERSARY PRESS

TOM BETHELL

It has become a commonplace, I know, to say that the recent Presidential campaign demonstrated the increasingly indistinguishable nature of media and government, to say that it has become impossible, finally, to discern that "the campaign" means anything more than the coverage of the campaign; and it is almost superfluous to point out, because it is done so often, that the media grow more powerful with every passing day, in inverse ratio to the ever-declining strength of the political parties themselves. But these points, well known as they are, exemplify the more general point that I want to make—one that is not so often pointed out—that the news media have now become a part of the government in all but formal constitutional ratification of the fact. For all intents and purposes, *The New York Times* or CBS News can best be understood as departments of the federal bureaucracy.

I do not wish to adopt an accusatory tone—to speak with the voice of Spiro Agnew. It may well be that the new media-government alliance is a good one, all things considered. It almost certainly is unavoidable, given the technology upon which it relies. It is, however, a new combination—one that could not have been foreseen by the framers of the Constitution—and my concern is simply to try and describe it, not an easy task, given that media and government alternately dance together in close embrace, and break apart to make confusing gestures of mutual defiance. Much of the time what we are witnessing is the equivalent of a marathon dance, in which media and government lean on each other because they need each other to survive and prosper.

Their partnership gives rise to strange illusions. One begins to suspect that things aren't quite as they seem in the phantasmagoria of the electronic screen, in the endless droning of the nightly news, which threatens to make media junkies of us all, primed for the fix of crisis, and its attendant escalation of interest and receptiveness to media soothsayers. Take Wa-

tergate, for example, that peculiar succession of events leading
nowhere but to the creation of more or less salable images.
Monotonously one reads in the columns of such contemporary
pundits as Joseph Kraft and Anthony Lewis that Watergate
was a "crisis," so much so that one begins to suspect that they
have some personal stake in the matter: the crisis from which
they helped to rescue us. They remind us of the crisis of Vietnam and the crisis of Watergate, which led to a general disenchantment with politicians and a loss of faith in government,
and more. But I do not believe that Watergate was a crisis at
all.

I feel this way because I don't know one person who didn't
thoroughly enjoy it from beginning to end. Friends of mine
were carrying portable televisions to work so as not to miss
any of the fun. Surely it was a melodrama, not a crisis. A surprisingly bloodless melodrama. There were no victims of Watergate, save a number of people in the White House, and a
few other odd characters, such as G. Gordon Liddy, still in
jail. But most of them seem to be ending up with books on
the best-seller lists, with publishing, television, and movie
"deals." With media deals, that is. And the journalists didn't
do too badly out of Watergate, either. Don't forget that. More
and more, in retrospect, Watergate seems to have involved a
nearly invisible sleight of hand, which deftly transmuted what
may not have been so very far from government-as-usual into
"crisis" into lecture-circuit appearances and Book-of-the-
Month Club success for all hands involved.

How, then, did it happen? Why is it that the media now
seem so often to assume the role of provoking this or that
"crisis," which may be only apparent? The conventional answer, I know, is that the news media's job is to police the government, to keep it honest, to blow the whistle, to defend the
people's right to know, to stand watchfully on the ramparts
of freedom and democracy. But that strikes me as being comparable to a good magician's patter—designed to distract.

What is the first thing one notices about the performance
of the media today? (By media let me stress I mean the Big
Media: the three television networks, the two wire services,
Time and *Newsweek,* and a handful of newspapers whose influence is disproportionately greater than their circulation,

such as *The New York Times* and *The Washington Post*.) I believe the most important element in their handling of the
news is something that one is at first in danger of not noticing
at all, because it is so reasonable-seeming and all-pervasive: I
refer to the way in which the news organizations in question
are above all relentlessly and strenuously impartial in their
presentation of political events. They don't take sides. Having chosen the only important side—that of big government
and all its works—the media can affect an olympian stance
with regard to mere squabbling of factions.

Coming to Washington as I did, just over a year after President Nixon's resignation, I think I half expected to find *The
Washington Post* a thinly disguised house organ for the Democratic party, reminiscent of the old days when most newspapers were controlled by this or that political party. I could not
have been more wrong. During the Presidential campaign, for
example, it was impossible to detect any bias in *The Post*'s
news columns, and there was scarcely any in the editorials,
either. The televised debates, for example, were always followed by photographs of the two candidates that were scrupulously identical in position and size. The same was true of
headlines. As for *The Post*'s final "endorsement," it was so
carefully balanced as to be ineffectual.

This "objectivity" of the Big Media is so carefully sustained
that, I believe, an intelligent observer coming to this country
from a far-off land might well conclude, after a good deal of
puzzlement, that the government itself ran the entire publicity
apparatus here, and, in deference to the people's will, did so
in a spirit of scrupulous fair-mindedness. (Editors might well
be appointed to their positions in the Media Branch of government after they had shown the requisite degree of wisdom
and impartiality in one of the other branches, much as judges
are appointed in fact.)

In the case of television, of course, such a judgment would
not be so far from the truth, inasmuch as the impartiality of
television news is dictated by the Fairness Doctrine of the
Federal Communications Commission, which is to say, by the
government. This is one of the most striking counter-examples
to the First Amendment decree that the government "shall
make no law . . . abridging the freedom of speech, or of the
press," but media people as a rule do not quibble with it, al-

though at other times they find the First Amendment as compelling and unalterable as the Ten Commandments.

They do well not to quibble. The Fairness Doctrine, and the resulting equable treatment of the news, result in all manner of unsuspected but delightful benefits to the media, and, less conspicuously to the government. Perhaps most important, the media instantly appear clothed in the robes of judicial impartiality—not as snapping prosecutor, haranguing defender. Not as being anti-Ford, anti-Carter, but as above the dirty political battle entirely. Walter Cronkite, it has often been said, has a credibility exceeding that of Presidents. As a result, he is from time to time urged to run for office himself. But he has sensibly declined, no doubt appreciating the extent to which his credibility stems from his position as umpire, not participant.

No doubt the influential newspapers assumed their present guise of impartiality as a result of the example provided by television. How much better, after all, to be perceived as impartial than as being the captive of this or that party. That is precisely what makes a newspaper influential. (Incidentally, the widespread, and I believe largely erroneous, public perception of *The Washington Post* as the nemesis of Richard Nixon may have been nice for the paper's immediate prestige and profits; but it had, I believe, a secondary and undesirable backlash in giving it the appearance of partisanship.)

Thus the "fairness" of the media automatically sets the media up as judges, but as judges of what? Not, as it turns out, of the political issues themselves, because to adjudicate such issues would inevitably result in the very partisanship the media above all avoids, but as judges of events that are perceived as having moral or ethical weight, questions of character, "leadership," and personality. The political issues themselves are not ignored, of course, but they get the "equal treatment," which tends to result in a zero sum. The questions of conscience get the full treatment, with the result that last year's campaign was perceived as a series of gaffes and missteps and exposures of ethical shortcomings. In response to this there has been, I believe, a kind of moral escalation in politics, with President-elect Carter emerging as a man who was able (but barely) to be holier than the media. (He had better be careful, though, because the media don't like looking up to anyone. If it is true, as one hears, that Carter doesn't like the press, he will do well to tread warily if he is going to engage in Nixonian confrontations with it. The press loves these confrontations more than anything—while pretending to deplore them—because, as I hope to show, the mechanics of confrontation tend to confirm the press in its pose as the custodian of conscience.)

The media's broad political impartiality also tends to validate the general framework of political discourse. The "equal and opposite" placement of Ford and Carter by the same token "rationalizes" the elimination of Eugene McCarthy from the debates. The FCC's Fairness Doctrine makes "equal treatment" of alternative candidates "impossible," and so their candidacies are treated as though they were impossible by the media, which in turn really does make them impossible. So at this point government and media agree to their mutually convenient roles.

There is, however, another and a more subtle side effect of the media's neutral status. And it is here that we get close to the point where the magician's bland patter distracts us. It results in the government being perceived, by and large as a monolithic entity, and one that is rather inclined toward wickedness and corruption (could it but get away with it), while the dispassionately critical press emerges triumphantly on the side of "the people." This has the effect of disguising the extent to which the actual evidence of corruption, when it is forthcoming, is provided by people who work for the government. As a matter of fact, the government is not monolithic at all. It wars with itself. This has always been true, but in recent years a new mechanism has played a critical role in amplifying this internal government struggling: a hidden coupling, or connection, between government and media whereby dissident opinion, contradictory evidence, hitherto "secret" documents, can appear in the hands of the media. The precise location of this connection, namely, the identity of the leaker, according to an interpretation of the First Amendment that its beneficiaries in the media have been strenuously promoting of late, is said to be immune from government scrutiny—as sacrosanct as the confessional.

Note that the media themselves urge the secrecy and integrity of this government-to-media connection. That is because it enables them to play a role in government. It gives them what they are pleased to call "policy significance," which is better than reprinting handouts. Journalists also enjoy the considerable fringe benefits of wealth and prestige that have accrued, in some cases, as a result.

Suppose, for a minute, that the Constitution was *not* tacitly interpreted (as it now is) in such a way as to countenance secrecy between media and government. Suppose that, as a result (knowing he would soon be identified by government investigators if he spoke to the press and subsequently tried to remain anonymous) Deep Throat had early on called a press conference to explain what he told Bob Woodward about goings-on in the White House. Would we, the people, be any the worse off? Or would the losers have been Woodward, Bernstein, *The Washington Post,* the media?

It was Watergate, of course, that saw the government-to-media connection working with maximum effectiveness, but we tend not to perceive it that way, becaue the "issue" was so rapidly and so effectively transformed into a contest between media and government: the bad guys of the government strenuously guarding their nefarious doings from view, versus the good guys of the press, the investigative journalists, who were stripping away the veils of secrecy. And yet the evidence of government corruption came from the government, either from well-placed insiders, such as Deep Throat, or from official investigators who leaked the evidence being accumulated in those investigations before their results were publicly declared. The great advantage the press had going for it was that its "policy decisions," made in an editor's office, were arrived at much more quickly than the cumbersomely slow formal investigations, thus enabling the press to proclaim the government's own findings ahead of government. As a result, government tended to appear indifferent to corruption within its boundaries, and the press, once again, came out looking like the savior of the republic.

This argument was lucidly presented by Edward Jay Epstein in an article in the July 1974 issue of *Commentary* entitled "Did the Press Uncover Watergate?"

> In keeping with the mythic view of journalism, the book [*All The President's Men*] never describes the "behind-the-scenes" in-

vestigators which actually "smashed the Watergate scandal wide
open"—namely the investigations conducted by the FBI, the federal prosecutors, the grand jury, and the Congressional committees. The work of almost all those institutions, which unearthed
and developed all the actual evidence and disclosures of Watergate, is systematically ignored or minimized by Bernstein and
Woodward. Instead, they simply focus on those parts of the prosecutors' case, the grand jury investigation, and the FBI reports that
were leaked to them.

It is perhaps superfluous to say that Epstein's article did
nothing to alter the mythic view of journalism, which was
subsequently fixed more firmly than ever by the arrival of
Robert Redford and his film crew in Washington. Certainly
Woodward and Bernstein have not found it necessary to answer Epstein's argument; after all, they never claimed that
they broke the case open. Here, as it happens, their principal
allies were Ron Ziegler and Richard Nixon, whose angry de-
nunciations of *The Post* contributed, more than anything else,
to the public perception of *The Post,* and not the federal investigators, as David taking Goliath.
. . . .
. . . Journalists in Washington today play an ex officio pol-
icy role that would have been unrecognizable in the bad old
days (recalled by some journalists with an understandable
shudder of distaste) when their badge of office was a green eye-
shade and a whiskey bottle on the desk. Armed, now, with a
novel interpretation of the First Amendment that has shifted
the locus of acceptable secrecy, they will not easily surrender
their new importance. It translates into wealth and social
status, after all. Proximity to power in Washington has always
conferred status, and today important journalists do not
merely have proximity, they have the real thing.

Sally Quinn, who writes about Washington society for *The
Washington Post,* touched on this in a recent article which
managed to give a more revealing picture of the press than
most press critics ever achieve. Discussing the "ins and outs of
Carter's Washington" she wrote:

> The press in general feels that no matter who wins or loses, the
> politicians will be gone in four or eight years, and they, the press,
> will be around forever. So they don't care how they fit in. It will be
> nice to make friends and cultivate sources, but there is a real an-
> ticipation of a new adversary relationship. The Carter types resent

the press. Not the way Nixon did, but they feel the press is "snotty," has gotten out of hand and needs to be put in its place. But the press is big socially in Washington these days, and Carter needs the press. There will be tentative mutual cultivation here.

I formed much the same impression some months ago when I went to the Kennedy Center in Washington for the premiere of the film *America at the Movies*. The party that was held beforehand somehow managed to dramatize much that I have been trying to say. The guest list had been broken down into a number of categories: Senate, House of Representatives, Supreme Court, Administration, Hollywood, Media. An occasional Hollywood figure would come strolling by, complete with retinue. Here and there an inconspicuous Administration figure or two might have been noticed by the alert observer. Congressmen and Senators were, it seemed, disconsolately munching popcorn in quiet corners of the room, when they could be recognized at all. (Was that Senator McIntyre? J. Bennett Johnston of Louisiana? Did it matter?)

But, ah, here in the very center of the room was a pair of familiar faces, ringed by a crowd which seemed to be keeping a respectful distance. Woodward of *The Post* and Schorr of CBS were engaged in earnest conversation. The keepers of the secrets? They were the center of attention. True, a Kissinger or a Moynihan could have competed on equal terms, but the media, on this occasion, held our undivided attention. What, one wondered, were Woodward and Schorr discussing? A loud band at the end of the room prevented one from hearing much of anything, but one felt it would be imprudent to overhear so much as a word of *this* particular conversation, lest one accidentally become privy to . . . how best to describe it? . . . state secrets!

From Harper's Magazine, 1977.

QUESTIONS

(1) What is the general theme—the topic sentence of the first paragraph and of the entire essay?

(2) How does the author define the term "media"? Does that appear to be a legitimate definition or should it be extended to include all aspects of public communication?

(3) What is the author's objection to the Fairness Doctrine that governs television news?

(4) What arguments are offered in support of the view that the press was given more credit for the Watergate exposure than it deserved? Is there a counter-argument?

(5) The quotation from Sally Quinn suggests a new adversary relationship between the press and the Carter administration. What is the presumed basis of the opposition?

(6) The author concludes half facetiously with an anecdote. What point is the story designed to illustrate?

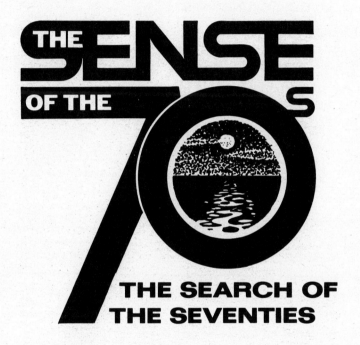

THE SENSE OF THE 70s

THE SEARCH OF THE SEVENTIES

The search for personal happiness had led in two directions, East and West. The Western road is exemplified by the "Me Decade" syndrome: the attempt to develop the autonomous inner self that is the goal of psychoanalysis and other forms of therapy. The Eastern way is reflected in the desire to lose the self, to merge the individual identity with a collective or communal one. Not surprisingly the latter route has taken on a specifically religious character. Many young people have chosen a life modeled on the practices and disciplines of Oriental religions or, in some cases, of early Christian and Judaic movements. The Eastern way is most clearly evident in the spread of such movements as Transcendental Meditation, Hare Krishna, Jesus communes, in the followers of the Reverend Sung Yung Moon and in the numerous gurus and yogis who have attracted large followings of young people throughout the country.

Why have so many been attracted to this apparently exotic, far-out mode of life? The answers range from rebellion to an intuitive sense that Western life has strained both the environment and the individual psyche to the limit. The selections that follow examine both the causes and consequences of these explorations in a realm about which little is known.

The opening selections offer two accounts of communal life. The first of these is June Jordan's discussion of a Christian commune in Georgia that follows, with edifying fidelity, the original teachings of Christ. The second selection focuses on The Farm, a remarkably successful experiment in communal living. Following these is Harvey Cox's sympathetic analysis of the appearance of Oriental religion in our society. Finally, William Irwin Thompson explores some of the truly extraordinary intellectual possibilities that may emerge from a marriage of Western science and Eastern mysticism; he suggests that the Eastern and Western searches have now reached a point of intersection.

A CHURCH WITHOUT WALLS

JUNE JORDAN

. . . the freedom, here, to become really friends with men, with my brothers . . . the freedom to fail. We are getting away from result-orientation and that kind of ego trip. I leave the success to God. And that gives you more freedom to just try more things, and then you have the support of the Fellowship here. Your work and your life are one thing.

Peggy, a member of a commune in Georgia

Koinonia (pronounced coin-o-NEE-a) means "community" in Greek. The Georgia commune called Koinonia is a 1400-acre farm which is regarded by its members as "a gift from God." The focus is threefold: to provide income for the community, to serve other people in need, and to deepen the fellowship among the believers. The land, the cinder-block and wood-frame housing, and the equipment are things not owned by anyone, except the entire group.

Founded 30 years ago, Koinonia has endured through a difficult history of Ku Klux Klan-inspired bombings, burnings, and boycotts of their produce. During the 1950s, this racially integrated community came under racist attack and slander by hostile neighbors who viewed the commune as "a nigger-loving, communist hotbed of troublemakers." As a result, the internal commitment was strengthened and a policy of outreach developed.

Of the 70 to 150 communards, most are "resident partners": married and unmarried men and women, black and white, who make an indefinite, long-term commitment to work for Christ through labor and community life at Koinonia. The commune provides its members with a subsistence-level allowance; a little under $200 a month for a family of four. Others are visitors and volunteers. Volunteers commit themselves for differing periods of participation and service: two weeks to two years. In return, they receive roughly $10 a week, plus bed

and board. Members divest themselves of material securities:
even life and health insurance policies are cashed in, and the
cash given away, so all are equal. The common ideal is the
ideal of investing yourself in people rather than material
goods. Thus, it is a truly Christian commune, and everyone is
welcome. Members maintain 30 to 40 head of cattle, raise peanuts, pecans, corn, grapes, and strawberries, as cash crops, and
have recently developed candy-making and a new sewing industry.

Plumbing, carpentry, equipment repair, housing construction, and a child-care center provide employment as well as
fulfilling practical needs. Previously indigent Southern blacks
rise from employee or coworker status to assume eventual, full
responsibility and complete control.

The pecans alone provide financial self-sufficiency. In addition, the Koinonia newsletter goes out to 30,000 friends
around the world, whose contributions of interest-free loans,
or outright gifts, sustain "The Fund of Humanity." In turn,
Koinonia uses these monies to sponsor its partnerships, to issue
interest-free loans and mortgages to its neighbors, and run an
adult literary and sex education program for the surrounding
impoverished population.

Nobody pretends that entry to a Christian commune con-
fers automatic, spontaneous answers to all questions. But
everyone is deeply involved with a sense of revolutionary commitment to Christian ideals.

"It's about brotherhood," says one member. "It obviously
means that someone who lives in Vietnam is my brother, that
God created them and loves them as much as me. And I have
no right to go to war, to kill that brother, or to pay taxes that
let somebody else kill my brother for me. . . . I wish all
women could be free the way I am, and have a supportive
body to be with them, whatever happens."

From Ms. Magazine, 1974.

QUESTIONS
(1) Peggy, the woman quoted at the beginning of the essay,
speaks of "getting away from result-orientation and that kind
of ego trip." How would you paraphrase her statement?

(2) What is the relation of the economical structure of the commune to its religious beliefs?

(3) Do you feel that the principles upon which the commune's priorities are based are too unrealistic to be extended to the outside world?

THE FARM

SUZANNE CHARLÉ

Spring has come to the Farm. Rows of cool green shoots of winter wheat have poked their way through the rust-colored Tennessee soil. The farm crew is busy planting onions and potatoes, while the mechanics preen the tractors and combines which will eventually harvest tons of soybeans, white potatoes and other produce—enough to feed the 900 folks living on what is, perhaps, the largest commune in the United States.

Things have not always been so hopeful. Five years ago when Stephen Gaskin, the spiritual leader of the Farm, led his caravan of 200 flower children from the psychedelic frenzy of San Francisco to the rolling countryside of central Tennessee in search of a religious and self-sufficient life, the soil was not so fertile, and the would-be farmers knew more about harvesting window boxes of cannabis than hundreds of acres of sorghum. And then there were the locals—good, God-fearing dirt farmers, who were less than happy with the arrival of their bearded neighbors in Day-Glo buses.

The first was not an easy year [in Summertown]. Stephen and some others were busted for growing grass and the vegetarian diet proved hard on some members.

But the Farmers were determined. Men apprenticed themselves out to farmers in the area, volunteering their labor in exchange for knowledge. They learned quickly which crops would take to the soil and which would not, which fertilizers and insecticides were necessary. And the women sought help from the state and deciphered which nutritional supplements were necessary for a balanced diet. Still others learned the art of midwifery—a very important calling in a community that uses no form of chemical or mechanical birth control and that takes pride in centering itself around children ("That's why we're doin' this," one father said, "for our kids").

And the Farm, with surprising speed, transformed itself from yet another doomed Utopia to a thriving community which has quadrupled its population in the past five years and attracts over 15,000 visitors annually. It has gained the admiration of state officials to the point where a number of teenagers, otherwise destined for detention homes, have been sent to spend time on the Farm. And, more important, it has gained the respect of local inhabitants: a congregation in Summertown has just donated its old church building to the Farm. The sheriff who arrested Stephen some years back maintains he wouldn't mind having his own son live on the Farm. "When I was young," he says, "if one of the farmers would get sick, all the neighbors would go ahead and catch his crop up, clear his land for him. They don't do that now, not here. But they still do that at the Farm. I had a fire out here last year, coming toward my house. And next thing I know, here they are—and I bet there were fifty of them—and they got the fire put out."

The fact that the Farm has met with so much success here in the heart of the Bible Belt is no fluke: the old values do not stop with neighborliness. The community considers itself a spiritual entity, and the religion taught by Stephen at Sunday meetings and practiced by all throughout the rest of the week is a curious blend of Eastern disciplines and Christianity.

Indeed, life here is possibly more traditional than in the surrounding fundamentalist towns. Men wear beards and women (referred to as "ladies" on the Farm) usually wear long skirts. By and large, they stick to traditional male/female roles. Even the speech of the Farmers is a curious patois of Biblical language and hip slang.

Perhaps the most glaring difference between the young people on the Farm and their counterparts elsewhere is their attitude about sex. Casual sex on the Farm is openly rejected and sex at an early age is discouraged. Couples living together are considered engaged, and those who have babies, married. Marriage itself is considered a holy and permanent state; the family is central to life on the Farm, and consequently "hanky-panky," as the Farmers call it, is *verboten*.

For those outside the Farm's gates, the concept of 900 people living in a community with no courts or written codes, all getting along, all working for the greater good, is not an easy one to comprehend. And yet this is what the Farm seems to have achieved. All material goods are held in common; those who live within the Farm's confines surrender all possessions to the Farm. No currency is used, people take what they need from the Farm store, children are educated at the Farm school and health needs are paid for by the Farm (the funds for these and other expenses incurred by the Farm come from money brought in by construction work in neighboring communities, sale of excess produce and money handed over by those joining the Farm). Everyone, residents claim, stands equal: the woman who is in charge of the Farm's budget—over $700,000 in 1975—is paid no salary and lives in the same type of house, eats the same food, as a man on the construction crew.

And while there are various levels of responsibility, there is, members claim, no hierarchy. If a person wants to work on the press, he or she must go and apprentice and, as the person's skill increases, so will the responsibilities. Assuming there are two people equally qualified for the same job, they will either share it or expand operations. And if a certain job is not being done, volunteers will be sought and found without pressure, say the Farmers. Everyone pitches in, even on jobs that the "square world" (Farmers' definition for the rest of humanity) would shun and find unpleasant, such as shoveling a ton of manure from truck to field. "We really be fair and loving," explains David Frohman, who does much of the photography for the Farm's books and pamphlets and who has, he says, spent many joyous hours shoveling cow dung. "Everybody here depends on everybody else. We can't have worries and be jockeying for social position."

The Farm, to be sure, is an idyllic community which has accomplished amazing things, and aims to accomplish more. It recently sent 30 tons of free food to British Honduras and has a crew seeking out a freighter so that similar missions can be carried out solely by the Farm. Several Farmers are being sent through medical school, and shows are being videotaped to spread the word of Stephen's teachings and the Farm's activities.

But all of this has been accomplished at a cost. The Farm is not an open society. Although they are free to visit, agnostics really have no place here, nor do those who believe that the individual comes before the group. The person who wants to live by himself in a house of his own should look elsewhere. This is a homogeneous community, one that accepts one man as its spiritual leader and its best example. Some people, long-term Farm citizens, find they can't take the thick communal ties, the simple life of the "voluntary peasant." And they have left this bit of Eden for the "square world," a place of quirks and violence, intense individualism and seemingly infinite diversity.

But for those who remain, this community, where all are one, is a very real and viable way to deal with this thing called life; it is, as one Farmer put it, "One way to make it sanely through a world that, from all appearances, is clearly going mad."

From *New Times Magazine*, 1976.

QUESTIONS

(1) How does the author account for the success of the Farm in the "heart of the Bible Belt"?

(2) What is the attitude of the Farmers toward modern sexual conduct?

(3) What are some of the disadvantages of life on the Farm?

(4) Compare the description of life on the Farm with that given in the essay "A Church Without Walls." In what respect are the lives on these two communes different? In what ways similar?

PLAYING THE DEVIL'S ADVOCATE, AS IT WERE

HARVEY COX

A flurry of recent court cases suggests we are facing another test of how genuine our pluralism is and whether we will guarantee freedom of religion to movements that were not foreseen when the First Amendment was written.

Do the recruitment and training methods of the Hare Krishna sect constitute illegal mind control? A Queens grand jury thinks so in the case of two individuals. But if the Krishna practices are illegal, what about the repetitious chanting and exclusion of family in Trappist and Carthusian novitiates? How are the courts to decide what is "religious" for purposes of tax exemption, freedom of expression, ministerial draft deferment, zoning ordinances?

For courts to declare that churches in residentially-zoned areas can be used only for clearly "religious" activities begs the question when one remembers that dancing, feasting, trances, vomiting, sexual intercourse and gazing for hours at the tip of one's nose have all been considered religious activities somewhere.

The courts have usually tried to sidestep the issue of "legitimate church use." Sensing, perhaps, that the power to define what is or is not a legitimate "religious" activity seems denied them by the Constitution, the courts, when they cannot avoid a decision, turn to some vague "man-in-the-street" idea of what "religion" should be: It involves prayer, and has something to do with a deity, etc. But a man-in-the-street approach would surely have ruled out early Christianity, which seemed both subversive and atheistic to the religious Romans of the day. The truth is that one man's "bizarre cult" is another's true path to salvation, and the Bill of Rights was designed to safeguard minorities from the man-on-the-street's uncertain capacity for tolerance.

The new challenge to our pluralism often comes from Ori-

ental religious movements, because their views of religion differ so fundamentally from ours.

Oriental thought does not make our Western distinction
between "science" and "religion," but sees a unified cosmos.
Consequently, when the Transcendental Meditation organization designed a "Creative Intelligence" course for the New
Jersey school system, the course was contested as a violation of
the separation of church and state.

Eastern spirituality does not always make a clear distinction
between religious and other types of behavior. This makes the
legal situation more complex, since the traditional focus of
our thinking on this subject has been on institutions, not persons. The result has been chaotic, even for homegrown religious minorities.

By deciding on the limits of religious freedom, the courts
have also been setting the perimeters of allowable personal
behavior. But, again, they have been doing so, albeit inexplic-
itly, on the basis of an ethic derived from one religious tradition. Although Mormons have adjusted to monogamy, some
of the newer movements encourage personal religious practices
that run counter to current taboos. Should the courts deny
freedom of expression in personal behavior because it goes
against standards derived from a more familiar religion?

Some Oriental religious movements bother us because they
pose a threat to the values of career success, individual competition, personal ambition and consumption, on which our
economic system depends. We forget that Christianity, taken
literally, could cause similar disquietude. Some psychiatrists
contend that young people who join Oriental religious movements or Jesus communes have obviously been "brainwashed,"
since they now share their money and have lost interest in becoming successful executives. That someone could freely
choose a path of mystical devotion, self-sacrifice and the sharing of worldly goods seems self-evidently impossible to them.
They forget that these "crazy" attitudes have also been taught
by St. Francis and the Baal Shem Tov.

Indeed, according to the Gospel of Mark, Jesus was a candidate for "deprogramming," since his own family thought he
was berserk and his religious leaders said he was possessed of
the devil. One can sympathize with the sadness of parents
whose offspring choose another way. But surely the rights of

adults so to choose must be safeguarded if the First Amendment means anything.

My real fear about new religious movements is not that harassment will drive them out of existence, but rather that it could push them into premature accommodation, and we would lose the critical perspective that religion can bring to a culture in need of renewal.

Some new religious groups answer the need young people feel today for a way of life not based on accumulation and competition. Others promise an experience of the holy, undiluted by the accommodations Christianity and Judaism have made to consumer culture. Thus, minority religious movements can also be seen as symptoms of a hunger seemingly too deep for our existing religious institutions to feed.

I doubt if many people will ultimately find answers in these movements. Most of those who try an Oriental path will eventually find it too exotic for the Western psyche. They will then turn, as some are doing already, to the neglected spiritual and critical dimensions of our own traditions. Meanwhile, minority movements need protection, in part because they help us to see what is missing in our own way of life.

American culture has an enormous capacity to domesticate its critics. It is not unique in that respect. Christianity was once an exotic cult, providing a way of life visibly different from the jaded society around it. After a short period of persecution, it accommodated to the culture so well it was eventually accepted as Rome's only legitimate religion. Christians then quickly turned to the persecution of other religions. The same thing could happen to today's "cultists."

A new test of America's capacity for genuine pluralism is under way. We could flunk it by driving unconventional religious movements into accommodation before their message can be heard. I hope not. It is important to preserve freedom of religion, not only for the sake of the minority immediately involved but also because the majority needs to hear what the minority is saying.

From *The New York Times*, 1977.

QUESTIONS

(1) In what sense is the author "playing the devil's advocate"?

(2) What distinctions between Eastern religions and our traditions cause misunderstanding between the two groups?

(3) The author suggests that some of the opposition to Oriental religion among Americans may have a more social than a religious basis. What are these social reasons?

(4) What is the potentially positive impact of the presence of these new religions?

(5) The author uses the word "pluralism" in the first and last paragraph of the essay. What is the meaning of this key term?

OF PHYSICS AND TANTRA YOGA

WILLIAM IRWIN THOMPSON

"I have always felt that it is better to be esoteric from within society than esoteric in some mysterious place hidden away in the Himalayas." As he mused in his tower overlooking the Starnbergersee, Professor von Weizsäcker seemed to be summing up his whole career. The latest act in that career is certainly in keeping with that conviction. Having established a Max Planck Institute for the study of the technological society, he has gone on to create a private Research Foundation for Eastern Wisdom and Western Science. Out of a friendship that developed with the Kashmiri yogi, Gopi Krishna, Weizsäcker has gathered together a small group of German scientists interested in research and intellectual exploration at the interface between East and West.

The wedding of the mystique of German science and the

mysticism of Indian yoga evokes all the archetypal images of an alchemical marriage; as you hear rumors of mysterious happenings in Starnberg, you go over expecting to see the salamander in the flames. Before I had gone to Germany, I had heard rumors from graduate students that the German physicists were conducting esoteric research with Gopi Krishna. Legend had it that when they would photograph him, he would irradiate the film so that only an outline of light would show up in the picture. But the American graduate students were simply projecting; the research that was going on with Swami Rama at the Menninger Institute in Kansas was being distorted into a science fiction film, and for that film German physicists were much more cinematic than Midwestern doctors. When I arrived in Starnberg, I discovered that one of the members of Weizsäcker's Research Foundation had taken a few EEG measurements of Gopi Krishna in meditation, but that there was no research being conducted on the scale of Wallace's work at Harvard or Kamiya's work at Langley Porter. Weizsäcker himself thought it silly to look upon the Research Foundation as anything more than a club, a *"Verein."* As we talked in his office, our conversation was drawn more in the direction of Wagar, Wells, and the Club of Rome than to the scientific explanation of yoga. What Weizsäcker had to say about yoga was in his introduction to Gopi Krishna's essay on kundalini.

But what Weizsäcker had to say about science, world affairs, and atomic research in Hitler's Germany was so fascinating that I almost forgot I had flown over to Germany to meet Gopi Krishna and the physicists around him. When I did meet Gopi Krishna later that day, the meeting was something of an anticlimax. Nothing could be further from the truth of Gopi Krishna's simple and unassuming manner than the American legends of initiatic wonder-working. To appreciate how normal Gopi Krishna is, you have to set him against a theatrical guru like Sri Chinmoy. When you go to see Sri Chinmoy, you come upon a resplendent figure in gold slippers and saffron robes. With his eyeballs rolled up and his lips curled into a blissful smile of nirbikalpa samadhi, you do not have a conversation with him, you have darshan with an exalted being who uses more subtle vibrations than the pathetic beating of the wind with the larynx. If you stare at this being

while he intones to his devotees, you will see a purple aura
emanating from his head and shoulders. And if you look into
the eyes of his disciples, you will see little reflections of Sri
Chinmoy, their doorway to the infinite; and with his smile
upon their lips, they will tell you that every morning they
rise to meditate gazing upon the photograph of their master in
samadhi. Since Sri Chinmoy was the only yogi I had ever
talked to, I was prepared for darshan when I was ushered into
Gopi Krishna's room in Starnberg.

But darshan it was not. Gopi Krishna rose from his desk,
and in his white turban, the seventy-year-old fair-skinned
Kashmiri stood tall and strongly present in a very physical
way. With a warm and solicitous smile, he motioned me to a
chair across from his little writing table. I sat down and looked
into his bright and clear eyes and saw a grandfatherly goodness but no purple aura's majesty. His accent was Indian, and
the dental sharpness of his speech was matched with a sharply
didactic manner. He gave me little set-pieces and mini-lectures
that answered questions I did not have and missed the questions I did have.

Months later, when I got to know him better on his own
soil in Kashmir, I realized that his didactic approach was
simply his defensive response to being questioned by academics. When he was relaxed and at home in Srinigar, he was
warm, very friendly, and an avatar of Kashmiri hospitality.
The cosmic theater of the kingly guru was missing, and the
humble pride of Gopi Krishna struck me quite differently
from the proud humility of Sri Chinmoy. The overall impression he created was one of goodness. Gopi Krishna was a good
man, a family patriarch and a village pandit, but not another
god-man of the Himalayas. If you were to translate the government clerk from Kashmir into American culture, you
would come up with a working-class sage: an old logger from
the Northwest with a love for books or a wizened and storied
fisherman from Maine. As you questioned him about other
yogis and other yogic traditions, you could see that, so much
like a working-class sage, he was suspicious and felt that the
famous yogis often did not know what it was all about. Like
an Eric Hoffer or an H. G. Wells, Gopi Krishna had all the
virtues and vices of a self-made man: free of authority figures,
he was bound to his own brand of authoritarianism. After

meditating on his own for fourteen years, he had discovered a physiological basis to religion and genius in the experience of the raising of kundalini. Now he could climb to higher levels of religious contemplation or go into an artistic trance to write 150 pages of rhyming poetry effortlessly.

Gopi Krishna is especially pleased with his new poetic gifts; and the fact that he can receive and transmit poetry written in languages he does not know convinces him of the quality of genius of this creative process. It is, perhaps, unfair to quote his poetry, but since he does claim that Kundalini Yoga is responsible for his transformation from an ordinary civil servant into a poet and sage of a new era of human evolution, the poetry must be taken into account.

> Those who adrift in fancy's golden realm
> Of harsh reality let go the helm
> And floating smoothly down the gliding stream
> Of thought, of the hidden future try to dream.
> Most often build its image on the shape
> Of present-day conditions, hard to escape.
> On their likes and dislikes, choice and desire
> Which often color mortals' thought entire
> And thus let their minds be enfettered by
> So much of earth they lose sight of the sky,
> One day to wake up with a sudden start
> To find their dream-world falling all apart.

In the Vedic tradition sacred knowledge is always transmitted in verse; and in Sanskrit the vibrations of the words are pitched in harmony with the vibrations of the cosmos; thus all Indian saints feel compelled to give authority to their utterances by means of poetry. With millennia of tradition behind him, an Indian sage simply cannot resist the temptation to write poetry. Unfortunately, whether it is the poetry of Sri Aurobindo, Paramahansa Yogananda, Sri Chinmoy, or Pandit Gopi Krishna, it is an artistic embarrassment. Of course, you can forgive a yogi his bad verses, but when he eagerly offers his poetry as proof that yoga is good not only for the soul but for the IQ and artistic ability as well, you can only wonder why illumination isn't light enough to see the poetry for what it is. In trying to prove the worth of the East to the West, yogis often only prove their total lack of understanding of the West.

Gopi Krishna wants to offer scientific proof for the claims of yoga, and in this effort he is more likely to secure an audience by working with Weizsäcker than by writing alone. Yogis we have always had with us; physicists interested in yoga we have not had. The first expression of Weizsäcker and Gopi Krishna's collaboration in the Research Foundation for Eastern Wisdom and Western Science is the publication of a small volume, *The Biological Basis of Religion and Genius*. Since the introduction by Weizsäcker is almost as long as the text itself, it is fair to look upon this book as a jointly authored work; certainly for most Westerners, it is the introduction that will arouse the greater interest.

If yogic physics seems to be an oxymoron, it is a figure of speech in a language that is now part of the traditions of German science. While our scientists are claiming to have cast a new cold and scientific light on man that resolves the ambiguous flesh tones into one ghastly pallor, the German physicists are pointing out that even the light of science still oscillates with a darkness we do not understand. In 1971 Heisenberg's *Physics and Beyond* appeared in English, and although Heisenberg is no yogi, his views on God and the "central order" would not positively reinforce a behaviorist:

> There was a hush as, high above us, he struck up the first great D-minor chords of Bach's Chaconne. All at once, and with utter certainty, I had found my link with the center. The moonlit Altmühl Valley below would have been reason enough for a romantic transfiguration; but that was not it. The clear phrases of the Chaconne touched me like a cool wind, breaking through the mist and revealing the towering structures beyond. There had always been a path to the central order in the language of music, in philosophy and in religion, today no less than in Plato's day and in Bach's. That I now knew from my own experience.

I had this passage in mind when I talked to Heisenberg in Munich after my visit with Weizsäcker and Gopi Krishna. When I asked him how it could be that science in his hands or Einstein's (a portrait of Einstein was on the wall over his left shoulder) could be so contemplative and in B. F. Skinner's hands so twisted out of shape as to become a weapon, he answered: "Scientists now work as stonemasons did once on cathedrals. They put the stones next to one another with great attention to detail and the work of the fellow next to them, but they have no sense of the architectonics of the whole. And sometimes they do not even have a sense of the purpose of a cathedral." His eyes under his great bushy eyebrows actually twinkled. He was too thin and bald to make a good Santa Claus, but decked out in the appropriate costume, the grand-fatherly Heisenberg was one of those archetypal wise old men whom Yeats had been able to celebrate but not emulate:

> One asks for mournful melodies;
> Accomplished fingers begin to play.
> Their eyes mid many wrinkles, their eyes,
> Their ancient, glittering eyes, are gay.

As Heisenberg reflected over the climax of physical science in his lifetime, he agreed with his colleague, Weizsäcker, that the great age of natural science was nearing its end. In finishing his own Unified Field Theory, he felt that an era was over. When he was a young musician, Heisenberg had felt that the great era of European music had reached its consummation and that the mind of Europe could be better raised to new heights in physics. His intuition had always been good, and now he intuitively felt that our culture was reaching its limit. The ecological limit on the growth of civilization, he main-tained, only expressed the outward sign of the limits to growth of the human spirit in the material dimensions it had been exploring since the Renaissance.

There was no sadness in Heisenberg's sense of the passing of the great age of natural science. He was a master surveying a satisfying life of full creation. He saw the limit and accepted it with humility.

Since Heisenberg felt that human culture could now reori-ent itself by making the limit part of its new bearings, I asked him if he felt that the direction Weizsäcker was taking into Eastern mysticism was a path others could take to move from an abusive technology to a more contemplative science. He answered that there was no question that the East had a knowledge we needed, that this knowledge was stronger than the West's feeble attempts to reduce consciousness to electron-ics and information theory, but he still felt that the new direc-tions would appear in the West. He was a Western man; as a musician and a scientist, he was more a follower of Pythagoras than of Patanjali.

The work of Heisenberg and Weizsäcker should demonstrate

that if there are "two cultures," they are not, as Lord Snow indicated, science and the humanities, but Archimedean and Pythagorean forms of knowledge. On the Archimedean side we have all the technological attempts, whether agricultural, industrial, or military, to alter and control nature; on the Pythagorean side we have all the cosmological thinkers for whom art, religion, and science are different idioms in a single language of contemplation. Within the Archimedean ranks are Bacon, Harvey, Lavoisier, Pasteur, Teller, and von Braun; within the Pythagorean ranks are Kepler, Descartes, Pascal, Newton, Faraday, Whitehead, Einstein, Schrödinger, Heisenberg, and Weizsäcker. There are two cultures, but the dividing line cuts at right angles across the boundary between science and the humanities; for if contemplative mysticism can appear in science, superstition and priestcraft can as well. Certainly the science of Skinner bears the same relation to the scientific tradition as the Inquisition does to Christianity.

Weizsäcker's interest in yoga, like Schrödinger's interest in Vedanta before him, grew out of his own meditations on the psychological implications of the quantum theory. If subatomic particles are more mathematical *forms* than discrete pieces of *material,* and if the *modes* of perceiving these forms through laboratory instruments and mathematics alter the material itself, then, as Heisenberg would say, we no longer have a science of nature, but a science of the mind's knowledge about nature. As Pythagoras said, "All is number." Although we have only a few phrases and many legends of Pythagoras, men as different in religious temperament as Whitehead and Russell are willing to accept his apotheosis. Whitehead's celebration in particular is worth recalling:

> The field is now open for the introduction of some new doctrine of organism which may take the place of the materialism with which, since the seventeenth century, science has saddled philosophy. It must be remembered that the physicists' energy is obviously an abstraction. The concrete fact, which is the organism, must be a complete expression of the character of a real occurrence. Such a displacement of scientific materialism, if it ever takes place, cannot fail to have important consequences in every field of thought.
>
> Finally, our last reflection must be, that we have in the end come back to a version of the doctrine of old Pythagoras, from whom mathematics, and mathematical physics, took their rise. He discovered the importance of dealing with abstractions; and in par-

ticular directed attention to number as characterizing the periodic-
ities of notes of music. . . .

Truly, Pythagoras in founding European philosophy and European mathematics, endowed them with the luckiest of lucky
guesses—or, was it a flash of divine genius, penetrating to the in-
most nature of things?

If mathematical form becomes more basic than matter itself,
then it follows that science, the cultural process in which the
mind develops *modes* for the knowing of *forms,* is an inseparable part of nature. The subjective-objective distinction col-
lapses. It does little good, then, to talk confidently of "facts"
when you do not understand the *structure* of consciousness
through which one can entertain the *content* of facts.

The difficulty always arises when one confidently thinks in
terms of a subjective "inside" world and an objective "outside"
world. We are not standing outside nature and observing it
through a window. We ourselves are a part of the nature we
seek to describe, and through what Whitehead calls "the with-
ness of the body" we can discover the correspondence between
neurons and neutrinos.

The mechanists seek to reduce consciousness to electrochemical behavior; the mystics seek to show that "behavior" is an
abstraction taken out of context. If there is a structure to consciousness (the way in which the brain processes information),
and this can be expressed scientifically in mathematics; and if
there is a structure to matter, and this can be scientifically
expressed in the mathematics of the quantum theory, then the
forms of one relate to the forms of the other through pure
form, the structure of structures, the Logos. In other words, it
is not the case that consciousness is created out of behavior;
behavior is a construct built up out of consciousness. It is not
"In the beginning was the flesh, and the flesh developed
words," but "In the beginning was the Word and the Word
was made flesh."

The way that Weizsäcker would express this is to point out
that our consciousness of nature is a real event in the "history
of nature." Unfortunately, we discover the force of consciousness most often in negative ways: we discover the nature of
matter by taking it apart; we gain information about events
through their vanishing. In terms of information theory, an
increase in information generates an increase in entropy else-

where in the system. The "feedback" of consciousness to nature is called culture; when culture reaches a certain point in the "negative feedback loop," it can destroy nature. We can see this effect in the earth's ecosystem, for our culture is changing the earth's atmosphere and weather. The point of maximum information, or maximum civilization, will correspond with entropy, and we will reach the end of history—which is precisely what the ecologists and the mystics have been prophesying. If the mind is, therefore, an energy state in which the increase of information is generating an increase in entropy in the surrounding system, then, for all practical purposes, the mind has to be looked upon as a very real event in the physical system.

According to the Second Law of Thermodynamics, all physical systems are moving toward maximum molecular chaos; according to evolution, some organic systems are moving toward maximum molecular organization. The evolution of man created an order on one level that generated disorder on lower levels in the plant and animal kingdoms. Now the cultural evolution of consciousness through science is generating disorder on the lower levels of human culture. Through genetic engineering, behavioral modification, and electronic stimulation of the brain, there is an increase in information which generates an increase in entropy in the cultural system. Traditions come apart as they are touched by the new kinds of science and technology that are beyond the control of their political and religious institutions. Paolo Soleri has characterized the evolutionary process as one of complexification and miniaturization, and this process seems to be holding true for culture. As our scientific knowledge has reached incredible levels of complexification, it has miniaturized itself into an increasingly smaller elite. Thus the growth of knowledge has a negative feedback loop not only to nature, but also to culture.

Now the yogis would claim that just as there is a negative feedback of consciousness to nature and culture, so, in terms of the laws of symmetry, is there a positive feedback. But before we can observe the positive feedback of consciousness to the body of the planet, we must first observe it in our own bodies. When a yogi stops his heart or alters other physical conditions hitherto thought to be part of the involuntary nervous system, he demonstrates that "matter" is subordinate to "mind." When a devout Christian develops the stigmata on Good Friday, he demonstrates the same priority of consciousness. Symbol is clearly dominant, for how is it that the devotee selects the right cells in the right symbolic spots, and does not miss and bleed from the cheek or forearm? When Swami Rama stopped his heart for seventeen seconds at the Menninger Institute under conditions of precise scientific observation, he closed a chapter of Western medicine and showed that the old Cartesian split between the *res extensa* and the *res cogitans* had been carried over into our medical textbooks in terms of the autonomic and voluntary nervous systems. This is only the first of many anomalies now being registered; as the anomalies accumulate, they will force the community of scientists to generate a new "paradigm" and Whitehead's prophesy will come true. The yogis insist that when the consciousness of mankind is raised to this new level, then matter will be spiritualized and the positive feedback to the body of the earth will be visible. Consciousness will then surround nature and culture to give us "a new heaven and a new earth." Of course, the Second Law will still remain to demand its price, and that is why many evolutionary thinkers feel that this transformation cannot be anything but apocalyptic.

From *Passages About Earth*, 1973.

QUESTIONS

(1) Read again the contrasting descriptions of Sri Chinmoy and Gopi Krishna in the second, third and fourth paragraphs. Which one of the two men appears to be more "religious"? How does the author regard the yogis? Does he favor one over the other?

(2) Look up the meaning of the word *oxymoron*. How does the dictionary definition clarify the author's comment" . . . yogic physics seems to be an oxymoron"?

(3) The author argues that the increasing complexity of scientific thought represents a threat to the order not only of nature but of society as well. As scientific knowledge advances

beyond the ability of the culture to assimilate the information, the gap between science and culture widens. According to the author, what is the consequence of such a development?

(4) The author's reference to "the old Cartesian split between the *res extensa* and the *res cogitans*" (final paragraph) is to the distinction made by the philosopher Descartes between the objective world (matter, *res extensa*) and the subjective world (mind, *res cogitans*). How does the view of yogic physics, which sees the eventual spiritualization of matter, contradict this idea?

THE SENSE OF THE 70s PEOPLE

The sixties—the age of the charismatic hero: the Kennedys, Martin Luther King, Malcolm X. All bright blazing stars that symbolized the decade. All dead before it was concluded. Other charismatic heroes of that time have gone into hiding— some figuratively and some, like Abbie Hoffman, quite literally. Still others drove themselves to a self-destructive conclusion. Janis Joplin is a case in point. Her death in 1970 from an overdose of heroin constitutes an epitaph of the sixties. As Ellen Willis trenchantly writes in the essay reprinted here, Janis Joplin was not a victim of her age but a casualty. The distinction is an important one.

The heroes of the seventies are of the new breed, dedicated to underplaying the charismatic. They match in their style the tendency of the decade to retreat to the shadows of private life rather than court the spotlight (and the sniper's scope) as their predecessors did. But their achievement is not any the less for the change of style. Hank Aaron is surely as great an athlete as Joe Namath; Jerry Brown as astute a politician as John Lindsay at his best; and Jimmy Carter as significant a figure in American history as John F. Kennedy.

The *People* of the seventies have worked quietly but effectively toward their goals. A good example of the process is evident in George Plimpton's stark understated account of Aaron's record-breaking 715th home run. Plimpton's prose style matches the modesty of his subject. On the other hand, quite the opposite is the style in Hunter Thompson's raucous rambunctious account of his first encounter with Jimmy Carter—in which the self-styled *gonzo* journalist finds himself surprised by Carter's quiet effectiveness.

All of which is not to say that charisma is dead entirely. Elsewhere in this book is a report of an attempt to revive it

by the charismatic hero of pop culture, Boy Dylan. (See "On
Tour with the Rolling Thunder Revue.") And as Gloria
Steinem indicates—and her own outrageous aphorisms vividly
illustrate—Florynce R. Kennedy carries on the fight for social
justice and equal rights with a flamboyant charm that overwhelms all obstacles. Nevertheless, the seventies is, in the last
analysis, a private decade. The final selection summarizes that
celebration of the private life in the brief tribute paid by a
daughter to her immigrant father, Morris Heller.

JANIS JOPLIN

ELLEN WILLIS

Janis Joplin was born in 1943 and grew up in Port Arthur, Texas. She began singing in bars and coffeehouses, first locally, then in Austin, where she spent most of a year at the University of Texas. In 1966, she went to San Francisco and got together with a rock band in search of a singer, Big Brother and the Holding Company. The following summer Big Brother performed at the Monterey Pop Festival; Janis got raves from the fans and the critics and from then on she was a star. "Cheap Thrills," Big Brother's first major album (there had been an early record on a small-time label), came out in July 1968. By then there were tensions between Janis and the group, and she left soon afterward.

With her new backup band she made another album, "I Got Dem Ol' Kozmic Blues Again Mama!" But the band never quite jelled, and in the spring of 1970, Janis formed another, Full-Tilt Boogie. They spent most of the summer touring, then went to Los Angeles to record an album, "Pearl." It was Janis's last. On October 4th, 1970, she died of an overdose of heroin.

The hippie rock stars of the late sixties merged two versions of that hardy American myth, the free individual. They were stars, which meant achieving liberation by becoming rich and famous *on their own terms;* and they were, or purported to be, apostles of cultural revolution, a considerably more ambitious and romantic vision of freedom that nevertheless had a similar economic foundation. Young Americans were in a sense the stars of the world, drawing on an overblown prosperity that could afford to indulge all manner of rebellious and experimental behavior. The combination was inherently unstable—Whitman's open road is not, finally, the Hollywood Freeway, and in any case neither stardom nor prosperity could deliver what it seemed to promise. For a fragile historical moment rock transcended those contradictions; in its aftermath our pop heroes found themselves grappling, like the rest of us, with what are probably enduring changes in the white American consciousness—changes that have to do with something very like an awareness of tragedy. It is in this context that Janis Joplin developed as an artist, a celebrity, a rebel, a woman, and it is in this context that she died.

Joplin belonged to that select group of pop figures who mattered as much for themselves as for their music; among American rock performers she was second only to Bob Dylan in importance as a creator/recorder/embodiment of her generation's history and mythology. She was also the only woman to achieve that kind of stature in what was basically a male club, the only sixties culture hero to make visible and public women's experience of the quest for individual liberation, which was very different from men's. If Janis's favorite metaphors—singing as fucking (a first principle of rock and roll) and fucking as liberation (a first principle of the cultural revolution)—were equally approved by her male peers, the congruence was only on the surface. Underneath—just barely—lurked a feminist (or prefeminist) paradox.

The male-dominated counterculture defined freedom for women almost exclusively in sexual terms. As a result, women endowed the idea of sexual liberation with immense symbolic importance; it became charged with all the secret energy of an as yet suppressed larger rebellion. Yet to express one's rebellion in that limited way was a painfully literal form of submission. Whether or not Janis understood that, her dual persona —lusty hedonist and suffering victim—suggested that she felt it. Dope, another term in her metaphorical equation (getting high as singing as fucking as liberation) was, in its more sinister aspect, a painkiller and finally a killer. Which is not to say that the good times weren't real, as far as they went. Whatever the limitations of hippie/rock star life, it was better than being a provincial matron—or a lonely weirdo.

For Janis, as for others of us who suffered the worst fate that can befall an adolescent girl in America—*unpopularity*—a crucial aspect of the cultural revolution was its assault on the rigid sexual styles of the fifties. Joplin's metamorphosis from the ugly duckling of Port Arthur to the peacock of Haight-Ashbury meant, among other things, that a woman who was not conventionally pretty, who had acne and an intermittent

weight problem and hair that stuck out, could not only invent
her own beauty (just as she invented her wonderful sleazo-
freak costumes) out of sheer energy, soul, sweetness, arrogance,
and a sense of humor, but have that beauty appreciated. Not
that Janis merely took advantage of changes in our notions of
attractiveness; she herself changed them. It was seeing Janis
Joplin that made me resolve, once and for all, not to get my
hair straightened. And there was a direct line from that sort of
response to those apocryphal burned bras and all that followed.

Direct, but not simple. Janis once crowed, "They're paying
me $50,000 a year to be like me." But the truth was that they
were paying her to be a personality, and the relation of public
personality to private self—something every popular artist has
to work out—is especially problematic for a woman. Men are
used to playing roles and projecting images in order to compete and succeed. Male celebrities tend to identify with their
maskmaking, to see it as creative and—more or less—to control
it. In contrast, women need images simply to survive. A
woman is usually aware, on some level, that men do not allow
her to be her "real self," and worse, that the acceptable masks
represent men's fantasies, not her own. She can choose the
most interesting image available, present it dramatically, indi-
vidualize it with small elaborations, undercut it with irony.
But ultimately she must serve some male fantasy to be loved—
and then it will be only the fantasy that is loved anyway. The
female celebrity is confronted with this dilemma in its starkest
form. Joplin's revolt against conventional femininity was
brave and imaginative, but it also dovetailed with a stereotype—the ballsy, one-of-the-guys chick who is a needy, vulnerable cream puff underneath—cherished by her legions of hip
male fans. It may be that she could have pushed beyond it and
taken the audience with her; that was one of the possibilities
that made her death an artistic as well as human calamity.
There is, for instance, the question of her bisexuality. People
who knew Janis differ on whether sexual relationships with
women were an important part of her life, and I don't know
the facts. In any case, a public acknowledgment of bisexual
proclivities would not necessarily have contradicted her image; it could easily have been passed off as more pull-out-the-
stops hedonism or another manifestation of her all-encom-

passing need for love. On the other hand, she could have used it to say something new about women and liberation. What makes me wonder is something I always noticed and liked about Janis: unlike most female performers whose act is intensely erotic, she never made me feel as if I were crashing an orgy that consisted of her and the men in the audience. When she got it on at a concert, she got it on with everybody.

Still, the songs she sang assumed heterosexual romance; it was men who made her hurt, who took another little piece of her heart. Watching men groove on Janis, I began to appreciate the resentment many black people feel toward whites who are blues freaks. Janis sang out of her pain as a woman, and men dug it. Yet it was men who caused the pain, and if they stopped causing it they would not have her to dig. In a way, their adulation was the cruelest insult of all. And Janis's response—to sing harder, get higher, be worshiped more—was rebellious, acquiescent, bewildered all at once. When she said, "Onstage I make love to 25,000 people, then I go home alone," she was not merely repeating the cliché of the sad clown or the poor little rich girl. She was noting that the more she gave the less she got, and that honey, it ain't fair.

Like most women singers, Joplin did not write many songs; she mostly interpreted other people's. But she made them her own in a way few singers dare to do. She did not sing them so much as struggle with them, assault them. Some critics complained, not always unfairly, that she strangled them to death, but at her best she whipped them to new life. She had an analogous adversary relationship with the musical form that dominated her imagination—the blues. Blues represented another external structure, one with its own contradictory tradition of sexual affirmation and sexist conservatism. But Janis used blues conventions to reject blues sensibility. To sing the blues is a way of transcending pain by confronting it with dignity, but Janis wanted nothing less than to scream it out of existence. Big Mama Thornton's classic rendition of "Ball and Chain" carefully balances defiance and resignation, toughness and vulnerability. She almost pities her oppressor: "I know you're gonna miss me, baby . . . You'll find that your whole life will be like mine, all wrapped up in a ball and chain." Her singing conveys, above all, her determination to survive abuse. Janis makes the song into one long frenzied, despairing protest. Why, why, *why*, she asks over and over, like a child unable to comprehend injustice. "It ain't fair . . . this can't be . . . I just wanted to hold you . . . All I ever wanted to do was to love you." The pain is overwhelming her, "draggin' me down . . . maybe, maybe you can help me— c'mon *help me.*" There are similar differences between her recording of "Piece of My Heart" and Erma Franklin's. When Franklin sings it, it is a challenge: no matter what you do to me, I will not let you destroy my ability to be human, to love. Joplin seems rather to be saying, surely if I keep taking this, if I keep setting an example of love and forgiveness, surely he has to understand, change, give me back what I have given.

Her pursuit of pleasure had the same driven quality; what it amounted to was refusal to admit of any limits that would not finally yield to the virtue of persistence—*try just a little bit harder*—and the magic of extremes. This war against limits was largely responsible for the electrifying power of Joplin's early performances; it was what made *Cheap Thrills* a classic, in spite of unevenness and the impossibility of duplicating on a record the excitement of her concerts. After the split with Big Brother, Janis retrenched considerably, perhaps because she simply couldn't maintain that level of intensity, perhaps for other reasons that would have become clear if she had lived. My uncertainty on this point makes me hesitate to be too dogmatic about my conviction that leaving Big Brother was a mistake.

I was a Big Brother fan. I thought they were better musicians than their detractors claimed, but more to the point, technical accomplishment, in itself, was not something I cared about. I thought it was an ominous sign that so many people did care—including Janis. It was, in fact, a sign that the tenuous alliance between mass culture and bohemianism—or, in my original formulation, the fantasy of stardom and the fantasy of cultural revolution—was breaking down. But the breakdown was not as neat as it might appear. For the elitist concept of "good musicianship" was as alien to the holistic, egalitarian spirit of rock and roll as the act of leaving one's group the better to pursue one's individual ambition was alien to the holistic, egalitarian pretensions of the cultural revolutionaries. If Joplin's decision to go it alone was influenced by all the obvious professional/commercial pressures, it also reflected a conflict of values within the counterculture itself—a conflict that foreshadowed its imminent disintegration. And again, Janis's femaleness complicated the issues, raised the stakes. She had less room to maneuver than a man in her position, fewer alternatives to fall back on if she blew it. If she had to chose between fantasies, it made sense for her to go with stardom as far as it would take her.

But I wonder if she really had to choose, if her choice was not in some sense a failure of nerve and therefore of greatness. Janis was afraid Big Brother would hold her back, but if she had thought it was important enough, she might have been able to carry them along, make them transcend their limitations. There is more than a semantic difference between a group and a backup band. Janis had to relate to the members of Big Brother as spiritual (not to mention financial) equals even though she had more talent than they, and I can't help suspecting that that was good for her not only emotionally and socially but aesthetically. Committed to the hippie ethic of music-for-the-hell-of-it—if only because there was no possibility of their becoming stars on their own—Big Brother helped Janis sustain the amateur quality that was an integral part of her effect. Their zaniness was a salutary reminder that good times meant silly fun—remember "Caterpillar"?—as well as Dionysiac abandon; it was a relief from Janis's extremism and at the same time a foil for it. At their best moments Big Brother made me think of the Beatles, who weren't (at least in the beginning) such terrific musicians either. Though I'm not quite softheaded enough to imagine that by keeping her group intact Janis Joplin could somehow have prevented or delayed the end of an era, or even saved her own life, it would have been an impressive act of faith. And acts of faith by public figures always have reverberations, one way or another.

Such speculation is of course complicated by the fact that Janis died before she really had a chance to define her post-San Francisco, post-Big Brother self. Her last two albums, like her performances with the ill-fated Kozmic Blues band, had a tentative, transitional feel. She was obviously going through important changes; the best evidence of that was "Me and Bobby McGee," which could be considered her "Dear Landlord." Both formally—as a low-keyed, soft, folkie tune—and substantively—as a lyric that spoke of choices made, regretted and survived, with the distinct implication that compromise could be a positive act—what it expressed would have been heresy to the Janis Joplin of *Cheap Thrills*. "Freedom's just another word for nothing left to lose" is as good an epitaph for the counterculture as any; we'll never know how—or if— Janis meant to go on from there.

Janis Joplin's death, like that of a fighter in the ring, was not exactly an accident. Yet it's too easy to label it either suicide or murder, though it involved elements of both. Call it rather an inherent risk of the game she was playing, a game whose often frivolous rules both hid and revealed a deadly serious struggle. The form that struggle took was incomplete, shortsighted, egotistical, self-destructive. But survivors who give in to the temptation to feel superior to all that are in the end no better than those who romanticize it. Janis was not so much a victim as a casualty. The difference matters.

From *Rolling Stone*, 1976.

QUESTIONS

(1) What "two versions of . . . American myth" are represented by rock stars?

(2) What is the connection, according to the author, between the personality and popularity of Joplin and women's liberation?

(3) What was the basis of Joplin's appeal to men? To women?

(4) What is the basis of the thesis that Janis Joplin made a mistake in breaking with the group, Big Brother and the Holding Company?

(5) In the author's view, why is the line "Freedom's just another word for nothing left to lose" an appropriate epitaph for the counter culture?

(6) What is the author implying about the difference between the words "victim" and "casualty"? Is the distinction a real one?

JERRY BROWN

RICHARD REEVES

"I am going to starve the schools financially until I get some educational reforms," said the Governor of California, Edmund G. Brown, Jr.

"What reforms? What do you want?" said Jack Rees, the executive director of the California Teachers Association.

"I don't know yet."

Jerry Brown is different. He is the most interesting politician in the United States. And, at the moment, he is one of the most popular, phenomenally popular in his own state where polls show that only 7 percent of voters disapprove of his performance in office. Although he is not a particularly likable young man, he has piqued the imagination of Californians by choosing to sleep on a mattress on the floor of a bare, $250-a-month apartment in Sacramento rather than in a $1.3-million mansion, by trading in a bulletproof Cadillac limousine for a Plymouth Satellite and by roaming around state government asking hostile and irreverent questions like this one of the University of California's Board of Regents: "Why is it better to have a smaller number of students in each class?"

The people of California thought they were just electing the son of a former Governor, Edmund G. Brown, Pat Brown's kid, another liberal Democrat like his old man. Instead, they have inherited this loner who sometimes sounds like an erudite George Wallace, attacking big-government spending, "government gibberish," "the bureaucratic maze" and saying that it's about time some people on welfare picked up shovels and went to work. And they love it. Jerry Brown is popular not so much because he is telling them what they want to hear, but because he is saying what they are saying these days. He has a perfect ear for the grumbling anti-politics of America, and he is in tune with the strain of rhetorical conservatism and operational liberalism that has always run through American politics. (A lot of Americans are against big spending and against cutting Medicare.)

But Brown is not at all like Wallace or anyone else in American politics. He is almost impossible to classify as liberal or conservative—it is hard to classify a governor with a special assistant like Jacques Barzhagi, a former French sailor with a shaved head who has opened meetings of California cabinet members with a touch of Zen: "How is the Governor different from a shoemaker?" Intellectually, Governor Brown may be farther left than anyone holding high executive office in the United States: He calls on his staff to work "in the spirit of Ho Chi Minh" and he has proposed equal pay raises for all California state employees because he is willing to consider seriously the proposition that janitors should earn as much as judges. Emotionally, he is extremely conservative: At twice-a-week cabinet meetings that sometimes last until 2 A.M., in the style of college bull sessions, he has said, "Hot lunches for school children? No one ever gave me a hot lunch!" and "I don't believe in disability benefits for pregnant women. Giving life is not a disability."

"Jerry has no ideology," said his executive assistant, Gray Davis, quite accurately. Rather, Brown, a very serious man who tends to think each man is an island, has an individual philosophy, an evolving cerebral mix of the teachings of St. Ignatius and Thomas Aquinas, Buddhism, Existentialism, and Machiavelli.

On his first day as Governor in January, 1975, Brown was asked by Davis whether he wanted to issue a statement of objectives, to which he answered, "What do you mean?" Well, said Davis, what are we trying to do? "It'll emerge," said the Governor of California.

When I asked Brown the same question after he had been in power six months and produced a couple of pretty solid achievements, including farm-labor laws that might just end decades of wrath in California fields, he answered: "Reduce the sum of human misery a bit, I guess. Help people expand their lives a little bit, give them an awareness of their own potential." Then he stopped for a moment and said, "Do you think that what you do or what I do will really make a difference in the long run?"

What he does in the next few years might make a difference. In his own mind, I think, he has set himself an incredibly ambitious objective: Jerry Brown would like to lead people into

changing their values, American values. He wants Americans
to question materialism. Ho, Mao Tse Tung and Gandhi are
political idols of his not because of their ideology but because
of the ascetic and spiritual quality of their leadership: They
were able to motivate large numbers of people with visions of
a better life not linked to material reward.

What does that mean? One thing it means is that other California politicians should read a book called *Small Is Beautiful—Economics as If People Mattered,* a minor underground
classic by an English socialist, E. F. Schumacher, the former
chief economist of the British Coal Board. Brown is a student
of the book. He is in fact a student of many books, *prima facie*
evidence that he is a politician aberrant. When I mentioned
Schumacher, he seemed annoyed at the possible suggestion
that his thinking was not original, and he ended that part of
our conversation with, "I had those ideas before I read the
book."

He probably did. Obviously, he has a complex and searching mind, an extraordinary mind for a politician. But, in a
month around Brown, Schumacher's work—particularly a 1966
essay titled "Buddhist Economics"—was the most trustworthy
guide I could find to the current that runs through the individualistic political philosophy, rhetoric and action of Governor Brown. Some excerpts from *Small Is Beautiful* could
have come from a long conversation with Jerry Brown:

> The substance of man cannot be measured by Gross National
> Product. For the modern economist, this is very difficult to under-
> stand. He is used to measuring the "standard of living" by the
> amount of annual consumption, assuming all the time that a man
> who consumes more is "better off" than a man who consumes less.
> A Buddhist economist would consider this approach excessively
> irrational: Since consumption is merely a means of human well-
> being, the aim should be to obtain the maximum of well-being
> with the minimum of consumption. Thus, if the purpose of cloth-
> ing is a certain amount of temperature comfort and attractive
> appearance, the task is to attain this purpose with the smallest pos-
> sible effort—that is, with the smallest annual destruction of cloth
> and with the help of designs that involve the smallest possible in-
> put of toil. The ownership and consumption of goods is a means to
> an end, and Buddhist economics is the systematic study of how to
> attain given ends with the minimum means. . . .
> There is the immediate question of whether "modernization,"

as currently practiced without regard to religious and spiritual
values, is actually producing agreeable results. As far as the masses
are concerned, the results appear to be disastrous—a collapse of the
rural economy, a rising tide of unemployment in town and country, and the growth of a city proletariat without nourishment for
either body or soul.

It is remarkable that a politician who reads stuff like that,
much less thinks it, could be elected to govern 22 million
Americans. The secret, of course, is to be Pat Brown's kid. Nobody ever gave Jerry Brown a free hot lunch at school, but he
practically inherited the governorship without political trial
or conditioning. This Governor has none of the mellow hearti-
ness of professional politicians, but he also did not begin with
their conditioned caution or share their assumptions of what
is possible in American politics. Officially challenging materialism is a young man's vision, and Brown is a very young
man. By very young, I mean that Brown is even younger than
his 39 calendar years. He has had limited life experience—
Governor's son, Jesuit seminarian from 1956 to 1960, student
and law clerk until he was 28 years old in 1965, and a high
state official after practicing law for five years. He is sometimes
portrayed as a veteran of the movements of the 1960s, a veteran who was at Berkeley during the Free Speech Movement,
went to Mississippi in 1962, marched with Cesar Chavez and
the United Farm Workers, but that list is stretching things a
bit. His involvements were brief and limited, and he empha-
sizes that he was "an observer—never a participant."
. . . .
. . . "If he ran again today, he'd get 65 percent of the vote,
more," said Ed Salzman, editor of the *California Journal.* A
state Republican leader put it this way: "He's been good. People are after me to attack, but what am I supposed to attack
him on? He's doing a real good job of getting to that silent
majority vote, and if I attack him, I just make them mad."
Brown calls it all "oneness with the people." "To be a
leader you have to be at one with the people you lead. You
have to feel it." This time he reaches back to Lao-tze, the
founder of Taoism, offering Chinese that translates into: "You
can't go across the grain." Can he, a loner, a man without attachment except to ideas, really be at one with the people out

there, people worrying about children and lousy jobs, mortgages and money? "It is my impression that I can," he said,
pausing, then adding, "And I'm perfectly willing to test it."

It was a very good answer. He will probably test it again:
Value-changing politics cannot stop at the border of California. A couple of years ago, just after Brown moved to Hollywood Hills, he stopped his car on one of the winding little
roads there when he saw a new neighbor and old friend, Paul
Schrade, a liberal activist and former Western regional director of the United Auto Workers.

"Hey, Paul," Brown said, "we have to get together and talk
about taking over the state of California."

"Just California?" Schrade asked. "What about the country?"

"Yeah, but I have to wait until 1976," Brown said and drove
off.

It seems that 1976 will be much too soon to tell whether
Jerry Brown's difference will make a difference in California.
Kline calls the exercise "The Great Attempt," but then con-
cedes it could end as "The Spectacular Failure." If Brown does
fail, it will probably be for the wrong reasons, just as he succeeded for the wrong reasons. He got where he is not because
of his ideas but because he was Pat Brown's son and if he fails
it could be because of flaws in his own personality and because
he became a prisoner of his own popularity and ambition.
The ideas, the real commitment to nonmaterialist reform, may
never be fairly tested.

There is a sense of tragedy about Jerry Brown. He is *too*
popular and his deep, cold ambition may drive him too far in
trying to hold the acclaim of both left and right. And his feel
for "the people" is for people in the abstract, not for individual human beings. Stepping outside Brown's small circle of
friends and assistants, it is very difficut to find anyone who
knows him and says they *like* him—the people out there who
like him have never met him.

Brown, in fact, is beginning to show signs of trying to remain all things to all sides. When the conservative *Oakland
Tribune* discovered state memoranda proposing discussion of
a community jobs program for welfare recipients, a state-
owned bank like New York's, and cooperative food markets,
the newspaper headlined in red: "Governor's Secret Worker-
State Plan." Co-ops, according to the *Tribune,* were "com-

munes" and the paper demanded and got the dismissal of the proposals' author, Employment Development Director James Lorenz, the founder of California Rural Legal Assistance. Then, to placate conservatives, Brown announced he would form an informal council of economic advisers including the *Tribune*'s publisher, the presidents of the Bank of America and Standard Oil of California, and David Packard, the first finance chairman of President Ford's 1976 campaign committee.

Brown does not think in terms of individuals and their problems. When he took over as Governor, he made a series of late-night phone calls—he is a classic "night person," often working or talking until dawn—to friends and acquaintances asking them to come to Sacramento for a few weeks and help him get started. Everyone turned him down. "What's *wrong* with these people?" he blurted out one night. What was wrong was that they had families and jobs that they could not just up and leave. Later, when he heard that Lieutenant Governor Mervyn Dymally was complaining that he never saw the Governor, Brown said, "That's nonsense. I saw him yesterday"— they had walked past each other at Los Angeles International Airport. He refuses to answer the calls of his largest contributors—"He things we're unclean because we gave a politician, him, some money," one said. Because he despises the ceremonial, he refused to step outside his office one day last month to say a few words and shake a few hands of 400 officers from senior citizen organizations around the state.

There are a lot of people, some of them quite powerful, waiting in line to be the second to kick Jerry Brown on his way down. Of course, none of them has the guts to be first—not when he's on top. But if he slips, he has no network and few friends, no personal or political power base to stop the fall.

Politicians, like any other establishment, have the patience and procedures to punish aberrant behavior. Congressman Philip Burton, the chairman of the House Democratic Caucus, is not likely to forget that Brown did not even bother to answer his letter recommending the appointment of his brother, Robert Burton, to a state commission. State legislators, too, will still be there if Brown stumbles—a fading Governor could find his desk piled with popular bills, giving him the unhappy choice of vetoing or raising taxes.

"We're protecting him now," said Assembly Speaker Leo McCarthy, a political friend at the moment. "I'm killing bills like tax exemptions and deductions for veterans and senior citizens that could embarrass him. But he'd better be much more sensitive to us a year from now or there will be problems. He could talk to us more. At least he could let us know when someone from our counties is being appointed to a judgeship or state job."

If things don't work out, Jerry Brown will be alone, on his own—which is the way he always wanted it.

From Old Faces of 1976, 1976.

QUESTIONS

(1) What is the author's attitude toward Brown? What kind of a man does he see him as being?

(2) How does the author develop the statement "Jerry Brown is different"?

(3) What are some of the positions Brown has taken that make it difficult to classify him either as a liberal or a conservative?

(4) To what does the author ascribe the popularity of Brown with the California voters?

(5) Do you agree with the proposition that most Americans are conservative in theory and liberal in practice?

(6) In what sense might the concluding paragraphs of the essay be described as ominous?

THE HITTER

GEORGE PLIMPTON

Aaron came up for the second time in the fourth inning. He had yet to swing the bat off his shoulder at a ball. Downing's first pitch was a change-up that puffed in the dirt in front of the plate. The umpire, Satch Davidson, looked at it suspiciously through the bars of his mask and tossed it out. He signaled to Frank Pulli, the first-base umpire, to throw in another of the specially marked balls, this one identified with a 12, stamped twice in invisible ink, and two 2s. Downing polished it up a bit, turned, and as the clock on the scoreboard showed 9:07 he wheeled and delivered a fast ball, aiming low and expecting it to tail away on the outside corner.

The ball rose off Aaron's bat in the patented trajectory of his long hits, ripping out over the infield, the shortstop instinctively bending his knees as if he could leap for it, and it headed for deep left center field.

From behind the plate Satch Davidson leaned over the catcher Joe Ferguson's shoulder, and as the two stood up to watch the flight of the ball going out, the umpire said, "Fergie, that might be it." The catcher said, "I think so too."

Out in left center field Jimmy Wynn, who often plays with a toothpick working in his mouth, and Bill Buckner converged on the ball. The pair of them had a vague hope that if the ball was going over, somehow Buckner was going to scale the fence and get to the ball before anyone else; he would toss it back over the fence, and the two of them were going to spilt the reward. Afterward, his toothpick whisking busily in his mouth, Wynn admitted that the two of them would doubtless have given the ball to Aaron: "We wanted him to get it over with, so he could be a human being again."

At the time, though, Buckner made a leap up the fence, scaling up it with his spikes in the wire mesh until, spread-eagled for an instant like a gigantic moth against a screen door, he saw that he had no chance, and he dropped back down.

Aaron never saw the ball clear the fence. As he had done those countless times, he looked toward first base as he ran, dropping his bat neatly just off the base path, and when he saw the exultation of the first-base coach, Jim Busby, he knew for sure that the long chase was over.

THE PITCHER

Downing went to the empty Dodger locker room and dressed. A taxi was ordered for him and he stood out in the stadium tunnel waiting for it. The game was still on and Milo Hamilton's voice murmured from the amplifying system in the visiting-team locker room. I was coming along the the tunnel and I happened to spot him. He was in a coal black jump-suit outfit, with a black felt belt looped around his waist, and he was wearing black shoes polished to a glisten. I went up and said I was sorry that it had happened to him. He has a very cheery voice which seems to bely the gravity of any situation one might connect him with . . .

"Well, that's that," he said. "I didn't have the rhythm and the fast ball wasn't doing what it was supposed to, which is to drop slightly. I threw a change-up, low, and then I threw a fast ball right down the middle—the best possible pitch if it had done what it was supposed to. There was a man on base. Since my fast ball sinks—usually!—there was every reason to believe he would bang it along the ground for a double-play possibility. That's what Satchel Paige always said: 'With men on base, throw the ball low and let the infielders do the work for you.' What did I think when he hit it? 'Damn, there goes our lead!' So I went and sat in the dugout. Nobody said anything about the home run. Why should they? We're all grown men. We don't have to console each other. One or two people came by and said, 'We'll get the runs back for you.' "

It was awkward talking to him—one wanted to commiserate and assure him that the whole thing was nonsense, and yet one had the notebook that flipped back on itself, and the pencil poised.

"What about the catcher?" I asked merrily. "I mean he was the guy who called for the pitch."

Downing laughed. "I'm the guy who's going to have to live with the ramifications. It was a fine call—a good idea."

I asked him if all the pregame commotion had bothered him—the fireworks banging away. He grinned. "So those were fireworks. I was wondering. I couldn't see from the bullpen."

A photographer appeared with a small souvenir placard handed out by the Braves testifying that the bearer had been on hand to see the record home run hit. It had a picture of Aaron and the number 715. The photographer wanted Downing to pose with it, hold it up, and smile.

Downing shook his head quickly. "I don't think that would prove anything." He looked up and down the tunnel for his taxi.

"Is it going to bother you much?" I asked.

"I've been around too many great athletes, and observed them, to kick the water cooler and throw things," he said. "If Whitey Ford had a bad day, he never made excuses or made life embarrassing for others. A lot of players think that if they throw a bat, they're showing that they're competitive. But that's not what I think. A pitcher has to maintain composure. I'm more concerned about my next start," he went on. "This thing is over. It's history. It won't bother me. There's only one home run hit off me that's ever stayed in my mind. That was the grand-slam home run that Ken Boyer hit off me in the sixth inning of the 1964 World Series that beat the Yankees 4–3 and turned the whole series around. I threw him a change-up, and there was a lot of second-guessing that I had thrown him the wrong pitch, that I should have challenged him. I thought about that for a long time. I was 23 at the time. It was a technical consideration. This one? It's more emotional. Well, pitchers don't ever like to give up home runs. But," he said in the cheery voice, "I'm not giving myself up to trauma. People will be calling to see if I've jumped out the window yet. I'm not going to wake up in the middle of the night and begin banging on the walls, and looking over the sill down into the street. The next time I pitch against him I'll get him out."

A distant roar went up from the crowd. The Braves were having a good inning.

"Your team has made six errors."

"That so? They must be pressing," Downing said. "Everybody's edgy tonight." He craned his head, looking for his taxi.

From One for the Record, 1974.

QUESTIONS

(1) Notice the detail of the author's description. How does the plain recounting of details help to recreate the atmosphere of suspense?

(2) Reread the description of the outfielder trying to catch the ball. What emotion does the image of a giant moth convey to you?

(3) What does the description suggest about the character of Hank Aaron? How is this suggestion conveyed?

THE VERBAL KARATE OF
FLORYNCE R. KENNEDY, ESQ.

GLORIA STEINEM

Like many people all over the country, I knew a little about the Flo Kennedy legend long before I met her in the flesh. In fact, the name "Flo" alone was enough to evoke images of outrageous and creative troublemaking in almost any area, from minority hiring to ban-the-bomb. Just as there was only one Eleanor or Winston, one Stokely or Marilyn or Mao, there was only one Flo.

Of course, her fame was more limited. But for those who had been in the Black Movement when it was still known as

Civil Rights, or in the Consumer Movement that predated Ralph Nader, or in the Women's Movement when it was still supposed to be a few malcontents in sneakers, or in the Peace Movement when there was more worry about nuclear fallout than about Vietnam, Flo was a political touchstone—a catalyst in the lives of people who knew her, and a source of curiosity to those who did not.

For one thing, she was a lawyer—one of the few women and even fewer black people to get into and out of Columbia Law School in the fifties—though she had not even finished working her way through college until she was over 30 years old. (Ironically, Columbia at first turned her down because she was a woman: then relented because she threatened to denounce the Law School as racist. "But, it was clearly prejudice against women," Flo remembers. "My white girlfriend from Barnard had better grades than I did, and she got nowhere.") For another thing, she was always taking unpopular cases and feeding or housing a variety of social strays—long before such unconventional behavior was common at all, especially among lawyers.

At 42, she married a Welsh writer 10 years her junior, whom she recalls fondly, though accurately, as someone who was very kind and talented when he was sober, which wasn't often. Eventually, his drinking caused their separation and, a few months later, his death. Though she had very little money and generous habits that made it impossible to keep even the small fees she earned, Flo turned all her husband's money and future royalty rights over to his mother. Whether it's a bowl of her homemade chili, a bed for the night, bail money, or free legal and life-fixing advice, the real instances of Flo's generosity probably exceed their own legend.

By the time I met her in 1969, she had become well known as a founder of the National Organization for Women—though, characteristically, she had left to form other feminist groups when NOW's rough early days were over and the going got too tame. Because we both wanted to emphasize racism and sexism as parallel problems of caste, we ended up speaking together in what Flo referred to as our "Topsy and Little Eva" team. Several times each month, we would go off to campuses and communities in Texas or Michigan or Oregon, with Flo describing herself as "tired and middle-aged" as I tried to keep up with her energetic, nonstop, and generous-hearted pace.

Since then, she has written two books—*Abortion Rap,* with Diane Schulder, published by McGraw-Hill; and *The Pathology of Oppression,* which she is polishing for publication soon by Viking. She has also founded the Feminist Party, whose chapters spring up wherever Flo pauses to give out a pamphlet or two; disrupted several major political events in a very issue-oriented and mind-expanding way; launched a suit to deprive the Catholic Church of its tax-exempt status on the grounds that it spends illegal amounts of its money to influence legislation, particularly on abortion.

And since then, I have found that—like so many others—I can't talk for more than an hour or so without quoting the infinitely quotable Flo. By combining a high-style street rap and political insight, Flo has become one of the few feminists who make humor work *for* change, not against it.

THE MILITARY

"They call us militants, but General Westmoreland, General Abrams, General Motors and General Dynamics—they're the real militants. We don't even have a helicopter."

"We ought to give the Pentagon budget to the Department of Health, Education, and Welfare, and the HEW budget to the Pentagon. Then we'd have enough money to cure cancer and sickle-cell anemia and muscular dystrophy, and we'd only have telethons for Pentagonorrhea."

"The draft is very new in this country, and a lot of people want to eliminate it. But as soon as women start talking about their rights, somebody says they should get drafted. It's as if men are saying, 'If you don't let me hold the door open for you, I'll slam it on your hand.' "

"Angela Davis is accused—only *accused*—of buying a gun for somebody, and what happens? She spends months in solitary confinement and hundreds of thousands of dollars on legal defense before she can go free. Lieutenant Calley is convicted of slaughtering kids and women in Vietnam, and what happens? He gets confined to very comfortable quarters, not even sent to jail—and Nixon defends him in public. It makes you wonder: does femocide pay?"

ON RESEARCH

"If you're lying in a ditch with a truck on your ankle, you don't send somebody to the library to find out how much the truck weighs. You get the truck *off*."

MOTHERHOOD

"Being a mother is a noble status, right? Right. So why does it change when you put 'unwed' or 'welfare' in front of it?"

OPPRESSION

"Oppression has at least four dimensions: The personal or psychological—like when you yourself believe that you're a big zero because society keeps telling you so. The private—like when some employer tries to make out with you when you ask for a job. The public—like when the government takes the money you need for child-care centers, and uses it to kill people in Indochina. And the cultural—like when the history books attribute everything we did and invented to some guy we worked for."

"Niggerization is the result of oppression—and it doesn't just apply to black people. Old people, poor people, and students can also get niggerized. Sure, there are differences in degree, but we've got to stop comparing wounds and go out after the system that does the wounding."

"If you've been hit a lot, you tend to stay sore for a while. Trying to help an oppressed person is like trying to put your arm around somebody with a sunburn."

"As the struggle intensifies, the oppressor tends to pick more attractive agents—frequently from among the oppressed."

EMPLOYMENT

"There are very few jobs that actually require a penis or vagina. All other jobs should be open to everybody."

"People always ask if a woman can be a wife and mother and have a career at the same time. Why don't they ask if she can be a hostess, chauffeur, cook, gardener, nurse, seamstress, social secretary, purchasing agent, baby machine, and courtesan—and a wife and mother too?"

REVOLUTION

"Some people say they won't work 'inside the system'—they're 'waiting for the revolution.' Well, when the ramparts are open, honey, I'll be there. But until then, I'm going to go right on zapping the business and government delinquents, the jockocrats, the fetus fetishists, and all the other niggerizers any way I can. The biggest sin is sitting on your ass."

"You can't dump one cup of sugar into the ocean and expect to get syrup. If everybody sweetened her own cup of water, then things would begin to change."

TACTICS

"Unity in a Movement situation can be overrated. If you were the Establishment, which would you rather see coming in the door: one lion or five hundred mice?"

"Loserism is when oppressed people sit around and think up reasons why they can't do something. Well, just *do* it. Thinking up reasons why you can't is the Establishment's job."

"You don't cure malaria by getting in bed with the malaria patient, and you don't cure poverty by going to live in the ghetto. You go to Wall Street and Washington and put pressure on the people who've got the cure."

"If the ass is protecting the system, ass-kicking should be undertaken regardless of the sex, ethnicity, or charm of the ass involved."

"If you've had a broken leg, you don't get up and win the Olympics. The first step is to get out of bed."

"The innocence of good people is inexcusable. Naïveté is a luxury only the pigocrats can afford."

"When you spit on someone at a cocktail party, you don't want to drown him. You just want to let him know you don't like him."

"We've got to stop sucking and begin to bite."

"Don't agonize. Organize."

MARRIAGE

"Going in and out of a closet, your mind is on what you really want in there. But the minute the door locks, all you want is out."

POWER

"Women have at least three kinds of power: Dollar Power, to boycott with; Vote Power, to take over structures with, and maybe even get somebody elected; and Body Power, to get out and support our friends and make a damned nuisance of ourselves with everybody else."

"We don't say a word when Madison Avenue makes millions off us, but we get all resentful and suspicious when some-

body in the Movement gets attention or makes a dime. That's
Nigger Nobility. If you have to lose to prove you're a good
person, we'll never get anywhere."

"Powerlessness is a dirty word."

REPRODUCTIVE FREEDOM

"If men could get pregnant, abortion would be a sacrament."

ON BEING A LAWYER

"Most lawyers are like whores. They serve the client who puts
the highest fee on the table. The biggest law firms serve the
richest johns."

"I don't practice law much any more. Even if you're honest,
the law is still a one-ass-at-a-time proposition—and what we
have to do is stop the wringer."

WOMEN WHO LIKE THINGS THE WAY THEY ARE

"Women who say they're contented just having a nice husband and two beautiful children—fine; I'm glad. Of course, I
always wonder what happens if one of the children *isn't* beautiful . . . and if housework is so rewarding, why don't men do
it, too? But this Movement isn't about getting some woman to
leave her husband. It's about social justice."

"Just because you're not feeling sick doesn't mean you
should close the hospitals."

SISTERHOOD

"Divide and conquer—that's what they try to do to any group
trying to make social change. I call it D&C. Black people are
supposed to turn against Puerto Ricans. Women are supposed

to turn against their mothers and mothers-in-law. We're all supposed to compete with each other for the favors of the ruling class."

"We criticize each other instead of the oppressor because it's less dangerous. The oppressor fights back."

"In the name of elitism, we do a crabs-in-a-barrel number, and pull down any of our number who get public attention or a small success. As long as we're into piranha-ism and horizontal hostility, honey, we ain't going to get nowhere."

SEX

"Okay, roses are beautiful, fragrant, and desirable. But how much shit should you have to walk over to get one rose?"

THE PRESS

"In a jockocratic society, you can turn on the TV and find out the score of some basketball game in Alaska—but you can't find out how many states have ratified the Equal Rights Amendment. You can turn on the radio, and hear every score in the country repeated all day long—but you don't hear how many women died from illegal abortions."

"Take a look at your local Weird Herald. On the Woman's Page, are they telling you how to make aprons out of artichokes and artichokes out of aprons? Well, protest! Picket! And if that doesn't work, try boycotting their biggest advertiser. That should turn the trick."

ON HERSELF

"My parents gave us a fantastic sense of security and worth. By the time the bigots got around to telling us we were nobody, we already *knew* we were somebody."

"When we first moved to Kansas City, some Ku Klux Klansmen gave us ten minutes to get out of the neighborhood. My father went out with a shotgun and said, 'I'll shoot the first man who steps on this porch. After that, you can get me.' And you know, those Klansmen never came back?"

"At my age and in my condition, I'm going to do what I want—I haven't got time for anything else."

"I may seem radical, but I'm not. I'm just a worm, turning."

"I know we're termites. But if all the termites got together, the house would fall down."

"You've got to rattle your cage door. You've got to let them know that you're in there, and that you want out. Make noise. Cause trouble. You may not win right away, but you'll sure have a lot more fun."

Irene Davall and Susan Margolis—writers and Feminist Party organizers from New York and California respectively—helped with the collection of these quotes. All words and phrases not to be found in any dictionary were coined by Flo herself.

From Ms. Magazine, 1973.

QUESTIONS

(1) What are the characteristics of Flo Kennedy that clearly emerge from Gloria Steinem's sketch?

(2) Look at the Kennedy aphorisms under "Oppression." On the basis of these alone how would you characterize her attitudes toward race, feminism, government and the dominant points of view in our society?

(3) Summarize the tactics of Flo Kennedy as represented by the aphorisms listed under "Tactics."

(4) Define the following terms coined by Flo Kennedy: niggerization, jockocrats, loserism, piranha-ism and Pentagonnorhea.

RIDING THE UNDERGROUND RANGE WITH ABBIE

KEN KELLEY

One April day in San Francisco last year, I was awakened at the crack of noon by the trill of my doorbell. A postman with an American-flag lapel pin handed me a letter with four cents' postage due. Inside was a cryptic note: "Hi! Greeting from The Underground! Wanna rendez-vous? Go to a pay phone and call ———, 11 P.M., April 15. 11:05 will be too late. Your old pal, Abbie." The postmark was Seattle; the area code, Miami. I pictured a coast-to-coast tunnel of radical molework.

For the next three days, I found myself reliving old memories of Abbie Hoffman. It had been more than a year since I had last seen him, just before he vanished in the wake of his cocaine bust. I remembered the first time I had met him, in 1968. It was in New York's Tompkins Square, when the Lower East Side teemed with the flotsam and jetsam of flower children not yet wilted. A demonic apparition had popped out of the hordes, its head a mass of friz, and parked itself in front of me.

"I'm Abbie. Wanna see my tongue?"

Nobody had ever asked me that before. Before I could muster a "Shucks," a wondrous membrane slowly unfurled itself, wet, flat and craggy. I knew it was the beginning of a life-long friendship.

At the appointed hour, I walked to a nearby phone booth and dialed the number. Instead of Abbie's Boston pool-hall twang, I heard a friendly, businesslike female voice. She was, she said, also at a pay phone, and "our friend" wanted to see me. If I wanted to meet him, I was to go to a certain department-store parking lot in Phoenix in exactly one week, at three P.M.

Now, there are no doubt less interesting places for hanging around to meet an underground fugitive than a suburban department store in the Arizona desert, but after three hours of waiting, I was becoming bored. Then I noticed a white

T-bird, late model, pull up near me. Opening the door, a tall, slender, flaxen-haired woman beckoned. I nervously plopped myself into the front seat without a word. She wheeled out like a pro.

"Ken, my name is Angel," she said after a few minutes on the road. It was the same mystery voice from the Miami phone. I was to find out later that she had been a highly paid fashion model before taking up with Abbie. She handed me a black kerchief. "I know this sounds weird, but you have to put this on and slouch down in your seat."

Perhaps half an hour later, we turned left, went another 100 yards or so and turned left again. She shut off the ignition. "Take that thing off, keep your eyes averted and follow me." We walked up two flights of concrete stairs. A typical American Highway Gothic motel room, empty. "Wait here, on the bed," she instructed, and walked into an adjoining room. I heard the doorknob click. I opened my eyes and in strode a handsome, auburn-haired, seersuckered dead ringer for an associate professor of philosophy at Bryn Mawr. The professor smiled, half-yawned and, in a familiar brogue, said, "Oh, shit, they told me *Clarence* Kelley [of the FBI] was out here. I guess he'll have to wait till the Ks come around again next year."

"Abbie!" I whispered loudly.

"How'd you know it was me?"

"I'd recognize that tongue anywhere," I said.

"This is only one of about seven disguises I have down."

He wasn't kidding. Over in a corner was an antique steamer trunk, which Abbie proceeded to open with some ceremony. Inside he had stashed an assortment of costumes suitable for Madame Tussaud's. For formal occasions ("such as Rockefeller's funeral"), a dark-blue tuxedo with tails and satin cummerbund. For more casual attire, a simple silk pinstripe, black. Abbie stopped me before I could inspect the final item of apparel—he wanted to model it personally. Faster than Clark Kent in a phone booth, he emerged from the bathroom sporting three proud sergeant's stripes on his sleeve: a New York City policeman posed menacingly before me. "I just got promoted last week!" he shouted. "Now, up against the wall!"

Inside a compartment of the trunk was his "Head Kit"—a huge assortment of make-up, wigs and beards, face putty, eyebrow paste-ons, a *yarmulke,* even a stretchy pink fake scalp for the Telly Savalas look.

Abbie chose to remain in his police uniform for the duration of my visit. We had an auld-lang-syne chat for the next couple of hours. Somewhere in the course of it, I said, "Say, why don't we do an interview? You know, sit down for three straight days of Q. and A. I bet that *Playboy.* . . ."

"We'll see. I have to consult my collective, you know, before I can give you a yes or no. I'm a full-fledged Commie now."

Then a treat—in the motel kitchenette, Abbie fixed a sumptuous five-course French meal that would rate a couple of stars from Michelin, presented with a flourish.

Abbie, Angel and I sat around briefly after the meal. Abbie informed me that I was taking a nine-o'clock flight back to San Francisco in the morning, that Angel would drive me and that when he figured out his plans, he would let me know in the same way that this meeting had been arranged. Meantime, I should put out a feeler to *Playboy,* but I was to select only one editor at the magazine, swear him to secrecy and communicate with him only in person or by mail. Abbie then swept Angel up in his arms and exited stage left.

Memorial Day weekend, I found myself in San Diego in the engaging presence of my two scofflaw friends. While it did not seem particularly frightening or different for me to walk around publicly with Abbie, he wanted to practice a day of being "normal," since the major problem he had with his friends from the past was *their* paranoia. It was an enjoyable, relaxed day that ended in another motel room, this one with sauna and whirlpool.

But behind this deliberately cheerful and relaxed vibration, I could sense Abbie's terrible uneasiness. His humor was more manic than usual—and his normal pace left most people breathless. There was a choppiness to his gestures; a haunted look would enshroud his eyes from time to time. I couldn't figure out why, but Abbie scared me. I soon found out. While he went downstairs to buy an after-dinner cigar, Angel told me about her past month with him. The pressure of meticulously preparing a tape to be shown on public television had wiped him out. On an impulse, he had taken Angel for a week-end fling in Las Vegas. It was there, she said, that Abbie had lost all his marbles. For 17 hours straight, he screamed his real name at the top of his lungs over and over again within ear-shot of hotel residents. Angel barely survived the ordeal herself.

Given his condition, the three of us agreed that we should find a spot for the interview that would be sunny, warm and relaxing.

"Why not Mexico?" I asked jokingly, as we were only an hour's drive from the border. To my startled chagrin, he looked at me with the old why-not gleam in his eye—why not do something a bit daring, unpredictable? Spontaneity ruled the moment.

So we packed our suitcases, beat the motel bill—I wanted to pay it, but Abbie insisted it would be "good practice" not to— and headed for a downtown bookstore.

As we got into the T-bird, I felt a strange pulsation under my seat, kind of a lilting back and forth. We parked and I went into a bookstore to look for a Mexico-on-five-dollars-a-day book. When I emerged, a surreal scene greeted me. Abbie was clutching a large Siamese cat by the nape of the neck, trot-ting after a slinky-haired woman who obviously thought him daft. I inquired as to what the hell was going on.

"This cat, this goddamn cat came out from under the seat!" Abbie yelled. "So I figured it belonged to someone around here. Then this girl that I'm *sure* is Cher came out of that shop, and this looks like a cat she would own. . . ."

"C'mon, Abbie, what would Cher be doing in San Diego?"

"I dunno—getting married to a sailor?"

We deposited the cat on the sidewalk and headed for Tiju-ana, stopping for a Baskin-Robbins sugar hit first. The border crossing was a cinch and we did a little shopping in town for some tequila, cigarettes and perfume that Angel claimed could be bought only there and in Aix-en-Provence.

We decided to head for the eastern shore of the Gulf of California—lots of beaches, small towns and sun.

We were all pretty tired when we arrived at a town called Guaymas. We drove until we came to a hotel right on the ocean with an alluring stretch of beach. Abbie went to sleep immediately and Angel and I decided to head into town for a little local culture.

We walked around town for 45 minutes and then heard the strains of rock 'n' roll emanating from a distant courtyard. We paid our way in and began dancing in a large, crowded room off the courtyard.

Suddenly a scuffle broke out on the other side of the room. Instinctively, I ducked and moved to a corner with Angel, though the distance between us and the commotion was a good 50 yards. I felt a whizzing pass in front of my lips, very close. I turned just in time to see Angel clutch her hands to her face. At her feet was an unopened can of beer, the top rim bloody. She took away her hand and a long, ugly scarlet gash started to ooze to the left of her eye, slanting down to her ear. She was in a state of shock, as was I. Complete pandemonium broke loose, everyone wanting to help, offering advice in a high-pitched Spanish staccato. I maneuvered her into the back room and someone called the Red Cross.

Two soldiers in full military regalia showed up, ushered us into a jeep and drove breakneck through the narrow cobblestone streets to the Red Cross Center. Inside, we found there was no doctor on duty—but a very crisp and reassuring nurse showed us into a makeshift operating room. Angel lay on the one cot in the room, clutching my hand fiercely. The problem was to prevent the nurse from stitching up the wound on the outside and leaving a scar. Angel's modeling career would end unless I kept a constant eye on the nurse to make sure she understood what we wanted—inside stitching, yes, but only a butterfly bandage on top.

An ungodly series of yelps and thuds commenced in the hallway outside and five brown-shirted Mexican gendarmes hustled in a bloody specimen. He was kicking and screaming, so they began to beat him with truncheons a few feet away from us until he subsided into a bloody heap. A few minutes later, there was another commotion and another unfortunate was dragged in, this one in even worse shape, with bullet wounds in his stomach and legs. The victim's mother came in, waving her hands frantically in the air, tears streaming down her face. One of the cops turned menacingly toward her. Jesus, I thought, now they're going to beat *her* into a pulp. At that moment, a nun walked in and interposed herself between them. She was a large nun. A typical Saturday night in the country, I figured.

The stitch job was completed and Angel and I returned to the hotel.

Now the real fear set in, a fear that transcended even the night's terrors. How would Abbie react? Would he pull another Las Vegas? We decided to let sleeping Abbies lie, and Angel said she would sleep in the back of the car while I tiptoed into the room. I managed maybe 15 minutes of light dozing, then heard him yawn and start.

"Where's Angel?"

I jumped up, ran to the basin and splashed water in my bleary eyes and recapitulated the story as fast as I could, trying to sound calm. I don't think I sounded calm. Abbie ran out to Angel in the car and they had a talk while I chain-smoked Fiesta cigarettes. In half an hour, he came back to the room. He was shaken and I smelled trouble. "We have to get back to the States right away," he said. "Go check on flights for you and Angel—I'll drive the car."

I knew there was a small airport in Guaymas and I trudged into the hotel lobby to get the clerk to place a call to the airlines. As I approached the desk, I did a double take. Surely this experience had finally taken its toll and I was a goner. The lobby was filled with Americans, and very unusual Americans, at that. Liza Minnelli, Burt Reynolds. A groggy-looking Gene Hackman. I cornered one of the crew—I wasn't hallucinating—and found that the cast of *Lucky Lady* was staying at that hotel on location.

I was strictly on automatic pilot. I was told there was a plane available in about two hours and booked two seats on it. I prayed that Abbie wouldn't pick that moment to stumble into the lobby. My prayer was answered: He waited fully 20 seconds after Liza had gone out the exit. The sun was rising and before I could head him off, he strolled out onto the veranda. All those Americans around—What's up? It took him all of several seconds to discover he was on location. Hollywood! Movies! His glitterbug went haywire. Inside of ten minutes, he had persuaded the entire crew that he was in pictures himself, a Hollywood film producer, but most of the cast concluded he was an obnoxious creep. An hour and a half to go,

King started to smile again, but his mouth suddenly froze and I looked to my right just in time to see Dean Rusk's swollen face about 18 inches away from my own. King reached out to shake his hand. "Congratulations, sir," he said. "We're all very proud of you."

"Balls," I muttered.

After Rusk had gone inside, King stared at me and shook his head sadly. "Why can't you give the old man some peace?" he said. "He's harmless now. Jesus, you'll get us in trouble yet."

"Don't worry," I said. "He's deaf as a rock."

"Maybe so," King replied. "But some of those people with him can hear okay. One of the women over there at the ceremony asked me who you were and I said you were an undercover agent, but she was still pissed off about what you said. 'You should have Senator Kennedy teach him some manners,' she told me. 'Not even a government agent should be allowed to talk like that in public.' "

"Like what?" I said. "That stuff about the blood on his hands?"

King laughed. "Yeah, that really jolted her. Jesus, Hunter, you gotta remember, these are genteel people." He nodded solemnly. "And this is their turf. Dean Rusk is a goddamn national hero down here. What are his friends supposed to think when the senator comes down from Washington to deliver the eulogy at the unveiling of Rusk's portrait, and he brings some guy with him who starts asking people why the artist didn't paint any blood on the hands?"

"Don't worry," I said. "Just tell 'em it's part of my deep cover. Hell, nobody connects me with Kennedy anyway. I've been careful to stay a safe distance away from you bastards. You think I want to be seen at a ceremony honoring Dean Rusk?"

"Don't kid yourself," he said as we walked inside. "They know you're with us. You wouldn't be here if they didn't. This is a very exclusive gathering, my boy. We're the only ones on the guest list without some kind of *very* serious title: they're all either judges or state senators or the Right Honorable this, the Right Honorable that . . ."

I looked around the room, and indeed there was no mistaking the nature of the crowd. This was not just a bunch of

good ol' boys who all happened to be alumni of the University
of Georgia Law School; these were the *honored* alumni, the
ranking 150 or so who had earned, stolen or inherited enough
distinction to be culled from the lists and invited to the unveiling of Rusk's portrait, followed by a luncheon with Senator Kennedy, Governor Carter, Judge Crater and numerous
other hyper-distinguished guests whose names I forget. . . .
And Jimmy King was right: this was not a natural habitat for
anybody wearing dirty white basketball shoes, no tie and nothing except *Rolling Stone* to follow his name on the guest list
in that space reserved for titles. If it had been a gathering of
distinguished alumni from the University of Georgia Medical
School, the title space on the guest list would have been in
front of the names, and I would have fit right in. Hell, I could
even have joined a few conversations and nobody would have
given a second thought to any talk about "blood on the
hands."

Right. But this was law day in Georgia, and I was the only
Doctor in the room. . . . So I had to be passed off as some
kind of undercover agent, traveling for unknown reasons with
Senator Kennedy. Not even the Secret Service agents understand my role in the entourage. All they knew was that I had
walked off the plane from Washington with Teddy, and I had
been with them ever since. Nobody gets introduced to a Secret
Service agent; they are expected to *know* who everybody is—
and if they don't know, they act like they do and hope for the
best.

It is not my wont to take undue advantage of the Secret
Service. We have gone through some heavy times together, as
it were, and ever since I wandered into a room in the Biltmore
Hotel in New York one night during the 1972 campaign and
found three SS agents smoking a joint, I have felt pretty much
at ease around them. . . . So it seemed only natural, down in
Georgia, to ask one of the four agents in our detail for the
keys to the trunk of his car so I could lock my leather satchel
in a safe place, instead of carrying it around with me.

Actually, the agent had put the bag in the trunk on his
own, rather than give me the key. . . . But when I sat down
at our table in the cafeteria and saw that the only available
beverage was iced tea, I remembered that one of the things in

my satchel was a quart of Wild Turkey, and I wanted it. On
the table in front of me—and everyone else—was a tall glass of
iced tea that looked to be the same color as bourbon. Each
glass had a split slice of lemon on its rim: so I removed the
lemon, poured the tea into Paul Kirk's water glass, and asked
one of the agents at the next table for the key to the trunk. He
hesitated for a moment, but one of the law school deans or
maybe Judge Crater was already talking into the mike up
there at the speakers' table, so the path of least disturbance
was to give me the key, which he did. . . .

And I thought nothing of it until I got outside and opened
the trunk. . . .

Cazart!

If your life ever gets dull, check out the trunk of the next
SS car you happen to see. You won't need a key; they open
just as easily as any other trunk when a six-foot whipsteel is
properly applied. . . . But open the bugger *carefully,* because
those gentlemen keep about 69 varieties of instant death inside. Jesus, I was literally staggered by the mass of weaponry in
the back of that car: there were machine guns, gas masks,
hand grenades, cartridge belts, tear gas canisters, ammo boxes,
bulletproof vests, chains, saws and probably a lot of other
things. . . . But all of a sudden I realized that two passing
students had stopped right next to me on the sidewalk and I
heard one of them say, "God almighty! Look at *that* stuff!"

So I quickly filled my glass with Wild Turkey, put the bottle back in the trunk and slammed it shut just like you'd slam
any other trunk . . . and that was when I turned around to
see Jimmy Carter coming at me with his head down, his teeth
bared and his eyes so wildly dilated that he looked like a
springtime bat. . . .

What? No. That was later in the day, on my third or fourth
trip to the trunk with the iced-tea glass. I have been sitting
here in a frozen, bewildered stupor for 50 or 55 minutes trying
to figure out where that last image came from. My memories
of that day are extremely vivid, for the most part, and the
more I think back on it now, the more certain I am that whatever I might have seen coming at me in that kind of bent-
over, fast-swooping style of the springtime bat was *not* Governor Carter. Probably it was a hunchbacked student on his way
to final exams in the school of landscaping, or maybe just try-

ing to walk fast and tie his shoes at the same time. . . . Or it could have been nothing at all; there is no mention in my notebook about anything trying to sneak up on me in a high-speed crouch while I was standing out there in the street.

According to my notes, in fact, Jimmy Carter had arrived at the cafeteria not long after Kennedy—and if he attracted any attention from the crowd that had come to see Teddy I would probably have noticed it and made at least a small note to emphasize the contrast in style—something like: "12:09, Carter suddenly appears in slow-moving crowd behind TK. No autographs, no bodyguards & now a blue plastic suit instead of Levi's///No recognition, no greetings, just a small sandy-haired man looking for somebody to shake hands with. . . ."

That is the kind of note I would have made, if I'd noticed his arrival at all, which I didn't. Because it was not until around ten o'clock on the night of the New Hampshire primary, almost two years later, that there was any real reason for a journalist to make a note on the time and style of Jimmy Carter's arrival for any occasion at all, and especially not in a crowd that had come to rub shoulders with big-time heavies like Ted Kennedy and Dean Rusk. He is not an imposing figure in any way: and even now, with his face on every TV screen in the country at least five nights a week, I'd be tempted to bet $100 to anybody else's $500 that Jimmy Carter could walk—by himself and in a normal noonday crowd—from one end of Chicago's huge O'Hare Airport to the other, without being recognized by anybody. . . .

Or at least not by anybody who had never met him personally, or who had not seen him anywhere except on TV. Because there is nothing about Carter that would make him any more noticeable than anyone else you might pass in one of those long and crowded corridors in O'Hare. He could pass for a Fuller Brush man on any street in America. . . . But if Jimmy Carter had decided, 15 years ago, to sign on as a brush and gimcrack salesman for the Fuller people, he would be president of the Fuller Brush Company today and every medicine chest in the country would be loaded with Carter-Fuller brushes. . . . And if he had gone into the heroin business, every respectable household between Long Island and Los Angeles would have at least one resident junkie.

Ah. . . . but that is not what we need to be talking about right now, is it?

The only thing I remember about the first hour or so of that luncheon was a powerful sense of depression with the life I was drifting into. According to the program, we were in for a long run of speeches, remarks, comments, etc., on matters connected with the law school. Carter and Kennedy were the last two names on the list of speakers, which meant there was no hope of leaving early. I thought about going back to the beer parlor and watching a baseball game on TV, but King warned me against it. "We don't know how long this goddamn thing is gonna last," he said, "and that's a hell of a long walk from here, isn't it?"

. . . .

I am still not sure when I began listening to what Carter was saying, but at some point about ten minutes into his remarks I noticed a marked difference in the style and tone of the noise coming from the speakers' table and I found myself listening, for the first time all day. Carter had started off with a few quiet jokes about people feeling honored to pay ten or twelve dollars a head to hear Kennedy speak, but the only way he could get people to listen to him was to toss in a free lunch along with his remarks. The audience laughed politely a few times, but after he'd been talking for about 15 minutes I noticed a general uneasiness in the atmosphere of the room, and nobody was laughing anymore. At that point we were all still under the impression that Carter's "remarks" would consist of a few minutes of friendly talk about the law school, a bit of praise for Rusk, an introduction for Kennedy, and that would be it. . . .

But we were wrong, and the tension in the room kept increasing as more and more people realized it. Very few if any of them had supported Carter when he won the governorship, and now that he was just about finished with his four-year term and barred by law from running again, they expected him to bow out gracefully and go back to raising peanuts. If he had chosen that occasion to announce that he'd decided to run for president in 1976, the reaction would almost certainly have been a ripple of polite laughter, because they would know he was kidding. Carter had not been a bad governor, but so what? We were, after all, in Georgia; and, besides that, the South already had one governor running for president. . . . Back in the spring of 1974 George Wallace was a national power; he had rattled the hell out of that big cage called the Democratic National Committee in 1972, and when he said he planned to do it again in 1976 he was taken very seriously.

So I would probably have chuckled along with the others if Carter had said something about running for president at the *beginning* of his "remarks" that day, but I would not have chuckled if he'd said it at the end. . . . Because it was a king hell bastard of a speech, and by the time it was over he had rung every bell in the room. Nobody seemed to know exactly what to make of it, but they knew it was sure as hell not what they'd come there to hear.

I have heard hundreds of speeches by all kinds of candidates and politicians—usually against my will and for generally the same reasons I got trapped into hearing this one—but I have never heard a sustained piece of political oratory that impressed me any more than the speech Jimmy Carter made on that Saturday afternoon in May 1974. It ran about 45 minutes, climbing through five very distinct gear changes while the audience muttered uneasily and raised their eyebrows at each other, and one of the most remarkable things about the speech is that it is such a rare piece of oratorical artwork that it remains vastly impressive, even if you don't necessarily believe Carter was sincere and truthful in all the things he said. Viewed purely in the context of rhetorical drama and political theater, it ranks with General Douglas MacArthur's "old soldiers never die" address to the Congress in 1951—which still stands as a masterpiece of insane bullshit, if nothing else.

There were, however, a lot of people who believed every word and sigh of MacArthur's speech, and they wanted to make him president—just as a lot of people who are still uncertain about Jimmy Carter would want to make him president if he could figure out some way to deliver a contemporary version of his 1974 Law Day speech on network TV. . . . Or, hell, even the same identical speech; a national audience might be slightly puzzled by some of the references to obscure judges, grade-school teachers and backwoods Georgia courthouses, but I think the totality of the speech would have the same impact today as it did two years ago.

But there is not much chance of it happening. . . . And that brings up another remarkable aspect of the Law Day speech: it had virtually no impact at all when he delivered it, except on the people who heard it, and most of them were more stunned and puzzled by it than impressed. They had not come there to hear lawyers denounced as running dogs of the status quo, and there is still some question in my own mind—and in Carter's too, I suspect—about what he came there to say. There was no written text of the speech, no press to report it, no audience hungry to hear it, and no real reason for giving it—except that Jimmy Carter had a few serious things on his mind that day, and he figured it was about time to unload them, whether the audience liked it or not. . . .

Which gets to another interesting point of the speech: although Carter himself now says, "That was probably the best speech I ever made," he has yet to make another one like it—not even to the extent of lifting some of the best images and ideas for incorporation into his current speeches—and his campaign staff attached so little importance to it that Carter's only tape recording of his Law Day remarks got lost somewhere in the files and, until about two months ago, the only existing tape of the speech was the one I'd had copied off the original, before it was lost. I've been carrying the bastard around with me for two years, playing it in some extremely unlikely situations for people who would look at me like I was finally over the hump into terminal brain damage when I'd say they were going to have to spend the next 45 minutes listening to a political speech by some ex-governor of Georgia.

It was not until I showed up in New Hampshire and Massachusetts for the 1976 primaries and started playing my tape of the Law Day speech for a few friends, journalists and even some of Carter's top staff people who'd never heard it that Pat Caddell noticed that almost everybody who heard the speech was as impressed by it as I was. . . . But even now, after Caddell arranged to dub 50 tape copies off of my copy, nobody in Carter's brain trust has figured out what to do with them.

I am not quite sure what I would do with them, myself, if I were Carter, because it is entirely possible that the very qualities that made the Law Day speech so impressive for me would have exactly the opposite effect on Carter's new national constituency. The voice I hear on my tape is the same one all those good conservative folk out there on the campaign trail have found so appealing, but very few of them would find anything familiar in what the voice is saying. The Jimmy Carter who has waltzed so triumphantly down the middle of the road through one Democratic primary after another is a cautious, conservative and vaguely ethereal Baptist Sunday school teacher who seems to promise, above all else, a return to normalcy, a resurrection of the national self-esteem, and a painless redemption from all the horrors and disillusion of Watergate. With President Carter's firm hand on the helm, the ship of state will once again sail a true and steady course, all the crooks and liars and thieves who somehow got control of the government during the turmoil of the sixties will be driven out of the temple once and for all, and the White House will be so overflowing with honesty, decency, justice, love and compassion that it might even glow in the dark.

It is a very alluring vision, and nobody understands this better than Jimmy Carter. The electorate feels a need to be cleansed, reassured and revitalized. The underdogs of yesteryear have had their day, and they blew it. The radicals and reformers of the sixties promised peace, but they turned out to be nothing but incompetent troublemakers. Their plans that had looked so fine on paper led to chaos and disaster when hack politicians tried to implement them. The promise of Civil Rights turned into the nightmare of busing. The call for law and order led straight to Watergate. And the long struggle between the Hawks and the Doves caused violence in the streets and a military disaster in Vietnam. Nobody won, in the end, and when the dust finally settled, "extremists" at both ends of the political spectrum were thoroughly discredited. And by the time the 1976 presidential campaign got under way, the high ground was all in the middle of the road.

Jimmy Carter understands this, and he has tailored his campaign image to fit the new mood almost perfectly. . . . But back in May of 1974 when he flew up to Athens to make his "remarks" at the Law Day ceremonies, he was not as concerned with preserving his moderate image as he is now. He was thinking more about all the trouble he'd had with judges, lawyers, lobbyists and other minions of the Georgia establishment while he was governor—and now, with only six more months in the office, he wanted to have a few words with these people.

There was not much anger in his voice when he started talking, but halfway through the speech it was too obvious for anybody in the room to ignore. But there was no way to cut him short, and he knew it. It was the anger in his voice that first caught my attention, I think, but what sent me back out to the trunk to get my tape recorder instead of another drink was the spectacle of a Southern politician telling a crowd of Southern judges and lawyers that "I'm not qualified to talk to you about law, because in addition to being a peanut farmer, I'm an engineer and nuclear physicist, not a lawyer. . . . But I read a lot and I listen a lot. One of the sources for my understanding about the proper application of criminal justice and the system of equities is from Reinhold Niebuhr. The other source of my understanding about what's right and wrong in this society is from a friend of mine, a poet named Bob Dylan. Listening to his records about 'The Lonesome Death of Hattie Carroll' and 'Like a Rolling Stone' and 'The Times They Are A-Changin',' I've learned to appreciate the dynamism of change in a modern society."

At first I wasn't sure I was hearing him right and I looked over at Jimmy King. "What the hell did I just hear?" I asked.

King smiled and looked at Paul Kirk, who leaned across the table and whispered, "He said his top two advisers are Bob Dylan and Reinhold Niebuhr."

I nodded and got up to go outside for my tape recorder. I could tell by the rising anger in Carter's voice that we were in for an interesting ride. . . . And by the time I got back he was whipping on the crowd about judges who took bribes in return for reduced prison sentences, lawyers who deliberately cheated illiterate blacks, and cops who abused people's rights with something they called a "consent warrant."

"I had lunch this week with the members of the Judicial Selection Committee and they were talking about a 'consent search warrant,' " he said. "I didn't know what a consent search warrant was. They said, 'Well, that's when two policemen go to a house. One of them goes to the front door and knocks on it and the other one runs around to the back door and yells 'come in.' "

The crowd got a laugh out of that one, but Carter was just warming up and for the next 20 or 30 minutes his voice was the only sound in the room. Kennedy was sitting just a few feet to Carter's left, listening carefully but never changing the thoughtful expression on his face as Carter railed and bitched about a system of criminal justice that allows the rich and the privileged to escape punishment for their crimes and sends poor people to prison because they can't afford to bribe the judge. . . .

. . . .

So this will have to be it, . . . I would need a lot more time and space than I have to properly describe either the reality or the reaction to Jimmy Carter's Law Day speech, which was and still is the heaviest and most eloquent thing I have ever heard from the mouth of a politician. It was the voice of an angry agrarian populist, extremely precise in its judgments and laced with some of the most original, brilliant and occasionally bizarre political metaphors anybody in that room will ever be likely to hear.

The final turn of the screw was another ugly example of crime and degradation in the legal profession, and this time Carter went right to the top. Nixon had just released his own, self-serving version of "the White House tapes," and Carter was shocked when he read the transcripts. "The Constitution charges us with a direct responsibility for determining what our government is and ought to be," he said. And then, after a long pause, he went on: "Well. . . . I have read parts of the embarrassing transcripts, and I've seen the proud statement of a former attorney general who protected his boss, and now brags of the fact that he tiptoed through a minefield and came out. . . . quote, clean, unquote." Another pause, and then: "You know, I can't imagine somebody like Thomas Jefferson tiptoeing through a minefield on the technicalities of the law, and then bragging about being *clean* afterwards. . . ."

Forty-five minutes later, on our way back to Atlanta in the governor's small plane, I told Carter I wanted a transcript of his speech.

"There is no transcript," he said.

I smiled, thinking he was putting me on. The speech had sounded like a product of five or six tortured drafts. . . . But

he showed a page and a half of scrawled notes in his legal pad
and said that was all he had.

"Jesus Christ," I said. "That was one of the damnedest
things I've ever heard. You mean you just winged it all the
way through?"

He shrugged and smiled faintly. "Well," he said, "I had a
pretty good idea what I was going to say, before I came up
here—but I guess I was a little surprised at how it came out."

Kennedy didn't have much to say about the speech. He said
he'd "enjoyed it," but he still seemed uncomfortable and preoccupied for some reason. Carter and I talked about the time
he invited Dylan and some of his friends out to the governor's
mansion after a concert in Atlanta. "I really enjoyed it," he
said with a big grin. "It was a real honor to have him visit my
home."

I had already decided, by then, that I liked Jimmy Carter—
but I had no idea that he'd made up his mind, a few months
earlier, to run for the presidency in 1976. And if he had told
me his little secret that day on the plane back to Atlanta, I'm
not sure I'd have taken him seriously. . . . But if he had told
me and if I had taken him seriously, I would probably have
said that he could have my vote, for no other reason except
the speech I'd just heard.

From *Rolling Stone*, 1976.

QUESTIONS

(1) In his opening paragraphs, the author is obviously trying
to offer a contrasting description of Jimmy Carter and Ted
Kennedy. What is the distinction between the two men?

(2) What is the effect of the author's intrusion of his own personality into his account? Does it add to or detract from the
story?

(3) Why was the author attending the Law Day dinner?

(4) What are the characteristics of Carter's speech that most
impressed the author?

(5) What was the reaction of the audience to the speech?

(6) What picture of Jimmy Carter emerges from the narrative? Is it a positive one?

(7) This article was written well before the nomination and election of Carter, and it created a stir when it first appeared in *Rolling Stone*. Why do you think it elicited a strong reaction?

ABOUT MORRIS HELLER

JANET HELLER

My father, Morris Heller, will soon be 82. Each weekday he leaves the small real estate office he shares with my brother to take a three-mile walk through the town of Cedar Grove, N.J. If, for some reason, he is off schedule or neglects to make the tour, concern is expressed among those accustomed to seeing and greeting him.

He is in excellent health, reads four newspapers a day and is up-to-date on business trends and politics. Nor does he overlook his patriarchal duties. When articles appear that he thinks might improve the quality of my life or that of my children, we receive them in the mail and later a follow-up phone call soliciting our response.

Father was born in the Ukraine in Russia. He arrived at Ellis Island in 1911 at the age of 16. His grandchildren find it hard to believe that he never saw a train until the day his mother gathered up her children to make the trip by rail to the Netherlands. One-way passage across the Atlantic in those days cost $28 and the family somehow survived the rigors of the two-week sea voyage.

Once settled in New Jersey, Father initially found work in a factory producing fans. Eager to learn English, he didn't discover for several days that his co-workers were speaking Swedish. To this day he regrets that he speaks three languages with an accent—managing Russian with a Yiddish accent, Yiddish with a Russian, and English with a mixture of both.

As children growing up in a small town, my brother and I were the only ones whose father was "different." He couldn't sing the national anthem or remember the words of the Pledge of Allegiance and found it difficult to comprehend the intricacies of football and baseball.

Yet, he was a very special parent. On rainy days he was always waiting for us at the school door, rubbers in hand; if we were ill he was there to take us home. He worked in town and was available to take us to music and dancing lessons or on little drives. When I was a small child he planted beside my window a beautiful oak tree that grew to be taller than our home.

And, for a man who never owed a nickel to anyone and never bought anything on the installment plan, he boldly purchased a grand piano for me when I was ten and spent years paying off the debt.

Family is everything to him. He keeps his grandchildren enthralled with stories about the old country. Imagine, never tasting ice cream or chocolate or seeing an orange until the age of 16!

The primitiveness of his youth, the descriptions of the village where families shared their homes with domestic animals, the unavailability of luxuries that we deem essentials today— these seem more fiction than fact. But it is still vivid to him as is the memory that what relieved the searing poverty was the dream of emigrating to America.

Nor can the grandchildren envision how difficult life was for the countless immigrants who once in America continued to suffer hardships. Father worked ten hours a day in an unheated factory (60 hours a week for $7), walked miles every day to save a few pennies, and lined his thin jacket with newspapers to keep out the cold.

Yet the desire to make something of himself was overwhelming. He entered New York University with a high school certificate at the age of 20 and worked his way through six years of night school, ultimately receiving a diploma and the sense of pride that went with it.

It is always an accomplishment to live a productive and disciplined life and enjoy the respect and love of others. But to

be old with grace, dignity and good health is a dream few
realize.

Father is still full of energy and enthusiasm. He is gentle,
courtly and good-humored. He blushes when an off-color remark is made and finds many current social trends incomprehensible. He has never smoked and maintains that liquor
gives him palpitations. Yet he somehow manages to view the
behavior of his children and grandchildren with tolerance
and, when necessary, benign disapproval, realizing that our
lives have been rooted in a different soil.

When he calls, the question is always the same: "Is everything under control?" And more often than not it is, simply
because he cares and isn't afraid to show how much we matter
to him.

From The New York Times, 1976.

QUESTIONS

(1) What are the characteristics of Morris Heller that would
make his neighbors particularly conscious of his absence?

(2) What kind of a father is he?

(3) Notice the simplicity of the style of the author. How is
that simplicity particularly appropriate in this case?

THE SENSE OF THE 70's

POP CULTURE

Popular music, television, and motion pictures constitute a kind of triumvirate in our society, ruling and shaping the imaginations of virtually all of its citizens. The extent of their appeal and the ramifications of it have been the subject of increasingly more thoughtful and considered commentary. It becomes clear under close scrutiny that popular culture holds a mirror up to society, revealing both the appearance of reality and, inadvertently, the wishes, lies, and dreams underlying that reality; and, as a consequence, it causes us to superimpose on the real world the fantasies of popular culture.

Reprinted here, for example, is an essay entitled "The Scary World of TV's Heavy Viewer." The article reports the results of a study showing that people who watch television as much as four hours a day tend to derive their notions of the real world from television rather than the other way around. As a result they assume that the world is a more dangerous place than in fact it is. As if in tribute to this reality-transforming power of television, John Leonard, in "Nausea in the Afternoon," offers a hallucinatory vision of Marx and Freud appearing on a TV game show.

But for all its pervasive power, even TV has not been able to generate the intensity of reaction of rock music. Born in the fifties, reaching explosive prominence in the sixties, rock continues to exert its extraordinary power on the life style of the time. Some sense of its appeal is evident in Nat Hentoff's kaleidoscopic coverage of the Joan Baez-Bob Dylan Rolling Thunder Revue Tour in 1975. Dylan's all but mythical status is reflected in Hentoff's ironic but respectful portrait.

Nor can TV's miniature twenty-inch world satisfy the larger appetites of its audience. For the more powerful, consuming myths of our time, movies remain the dominant source. As evidence of their continuing hold on our collective imagination, the seventies witnessed the remake of one of the most popular visual fantasies of all time, *King Kong*. Wallace Markfield's rhapsodic tribute to the original ("The Kong and I") testifies to the strength of that hold.

As if in competition with these powerful magnets, some American novelists have explored sexual self-revelation as a means of calling attention to themselves ("The Writer as Sexual Show-Off").

The popularity of the writer-as-performer is matched by the popularity of the performer-as-writer as in the case of the comedian George Carlin, who sees himself primarily as a writer. Thus the line between traditional culture and popular culture becomes increasingly less clear—for better and for worse.

NAUSEA IN THE AFTERNOON

JOHN LEONARD

It has drizzled on you for a month; charity shrinks. You're
trapped in New York City over a long summer weekend; hope
doesn't spring, it autumns. You wander into a midtown Chinese bar for a pisco sour and the Mets game: faith moves bow-
els. And, naturally, it is raining even in Montreal; a washout
with a French accent. But the bartender has taken so much
trouble to achieve a pisco sour, and the color TV set is already
warmed up, and although you've already done a column
about daytime TV you were sick at the time and maybe you
missed some nuances—so you watch:
  (a) *Three on a Match,* and/or *Let's Make a Deal*
  (b) *The Newlywed Game,* and/or suicide.
You don't remember which host afflicted which game show,
for the same reason that you don't remember which urea de-
rivative was responsible for which custom-compounded plastic. They all make the pisco sour.

Does anybody know what's going on on NBC and ABC
while decent people are supposed to be eating lunch? Con-
scripts, refugees, miscreants, the flotsam of an affluent society
are press-ganged into embarrassing themselves for half an
hour in front of *millions* of analgesiacs. Bastards-of-ceremony
whip them into giggledom. Dashboards and control panels
elaborated unto gimcrackery swallow, spit, hiccough and
vomit. Klaxons admonish. Categories—"Famous Bald Heads"
is my personal favorite—flap like lapwings around the studio.
Simpletons sigh, simper, seethe and savage one another. Never
before have greed and speed conspired at such a stupefying
tryst. Who wrote *Aunt Jemima's Cookbook?* I'm sorry, your
thyme is upchuck.

Three on a Match is so complicated—their tic-tac-toe had to
go into systems analysis to find out why it hates itself—that
even the advertising agencies can't figure it out. Therefore
there isn't any advertising, unless you count commercials for
how NBC intended to cover the political conventions and why

drunks shouldn't drive. It's like watching an Apollo lift-off, only with rubber bands. But it's a great mistake to switch channels. On ABC, they're making a deal. Some weirdo prowls up and down the aisles, waving hundred-dollar bills, asking members of the studio audience whether they've got a whale tooth or Linda Kasabian's autograph or Spanish fly. If they do have it, they can either keep the cash or opt for the unseen. The unseen—a Polaris submarine, Dean Martin's bladder, thirty-four years on the jungleboat at Disneyland, capital punishment—sits behind a curtain. Zowie.

Neither program is in a class with *The Newlywed Game,* ABC's midday answer to the Salem witch trials. To qualify as contestants you must be a recently married couple within pogo-sticking distance of Los Angeles; otherwise, skyjack a lapwing. A bunch of men troop onto the stage and guess how their wives would respond to such questions as, "Last night, your hugging and kissing were (1) heavyweight, (2) middleweight, (3) lightweight." I'm *serious.* I'm *always* serious. This was a *real* question. Then of course the wives appear and prove their husbands dunderheads. The sexes are reversed for the next round of hugger-muggering. Cute enough to make your teeth ache.

I wish Karl Marx were alive to watch *The Newlywed Game.* I wish Sigmund Freud were alive to do the same thing. I wish the two of them were newlywed, living at Malibu on a rented surfboard, so they qualified for the program. I'd like to see the Hegelian dialectic interpreted as a sex act, Hamlet pedaling his Oedipal cycle all the way to the United Fruit Company, workers risible, *Das Kapital mit Traumdeutung.* Hell, I'd like to see Simone de Beauvoir and Jean-Paul Sartre glaring at each other because they blew their big chance at free dining-room furniture. Id Kant happen, *Herren,* you will say. But it does, every weekday at 2 P.M., and the days get weaker by the minute.

From *This Pen For Hire,* 1972.

QUESTIONS

(1) John Leonard's style is as important as his direct assertions in making his point about daytime television. It is designed to be satiric, allusive and punning. Notice the use of the pro-

noun "you" in the opening paragraph. Notice also the regularity of the first three sentences—each one a compound sentence. What is the effect of these features on the reader?

(2) The third paragraph offers a scathing, pun-filled summary of the world of game shows. It also offers you an opportunity to observe the importance of verbs in vivid writing. Notice the profusion of lively verbs such as "press-ganged" or a series such as "sigh, simper, seethe and savage." Locate in the essay other examples of vivid verbs.

(3) This essay is filled with puns that rely on the reader's acquaintance with the general culture. Explain as many of the following as you can: ". . . your thyme is upchuck"; ". . . had to go into systems analysis"; "Id Kant happen, *Herren*," "workers risible," and "pedaling his Oedipal cycle."

(4) The final paragraph invokes the name of Marx and of Freud in order to contrast serious achievement with the frivolous nature of the TV shows. Why is the contrast funny?

THE SCARY WORLD OF TV'S HEAVY VIEWER

GEORGE GERBNER AND LARRY GROSS

Many critics worry about violence on television, most out of fear that it stimulates viewers to violent or aggressive acts. Our research, however, indicates that the consequences of experiencing TV's symbolic world of violence may be much more far-reaching.

We feel that television dramatically demonstrates the power of authority in our society, and the risks involved in breaking society's rules. Violence-filled programs show who gets away with what, and against whom. It teaches the role of victim, and the acceptance of violence as a social reality we must learn to live with—or flee from.

We have found that people who watch a lot of TV see the real world as more dangerous and frightening than those who watch very little. Heavy viewers are less trustful of their fellow citizens, and more fearful of the real world.

Since most TV "action-adventure" dramas occur in urban settings, the fear they inspire may contribute to the current flight of the middle class from our cities. The fear may also bring increasing demands for police protection, and election of law-and-order politicians.

Those who doubt TV's influence might consider the impact of the automobile on American society. When the automobile burst upon the dusty highways about the turn of the century, most Americans saw it as a horseless carriage, not as a prime mover of a new way of life. Similarly, those of us who grew up before television tend to think of it as just another medium in a series of 20th-century mass-communications systems, such as movies and radio. But television is not just another medium.

TV: THE UNIVERSAL CURRICULUM

If you were born before 1950, television came into your life after your formative years. Even if you are now a TV addict, it will be difficult for you to comprehend the transformations it has wrought. For example, imagine spending six hours a day at the local movie house when you were 12 years old. No parent would have permitted it. Yet, in our sample of children, nearly half the 12-year-olds watch an average of six or more hours of television per day. For many of them the habit continues into adulthood. On the basis of our surveys, we estimate that about one third of all American adults watch an average of four or more hours of television per day.

Television is different from all other media. From cradle to grave it penetrates nearly every home in the land. Unlike newspapers and magazines, television does not require literacy. Unlike the movies, it runs continuously, and once purchased, costs almost nothing. Unlike radio, it can show as well as tell. Unlike the theater or movies, it does not require leaving your home. With virtually unlimited access, television both precedes literacy and, increasingly, preempts it.

Never before have such large and varied publics—from the nursery to the nursing home, from ghetto tenement to penthouse—shared so much of the same cultural system of messages and images, and the assumptions embedded in them. Television offers a universal curriculum that everyone can learn.

Imagine a hermit who lives in a cave linked to the outside world by a television set that functioned only during prime time. His knowledge of the world would be built exclusively out of the images and facts he could glean from the fictional events, persons, objects and places that appear on TV. His expectations and judgments about the ways of the world would follow the conventions of TV programs, with their predictable plots and outcomes. His view of human nature would be shaped by the shallow psychology of TV characters.

TV HERMITS

While none of us is solely dependent upon television for our view of the world, neither have many of us had the opportunity to observe the reality of police stations, courtrooms, corporate board rooms, or hospital operating rooms. Although critics complain about the stereotyped characters and plots of TV dramas, many viewers look on them as representative of the real world. Anyone who questions that assertion should read the 250,000 letters, most containing requests for medical advice, sent by viewers to "Marcus Welby, M.D." during the first five years of his practice on TV.

If adults can be so accepting of the reality of television, imagine its effect on children. By the time the average American child reaches public school, he has already spent several years in an electronic nursery school. At the age of 10 the average youngster spends more hours a week in front of the TV screen than in the classroom. Given continuous exposure to the world of TV, it's not surprising that the children we tested seemed to be more strongly influenced by TV than were the adults.

At the other end of the life cycle, television becomes the

steady and often the only companion of the elderly. As failing
eyesight makes reading difficult, and getting around becomes
a problem, the inhabitants at many nursing homes and retirement communities pass much of the day in the TV room,
where the action of fictional drama helps make up for the in-
action of their lives.

To learn what they and other Americans have been watching we have been studying the facts of life in the world of
evening network television drama—what that world looks like,
what happens in it, who lives in it, and who does what to
whom in it. We have explored this world by analyzing the
content of the situation comedies, dramatic series, and movies
that appear in prime time, between eight and 11 P.M.

THE SIMPLE WORLD OF TV PLOTS

Night after night, week after week, stock characters and dramatic patterns convey supposed truths about people, power
and issues. About three fourths of all leading characters on
prime-time network TV are male, mostly single, middle and
upper-class white Americans in their 20s or 30s. Most of the
women represent romantic or family interests. While only one
out of every three male leads intends to or has ever been married, two out of every three female leads are either married,
expected to marry, or involved in some romantic relationship.

Unlike the real world, where personalities are complex, motives unclear, and outcomes ambiguous, television presents a
world of clarity and simplicity. In show after show, rewards
and punishments follow quickly and logically. Crises are re-
solved, problems are solved, and justice, or at least authority,
always triumphs. The central characters in these dramas are
clearly defined: dedicated or corrupt; selfless or ambitious; efficient or ineffectual. To insure the widest acceptability, (or
greatest potential profitability) the plot lines follow the most
commonly accepted notions of morality and justice, whether
or not those notions bear much resemblance to reality.

In order to complete a story entertainingly in only an hour
or even a half hour, conflicts on TV are usually personal and
solved by action. Since violence is dramatic, and relatively
simple to produce, much of the action tends to be violent.

As a result, the stars of prime-time network TV have for years been cowboys, detectives, and others whose lives permit unrestrained action. Except in comic roles, one rarely sees a leading man burdened by real-life constraints, such as family, that inhibit freewheeling activity.

For the past four years, we have been conducting surveys to discover how people are affected by watching the world of television. We ask them questions about aspects of real life that are portrayed very differently on TV from the way they exist in the real world. We then compare the responses of light and heavy viewers, controlling for sex, education, and other factors.

Anyone trying to isolate the effects of television viewing has the problem of separating it from other cultural influences. In fact, it is difficult to find a sufficiently large sample of non-viewers for comparison. For this article we have compared the responses of light viewers, who watch an average of two hours or less per day, and heavy viewers, who watch an average of four or more hours per day. We also surveyed 300 teenagers in the 6th, 7th, and 8th grades, among whom the heavy viewers watched six hours or more per day.

THE HEAVY VIEWER

Since the leading characters in American television programs are nearly always American, we asked our respondents: "About what percent of the world's population live in the United States?" The correct answer is six percent. The respondents were given a choice of three percent or nine percent, which obliged them either to underestimate or overestimate the correct percentage. Heavy viewers were 19 percent more likely to pick the higher figure than were the light viewers.

We next took up the subject of occupations, since the occupational census in prime time bears little resemblance to the real economy. Professional and managerial roles make up about twice as large a proportion of the labor force on TV as they do in the real world. To find out if this distortion had any effect on viewers, we asked: "About what percent of Americans who have jobs are either professionals or managers—like doctors, lawyers, teachers, proprietors, or other executives?"

When forced to make a choice between either 10 or 30 percent
(the correct figure is 20 percent), the heavy viewers were 36
percent more likely to overestimate.

One might argue, correctly, that heavy viewing of television
tends to be associated with lower education and other socioeconomic factors that limit or distort one's knowledge about
the real world. But when we controlled for such alternative
sources of information as education and newspaper reading,
we found that although they did have some influence, heavy
television viewing still showed a significant effect. For example, while adult respondents who had some college education
were less influenced by television than those who had never
attended college, heavy viewers within both categories still
showed the influence of television. We obtained similar results
when we compared regular newspaper readers with occasional
readers or nonreaders.

The only factor that seemed to have an independent effect
on the responses was age. Regardless of newspaper reading,
education, or even viewing habits, respondents under 30 con-
sistently indicated by their responses that they were more influenced by TV than those over 30. This response difference
seems especially noteworthy in that the under-30 group on the
whole is better educated than its elders. But the under-30
group constitutes the first TV generation. Many of them grew
up with it as teacher and babysitter, and have had lifelong
exposure to its influence.

DIET OF VIOLENCE

Anyone who watches evening network TV receives a heavy
diet of violence. More than half of all characters on prime-
time TV are involved in some violence, about one tenth in
killing. To control this mayhem, the forces of law and order
dominate prime time. Among those TV males with identifi-
able occupations, about 20 percent are engaged in law enforcement. In the real world, the proportion runs less than one
percent. Heavy viewers of television were 18 percent more
likely than light viewers to overestimate the number of males
employed in law enforcement, regardless of age, sex, education, or reading habits.

Violence on television leads viewers to perceive the real world as more dangerous than it really is, which must also influence the way people behave. When asked, "Can most people be trusted?" the heavy viewers were 35 percent more likely to check "Can't be too careful."

When we asked viewers to estimate their own chances of being involved in some type of violence during any given week, they provided further evidence that television can induce fear. The heavy viewers were 33 percent more likely than light viewers to pick such fearful estimates as 50-50 or one in 10, instead of a more plausible one in 100.

While television may not directly cause the results that have turned up in our studies, it certainly can confirm or encourage certain views of the world. The effect of TV should be measured not just in terms of immediate change in behavior, but also by the extent to which it cultivates certain views of life. The very repetitive and predictable nature of most TV drama programs helps to reinforce these notions.

Victims, like criminals, must learn their proper roles, and televised violence may perform the teaching function all too well [see "A Nation of Willing Victims," *Psychology Today,* April 1975]. Instead of worrying only about whether television violence causes individual displays of aggression in the real world, we should also be concerned about the way such symbolic violence influences our assumptions about social reality. Acceptance of violence and passivity in the face of injustice may be consequences of far greater social concern than occasional displays of individual aggression.

Throughout history, once a ruling class has established its rule, the primary function of its cultural media has been the legitimization and maintenance of its authority. Folk tales and other traditional dramatic stories have always reinforced established authority, teaching that when society's rules are broken retribution is visited upon the violators. The importance of the existing social order is always explicit in such stories.

We have found that violence on prime-time network TV cultivates exaggerated assumptions about the threat of danger in the real world. Fear is a universal emotion, and easy to exploit. The exaggerated sense of risk and insecurity may lead to increasing demands for protection, and to increasing pressure for the use of force by established authority. Instead of threatening the social order, television may have become our chief instrument of social control.

From *Psychology Today Magazine*, 1976.

QUESTIONS

(1) The authors argue that television is not just another medium but a profoundly pervasive influence on the lives of many Americans. What evidence do they offer to support this contention?

(2) "Television presents a world of clarity and simplicity." Do you find this statement to be an accurate one? Is there any TV show that you watch in which the characters' lives are presented with the complexity of real life? If so, how does that show represent the reality of its world?

(3) Which age groups in our society spend the most time watching television? How does television programming reflect the interests of these groups?

(4) In the study the authors conducted, they found a significant tendency among heavy viewers to view reality as corresponding in some sense to the world as it is presented on television. What examples of this outlook are cited by the authors? Are they all equally convincing?

(5) What is the basis of the authors' argument that TV is shaping a self-image among Americans as passive victims?

(6) In their conclusion, the authors argue that "television may have become our chief instrument of social control." What are the logical steps of their argument? What is the initial hypotheses of their thesis?

(7) How many hours a day do you spend watching television? How applicable are the authors' comments to your TV habits?

THE KONG AND I

WALLACE MARKFIELD

Though a bunch of wise guys chanted, "Biff, Boom, Bam/He dies for our sins in Vietnam," though one kook sought to tear a strip of Styrofoam skin from the great dead gorilla crumpled under the World Trade Center, those 5,000-odd people who showed up in New York City last June for work as unpaid extras in Dino De Laurentiis's remake of *King Kong* impressed me with their essential solemnity and sweet-tempered patience. Punished by the dank heat, the ferocious smoky arc lights, they nevertheless endured a good two hours of running up and down, back and forth between chalk lines while roaring a concerted acclaim for imaginary helicopters come to blast Kong off the North Tower. And even at midnight, after the last tedious take of the shot which closes the movie ("Camera pulls away and up from the bleeding Kong, the weeping sequined girl"), hundreds lingered, congregating by the 40-foot corpse to swap rumors.

I heard that this time Kong would have a mate and be as docile and domestic as Dagwood Bumstead; that this time Fay Wray, playing a Margaret Mead-type anthropologist, would willingly, gladly hop into his palm; that this time he would be captured by the CIA and freed by terrorists; that this time he would deal more severely with the city than he had in 1933 —bringing down the Verrazano bridge, kicking the Statue of Liberty to pieces and using her torch upon a Staten Island shopping center.

Standing apart from this speculation, I felt suddenly cranky. I found myself glaring at the new Kong, fighting down a compulsion to cry out, "Abomination!" or "Effete affront!" or "Pipsqueak pretender!" "Who needs this, who wants this?" I said to myself. "Another Vistavision, Sensurround rip-off with yet another sneaky PG peek at bare breasts. Yes, and with $25 million worth of overblown technology that will still be light-years away from the hand-tooled $430,000 wizardry of Willis O'Brien and Marcel Delgado and Orville Goldner. Oh, Dino,

oh, Paramount, oh, Gulf and Western, oh, cold-hearted conglomerate, take pity. Abort this enterprise entirely or turn it
into a trailer for a reissue of the original *King Kong*. Let me
and mine grow old grooving on foot-by-foot, frame-by-frame
memories of a wonder, a milestone, a work of art, an act of
love!"

The lights were doused. "Big Guy go beddy-bye," an assistant director crooned into a megaphone, "but Big Guy thanks
you wonderful, wonderful people." Whereupon a hefty moon-
faced fellow was pushed forward by several hands. "We are
from . . . N.Y.U." he announced. "We are majoring in film
and as N.Y.U. film majors we wonder if the changes will alter
the tone or tonal qualities of the original. Which. . . ." He
released a long, flutey breath. "Which we venerate as a classic." "You'll have a classic," the assistant director said. "And
the changes . . . oh, they'll add depth and dimension to big
guy's character."

"Once, in Film Quarterly, our instructor perceived and apprehended . . . ," I heard a student piping. In my time and
on my Brooklyn block, I reflected bitterly, we candy-store
intellectuals perceived and apprehended *King Kong* for ourselves—and usually in some derelict theater located two fares
away between a penny arcade and a tattoo parlor.

The current Kong was vacuumed, sprayed and covered with
sailcloth. And as I walked off, I spotted the film majors drumming their chests and making simian sounds, testing one another on the exact pitch and intonation Robert Armstrong
had used when he said, "There's one thing we haven't thought
of: airplanes. . . . We're millionaires, boys—I'll share it with
all of you! . . . He's always been king of this world—but we'll
teach him fear."

Come on, come off it, I wanted to tell these cavorting cultists, these cïnéastes. I'll warrant I've seen *King Kong* more
often, wept over it more copiously. Whose obsession surpasses
mine? Which of you ever memorized the map of Skull Island—
reef, peninsula and precipice? Dreamed, recurrently, of raising
a window shade and beholding the eye of Kong? Paid homage
to him in his first short story and in each of his three novels?

I held my tongue, but only because I had a train to make.
For after all these years I'm still delighted to talk Kong-lore,
still capable of keen interest, even exaltation, when I hear him

celebrated as the Natural Child, the Last Romantic, the Noble
Savage, the Oppressed Proletarian seeking to expropriate the
expropriators, the Black Man entering modern history in
chains, the Third World Emissary. To this day the sight of his
name in some film chronicle so turns me on that my nostrils
quiver and I end up underscoring lines like "Kong's death
stirs memories of a similar event on Golgotha" and "Kong
endures as self-image of man divided within (or against) himself, opposing the rational to the irrational, the civilized to
the natural, the mechanical to the physical, the technological
to the magical-fantastic, and the European to the Afro-Asian."

Yet if "King Kong" is as much race memory as movie to me,
I must also live with the fact that Merian C. Cooper and
Ernest B. Schoedsack, the adventurous, tough-minded men
who made it, would nearly tear their heads off laughing when
critics called them "film poets" and "Merlins springing myths
from the camera box." At such times, contemporaries claim,
they pranced, capered and simultaneously bellowed the iron
rule of Cooper-Schoedsack Productions: "Keep it distant, difficult and dangerous."

And while studios built back-lot Babylons, Cooper, a World
War I flying ace enamored of suicide missions, and Schoedsack,
a crackerjack cameraman bored by anything less than bom-
bardments, shot their first feature, *Grass* (1925), in northern
Persia, migrating with Baktyari tribesmen across the awesome
Zardeh Kuh mountains. But they ran out of money long before *Grass* could be worked into an "epic about man, not a
travelogue about tribesmen." It packed enough spectacular
footage, though, to please the likes of Jesse L. Lasky at Paramount; on the strength of that, and a 50-word synopsis, he
backed their next try.

Bursting now with notions of a "natural drama," they went
off looking for nothing less than a jungle which was (1) 90
river crossings from nowhere, and (2) infested with beasts
cruel and cunning enough to be propitiated by the natives.
Months later, blind luck and a bark canoe brought them to
just such a jungle in the Nan Province of northeast Siam. One
of the Lao villagers they got to know well was Kru, an engaging, eminently photogenic farmer. They turned their two out-
dated cameras loose on him and cooked up a thin story: Kru,
land-hungry and a little rash, plants his rice dangerously close

to the jungle, is thereafter harassed by leopards, then tigers, then, finally, a great thundering herd of rogue elephants.

Cooper and Schoedsack settled on the title "Chang," a Lao word for elephant, because its single harsh syllable "kept resounding in our ears like a gong." Disdaining advice from older Hollywood hands ("Give people a *Nanook of the North,* only cuter, happier"), they honed their 30 reels to 63 lacerating minutes, which conveyed, as though through Kru's skin and nerves, the presence of something unknown and still unnamed, something malign and indestructible and everlastingly astir in the jungle. . . .

"From baboons I went to gorillas, from gorillas to the gorilla of gorillas—a throwback, a magnificent brute standing—hey, why not?—forty, fifty feet tall, a savage god who's been brought here by modern man and turned into a spectacle. I had him in Madison Square Garden or Yankee Stadium, where some drunken keepers try to make him dance with electric prods. He breaks loose. The teenie-tinies pursue. He sees only one place to hide—top of the Empire State Building. And there, the teenie-tinies get him with a fleet of warplanes."

But Cooper had a powerful hunch that he needed to deepen and enrich the fantasy for a Depression audience, that he would otherwise run the risk of having his gorilla transformed into a monstrous metaphor for the contradictions of capitalism. He needed, besides, a plausible answer to a question which would inevitably be on the mass mind: "If it took warplanes to finish the bastard, then how had he been captured in the first place?"

During the months that followed, Cooper tapped his Boy's Life imagination and set about opening the escape valve to the last thread. Out of the pulps, which pleased him nearly as much as Pinter pleases today's theologians of the cinema, he invented a lost world—something akin to Komodo, an Indonesian island which his naturalist friend, Douglas Burden, had described as "a tumble of jagged volcanic peaks abounding in varanus lizards, vicious carnivores attaining a length of 10 feet, and a weight of 250 pounds."

He invested this lost world with dinosaurs so large and so low on the evolutionary scale that they would speak to people of "a time when the earth still seemed to be warm from creation, when any manner of improbable beasts lumbered across

the firmament. Why not, therefore, one beast more powerful
than all the others and more intelligent—one beast giving a
hint, a suggestion, a prefiguration of the dawn of man." (From
Burden, Cooper first heard of an East Indies word for gorilla:
"Kong." He loved the word, and threw in King to suggest size
and supremacy.)

His biggest worry now was working out a way for the
teenie-tinies to take Kong. After rejecting permutations and
combinations of pits, snares and deadfalls; earthquakes, tidal
waves and tropical fevers; poisoned darts, flame-throwers and
radio beams, he caught hold of an idea: King, like the kings of
classic drama, ought to have a weakness. Why not, then, make
it a weakness for blondes? Let Kong only lay eyes on his first
blonde—a vulnerable, fragile, achingly beautiful Snow Queen,
a Madonna—and he would be suddenly gentled and, once gentled, humanized, and once humanized, undone.

All through the summer of 1931, Cooper strove to peddle
his plot. He found out from Paramount, then M-G-M, then
Warner Bros., that he would have been better off, in such hard
times, dreaming up something suited to Maurice Chevalier
and Jeanette MacDonald, Wallace Beery and Marie Dressler,
Johnny Downs and Mary Carlisle, James Cagney and Joan
Blondell. For nowadays, he was told, the hard-nosed bankers
from whom studio heads had to wheedle financing weren't
exactly about to OK a costly production starring a surreal
gorilla and this Fay Wray, whose face people had seen in so-so
parts maybe three times and wouldn't recognize anyway because it would be under a blonde wig.

What's more, word reached him that back in Hollywood his
"ape thing" was inspiring a multitude of jokes; according to
legend, around this time, Adolph Zukor called from the Coast
to say, "You know what a 50-foot gorilla would see in a 5-foot
girl? His lunch!"

Then, in September, Cooper's old friend from Paramount,
David O. Selznick, now R.K.O.'s production chief, asked him
for a favor. He wondered if Cooper would recommend an
executive assistant, someone nutty and nervy enough to have
a go at salvaging what was left of the most mismanaged, debt-
ridden, overextended studio in Hollywood.

One of the first things Cooper did after he joined R.K.O.
was to send for a special-effects technician named Willis

O'Brien and tell him that *Creation*, his first big-budget job, had to be shelved because it would take millions to complete —and because after screening the unfinished footage, Cooper could see nothing in it except "a lot of animals walking around." Nonetheless, he thought that O'Brien, if no great shakes as director or scenarist, was one "helluva terrific" technician. Why, just the look of those dinosaurs—especially the movements! He had never seen anything so lifelike and fluent.

O'Brien explained that his beasts were built to exact scale, with diligently detailed hides, nails and hair, with joints, limbs and digits that could articulate. Furthermore, he had perfected a painstaking process called stop motion. You take, say, a miniature pterodactyl, put it into position with its wings furled, and shoot a single frame of that position. Then you open the wings a fraction of an inch and shoot the next frame. It may take hundreds of stills to record the beat of one wing, but when these stills are spliced together and projected, you have the illusion of flight—an illusion abetted by the fallible human eye, which is too slow to catch the separation of movements.

For once in his movie life, it struck Cooper that he might manage beautifully on a studio lot, that O'Brien's marvelous miniatures and camera craft might give him his prehistoric animal kingdom. And whatever bogs and fens and rain forests he wanted for his lost world could be created by O'Brien's crew of artists—"only the best in the industry; if da Vinci had had them, 'The Last Supper' wouldn't be peeling off the Sistine Chapel."

He put his plan before R.K.O.'s board of directors, which received it with a passionate "Uh-huh." Only pleading and pressure from Selznick, plus a few dozen of his characteristic, closely reasoned, monograph-sized memos, budged the board to authorize one sample reel.

A little before Thanksgiving, 1932, nearly a year later, Cooper entered the R.K.O. board room, handed this reel to a projectionist, took a chair and said, "Gentlemen, I want you to see the greatest thing your eyes have ever beheld . . . !" When the lights came on, all present pumped his hand. By unanimous voice vote it was agreed that he should immediately start work on Feature Production 601, tentatively titled *The Eighth Wonder*.

After an emotional moment, Cooper rose to give thanks, brushing a bit of suspicious moisture from his eyes as he mumbled, "Shocked and surprised, surprised and overwhelmed, overwhelmed and dumbfounded."

There is no record of his mentioning at the time how he had months ago helped Selznick steal Schoedsack away from Paramount; or that he had already picked Schoedsack's wife, Ruth Rose, to write the scenario for *The Eighth Wonder;* or that he had assigned Schoedsack to *The Most Dangerous Game,* a thriller which, by crazy coincidence, paired Fay Wray and Robert Armstrong, and whose set had been designed so that every last tree could be used for Kong's domain.

When Selznick reminded Cooper and Schoedsack that the shooting schedules of *The Most Dangerous Game* and *The Eighth Wonder* conflicted and demanded to know exactly how they proposed shuttling between the two productions without killing themselves and their stars, they replied, hey, they were just going to ask him the same thing. First Selznick said something scatalogical. Then he grinned and went on to say, "What sublime chutzpah!"

It satisfied something in Cooper's and Schoedsack's cantankerous natures to play lumpen lugs, to bluster that *The Eighth Wonder* would contain no hidden meanings, no florid symbolism, no enigmatic German Expressionist shadows left over from Todd Browning's *Freaks* or James Whale's *Frankenstein,* no points that couldn't be grasped as easily as a banana, no deep-dish, upper-case, high-minded bits of directorial business. To restrain themselves, they went around the set needling one another with cracks like "My dear colleague, what a ravishing piece of craftsmanship!" and "Today it appears you are anxious to advance the art of the cine-mah" and "Might we, do you suppose, have been seduced here by an effect a wee bit too aggressively recondite?"

Forty years later, in fact, Cooper and Schoedsack would still be insisting that *King Kong* couldn't hold a candle to *Chang,* that it was only a good studio job produced under "sleeper" conditions on a skimpy "B budget," a philistine enterprise which the Existentialists and the *Cahiers du Cinéma* crowd had mysteriously decided to move into the museum.

They took a Jungle Jim fantasy out of Edgar Rice Burroughs by way of H. Rider Haggard and made it yield images

that are now permanently fused into the American psyche
with a power that never diminishes. Yet they managed this
with such artful artlessness that the most fanatic *King Kong*
buffs wonder now and then whether somehow it isn't all in
their minds, whether, at bottom, *King Kong* might not just be
exactly what it pretends to be.

And what it pretends to be is a resolutely old-fashioned
spellbinder, stocked with characters who present themselves
as clearly as placards, and flavored with a Victorian blend of
manly virtue, earnestness and high moral purpose. There is
even a filigreed parchment scroll following the opening cred-
its that bears an illuminated epigraph (written by Cooper,
who could find nothing in the Bible that exactly suited him):
"And the Prophet said: 'And lo! the Beast looked upon the
face of Beauty. And it stayed its hand from killing. And from
that day it was as one dead.' "

Whereupon we glimpse Manhattan through a fog which
could have rolled right off Gustav Doré's sketch pad and get
the equivalent, over the next 20 minutes, of a prologue. One
night, in the winter of 1933, a theatrical agent stops beside a
tramp steamer moored on the dismal Hoboken docks. This is
the Venture, and it has been chartered by Carl Denham (Robert Armstrong), a fearless producer-director-cameraman, for a
"crazy voyage to Lord knows where" with three times the
crew any steamer ever carried.

Jack Driscoll (Bruce Cabot), the first mate, calls him
aboard. The brash, bellicose Denham is "getting wild," for
he needs an actress—and before morning if the ship is to dodge
an impending monsoon and a fire marshal who would spot the
strange cargo of high-powered rifles and oversize gas grenades.
But the agent, a too solid citizen, won't throw one lone woman
among "the toughest mugs I ever looked at."

Denham, in bitter irony, sounds off as Schoedsack once did
on the set of *Rango*. "I go out and sweat blood to make a swell
picture, and then the critics and exhibitors all say [mincingly]
'If this picture had a love interest, it would gross twice as
much.' All right, if the public wants a girl, this time I'm goin'
to give 'em what they want. . . . I'm goin' out to get a girl
. . . even if I have to [as if with ashes in his mouth] *marry*
one!"

The Bowery. A quick, unsentimental shot of frumpy, whin-

ing women on a soup-kitchen line nails down the times as
cleanly and as perfectly as a single hammer blow. Denham
gives the line a harsh, derisive glance. Someone cries out—the
very softest, saddest, tinkliest of cries. Turning, Denham con-
fronts a starving, anguished girl (Fay Wray) on the verge of
snitching an apple. He pays off the grocer, and the slum flower
swoons; a shade reluctantly, he catches her.

Inside a crummy luncheonette, she tells him that she is Ann
Darrow, that she is an orphan, that she worked as an extra at
Paramount's Astoria Studio till it closed down. Denham offers
her a job. "It means money and adventure and fame and a
long sea voyage that starts at 6 o'clock tomorrow morning."
Her lashes flutter. She clearly thinks the worst; and the
thought, clearly, is far from unthinkable. "Say," Denham
croons, "you've got me wrong. I'm on the level . . . no funny
business. Just trust me and keep your chin up!"

She does, and takes an accidental smash on it from Jack
Driscoll the moment she boards the Venture—a cornball device even in that movie era, likewise a delicious foretaste of
sufferings to come. At sea, as Driscoll starts "goin' soft" on
Ann, Denham warns him against being unmanned: "sappy."
"You're a pretty tough guy, but if Beauty gets ya'. . . ." In 10
minutes—and about 50 lines—with a minimum of hanky-
panky, the characters reveal who they are, what they want and
how they see the world.

Now the Venture is somewhere in the Indian Ocean "way
west of Sumatra," and Denham, at last, hands the captain a
rough map of an island "you won't find on any chart"—an island whose outlines conform to Manhattan's. This island has
a great wall, "as strong today as it was centuries ago. The natives keep that wall in repair. They need it. There's something
on the other side. Something they call . . . Kong. Something
they fear . . . something monstrous, all-powerful . . . still
living, still holding that island in a grip of deadly fear."

The following day—a day as sunless and uncongenial as all
the other days at sea—Denham improvises a screen test for
Ann. He fits her out with a dove-white Arthurian gown and
bids her: "Look higher . . . still higher. . . . Now you see
it! It's horrible but you can't look away. You're helpless. . . .
If you could only scream. Scream, Ann, scream for your life!"

Throughout this prologue, the camera has taken a comfort-

able stance and held still, doggedly declining any panoramic
sweeps or searching close-ups or eccentric angles. Yet at the
very moment Ann's cries are building and building, it pulls
away from her and stays, seconds longer than it has thus far
stayed, on Driscoll, whose open, ardent, true-blue, love-smitten
gaze is so eerily close to Kong's. Here ends our tenuous contact with reality. For suddenly, Skull Island emerges out of a
fog bank, and Max Steiner's magnificent doomful score turns
wild and dissonant.

Denham rows ashore with Ann and a dozen armed sailors,
leads them in quiet scuttling unison toward the sound of
throbbing drums and hides behind some palm fronds. He
parts them, strains forward, squints, falls into a fit of rap-
turous ogling. "Holy cow," he cries, in a singularly weak, thin
voice, "what a show!" Then the camera backs off, and after a
sly shot over Denham's shoulder—a shot which once and for
all implicates us with this quintessential voyeur—we see some
islanders dancing in gorilla suits before a colossal wooden
wall while midwives drape garlands of flowers and shells about
a dazed adolescent girl.

Possibly the sequence that follows—cringing natives, a witch
king rattling gourds, the very big, very, very black chief leering
at blond Ann and going, "Kow bisa para Kong"—is everything
some critics and most human-relations experts have called it:
"flagrantly racist" . . . "heinous stereotyping" . . . "a tab-
leau of Wilshire Boulevard Swahilis" . . . "the usual de-
praved darkies mouthing Hollywood's time-tested nonsense
syllables as they lay rapacious hands on a fair white maiden."

But we'd do well, I think, to read no meaning into their
blackness—or, for that matter, into Kong's. ("You know,"
Cooper once told a film scholar, "sometimes a black gorilla
is only a black gorilla.") The Skull Islanders, it happens,
spoke a scrupulously coached Australasian-based language;
the same natives who cringe before Denham stand up to Kong
with spears (one small boy, as I remember, even lands a hay-
maker on Kong's shin); the witch king and the chief, when
last seen, are moving sorrowfully among the dead and covering them with shields; and the hands they lay on Ann are far
from rapacious. Indeed, their implacable indifference when
they deliver Ann to Kong's phallic altar serves to augment her

screams, to make her desolation all the more total and terrifying.

These scenes are so visually alive, so finely timed and related that even the habitually ungenerous D. W. Griffith was
heard to praise them: "Primitive but perfect, perfect like the
wheel. . . ."

First there is the nightmarishly langorous binding of each
of Ann's wrists. Then there is the somnambulistic ballet when
the witch king and his men withdraw. And then the gates
start slowly to close. And for an instant Ann is framed between
them. And the massive bolt slides through one, two, three
hoops in the gate, and through two more hoops in the retaining wall. And the chief intones the name of Kong three times,
and then sounds the tocsin gong. And something prodigious
moves through the jungle. And Ann sighs like a sleeper, and
gives a long tremor of anguish.

And Kong.

God knows, I love this big, dumb, gallant bull gorilla—and
with such passionate intensity I shall most likely be saying
unto the millennium that he is a representative figure of the
times; that his fate is somehow, somehow linked with mine;
that he is what I would be if I only . . . well, if I only stood
50 feet tall and had the will and nerve to take on civilization,
to bring it to a grinding halt.

I must confess that whenever the original Kong crosses the
light of the TV screen, he renders me helpless. One bellow
from him, and I instantly shed decades of training in the vocabulary of cinema to gibber either, "Holds up and wears
well," or "Still works and comes across." By the time he lays
a paw on Ann, I'm grinning a goofy grin, and while my wife
wails, "You're starting? He's starting!" I commence to rock
and sway in the Barcalounger, turning hot-faced and light-
headed, chokey and sniffly.

Next I wait for Driscoll's knife to prick Kong's middle finger. Kong, the potentate, the powerhouse, blows on it, puts it
to his mouth, sucks it, flutters it, and cocks his head to study it.
There is a very close close-up of his eyes; they are as wistful
and stricken as Chaplin's. At this moment, I hiccup, flinch
and muffle my sobs with noisy yawning.

And when Denham lobs the first gas grenade and Kong clutches his throat—the throat that will be leaking blood atop the Empire State Building—I inevitably clutch mine.

I send subliminal messages to Denham, calling him "Pig-eye," "Cold-heart" and "Rotten-louse," quoting D. H. Lawrence at him: "The essential American soul is hard, stoic, isolate and a killer."

When Kong snaps his chrome steel chains, I mutter, "Good, good for you, old rough beast. You are altogether your own gorilla. You have endured and prevailed against whatever Denham and his kind did to you down in the hold of the Venture."

And nowadays, when he caresses Ann, then sets her down, then half turns to receive the benediction of bullets, I'm too spent to utter Lear's "Never, never, never, never, never!" If I have the voice, I content myself instead with, "Well, this is only the highest moment in movies."

What must Cooper and Schoedsack have felt? I ask myself. What manner of men were these, to cradle a brute, an effigy, with such compassion?

I know only that Cooper, sometime around the 50th week of the making of "King Kong," growled, "We should kill the sonofabitch ourselves" and then sat in front of Schoedsack, at the controls of the Navy biplane which fires that last murderous burst into Kong.

From *The New York Times Magazine*, 1976.

QUESTIONS

(1) What is the author's attitude toward the film students who question the assistant director of *King Kong*?

(2) Why do the critics' comments of the original *King Kong* strike the film's creators as being terribly funny?

(3) What is the author's response to the charge that the original film is racist?

(4) What is the author's own explanation for the power the film holds over him?

(5) What is the tone of the essay in which the author describes his reactions to the death of King Kong?

(6) What is the point of the last anecdote of the essay?

THE WRITER AS SEXUAL SHOW-OFF

ALFRED KAZIN

So there was Norman Mailer, walking bottomless around the party with the solemnity of a lecturer before a women's club. The sight was in no way remarkable, but imagine the contrast between so many fully clothed people and, in the middle, Norman without his shorts! His then wife, a Latin-looking beauty and naked, looked sour. Norman walked up to her every few minutes like a pitcher leaving the mound to confer with his catcher. She whispered. He shook his head. Something new was needed. She looked more and more impatient. To my great delight, I heard her say: "S——, Norman! These bourgeois characters are just too timid for us."

I knew what Norman was going through. A deeply serious writer with a mission to teach the freer life, to indoctrinate the lesson of *The White Negro*—"One is a rebel or one conforms" —to bring his audience up to his own brave level, he was also advancing his fortunes *as a writer*. The "braver" you showed yourself sexually—the more "advanced" and "fearless" and "trailblazing" you showed yourself in public—the more attention and admiration. Sex in public—even just your genitals in public—is no longer sex, but publicity. Of course for a writer, an advance man of human intelligence, the publicity is different from the kind Xaviera Hollander gets. When Mailer said once-dirty words from the stage of the YMHA, and got the apoplectic old *Yiddishe* manager to order the curtain down, Mailer was doing this for you and me. There was a mission involved: to awaken the victims of our repressive sexual-economic system. And no matter how many books a man writes in our system, he still has to give interviews, to sacrifice his valuable working time (for of course no sensible writer will allow any interviewer to print the interview raw; he has to rewrite it). A writer has to make his mission and his meaning perfectly clear by presenting himself, explaining himself, by offering himself up all over again.

So to the man from *Rolling Stone,* after two very lengthy interviews, Mailer wearily summarized in 1975 what he had been saying ever since he had discovered the glamour of his own wickedness twenty years before: "The ambition of a writer like myself is to become consecutively more disruptive, more dangerous, and more powerful."

And it's not just self-advertising. For a nationally famous, big-market writer on everything and anything like Mailer, all pro, with more than a dozen books behind him, a much-questioned novelist whose million-dollar advance for his much-promised big big novel made a lead story in *The Times,* does have a special connection with his audience. Mailer is the one American novelist since Hemingway and Fitzgerald who has had some influence on the manners of his readers. Who can honestly say that sex-as-show, sex-as-ideology, is not intensely meaningful to a writer who is the prisoner not just of sex but of all his many ideas about it? Parading without his shorts in front of his dazed readers can be important. It turns the novelist into the all-out public character that in our disturbed, confused culture readers actively require of a writer. A bad fight with your wife gets you on the front page of the *News,* a million-dollar advance, a prominent story in *The Times.* Readers have come to expect such things of a favorite novelist in order to feel that they are connecting with his books.

Hemingway made fun of Scott Fitzgerald's sexual anxieties —he may even have invented them—in order to put down Fitzgerald's novels. Mailer once married an ex-girlfriend of Henry Luce. Nine hundred professors once came out to hear a paper at the Modern Language Association by a professor rumored to have been the lover of Herzog's wife.

The connections between sexual rumor and literary promotion are prodigious. "Was Nabokov ever that way about a Lolita?" This is a silly question to anyone who knows Nabokov's profoundly ironic mind, especially in *Lolita*. But it was one provoked by the superficial "scandal" of the book. Was that only twenty years ago? Nabokov has been invisible for years. No one has ever seen Thomas Pynchon except his agent, and J. D. Salinger will call out the cops against anyone who comes within seven miles of him. Poor old James Joyce thought that the artist should be like God in His creation—present everywhere, but invisible. No one will ever see Louis Auchincloss or Eudora Welty or Bernard Malamud promoting himself or herself as a sexual hero. But these writers don't believe that sex is Courage, Ideology, Revelation. Nor are they supersellers, household words, public figures playing the role so often played by confessional prima donnas like Mark Twain, Hemingway, Thomas Wolfe, Fitzgerald—and lesser but no less self-absorbed characters like Mailer, Gore Vidal, Philip Roth, and—going rapidly downhill—Erica Jong.

But to get back to Mailer. The public man known as "Norman Mailer" has for some time now been what you get most out of Mailer's work. Hemingway was the absolute self-creation in this department, as was "Mark Twain" before him—and Mark got his name protected legally. So Mailer, notoriously obsessed by Hemingway—whose own trademark was "grace under pressure," a show of guts at all cost—has been driven by the same need to present himself as a breakthrough in all matters sexual, as an "advance scout." Mailer's military imagery about bed has affected more new novelists than Vietnam.

You think it is easy and natural for a Harvard graduate, worrying about middle-age, brought up in Jewish Brooklyn among some of the most anxiously moral people on earth, to walk around a party without his shorts? Only a need to relieve the benighted middle class of its inhibitions can do it. And all this "revolutionary" cultural-sexual incitement is Mailer's bridge to his real audience—the educated bourgeois professionals, mostly white and more often Jewish than not, who support the book trade and the psychoanalysts, and who cannot bear to be thought bourgeois, square, out of it. Disaffection of a strictly cultural-introverted kind is ripe in this class—just now especially among women—and the sounds of incipient *personal* revolution are heard in the bedroom. If the young in the sixties played revolution by seizing the univer-

sity, the middle-aged professionals, unable and probably un-
willing to do anything about their jobs, liked to talk about
sex as revolution. It is now more usually consumer research.
My car gives me this, my washing machine gives me that, my
bed partner gives me what? The boldest character in Updike's
Couples was the wife who arranged it so that she could get
tanned and laid at the same time.

But Mailer's romantic rebellion about sex as the last frontier is as archaic as his belief that sexual showing off makes
him the bravest possible writer—and therefore the guru to our
generation. Fifteen years ago, when Mailer had set out to be
the greatest possible novelist instead of a wildly high-priced
observer of conventions and prize fights, Mailer wrote proudly
about the long, big novel he has been promising us:

> Let me finish with a word about the new book. . . . By present
> standards of publishing practice, it will be, if I can do it, an un-
> publishable work. Since it is likely to take ten years—what with a
> side-effort or two to pick up some money—I do not have the confi-
> dence that you will see it in its completed form, except as an out-
> law of the underground like *Tropic of Cancer, Ulysses,* or Sade's
> *The Hundred and Twenty Days of Sodom.* If it is to have any ef-
> fect, and I can hardly look forward to exhausting the next ten
> years without hope of a deep explosion of effect, the book will be
> fired to its fuse by the rumor that once I pointed to the farthest
> fence and said that within ten years I would try to hit the longest
> ball ever to go up into the accelerated hurricane air of our Ameri-
> can letters. For if I have one ambition above all others, it is to
> write a novel which Dostoevsky and Marx; Joyce and Freud;
> Stendhal, Tolstoy, Proust and Spengler; Faulkner, and even old
> moldering Hemingway might come to read, for it would carry
> what they had to tell another part of the way.

Mailer's present million-dollar advance will not allow him
to keep his big novel "unpublishable," "an outlaw of the underground." Whatever happens, Mailer has stamped his bravado, his public character, all too successfully into the minds
of his middle-class audience. There is no longer any romantic
revolutionary connection to be made between sex and the
middle class; the "advance scouts" have returned to discover
that what the middle class wants is liberation from parents,
spouses, monogamy. Mailer went to see *Last Tango in Paris*
and got mad at the *audience:*

After years of resistance to the Vietnamese War—now, bring on the Caribbean. Amazing! . . . the egocentricity of the Fascist mouth is on the national face. Perhaps it is the five-dollar admission, but this audience has an obvious obsession with sex as the confirmed core of a wealthy life. It is enough to make one ashamed of one's own obsession (although where would one delineate the difference?).

When it comes to literary sex nowadays, there is no divine light at the end of the tunnel. It is the expression of a fondly self-absorbed, personal complaint, usually from long-suppressed "minorities"—Jews, women, homosexuals. Mailer said that the one role in life he found totally unsupportable was the "nice Jewish boy." The tumultuous sale of *Portnoy's Complaint*—the one great sale Philip Roth has had—was of course due to the long-awaited revolt by a Jewish boy against his overloving mamma. *Portnoy* was a "young" book, loved by the young, feared and execrated by older Jews as if Roth were Hitler. The Zionist publicist Marie Syrkin was reminded of the anti-Semitic ravings of Streicher. The real point of the book was made by the Jewish mother who said: "Other people have children, I have enemies." *Portnoy* was the Jewish children's crusade. But when attacked, Roth responds to papa and mamma types not with joyously fresh provocations, but by academically comparing himself to other authors. He is the greatest possible explainer of himself, his literary intentions, his literary affinities. In a just-published book, *Reading Myself and Others,* he interviews himself so often and solemnly, especially to deliver himself from the supposed sexual scandalousness of *Portnoy,* that I willingly grant he is as good a Jew as Kafka and Saul Bellow and no threat to Israel.

Enter Gore Vidal, who also constantly interviews himself and presents himself, but is definitely not interested in being better than he should be. Vidal is a hard-boiled, professionally disenchanted, unstoppably fluent pro who has published fourteen novels, dozens of plays and television scripts and movie treatments. He sells and sells, then constantly publishes literary essays attacking his contemporaries. Vidal, who likes to say that "with an ax, I took on the heterosexual dictatorship of the country," gets more literary mileage out of his sex life than anyone since Oscar Wilde and Jean Cocteau. "The love that dare not speak its name" (in the nineteenth century) cannot, in the twentieth, shut up.

But unlike Mailer, whom Vidal hates as "sweaty, serious," Vidal presents himself as professionally cool, skeptical, detached in a patrician sort of way. He also does a lot of self-packaging. In interviews with him and stories about him—in *Oui, Vogue, Penthouse, Fag Rag, Paris Review, The Washington Post, Esquire, Newsweek, Village Voice*—he explains somewhat truculently, as he does in so many of his books, that he knows the upper crust as no other American writer knows it. He was born at West Point, his grandfather was a U.S. Senator, he once had a stepfather (Hugh Auchincloss) who later became Jackie Bouvier Kennedy Onassis's stepfather, he even claims descent from Roman soldiers and a medieval troubadour. And "In youth I never missed a trick. . . . I tried everything . . . I could no more go to bed with somebody whose work I admired than I could . . . well, make love to a mirror. Fame in others switches off desire."

Vidal constantly features, presents, explains himself; in his books and out of them. The picture he draws is of a haughty, dogged insolence, with a dab of vague wickedness and not so vague snottiness toward most other American writers, past and present. Nobody else knows how to write good clear English any longer. Nobody else knows so much about the real power centers in America. Nobody else knows so much about where the Kennedy skeletons are hidden. And nobody else hates all the Kennedys so much. Yet since he is a tremendous seller, lives in Italy like a prince—both in Rome and along the Tyrrhenian Sea—and comes on as a Tory anarchist, a real bad socking radical with no respect whatsoever for the rich who steal us blind or for their poor dumb victims, he wonders why he *is* so popular. "I write books that say things Americans detest yet are drawn to, so it must be that in some way I am, if nothing else, a mirror image of the reader, just as Nixon is a mirror image of the voter."

The reason for Vidal's popularity is that he is both a natural entertainer in the Somerset Maugham class and a great hater, a witty subversive, a transposer of all things out of their expected order. He inverts all topics, whether in ancient Rome (*Julian*), early America (*Burr*), or Hollywood (*Myra Breckinridge*), by turning expected relationships upside down.

This gives the mischief, the topsy-turvy quality, to a middle-class, middle-brow audience that by now finds nothing more natural than sex as disruption to established ideas. In Vidal's fiction men turn themselves into women, then become men again; old heroes like Washington are shown up as dopes; Jefferson as a phony, but traitorous nutty Aaron Burr comes on as witty and sexy as Gore Vidal. Incest and homosexuality somehow seem more natural, more kindly and folksy and human than marriage. And pressing all these transpositions and rearrangements together is a style as clearly addressed to the last row as Maugham's, as extravagantly barbed as Mencken's. Plus, above all, the cold rage of a man who despite his good looks, talent, money, and doting publisher, still sees himself as an outsider, determined to assert his superiority against a literary scene made up of boring lower-class types who don't know enough to respond to his whiplash.

What whiplash? The whiplash of an enormously clever and gifted man who despite all the sexual sophistication, indifference, cynicism of our time *still* feels himself marked off from other men. So in Vidal's books and interviews all possible rivals are marked down as dopey, scruffy, inelegant. How the opposition gets it from Vidal! Of all literary shrews, Vidal is undoubtedly the sharpest, comes on as the maximum snob *and* radical—and always brings the subject back to himself:

> Every year there is a short list of the OK writers. Today's list consists of two Jews, two Negroes, and a safe gloating goy of the old American establishment . . . just to show that there is no prejudice. . . . Only the poor old homosexualists are out.

> Even those who dislike Tennessee Williams must give him credit for castrating a hero here, eating one there.

> But then how can the doings of a banker who is white and gentile and rich be *relevant* when everyone knows that the only meaningful American experience is to be Jewish, lower-middle-class and academic?

> From the beginning, Louis [Auchincloss] was a writer. . . . In other words, a sissy by the standards of the continuing heterosexual dictatorship that has so perfectly perverted in one way or another just about every male in the country. . . . At least he did not have to apologize for his class because, pre-Camelot, no American writer had a clue to who or what an Auchincloss was.

In my first years as a writer, I was often pleased to be identified with the protagonist of *The City and the Pillar*—a male prostitute. After all, that was a *real* identity. . . .

The "sexual elite" is the "creative elite"? The "braver" you are in print, the better writer? One wonders, for here at last is Erica Jong, as commonplace a mind as ever appeared on the best-seller lists, but a woman novelist who obviously speaks for all the oppressed women writers in this country, a woman not afraid to speak up for the long-concealed, male-suppressed raunchiness *that is just as natural to women as it is to men.*

When her first novel, *Fear Of Flying*, was published in October, 1973, it sold just 8,000 copies before Christmas. Then John Updike, a superior novelist, and one known not to be afraid of flying, reviewed *F. of F.* in *The New Yorker* so glowingly, charmingly, and appetizingly, that it was not clear from Updike's excitement whether he was reviewing Jong or tasting her. "It has class and sass, brightness and bite." The sales went up and up. Henry Miller came out of his retirement in the suburban mansion in Pacific Palisades bought with the countless paperbacks of *Tropic of Cancer* to tell an audience that connects his name with SEX as easily as it does GM with automobiles—"It is rare these days to come upon a book written by a woman which is so refreshing, so gay and sad at the same time, and so full of wisdom about the eternal man-woman problem."

The sales went up again. Jong was photographed sitting in bed with Henry Miller, holding hands: Youth being happily instructed by Age. She looked as demure as she had at Columbia when she was doing her master's on sexual slang in the English Renaissance. Holt, Rinehart and Winston was to sell 50,000 copies of the hardback edition of *F. of F.* The NAL paperback, which has now printed 3.5 million, is expected to reach 5 million.

It turned out that sexist old Henry Miller and the millions of embattled wives in the United States were agreed. *F. of F.* was not just another Dissatisfied Wife novel, but a breakthrough, with all the concealed words and parts *negligently spelled out by a woman,* right up front. Jong was not, like Jacqueline Susann, furnishing sexual gossip for Woolworth shopgirls about remote movie stars and TV executives. She was writing about the literate, psychoanalytically oriented,

often well-read middle-class and professional women who had
at last found someone to say, for them, that they are just as
demanding about sex—and just as weary of monogamy—as
men. And—more!—that psychoanalysts could be just as boring
and unreasonable husbands as other men.

And more, more—there was Erica's sweet, confiding blond
prettiness as she admitted, in interview after interview, that
yes, the book was autobiographical enough and that Isadora
Wing's lovable weaknesses could be hers. But, she always
added, though fluttery on the outside and unable to live without a man, she is determined to live and write in defiance of
her own regrettable weakness. "Honesty is What Counts,"
read the caption beside her photograph in the New York *Post*.
All her "confessions" were as sweet as an old-fashioned sixteen-year-old's. *The age of Mailer was over.* Good-by to the
sexual Apache as radical forerunner of God knows what revolution. Swinging sex, as he had noticed at *Last Tango,* was
bourgeois to the hilt. Even adultery could be domestic.

Here is Erica Jong's triumph. What's to fear in a regular
girl who confides to her readers that she is always looking for
love but determined not to be dominated by One Man? Who
can resent such a nice, pretty Jewish girl who in interview
after interview tells every woman in America that Her problem is Erica's problem? Touchingly, she gets letters by the
bushel—from men, too!—who treat her as if she were a sex
maven. "Could it be some intuition of this connection between the muse and the genitals that makes readers write to
writers for sexual advice? I suspect so."

There is the extra fillip that adds to Erica Jong's sales. She
is living proof that Creativity Is Easy. From now on English
majors will be able to give a high-class flavor to sexual remi-
niscences. *F. of F.* abounds in quotations from Byron, Auden,
Colette, Plath, Freud, etc., etc. Yet the central fantasy described in the book is vulgar. The now-celebrated opening of
F. of F. spoke dreamily of the ideal passage between a man
and a woman as a "zipless f——." (The paperback cover of
F. of F. is a woman's dress zipped halfway down to show a
delicious torso and the promising curve of a breast.) But the
"zipless f——" represented the real dream behind the book—
passion without involvement, no sweat, no strain, no tears.
This dream is our dream. In the same way, the book represents

fiction that is "blunt" and "creamy" but without involvement. Unlike Mailer, Roth, Vidal, who are pros with a respect for the intricacies of narrative, Jong is so blissfully self-centered that she comes on as *True Stories* mixed with Masters and Johnson:

> What *was* it about marriage anyway? Even if you loved your hus-band, there came that inevitable year when f——ing him turned as bland as Velveeta cheese: filling, fattening even, but no thrill to the taste buds, no bittersweet edge, no danger. And you longed for an overripe Camembert, a rare goat cheese, luscious, creamy, cloven-hoofed.

> The diaphragm has become a kind of fetish for me. . . . Somehow the idea of bearing *his* baby angers me. Let him bear his own baby! If I have a baby, I want it to be all *mine*.

You, too, can write!

> Imagine the lost continent of Atlantis and all the submerged islands of childhood right there waiting to be found. The inner space we have never adequately explored. The worlds within worlds within worlds. And the marvelous thing is that they are waiting for us. If we fail to discover them, it is only because we haven't yet built the right vehicle—spaceships or submarines or poems—which will take us to them.

> My writing is the submarine or spaceship which takes me to the unknown worlds within my head. And the adventure is endless and inexhaustible.

And not to forget the nice Jewish girl. Sexual show-offs are often worried about the pieties they need to profane. It is no accident that so many Jewish writers, and especially Jewish women writers, now make like professional swingers.

> . . . I began to feel intensely Jewish and intensely paranoid (are they perhaps the same?) the moment I set foot in Germany.

> Suddenly people on buses were going home to houses where they treasured clever little collections of gold teeth and wedding rings. . . .

> Sometimes, wandering around aimlessly, riding the Strassenbahn, stopping for beer and pretzels in a cafe . . . I would have the fantasy that I was the ghost of a Jew murdered in a concentration camp on the day I was born.

It is all so *normal,* so familiar, confiding, *acceptable.* There is nothing to fear but fear itself. Here is the text of the full-page ad in *Publishers Weekly* for her new book of poems, *Loveroot* (30,000 copies in print):

> I, Erica Jong
> in the midst of my life,
> having had two parents,
> two sisters,
> two husbands,
> two books of poems,
> & three decades of pain . . .
> declare myself now
> for joy.

The ad is actually the beginning of the first poem in the book, but it really is an ad and not a poem. Mailer called a book *Advertisements for Myself,* but the "myself" was like Don Quixote, off to cleanse the world of all the dominations and powers. "Myself" in *Loveroot* is "myself" the woman celebrating "myself" the author, because "myself" is so cuddly. There hasn't been so much public exploitation of a woman's parts, a woman's fantasies, a woman's "chemistry," a woman's idlest daydreams, since cosmetics ads were invented. But as usual, public sex is a fake—when it is not just boasting about how "brave" one is. The idea is to capture the attention—and if there is enough self-fascination, easy does it. In a poem called "Menstruation in May," Jong ends up: *The poems keep flowing monthly / like my blood / The word is flesh, I say, still unconvinced / The flesh is flesh. The word is on its own.*

Not in these books.

From *New York Magazine,* 1975.

QUESTIONS

(1) According to Kazin, what is the purpose of the sexual self-revelation of writers such as Norman Mailer?

(2) Paraphrase the sentence, " 'The love that dare not speak its name' (in the nineteenth century) cannot, in the twentieth shut up."

(3) Trace the theme of this essay as is reflected in the discussion of Mailer, Philip Roth, Gore Vidal and Erica Jong. How is the theme varied in the comments on each writer?

(4) What point is the author trying to make in commenting on the fact that three of these writers are Jewish?

(5) In the view of the author which one of these authors has the least literary merit? Which one has the most?

(6) What is the connection between the sexual revelations and the popularity of the books in which they appear? In what sense does that popularity defeat the writers' apparent intention rather than fulfill it?

(7) One of Erica Jong's poems ends with the line, "The word is on its own." How would you interpret Kazin's reply, "Not in these books"?

THE PILGRIMS HAVE LANDED ON KEROUAC'S GRAVE: ON THE ROAD WITH THE ROLLING THUNDER REVUE

NAT HENTOFF

Backstage at the Rolling Thunder Revue, Allen Ginsberg (who has just dedicated his book of *First Blues* to "Minstrel Guruji Bob Dylan") asks the convener of these revels, these winds of the old days, "Are you getting any pleasure out of this, Bob?"

The convener, who can use words as if they were fun-house mirrors when he's pressed, fingers his gray cowboy hat and looks at the poet. The first he had ever heard of Allen Ginsberg and the kind of people he hung out with was in *Time* around 1958 while he was still a kid in Minnesota. ("I'm Allen Ginsberg and I'm crazy." "My name is Peter Orlovsky and I'm crazy as a daisy." "My name is Gregory Corso and I'm not crazy at all." That had broken up the kid in Minnesota.)

Now, here on the road with this hooting, rocking carnival of

time present and time past, both perhaps present in time future, is Allen, who has survived serene and curious, in a business suit.

"Pleasure?" Dylan finds the word without taste, without
succulence. "Pleasure? I never seek pleasure. There was a time
years ago when I sought a lot of pleasure because I'd had a lot
of pain. But I found there was a subtle relationship between
pleasure and pain. I mean, they were on the same plane. So
now I do what I have to do without looking for pleasure from
it."

"He is putting you on," said a friend to whom Ginsberg,
later in the tour, had described Dylan's exorcism of the pursuit of pleasure.

"No," Ginsberg said firmly. "Bob's attitude is very similar
to the Buddhist view of nonattachment. The belief that seeking pleasure, clinging to pleasure, evokes pain. It stunned me
when Bob said that. It meant that he's reached a philosophical
level very few come close to. And it's a long-range, practical,
workable, philosophical level. Bob has grown an awful lot.
He's alchemized a lot of the hangups of his past. Like his insecurity, which has now become," Ginsberg laughs, "an acceptance of and an ability to work with continuous change."

On the other hand, a musician in Minstrel Guruji's band
tells of an epiphany early in the tour:

"Joan and Bob are doing a duet. I forget the name of it,
it's one of his old tunes. She's really moving. I mean dancing.
She starts doing the Charleston and the audience is digging
it and we're digging it. Dylan though, he's plunking his guitar,
moving his eyes around quick, like he does, looking at Joanie,
looking at us, looking at the audience. Like, 'What the hell is
she doing that's going over so damn big?' It's over, and Joan
walks offstage, grinning, sees a friend in the wings, and says to
him, 'You won't be hearing *that* number again from this little
old duo on this tour.' And laughs because neither the friends
nor the others standing there can figure out what she's talking
about. But she's right. Bob's never called for that tune since.
He couldn't stand the competition. Big as he is, in some ways
he's still a kid scrabbling for his turf."

"Not true," says Joan Baez of the kid characterization. "Or,
not as true as it used to be." She had once described Dylan as
"a huge ego bubble, frantic and lost, so wrapped up in ego, he

couldn't have seen more than four feet in front of him." But now, "Bob has learned how to share," Joan told me one night after a three-and-a-half-hour show in Waterbury, Connecticut, at an old rococo movie theater that reminded me of Depression nights as a boy when we would go to just such a place to feel good anyhow and come home with some dishes besides. No dishes this time, but the most mellow feelings I've had from a concert since the Duke Ellington band on an exceptionally good night. The kicks were from the genuine mutual grooving of the music makers; but it was Dylan, as shaper of the thunder, who was responsible for lifting the audience and keeping it gliding.

A bounteous dispenser of thunder was Dylan this time around. At least three and a half hours *every* night, sometimes longer. (The first concert in Toronto, one of the tour's more exalted evenings, ran close to five hours.) And yet always, or nearly always, the pacing, though relaxed, didn't go slack.

The right mix of a backup band, driving strong but sinuously so it never sounded like an assault. If you could keep T-Bone Burnett, Steve Soles, Howie Wyeth, Mick Ronson, Luther Rix and David Mansfield together—I was thinking as a once and former A&R man—you could have one hell of a house insurance band. Especially with Mansfield, 19 and the kind of natural whom conservatory students prone to neurasthenia should never be allowed to hear or see. Mandolin, pedal steel, dobro, violin—Mansfield makes them all sing, for God's sake, as if he were the sorcerer, not the apprentice he looks like.

Up front Rob Stoner, who doesn't get in the way, and the authentically raffish Bob Neuwirth who may, he says, be in the movies soon. Finally a Rhett Butler for our time. Put another way, I think you have to see Neuwirth to remember his singing.

Then the substars. Ronee Blakley, who earnestly needs direction, as her albums and her musical aimlessness on this tour rather painfully indicate. Roger McGuinn, who has become a large, jolly, historic rocker, almost right for a Christmas mime show. And surprisingly, most impressive of all in the second line some nights, Jack Elliott. With his rambling white cowboy hat and folk collector's glasses, Jack is real serious, however idiosyncratic, and on this tour quite moving in his seriousness. Watching and feeling what "Pretty Boy Floyd," let's say, still means to him, I started thinking of Cisco Houston. Not that they sang alike, Cisco being more of an original, but they trained a lot of memories. And Jack is still spreading seeds.

All the way up front, Joan Baez and, as she calls him, The Kid. Her voice has lowered and so the bodiless sound of medieval caroling in a cathedral is also gone. But now there is more warmth and flesh and survivor's humor ("Love is a pain in the ass"); and still that surging vibrato which is so strong that when Joan sings a cappella, the vibrato becomes her rolling rhythm section.

In her duets with Dylan, Joan, most of the time, is a secondary strand. She could overpower him because her timbre penetrates deeper and because she is more resourceful with her voice than he is, but Joan is content to orchestrate Dylan. And Dylan—less coiled, even dancing from time to time—cannot ever be called relaxed but now is so in charge that even he believes he's in charge. His singing, therefore, is more authoritative than ever before. That is, the anxiety in his delivery has to do with the story he's telling rather than with the way he's telling it.

. . . .

Joan, in faded jeans and multicolored, boldly striped cotton shirt, is talking with amused affection about Dylan, about the tour, about herself. The Ghost of Johanna still marvels at the sparks that never cease coming from this "savage gift on a wayward bus." Throughout the tour, although Lord knows she knew his numbers well, Joan would slip into the audience to hear Dylan's sets or, if she were weary, she'd sit down backstage to listen.

"Bob has so powerful an effect on so many lives," Joan says. She has been saying this for some 13 years; and at the beginning, before his pop beatification, she pushed mightily to press that savage gift on those who had come to pay homage only to her. Dylan was the "mystery guest" unveiled at her concerts, lurching onstage to break the spell of high-born doom across the seas in someone else's history as he rasped about freak shows right outside.

"I'm still deeply affected by his songs," Joan says. And by

him? "Well, of course, there's that *presence* of his. I've seen
nothing like it except in Muhammad Ali, Marlon Brando and
Stevie Wonder. Bob walks into a room and every eye in the
place is on him. There are eyes on Bob even when he's hiding.
All that has probably not been easy for him." She says this
entirely without her usual irony.

"Sometimes," Dylan says to me on the phone in 1966, "I
have the feeling that other people want my *soul*. If I say to
them, 'I don't *have* a soul,' they say, 'I know that. You don't
have to tell me that. Not me. How dumb do you think I am?
I'm your *friend*.' What can I say except that I'm sorry and feel
bad? I guess maybe feeling bad and paranoia are the same
thing."

Onstage, all during the Rolling Thunder Revue, Joan had
put her arm around Dylan's shoulders, wiped the sweat off his
forehead, kissed his cheek, and looked into his eyes, giving
rise to a frisson of voyeurism among those in the audience
who yearn for *Diamonds & Rust* to have a sequel, several se-
quels, for where else these days can you find that old-time
mysterious rhapsody in the romances of the famous? "It's on
again," a woman behind me whispers eagerly as Dylan and
Baez intertwine in close harmony onstage. "It's on again."
    Later I ask the question and Joan laughs. "This is a *musical*
tour for me. Actually, I don't see much of Bob at all. He
spends most of his time on that movie he's making. The movie
needs a director. The sense I get of it so far is that that movie
is a giant mess of a home movie."
    Joan, sitting back on the couch, as spontaneously straight-
forward as Dylan is cabalistically convoluted. And as he figures in who knows how many sexual fantasies of how many
genders, so she is erotic, still freshly erotic, but probably stars
in somewhat straighter fantasies. But who knows?
    And she is funny, especially in self-defense. As on the day
she showed up for her first rehearsal for the Rolling Thunder
Revue.
    "I'd like to hear that song off your new album," Dylan asks
the once and former girl on the half-shell. "You know, 'Diamonds & Rust.'"

"You want me to do *that* on the show?" Joanie looks at him in solemn question.

"Yeah." There is a distinct collector's gleam in Dylan's eyes. "Yeah, I do."

"You mean," the ex-madonna grabs Dylan by the chin and looks him in the eye, "that song I wrote about my ex-husband."

Dylan has been aced. "I have to keep him spinning," Joan says of the rout, "in order to keep my balance."

"Those duets," Joan says of what she's sometimes been thinking while also wiping Dylan's brow and looking into his eyes, "are a hazard. It's hard singing with him because he's so devilish.

. . . .

"I am not able to tell you any details," says Allen Ginsberg, "but this tour may not end as all other tours have. There is some desire among us to have a kind of permanent community and Dylan is stepping very, very slowly to find out if that can work. Recordings would be one way and there may be other ways. One must proceed slowly and soberly—unlike the Beatles when they tried to expand their sense of community. Remember John Lennon trying to put together that whole Apple enterprise as a sort of umbrella organization for all kinds of collective work? But he didn't have the right personnel and so it wasn't done soberly and practically enough. This would be. Keep watching. The thing is to keep the Rolling Thunder spirit alive."

Joan Baez's denunciation of class segregation aboard the Rolling Thunder Revue has appeared in the troupe's internal newspaper. Her sketch of some nameless star, lying on the ground with blood pouring out of his head, was not printed and has disappeared. But the accusatory text reads:

"We strongly suggest that the security people, the bus drivers and the crew be treated more like human beings and less like bastard children because without them one of the principals might be left dead in the wake of the Rolling Thunder Revue.

"[Signed], Joan Baez and a large supporting cast."

Did it work? I ask.

"Well," says the ceaseless strategist of nonviolent direct

action, "things kind of came together a bit after that. A lot of
people, each in his or her own way, began committing small
acts of civil disobedience—like taking the bus driver to their
table. So the tone has changed and the segregation has lessened." Some people, I am buoyed to see, are still overcoming.

The tour is old enough for retrospection.

"When you got that call from Bob," an old acquaintance
visiting Joan backstage says, "I suppose you got on the plane
without even knowing what you were going to get paid."

Joan looks at the questioner as if the latter has just asked
if the tooth fairy has gotten over its cold. "When I got that
call," Joan says, "I had already planned my fall tour. So I told
the people dealing with the money that although it seemed
like fun, they'd have to make it worth my while to change my
plans. Well, after my lawyers got involved and we worked out
a contract, a very detailed contract, they made it worth my
while. Sure, I'm glad I came. This tour has integrity. And
that's because of Bob."

"Tell me," the acquaintance asks, "what are his children
like?"

Joan hoots, "I've *never* seen any of them. They're like mythology. It does gather around him, mythology. And he certainly helps it gather. Mythology and confusion. Like some of
the songs. *I* know who 'Sad-Eyed Lady of the Lowlands' is,
no matter who *he* says it is."

"But at least we all know who 'Sara' is," the visitor observes.

"Dylan says," Ginsberg has overheard, "that song is about
Sarah in the Bible." And Ginsberg laughs.

Mythology has become palpable. Sara Lowndes Dylan has
joined the Rolling Thunder Revue, and with her are several
Dylan children and a nanny. Allen Ginsberg is impressed.
"Sara is very intelligent, very funny and I would say queenly.
She's sort of aristocratic looking, like an old-time New York
young Jewish lady who's been around a lot in the theater,
which she has been. Sara and Joan," Ginsberg chuckles, "have
had time to compare notes on Dylan."

"No, I had *never* known her before," Joan says of Sara, "and
yes, we have been comparing notes, and that is all I'm going to
tell you about that. But I will say that for me, Sara is the most

interesting female on this tour. Why? Because she's not a bore. That's the best thing I can say about anybody."

Sara Lowndes Dylan has become part of the Rolling Thunder Acting Company, adding her skills and fantasies to what Allen Ginsberg estimates to be more than 100 hours of film already in the can for the giant kaleidoscope being shot by Lombard Street Films, which is being financed—I am told for nonattribution by those close to Zeus—by Dylan himself. At least five or so complete concerts have been preserved and some special numbers, such as "Isis," have been filmed more times than that. And there have been scores of scenes enacted by diversely mixed members of the troupe. Sara Dylan, for instance, has now portrayed a madam in a bordello in which one of the nubile employees is enacted by Joan Baez in a brazen French accent.

Joan, at first rather standoffish about what she had earlier regarded as a huge mess of a home movie, has now become more involved. In another scene, for instance, she and Dylan are in a bar and the bartender is Arlo Guthrie. "My God, she has a lot of energy," says cinéaste Allen Ginsberg. "And what a marvelous mime."

Also intermittently involved are members of the band, virtuosic David Mansfield among them. As an educational insert in the bordello sequence, Allen Ginsberg is seen in his business suit, taking Mansfield (playing a chaste 14-year-old) to lose his cherry, as Ginsberg puts it in the old-time vernacular. This being, in part, a musical, Mansfield of course has his violin along.

Like many of the scenes in this gargantuan movie—which will purportedly be cut and edited in the spring by Dylan and Howard Alk, who worked with Dylan on *Eat the Document*— the bordello section started as quite something else. Ginsberg had suggested a scene involving a number of women in the troupe, in part because he is much taken with the notion that the dominant theme in the Rolling Thunder Revue is respect for the "mother goddess, eternal woman, earth woman principle." He points to the songs in the show, such as "Isis" and "Sara," and notes as well that Sara Dylan has diligently researched this theme in such works as Robert Graves's *The White Goddess*.

The women having assembled, there was much discussion as
to the roles they would play—perhaps the graces or the goddesses of the nine muses. Somehow, however, as Sara Lowndes
Dylan said, "After all that talk about goddesses, we wound up
being whores."

"Nonetheless," says Allen, "Sara, as the madam, did talk
about Flaubert."

Dylan is consumed by this film. He conceives a good many
of the situations, advises on the transmutation of others, does
some of the directing, peers into the camera and works, picking up technique, with the film crew.

One day after much shooting, Ginsberg, wondering how
Dylan keeps track of the direction of all this footage, asks him.
Dylan wishes he hadn't.

"I've lost the thread," Dylan, with some bewilderment, ad-
mits to Ginsberg.

A couple of days later, Ginsberg asks Dylan if the thread
has been relocated. The singing filmmaker nods affirmatively.

"So what *is* the thread of the film?" the poet asks.

"Truth and beauty," says his ever-precise friend.

Along with the Dylan children and their nanny, Joan Baez's
six-year-old son, Gabriel, is now on hand, together with Joan's
mother and a nursemaid for Gabriel. What would Kerouac
have made of this way of doing the road?

Also suddenly, triumphantly materialized—a climactic re-
affirmation of the eternal-woman principle—Bob Dylan's
mother, Beatty Zimmerman.

"A regular chicken soup Jewish mother," Allen Ginsberg
says approvingly. "With a lot of spirit."

Toronto. A cornucopian concert with Gordon Lightfoot
and Joni Mitchell added to the Astartean cast. And also added
in the fertile finale, "This Land Is Your Land"—Bob Dylan's
mother.

Seated at the back of the stage, Beatty Zimmerman pulled
up and onto stage center and begins to dance and wave to the
audience, none of whom, she is sure, knows who she is.

It is getting near the start of the second chorus and Joan
Baez, chronically gracious, pulls Mrs. Zimmerman toward the
lead mike, the principals' mike. "All of a sudden," Joan says,

"Dylan kicks me in the ass. Gently. It was his way of saying, 'I think I'd rather sing this chorus than have my mother do it.' So I had to gracefully Charleston Mrs. Zimmerman back a few steps and then leap to the mike and sing with Bob."

And there, back a few steps, is Mrs. Zimmerman, arms flailing, dancing to Woody's song and the music of Woody's children and the music of her own child, of all things. The first time she's ever been onstage with that child.

"Sara, Joan, his children, his mother," Allen Ginsberg meditates, "he's getting all his mysteries unraveled."

Not quite. Not yet. Earlier in the tour, listening to him as he chants what I took—wrongly, it turns out—to be kaddish for "Sara," there is that mysterious, demonic force, in and beyond the words, that will last a long while beyond the tour. That cracking, shaking energy which reminds me of another *klezmer* on the roof, another Tateh in ragtime, Lenny Bruce. But Lenny, who certainly had his act together, never learned how to get his defenses together. Dylan, on the other hand, has developed a vocation for self-protection. If he has a mania, it is for survival. ("I'm still gonna be around when everybody gets their heads straight.") And part of the way of survival is keeping some of his mysteries damn well raveled.

One morning, as the caravan is about to break camp, a rock musician says, "You know what makes him different. He sees the end of things. The rest of us, we're into something, it's as if it's going to last forever. Dylan, he's in just as deep, but he *knows* it's not going to last."

I am mumbling about a stiff singer who phrases, however authoritatively, like a seal and plays nothing guitar on the side. Why, then, do I once again (unlike the 1974 tour) find him powerful? "It doesn't matter whether he's musical at all," I am instructed by Margot Hentoff, a writer on these matters. "He has in his voice that sense of the fragility of all things, that sense of mortality which everybody tries to avoid acknowledging but is drawn toward when they hear it. He's got it and nobody else has."

It was my wife (quoted in a *New York Times* epitaph I had written of the 1974 tour) who had greatly annoyed Dylan, a

friend of his told me. "He's not 'The Kid' anymore," she had
said in print, "so what can he be now?"

A year later, having come upon the Rolling Thunder Revue, she has an answer: "a grown-up. Maybe a suspicious, secretive, irritating grown-up. But no longer a kid. He's lost
that. And now, as he grows older, he'll get still more powerful
because he'll reach the further knowledge that there is no way
out of loss, and so he'll have a new truth to talk about."

Late one night, at the Other End, before the trail boss was
quite ready to get the wagon train going, Dylan and Bob
Neuwirth and the rest of the gang are elevating their discourse.

"Hey, poet, sing me a poem!" one of them yells to Dylan.

"Okay, poet," says the Minstrel Guruji.

Delighted, Allen Ginsberg is saying, "It's like in a Dosto-
evsky novel, the way they've taken to calling each other
'poet.' It's no more 'Okay, cowboy.' It's 'Okay, poet.' They're
using 'poet' as an honorific, practical thing, and that means
they've grown old enough to see that poetry is tough, that it's
a lasting practice bearing fruit over decades.

"Dylan has become much more conscious of himself as a
poet," Ginsberg adds. "I've watched him grow in that direction. Back in 1968, he was talking poetics with me, telling me
how he was writing shorter lines, with every line meaning
something. He wasn't just making up a line to go with a
rhyme anymore; each line had to advance the story, bring the
song forward. And from that time came some of the stuff he
did with the Band—like 'I Shall Be Released,' and some of his
strong laconic ballads like 'The Ballad of Frankie Lee and
Judas Priest.' There was to be no wasted language, no wasted
breath. All the imagery was to be functional rather than orna-
mental. And he's kept growing from there.

"Like he's been reading Joseph Conrad recently. *Victory* in
particular. I found out when we were talking about the narrative quality of some of the newer songs—'Hurricane' and
'Joey' and 'Isis.' Bob related the way those songs developed to
what he'd been learning about narrative and about characterization from Conrad. The way characterization and mood
shape narrative. Now he's asking about H. P. Lovecraft. I
wonder what that's going to lead to?"

It is near the end. In Toronto, Joan Baez is backstage. On-stage, Dylan is beginning his acoustic set. A member of Gordon Lightfoot's band begins to move some equipment. Baez glares at him and he stops.

"The jerk didn't know any better," she says later, "but I didn't want to miss a note. I didn't want to miss a word. Even after all these shows, the genius of The Kid was still holding it all together. I'd heard it all, every night, and here I'm sitting again as close to him as I can get. And not only me. You look around and you see every member of the band and the guys in the crew listening too."

What is it? What is it he has? I ask.

"It's the power," Joan says. "It's the power."

"Oh, I'm hurtin'." It is the next morning. Bob Neuwirth groans and coughs in a most alarming manner. "This is a rolling writers' show," Neuwirth manages to say. "Nobody on this tour who isn't a writer. *Oh, I'm really hurtin'.* Even the equipment guys, the bus drivers, they're all jotting things down. It's a goddamn rolling writers' convention. *Oh my God, I can't even cough.* It's going to be such a drag when this tour is over."

Joan Baez, mildly sympathetic when she's not laughing, says to the audibly aching Neuwirth, "Do let me describe what happened to you last night. Everybody has his own way of dealing with anxieties," she explains to me, "and his way was to get himself black and blue. He got very, very drunk and ornery and for an hour and a half four very large security guards were wrestling him in the hall because they didn't want him to leave the hotel and go wreck Gordon Lightfoot's house where we were having a party. Well, he got there anyhow and he did wreck the house just a little. But everybody had a grand time, and now Neuwirth feels fine too, except he can't walk very well.

"You see, it's going to be rough for all of us when this is over. And Neuwirth's way of handling that was to have an early blowout. God, it's depressing at the end."

At the beginning, in Plymouth, Massachusetts, Elliott Adnopoz (long since transubstantiated into his vision, Ramblin' Jack Elliott) sees an old friend, the replica of the *Mayflower,* on whose rigging he, an expert sailor, had actually worked years before. Climbing to the top of the mizzenmast, Elliott explodes with a long, joyous, "Ahoy!" and waves to the Minnesota poet in the cowboy hat below as Allen Ginsberg proclaims, "We have, once again, embarked on a voyage to reclaim America."

At least it is steady work, especially for a minstrel.

From Rolling Stone, 1976.

QUESTIONS

(1) What is the point of the opening anecdotes about Allen Ginsberg, Joan Baez, and Bob Dylan? Do they present contradictory images of Dylan?

(2) What are the differences in the personalities of Joan Baez and Bob Dylan?

(3) What is *the joke* in the exchange between Dylan and Baez over the song "Diamonds and Rust"?

(4) Hentoff's technique in this essay provides a series of fleeting impressions that in their totality will add up to an overall sense of the experience of being on the tour. How would you characterize that experience from reading Hentoff?

(5) What does the incident in which Dylan's mother is on stage tell you about the personality of Bob Dylan?

(6) What does the incident involving Bob Neuwirth (second from final paragraph) suggest about the emotional involvement of those on the tour?

(7) How does the final anecdote reflect both the illusions and the reality that surrounded the tour? What is the author's tone at the conclusion?

GEORGE CARLIN FEELS FUNNY

MARK GOODMAN

From the outside, George Carlin's home looks like any one of a thousand modest residences perched high on Southern California's Pacific Palisades. That's from the outside. Inside, the living room appears fairly normal at first—until you notice a fully clothed wooden Indian reclining in a modern, egg-shaped chair. Next to the wooden Indian, presumably awaiting the drill, sits a doll in a dentist's chair. A mannequin's torso rests on the bar; it is clothed in a sweat shirt emblazoned with the seven words deemed by Carlin (and surely the F.C.C.) the most abominable in the ears of the American audience. On the balcony stands a telescope through which, Carlin claims, the viewer can enjoy the splendors of Osaka. Over the mantel there is a photo of Carlin being busted by four cops in Milwaukee. And, finally and most gloriously, there is a full-sized cardboard cutout of Carlin's former square self, bedecked with enormous wooden rosary beads and crucifix.

Where, you may ask, is George Carlin these days? Where are all our old favorites: sportscaster Biff Barf, with his spotlight on sports; Al Sleet, the Hippy-Dippy Weatherman; and the wonderful WINO disc jockey Willie Wise? Well, Carlin is alive and thrivin', man. Oh, not entirely; you can still catch him guest-hosting *The Tonight Show* on occasion. But since 1969, when the resident comedian of the American middle class decided to go "NYAAH, NYAAH!" to straight entertainment, his main gig has been the college concert circuit and coincident recordings. Hence George Carlin: high-school dropout, Catholic Church dropout, Air Force dropout—now a middle-class dropout. "I didn't really change into somebody new," he says. "I just changed back to my real self. I had been hiding behind my characters for years for the benefit of the baldheads and the blue hairs, and I found I just couldn't relate to them. I said, 'Screw it, it's time to drop out completely, time to go on the concert tour with my soul, my gut, and not *just* be funny.'"

He is as funny as ever, but instead of crisp, flashy, six-to-eight-minute character sketches, Carlin now does ninety—count 'em, ninety—minutes of canny, wildly discursive, none-too-divine comedy on the American condition. The profane accent is on dope, race and sex. In short, Carlin is happily doing the same *shtik* for which his forebear, Lenny Bruce, was hounded to his grave less than ten years ago. Yet Carlin, at thirty-seven, has not become a martyred mendicant, trading toilet poems for bread. Whereas Lenny was forced to sink his meager savings into debilitating First Amendment battles, George scarcely knows what to do with the $1,000,000 or so he made in 1973, much less the like sum he'll have earned in 1974.

The times have clearly changed in Carlin's favor: most of the machine-gun emplacements have been removed from our campuses; the cops are concerned less with politically inspired confrontation than with the muggers at their backs; and Middle America is acutely aware that the deleted expletive is much more dangerous than a dirty word up front. And while Bruce is admittedly Carlin's main man, in fact helped give him his start back in 1960, Carlin also notes some key differences. "I learned my sense of double standards from Lenny," he says. "We shared the same attitudes, and he influenced me a lot while I was developing. But it's obvious that our comedy was different. There's more of a gentleness in my comedy than there was in his. Lenny really came down hard, and he came down especially hard on the Catholic Church, so the church and the Irish police hierarchy got together to go after him."

That was Lenny's sin, then, blasphemy, not obscenity? George Carlin, as lapsed a Catholic as ever tempted hellfire, thinks so, and he may be right. When Lenny Bruce, the heretic Jew, told Chicago audiences that the Dodge Company was going to raffle off a 1964 Catholic Church, there were sure some tongues cluckin' out there, Father. And Carlin? Well, fallen from grace or not, he is still one of their own, and the Irish on both sides of the Atlantic have long since resigned themselves to catching unholy hell from their mad, mordant strays: Joyce, Shaw, O'Casey, Wilfrid Sheed, Jimmy Breslin, to name but a few. George has done his penances, you see, he's earned the right to poke a bit of fun.

I used to be an Irish Catholic. . . . I was worried about sin, especially the sin of "wanna". . . . "Wanna" was a sin all by itself.
. . . It was a sin to wanna feel up Ellen, a sin to plan to feel up
Ellen, a sin to figure out a place to feel up Ellen, a sin to take
Ellen to the place to feel her up, a sin to try to feel up Ellen and
a sin to, you know, *feel up* Ellen. Six sins in one. . . . And then
confession. In my diocese in New York, when Puerto Ricans started
moving in they made a rare display of tokenism for the fifties—
they brought in Father Rivera. All the Irish guys heavily into
puberty went to him for confession because he didn't seem to take
the sins personally. It was three Hail Mary's and back on the
street with Father Rivera—he was known as a light penance. But
he wasn't ready for the way Irish boys confessed. "Bless me, Fodder,
for I have sinnned. I have touched myself in an impure manner. I
was impure, impurity, impureness. Thought, word and deed, body,
touch, impure; sex, dirty, impure legs, impureness, touch, impure,
dirty, bodies, sex, rub. And covet, Fodder, heavy on the covet."
"Das okay, mane, tres Santa Marías."

There are those who suggest that Carlin should do, if not
eternity, at least one-to-five for Ripping Off. The overage
hippy was highly suspect, especially in the strident sixties.
Carlin fields such notions easily, intelligently—he's heard it before, and it really doesn't bother him. He settles his ectomor-
phic body into the sofa, alternately pulling on a beer and a
roach. The Carlin you see at home is precisely the Carlin you
see onstage. "I always was a street person," he says. "The record of my life shows a pattern of rebellion, and that attitude
carried over when I got started in the Greenwich Village coffeehouses, like the Café Au Go Go. I went straight for television because I had decided that I wanted to be an actor. But
among other things, I came to realize that what I really am is
a writer, a writer who can perform his own work. I wanted to
try to achieve total self-expression, not ego gratification or the
solace of a lavish show-business life-style. My bit is to originate
my own material, not just memorize scripts. I wanted to do
my own stuff and relate it to an audience. So where do you
find your audiences? In the coffeehouses and on the campus."
Truth be told, although Carlin is a wealthy dude now, his
controversial conversion from tuxedoed comic to tie-dyed
freako cost him plenty at the time. He was booted out of Las
Vegas' Frontier Hotel, ostensibly for profanity but in reality
for offending a high-toned customer; busted during a Milwaukee Summer Festival in 1970 for doing the seven-words-

you-don't-say-on-TV routine before a G-rated audience;
dropped like a bad habit from Hugh Hefner's Playboy Clubs.
Nor was it clear in the late sixties that there was a youthful
comic field to be exploited. Says Carlin: "If anyone had tried
to use comedy as a means of statement in the sixties—well, I
think, the kids would have been distracted. Other voices were
saying it plainer, both radical spokesmen and rock musicians.
Anyway, my comedy is timeless, and varied. Mort Sahl is all
topical, Jonathan Winters all invention. I do both, plus a bit
of the childhood stuff that Cosby raised to such heights."

George Carlin was raised in the uppermost white reaches of
Manhattan's West Side, Morningside Heights. It includes such
cultural centers as Columbia University, Juilliard School of
Music and Union Theological Seminary. It also borders on
black and Puerto Rican cultural centers, and the curious ad-
mixture forms the foundation of Carlin's raunchy, ethnic-
oriented street comedy. "At least I was brought up in a progressive Catholic school," he says. "It could have been Our
Lady of Great Agony, or St. Rita Moreno, but Father Ford
had somehow talked the diocese into trying new procedures at
Corpus Christi, like the Dewey method. The nuns were reasonable; there was no Sister Mary discipline with the steel
ruler. . . . WHACK! YAAAGH! You fall behind two years
in penmanship. Anyway, we had so much freedom in the
school that by eighth grade many of us had lost our faith.
They made little questioners out of us. The priests would fall
back on, 'Ah, it's a mystery, my son.' 'Oh, tanks, Fodder, a
mystery you say. Hey, Roger, what's he talkin' about, a mystery?' "
George's father died when he was young; he lived with his
mother, who had the comparatively worldly job of executive
secretary to the president of the Association of National Ad-
vertisers. And there was his older brother Patrick. "From
grade school I went to Cardinal Hayes, a big-league Catholic
high school, big jock, big band. I got into the band my first
year—I played trumpet. I figured out there was no way you
could march, read music and play an instrument at the same
time, so I just didn't play my instrument. Who wants to march
like a jerk? Anyway, by May I had failed five subjects: neither

my brother nor I took school very seriously. I ran away from
home with three buddies, and when I finally came back the
first thing my mother said was, 'Well, at least you came home
on Ascension Day.' "

Most of George's intellectual gifts and restless energies were
consecrated to Hanging Out—with his Irish buddies, with the
blacks and Puerto Ricans seeping into the area, and later with
the Italians down on Fourteenth Street. These neighborhoods
were George Carlin's classrooms, his laboratories.

> We called our neighborhood White Harlem, because that
> sounded *bad*. Morningside Heights was the real name, but that
> sounded faggy. . . . Fag didn't mean the same thing in those days;
> fag meant sissy. A fag wouldn't stay out late or go steal off trucks.
> . . . "Go home, fag, it's ten o'clock, hey, look, the fag's going
> home. . . ." We knew what a queer was, he was a *queer,* that was
> the word after homo, remember? So there was a big difference be-
> tween a fag and a queer. A fag was a guy who wouldn't go down-
> town and beat up queers. . . .

George suffered several unsuccessful bouts with high school;
Spencer Tracy types kept coming around to the Carlin house
telling him what a fine mind he had if he would only apply
himself. Trouble was, Carlin knew all that and didn't care.
"I always knew I wanted to be a movie actor or a comic or a
TV star, some kind of entertainer. I thought disc jockey was
probably the best."

He then went into the Air Force. It taught him, to its ultimate chagrin, to operate B-47 bomber navigation systems, and
dispatched him to Barksdale Air Force Base near Shreveport,
Louisiana. As Carlin fondly recalls, "The first thing I became
was a fuck-up. I got a couple of Article Fifteens, two courts-
martial, but I never did any time. The Air Force was pretty
loose." The only thing he didn't befoul was his part in a local
theatre production of *Golden Boy,* which landed him a spot
in town as a D.J.

"I spent most of my time in the Air Force as a spade, a
voluntary nigger. I gravitated toward the urban blacks rather
than the rural red-necks. The whites didn't take to me until
I became a D.J. Then they said, 'Okay, he's a nigger-lover, but
he's all right, he'll play your requests.' "

When Carlin got out, a pal from Shreveport, Homer Odom,

got him a job with WEZE in Boston, an ABC affiliate. George laughs, sucks on his beer. "I used to borrow the station's mobile unit and run down to New York on weekends. Once I came back on Monday and found them frantic, man. They said, 'Where the hell have you been? There was a breakout at Walpole penitentiary this weekend.' That's hot news, all right. I shrugged and said, 'Wait till next week's break and catch that one.' They didn't see the humor in that and fired me, but that was okay."

Carlin found his way to Fort Worth and latched on as D.J. on the seven-P.M.-to-midnight show for KXOL, the number one Top Forty station in town. "I really dug that. I answered my own phones, you know, the requests, and it put me in touch with the kids. It was a nice way of keeping a rapport with my own childhood." One day a buddy from Boston showed up—Jack Burns, now of Burns and Schreiber. "I got him the job of newsman on my show," says Carlin, "and after hours we started working a local coffeehouse called The Cellar. We were loose and dirty in an ungainly way, but the audiences laughed their asses off. Finally we decided to pack up and give California a try."

They found a morning slot on KDAY in Los Angeles as a comedy team. "We were insane, and it was a funny show, but we had to open the station at six A.M., which was a drag. Sometimes we'd be as much as fifteen minutes late, all hung over, so we'd break in like, '—oudy today, chance of drizzle in the late afternoon,' so the listeners would just assume there was something wrong with their radios."

They played nights at the Cosmo Alley Coffeehouse, where an agent named Murray Becker offered to manage their act. "He knew Bruce and Sahl from the old days, and since we did imitations of them in the show, he got them both to come over. Lenny loved it and got us a contract with G.A.C. [now Creative Management Associates]. We lighted out for Chicago and played the Cloister with Bobby Short. Then Hefner saw us and put us in the Playboy Club."

By October, 1961, they were on *The Tonight Show* with Jack Paar. "We really couldn't believe it. I mean, look, in February we were sitting in our underwear in Fort Worth watching Jack Paar on the tube and fantasizing what it would be like to be on his show. And six months later we were really on the show."

Burns and Carlin became a staple on the Midwest nightclub circuit. On that tour—at the Dayton Racquet Club to be exact—George met and married Brenda Hosbrook. Yes, George Carlin, hip, funky, down-home urban freak, is happily married to a slender, pleasant blond with short-clipped hair, and is the father of a stunning eleven-year-old girl named Kelly. But if that partnership has held up, Burns and Carlin foundered early. "We just weren't innovating anymore," says George. "I'd always known I really wanted to do a single anyway."

The Carlins settled with George's mother in New York, and he started all over again—this time in the savage beat jungle of Greenwich Village. He worked the Café Au Go Go with other no-names like Richard Pryor and José Feliciano for five to ten dollars a night. Carlin persevered, and finally put together a routine suitable for television: the Indian drill sergeant.

"It was a standard fish-out-of-water gimmick, the thing that Bob Newhart was doing so well then. The idea was that if the Indians were good fighters, they must have been organized, and military organization means N.C.O.'s. So it was this: 'All right, you bucks, listen up to the word. There's gonna be a massacre tonight at twenty-one hundred; we'll meet down at the bonfire, dance around a little, and then move out.'"

Carlin got his shot on *Merv Griffin* in the summer of 1965, and the drill sergeant was a hit. He was arriving in the wake of a gilt-edged renaissance in stand-up comedy, with TV and 33⅓ r.p.m. records providing the momentum. In those days every college man worth his Bass Weejuns could do Winters and Newhart and the Steve Allen gallimaufry and of course Bruce and, with the aid of some razor-tongued witch from Manhattan Music and Art, Nichols and May. Carlin wanted all of that, wanted it badly, not just for the booty and the fame, but for the intellectual cachet he knew he deserved. "I wasn't very well educated, but I saw this beautiful stream of intelligent comedy coming out of those people, and it really got to me." So when Merv Griffin and others came back for more and more, Carlin, veteran of the disc-jockey wars, was

ready for them. Even today, Carlin has not completely severed
his ties with Wonderful, Wonderful WINO.

> This is Scott Lame with the boss sounds from the boss station in
> the boss town that my boss told me to play. . . . Here's a hot new
> sound from Crosby, Stills, Nash, Young, Merrill Lynch, Pierce,
> Sacco and Vanzetti. . . . It's moving fast, I say fast, it was re-
> corded at nine this morning, number three by noon, number one
> by three and now it's a . . . Golden Oldie! Super gold to make
> you feel old! And now, WINO news round the world from Bill
> Bleeper. . . . Saigon! Bleep-bleep-bleep-bleep-bleep. . . . Bangkok!
> Bleep-bleep-bleep-bleep-bleep. . . . Paris! Bleep-bleep-bleep-bleep-
> bleep. . . . And now the late sports with Biff Barf . . . ! This is
> Biff Barf with the Sportlight Spotlight, spotlighting sports, pickin'
> 'em up and barfin' 'em back at you. Now some scores from the
> Far West. . . . Guam Prep forty-five, Marshall Islands fourteen
> . . . Mindanao A. and M. twenty-seven, Molokai ten . . . Cal
> Tech fourteen point five, M.I.T. three to the fourth power . . .
> and a partial score—Stanford twenty-nine. Now over to Al Sleet,
> your Hippy-Dippy Weatherman. . . . Hey, man, *qué pasa*. . . .
> The present temperature is sixty-eight degrees at the airport, which
> is pretty stupid, man, 'cause I don't know anyone who lives at the
> airport. . . . Tonight's forecast: dark, continued mostly dark,
> with scattered light by midmorning. . . .

The *Merv Griffin*'s piled up, thirty-one of them; there were
Tonight Show's, eventually forty-two of them. There was the
NBC Kraft Summer Music Hall with John Davidson, and another summer replacement show with Buddy Greco, and an
unheard-of twelve minutes on *Ed Sullivan*. With it all came
more sketches, more characters.

> Welcome to *The Divorce Game,* where some lucky couple will
> win a divorce right here, brought to you by National Van Lines.
> If your home is breaking up, let National break it up for you. Now
> here's your host, Dom Decree. . . . Good evening, folks. In just a
> little while we're going to play our home divorce game, where we
> call a housewife at random and tell her that her husband is down-
> town drinking with . . . *ANOTHER WOMAN!* But now it's
> time to meet our couple from yesterday, Raoul and Congolia
> Breckinridge. . . . You awarded them a divorce right here on the
> show, and now we're going to play for custody of the *CHILDREN!*

Carlin was resoundingly successful—and increasingly unhappy. First came his disaffection with acting. "I had been
thinking in terms of a half-hour comedy series that would last
for five years. I kept visible and was jacking around audition-
ing for acting parts. Then I started to realize that I was un-

comfortable in them. I did an episode of *That Girl* and a bit
in a Doris Day movie, *With Six You Get Egg Roll*. I was terrified. I hated the loss of independence and, frankly, I just
didn't know how to do it. It was, 'Okay, George, let's try it
again, you come in over there and fall down,' or whatever. I
was too nervous, always afraid I was going to do it wrong."

A bigger problem was the nightclub circuit. "There was this
growing disenchantment with my audiences. My basic experience had been post-folk, early-rock freak audiences. Now here
I was—because of the TV success—back into the middle-class
show-biz world. I have nothing against the audience as folks—
even though I don't always agree with the way they think—
but they sure as hell aren't my kind of audience. They're on
trial as much as we are, you can see that in their body language. They're tense, worried about how to act, when to
laugh. I was just stitching characters together for them; I
couldn't reach them, person-to-person. They liked it, but I
didn't."

They, as it happened, didn't always like it. There was the
first Las Vegas incident at the Frontier in 1968, during a
Howard Hughes golf tournament. Carlin, still clean-shaven
and in a tux, did a number about different types of posteriors,
"the boldest thing I had at the time." A Hughes executive's
wife took offense, and Carlin was suspended with a year to go
on his contract. "That," he says, "is what you call an early-
warning system." When he came back the next year, he was
arrayed in a beard, long hair and a vest, "what they call formal
funky."

By then he had a mild scatological routine with an obvious
drug pun for a kicker. It did not go down, and Carlin got
riled. "I started in on, 'Hey, you bunch of ass holes with your
mortgages around your necks. . . .' That kind of stuff. The
management asked me not to come back." In between Vegas
dates was an even more bizarre performance at the Copa-
cabana. "I had avoided the Copa for years, and I quickly realized why. They wouldn't let me wear civies—I had to wear a
tux. And that audience—even my old thirty minutes didn't
work. Finally I just did weirdness, like lying on the floor and
describing the underside of the piano. Or telling them I was
a Dada comedian. I'd say, 'I don't know if you're familiar with
the Dada school of philosophy; it concerned itself in part with

the rejection of a performer by his audience. The point is that it's as difficult to gain your complete rejection for thirty minutes as it is to gain your acceptance, and I can go either way.' "
C.M.A., Carlin's agency, was understandably concerned, and some high-powered agency wheels arrived one night to check out the peculiar goings-on. They shouldn't have. Carlin harangued them from the stage: "I don't belong here, man, put me in the *colleges*. These places went out of style twenty-five years ago, they just forgot to close. I'm sure you all saw Dennis Morgan kicking George Raft out upstairs as you came in, and if Cesar Romero dances past me again I'm really going to be pissed."

Well, you don't do that at the Copa, and you don't insult Hughes execs' wives in Vegas. Carlin was finished in big-time nightclubs—including Hugh Hefner's. At the Lake Geneva Playboy Club he emboldened his social commentary and was rewarded with the stock reactionary catchphrases of the period: "Who are you to criticize our country?" and, "Have you ever been shot at?" As Carlin remembers, "People were coming up to the hotel desk and asking for my room number. The manager said, 'I can't guarantee your safety, you'll have to leave.' So I went down to Chicago to see Hef, the man who was so big on non-censorship. He said to me, 'George, there are two Hefners. One would be there in the audience laughing, but the other has to live with those people.' He didn't even pay me for the remaining shows."

Carlin's head was not completely turned around by externals; his conversion (or reversion) was abetted from within by the tablets of California Sunshine that occasionally burst in his brain. "That changed my life," George says. "It made it possible for me to act on some of the things that I was feeling. I noticed on one trip that I found myself not getting mad at little things—like waiting for elevators. It allowed me to view my talent and my craft in a different way. I saw that I was an observer of life and of the people around me, that I could turn these observations into funny routines, not just shoot for laughs per se."

Carlin was careful not to go too far with the acid, but he was doing eight or ten joints a day at the time and was thus, like Lenny Bruce, highly vulnerable. Indeed, his near-miss in Milwaukee was chillingly reminiscent of the Night of the Long Sticks at Chicago's Gate of Horn when Bruce was busted hard—and spent four hours in jail with George, who was himself rousted out of the Horn on a drunk-and-disorderly charge.

"It was a big festival on a lakefront—three bands a night, maybe sixty thousand people. I did my regular show, which included the seven words you can't say on TV. Pretty soon Brenda came out on the stage and told me that there were cops waiting to arrest me. So Brenda and some of our people walked the cops around while I divested myself of any embarrassing impedimenta. I sneaked into my dressing room just before they broke in and searched me. Then four cops dragged me off. Three were winking, but the fourth took pique. He was morally offended. He said there were parents and children hearing those words.

"I was charged with disorderly conduct and profanity. William Coffin came out to take my case. The state prosecutor threw it out, but the cop insisted on taking it to the city prosecutor. The municipal judge threw it out too." This was 1970, many light-years away from Bruce's dark struggle. But Carlin realized that he was faced with the residue of the same problem: he was saying things, very publicly, that a lot of people still did not want to hear.

> I was asked on a talk show about the dope problem. I said, "Yes, there are definitely too many dopes around. . . ." But there is a drug problem . . . it's all those *DRUG*stores, all-night *DRUGS,* we deliver *DRUGS, DRUG*stores. . . . The pharmacist is always stoned, you can see it in his eyes, man, how come he can't fill the prescription right away? He says, "Come back in an hour, I can't even read the bastard. . . ." It's no accident we're drug-oriented, the drug companies made it that way and they like it that way. They start us early on the oral habit, little orange-flavored aspirin for children. . . . "Something wrong with your head, son, put this in your mouth." Got it? Head bad, into mouth, *POP!* these little orange things, *THERE'LL BE OTHER COLORS SOME-DAY.* . . .
>
> Commercials worry me. Five-day deodorant pads have to be the strangest product of the business mind. Sounds like a curse. . . . Tell the truth, how many of you thought you *had* to wear them? "I been wearing these mothers for two years. . . ." Or Scope. Anyone ever sent someone a bottle of Scope? Seems like a cruel

thing to do. . . . Think of the borderline psychotic, he just needs
one more thing to go wrong. He goes down to his mailbox, finds a
bottle of Scope . . . *YAAAAGHH!* Up on the roof with the mag-
num . . . *BLOOEY!*

George Carlin's words have a bite, to be sure, but it's a love
bite, as harmless and pixilated and full of care as Carlin himself. Laughter is his rod and staff; he has no use for punditry
or politics. "I worked on the Jess Unruh campaign against
Reagan," he recounts. "I found myself speaking at an Elks
club one night, when they still had the black restrictions.
That's not where we're at, folks."

Carlin, with a microphone and a glib Gaelic street tongue
and an uncanny ear, conveys what is true and what is not true.
It is by now literary canon that one must be mad to survive in
a mad world: the Yossarian syndrome. Clearly George Carlin
believes that, and more: he considers this disastrous human
condition a personal burden. A gladsome burden, a risible
burden; but a burden nonetheless. I think Carlin engraved his
own epitaph within the covers of his album *Class Clown*. It is
a parable, author anonymous, which reads: "In ancient times
there was a country whose harvest came in and it was poisonous. Those who ate of it became insane. 'There is but one
thing to do,' said the king. 'We must eat the grain to survive,
but there must be those among us who will remember that
we are insane.' "

From Esquire Magazine, 1974.

QUESTIONS

(1) Which decoration in George Carlin's home is most revealing of his personality?

(2) How does Carlin distinguish his comedy from that of
Lenny Bruce?

(3) Why does Carlin think of himself as a writer rather than
as a comic or as an actor?

(4) Like many comics, Carlin draws upon the experiences of
his childhood for his routines. What is particularly distinctive
about Carlin's background?

(5) Why was Carlin dissatisfied with his role as a nightclub comedian?

(6) What does the author mean by the term the "Yossarian syndrome"? Who is Yossarian?

(7) Paraphrase the parable quoted at the conclusion of the essay.

Rights, realities, roles, relationships, responsibilities: they were all questioned; they all changed. Perhaps the most visible changes in the decade were those which redefined the nature and limits of male and female, as people tried to understand better the connections between sexuality and *person*-ality.

All over America, men and women acted out one of the major themes of the decade: "going public." Now all is to be told; all is to be shown; all is to be admitted. In the age of exposure, that most private experience, at its best and its worst, went public, and sex became the growth industry of the seventies.

What does it mean to be a woman or a man? Half a generation ago these were not even questions. Then half a decade ago those questions were being shouted because the old answers seemed inadequate or even harmful. The oldest and most basic human division suddenly became an unfinished, unsettled, and unsettling matter. Nothing seemed as self-evident as it once had. Homosexual and heterosexual, the revolution didn't change the terms of the human struggle—for self-definition, for self-respect, for the nourishing connection. But the new freedom of sexual expression meant that the struggle would now go on in the open.

In the seventies living together became a style, but getting together remained a problem. If the old roles no longer worked, if they ever did, what were the new roles in which to make public one's private feelings? As with most important questions, however, even if they are loudly shouted, the answers remain elusive.

The selections which follow are not offered as answers. That would be foolhardy. Rather, they are statements about sexual identity and human feelings. Funny, bitter, painful, factual, and again funny, positive and doubtful: they are examples of the ways in which men and women can define themselves, for themselves and for each other.

Joyce Maynard may have been the youngest author ever to make a best-seller list. Her "autobiography," *Looking Back,* was published when she was nineteen. In it she chronicles her generation, the one that always had the whole world and outer space in the living room. In the selection reprinted here, she describes the shaky survival of an old-fashioned virtue in a revolutionary time. This is her story of how she learned, when she arrived in college, that *V* was the scarlet letter.

The essays by Alan Alda, an actor, and Julius Lester, a poet and a teacher, one white and one black, both appeared in *Ms.* magazine. That fact in itself says that the new sexual definitions might lead, not to further divisions, but to better connections.

Woody Allen is a genius, and the products of genius are sometimes hard to classify. His essay, "The Whore of Mensa," is a nostalgic look at old detective stories, sexual clichés, and male fantasies. His radical inversion of the body-mind problem is itself a symbol for the crazy mix-up on which the stories, the clichés, and the fantasies were built in the first place.

Nora Ephron writes with brilliant humor and Adrienne Rich with painful feeling about the experience of being a woman. Despite their very different styles, they have in common the clarity, the integrity, and the courage which make writing memorable.

In a brief profile of Elaine Noble, Laura Shapiro touches all of the highlights of the decade's new sexual definitions. Ms. Noble is a conscientious, hard-working career person, a member of the Massachusetts House of Representatives. She is one of the many women challenging the old concepts of who is fit for what job. Elaine Noble also happens to be a lesbian.

Sally Kempton's "Cutting Loose" is one of the classic texts of the seventies: an intensely personal disclosure as a means to the understanding of a public issue. If we had to define *the* style of the decade, that would be it. Sally Kempton uses herself, mercilessly, in an effort to understand the meanings of "liberation" for herself and then for every woman. Along the way she redefines the battle of the sexes as a guerilla war for that liberation.

Although sex went public in the seventies, that did not

mean that individuals no longer faced private choices. But it did mean that they might be able to understand better their own feelings by having the chance to read some honest reports from others struggling with the demand of gender and the sense of self.

LOOKING BACK: VIRGINITY

JOYCE MAYNARD

For about three weeks of my freshman year at college I had two roommates instead of one—the girl in the bottom bunk and her friend, who made our quarters especially cramped because, in addition to being six feet tall with lots of luggage, he was male. We slept in shifts—they together, until I came back to the room at night, then he outside in the living room on the couch, until she got up, then he in her bed and I in mine, or I in hers and he in mine, because it was easier for me to get out from the bottom without waking him, and he needed his sleep. . . . We never made it a threesome, but the awkwardness was always there (those squeaking bedsprings . . .), as it was for many girls I knew, and many boys. Coming back to the room and announcing my presence loudly with a well-directed, well-projected cough or a casual murmur, "Hmmm—I think I'll go to my room now," it occurred to me that it wasn't my roommate but I—the one who slept alone, the one whose only pills were vitamins and aspirin—I was the embarrassed one. How has it happened, what have we come to, that the scarlet letter these days isn't *A,* but *V?*

In the beginning, of course, everyone's a virgin. You start on equal footing with everyone else (sex is something comic and dirty—the subject of jokes and slumber-party gossip), but pretty soon the divisions form. (Sex is still dirty, but less unthinkable, sort of thrilling.) There's the girl with the older boy friend (he's in ninth grade); the girl who went away to summer camp and fell in love; the girl who kisses boys right out there on the dance floor for all the junior high to see. (That's the point, of course. If she wanted it to be a secret, she'd have gone out to the Coke machine with him, the way the other couples do.) But everybody's still a virgin. The question isn't even asked.

The first to go is usually a secretarial student, the one who started wearing bras in fourth grade, the one who pierced her ears in sixth, the one who wears purple eyeshadow to school. She doesn't talk about it, but she doesn't make a big thing of keeping it quiet either, so word gets around, and all the *good* girls whisper about her—they knew it all the time, what can you expect? She's probably older anyway, she must have stayed back a couple of years. . . .

Then, maybe in tenth grade, or eleventh, (if you live in a city, make that ninth), it's a good girl, one of your crowd. (You know because she called her best friend up the next day and—promise not to tell—told her.) At first you think it was a mistake: he took advantage of her, she didn't know what was happening—and you feel terribly, terribly sorry for her and wonder how she'll ever face him again. But she does; in fact, she's with him all the time now—*doing it again* most likely. You stare at her in the halls ("she doesn't *look* any different") and, though she's still your friend—you still pass notes in math class—there's a distance between you now. Woman of the world and little girl—hot ticket and (for the first time, the word sounds slightly unpleasant) *virgin*.

After that, the pattern becomes more common. The girl, when she breaks up with that first boy, can hardly hold out on his successor. And her ex-boy friend's new girl friend, naturally, has an expectation to satisfy if she wants a date to the prom. More and more girls are, in the words of those who aren't, *going all the way*. As for the ones who still baby-sit on Friday nights, or the ones whose dates are still getting up the courage to kiss them good night, they spend their time speculating—"does she or doesn't she?" (It's always the *girl* who does; not a combined act at all so much as an individual one.) The group of shocked guessers gets smaller and smaller until they—you, if you're still one of them—realize that the ones to be whispered about, stared at, shocked by, aren't the others now but themselves. It's hard to say at what point the moment occurs, but suddenly virginity isn't fun anymore. The days when it was taken for granted are long gone; so are the days when it was half and half (The Virgins vs. the Nons). The ones who *aren't* now take that for granted, and as for the ones who are, well—they don't talk about it much. Virginity has become not a flower or a jewel, a precious treasure for Prince Charming or a lively, prized and guarded gift, but a dusty relic—an anachronism. Most of all, it's an embarrassment.

So here we have this baffled, frightened virgin (she's third person now; I can't help wanting to disassociate myself from her category and all it seems to represent). She may not really be a prude or an iceberg (maybe nobody's ever tried . . .) but that's how the world views her. She's on the same team with Sensible Orthopedic Shoes and Billy Graham and Lawrence Welk and the Republican party. Old ladies—her grandmother's friends—love her (she can get a date with their favorite nephews any time) and wonder sadly why there aren't more girls around like that. A certain kind of man (boy) is very fond of her, too. He's the timid type—just as glad, really, not to feel that he's expected to perform. (He's an embarrassed virgin too, and the last thing these two need is each other, perpetuating the breed—as their nonvirginal contemporaries, in lovemaking, perpetuate the race—by nonperformance.) The sexual revolution is on, but the virgin isn't part of it.

The sexual revolution. It's a cliché, but it exists all right, and its pressures are everywhere. All the old excuses ("I might get pregnant," "I'm not that kind of girl") are gone. Safe and increasingly available contraceptives (for anyone brave and premeditative enough to get them) make premarital sex possible; changing moral standards, an increased naturalness, make it commonplace; elegant models of sexual freedom—Julie Christie, Catherine Deneuve—have made it fashionable. Consider a virgin in the movies. Is there a single pretty young heroine who doesn't hop unself-consciously into bed? (Who is there left for her to identify with—Doris Day?) Then there are magazines, filled with discussions of intricate sexual problems (the timing of orgasms . . . do I get one? do I give one?) while the virgin remains on a whole other level—her fears compounded. (Our old, junior high notion of sex was that it got done to you; the girl with the purple eyeshadow just let it happen. Today all kinds of problems in technique make the issue much more complicated for an inexperienced, media-blitzed girl: not just *will I* but *can I*.) The people who've been making nice, simple love for years now, while the virgin became more and more unique, have, quite understandably, gone on to other things. There is foreplay and afterplay and the 999 positions of the *Kamasutra*. . . . The train has left the station before the virgin's bought her ticket or even, maybe, packed her bags.

There are other pressures too, less remote than the images on a screen or the words on a page. Though individuality is officially admired, "Peer-group pressure" (a fifties concept) is very real when it comes to sex. Other girls assume a friend's sexual experience. So, more importantly, do the men she goes out with. The death of the formal date (with dinner and the theater, high heels and a good-night kiss afterward) has put a new ambiguity on male-female relationships. Just sitting around, talking and listening to music, while it may be lots more real and honest and all those other good 1973-type adjectives, is also lots more difficult for a virgin to cope with. If this is someone she likes—but doesn't love—there isn't any way for her to demonstrate simple fondness. The kiss that once said "I like you" now seems a promise of something more to come. And if, perhaps, she's decided that yes, this is someone she would sleep with, she may discover (final irony) that he isn't eager, when he finds out she's a virgin, to be the first. The situation seems unresolvable: virginity is a self-perpetuating condition. (Like the unskilled, unemployed worker, the virgin hears—time and again—"Come back when you've got some experience.") The only way out seems to be the crudest, most loveless and mechanical way possible: almost a reverse prostitution. It happens—as once young boys would be initiated in a brothel—because the idea now, for the late-bloomer, the high school baby-sitter—the idea is to get it over with as quickly, painlessly and forgettably as possible.

If it hasn't happened before, the pressure is really on at college. I'm looking back now to the beginning of my freshman year. What I should remember is my first glimpse of the college campus, freshman assembly, buying notepads and textbooks and writing my name and my dorm on the covers. Instead, my memory of September blurs into a single word: sex. Not that Yale was the scene of one continuous orgy. But we surely were preoccupied. Ask a friend how things were going and he'd tell you whether or not he'd found a girl. Go to a freshman women's tea or a Women's Liberation meeting and talk would turn, inevitably, to contraceptives and abortions. Liberated from the restrictions imposed by parents and curfews and car seats (those tiny Volkswagens), we found ourselves suddenly sharing a world not with the junior high and the ninth grade, but with college seniors and graduate students—

men and women in their twenties. Very quickly, we took on
their values, imitated their behavior and, often, swallowed
their pills.

September was a kind of catching-up period for all the people who hadn't cut loose before. All that first week, girls
trooped up the stairs at 3 and 4 A.M., and sometimes not at all.
Fall, for the freshmen, at least, was a frantic rush of pairing
off, with boys running for the girls and, strangely enough
(there were so few of us, so many boys to go around) the girls
rushing for the boys and the couples, finally, rushing for the
beds as if this were musical chairs and if you didn't hurry
you'd be left standing up. It was maybe the last chance to be
clumsy and amateurish and virginal. After that, you entered
the professional league where, if you weren't a pro, you had
a problem.

I don't mean to reinforce the embarrassment, to confirm the
hopelessness of the virgin's situation—"yes, things are pretty
bad, aren't they?"—or to frighten anyone about to embark
upon the brave new world of college or job-and-apartment.
Because as a matter of fact there shouldn't be anything scary
or hopeless or embarrassing about virginity any more than
there should be anything scary, hopeless or embarrassing
about the loss of it. I'm not *for* virginity or *against* premarital
sex, and I'm certainly not defending virginity for its own
sake—the I'm-saving-it-for-my-husband line. Whether or not
you're a virgin isn't the point; the question is what *kind* of a
virgin or a nonvirgin you are, and whether you are what you
are by choice or by submission to outside pressures. (Plenty of
"freely consenting" adults are really victims of a cultural,
everybody's-doing-it type of forced consent.) Some women can
easily and naturally love a man or want to be close to him,
maybe even without love. I have a friend like that—a girl I
used to think of as promiscuous and hypocritical when she said
of each boy friend (and sometimes two at once), "I love him."
I see now this was quite genuine. She has a giving and sharing
nature and she loves very easily. She isn't racking up points in
her sexual relationships; she truly wants to know as many people as she can. Not everyone can be that way; knowing someone means being known, giving up privacy in a manner that's
difficult for many people. These days one's privacy is no longer
one's own. Even the act of refusing to give it up is intruded

upon. It's no longer just the nonvirgin who subjects herself to
intense scrutiny; now it's the virgin whose very refusal is
scrutinized, maybe even more closely than her surrender
would be. People don't talk much about who's on the pill or
who's sleeping together, but there's endless speculation about
who isn't. "What's the matter with her?" they ask. Is she
frigid? Lesbian? Big-brother types offer helpful advice, reasoning that if she isn't interested in them except as a friend, something must indeed be wrong with her. Her abstinence, in
short, is fair game for everyone.

Privacy—and freedom—can be maintained only by disre-
garding the outside pressures. Freedom is choosing, and sometimes that may mean choosing not to be "free." For the embarrassed virgin, unsure now whether her mind is her own ("Do
I really want to go to bed with him, or do I simply want to be
like everybody else?")—for her, there's a built-in test. If she
really wants to, on her own, she won't have to ask herself or
be embarrassed. Her inexperience and clumsiness will have,
for him, a kind of coltish grace. Our grandparents, after all,
never read the *Kamasutra,* and here we are today, proof that
they managed fine without it.

From *Looking Back,* 1972.

QUESTIONS

(1) Why does the author delay the words "he was male" until
the end of the sentence?

(2) What does the detail "with lots of luggage" contribute to
the effect Maynard wants?

(3) What does she mean that her only "pills" were vitamins
and aspirins?

(4) Do the details about the "secretarial student" give a complete picture? Is it fair? Is there a class prejudice connected
with the assumed sexual standard? Is the situation different
in a big city?

(5) Why does Maynard italicize certain words and phrases?
Are they more effective with that emphasis?

(6) Does the author use any other puns besides "The Virgins" and "The Nons"?

(7) What relationships does the author establish between the pressures of the sexual revolution and a media-blitz? What names would you substitute for hers?

(8) In what way does the author indicate that remaining a virgin upsets or reverses all the old-fashioned ideas about sexual experience and initiation?

(9) Do the repeated and connected words—"embarrassed," "purple eyeshadow," "lots of luggage" and "packed her bags," "pills," *Kamasutra*—involve the reader in the progress of the essay?

(10) How would you describe the tone of her statements about her freshman September? Is it more comic than rueful? Or vice versa?

(11) Is her statement about free choice a logical development of her previous observations about "peer pressure" and "media-blitz"?

(12) Are "privacy—and freedom" properly explained in this essay? Are they properly defended?

WHAT EVERY WOMAN SHOULD KNOW ABOUT MEN

ALAN ALDA

Everyone knows that testosterone, the so-called male hormone, is found in both men and women. What is not so well known is that men have an overdose.

Until now it has been thought that the level of testosterone in men is normal simply because they have it. But if you consider how abnormal their *behavior* is, then you are led to the hypothesis that almost all men are suffering from *testosterone poisoning*.

The symptoms are easy to spot. Sufferers are reported to show an early preference (while still in the crib) for geometric shapes. Later, they become obsessed with machinery and objects to the exclusion of human values. They have an intense need to rank everything, and are obsessed with size. (At some point in his life, nearly every male measures his penis.)

It is well known that men don't look like other people. They have chicken legs. This is symptomatic of the disease, as is the fact that those men with the most aviary underpinnings will rank women according to the shapeliness of *their* legs.

The pathological violence of most men hardly needs to be mentioned. They are responsible for more wars than any other leading sex.

Testosterone poisoning is particularly cruel because its sufferers usually don't know they have it. In fact, when they are most under its sway they believe that they are at their healthiest and most attractive. They even give each other medals for exhibiting the most advanced symptoms of the illness.

But there is hope.

Sufferers can change (even though it is harder than learning to walk again). They must first realize, however, that they are sick. The fact that this condition is inherited in the same way that dimples are does not make it cute.

Eventually, of course, telethons and articles in the *Reader's Digest* will dramatize the tragedy of testosterone poisoning. In the meantime, it is imperative for your friends and loved ones to become familiar with the danger signs.

Have the men you know take this simple test for—

THE SEVEN WARNING SIGNS OF TESTOSTERONE POISONING

(1) *Do you have an intense need to win?* When having sex, do you take pride in always finishing before your partner? Do you

always ask if this time was "the best"—and gnaw on the bed-post if you get an ambiguous answer?

(2) *Does violence play a big part in your life?* Before you answer, count up how many hours you watched football, ice hockey, and children's cartoons this year on television. When someone crosses you, do you wish you could stuff his face full of your fist? Do you ever poke people in your fantasies or throw them to and fro at all? When someone cuts you off in traffic, do violent, angry curses come bubbling out of your mouth before you know it? If so, you're in big trouble, fella, and this is only question number two.

(3) *Are you "thing" oriented?* Do you value the parts of a woman's body more than the woman herself? Are you turned on by things that even *remind* you of those parts? Have you ever fallen in love with a really great doorknob?

(4) *Do you have an intense need to reduce every difficult situation to charts and figures?* If you were present at a riot, would you tend to count the crowd? If your wife is despondent over a deeply felt setback that has left her feeling helpless, do you take her temperature?

(5) *Do you tend to measure things that are really qualitative?* Are you more impressed with how high a male ballet dancer can leap than with what he does while he's up there? Are you more concerned with how long you can spend in bed, and with how many orgasms you can have, than you are with how you or your partner feels while you're there?

(6) *Are you a little too mechanically minded?* Would you like to watch a sunset with a friend and feel at one with nature and each other, or would you rather take apart a clock?

(7) *Are you easily triggered into competition?* When someone tries to pass you on the highway, do you speed up a little? Do you find yourself getting into contests of crushing beer cans—with the beer still in them?

If you've answered yes to three or fewer of the above questions, you may be learning to deal with your condition. A man answering yes to more than three is considered sick and not someone you'd want to have around in a crisis—such as raising children or growing old together. Anyone answering yes to all seven of the questions should seek help immediately before he kills himself in a high-wire act.

WHAT TO DO IF YOU SUFFER FROM TESTOSTERONE POISONING

(1) *Don't panic.* Your first reaction may be that you are sicker than anyone else—or that you are the one man in the world able to fight it off—or, knowing that you are a sufferer, that you are the one man ordained to lead others to health (such as by writing articles about it). These are all symptoms of the disease. Just relax. First, sit back and enjoy yourself. Then find out how to enjoy somebody else.

(2) *Try to feel something.* (Not with your hands, you oaf.) Look at a baby and see if you can appreciate it. (Not how *big* it's getting, just how nice she or he is.) See if you can get yourself to cry by some means other than getting hit in the eye or losing a lot of money.

(3) *See if you can listen while someone is talking.* Were you the one talking? Perhaps you haven't got the idea yet.

(4) *Practice this sentence:* "You know, I think you're right and I'm wrong." (Hint: it is useful to know what the other person thinks before you say this.)

FOR WOMEN ONLY: WHAT TO DO IF YOU ARE LIVING
WITH A SUFFERER

(1) Remember that a little sympathy is a dangerous thing. The sufferer will be inclined to interpret any concern for him as appropriate submissiveness.

(2) Let him know that you expect him to fight his way back to health and behave like a normal person—for his own sake, not for yours.

(3) Only after he begins to get his condition under control and has actually begun to enjoy life should you let him know that there is no such thing as testosterone poisoning.

From Ms. Magazine, 1975.

QUESTIONS

(1) What kind of television announcement or newspaper statement is Alda parodying in this essay?

(2) Does the fact that Alda is best known for playing a doctor on a popular television series have any bearing on the style and the effect of this selection?

(3) Is the statement "They are responsible for more wars than any other leading sex" effective argumentation?

(4) Can a woman suffer from "testosterone poisoning"?

(5) Is the statement "Sufferers can change (even though it is harder than learning to walk again)" an exaggeration?

(6) Does the proposed treatment seem to fit the described disease?

A FEW WORDS ABOUT BREASTS

NORA EPHRON

I have to begin with a few words about androgyny. In grammar school, in the fifth and sixth grades, we were all tyrannized by a rigid set of rules that supposedly determined whether we were boys or girls. The episode in *Huckleberry Finn* where Huck is disguised as a girl and gives himself away by the way he threads a needle and catches a ball—that kind of thing. We learned that the way you sat, crossed your legs, held a cigarette, and looked at your nails—the way you did these things instinctively was absolute proof of your sex. Now obviously most children did not take this literally, but I did. I thought that just one slip, just one incorrect cross of my legs or flick of an imaginary cigarette ash would turn me from whatever I was into the other thing; that would be all it took, really. Even though I was outwardly a girl and had many of the trappings generally associated with girldom—a girl's name, for example, and dresses, my own telephone, an autograph book—I spent

the early years of my adolescence absolutely certain that I
might at any point gum it up. I did not feel at all like a girl.
I was boyish. I was athletic, ambitious, outspoken, competitive, noisy, rambunctious. I had scabs on my knees and my
socks slid into my loafers and I could throw a football. I
wanted desperately not to be that way, not to be a mixture of
both things, but instead just one, a girl, a definite indisputable
girl. As soft and as pink as a nursery. And nothing would do
that for me, I felt, but breasts.

I was about six months younger than everyone else in my
class, and so for about six months after it began, for six
months after my friends had begun to develop (that was the
word we used, develop), I was not particularly worried. I
would sit in the bathtub and look down at my breasts and
know that any day now, any second now, they would start
growing like everyone else's. They didn't. "I want to buy a
bra," I said to my mother one night. "What for?" she said.
My mother was really hateful about bras, and by the time my
third sister had gotten to the point where she was ready to
want one, my mother had worked the whole business into a
comedy routine. "Why not use a Band-Aid instead?" she
would say. It was a source of great pride to my mother that
she had never even had to wear a brassiere until she had her
fourth child, and then only because her gynecologist made
her. It was incomprehensible to me that anyone could ever be
proud of something like that. It was the 1950s, for God's sake.
Jane Russell. Cashmere sweaters. Couldn't my mother see
that? *"I am too old to wear an undershirt."* Screaming. Weeping. Shouting. "Then don't wear an undershirt," said my
mother. "But I want to buy a bra." "What for?"
I suppose that for most girls, breasts, brassieres, that entire
thing, has more trauma, more to do with the coming of adolescence, with becoming a woman, than anything else. Certainly more than getting your period, although that, too, was
traumatic, symbolic. But you could see breasts; they were
there; they were visible. Whereas a girl could claim to have
her period for months before she actually got it and nobody
would ever know the difference. Which is exactly what I did.
All you had to do was make a great fuss over having enough
nickels for the Kotex machine and walk around clutching

your stomach and moaning for three to five days a month about The Curse and you could convince anybody. There is a school of thought somewhere in the women's lib/women's mag/gynecology establishment that claims that menstrual cramps are purely psychological, and I lean toward it. Not that I didn't have them finally. Agonizing cramps, heating-pad cramps, go-down-to-the-school-nurse-and-lie-on-the-cot cramps. But, unlike any pain I had ever suffered, I adored the pain of cramps, welcomed it, wallowed in it, bragged about it. "I can't go. I have cramps." "I can't do that. I have cramps." And most of all, gigglingly, blushingly: "I can't swim. I have cramps." Nobody ever used the hard-core word. Menstruation. God, what an awful word. Never that. "I have cramps."

The morning I first got my period, I went into my mother's bedroom to tell her. And my mother, my utterly-hateful-about-bras mother, burst into tears. It was really a lovely moment, and I remember it so clearly not just because it was one of the two times I ever saw my mother cry on my account (the other was when I was caught being a six-year-old kleptomaniac), but also because the incident did not mean to me what it meant to her. Her little girl, her firstborn, had finally become a woman. That was what she was crying about. My reaction to the event, however, was that I might well be a woman in some scientific, textbook sense (and could at least stop faking every month and stop wasting all those nickels). But in another sense—in a visible sense—I was as androgynous and as liable to tip over into boyhood as ever.

I started with a 28AA bra. I don't think they made them any smaller in those days, although I gather that now you can buy bras for five-year-olds that don't have any cups whatso-ever in them; trainer bras they are called. My first brassiere came from Robinson's Department Store in Beverly Hills. I went there alone, shaking, positive they would look me over and smile and tell me to come back next year. An actual fitter took me into the dressing room and stood over me while I took off my blouse and tried the first one on. The little puffs stood out on my chest. "Lean over," said the fitter. (To this day, I am not sure what fitters in bra departments do except to tell you to lean over.) I leaned over, with the fleeting hope

that my breasts would miraculously fall out of my body and
into the puffs. Nothing.

"Don't worry about it," said my friend Libby some months
later, when things had not improved. "You'll get them after
you're married."

"What are you talking about?" I said.

"When you get married," Libby explained, "your husband
will touch your breasts and rub them and kiss them and they'll
grow."

That was the killer. Necking I could deal with. Intercourse
I could deal with. But it had never crossed my mind that a
man was going to touch my breasts, that breasts had something to do with all that, petting, my God, they never mentioned petting in my little sex manual about the fertilization
of the ovum. I became dizzy. For I knew instantly—as naïve as
I had been only a moment before—that only part of what she
was saying was true: the touching, rubbing, kissing part, not
the growing part. And I knew that no one would ever want to
marry me. I had no breasts. I would never have breasts.

My best friend in school was Diana Raskob. She lived a
block from me in a house full of wonders. English muffins, for
instance. The Raskobs were the first people in Beverly Hills
to have English muffins for breakfast. They also had an apri-
cot tree in the back, and a badminton court, and a subscrip-
tion to *Seventeen* magazine, and hundreds of games, like Sorry
and Parcheesi and Treasure Hunt and Anagrams. Diana and
I spent three or four afternoons a week in their den reading
and playing and eating. Diana's mother's kitchen was full of
the most colossal assortment of junk food I have ever been exposed to. My house was full of apples and peaches and milk
and homemade chocolate-chip cookies—which were nice, and
good for you, but-not-right-before-dinner-or-you'll-spoil-your-
appetite. Diana's house had nothing in it that was good for
you, and what's more, you could stuff it in right up until dinner and nobody cared. Bar-B-Q potato chips (they were the
first in them, too), giant bottles of ginger ale, fresh popcorn
with melted butter, hot fudge sauce on Baskin-Robbins jamoca
ice cream, powdered-sugar doughnuts from Van de Kamp's.
Diana and I had been best friends since we were seven; we
were about equally popular in school (which is to say, not par-

ticularly), we had about the same success with boys (extremely intermittent), and we looked much the same. Dark. Tall. Gangly.

It is September, just before school begins. I am eleven years old, about to enter the seventh grade, and Diana and I have not seen each other all summer. I have been to camp and she has been somewhere like Banff with her parents. We are meeting, as we often do, on the street midway between our two houses, and we will walk back to Diana's and eat junk and talk about what has happened to each of us that summer. I am walking down Walden Drive in my jeans and my father's shirt hanging out and my old red loafers with the socks falling into them and coming toward me is . . . I take a deep breath . . . a young woman. Diana. Her hair is curled and she has a waist and hips and a bust and she is wearing a straight skirt, an article of clothing I have been repeatedly told I will be unable to wear until I have the hips to hold it up. My jaw drops, and suddenly I am crying, crying hysterically, can't catch my breath sobbing. My best friend has betrayed me. She has gone ahead without me and done it. She has shaped up.

Here are some things I did to help:
Bought a Mark Eden Bust Developer.
Slept on my back for four years.
Splashed cold water on them every night because some French actress said in *Life* magazine that that was what *she* did for her perfect bustline.
Ultimately, I resigned myself to a bad toss and began to wear padded bras. I think about them now, think about all those years in high school I went around in them, my three padded bras, every single one of them with different-sized breasts. Each time I changed bras I changed sizes: one week nice perky but not too obtrusive breasts, the next medium-sized slightly pointy ones, the next week knockers, true knockers; all the time, whatever size I was, carrying around this rubberized appendage on my chest that occasionally crashed into a wall and was poked inward and had to be poked outward—I think about all that and wonder how anyone kept a straight face through it. My parents, who normally had no restraints about needling me—why did they say nothing as

they watched my chest go up and down? My friends, who
would periodically inspect my breasts for signs of growth and
reassure me—why didn't they at least counsel consistency?

And the bathing suits. I die when I think about the bathing
suits. That was the era when you could lay an uninhabited
bathing suit on the beach and someone would make a pass at
it. I would put one on, an absurd swimsuit with its enormous
bust built into it, the bones from the suit stabbing me in the
rib cage and leaving little red welts on my body, and there I
would be, my chest plunging straight downward absolutely
vertically from my collarbone to the top of my suit and then
suddenly, wham, out came all that padding and material and
wiring absolutely horizontally.

Buster Klepper was the first boy who ever touched them. He
was my boyfriend my senior year of high school. There is a
picture of him in my high-school yearbook that makes him
look quite attractive in a Jewish, horn-rimmed-glasses sort of
way, but the picture does not show the pimples, which were
air-brushed out, or the dumbness. Well, that isn't really fair.
He wasn't dumb. He just wasn't terribly bright. His mother
refused to accept it, refused to accept the relentlessly average
report cards, refused to deal with her son's inevitable destiny
in some junior college or other. "He was tested," she would
say to me, apropos of nothing, "and it came out a hundred
and forty-five. That's near-genius." Had the word "under-
achiever" been coined, she probably would have lobbed that
one at me, too. Anyway, Buster was really very sweet—which
is, I know, damning with faint praise, but there it is. I was the
editor of the front page of the high-school newspaper and he
was editor of the back page; we had to work together, side by
side, in the print shop, and that was how it started. On our
first date, we went to see *April Love,* starring Pat Boone. Then
we started going together. Buster had a green coupe, a 1950
Ford with an engine he had hand-chromed until it shone,
dazzled, reflected the image of anyone who looked into it,
anyone usually being Buster polishing it or the gas-station attendants he constantly asked to check the oil in order for
them to be overwhelmed by the sparkle on the valves. The
car also had a boot stretched over the back seat for reasons I

never understood; hanging from the rearview mirror, as was
the custom, was a pair of angora dice. A previous girl friend
named Solange, who was famous throughout Beverly Hills
High School for having no pigment in her right eyebrow, had
knitted them for him. Buster and I would ride around town,
the two of us seated to the left of the steering wheel. I would
shift gears. It was nice.

There was necking. Terrific necking. First in the car, overlooking Los Angeles from what is now the Trousdale Estates.
Then on the bed of his parents' cabana at Ocean House. Incredibly wonderful, frustrating necking, I loved it, really, but
no further than necking, please don't, please, because there I
was absolutely terrified of the general implications of going-a-
step-further with a near-dummy and also terrified of his finding out there was next to nothing there (which he knew, of
course; he wasn't that dumb).

I broke up with him at one point. I think we were apart for
about two weeks. At the end of that time, I drove down to see
a friend at a boarding school in Palos Verdes Estates and a
disc jockey played "April Love" on the radio four times during the trip. I took it as a sign. I drove straight back to Griffith
Park to a golf tournament Buster was playing in (he was the
sixth-seeded teen-age golf player in southern California) and
presented myself back to him on the green of the 18th hole. It
was all very dramatic. That night we went to a drive-in and I
let him get his hand under my protuberances and onto my
breasts. He really didn't seem to mind at all.

"Do you want to marry my son?" the woman asked me.

"Yes," I said.

I was nineteen years old, a virgin, going with this woman's son,
this big strange woman who was married to a Lutheran minister
in New Hampshire and pretended she was gentile and had this
son, by her first husband, this total fool of a son who ran the hero-
sandwich concession at Harvard Business School and whom for
one moment one December in New Hampshire I said—as much
out of politeness as anything else—that I wanted to marry.

"Fine," she said. "Now, here's what you do. Always make sure
you're on top of him so you won't seem so small. My bust is very
large, you see, so I always lie on my back to make it look smaller,
but you'll have to be on top most of the time."

I nodded. "Thank you," I said.

"I have a book for you to read," she went on. "Take it with you when you leave. Keep it." She went to the bookshelf, found it, and gave it to me. It was a book on frigidity.

"Thank you," I said.

That is a true story. Everything in this article is a true story, but I feel I have to point out that that story in particular is true. It happened on December 30, 1960. I think about it often. When it first happened, I naturally assumed that the woman's son, my boyfriend, was responsible. I invented a scenario where he had had a little heart-to-heart with his mother and had confessed that his only objection to me was that my breasts were small; his mother then took it upon herself to help out. Now I think I was wrong about the incident. The mother was acting on her own, I think: that was her way of being cruel and competitive under the guise of being helpful and maternal. You have small breasts, she was saying; therefore you will never make him as happy as I have. Or you have small breasts; therefore you will doubtless have sexual problems. Or you have small breasts; therefore you are less woman than I am. She was, as it happens, only the first of what seems to me to be a never-ending string of women who have made competitive remarks to me about breast size. "I would love to wear a dress like that," my friend Emily says to me, "but my bust is too big." Like that. Why do women say these things to me? Do I attract these remarks the way other women attract married men or alcoholics or homosexuals? This summer, for example. I am at a party in East Hampton and I am introduced to a woman from Washington. She is a minor celebrity, very pretty and Southern and blond and outspoken, and I am flattered because she has read something I have written. We are talking animatedly, we have been talking no more than five minutes, when a man comes up to join us. "Look at the two of us," the woman says to the man, indicating me and her. "The two of us together couldn't fill an A cup." Why does she say that? It isn't even true, dammit, so why? Is she even more addled than I am on this subject? Does she honestly believe there is something wrong with her size breasts, which, it seems to me, now that I look hard at them, are just right? Do I unconsciously bring out competitiveness in women? In that form? What did I do to deserve it?

As for men.

There were men who minded and let me know that they

minded. There were men who did not mind. In any case, *I* always minded.

And even now, now that I have been countlessly reassured that my figure is a good one, now that I am grown-up enough to understand that most of my feelings have very little to do with the reality of my shape, I am nonetheless obsessed by breasts. I cannot help it. I grew up in the terrible fifties—with rigid stereotypical sex roles, the insistence that men be men and dress like men and women be women and dress like women, the intolerance of androgyny—and I cannot shake it, cannot shake my feelings of inadequacy. Well, that time is gone, right? All those exaggerated examples of breast worship are gone, right? Those women were freaks, right? I know all that. And yet here I am, stuck with the psychological remains of it all, stuck with my own peculiar version of breast worship. You probably think I am crazy to go on like this: here I have set out to write a confession that is meant to hit you with the shock of recognition, and instead you are sitting there thinking I am thoroughly warped. Well, what can I tell you? If I had had them, I would have been a completely different person. I honestly believe that.

After I went into therapy, a process that made it possible for me to tell total strangers at cocktail parties that breasts were the hang-up of my life, I was often told that I was insane to have been bothered by my condition. I was also frequently told, by close friends, that I was extremely boring on the subject. And my girl friends, the ones with nice big breasts, would go on endlessly about how their lives had been far more miserable than mine. Their bra straps were snapped in class. They couldn't sleep on their stomachs. They were stared at whenever the word "mountain" cropped up in geography. And *Evangeline,* good God what they went through every time someone had to stand up and recite the Prologue to Longfellow's *Evangeline:* ". . . stand like druids of eld . . . / With beards that rest on their bosoms." It was much worse for them, they tell me. They had a terrible time of it, they assure me. I don't know how lucky I was, they say.

I have thought about their remarks, tried to put myself in their place, considered their point of view. I think they are full of shit.

From Crazy Salad, 1972.

QUESTIONS

(1) How do the contrasts given in the first paragraph help to establish the theme of the essay?

(2) Is "becoming a woman" the theme of the essay? In what ways? In how many senses?

(3) What significant contrasts does Ephron make in the opening paragraphs between childhood and womanhood?

(4) How do the details presented convey her feelings about her mother?

(5) How does the fact that she is "six months younger" prepare the reader for her encounters with Libby and Diana? Why is it necessary to establish that fact first?

(6) What do the details reveal about Nora Ephron's feelings for and about Diana Raskob? How do they prepare the reader for the climax of that friendship?

(7) Do the names sound real? Better than real?

(8) Is there a pattern of adult-children relationships in the essay?

(9) How do the questions in the third paragraph from the end, "And even now . . . ," change the tone of the essay?

(10) The essay is based on contrasts. Why is the contrast in the next to last paragraph so effective?

(11) Is the stylistic contrast the reason the last sentence is so effective?

BEING A BOY

JULIUS LESTER

As boys go, I wasn't much. I mean, I tried to be a boy and spent many childhood hours pummeling my hardly formed ego with failure at cowboys and Indians, baseball, football, lying, and sneaking out of the house. When our neighborhood gang raided a neighbor's pear tree, I was the only one who got sick from the purloined fruit. I also failed at setting fire to our garage, an art at which any five-year-old boy should be adept. I was, however, the neighborhood champion at getting beat up. "That Julius can take it, man," the boys used to say, almost in admiration, after I emerged from another battle, tears brimming in my eyes but refusing to fall.

My efforts at being a boy earned me a pair of scarred knees that are a record of a childhood spent falling from bicycles, trees, the tops of fences, and porch steps; of tripping as I ran (generally from a fight), walked, or simply tried to remain upright on windy days.

I tried to believe my parents when they told me I was a boy, but I could find no objective proof for such an assertion. Each morning during the summer, as I cuddled up in the quiet of a corner with a book, my mother would push me out the back door and into the yard. And throughout the day as my blood was let as if I were a patient of 17th-century medicine, I thought of the girls sitting in the shade of porches, playing with their dolls, toy refrigerators and stoves.

There was the life, I thought! No constant pressure to prove oneself. No necessity always to be competing. While I humiliated myself on football and baseball fields, the girls stood on the sidelines laughing at me, because they didn't have to do anything except be girls. The rising of each sun brought me to the starting line of yet another day's Olympic decathlon, with no hope of ever winning even a bronze medal.

Through no fault of my own I reached adolescence. While the pressure to prove myself on the athletic field lessened, the overall situation got worse—because now I had to prove my-

self with girls. Just how I was supposed to go about doing
this was beyond me, especially because, at the age of 14, I was
four foot nine and weighed 78 pounds. (I think there may
have been one 10-year-old girl in the neighborhood smaller
than I.) Nonetheless, duty called, and with my ninth-grade
gym-class jockstrap flapping between my legs, off I went.

To get a girlfriend, though, a boy had to have some asset
beyond the fact that he was alive. I wasn't handsome like Bill
McCord, who had girls after him like a cop-killer has policemen. I wasn't ugly like Romeo Jones, but at least the girls noticed him: "That ol' ugly boy better stay 'way from me!" I was
just there, like a vase your grandmother gives you at Christmas
that you don't like or dislike, can't get rid of, and don't know
what to do with. More than ever I wished I were a girl. Boys
were the ones who had to take the initiative and all the responsibility. (I hate responsibility so much that if my heart
didn't beat of itself, I would now be a dim memory.)

It was the boy who had to ask the girl for a date, a frightening enough prospect until it occurred to me that she might say
no! That meant risking my ego, which was about as substantial as a toilet-paper raincoat in the African rainy season. But
I had to thrust that ego forward to be judged, accepted, or
rejected by some girl. It wasn't fair! Who was she to sit back
like a queen with the power to create joy by her consent or
destruction by her denial? It wasn't fair—but that's the way it
was.

But if (God forbid!) she should say Yes, then my problem
would begin in earnest, because I was the one who said where
we would go (and waited in terror for her approval of my
choice). I was the one who picked her up at her house where I
was inspected by her parents as if I were a possible carrier of
syphilis (which I didn't think one could get from masturbat-
ing, but then again, Jesus was born of a virgin, so what did I
know?). Once we were on our way, it was I who had to pay
the bus fare, the price of the movie tickets, and whatever she
decided to stuff her stomach with afterward. (And the smallest
girls are all stomach.) Finally, the girl was taken home where
once again I was inspected (the father looking covertly at my
fly and the mother examining the girl's hair). The evening
was over and the girl had done nothing except honor me with
her presence. All the work had been mine.

Imagining this procedure over and over was more than enough: I was a sophomore in college before I had my first date.

I wasn't a total failure in high school, though, for occasionally I would go to a party, determined to salvage my self-esteem. The parties usually took place in somebody's darkened basement. There was generally a surreptitious wine bottle or two being passed furtively among the boys, and a record player with an insatiable appetite for Johnny Mathis records. Boys gathered on one side of the room and girls on the other. There were always a few boys and girls who'd come to the party for the sole purpose of grinding away their sexual frustrations to Johnny Mathis's falsetto, and they would begin dancing to their own music before the record player was plugged in. It took a little longer for others to get started, but no one matched my talent for standing by the punch bowl. For hours, I would try to make my legs do what they had been doing without effort since I was nine months old, but for some reason they would show all the symptoms of paralysis on those evenings.

After several hours of wondering whether I was going to die ("Julius Lester, a sixteen-year-old, died at a party last night, a half-eaten Ritz cracker in one hand and a potato chip dipped in pimiento-cheese spread in the other. Cause of death: failure to be a boy"), I would push my way to the other side of the room where the girls sat like a hanging jury. I would pass by the girl I wanted to dance with. If I was going to be refused, let it be by someone I didn't particularly like. Unfortunately, there weren't many in that category. I had more crushes than I had pimples.

Finally, through what surely could only have been the direct intervention of the Almighty, I would find myself on the dance floor with a girl. And none of my prior agony could compare to the thought of actually dancing. But there I was and I had to dance with her. Social custom decreed that I was supposed to lead, because I was the boy. Why? I'd wonder. Let her lead. Girls were better dancers anyway. It didn't matter. She stood there waiting for me to take charge. She wouldn't have been worse off if she'd waited for me to turn white.

But, reciting "Invictus" to myself, I placed my arms around her, being careful to keep my armpits closed because, somehow, I had managed to overwhelm a half jar of deodorant and a good-size bottle of cologne. With sweaty armpits, "Invictus," and legs afflicted again with polio, I took her in my arms, careful not to hold her so far away that she would think I didn't like her, but equally careful not to hold her so close that she could feel the catastrophe which had befallen me the instant I touched her hand. My penis, totally disobeying the lecture I'd given it before we left home, was as rigid as Governor Wallace's jaw would be if I asked for his daughter's hand in marriage.

God, how I envied girls at that moment. Wherever *it* was on them, it didn't dangle between their legs like an elephant's trunk. No wonder boys talked about nothing but sex. That thing was always there. Every time we went to the john, there *it* was, twitching around like a fat little worm on a fishing hook. When we took baths, it floated in the water like a lazy fish and God forbid we should touch it! It sprang to life like lightning leaping from a cloud. I wished I could cut it off, or at least keep it tucked between my legs, as if it were a tail that had been mistakenly attached to the wrong end. But I was helpless. It was there, with a life and mind of its own, having no other function than to embarrass me.

Fortunately, the girls I danced with were discreet and pretended that they felt nothing unusual rubbing against them as we danced. But I was always convinced that the next day they were all calling up all their friends to exclaim: "Guess what, girl? Julius Lester got one! I ain't lyin'!"

Now, of course, I know that it was as difficult being a girl as it was a boy, if not more so. While I stood paralyzed at one end of a dance floor trying to find the courage to ask a girl for a dance, most of the girls waited in terror at the other, afraid that no one, not even I, would ask them. And while I resented having to ask a girl for a date, wasn't it also horrible to be the one who waited for the phone to ring? And how many of those girls who laughed at me making a fool of myself on the baseball diamond would have gladly given up their places on the sidelines for mine on the field?

No, it wasn't easy for any of us, girls and boys, as we forced our beautiful, free-flowing child-selves into those narrow, constricting cubicles labeled *female* and *male*. I tried, but I wasn't good at being a boy. Now, I'm glad, knowing that a man is nothing but the figment of a penis's imagination, and any man should want to be something more than that.

From *Ms. Magazine*, 1973.

QUESTIONS

(1) Do the details in the first paragraph "prove" the author's failure to be a boy? What does he imply are the standards of a boy's success?

(2) Is Julius Lester's "jockstrap" in the fifth paragraph the same kind of "symbol" as Nora Ephron's "28AA bra"? What does each article of clothing represent to the particular author?

(3) Are his descriptions of a date and a party accurate?

(4) Is the "jockstrap" in the fifth paragraph a way of setting up the reader for the "catastrophe" in the dance?

(5) How many specific failures does Lester include in his "autobiography"? Despite all the failures listed, can you think of the man who wrote the essay as a failure?

(6) Why is the next to last paragraph important? Why does it come before he presents his conclusion? (Notice that he shifts to questions because he is not describing his own experience.)

(7) The essay implies that there are alternatives to forcing a child into "constricting cubicles labeled *female* and *male*." What are some of the alternatives?

THE WHORE OF MENSA

WOODY ALLEN

One thing about being a private investigator, you've got to learn to go with your hunches. That's why when a quivering pat of butter named Word Babcock walked into my office and laid his cards on the table, I should have trusted the cold chill that shot up my spine.

"Kaiser?" he said. "Kaiser Lupowitz?"

"That's what it says on my license," I owned up.

"You've got to help me. I'm being blackmailed. Please!"

He was shaking like the lead singer in a rumba band. I pushed a glass across the desk top and a bottle of rye I keep handy for nonmedicinal purposes. "Suppose you relax and tell me all about it."

"You . . . you won't tell my wife?"

"Level with me, Word. I can't make any promises."

He tried pouring a drink, but you could hear the clicking sound across the street, and most of the stuff wound up in his shoes.

"I'm a working guy," he said. "Mechanical maintenance. I build and service joy buzzers. You know—those little fun gimmicks that give people a shock when they shake hands?"

"So?"

"A lot of your executives like 'em. Particularly down on Wall Street."

"Get to the point."

"I'm on the road a lot. You know how it is—lonely. Oh, not what you're thinking. See, Kaiser, I'm basically an intellectual. Sure, a guy can meet all the bimbos he wants. But the really brainy women—they're not so easy to find on short notice."

"Keep talking."

"Well, I heard of this young girl. Eighteen years old. A Vassar student. For a price, she'll come over and discuss any subject—Proust, Yeats, anthropology. Exchange of ideas. You see what I'm driving at?"

"Not exactly."

"I mean, my wife is great, don't get me wrong. But she won't discuss Pound with me. Or Eliot. I didn't know that when I married her. See, I need a woman who's mentally stimulating, Kaiser. And I'm willing to pay for it. I don't want an involvement—I want a quick intellectual experience, then I want the girl to leave. Christ, Kaiser, I'm a happily married man."

"How long has this been going on?"

"Six months. Whenever I have that craving, I call Flossie. She's a madam, with a master's in comparative lit. She sends me over an intellectual, see?"

So he was one of those guys whose weakness was really bright women. I felt sorry for the poor sap. I figured there must be a lot of jokers in his position, who were starved for a little intellectual communication with the opposite sex and would pay through the nose for it.

"Now she's threatening to tell my wife," he said.

"Who is?"

"Flossie. They bugged the motel room. They got tapes of me discussing *The Waste Land* and *Styles of Radical Will*, and, well, really getting into some issues. They want ten grand or they go to Carla. Kaiser, you've got to help me! Carla would die if she knew she didn't turn me on up here."

The old call-girl racket. I had heard rumors that the boys at headquarters were on to something involving a group of educated women, but so far they were stymied.

"Get Flossie on the phone for me."

"What?"

"I'll take your case, Word. But I get fifty dollars a day, plus expenses. You'll have to repair a lot of joy buzzers."

"It won't be ten Gs' worth, I'm sure of that," he said with a grin, and picked up the phone and dialed a number. I took it from him and winked. I was beginning to like him.

Seconds later, a silky voice answered, and I told her what was on my mind. "I understand you can help me set up an hour of good chat," I said.

"Sure, honey. What do you have in mind?"

"I'd like to discuss Melville."

"*Moby Dick* or the shorter novels?"

"What's the difference?"

"The price. That's all. Symbolism's extra."

"What'll it run me?"

"Fifty, maybe a hundred for *Moby Dick*. You want a comparative discussion—Melville and Hawthorne? That could be arranged for a hundred."

"The dough's fine," I told her and gave her the number of a room at the Plaza.

"You want a blonde or a brunette?"

"Surprise me," I said, and hung up.

I shaved and grabbed some black coffee while I checked over the Monarch College Outline series. Hardly an hour had passed before there was a knock on my door. I opened it, and standing there was a young redhead who was packed into her slacks like two big scoops of vanilla ice cream.

"Hi, I'm Sherry."

They really knew how to appeal to your fantasies. Long straight hair, leather bag, silver earrings, no make-up.

"I'm surprised you weren't stopped, walking into the hotel dressed like that," I said. "The house dick can usually spot an intellectual."

"A five-spot cools him."

"Shall we begin?" I said, motioning her to the couch.

She lit a cigarette and got right to it. "I think we could start by approaching *Billy Budd* as Melville's justification of the ways of God to man, *n'est-ce pas?*"

"Interestingly, though, not in a Miltonian sense." I was bluffing. I wanted to see if she'd go for it.

"No. *Paradise Lost* lacked the substructure of pessimism." She did.

"Right, right. God, you're right," I murmured.

"I think Melville reaffirmed the virtues of innocence in a naïve yet sophisticated sense—don't you agree?"

I let her go on. She was barely nineteen years old, but already she had developed the hardened facility of the pseudo-intellectual. She rattled off her ideas glibly, but it was all mechanical. Whenever I offered an insight, she faked a response: "Oh, yes, Kaiser. Yes, baby, that's deep. A platonic comprehension of Christianity—why didn't I see it before?"

We talked for about an hour and then she said she had to go. She stood up and I laid a C-note on her.

"Thanks, honey."

"There's plenty more where that came from."

"What are you trying to say?"

I had piqued her curiosity. She sat down again.

"Suppose I wanted to—have a party?" I said.

"Like, what kind of party?"

"Suppose I wanted Noam Chomsky explained to me by two girls?"

"Oh, wow."

"If you'd rather forget it . . ."   •

"You'd have to speak with Flossie," she said. "It'd cost you."

Now was the time to tighten the screws. I flashed my private-investigator's badge and informed her it was a bust.

"What!"

"I'm fuzz, sugar, and discussing Melville for money is an 802. You can do time."

"You louse!"

"Better come clean, baby. Unless you want to tell your story down at Alfred Kazin's office, and I don't think he'd be too happy to hear it."

She began to cry. "Don't turn me in, Kaiser," she said. "I needed the money to complete my master's. I've been turned down for a grant. *Twice*. Oh, Christ."

It all poured out—the whole story. Central Park West upbringing, Socialist summer camps, Brandeis. She was every dame you saw waiting in line at the Elgin or the Thalia, or penciling the words "Yes, very true" into the margin of some book on Kant. Only somewhere along the line she had made a wrong turn.

"I needed cash. A girl friend said she knew a married guy whose wife wasn't very profound. He was into Blake. She couldn't hack it. I said sure, for a price I'd talk Blake with him. I was nervous at first. I faked a lot of it. He didn't care. My friend said there were others. Oh, I've been busted before. I got caught reading *Commentary* in a parked car, and I was once stopped and frisked at Tanglewood. Once more and I'm a three-time loser."

"Then take me to Flossie."

She bit her lip and said, "The Hunter College Book Store is a front."

"Yes?"

"Like those bookie joints that have barbershops outside for show. You'll see."

I made a quick call to headquarters and then said to her, "Okay, sugar. You're off the hook. But don't leave town."

She tilted her face up toward mine gratefully. "I can get you photographs of Dwight Macdonald reading," she said.

"Some other time."

I walked into the Hunter College Book Store. The salesman, a young man with sensitive eyes, came up to me. "Can I help you?" he said.

"I'm looking for a special edition of *Advertisements for Myself*. I understand the author had several thousand gold-leaf copies printed up for friends."

"I'll have to check," he said. "We have a WATS line to Mailer's house."

I fixed him with a look. "Sherry sent me," I said.

"Oh, in that case, go on back," he said. He pressed a button. A wall of books opened, and I walked like a lamb into that bustling pleasure palace known as Flossie's.

Red flocked wallpaper and a Victorian décor set the tone. Pale, nervous girls with black-rimmed glasses and blunt-cut hair lolled around on sofas, riffling Penguin Classics provocatively. A blonde with a big smile winked at me, nodded toward a room upstairs, and said, "Wallace Stevens, eh?" But it wasn't just intellectual experiences—they were peddling emotional ones, too. For fifty bucks, I learned, you could "relate without getting close." For a hundred, a girl would lend you her Bartók records, have dinner, and then let you watch while she had an anxiety attack. For one-fifty, you could listen to FM radio with twins. For three bills, you got the works: A thin Jewish brunette would pretend to pick you up at the Museum of Modern Art, let you read her master's, get you involved in a screaming quarrel at Elaine's over Freud's conception of women, and then fake a suicide of your choosing —the perfect evening, for some guys. Nice racket. Great town, New York.

"Like what you see?" a voice said behind me. I turned and suddenly found myself standing face to face with the business end of a .38. I'm a guy with a strong stomach, but this time it did a back flip. It was Flossie, all right. The voice was the same, but Flossie was a man. His face was hidden by a mask.

"You'll never believe this," he said, "but I don't even have a college degree. I was thrown out for low grades."

"Is that why you wear that mask?"

"I devised a complicated scheme to take over *The New York Review of Books,* but it meant I had to pass for Lionel Trilling. I went to Mexico for an operation. There's a doctor in Juarez who gives people Trilling's features—for a price. Something went wrong. I came out looking like Auden, with Mary McCarthy's voice. That's when I started working the other side of the law."

Quickly, before he could tighten his finger on the trigger, I went into action. Heaving forward, I snapped my elbow across his jaw and grabbed the gun as he fell back. He hit the ground like a ton of bricks. He was still whimpering when the police showed up.

"Nice work, Kaiser," Sergeant Holmes said. "When we're through with this guy, the F.B.I. wants to have a talk with him. A little matter involving some gamblers and an annotated copy of Dante's *Inferno.* Take him away, boys."

Later that night, I looked up an old account of mine named Gloria. She was blond. She had graduated *cum laude.* The difference was she majored in physical education. It felt good.

From Without Feathers, 1974.

QUESTIONS

(1) Exactly who or what is Allen making fun of: pornography, intellectuals, private detective stories, old movies, New Yorkers, all of the above?

(2) What clichés does Allen use to make fun of clichés?

(3) Define parody. How does Allen use it in the essay?

(4) Is this an essay or a piece of "creative writing"? Does one exclude the other?

(5) Could the "essay" be used as the shooting script for a scene in a movie? Would anything have to be changed? What substitutions might be necessary?

ELAINE NOBLE, REP.

LAURA SHAPIRO

The Massachusetts House of Representatives is full of men—
men walking around the chamber, inching between the desks
that stretch in long curved rows, guffawing together or beckoning to one another or standing at the microphone droning.
The entire Massachusetts State House, in fact, is full of men,
and pictures of men line its walls. Centuries of democracy here
in the cradle of liberty have given birth to a predictably runt-
ish litter of lawmakers—men who snuffle suspiciously around
anything shaped like a reform bill and debate with real enthusiasm a proposal to install a kitchenette for senators.
Women are not a terribly popular issue in the State House
(although there's always a lot of hilarity during the annual
debate on whether to allow married women to keep their
names), but a handful have been elected, and if you peer over
the edge of the visitors' gallery in the House of Representatives
you can pick some out. Most of them sit quietly at their desks,
studying papers or listening politely to the droning male at
the microphone. One is applying makeup.

Another one, however, catches your eye. In fact, she seems to
have caught everyone's eye: she jumps up from her desk and
in a few athletic strides bounds over to a white-haired representative, who greets her with a delighted smile. Perching on
the desk behind him, she leans forward intently to talk. She's
brightly and casually dressed in a lavender turtleneck under a
print blouse that swings open; her dark blond hair is clipped
neatly around her lively face. Her name is Elaine Noble, and
when she first entered the House of Representatives in 1974
some of her colleagues talked about refusing to seat her. She
is a lesbian. Now they watch her fondly, grin at her, vote for
her bills and offer to be quoted in admiration of her. To them,
she may be queer but she's a natural politician—and they can
recognize one of their own.

Elaine Noble has used her lesbianism from the beginning
of her career the way Jimmy Carter uses God: as an asset

clearly beyond her control, but very impressive once people get over the shock. One of her better friends in the State House is the extremely powerful chairman of the Senate Ways and Means Committee, Senator James Kelly, and while it seems an unlikely alliance (he's the compleat Massachusetts wheeler-dealer, short, stout and important, and in love with the perquisites of power) it is in fact a friendship in the great political tradition. Kelly, whose office is full of family portraits, can be seen these days breakfasting at the Ritz with his young women friends. Noble shepherds him around both gay and straight nightspots, and when Lily Tomlin came to Boston to volunteer two performances toward Noble's reelection campaign, Noble called out cheerfully to him by name as she perched onstage with Tomlin. "She has," says Kelly cautiously, "an interesting personality with men." Aging, too-nattily dressed, Kelly is enjoying a little mid-life mania and Noble makes a charming and titillating contribution. "Most women in this building are afraid of me," Kelly said one day in his office. "Most men are too. Very few people approach me as an equal. Elaine does—I can relax with her. It's such a comfortable relationship with her . . . there's no possibility of sex."

For any other woman in the legislature to escort Senator James Kelly drinking and dancing would be unthinkable, but Noble's lesbianism gives her a tremendous advantage. On the House floor she is for all intents and purposes neuter—no more sexually or emotionally threatening than another man, but much smarter, wittier and better company than most. "She has a wonderful warm personality, and she isn't so into the gay things that she can't have a beer with you," pointed out a former representative who had worked on a committee with her. "She can get along. And politics is getting along."

In the beginning there wasn't much getting along. Noble was a tremendous favorite with the press from the day she won the election—filmed, photographed, invited to speak, interviewed all over the country—but making her way around the State House those first months she didn't feel very popular. There was the slimy little plan to stop her from being seated, on the grounds that homosexuality is still illegal in Massachusetts; Noble's liberal colleagues nipped that one in the bud by threatening to raise a "Let-him-who-is-without-sin" response. There were the looks and leers. "Hey Elaine—how 'bout going straight for a night?" "You ain't really gay are you? What a waste." "Bet I could change your mind." There was the coy request that she wear a bra in the House chamber. And after she gave her first speech on the House floor, in support of a gay rights bill, she returned to her seat to listen to her colleagues label it a bill for sin, sickness, degradation and the befouling of small children. Finally one day, after a particularly sleazy attack, she stood up and asked politely, "Does the Representative feel that homosexuality is catching? And if so, is he afraid he'll catch it?"

As she recalled the tensions of her debut in the House, Noble grinned. "I enjoy like hell being around people who don't think like me at all," she said from a seat in the House gallery, gazing down at the men. "I enjoy a good fight, too. I can always walk out of that chamber when it's too much. Oh, they'd rather forget my lesbianism, but they found out I didn't have horns."

She pointed out a young representative. "An older representative was talking to him one day and said he should cut his hair; he said, if you were my son, I'd make you cut your hair. I went up to the kid and I told him that representative wears a wig. Get him on that, I said. He was really grateful. He said the man freaked out. Now I've got my people helping him in his district, and he voted for my gay bill."

Noble was political long before she got into politics—she had to be. Born in 1944 and raised in a Pennsylvania salt mining town ("We were the poor kids, and we were supposed to be dumber, too"), she got a scholarship to Boston University, where she received a degree in speech education. For a time she led a classic lesbian double life—working in an advertising department, lying constantly about her social life, and going home to her lover at night. The tension became too much, and she ended up in the hospital with a case of bleeding ulcers. She knew she couldn't continue with her old life, but coming out—even more so in the sixties than now—had its own terrors. She plunged, and suddenly she wasn't respectable anymore, suddenly she was a sort of poison to people. The gay community took her in. By 1970 she had helped set up the Boston branch of Daughters of Bilitis, she was working on her master's degree and she had begun teaching at Emerson

College; but while she identified most passionately with the
women's movement, as a feminist she was all dressed up with
no place to go. The local chapter of the National Organization
for Women was distinctly unready for lesbian feminists. "They
let us march in the Women's Equality Day parade, but we
weren't welcome," Noble said; the memory still makes her jaw
tighten. With the other lesbians she began to build what
would become her first power base—a gay speakers' bureau, a
gay radio show, a gay feminists' organization. It worked—two
years later lesbians were demonstrating, lobbying and cospon-
soring legislation with NOW, and Noble herself had been
elected to the three-person steering committee of the Massachusetts Women's Political Caucus. By the time she was appointed to the Governor's Commission on the Status of
Women in 1973 she had gained the newspaper epithet of
"leading lobbyist" (not to mention "gay spokesman").

Like every political success, Noble was backed by the right
people—in this case, a handful of astute, courageous political
feminists who were well established in the mainly straight and
suburban leadership of NOW and the Caucus, but who also
firmly supported lesbianism. Even with women whose liberation was less sophisticated and a little more nervous, however,
Noble proved to be smash hit. At a time when lesbians were
still considered hairy and unattractive to have around, she
was nicely dressed, smart, literate, funny and committed. It
gave some pizazz to a meeting when she showed up, high-
spirited and energetic. She was obviously one of the Most
Popular, and it became increasingly evident that she would
be Most Likely to Succeed.

In those heady McGovern years more and more women
were starting to run for office, and towards 1973 Noble herself
began mentioning it to friends. During the 1972 elections she
had helped organize the sizable and powerful gay community
in the Boston district of a young, very smart, very liberal candidate named Barney Frank. She was good at it, and when a
new district was created adjoining his, Frank and some of her
other supporters urged her to run. It wasn't another gay district; on the contrary, it was made up of poor and working-
class families, ethnic minorities, students and the elderly. But
they had never been represented by anyone whom they felt
cared about them, and Noble managed to convince them that

her background in education, her organizing, her community
work and her solid liberalism were at least as real as her sex
life. She had little outstanding opposition and won handily.

Neglected for years, the streets of her district are shabby and
littered, but Noble proudly points out the traffic signals, street-
lights and new parking regulations she has won; she also
points to the crime-ridden river area that has begun to be
dredged and rehabilitated, watching her yell out cheerfully to
the barber and the drugstore owner, who greet her with raucous, genuine pleasure, is to see her in the politicking she loves
best. ("Representative! I heard ya on Avi Nelson's show! Terrific!") As she waits for change in a drugstore, people come up
to grin hello, or ask a favor or offer advice ("Representative,
y'know, you can get federal funds to paint the hydrants this
year, if you paint them Bicentennial colors"). On the street
she's clearly a favorite but when she steps into the community
center—a storefront that used to be her campaign headquarters
—the atmosphere changes a bit. The tough-minded working-
class women who run the center, who indeed run the whole
neighborhood, feel very strongly that it was their support that
made her a legitimate candidate and put the district solidly
behind her; and they have no intention of letting her forget
the community to become a media/feminist/gay celebrity. Noble resents it when they accuse her of neglecting the district
for her national speaking engagements ("I work my ass off for
them," she said firmly) but she sits down quietly to discuss a
few local problems while the children crawl over her.

Some of the local feminists who helped put Noble in office
also are critical. They feel betrayed by at least one of her political maneuvers, the legislative fight over the state Equal
Rights Amendment. When the bill was about to come before
the House, Noble was accused of "waffling" and "hesitating"
instead of pitching in and fighting.

Noble gets livid when the subject of the ERA comes up.
"We did not have the votes," she emphasized. "A lot of people took my saying that as being antifeminist, but I wasn't
going to be a martyr. The women in the State House weren't
going to hang alone on this one—we just wanted a coherent
strategy, we wanted the lobbyists to be up there with us every
day. We weren't going to do it alone, and I only verbalized

what the other women in the legislature would have loved to tell those women."

The feminist legislators organized a lobbying strategy that essentially involved talking to everyone, especially the nean-derthal contingent. "You can't ever afford politically to say, oh he isn't with us," stressed Noble. "Those women were used to talking to the converted, to their own inner circle or the legislators who agreed with them. We talked to the people who had always been avoided before, and the people on the outside didn't know what we were doing."

That, of course, has been her strategy all along—winning over the people most likely to hate and fear her. "It's viewed as treason, but women have to learn this. You have to pay some homage to the old order. And I've gotten to like some of those old shits. They can reason. I was a pompous ass to think they couldn't."

The ERA passed, and Noble went on to get funding for a legislative commission to study its effect on Massachusetts laws. More radical women still feel she hasn't done enough hell-raising on feminist bills, and liberals are still waiting for her to speak before the House on something besides gay rights legislation; nobody, however, denies that her political future looks just fine. Her opposition in November was only nomi-nal, but a massive House cut is scheduled for next term that will probably eliminate her district, and it's doubtful she would choose to run against her neighboring legislator, Barney Frank. So she's got to move up. Some people think she could climb as far as the U.S. Senate: they see her having the appeal of Bella Abzug—tough, idealistic, committed—with none of the overt belligerence and aggression that hurt Abzug so badly in the press and with her colleagues. Noble makes lots of friends, and with frequent hugs and a great deal of understanding she manages to keep most of them. That's the way it all starts, no matter whom you sleep with.

From *Rolling Stone*, 1977.

QUESTIONS

(1) What kinds of contrasts does the author make in the first paragraph?

(2) How do the verbs—"guffawing," "beckoning," "droning," "have given birth to,"—combine to determine the reader's response?

(3) Why is the sentence at the end of the second paragraph: "To them, she may be queer but she's a natural politician—and they can recognize one of their own," so effective? How does Shapiro use identification and contrast to make her point? Is there any pun on "natural"?

(4) How do the details of Representative Noble's first days in the Massachusetts House help to get the reader's sympathy and respect in the same way they did her colleagues'?

(5) At one point the interviewer sets Representative Noble in "a seat in the House gallery, gazing down at the men." How does the setting affect the action?

(6) Why doesn't Shapiro begin her profile: "Elaine Noble was born in 1944 and went to . . . "?

(7) Is the use of the cliché "all dressed up with no place to go" effective? Why? Are "Most Popular" and "Most Likely To Succeed" in the same category?

(8) A reference to children appears in the fifth paragraph of this essay, and a description of children appears in the eleventh paragraph. What does this repetition accomplish? What point is being made indirectly by the second reference, "while the children crawl over her"?

(9) Why is the Representative's own statement, "I was a pompous ass to think they couldn't," an important part of Ms. Shapiro's presentation of Ms. Noble?

(10) Why is the reference to "frequent hugs" included in the next to last sentence? How does it affect the tone of the article?

OF WOMAN BORN

ADRIENNE RICH

"Vous travaillez pour l'armée, madame?" (You are working for the army?), a Frenchwoman said to me early in the Vietnam war, on hearing I had three sons.

April 1965
> Anger, weariness, demoralization. Sudden bouts of weeping. A sense of insufficiency to the moment and to eternity . . .
> Paralyzed by the sense that there exists a mesh of relations, between e.g. my rejection and anger at [my eldest child], my sensual life, pacifism, sex (I mean in its broadest significance, not merely physical desire)—an interconnectedness which, if I could see it, make it valid, would give me back myself, make it possible to function lucidly and passionately—Yet I grope in and out among these dark webs—

> I weep, and weep, and the sense of powerlessness spreads like a cancer through my being.

August 1965, 3:30 A.M.
> Necessity for a more unyielding discipline of my life.
>> Recognize the uselessness of blind anger.
>> Limit society.
>> Use children's school hours better, for work & solitude.
>> Refuse to be distracted from own style of life.
> Less waste.
> Be harder & harder on poems.

Once in a while someone used to ask me, "Don't you ever write poems about your children?" The male poets of my generation did write poems about their children—especially their daughters. For me, poetry was where I lived as no-one's mother, where I existed as myself.

The bad and the good moments are inseparable for me. I recall the times when, suckling each of my children, I saw his eyes open full to mine, and realized each of us was fastened to the other, not only by mouth and breast, but through our mutual gaze: the depth, calm, passion, of that dark blue, maturely focused look. I recall the physical pleasure of having my full breast suckled at a time when I had no other physical pleasure in the world except the guilt-ridden pleasure of addictive eating. I remember early the sense of conflict, of a battleground none of us had chosen, of being an observer who, like it or not, was also an actor in an endless contest of wills. This was what it meant to me to have three children under the age of seven. But I recall too each child's individual body, his slenderness, wiriness, softness, grace, the beauty of little boys who have not been taught that the male body must be rigid. I remember moments of peace when for some reason it was possible to go to the bathroom alone. I remember being uprooted from already meager sleep to answer a childish nightmare, pull up a blanket, warm a consoling bottle, lead a half-asleep child to the toilet. I remember going back to bed starkly awake, brittle with anger, knowing that my broken sleep would make next day a hell, that there would be more nightmares, more need for consolation, because out of my weariness I would rage at those children for no reason they could understand. I remember thinking I would never dream again (the unconscious of the young mother—where does it entrust its messages, when dream-sleep is denied her for years?)

For many years I shrank from looking back on the first decade of my children's lives. In snapshots of the period I see a smiling young woman, in maternity clothes or bent over a half-naked baby; gradually she stops smiling, wears a distant, half-melancholy look, as if she were listening for something. In time my sons grew older, I began changing my own life, we began to talk to each other as equals. Together we lived through my leaving the marriage, and through their father's suicide. We became survivors, four distinct people with strong bonds connecting us. Because I always tried to tell them the truth, because their every new independence meant new freedom for me, because we trusted each other even when we wanted different things, they became, at a fairly young age, self-reliant and open to the unfamiliar. Something told me that if they had survived my angers, my self-reproaches, and still trusted my love and each others', they were strong. Their lives have not been, will not be, easy; but their very existences seem a gift to me, their vitality, humor, intelligence, gentleness, love of life, their separate life-currents which here and there stream into my own. I don't know how we made it from their embattled childhood and my embattled motherhood into a mutual recognition of ourselves and each other. Probably that mutual recognition, overlaid by social and traditional circumstance, was always there, from the first gaze between the mother and the infant at the breast. But I do know that for years I believed I should never have been anyone's mother, that because I felt my own needs acutely and often expressed them violently, I was Kali, Medea, the sow that devours her farrow, the unwomanly woman in flight from womanhood, a Nietzschean monster. Even today, rereading old journals, remembering, I feel grief and anger; but their objects are no longer myself and my children. I feel grief at the waste of myself in those years, anger at the mutilation and manipulation of the relationship between mother and child, which is the great original source and experience of love.

On an early spring day in the 1970s, I meet a young woman friend on the street. She has a tiny infant against her breast, in a bright cotton sling; its face is pressed against her blouse, its tiny hand clutches a piece of the cloth. "How old is she?" I ask. "Just two weeks old," the mother tells me. I am amazed to feel in myself a passionate longing to have, once again, such a small, new being clasped against my body. The baby belongs there, curled, suspended asleep between her mother's breasts, as she belonged curled in the womb. The young mother—who already has a three-year-old—speaks of how quickly one forgets the pure pleasure of having this new creature, immaculate, perfect. And I walk away from her drenched with memory, with envy. Yet I know other things: that her life is far from simple; she is a mathematician who now has two children under the age of four; she is living even now in the rhythms of other lives—not only the regular cry of the infant but her three-year-old's needs, her husband's problems. In the building where I live, women are still raising children alone, living day in and day out within their individual family units, doing the laundry, herding the tricycles to the park, waiting for the husbands to come home. There is a baby-sitting pool and a children's playroom, young fathers push prams on weekends, but child-care is still the individual responsibility of the individual woman. I envy the sensuality of having an infant of two weeks curled against one's breast; I do not envy the turmoil of the elevator full of small children, babies howling in the laundromat, the apartment in winter where pent-up seven-

and eight-year-olds have one adult to look to for their frustrations, reassurances, the grounding of their lives.

From *Of Woman Born*, 1976.

QUESTIONS

(1) How do you think Ms. Rich felt when the Frenchwoman asked her if she is working for the army? Does the essay offer any answer(s) to the question?

(2) Instead of attempting an immediate answer, Rich goes to her journal. Are the old diary entries a good preparation for the essay that follows?

(3) What is (are) the theme (themes) of the diary entries? Notice that in the essay she refers to her own feelings on "re-reading old journals."

(4) What are some of the implications of Rich's statement: ". . . poetry was where I lived as no-one's mother, where I existed as myself"?

(5) Are little boys taught "that the male body must be rigid"? If so, by whom? In what ways? Why? Do those who teach that conceive of one part of the male anatomy as the entire body?

(6) "I remember moments of peace when for some reason it was possible to go to the bathroom alone." How does that one detail stand for a whole way of life?

(7) How many examples of cause and effect can you find in the essay? Do they have a common denominator? What kind of connection does the author make between "then" and "now"?

(8) Would "Drenched with Memory" be a good title for this selection? If yes, why? If no, why?

CUTTING LOOSE

SALLY KEMPTON

Once another woman and I were talking about male resistance to Woman's Liberation, and she said that she didn't understand why men never worry about women taking their jobs away but worry only about the possibility that women may stop making love to them and bearing their children. And once I was arguing with a man I know about Woman's Liberation, and he said he wished he had a motorcycle gang with which to invade a Woman's Liberation meeting and rape everybody in it. There are times when I understand the reason for men's feelings. I have noticed that beyond the feminists' talk about the myth of the vaginal orgasm lies a radical resentment of their position in the sexual act. And I have noticed that when I feel most militantly feminist I am hardly at all interested in sex.

Almost one could generalize from that: the feminist impulse is anti-sexual. The very notion of women gathering in groups is somehow anti-sexual, anti-male, just as the purposely all-male group is anti-female. There is often a sense of genuine cultural rebellion in the atmosphere of a Woman's Liberation meeting. Women sit with their legs apart, carelessly dressed, barely made-up, exhibiting their feelings or the holes at the knees of their jeans with an unprovocative candor which is hardly seen at all in the outside world. Of course, they are demonstrating by their postures that they are in effect off duty, absolved from the compulsion to make themselves attractive, and yet, as the world measures these things, such demonstrations could in themselves be seen as evidence of neurosis: we have all been brought up to believe that a woman who was "whole" would appear feminine even on the barricades.

The fact is that one cannot talk in feminist terms without revealing feelings which have traditionally been regarded as neurotic. One becomes concerned about women's rights, as Simone de Beauvoir noted, only when one perceives that there are few personal advantages to be gained from accepting the traditional women's roles. A woman who is satisfied with her life is not likely to be drawn into the Woman's Liberation movement: there must be advantages for her as a woman in a man's world. To be a feminist one must be to some degree maladjusted to that world, one must be, if you will, neurotic. And sometimes one must be anti-sexual, if only in reaction to masculine expectations. Men do not worry about women taking their jobs because they do not think that women could do their jobs; most men can only be threatened by a woman in bed. A woman who denies her sexuality, if only for an evening, denies her status as an object of male attention, as a supplicant, successful or not, for male favor. For a woman to deny her sexuality is to attack the enemy in his most valuable stronghold, which is her own need for him.

I became a feminist as an alternative to becoming a masochist. Actually, I always was a masochist; I became a feminist because to be a masochist is intolerable. As I get older I recognize more and more that the psychoanalytical idea that women are natural masochists is at least metaphorically correct: my own masochism derived from an almost worshipful respect for masculine power. In my adolescence I screwed a lot of guys I didn't like much, and always felt abused by them, but I never felt free to refuse sex until after the initial encounter. My tactic, if you can call it a tactic, was to Do It once and then to refuse to see the boy again, and I think I succeeded, with my demonstrations of postcoital detachment, in making several of them feel as rejected by my lovemaking as I had felt by their desire to make love to me without love. Yet I felt in those years that I had irretrievably marked myself a sexual rebel, and I was given to making melodramatic statements like "I'm not the kind of girl men marry." Years later I realized that I had been playing a kind of game, the same game boys play at the age of sexual experimentation, except that, unlike a boy, I could not allow myself to choose my partners and admit that I had done so. In fact, I was never comfortable with a lover unless he had, so to speak, wronged me. Once during my senior year in high school I let a boy rape me (that is not, whatever you may think, a contradiction in terms) in the bedroom of his college suite while a party was going on next door; afterward I ran away down the stairs while he followed, shouting apologies which became more and

more abject as he realized that my revulsion was genuine, and
I felt an exhilaration which I clearly recognized as triumph.
By letting him abuse me I had won the right to tell him I
hated him; I had won the right to hurt him.

I think most American adolescents hate and fear the opposite sex: in adolescence it seems that only one's lovers can hurt
one, and I think that even young people who are entirely
secure in other relations recognize and would, if they could,
disarm the power the other sex has for them. But for adolescent boys, sexual success is not the sole measure of worth. It is
assumed that they will grow up and work, that their most important tests will come in areas whose criteria are extra-sexual.
They can fail with girls without failing entirely, for there remains to them the public life, the male life.

But girls have no such comfort. Sex occupies even the economic center of our lives; it is, we have been brought up to
feel, our lives' work. Whatever else she may do, a woman is a
failure if she fails to please men. The adolescent girl's situation is by definition dependent: she *must* attract, and therefore, however she may disguise it, she must compromise the
sticky edges of her personality, she must arrange herself to
conform with other people's ideas of what is valuable in a
woman.

I was early trained to that position, trained, in the traditional manner, by my father. Like many men who are uncomfortable with adult women, my father saw his daughter as a
potential antidote to his disappointment in her sex. I was
someone who could be molded into a woman compatible with
his needs, and also, unlike my mother, I was too impression-
able to talk back. So I became the vessel into which he fed his
opinions about novels and politics and sex; he fed me also his
most hopeful self-image. It reached a point where I later suspected him of nourishing a sort of eighteenth-century fantasy
about our relationship, the one in which the count teaches his
daughter to read Virgil and ride like a man, and she grows up
to be the perfect feminine companion, parroting him with
such subtlety that it is impossible to tell that her thoughts and
feelings, so perfectly coincident with his, are not original. I
had three brothers, as it happened, and another sort of man
might have chosen one of them to mold. But my father had
himself a vast respect for masculine power. Boys grow up and

have to kill their fathers, girls can be made to understand their place.

My father in his thirties was an attractive man, he was witty by adult standards and of course doubly so by mine, and he had a verbal facility with which he invariably demolished my mother in arguments. Masculine power in the intellectual classes is exercised verbally: it is the effort of the male supremacist intellectual to make his woman look clumsy and illogical beside him, to render her, as it were, dumb. His tactic is to goad the woman to attack him and then, resorting to rationality, to withdraw himself from the battle. In my childhood experience, subtlety appeared exclusively a masculine weapon. I never saw a woman argue except straightforwardly, and I never saw a woman best a man in a quarrel. My mother tried, but always with the conviction of ultimate failure. She attacked with pinpricks to begin with; in the end, maddened invariably by my father's ostentatious mental absence, she yelled. He was assisted in these struggles by his natural passivity. Withdrawal came easily to him; he hated, as he told us over and over again, scenes. My mother, it seemed to me, was violent, my father cool. And since it also seemed to me that he preferred me, his daughter who never disagreed with him, to his wife who did (that was a fantasy, of course, but one to which my father devoted some effort toward keeping alive), I came to feel that male power, because uncoercible, could only be handled by seduction, and that the most comfortable relation between men and women was the relation between pupil and teacher, between parent and child.

My father taught me some tricks. From him I learned that it is pleasant and useful to get information from men, pleasant because it is easier than getting it for yourself, and useful because it is seductive: men like to give information and sometimes love the inquirer, if she is pretty and asks intelligently. From him I also learned that women are by definition incapable of serious thought. This was a comforting lesson, although it made me feel obscurely doomed, for if I was to be automatically barred from participation in the life of high intellect, there was no reason why I should work to achieve it, and thinking, after all, is difficult work. When I was fifteen my father told me that I would never be a writer because I wasn't hungry enough, by which I think he meant that there would

always be some man to feed me. I accepted his pronounce-
ment as I accepted, at that age, all pronouncements which had
an air of finality, and began making other career plans.

My task, it seemed to me, was to find a man in whom there
resided enough power to justify my acting the child, that is,
to justify my acceptance of my own femininity. For I regarded
myself as feminine only in my childlike aspect; when I presented myself as a thinking person I felt entirely sexless. The
boys in my class regarded me as an intellectual and showed an
almost unanimous disinterest in my company. When I was in
the eighth grade I lived in trepidation lest I be cited as class
bookworm, and defended myself against that threat by going
steady with what surely must have been the dumbest boy in
our set. He was no fonder of me than I was of him; we needed
each other because you had to be part of a couple in order to
get invited to parties.

I did not get the opportunity to demonstrate my skill as a
child-woman until I became old enough to go out with college
boys. My training had equipped me only to attract intelligent
men, and a boy who was no brighter than I held no power for
me. But for a man who could act as my teacher I could be
submissive and seductive—I *felt* submissive and seductive; my
awe of the male mind translated easily into an awe of the male
person.
. . . .
. . . I picked up some interesting lore from men, while I
was studying to please them. I learned about Eliot from one
boy, and about Donne from another, and about Coltrane from
a third. A lover turned me on to drugs and also showed me
how you were supposed to act when you were high—that is, as
if you were not high. I was not surprised that he was better
at this than me, cool was beginning to seem more and more a
masculine talent, and I had even taken to physical retaliation
in arguments, having given up the idea that I would ever win
anything by verbal means. I went to Sarah Lawrence instead
of Barnard because my boyfriend thought Sarah Lawrence was
a more "feminine" school. My parents got divorced and I sided
with my father, at least at first, because his appeared to me to
be the winning side. Men, I believed, were automatically on
the winning side, which was why my oldest brother could afford to withdraw in moral outrage from my father's advances;

there was for *him* no danger of branding himself a loser by consorting with my mother. Yet I envied him his integrity. How could I maintain integrity when I was willing to sell out any principle for the sake of masculine attention?

I went to Sarah Lawrence and got to love it without ever taking it very seriously, which I also supposed was the way the boys I loved in those days felt about me. In fact, Sarah Lawrence appeared to me and to most of my friends there as a sort of symbol of ourselves: like the college, we were pretty and slightly prestigious and terribly self-serious in private, but just as we laughed at the school and felt embarrassed to be identified with it publicly (I always felt that if I had been a real student I would have gone to Barnard), so we laughed publicly at our own aspirations. "I like Nancy," a Princeton boy said to me, "except she always starts talking about Kafka promptly at midnight." And I laughed, god how I laughed, at Nancy—how *Sarah Lawrency* to carry on about Kafka—and, by implication, at myself. For I too expressed my intellectualism in effusions. Men expected the effusions, even found them charming, while treating them with friendly contempt. It was important to be charming. A passion for Marxism, stumblingly expressed, an interpretation of *Moby Dick,* these tokens we offered our lovers to prove we were not simply women, but people. Yet though we displayed strong feelings about art and politics, we behaved as if we had not really done the reading. To argue a point logically was to reveal yourself as unfeminine: a man might respect your mind, but he would not love it. Wit, we believed, is frightening in a woman.

In my senior year I met a girl who knew the editor of *The Village Voice,* and after graduation she got me a job there. I went to work as a reporter without having the slightest notion of how to conduct an interview and so, to cover myself, I made up a couple of pieces out of whole cloth. They were about drugs and hippies and homosexuals, the sort of scene pieces *The Voice* later specialized in, but nobody much was writing about that stuff in 1964, and I got several book offers and invitations to cocktail parties, and my father's friends started writing me letters full of sports analogies, saying it was time I entered a main event. In fact, I felt terribly guilty about writing those pieces because they seemed frivolous and sensationalistic, the sort of thing empty-headed girl reporters did when they were too dumb to write about politics, but on the other hand they got me attention, which writing about politics would never have done. I agonized all summer, publicly and privately, over this dilemma, often spending hours telling big strong male reporters how unworthy I felt. They seemed to like it.

I had never thought of myself as ambitious; actually, I think I was too convinced of my basic incompetence to be constructively ambitious, but I quickly saw that a lady journalist has advantages denied to men. For one thing, she never has to pick up a check. For another thing, if she is even remotely serious, people praise her work much more than they would praise the work of a comparably talented man; they are amazed that a woman can write coherently on any subject not confined in interest to the readers of a woman's magazine. And finally, people tell her things they would not tell a man. Many men think the secrets they tell a woman are automatically off the record. They forget that the young woman hanging on their every word is taking it all down—often they confuse her attention with sexual interest. (That is not such an advantage. Some men, rock stars for instance, simply assumed that sex was what I had come for. They would expend a little flattery to assure me that they regarded me as a cut above other groupies, and then they would suggest that we get down to balling. They were often nasty when I refused.)

At any rate, the work was nice, and it gave me a higher status as a sexual object than I had ever had before. But it was also scary. If I was to do well at it I had to take it seriously, and the strongest belief I had retained from my childhood was my idea that nothing I could achieve was worth taking seriously. In the Autumn of 1964 I fell in love with a boy who was not sure he was in love with me, and by the time he decided he was I had quit my job and moved with him to Boston. He styled himself a revolutionary and thought the content of my work hardly worth the effort it took to produce it; I accepted his opinion with relief, telling myself that in any case I had not the emotional energy to handle both a lover and a job. My feeling for him evaporated fairly soon after I discovered that it was reciprocated, though I lived with him for several months after that, partly out of guilt and partly because living with a man made me feel grown-up in a way holding a job never could have done. But finally I left him and took a job as a staff writer on a national magazine, a classy job but underpaid. Instead of complaining about the salary, I took to not showing up for work, justifying my laziness by telling myself that I was selling out anyway by taking an up-town job and that the sooner I rid myself of it, the sooner I would regain my integrity.

In the meantime I had met a grown-up man who was powerful and smart and knocked out by my child act. We spent a few months seducing each other—"You're too young for me," he would say, and I would climb upon his lap, figuratively speaking, and protest that I was not. It was no more disgusting than most courtships. In the end we got married.

Of course, I had to marry a grown-up, a father figure if you will, and my husband, as it turned out, had to marry a child. That is, he had to have an intelligent woman, but one whose intelligence had been, as it were, castrated by some outside circumstances. My youth served that purpose; my other handicaps had not yet emerged.

Anyway, our romantic personae lasted about a year. For a year he was kind to me and listened to my problems and put up with the psychosomatic diseases which marriage had induced in me, and for a year I brought joy and spontaneity into his drab grown-up existence. Then he began to get tired of being a father and I to resent being a child, and we began to act out what I think is a classic example of contemporary marriage.

It had turned out, I realized with horror, that I had done exactly what middle-class girls are supposed to do. I had worked for a year in the communications industry, and my glamorous job had enabled me to meet a respectable, hard-working man who made a lot of money at *his* glamorous job, and I had settled down (stopped screwing around) and straightened myself out (went into analysis), and all that was missing was babies. I defended myself by assuming that we would be divorced in a year, and sneered a lot at Design Research furniture and the other symbols of middle-class marriage, but still I could not escape the feeling that I had fallen not just into a trap but into a cliché. On the other hand, I loved my husband, and I was still a writer, that is to say, a privileged woman with a life of her own. I could afford, as I began to at that time, to read feminist literature without really applying it to my own situation.

My husband, although he is nice to women, is a male supremacist, very much in the style of Norman Mailer. That is, he invests women with more or less mystical powers of control over the inner workings of the world, but thinks that feminine power is strongest when exercised in child rearing and regards contraception as unnatural. When I had my first stirrings of feminist grievance, he pronounced the subject a bore; I used to follow him from room to room, torturing him with my recitals of the sexist atrocities I was beginning to find in my favorite novels, and when I complained that magazines were paying me less than they paid men, he accused me of trying to blame the world for my own crazy passivity. But we were engaged at that time in the usual internal power struggle, and my feminism seemed to both of us more an intellectual exercise than a genuine commitment. It was not until many months later that he began to accuse me of hating men.

We already knew that he hated women, even that he had good reasons for hating women, but I had up to that time put on such a good display of being cuddly, provocative, sexually uninhibited and altogether unlike those other women that the subject of my true feelings about men had never come up. He knew that I had a compulsion to seduce men, which argues a certain distrust of them, but as the seductions, since our marriage, were always intellectual rather than sexual, they could, if you didn't want to consider their implications, be put down simply to insecurity. I don't think even I realized how I felt. Once I told my husband about a rigmarole a friend and I had made up to dismiss men we didn't like—we would go through lists of names, pointing our fingers and saying, "Zap, you're sterile," and then collapse into giggles; my husband, who has a psychoanalytical turn to mind, thought that was Terribly Revealing and I agreed that it was, but so what? And also, I agreed that it was Terribly Revealing that I liked to pinch and bite him, that I made small hostile jokes and took an almost malicious pleasure in becoming too involved in work to pay attention to him (but only briefly; I never for very long attempted to work when he had other plans), that I would go into week-long depressions during which the bed never got made nor the dishes washed. But the degree of my hostility

didn't reveal itself to me until a pattern began to emerge
around our quarrels.

We had, since early in the marriage, periodically engaged in
bitter fights. Because my husband was the stronger, and because he tends to be judgmental, they usually started when he
attempted to punish me (by withdrawing, of course) for some
offense. I would dispute the validity of his complaint, and the
quarrel would escalate into shouts and blows and then into
decisions to terminate the marriage. In the first year my husband always beat me hollow in those battles. I used to dissolve
into tears and beg his forgiveness after twenty minutes; I
could not bear his rejection and I had no talent at all for conducting a quarrel. I won only when I succeeded in making
him feel guilty; if he behaved badly enough I automatically
achieved the moral upper hand for at least a week following
the quarrel. But after a while, the honeymoon being over, he
began to refuse to feel guilty and I began to resent his superior force. Things rested there until, in the third year of
our marriage, we went to live in Los Angeles because of my
husband's work. During the year we spent away from home I
found that I could not work, and that he was always working,
and we suddenly found ourselves frozen into the textbook attitudes of male-female opposition. We fought continually, and
always about the same things. He accused me of making it
impossible for him to work, I accused him of keeping me dangling, dependent upon him for all emotional sustenance, he
accused me of spending too much money and of keeping the
house badly, I accused him of expecting me continually to
subordinate my needs to his. The difficulty, I realized over and
over again without being able to do much about it, was that I
had gotten myself into the classic housewife's position: I was
living in a place I didn't want to be and seeing people I didn't
like because that was where my man was, I was living my
husband's life and I hated him for it. And the reason this was
so was that I was economically dependent upon him; having
ceased to earn my living I could no longer claim the bread-
winner's right to attention for my special needs.

My husband told me that I was grown-up now, twenty-six
years old, there were certain realities which I had to face. He
was the head of the household: I had never questioned that.
He had to fulfill himself: I had never questioned that. He

housed and fed me and paid for my clothes, he respected my opinions and refused all his opportunities to make love to other women, and my part of the bargain should have become clear to me by now. In exchange for those things, I was supposed to keep his house and save his money and understand that if he worked sixteen hours a day for a year it was no more than necessary for his self-fulfillment. Which was all quite true. Except that it was also necessary for his fulfillment that I should be there for those few hours when he had time for me, and not complain about the hours when he did not, and that I should adapt myself to his situation or else end the marriage. It never occurred to him to consider adapting himself to mine, and it never occurred to me. I only knew that his situation was bad for me, was alien, was in fact totally paralyzing, that it kept me from working, that it made me more unhappy than I had been in my life.

I knew that I was being selfish. But he was being selfish also, the only difference being that his selfishness was somehow all right, while mine was inexcusable. Selfishness was a privilege I had earned for a while by being a writer, that is, a person who had by male standards a worthwhile place to spend her time. As soon as I stopped functioning as a writer I became to my husband and to everyone else a mere woman, somebody whose time was valueless, who had no excuse for a selfish preoccupation with her own wants.

I used to lie in bed beside my husband after those fights and wish I had the courage to bash in his head with a frying pan. I would do it while he slept, since awake he would overpower me, disarm me. If only I dared, I would mutter to myself through clenched teeth, pushing back the realization that I didn't dare not because I was afraid of seriously hurting him— I would have loved to do that—but because even in the extremity of my anger I was afraid that if I cracked his head with a frying pan he would leave me. God, how absurd it was (god, how funny, I would mutter to myself, how amusing, oh wow, what a joke) that my whole life's effort had been directed toward keeping men from leaving me, toward placating them, submitting to them, demanding love from them in return for living in their style, and it all ended with me lying awake in the dark hating my husband, hating my father, hating all the men I had ever known. Probably I had always hated them.

What I couldn't figure out was whether I hated them because I was afraid they would leave me or whether I was afraid they would leave me because I hated them.

Because one cannot for very long support such a rage without beginning to go crazy, I tried to think of the problem in political terms. It seemed to me too easy to say that my hatred for men was a true class hatred, that women hate men because women are an oppressed class hungering for freedom. And yet wherever there exists the display of power there is politics, and in women's relations with men there is a continual transfer of power, there is, continually, politics. There are political analogies even to our deepest, our most banal fantasies. Freud maintains that the female terror of the penis is a primary fear, and that the male fear of castration by the vagina is merely a retaliatory fantasy, a guilty fear of punishment. The serf fears the overlord's knout, the overlord, guilty, fears the serf's revenge. Women are natural guerrillas. Scheming, we nestle into the enemy's bed, avoiding open warfare, watching the options, playing the odds. High, and made paranoiac by his observance of my rage, my husband has the fantasy of woman with a knife. He sees her in sexual ecstasy with her eyes open to observe the ecstasy of her partner, with her consciousness awake, her consciousness the knife. It had often been my private boast that even in moments of greatest abandon, I always kept some part of my mind awake: I always searched for clues. Is he mine now, this monster? Have I disarmed him, and for how long? Men are beasts, we say, joking, parodying the Victorian rag, and then realize to our surprise that we believe it. The male has force almost beyond our overpowering, the force of laws, of science, of literature, the force of mathematics and skyscrapers and the Queensboro Bridge; the penis is only its symbol. We cannot share men's pride in the world they have mastered. If you follow that symbolism to its conclusion, we are ourselves that conquered world.

It is because they know that this is true, know it in their bones if not in their heads, that men fear the hatred of women. For women are the true maintenance class. Society is built upon their acquiescence, and upon their small and necessary labors. Restricted to the supportive role, conditioned to excel only at love, women hold for men the key to social order. It is a Marxist truism that the original exploitation, the enslavement which set the pattern for everything which came later, was the enslavement of women by men. Even the lowest worker rests upon the labor of his wife. Where no other claim to distinction exists, a man defines himself by his difference from the supportive sex; he may be a less than admirable man, but at least he is a man, at least he is not a woman.

And if women have fought, they have fought as guerrillas, in small hand-to-hand skirmishes, in pillow wars upon the marriage bed. When they attack frontally, when they come together in groups to protest their oppression, they raise psychic questions so profound as to be almost inadmissible. . . . When men imagine a female uprising they imagine a world in which women rule men as men have ruled women: their guilt, which is the guilt of every ruling class, will allow them to see no middle ground. And it is a measure of the unconscious strength of our belief in natural male dominance that all of us, men and women, revolt from the image of woman with a whip, that the female sadist is one of our most deep-rooted images of perversion.

And although I believe this male fantasy of feminine equality as a euphemism for feminine dominance to be evidence of the oppressors' neurosis rather than of any supporting fact, it was part of the character of my resentment that I once fancied wresting power from men as though nothing less than total annihilation would satisfy my rage. The true dramatic conclusion of this narrative should be the dissolution of my marriage; there is a part of me which believes that you cannot fight a sexist system while acknowledging your need for the love of a man, and perhaps if I had had the courage finally to tear apart my life I could write you about my hardworking independence, about my solitary self-respect, about the new society I hope to build. But in the end my husband and I did not divorce, although it seemed at one time as if we would. Instead I raged against him for many months and joined the Woman's Liberation Movement, and thought a great deal about myself, and about whether my problems were truly all women's problems, and decided that some of them were and that some of them were not. My sexual rage was the most powerful single emotion of my life, and the feminist analysis has become for me, as I think it will for most women of my generation, as significant an intellectual tool as Marxism was for generations of radicals. But it does not answer every question. To discover that something has been wrong is not necessarily to make it right: I would be lying if I said that my anger had taught me how to live. But my life has changed because of it. I think I am becoming in small ways a woman who takes no shit. I am no longer submissive, no longer seductive; perhaps it is for that reason that my husband tells me sometimes that I have become hard, and that my hardness is unattractive. I would like it to be otherwise. I think that will take a long time.

My husband and I have to some degree worked out our differences; we are trying to be together as equals, to separate our human needs from the needs imposed upon us by our sex roles. But my hatred lies within me and between us, not wholly a personal hatred, but not entirely political either. And I wonder always whether it is possible to define myself as a feminist revolutionary and still remain in any sense a wife. There are moments when I still worry that he will leave me, that he will come to need a woman less preoccupied with her own rights, and when I worry about that I also fear that no man will ever love me again, that no man could ever love a woman who is angry. And that fear is a great source of trouble to me, for it means that in certain fundamental ways I have not changed at all.

I would like to be cold and clear and selfish, to demand satisfaction for my needs, to compel respect rather than affection. And yet there are moments, and perhaps there always will be, when I fall back upon the old cop-outs. Why should I trouble to win a chess game or a political argument when it is so much easier to lose charmingly? Why should I work when my husband can support me, why should I be a human being when I can get away with being a child?

Woman's Liberation is finally only personal. It is hard to fight an enemy who has outposts in your head.

From *Esquire Magazine*, 1970.

QUESTIONS

(1) What kind of relationships between public causes and personal feelings does Ms. Kempton establish in the first paragraph?

(2) In the second paragraph, Ms. Kempton uses the word "postures." Is the idea of "postures" important in the essay?

(3) Is the third paragraph the key to the essay, the clear statement of theme? Notice the connection between "stronghold" in the last sentence of this paragraph and "outposts" in the last sentence of the essay. What does that connection reveal about the theme of the essay?

(4) Make a list of the words in the essay that are related to war and violence, words like stronghold, outpost, rape, power, abuse, kill. What is the cumulative effect of these words upon the reader?

(5) Is the relationship with her father, which she describes, another form of the "willing rape" she experienced in the college suite?

(6) Why does she say that the idea that "women are by definition incapable of serious thought" was "a comforting lesson"? What does this say about respect and responsibility as values in gender-education? How does it prepare the reader for her statement: "My task . . . was to find a man in whom there resided enough power to justify my acting the child . . ."?

(7) What kind of statements does Kempton make about her early jobs and loves that establish a connection between one's public integrity (doing a good job) and one's private integrity (self-esteem rather than self-loathing)?

(8) Does she imply that we are all doomed to replay the parent-child game in our adult lives? How does she convey that feeling without shouting it?

(9) When she describes her struggles with her husband, does she sound like her mother struggling with her father? What details connect the two descriptions? Do any of the details seem related to the "permitted rape" she described?

(10) Kempton says: "What I couldn't figure out was whether I hated them because I was afraid they would leave me or

whether I was afraid they would leave me because I hated them." Is this statement of her doubt and confusion important to the essay? Does it help to involve the reader in her personal struggle?

(11) At what point does the metaphor of a war between the sexes emerge and clearly dominate the essay? Has it been implicit from the beginning?

(12) Kempton says, ". . . my hatred lies within me and between us, not wholly a personal hatred, but not entirely political either." Has she made us understand that? Has she made us feel that? Has she made us feel and understand the connections between the personal and the political throughout her essay?

THE SENSE OF THE 70s

OF THE 70s

SCENES OF
THE SEVENTIES

This section offers a collage of American life in this decade. It provides in fragmented fashion a commentary on the way we live and the way we die or, at least, the way we face the fact of death. The essays collected here reflect the fact that we are still a people on the move, a people for whom movement is an end in itself. Thus Lucian Truscott's "In the Vanguard" suggests that the box van has become more than a way of transportation; it has become a way of life. Jeff Greenfield's "The Iceman Arriveth" argues that the furious speed and violence (as well as, for the present, its racial exclusivity) are the sources of hockey's claim to be "the sport of the seventies."

Movement of another sort—the movement of a mind celebrated for its conservative cast—is evident in William F. Buckley's deliberations on the laws against marijuana. Buckley's position represents a rather dramatic shift but a consistent, logical one. Beyond both logic and consistency is the subject of the final selection. Gloria Emerson's *Winners and Losers* is a powerful and painful account of the impact of the Vietnam War on American life. Here again we see a movement of the spirit in the dignified grief of people who must contend with the fact of death and the unexpressed, but deeply felt, sense of waste.

These, then, are some scenes of the seventies.

IN THE VANGUARD

LUCIAN K. TRUSCOTT IV

A little over a year ago, I joined the rank of the vanners, leaving my standard passenger car behind for a noisy box on wheels. Like a lot of other people, I wanted economical transportation that could be used for something more than just a place in which to sit. So I bought my 1968 Dodge van, an old laundry delivery panel truck. It's outfitted with crank-open windows, a double bed that converts to a dinette, a propane stove, a double sink, a hanging closet and that quintessential piece of van equipment, a citizen's band (CB) radio. (My handle is "Catfish"; it used to be "Broadway Hustler.")

Driving is for me, next to fishing, the best drug in the world. Right there at the edge of the windshield is the road, there's no hood to clutter your vision, all that pavement running away beneath the wheels, engine purring under your right elbow, CB crackling and spitting with truckers keeping each other awake, and in the rear-view mirror the inside of the van looks like your living room—which goes a long way toward explaining the van's peculiar attraction. Even at 60 miles per hour in the middle of Utah, you've never really left home.

A van is a poor man's Porsche. After 1,000 miles, you discover you're not alone out there. Just east of Nashville, an International orange van whips by, going in the opposite direction. Blinking headlights, wild waving from the driver's window. At the service station just off the next exit, a guy in a California van, with magnesium wheels, proffers a joint. No one could miss the first time a van club breezes by, 20 brightly painted vans, chrome wheels flashing, CB antennas waving in the 70-miles-per-hour air. The first guy, the "wagon master," is running on the trucker's channel, and you heard him coming up behind you from about five miles back, checking up the line, talking with truckers heading east, asking if there are any cops (Smokey Bears) or radar traps (picture-takers) in our lane ahead. The last van, the "tail gunner," is on the same frequency, and occasionally he'll check in because somebody has dropped behind, or because a cop has been spotted on the back door, coming up from behind. Reach down for the channel knob on your CB, flip a few and you'll find the rest of the club chattering it up on one of the non-trucker channels, talking about their engines and beer supply, complaining about the heat, checking the range of the new "twin hustler" antennas just mounted on the side-view mirrors. When they spot you, loafing along in the right-hand lane, one of the vanners will break the club chatter long enough to say hello:

"Break. Ten. How 'bout that blue guy from that New York State. You gotcha ears on?"

"Ten-four. You got the Hudson River Catfish. Go ahead."

"Four-ten, guy. You got that old Coffee Cup outa that Memphis town comin' atcha. Where you headed?"

"We're goin' up to that Okie City tonight, guy. How 'bout it?"

"Ten-four there. Catfish. We be gettin' off that two-four exit, goin' up to those boonies for the weekend. Hope this weather holds, come on."

"Ten-four on the weather."

"How 'boutcha, Catfish?"

"You gotim, go ahead."

"Four-ten there, Catfish. You have yourself a good truckin' trip now, guy. Keep that rubber side down and that tin box up, have a good day today and a better day tomorrow. You got that Memphis Coffee Cup. We goin' thisaway."

"Ten-four. Coffee Cup. We put the good numbers on ya. We westbound and down."

Within 25 miles, they've pulled ahead, an orderly bumper-to-bumper streak of chrome and gaudy slabsides, wide black tires and 70 MPH CB babble. After a number of such occasions, I figured I was pretty close to the van culture. Not much is really said on the CB radio, and swapping stories at the gas pump doesn't go much further, but after several months driving around the country, what you get is a feeling, a sense of who vanners are and why the urge to buy a box on wheels and outfit it at the edges of the imagination both inside and out seems to be sweeping the country. The van is the hot rod of the 1970s, I thought. There is the same camaraderie among vanners that there was among those who stripped, lowered and grey-primered 1949 Fords in the fifties, or among the early owners of 1964 Pontiac GTOs, the dignified peel-out crowd. A van, I figured, is recession autoego.

Then, after 25,000 miles in one year, I made my way to L.A. to investigate the van culture at its roots. And I discovered just how far off base I really was.

Southern California is, of course, the cradle of autoculture. And, for reasons understood only by the true denizen, in the late 1960s attention turned to the van. Surfers, it is said, were the first to pick up used delivery trucks, to buy old mail trucks at auctions and, with lavish application of candy-pearl paint to the outside, with conservative trimming of the box skeleton in wood paneling and the parents' left-over burnt orange carpeting from the rec room, the once lowly van was transformed into Surfer Wagon, suitable for turning heads on the way over to the Redondo Beach pier. Which is, of course, what it is all about. Or is it?

In November of 1975, I found myself in the right front seat of Jerry Wesseling's "Old Glory," said to be the most famous van in all of Southern California. In L.A., this is like saying you're discussing poetry with Robert Lowell, or talking sports with Dick Young. Fame is not easily bestowed in a metropolitan area of over 11 million. I mean, there are folks in Beverly Hills driving one-of-a-kind custom Lamborghinis' Rolls that belonged to the Royal Family, and racing Porsches that took their classes at Le Mans. In L.A., everybody wants to be noticed. Self-image is as precious in L.A. as a good Martini is in N.Y. One's car is at least a third of one's identity, the other two-thirds residing in the housewithpoolandsaunaandjacuzzi, and one's wardrobe, which is faded blue denim.

Still, the urge to be noticed is not, I believe, the explanation of the Southern California van phenomenon. Vans are virtually everywhere you look: There are 62 separate van clubs in L.A. alone, 92 in the state of California, hundreds of vans a month are sold by Dodge, Ford and Chevrolet dealers from one end of L.A. to the other, a van custom shop opens every other week to service the growing cult, upholsterers and paint shops are overwhelmed with business. The van represents something deep within the soul of the Southern Californian and, by extension, of the American of the seventies: Southern Californians and Americans are increasingly insecure, and vans are cozy.

This thought struck me somewhere south of Whittier, California, while cruising on Interstate 605 at 65 MPH. At the wheel was Jerry Wesseling, a tall, blond and balding autofreak with a past peppered with slot-car racing and so many different cars he has virtually lost count. At 25, Jerry Wesseling has achieved oneness with the world of the gasoline-powered vehicle.

"This van is my hobby. It is my business. It is my life," said Wesseling, peering through darkly tinted windows at the traffic ahead. Reaching to the padded console above his head for his CB mike, he checked the Smokey report for the short stretch of 605 we would drive on our way over to Southgate for a meeting of the Southern California Van Council, the governing body of the 62 van clubs in the area. Wesseling is part owner of Ye Van Shoppe, a van customizing and supply house on Whittier Boulevard in the town whence came our 37th president. His van is famous because he has made it famous. It is red, white and blue with stars in the classic flag theme, but, strangely, it does not smack of late sixties easyriderism. Rather than an assault on the American Dream, Wesselings "Old Glory" *is* the American Dream. "This is a patriotic van," said Wesseling as he showed me his hopped-up, chrome-plated 340-cubic-inch Dodge Duster engine and the padded, pleated, crushed velvet "pleasuredrome" interior. "It is everything I ever wanted in a car."

From inside an automobile on a normal highway, one can choose from two frames of reference. The first is the "inside" frame of reference, wherein one is stationary within the car. The classical physical example is a fly buzzing around in the "dead" space within the driver's compartment. The second frame of reference is that of motion, of speed, when one looks outside the car and sees land going by at X MPH. One does not feel motion inside the driver's compartment, but thrust a hand out the window and one immediately feels the force of the wind, indicative of the motion of the car.

In California, there is a third frame of reference: The relation of one's car to the surrounding cars. On Highway 605, Wesseling and I were *surrounded* by cars all traveling at 65

MPH, three and four deep on a side, cars for as far as you could see ahead and behind. The astounding thing was the fact that the cars didn't move. Once in position on an L.A. freeway, a car seems fixed almost as if it were in a space on a parking lot. Thus, peering from the window at all the stationary cars around us had the effect of removing the second frame of reference, the sensation of motion, and of replacing it with the parking lot effect, the feeling that in Wesseling's van we were part of a larger whole, like riding a magic carpet or a moving walkway inside an airport. Removal of the sensation of speed—in order to sense motion one must look beyond the surrounding cars, strain past the pack to catch a glimpse of a building or a tree or a patch of ground, and watch it go by— adds to a general feeling of helplessness and insecurity. Wesseling, like other vanners I talked to, compensates for the parking lot effect by relaxing, by treating the inside of the van as if it were *not* in motion, as if it were *in fact* parked, rather than in effect parked. Thus the inside of the van becomes a literal living room as well as a figurative one. The ever-present bar, complete with cold beer, ice and mixed drinks, if you prefer, is actually used. If you have a TV, you watch it. If the TV isn't on, the stereo blares, removing the rushing noise of fast travel from the senses. Lean back on the plush sofa. Have a drink. Talk with the people seated just across the cocktail table in the swivel chairs. We'll be there in a little while. Forget that what we're really doing is traveling, and accept the reality that in L.A. travel is a third of life, that inside a van this third can be translated back to the living room at home, the stereo, the before-dinner drink, indirect lighting and smokeajoint scene.

My van had always seemed to me part of a romantic vision of myself. Looking in the rear-view mirror and seeing my living room was like looking in the mirror and seeing myself as the owner of a railroad in his private car at the end of the train. But to Jerry Wesseling and the other vanners I talked to, looking in their rear-view mirrors at the homey scenes they created in the backs of their vans was looking at themselves as they really are. Their vans are intensely accurate (if narcissistic) portrayals of their own personalities. Wesseling did every lick of work on his van, from the tufted black Naugahyde driver's compartment—"It's black because it's all busi-

ness up here and people will get it dirty"—to the red velvet
and dark wood bed/couch/bar scene in back—"Strictly pleasure, for laying back and digging the sounds." He made all of
his own furniture: bed, sofa, chairs, dressers. And yes, the van
really looked like home, with maybe a few extras like the
velvet, judged financially impractical at home but allowable
in the van because everything in a van is miniaturized.

Do Wesseling and the others live in their vans? Not literally.
Then what, exactly, are the vans used for if not for living?
Wesseling: "Look, man, a van is not a recreational vehicle.
These vans don't have showers and johns and most of them
don't carry cooking equipment, except on runs. I use my van
to get around. Back and forth to work, hanging out and cruising at night. The furthest I've ever been in my van was like
about a seven-hour caravan we made on one of the runs."

Well, now, what we have is a kind of hybrid, a cross between
a hot rod and a station wagon. In Southern California, the
van is designed for life on the freeways, for runs to friends'
houses, for cruising The Strip or Van Nuys Boulevard on
Wednesday night, the scene to make for more than 40 years if
one's life revolves around his wheels. Yet Wesseling's van, and
those I saw up on The Strip one Wednesday night, seemed to
me a departure from the old Southern California autofantasy
lifestyle—low riders, channeled Ford roadsters, sports cars you
have to shoehorn yourself into, fair-weather vehicles all. Wesseling's van appears radical, but only because of its paint job.
The rest is functional: The flared wheel-wells house the wide-
profile Mickey Thompson tires, a safety factor for the generally top-heavy vans. The hot 340 V-8 gives the van about the
same performance as any standard size American car with
stock equipment (my early Dodge lugs up steep hills behind
its stock slant-6).

Eric Pierce, the editor of *RV—Van World* magazine, which
claims a circulation of 150,000 after eight months, says vans
are "intensely practical vehicles. The van is lighter than a
standard car, it gets as good gas mileage and it's just as easy
to work on. The mini-van will probably be the next thing you
see—two-thirds the size of the current van, four-banger or V-6
engine, maybe mounted transverse with front-wheel drive, 25
miles per gallon. This concept will probably develop into a
sport van, lower, less boxy, with some sort of sculpted styling

and a laid-back windshield. The van is going to get closer and closer to becoming the station wagon of the 1980s, more of a family car."

The auto industry seems to agree. Ford recently opened a van body plant in Avon Lake, Ohio, and was relieved to discover that the spectacular climb in van sales has continued even during this sharp recession. Industry sales doubled to 350,000 between 1971 and 1975, and spokesmen hope they will hit 400,000 in the Bicentennial year. While Dodge vans are readily available, Ford and Chevrolet still can't produce enough to satisfy demand. It's not just an American phenomenon, either. Australia and England are both experiencing a van boom, and they make beautiful models which aren't currently available here.

The base price for a 1975 model van is under $4,000, and about $2,000 worth of factory options are available. Of course that's just the beginning, because when a vanner starts customizing his interior his stretched imagination is the only limit. So far, the big automakers have steered clear of the more exotic possibilities, but Eric Pierce is convinced that "within two years or so they'll be in the conversion business, offering specialized equipment as options. Right now the van is a workhorse vehicle that is being doctored into a passenger carrier. In two years, the equation will be turned around."

For the time being, there is a growing demand for professional van conversions. A converted van will typically have a fairly radical paint job complete with "bellyband" (the bright, offset color stripe around the middle of the van), a cassette stereo deck, paneling, carpeting, a convertible bed, icebox, bar and swivel high-backed seats for driver and passenger. It is possible today to walk into a major L.A. Ford, Chevrolet or Dodge showroom and buy a custom-converted van right off the floor. Or you can buy a raw van and take it to a custom conversion company. Four years ago in Southern California there were only 6 custom converters to choose from; now there are over 60. One of them, Wildwood, grossed about $2 million in 1975, up from $25,000 four years ago. Its partners have solved the problem of what to do with all that money by expanding to Michigan, a huge growth area for vans. In just over a year, the number of custom converters in Michigan went from 3 to 30.

in the driver's compartment that are able to face backward,
with a round, mirrored cocktail table in the middle. And wall-
to-wall mirrors, ceiling included. When Stewart finished, they
would both be out somewhere in the vicinity of $13,000. They
paid in cash.

From New Times Magazine, 1976.

QUESTIONS

(1) How does the statement in the second paragraph, "even at
sixty miles per hour in the middle of Utah, you've never really
left home," help to explain the attraction of the van?

(2) What is a "van club"?

(3) How does the CB serve as that "quintessential piece of
van equipment"?

(4) What is the desire "deep within the soul of the Southern
Californian" that the van craze represents? Do you agree with
the author on this point?

(5) What does the author mean by the "third frame of reference"?

(6) According to the author the interior of a van accurately
reflects the personality of its owner. Do you find this to be true
among the van owners you know?

(7) In the latter part of his essay, the author deals with the
economics and the sociology of owning a van. What explanation does he offer for popularity of vans among increasing
numbers of older people?

(8) The author is himself a van owner, yet he suggests a difference between his attitude and that of the typical van
owner? How is that difference suggested?

THE ICEMAN ARRIVETH: HOCKEY IS THE SPORT OF THE SEVENTIES

JEFF GREENFIELD

Hockey is the gilded stepchild of American sports, earning profit without honor in its adopted country. While it is the neo-official religion of Canada, where children in Sunday school believe the Stanley Cup is the silver chalice, hockey is the last major sport in the United States to be under-analyzed, under-appreciated. Both its adherents and its detractors seem too captivated by hockey's color, speed, physical brutality, and frequent bursts of violence to consider whether this fastest sport in the world has a fair share of cerebral pleasures, rather than being simply a battle fought on a sparkling plain where ignorant armies slash by night.

The commercial pleasures and potential of hockey are beyond doubt. A National Broadcasting Company vice-president calls hockey "the fastest-growing sport in the United States." Discount his enthusiasm by the twelve million dollars his network has invested in National Hockey League telecasts, and his statement remains true. The growth of hockey in the last five years is measurable from the major leagues to the diversions of our children.

Seven years ago, the National Hockey League had six teams, four of them in the United States, all followed fanatically by a white working-class audience. This fall, with the addition of Kansas City and Washington, the N.H.L. will consist of eighteen teams (fifteen of them in the U.S.), playing in houses before corporate executives, suburban adolescents, and the tradesmen of yore. Unlike their counterparts in other sports, these new hockey teams have drawn remarkably big crowds, even in the cities where the teams don't win.

In the 1972-73 season, the New York Islanders established in their first year an all-time N.H.L. record for failure: twelve wins, sixty losses, six ties. In that same season, the Islanders drew more than 12,000 per game. By contrast, the A.B.A. Nets a year later could not draw 10,000 per game, despite a first-place finish and the presence of basketball's most exciting player, Julius Erving. In Buffalo, Philadelphia, Atlanta, Minnesota, St. Louis, the story is the same: no sport sells out its games more frequently than N.H.L. hockey.

This enthusiasm has spread to the children of affluent America, whose collective economic power exceeds the gross national product of most United Nations member countries. This group provided much of the audience for the Mets in their early years of glorious failure. Today, they seem to have seized on hockey. More than 200,000 of our flowering manhood play organized hockey on some 9000 teams. And this is no casual commitment. It costs about $150 to outfit a young hockey player, and enough outfits were put together last year to sell almost $90,000,000 worth of hockey equipment. Nor is money the only parental cost. So overcrowded are ice rinks that teams of children practice around the clock, some gathering for five a.m. sessions. Ice rinks may be the growth industry of this decade: 133 of them have been built since 1970. The NBC official, who lives in Greenwich, Connecticut, says that "these kids don't want to grow up to be Mickey Mantle; they want to grow up to be Bobby Orr."

The young men of Greenwich have planted their fantasies in a solid financial basis. A decade ago, a major-league hockey player was lucky to earn $10,000 a year. When the competing World Hockey Association began play in 1972, the market turned from a buyer's monopoly to a seller's paradise. A talented young player with a good junior-hockey record now has the bargaining power of a service-station attendant with a direct pipeline to Kuwait. Denis Potvin, the nineteen-year-old who broke Bobby Orr's scoring record for defensemen in junior hockey, signed a three-year Islander contract for $500,000.

And for established stars the possibilities are limitless. In 1971, Ranger All-Star Brad Park held out for the outrageous sum of $30,000. The following year Park was paid $150,000. Teammate Walter Tkaczuk's salary rose over that same summer from $15,000 to $150,000. The average N.H.L. salary is now about $55,000, and even with a fragile peace between the

N.H.L. and W.H.A., the demand for topflight players guaran-
tees that huge contracts are a permanent part of big-time
hockey.

All this suggests that hockey is leaving its historic past as a
sacrament of the urban white working class, celebrated in
South Boston, Chicago's Bridgeport, New York's Bay Ridge,
but foreign to most Americans. But for all of the successes of
the sport, hockey in America has yet to be taken seriously as a
sport fully entitled to respectability. The late Jimmy Cannon,
whose New York *Post* columns were as influential as any sports
writing, suggested in a famous remark that hockey would be
better if they played it in the mud.

Cannon's implication—that hockey is a sport without pattern or reason—is widely shared, particularly (a highly distorted survey suggests) by those members of the literati who
view the New York Knickerbockers as a living embodiment of
some esoteric philosophical principle ("In the pick and roll,
you see, we have a Hegelian synthesis of strength—Willis
Reed—and finesse—Walt Frazier"). Watching a sport as fast, as
violent, as apparently helter-skelter as ice hockey, a refined or
confused observer is likely to relegate the sport to the twilight
zone of legitimacy, close to the jungles where dwell roller
derby and professional wrestling.

Not that a cerebral judgment is likely to impede the growth
of hockey. It has too many qualities that are in demand today.
With football, it shares a sense of constant danger and violence, a sense enhanced by the furious speed of the game, and
by the openness of the violence (in football the force of the
hitting is muted by the movement of twenty-two men across
ten yards of space). Like baseball, hockey provides a refuge for
the daydreams of ordinary mortals: hockey players are often
under six feet tall, and weigh less than two hundred pounds.
One of the most exciting players in the league, Montreal's
Yvan Cournoyer, is five feet seven inches tall; it is his speed
that sets him apart, not genetic accident.

And hockey has something else: it is a white refuge. There
is no black hockey player in either the National Hockey
League or the World Hockey Association, and a black spectator at a hockey match is a rarity. While this may change
within a decade—it must occur to some bright coach that a
Jim Brown on skates and armed with a stick would make a

formidable forward—the current segregated state of hockey provides the same unspoken assurances to Middle America as do restrictive covenants. Those who cling to such charming racial principles as "a black always chokes" will find it hard to sustain an argument in the face of Dick Allen, Bill Russell, Willis Reed, Paul Warfield, ad infinitum. Watching hockey, the spectator need never think about "them."

Whether hockey wins respect or merely enthusiastic followers may not matter much to hockey's establishment, without question the most parochial, suspicious, and unsophisticated of any major sport. The massive, badly planned expansion of 1967 clearly lowered the quality of N.H.L. play, but still brought millions of new fans to the game. Few of hockey's followers seem to mind much the thinking of men like Bobby Orr's manager, who censored a reference to the young star's drinking of a can of beer. (New York writers regularly noted Dave DeBusschere's post-game habit of six or eight beers, and no reports were received of towheaded youths storming the Knick dressing room crying, "Say it ain't so, Dave!") Still, some of the derisive treatment hockey receives from sports' lettered tribe seems to be a product of the unique difficulties of appreciating the game—a fault within ourselves, not in the stars, or coaches, or the game itself.

Fundamentally, hockey is an alien sport, imported from the frozen Canadian wasteland. Americans grow up with baseball, basketball, and football, games they more or less invented. As children, we stand in a rocky plot of grass and dream of DiMaggio or Musial or Williams or Mays. We play football in organized school teams, or with a 1965 Plymouth as the end zone. There is not a school yard in the nation without a hoop on a backboard; even the poorest child can grow up with visions of Oscar Robertson in his head. Ice hockey, on the other hand, was confined to the Northeast and upper Midwest until just a few years ago. (Significantly, Boston and its environs is one area in America where hockey has always been unquestioned king: during the eight straight title years of the Boston Celtics, the N.B.A. champions went some seasons with an attendance average of around fifty percent, while the then last-place Bruins sold out every game.)

Moreover, hockey is played by imported mercenaries. Other

sports draw their heroes from among us: from the Hill neighborhood of St. Louis came Yogi Berra and Joe Garagiola; from San Francisco's fishing families came the DiMaggio brothers. Pete Axthelm's *The City Game* suggests how thin the line is between those who went from playgrounds to professional stardom and those who fell back into a life of lost dreams.

Hockey stars? They come from Saskatoon and South Porcupine; Parry Sound and Sault Ste. Marie; Point Anne and Arthabaska. They come forward as provincials, high-school dropouts in a sports world where college, even if only by osmosis, has given other athletes a patina of sophistication. Many hockey players cannot even speak English. In such a world, the social concern of goalie Ken Dryden and the natural wit and glib tongue of Derek Sanderson are freakish. It is difficult to believe in the mental stimulation of a game whose principals are given to explanations like: "He's a super hockey player, aye?"

These barriers will soon fall. With five hundred high schools and 160 colleges now competing in hockey, and with more than thirty N.H.L. and W.H.A. clubs competing for talent, American campuses are already beginning to feed players into the major leagues; thirty-five N.H.L. players have attended college.

What will take longer—and what may never happen at all, if the guardians of hockey are content to let television rights and box-office receipts be the sole measure of success—is the growth in understanding of hockey as a game of skill and precision. While no game appears easier to understand than ice hockey, no game requires more time before the patterns of play begin to make sense.

Hockey is a game of unrelieved intensity. It is played on a frozen pit. Its players are totally without sanctuary. There is no time out, no surcease. So fast is the game that a forward line cannot skate for more than two minutes without exhausting itself; the fury continues while the lines are changed in the midst of the play. An intentional stoppage of play is always punished, either by a face-off deep in the territory of the offender, or by a delay-of-game penalty. New York Ranger Coach and General Manager Emile Francis puts it bluntly: "There's no place to go. When that puck is dropped, there's no way to take a pass and step out-of-bounds. There are boards, and they're pretty hard."

The rules of hockey are simple, purposeful, and geared to the continuation of movement and passing. As a precision game, hockey tries to deter easy offensive and defensive plays. A player cannot put himself in front of the opposing goal and wait for a pass to come to him, the way a Jabbar or Walton might basket-hang; instead, a team must carry or pass the puck into the attacking zone before the team itself is allowed to be in that territory. Otherwise the play is off side. (Similarly, a player can't wait just outside the blue line for a pass to come his way from the other end of the rink. *Any* pass across two lines is off side, unless the man taking the pass has been speedy enough to catch up with the puck from the same zone in which the pass was begun.)

The rule isn't complicated at all. But until a spectator watches enough games to absorb the rhythm of the game, he won't understand that the off-side rule structures the entire flow of the offensive game. The forward line must know each other's moves automatically; they must know when to stop before crossing the blue line if the puck carrier is likely to put a move on a defender before crossing the line. A centerman must be able to pass the puck in full flight so that it crosses the blue line an instant ahead of a winger. Once the puck is in the attacking zone, the defensemen move just inside the blue line at the "points." Their key job is to keep the puck from coming back across the line, because once that puck leaves the zone, the entire attacking team must retreat to center ice.

A second basic rule rewards an effective attack, just as the off-side rule protects the defense. A team pinned in its own zone must fight its way out. If it tries to fling the puck of danger from its half of the ice, the puck will be brought right back into the heart of its zone.

This rule dictates, among other things, what makes a good two-way hockey player. As Emile Francis points out, a hockey player must react the moment the puck changes hands. If a team permits its opponent to cross the red line in full possession of the puck and unimpeded by checks, that team can throw the puck into the attacking zone legally, and that is where goals are scored. The standards that determine a hockey

player's worth are also inextricably linked to the pattern of
rules: can a forward back-check well enough to prevent a puck
from reaching his zone? Can a defenseman outmuscle his opponent to keep the puck on side? It is as difficult to learn these
subtleties as it is to learn what to watch for on a football field
or basketball court. In fact, it is more difficult because the
game of hockey is played at nearly inhuman speed.

A hockey player rushing up ice travels at more than twenty-
five miles an hour; a slap shot hurls a frozen rubber disc toward a goalie at one hundred miles an hour. Everything that
happens in hockey—passing, stickhandling, checking, shooting—happens fast. Ironically, the very intensity that makes
hockey a dramatic, visually hypnotic game makes an appreciation of the game enormously difficult. Nothing looks
planned; everything seems to be happening at once. A give-
and-go in basketball, or a flea-flicker pass in football, is understandable; we can watch it develop. In hockey the give-and-go
is a staple of offensive strategy too, but because it happens in
the midst of furious rushes up and down the ice, it is likely to
be forgotten as the play continues.

"There's no set plays like in football, of course, because
hockey's too fast for that," Emile Francis says, "but there's a
pattern of play, and a system, and depending on where the
puck is, there's a particular job you've got to be doing. And
it has to come instinctively, so that there's an automatic reaction: the minute *this* happens, you do *that*."

This pace is the key reason that the cause of our mass ob-
sessions is not yet suited to conveying the nature of hockey; I
mean, of course, television. Even though hockey is an exact
opposite of baseball—a game of icy savagery and bounded terrain as opposed to a summer game of scope and leisure—
hockey shares with baseball the problem of being trivialized
by television. Just as the screen shrinks baseball, robbing it of
its warmth and spaciousness, television strips hockey of its
spatial frame of reference. NBC's Scotty Connal says as much:

"One of the problems is that it's difficult to relate to the
game if you've never seen it in person. I would hate to have to
learn hockey without having seen it in person. If you're a guy
in Wheeling, West Virginia, tuning in for the first time, it's
very difficult."

This is less the fault of NBC's coverage, which valiantly

tries to illustrate the flow of the game and the separate skills involved, than it is of hockey itself. When ten men move up and down a two-hundred-foot-long surface in ten seconds, a camera cannot take in all of what is going on. By contrast, a medium shot of a basketball court can take in an entire half court—enough to watch every play moving through an offensive pattern.

"You know when you watch a game in person how important peripheral vision is," says Connal. "You can see the puck coming out over the blue line, and out of the corner of your eye you'll see Brad Park in a fight."

Connal's point was illustrated in last season's St. Patrick's Day game between the Rangers and the Bruins. With a little less than eight minutes gone, we saw Ranger left winger Steve Vickers take a pass from a teammate and rush up ice with only Bobby Orr between Vickers and the goal—a textbook one-on-one play. What the camera did *not* show was Ranger defenseman Brad Park racing up the right side of the ice, fruitlessly pursued by Phil Esposito. An instant after Park came into view, he took Vickers' pass and scored. The television audience was denied a sense of anticipation because it could not see the full nature of the scoring threat.

There are also clear advantages of televised hockey: the instant replays in slow motion are the surest way to see exactly how a scramble in front of the net produced a goal, and arenas in Long Island and Washington are planning to install huge closed-circuit screens for their fans. Isolated shots can also teach a largely untutored audience that there is method to hockey madness.

"Say Boston's on a power play," explains NBC's Connal. "If you isolate on Esposito, you can show that the man in the slot is not a garbage man—he's got to be big and strong to fight off the defense." NBC also introduced an intermission feature called *Peter Puck,* in which a Hanna-Barbera animated puck explains rules and terms of hockey. This noble gesture would be better facilitated by adopting the format of the National Football League's *Playbook* feature, in which game footage in super-slow motion illustrates what technical terms mean. As of last March, the combination of viewer unfamiliarity and technical limits had combined to give the hockey ratings a third-place standing among Sunday sports telecasts.

This is going to change in the coming decade. The parents of children now playing hockey and the students in high schools and colleges where the sport is just beginning are a natural audience for hockey. This and hockey's appeal as an active and, for some, whites-only sport mean that the market for hockey has nowhere to go but up during the 1970s.

The *real* question is whether hockey will succeed simply because of its capacity for bloodshed or racial pride, or whether those who control the sport care enough about it to take on the job of communicating its less sensational, but ultimately more rewarding qualities.

From Esquire Magazine, 1974.

QUESTIONS

(1) In the opening sentence the author uses the phrase "profit without honor." The phrase is an example of a punning allusion. What famous phrase is he alluding to? How does the pun reinforce his basic theme?

(2) The concluding sentence of the first paragraph contains another punning allusion to a famous English poem, Matthew Arnold's "Dover Beach." Can you find it? Is the recognition of the allusion necessary to the understanding of the sentence? What is gained by the writer's use of such references?

(3) According to the author, what has been the principal objection to hockey as reflected in the comment "hockey would be better if they played it in the mud"?

(4) What are the two basic rules that a spectator must be aware of in order to appreciate fully a hockey game?

THE PERILS OF THINKING
OUT LOUD ABOUT POT

WILLIAM F. BUCKLEY

Just after the Associated Press made news out of a commentary
I wrote in *National Review* about the need for changing the
pot laws ("Buckley Alters/Position on Pot") I had a letter
from a young man who ran for Congress on the Republican
ticket last November and very nearly made it. "I am in substantial agreement, but admit I must lose the habit of *thinking* as cautiously as a politician must *speak*." I haven't heard
it said better. The public exercises, in particular over a politician, a genuine tyranny, the conservative justification for
which is: It is right that public figures should not express
themselves, concerning an issue of grave social moment, icono-
clastically. Translated, that means someone who wants to go
to Congress (particularly on a Republican label) shouldn't
say: "I haven't decided for sure what my position is on the
pot laws. There is a lot of medical evidence coming in, and
a lot of analysis being done, and I might find myself, in the
days to come, advocating certain reforms in the marijuana
laws." My friend worried about frozen habits of mind that
come from having run for office. "I must, at least when not
running for office, resist the habit of arresting my capacity to
think," he says.

What's the story on the marijuana laws?

The story is, I think, this: In the past four or five years,
millions of middle Americans (I call them that for convenience) suddenly found out that marijuana was something with
which their own children were experimenting. Up until that
time, roughly, marijuana was neatly packaged in the imagination with the hard stuff, heroin, opium, the more recently discovered LSD, that kind of thing, and on late-night movies you
would occasionally see Dick Powell tracking down the swarthy
drug peddlers to their native lairs in mysterious and perfidious
Egypt and Turkey and Iran. The domestic victims were the
social reprobates who hadn't learned any better, and the thing

to do was to flog them with the law, and wait for the strictures of Harry Anslinger to reach their untutored ears.

Then, as I say, dozens of millions of Americans began to discover that the people they were in favor of sending to jail included, by theoretical extension, their own sons. Along the way, some conspicuous icons were smashed. Several teenage sons of the most prominent families in America were busted. They weren't sent to jail, but were reprimanded and let out on probation, and Mr. and Mrs. America's teeth were on edge.

A liberal Congressman from New York, Mr. Edward Koch, at the beginning of this period proposed to a committee of the House of Representatives that a panel of experts be commissioned to study the latest available evidence on marijuana, with the view to recommending changes in the law if such changes were indicated. Mr. Koch might as well have asked the Congress to look into the question whether the laws against matricide should be reconsidered: no one, but no one stepped forward to co-sponsor the measure. The months went by, and one, then another, then a third, finally whole carloads of Congressmen changed their minds and in due course the Presidential Commission on Marijuana was impaneled, and last spring it came in with its recommendations. The commission said that the laws that call for imprisoning people caught smoking pot should be repealed, but that the people who sell pot should continue to be prosecuted and sent to jail. President Nixon (let's face it, this was election year, and by that time he could see that Counterculture George loomed as his probable adversary) pointedly snubbed the report, advising the public that under no circumstances would he advocate the decriminalization of marijuana use. The public has a way of compressing the meaning of positions that touch on major emotional issues. Eight years ago Senator Goldwater said that atomic defoliation was one way of exposing the trails down which the North Vietnamese were infiltrating into South Vietnam, but that he tended to oppose that way of doing it. The headlines had Senator Goldwater "advocating" the use of atomic "weapons" in Indochina. Mr. Nixon, two years after he reached the White House, used the word "bums" to describe those hopped-up militants who had taken to using bombs in order to terrorize the campus—young men and women, said the President, to be sharply distinguished from those who protested by peaceful means. He was forthwith described as having declared that student protesters were, as a class, "bums." The Presidential Commission has been denounced as being "pro" marijuana.

Even though Middle America has come to realize it and to accept it (there is really no alternative to accepting it)—that in all probability their sons and daughters, at some point in high school or in college, are going to experiment with marijuana—they feel it is important to compensate by reinforcing their public position against marijuana, and the symbol of that position is the permanence of the laws. Their feeling, by the way, is not intuitively lacking in social intelligence. It is lacking in a lot of things, but not necessarily that. In Connecticut there is a statute dating back to the seventeenth century which prescribes the death penalty for sodomy committed with an animal (the question was not even raised whether it is a consenting animal). Frankly, I do not know whether the crime is being committed, and I do not even know whether the Sex Institute at the University of Indiana keeps up to date on the matter, but I do know (a) that no one is being electrocuted in Connecticut for having committed that crime and (b) that no politician is running for office on the need to repeal that particular law. Better—the public is saying in effect—to ignore the law's existence rather than to set right something the mere mention of which is kind of grubby, and the cause for raised eyebrows at the expense of the reformer. Once upon a time it took great courage for a British feminist to speak with passion to the elderly members of the House of Commons pleading for repeal of the laws disabling illegitimate children. "There are no such people as illegitimate children, honorable sirs, there are only illegitimate parents," was the famous line. A few generations later, Greer Garson was portraying the reformer in a popular movie. But not even Paul Newman can raise the question of medieval attitudes toward sodomy without, well, raising public suspicions about the odd allocation of his reformist energies. It is something of the same thing with marijuana reform.

So the same people whose elected representatives really wanted to know what an expert panel thought about the use of marijuana by their children more or less concluded that merely to open up the question of changing the laws might be interpreted as laxity on the subject in general. And, in California, a referendum was placed on the ballot, asking the public to express itself on whether the laws against marijuana should be repealed. The proposition was torn to pieces on election day. The voters unquestionably went home thinking they had struck back at pot. There is a sense in which they did.

Here is how the antipot people feel about it, and I struggle now to avoid saying the obvious things because the obvious things are so well known, and so boring. A little bit less than obvious is this: the public tends to react toward syndromes. It is a perfectly excusable way to act and, by the way, a very economical way to act. If the same man who (let us take an example from the forties and fifties) on issue after issue has sided with the Soviet Union—on the need for the United States to initiate a second front before General Eisenhower thought we were ready, on the undesirability of admitting Chiang Kai-shek to the summit conferences, on the good reasons Stalin had for overrunning Czechoslovakia, on the mercenary and colonialist reasoning behind the Marshal Plan, on the agrarian purity of Mao's movement in Mainland China: if that man, with that record, comes out against America's developing a hydrogen bomb, then the typical newspaper reader is quite reasonably going to discount his advice as prompted primarily by his habit of siding with the Communists on all matters of public controversy. Even if it happened that on that one issue the advocate was motivated by reasons unrelated to the strategic purposes of Soviet foreign policy, the chances of his getting people to listen to his arguments are very small. I am neither surprised that this should be so, nor particularly dismayed. The public doesn't have the time, the resources, or the patience to treat all the arguments raised by every politician or opinion-maker discretely: it tends to situate them in the general context of that person's performance.

Accordingly, people who are neither ignorant nor unresourceful nor lazy tend to believe that those who have come out for the repeal of the tough marijuana laws are really up to something more than compassion for young people who are occasionally caught experimenting with the weed and are sent to jail. The advocates of reform—they reason—are really consistent agents of the counterculture. They are the ones

who, by and large, favor repeal of all the obscenity laws. They
want abortion on demand. They want amnesty for draft
dodgers. They want every known protection for criminal de-
fendants. They reject the ideals of America and the standards
of America. They are—the enemy.

I speak not about Archie Bunker, whose amiable stupidity
is, I think, the greatest intellectual rip-off in theatrical history.
It isn't Archie Bunker, for instance, who wrote to me after I
sided with those who have come out for decriminalization, to
say: "Polemics aside, that is the reason for the push for decriminalization. The young refuse to learn the value of hypocrisy, vice's tribute to virtue. Most of the pot users in the
country are getting away with it, no question about that, so
why can't they admit they already have what they want and
not pomposify their position by claiming the stamp of legal-
ity for their aberrations?" Not quite so sophisticated, but by
no means primitive is the lady from California who writes me,
"Let's not kid ourselves. The campaign to legalize marijuana
is a step toward legalizing hard drugs. Degrees of harmfulness
may be debated—about alcohol, ordinary smoking, driving
faster than the speed limit, and many other things. The importance of the law against marijuana is that it is a signpost
which indicates society believes marijuana to be harmful. Remove this and other signposts (against porno, for example),
and the jungle will certainly become more natural."

I think it is fair to say that the overwhelming majority of
those who are against any reform in the present marijuana
laws are, in fact, not in favor of the vigorous prosecution of
the marijuana laws. In other words, they are opposed to their
own children going to jail. In taking this ambivalent position
toward the law they are of course making a statement, irre-
spective of the lack of rigor or of consistency. That statement
says this: We desire that the supreme law of the land dig in
against marijuana. We recognize that to implement that law
rigorously is not feasible, and that if it were feasible it would
be cruel. We recognize also that every now and then there is
going to be the exemplary prosecution, the young man who
finds himself face to face with the literal-minded judge in the
provinces. It having been established that the young man was
indeed smoking marijuana when the arresting magistrate de-

tained him, the judge looks into the statute book under, "Marijuana, illegal possession of, . . ." adjusts his bifocals, notes that he is at liberty to give anywhere from one to five years, and settles on three years as a moderate application of the law. Next case.

Too bad, but that's life. After all, only one out of one hundred people who exceed the speed limit is caught and fined—is that a reason for eliminating the speed limit? Only one out of a thousand tourists bringing in a little extra loot is caught by the customs officials—does that mean you should repeal the customs laws? A few go all the way, for instance the student who writes me from Ohio Northern University: "It is the very leniency of the punishment which increases the number committing the crimes." He, of course, is wedded to the rationalist superstition that there is a correlation between the severity of the sentence and the incidence of the crime. Thus: double the fine (or the prison sentence) and you halve the offense. Curiously it is not the curmudgeons alone who are tempted by the argument. A Princeton student whom I greatly hurt by revising my position wrote, "I guess this area is just another in the series where a minority is allowed to push their will on the majority. I tell you, one of these days I'm going to kick back—but hard. Or, perhaps, that will be the next balloon [I was the first, he had already told me] that went down the drain. Oh, my soul, why canst thou not stop weeping." Because, I fear, the young gentleman's soul is besotted with sentiment, and needs to dry out under the analytical rays of reason.

Reason tells you, I think, several things at the expense of both sides of the controversy. At the expense of the diehards, it tells you simply this, that the public conscience will strain at a system of justice that is utterly capricious. I know people (a) who believe in law and order; (b) who believe in the strong antipot laws; (c) who know that their children have smoked pot, and would protect them against a magistrate dispatched to bring in said children as resolutely as if they were braves doing the work of Sitting Bull. At the expense of the doves, it tells you that the counterculture operates most deviously, its subversive purposes to perform.

What will happen, under the circumstances, is that those who oppose the repeal of the laws will gradually diminish their call for the law's implementation—rather like the jaded

bottle laws in the dry states. Inasmuch as there is no real economic imperative for the legalization of marijuana smoking,
there is no clear lobby for institutionalizing it, as was the case
with alcohol, so intimately related to the tavern, the nightclub, and the country club. Pot smoking has been a privately
exercised vice: why not keep it that way, the hardliners are
saying in effect. I doubt that in the future anyone running for
district attorney, or judge, will be substantially imperiled by
the charges of the opposition that he failed to prosecute, and
imprison, people who were smoking marijuana. The law's
desuetude: the untidy recommendation, in effect, of those
who would leave the laws alone, in order to ignore them. The
philosophers among them hope to make the subtle cultural
point: This Society Disapproves of Marijuana. The Archie
Bunkers are not aware of philosophy: but straddling a hypocrisy is a calisthenic one learns early in life: they have got
so they can do it before breakfast.

Those, I think, are the terms of the forthcoming treaty between the hawks and the doves. Senator Aiken suggested a few
years ago that we should assert simply that we had won the
war in Vietnam—and withdraw. We could use our great resources to mystify the ensuing situation, get all mixed up
about who was representing whom, and simply cling hard to
the illusion. The antimarijuana hawks take a position not dissimilar: hang on to the marijuana laws, ignore them as much
as you can, put up with the occasional moral inconvenience
of the law applied at the expense of the desultory victim—and
relax in the knowledge that the catechism is unchanged.

The others, and I am on their side at this point, reject the
uses of individual victims for the sustenance of a legal chi-
mera; and recoil against altogether cynical uses of the law.
Not because we are purer than the manipulators, but because
we fear the attrition of the law's prestige. There are very good
arguments for taking the law seriously. These arguments call
for modifying the crazy penalties currently prescribed for the
idiots who smoke marijuana.

From *Execution Eve*, 1973.

QUESTIONS

(1) "I must lose the habit of *thinking* as cautiously as a politician must *speak*." Why does the author quote this line in his

opening paragraph? What is the relationship of the line to the title of the essay?

(2) How does the author explain the attitude of those who oppose legalization of marijuana even though they are aware of its widespread use?

(3) How does the author explain his statement "the public tends to react toward syndromes"? Do you agree with his analysis?

(4) The author is at pains to represent the position of those opposing decriminalization as fair and reasonable, not the prejudice of "Archie Bunker." What reason might he have for taking such pains? Is it related to the fact that the author—well known for his conservative views—has adopted a position that is one opposed by most conservatives?

(5) In the last analysis, the author defends his position on the grounds that widespread violation of the law leads to a lack of respect for law itself. Do you find his reason convincing?

(6) The author frequently uses the technique of argument by analogy, that is, he compares one situation to a different one for the purposes of making a particular point. Does the technique add to or diminish the effectiveness of his argument?

WINNERS AND LOSERS

GLORIA EMERSON

The newest names are going up now on the war monuments in the South. In a small place called Fulton, Mississippi, between Tupaloosa and Birmingham, there stands off Route 78 a newly erected monument made of old uneven bricks of a

burned, darker red. On top, the flame rises from a curved and
split iron cup; it was this light that made me stop. The men of
the county who went to the last four wars, and are pinned to
them forever, are listed on granite slabs: nineteen for World
War I, ninety-two for World War II, two for Korea, sixteen
for Vietnam: Boozer, Clark, Coats, Davidson, Hall, Hodges,
Humphries, Izard, Jones, Palmer, Sanderson, Waddle, West,
Willis, Worthey and Yielding. Aron Yielding died in World
War II; twenty-odd years later Vietnam had Larry T. Yielding.

During the war, somewhere in the middle of it, there were
men in Washington, D.C., who were bothered by the rising
American casualties—not by the wounds they did not see, but
by the concern that perhaps the small towns might not keep
taking such losses stoically. It was in these places that people
knew the boy who had been killed in Chu Lai, could remember how well he played high school football, knew what his father did, the name of his mother's family and if they were
churchgoers. It wasn't the same in the cities, where if a soldier
from Detroit or Los Angeles or St. Louis got killed, people in
the neighborhood would be startled or made uneasy. In Washington the worry was that the small towns would start questioning the war, that the prominent citizens—the banker, the
biggest farmer, a principal—would begin to speak against it.

Once, in Missouri, a university student driving me to the
airport remembered what had happened in his tiny hometown
in that state when there was someone killed in Vietnam. The
neighbors took food to the house. It was always done at such
times. The neighbors went to the house carrying soup pots,
covered dishes and pies to leave on the kitchen table so the
woman would not have to cook for her family during the first
days, those first white nights of grieving.

The boy, who was gentle and plump, remembered it all. "I
bet they had enough food there to last three days," he said.

People used to say that it was in the small places where
Vietnam had cut the deepest, that it was in the small places
where the war had taken away so much. So this is where I
went: small places of all kinds, everywhere.

One of them was Bardstown, in a smooth and fat part of
Kentucky. Driving there, you can see the low white fences of
some fine stables. I liked the cold and the grass that promised

to be greener when it was warm again, a child's idea of green,
clear and shiny, not the greens of Vietnam, not the green of
the Army.

Few of us would find it an alien or puzzling place; the white
curtains in so many windows look as if women washed, ironed
and fluffed them up every week. The porches are still there,
but people sit inside at night to watch television. The archi-
tecture of the oldest houses is neo-Greek, New England Colonial, Cape Cod or Georgian. Families still live in some of
them, taking care of the blue or yellow poplar flooring, the
hand-carved mantels, the brass doorknobs and the curving
staircases. On Tuesdays it is ladies night—drinks half price for
them—at the Holiday Inn near Blue Grass Parkway, and its
Oak Dining Room, with the harsh air conditioning and all
the salad you want to eat, is considered by many a fancy and
special place to go for steaks. In the summer a sweet and yeasty
smell from the eleven bourbon distilleries in the county speaks
of money, melted, soaking the bright air. There are three factories, nine churches, an art gallery, a Catholic bookstore, a
swap shop, good bowling alleys and a diner still named for a
dead owner, Tom Pig, because there is no reason to change it.
An award is given to the Outstanding Citizen of the Year from
Nelson County at the annual ladies-night meeting of the
Chamber of Commerce in mid-January. The local newspaper,
the *Kentucky Standard,* runs a picture and announcement if a
young man joins the service. It has been like this for a long
time. Louisville is thirty-nine miles away; the population here
is 5,800; it is the second oldest city in Kentucky.

The town gives its assets, briskly, on a green sign on US
31E: Bardstown, Nelson County, Bourbon Center of the
World, Old Kentucky Home, St. Joseph Cathedral.

Just before North Third, a soft and wide street of old trees
and white-frame or red-brick houses, there is the building of
the Kentucky National Guard Unit based in Bardstown. The
war is here, in a small low-lying house with two crossed cannon barrels in front, looking precise and proper. In red and
yellow a sign tells you here is Battery C, 2d Howitzer Battalion, 138th Artillery. The entire battery, part of a five-hundred-
man battalion, was called to active duty May 13, 1968, by an
executive order that summoned 24,000 men to bolster U.S.
forces in Vietnam.

Even during that terrible week in June years ago when four men from Battery C were killed on one day in Vietnam—and a fifth did not live another week—no one ever defaced the 138th Artillery sign or said they could not stand the sight of it any more. In Bardstown they are very nice people, not given to messing up property or doing wild things. Nor could it be said that the reporters, with their notebooks and questions, their cameras and television crews, were made to feel ill-at-ease, even as they asked, so many times, how people felt. For a little while the Vietnam war made Bardstown famous for a new, unpleasant reason. The older people, in positions of prominence, were cordial and kept to their cheerful ways, perhaps trying to make the point that good Christians do not collapse in crises. Millie Sutherland makes marvelous chocolate sheet cake and wrote out the recipe for me. Her husband, Judge Sutherland, gave me two boxes of Kentucky Kernel Seasoned Flour, Ideal for Chicken, Chops, Steak, Fish, Oysters and Shrimp, which is made by his family's firm, with very precise instructions on how to make the best batter and gravy with it. It was the judge who called Bardstown "a place of wholesomeness, goodness."

The town has always been used to outsiders; it calls out to tourists—who are usually southern—and does not make fun of them when they come. What draws many people is My Old Kentucky Home State Park, one mile from downtown Bardstown, where each summer a cast of forty-six performs in an outdoor musical drama called *The Stephen Foster Story*. One small Kentucky newspaper called the performance "as merry as a mint julep." The performers sing "My Old Kentucky Home," "Old Folks at Home," "De Camptown Races," "Jeanie with the Light Brown Hair" and "Oh, Susanna." Some are not so sure that the composer wrote his most famous, very sentimental song in Bardstown in 1852 while visiting his father's cousin, Judge John Rowan, in his mansion inspired by Independence Hall in Philadelphia. But it sells more bourbon and country hams, more souvenirs and more meals, and fills the motels where the room clerks referred to the mayor as Gus and know if the corn is doing well. It is typical of Bardstown that there are taxis bearing signs that say "Heaven Hill creates a better atmosphere." It was quite some time before I realized that Heaven Hill is only a bourbon sold in Kentucky, but the point is that Bardstown wants things to be calm and pleasant, and believes its own atmosphere to be very nice.

The past is persistent here, claiming attention even under the plates and coffee cups at the Old Talbott Tavern, which calls itself the Oldest Western Stagecoach in America. For there are paper place mats in the restaurant to remind you that the tavern and inn was opened in 1779 during the Revolutionary War when it was used by General George Rogers Clark as his base. Provisions and munitions were brought overland from Virginia and stored in the cellars. In 1797 the exiled Duke of Orleans, Louis Phillippe, stayed here, feeling rather ill, with a large entourage. Later, when he was King of the French, he sent paintings and church furniture to the Catholic Bishop of Bardstown. The gifts included two paintings by Van Eyck, two by Van Dyck, one Murillo and one Reubens, which were hung in St. Joseph's, the first Catholic cathedral west of the Alleghenies upon its completion in 1819.

Not far from the packages of Old Kentucky Bourbon Candy, $2.95 a pound, on sale in the Old Talbott Tavern, is an eight-inch steel saw which was one of four instruments used by Dr. Walter Brashear in 1806 in the first successful amputation of a leg at the hop joint. The patient was a seventeen-year-old boy whose leg was mangled. Nowhere is his name to be found.

In the Old Court House Square there is the plaque to the surgeon who amputated "without any precedent to guide him," and another to John Fitch, who died penniless in Bardstown, giving him credit for demonstrating a working steam-powered boat more than twenty years before Robert Fulton.

There is the slave block with the notice that upon this stone slaves were sold before emancipation in 1863, and a tribute to Thomas Nelson, a member of the Virginia House of Burgesses and, later, the Continental Congress, a signer of the Declaration of Independence and Commander of the Virginia Militia, who in 1781 was "commended for selfless patriotism in ordering guns to fire on his own home, the British headquarters at Yorktown, 1781." Here, too, is a cool bronze reminder that Braxton Bragg's Army of twenty-eight thousand men camped here from September 20 to October 3, 1862, moved to Harrodsburg, then met Buell's Union Army in the Battle of Perryville, October 8. The language on the plaques is dry, sparse, correct. It is not intended to move the imagination, to depress people or make them proud.

The newest bronze plaque, put in the Court House Square in May 1970, says this: IN MEMORY Dedicated to those men who gave their lives in Vietnam 1969 for the preservation of freedom.

There are seven names on it. Five were National Guardsmen from Battery C whose deaths came from an enemy attack before dawn at Fire Support Base Tomahawk, near Phu Bai, in South Vietnam. Four died there, in a place women could never imagine, but one burned man lived for another five days. In the long war, twelve men from the Bardstown area were killed. The first died in February 1966 and another later that year. Three died in 1968. The last two died on June 24 and 25, 1969. But there was never such a day as June 19, 1969. Some of the dead were from villages close to Bardstown: Cox's Creek, Willisburg, Carrolltown and New Haven. In Bardstown, when you ask about the dead, people nod and speak of the Simpson boy, the McIlvoy boy, the Collins boy; even if they cannot clearly see their faces now, there is a father or a cousin whom they know.

There was only one widow left. The four others remarried. It made her feel more alone. Her name was Deanna Durbin before she married Ronald Earl Simpson, who was killed at Fire Support Base Tomahawk. Other reporters had been to see her. She wanted no more of it; she did not want to see me. A child, whom she named Cheryl Lynn, was born five days before her husband's body was flown home and buried at Bardstown Cemetery on July Fourth in a military service. There were soldiers from Fort Knox, who fired their rifles, and Masons in their white aprons. At the cemetery she sat under the funeral tent, clutching a yellow handkerchief, and afterward she was led away to a car, unsteady, holding the folded American flag.

The young husband is remembered as an easygoing, pleasant man, tall and dark-haired, who did not complain or ask questions when he was in Vietnam. However, Specialist 4 Simpson had been one of the one hundred and five plaintiffs in a lawsuit argued by Nathan R. Zahm, a lawyer from California, that it was unconstitutional to send National Guards-

men overseas. The case was moving slowly to the Supreme
Court, but the unit was shipped overseas one day before the
court met on October 26, 1968.

Mrs. Simpson did not know what had happened to the case.
Nothing about the war, its purpose or its weaponry, or the arguments over it, seemed clear, only that she could not forgive
the death of her husband, and the words used to justify it did
not calm her at all.

Sometimes Deanna Simpson thought of leaving Bardstown,
but it was always the house on West Forrest Street that held
her there. Ronald Earl Simpson had built it for them, close to
the home of his parents, and they had lived there during that
brief marriage, until at the age of twenty-two he was killed.
She did not know right away that it happened on a Thursday
in a place near Phu Bai. She was not sure what a fire base was.
She knew nothing until the following Monday that he was
missing in action. The notification of his death came two days
later.

The government said it was shrapnel, Mrs. Simpson said.
"They bombed the place where he stayed and threw grenades
into it," she said.

Two British reporters from BBC had come to Bardstown,
where they were looked on kindly as somewhat exotic but af-
fable fellows. To this day Deanna Simpson remembers how
Peter Taylor, one of the BBC men, told her of one man in
Bardstown who had shocked the British visitors by his reaction to the casualties. It was First Sergeant Pat Sympson of the
National Guard in Bardstown, the man who knew the Bardstown boys in Battery C and first trained them, who had even
spent ten months on active duty in Vietnam, although he was
not at Fire Support Base Tomahawk when the North Vietnamese sappers came through the wire and, at 2 A.M., half
asleep, the young men of Bardstown learned, at last, the real
purpose of being in Battery C.

"That man, that sergeant, he said 'Well, somebody's got to
get killed in a war,' " Mrs. Simpson said on the telephone.

First Sergeant Sympson was sitting behind his desk in an
office at the National Guard building. He had his souvenirs
arranged around the rim of the desk. There was a grenade and
a defused shell casing, which the sergeant said was from a
"pineapple." This is a nickname for an antipersonnel weapon.

The pineapple was a very small bomb compared to others. It looked like a perforated Sterno can with six steel spring-locked fins on the top and two hundred and fifty pellets in the casing. An American plane could drop a thousand pineapples over an area the size of four football fields. In a single air strike two hundred and fifty thousand pellets were spewed in a horizontal pattern over the land below, hitting everything on the ground. A long time ago I learned about the pineapple, looking at a Vietnamese, lying on a straw mat, whose body seemed to have a thousand cuts.

The sergeant did not want me there. He did not pretend otherwise. There was only one peculiar thing about him: not the face that made me think of rope, not the hair cut so close to the scalp, not the boots shined to a ferocious glare. It was a pair of pinkish earplugs inside a tiny plastic vial that hung from a breast pocket of his fatigues. They are issued to artillery crews, but in Vietnam I did not see anyone who used them; the men simply covered their ears with their hands, except if they had to handle the warm canisters. The earplugs made it seem as if Sergeant Sympson was not sitting in an office in a quiet town pushing papers, but in the field, standing by the heavy 155s as they turned down to fire point-blank at attacking enemy positions.

Do you think that too much attention has been paid to the deaths in Bardstown? It was the only question I needed to ask him.

Sergeant Sympson did not speak; perhaps he had been told to shut up. He only nodded his head, not once, but twice, the big head dipping up and down very slowly, making sure I would have nothing to write down or quote. Then the sergeant, with the tiny pink earplugs hanging in the little vial on his chest, rose from his desk and made it clear my time was up, that I was not to loiter. He escorted me to the door, and stood there until I went away.

The Army was wise about death: it understood that the dying soldier, the dead man, could not give them as much trouble, present as many delicate problems, pose such embarrassment as the people who loved or were bound to him. In the Vietnam war they worked a procedure that was quite perfect for their purposes, a better system than the sending of a telegram, although much more troublesome for the military, more dreadful for the men who had to inform the families.

When a man died in Vietnam, his next of kin were notified in person. The notification teams of two men each were from the nearest Army base. An officer informed the family of a dead, or missing, officer, and noncommissioned officers told the families of men whose rank was below first lieutenant. The rules and guidelines were strict: be sure to identify the next of kin correctly, the wife or parents; always ask a woman to sit down in case she faints; if there are children around, take the mother to another room, so they will not learn the death of their father from a stranger; do not touch the woman even if she cries out or trembles terribly. Never touch her. Neighbors can be called in to assist in cases of collapse or hysteria. The fathers of the dead are not expected to go beserk, or weep uncontrollably, so they were not automatically asked to sit down. There were no prescribed formal expressions of sympathy aside from the opening sentence: "The Secretary of Army has requested me to inform you . . ." The idea was to convey regret—deep, official, masculine regret—but not a regret that sounded too regretful, too mushy, as if the death had been a waste.

From Winners and Losers, 1972.

QUESTIONS

(1) The author uses the first section of the essay to create a sense of the atmosphere in Bardstown? How would you describe this atmosphere? Why is the sense of the atmosphere so important to the point of the essay?

(2) How does the description of the widow, Deanna Simpson, emphasize the major theme of the essay?

(3) What is the sergeant's attitude toward the author? Why does he refuse to say anything to her?

(4) What is the connection between the author's description of the procedure for informing the next-of-kin and the comment in the beginning of the essay dealing with the government's concern over the reactions in small towns to the war?

(5) How would you describe the tone of the last sentence of the essay? What is the effect on the reader?

THE SENSE OF THE 70's

OF THE

WORKING

"What do you do for a living?" That's the polite, opening question and it usually gets a polite, closed answer. "How does it feel?" "What does your work do to you, to your sense of yourself?" Those are impolite questions.

Good writing is often based on impolite questions that demand to be answered. Some of them addressed to others, the most important to oneself. Good writing about working includes who is doing it as well as what is done.

There are thousands of boring jobs. People are not boring, however, if they will speak about not only what they do, but how it feels when they do it. What any person does is particular. Another person might not want to do it (fight fires in a tough neighborhood), or not be able to do it (practice the art of surgery). But everyone can share the joy and the tedium, the frustration and the triumph, that go with working. Good writing is spreading facts and sharing feelings. That's why the selections that follow offer personal descriptions of what it is like to be on the job. The writers want to reveal the "living" that is being done, the lives that are being made.

Joe Flaherty changed jobs: from Irish dock worker to Irish writer. Then he used the second to recapture the first before it disappeared completely. He recreates the mad world of Local 1268 beautifully because he allows himself to see the truth, but see it lovingly.

Studs Terkel is an artist with a tape recorder. His *Working* captures the many voices of America and shows that getting "ordinary" people to talk about themselves, about how they feel about what they do and why, makes an "extraordinary" book. Anyone who says, "I'm only a ———, so I have nothing interesting to say," could start by reading Brett Hauser's thrilling adventures in the supermarket.

Jimmy Breslin, himself one of America's fine writers, reveals the roots of *Roots* in an affectionate, funny tribute from
one worker to another. In the process he reveals some of the
tricks of the writing trade.

Gail Sheehy became interested in prostitution as a social
phenomenon—who made the money, who controlled whom—
and then discovered that it was also a human tragedy. Part of
her book *Hustling* is a shocking disclosure of the politics and
economics of the flesh game. But another part is about people.
The selection reprinted here is a description of one girl, a girl
who came from Minnesota to New York to work for a living.

Charles Colson went to Washington to work for a living.
Then he went to jail. In between he did odd jobs, one of
them detailed here. A hundred years from now, if historians
are still compiling books, in the full story of Watergate they
will include this brief and funny anecdote. It tells more about
the people involved and their working habits than yards of
ponderous commentary by those who thought high office somehow changed small men into great figures.

Dennis Smith's firehouse is different from Charles Colson's
White House, very different. So are the workers and the work
done. Obviously there is no more serious work than that done
in the centers of power in the great political capitals; unless,
perhaps, it is the daily struggle of life and death on the streets
of any city.

Richard Selzer clearly loves his work, even though it involves pain and makes demands that push him to his mental
and physical edge. Yet he loves it so much that he writes about
it so that others can understand the love and understand also
the self-doubt and wonderment that go with it.

Selzer says he agrees with Emerson, "that the poet is the
only true doctor." He would also probably agree with Robert
Frost:

> Only where love and need are one,
> And the work is play for mortal stakes,
> Is the deed ever really done
> For Heaven and the future's sakes.

> From "Two Tramps in Mud Time"

THE MEN OF LOCAL 1268, GOD BLESS THEM ALL, THE LAST OF A BAD BREED

JOE FLAHERTY

Come St. Patrick's Day, even the most cynical Irishman gets a tear in his eye, dons the green, gargles too much, and warbles a little.

Gone for the day are the memories of working-class poverty, priests in the confessional boxes giving with the third degree for capers committed between the sheets (if you grew up in the fifties, these usually were felonies with no accomplices), and the specter of the "good" nuns beating the eight-times multiplication tables into your head for the greater glory of God and academic oneupmanship over those heathen who attended P.S. 130. The dark Irish romanticize the day in somewhat the same way ex-GI's wax poetic about the great doses of clap they caught in France.

Luckily for me, when I think of the Irish, my mind wanders down to the water's edge and shapes up with memories of the men with whom I worked in ILA Local 1268 of the Grain Handlers' Association. But be at ease. What follows is not a tale of populist Celts brimming with *machismo,* like the foam on a pint of Guinness, but a rosary of labor miseries that would make the beads of the Sorrowful Mysteries look, by comparison, like the bricks on the yellow road to Oz.

I came to be a grain trimmer by heritage, not accident. My father, John, was once the president of the local, and his brother Christy succeeded my father after his death. My brother Billy (now a cop) was a trimmer, and my first cousin Bobby was a hatch boss. So when I was discharged from the Army at the age of twenty, my Flaherty blood beckoned me to seek my fortune in the dusty holds of grain ships.

In my memory the local had a membership of 100 men at most—all Irish, with the exception of a couple Swedes, which was considered the height of integration in those days. But in fairness to the democracy of 1268 we were avant-garde in some areas.

We recognized Gay Lib before it officially came into existence. One of our members sauntered up the pier daily in black chinos and turtleneck, treading softly on white tennies, and carrying his work gear in an airline shoulder bag. The old-timers used to peer down from the ship, muttering Hail Marys to the effect that the Celtic sperm must have been diluted by the salt water in the crossing. But he was judged by his work (which was splendid), not by his sexual preference, and there were no closets in 1268. Indeed, the opposite was true. One day our homosexual dockwalloper showed up wearing a head-band with a pigeon feather stuck into it to celebrate the acquisition of a new lover, an Indian ironworker. He also rewrote ILA history when he succeeded in getting Tough Tony Anastasia's medical clinic on Court Street to pay for his nose bob. Hernias and hemorrhoids you can understand, but the ILA financially floating a nose bob?

Our union hall was located on Coenties Slip over a saloon (mark the symbolism), and our meetings were held on Saturday mornings around ten o'clock. The strategy was that the members could drink for only two hours before the meeting, but it failed since everyone had usually been out until 4 A.M. the night before, and two hours of boozing was enough to turn their breaths to gasoline and their personalities to napalm.

While other locals argued about the impending threat of automation or better working conditions, 1268 concerned itself with much meatier matters. Some stalwart with his brain adrift in a 90-proof Galway Bay would seize the floor and recount how thirteen years before some boss hadn't hired him (even though he had seniority) just because he had been a "few minutes" late for the shape, and, indeed, the reason for his tardiness had been that he was at the bedside of his Aunt Peg, who had taken a stroke in far off Rockaway during the night. Shillelagh sentimentalism was the rule. Of course, the truth of the matter was that the bastard had been three hours late for the shape and so crippled that he had come up the dock looking like Toulouse-Lautrec.

This would lead to a countercharge that the "cheap cur" hadn't chipped in for the collection for Paddy So-and-So's family when he died and so didn't deserve a day's work, which

would segue into an oration from an "old-timer" devoted to
the proposition that the "Johnny-come-latelys" were running
the job, which ricocheted into a j-c-l stating that if it weren't
for the young holding up the end of the dilapidated old fogies,
not an ounce of grain would be shoveled out of a ship. The
crowning culmination was a punch-out, and our union would
go into "trusteeship" to be ruled by the overlords of the ILA.

Of course, that never worked either. The bad blood of numerous families flowed through our ranks, spiced with ould
sod geographical hatreds. The Galway men were considered
"clannish." The Tipperary contingent, not being bold men of
the west, were effete, and the Irish-Americans, like me, genetic
disappointments to be endured. ("Sure, you wouldn't put a
pimple on your father's ass.")

But the ILA officers tried to forge a brotherhood among us.
On one occasion the union president, Captain Bradley himself, graced our humble union hall and pleaded for unity, explaining that ours was the most troublesome local on the wa-
terfront, and we had only 100 members. He went on to say
that locals with thousands of members lived in harmony. Finally, in the spirit of ecumenism, he began to utter the Lord's
Prayer. But in the midst of his negotiations with the Snapper
in the Sky, one of our members bounced through the door like
a massé cueball and loudly urged the captain to commit an
act with himself that would have been difficult for a man
many years his junior to execute. Brotherhood in 1268. Better
to try forging a connubial contract between Ian Paisley and
Bernadette Devlin.

Loading and unloading grain from ships and barges was an
arduous and dangerous profession. One had to walk through
mounds of rye or corn up to his knees, an exercise which
makes running along a sandy beach seem like a cakewalk. The
dangerous aspect was provided by the grain dust that used to
fill the hold, making a smoke screen so thick you couldn't
recognize a fellow worker at twenty feet. Then there were the
occasional pier rats who were so big from eating the grain and
chasing it with the polluted Hudson they could have pulled
Cinderella's carriage without that transformation hocus-pocus.

So one would assume that it would take young Spartans to
work at this profession. But preconceived notions were always
shanghaied in Local 1268. The majority of the grain handlers

were men who nowadays would be relegated to pushing a shuf-
fleboard stick in Kern City.

Their training habits were simple. For decades they had
drunk anything that was bottled. (Once on an Italian ship
Scat Whalen drank cruets of white vinegar which he'd found
on the galley table and pronounced it "a great Dago table
wine.") To a man they worked in the dusty hold with pipes
clenched between their teeth, and their regular diet could
have killed a mule, never mind a man. At noon the old-timers
would open their brown paper bags and start with a raw
onion for an appetizer. (The onion, like garlic with vam-
pires, was supposed to ward off the evil of the dust.) The main
course most often was four meat sandwiches on Wonder Bread,
with the sliced meat cut to the thickness of a beaver's tail and
embalmed inside a quarter pound of butter.

Le Pavillon for the grain trimmers was Ma Kane's bar in
Jersey City ("Ah, Jaysus, a great feed"), where you were served
a slice of corned beef so thin you could read the *Morning Telegraph* through it and a boiled potato the size of an incubator
baby.

As a novice trimmer another phenomenon was revealed to
me: Nobody was called by his Christian name. The Irish, being frustrated curates, baptized everyone with a nickname.
My father, I learned, had been known as Young Bush which
roughly meant top man. My uncle was the Bull for his pen-
chant to bellow orders. Another old-timer was called Shag, because of his amorous adventures in the old country; another
Tokens, because he paid the snapper's subway fare. The first
day I shaped I was sporting a beard and was so christened.
"By Christ," crooned an old harp, "he looks like Haile Selassie."

Then there were the father-and-son teams. One man was the
Horse, so named in Orwellian fashion for his capacity for hard
work. Naturally, his son was called the Pony. There was Big
Joe Taylor, who looked like the eighth dwarf, and his son Little Joe, who looked like the World Trade Center.

We also had a resident spiritualist, the hatch boss, Paddy
the Priest, who could forgive anything but moral slackness. A
young dude named Ace Gillen was quick to notice this, and
when the going in the hold got tough, he would retreat to a
clear corner and pull out a newly acquired string of rosary
beads. When the Priest reprimanded him for dogging his

work, Gillen would piously apologize, saying he had only taken a blow "to say the Angelus." Paddy, touched to find such devotion in the young, would exhort the rest of the gang to work harder to take up the slack for the "saint" in the corner of the hatch.

The Pied Piper of the young men on the pier was the General, an old rogue of grand dimensions. He was a small man with a button nose, white hair, and the most beguiling blue eyes I've ever seen. The truth was an intrusion he couldn't bear, and over a drink he would reminisce: "To be young again and move across the desert with Lawrence of Arabia. Now there was a man! We left a river of blood behind us as long as the Nile." He could recite the seductive splendors of harem girls and desert goats in the same breath, and his sexual fantasies would make anything Girodias has published look pale. He swore that the eleventh-century Irish chieftain Brian Boru had been such a broth of a boyo that when he got an erection it reached all the way across the land, and it took the men of six counties to jerk him off.

The pious old-timers constantly advised us youngsters of his corrosive nature. He was aware of this and always managed to find a moment for revenge. He was a notorious drinker, and when any of them inquired about his wife, they always put "poor" in front of her name. To one patronizing inquiry he replied: "The woman is in desperate straits. I came home drunk last night, and she stole the last penny out of my pockets. When I woke up this morning, I was shocked to find I had a hard-on. The first one in three years. I walked out to the kitchen, showed it to her, then tucked it in my pants and left for work. The poor woman won't see the likes of it for another three years."

But the gem of our polluted ocean was our labor committee, or "comitty" as the old-timers called it, or "comedy" as the perceptive saw it. It was headed by John J. Moriarty aka Calhoun (after Amos and Andy's mouthpiece) and John "Woodenhead" Regan.

Calhoun was granted intellectual status, because he read publications other than the racing form and smoked Parliament cigarettes. He also separated himself from the vulgar herd by daintily sipping Irish Mist while we indulged with a ball and a beer. When he condescended to our level and talked about horse racing, he referred to the classic in Kentucky as the "Darby" and wanted to know if a particular charger's bloodlines went "back to Blenheim, that magnificent English sire." He not only read the minutes of our meetings but wrote them to boot, which put him in the enviable position of Joyce with *Finnegans Wake*. How could we remove him from his post? We wouldn't have known what had gone on in the union for the last ten years.

Woodenhead was our great orator. In his best moments, when he was calling for a strike, he shaped up to William Jennings Bryan in his Cross of Gold speech. And, my God, did we strike! We struck when there was a gossamer layer of snowflakes on the hatch covers (removing snow . . . wasn't in our contract); we struck when friends weren't hired or were fired; we struck for clean drinking water, though in memory I can't recall anyone putting that foreign substance to his lips. Yearly on opening day at Aqueduct the gang could be found draped over winches, claiming that scurvy had hit the ship (pity the paltry imagination of city employees with their "Asian flu" slowdowns).

Woodenhead scaled high C one freezing night when we were unloading a barge for the United States Lines. The barge sprung a leak that was considerably smaller than the dribble of a near empty seltzer bottle, but Woodenhead, running around the deck wildly, turned the incident into a maritime tragedy. "Get those men out of that barge," he screamed. "My God, get those men up before they drown like rats! This will be worse than the *Titanic!* Get the Fire Department. Never mind the Fire Department, get a priest!" Two hours later, after a U.S. Lines official plugged the hole (with Fleers Double Bubble Gum, I presume) we went back to work, a lot warmer, a lot drunker. Like Gepetto, I have loved woodenheads ever since.

As I noted, it was a dangerous thing to fire a worker, because of the threat of a strike. I once played the lead in such a drama. A ship was late docking in Jersey one morning, and we idled our waiting hours ("up the streets") in a bar. When we returned to the ship, all carrying much ballast, an old-timer fell overboard. My drunken brain reacted as if I were in a bad two-reeler, and I dived (wearing work boots) to the rescue. Calhoun, spotting the victim and the hero's condition, ran to the foc's'le, pulled out his rosary, and started to pray for the repose of our soused souls. I started to scream for a heaving line, but some good Samaritan flung me a breast line so heavy it could have been used as a leash for a dinosaur. The line hit us both on the head, and we sunk, and I began to wonder about the merits of sober discretion over drunken valor.

When they finally fished us out, I conked out for three hours and, when I woke up, was told I was being fired for drunkenness. The boys rallied around my flag and delivered an oration to my gallantry, spiced with the threat that the whole damn gang might retire to the high stool if I was fired. Needless to say, I remained on the payroll, and Calhoun, his rosary temporarily squandered, profusely kissed me, like a French general, on both cheeks.

But no story about Local 1268 would be complete without a mention of my first cousin Tommy "Lulu" Fleming. ("That one was well named," the Bull used to mutter.) We were unloading a "dead" (mothballed) grain ship in Brooklyn, and Lulu was fired for that sin the Irish flesh is heir to. But true to his nature, Lulu didn't take it lying down. In fact, he rewrote employer-employee relations forever.

After he left the ship, we heard this strange whacking sound. When we looked over the side, it was even stranger than we'd thought. Lulu was chopping the lines that held the ship to the pier with a fire ax! The thought of a gang of grain trimmers afloat at sea in a ship without engines, endlessly damned to the wavy limbo of the Flying Dutchman, was enough to have the employer "reassess" his position. . . .

But one day he went too far. Lulu was working a hatch with Salty Murphy, who had gained Brooklyn immortality by swimming bare-assed with the seals in Prospect Park Zoo. Lulu and Salty had been under suspicion all day, because every time they descended the ladder the contents of their pockets chimed like the Bells of St. Mary, and it was finally discovered they were working on a wine load. Salty was spraying grain from the open part of the hatch under the decks where Lulu was directing the stream. All that could be heard from the hatch was the sound of "dead soldiers" breaking and loud cursing. When Lulu didn't appear from between decks for about a half hour, the boss inquired where he was, and Salty matter-of-factly replied: "I buried the bastard."

The ship immediately took on the appearance of a January white sale at Korvette's. The flow of grain was stopped, and everyone charged down into the hold with hand shovels to dig Lulu out of his grainy crypt. After an endless time of futile digging, dark imaginings of breaking the "news" to the family, and scores of mental mass cards being written out, lo and behold, the dust cleared. As if the giant stone had been rolled back, there in a far corner of the hatch sat the resurrected Lulu, sipping muscatel and laughing maniacally. Like the Father and His Son, Salty and Lulu ascended the ladder to take body and spirit to the heavenly reaches of a Jersey saloon, a chorus of curses giving them wings. But such exploits must be put in perspective. As Tough Tony Anastasia once said: "That goddamn whiskey mixes with the dust in their Irish heads and drives them all mad."

It is all gone now. Grain hasn't been loaded in this harbor for years. In a way it's a shame. I've never worked at a job I liked so much or with men I loved more. Every day was a trip to the circus, and never will such grand clowns be assembled under one tent again. As Frank Skeffington said in *The Last Hurrah,* "How do you thank a man for a million laughs?"

But it is possible the end was fitting. In the prissy labor field of today, composed of slick four-flushers and punky bureaucrats, these men would be lost. Like Sam Peckinpah's cowboys, their time has passed. These were the urban cowboys.

So may God bless them this St. Paddy's Day wherever they're scattered. And forgive and understand them, too. Their sins were unavoidable—like Willie Loman's, they came with the territory. As old Mike Regan used to say ruefully: "Ah, they're the last of a bad breed."

From Chez Joey, 1974.

QUESTIONS

(1) How do the first two paragraphs set the tone for the rest of the essay?

(2) The basic technique of the essay is that of wild comparisons. Which are the most effective? Does he make the life of

the small local seem equal to a much larger institution—a country, for example?

(3) Is his story really a "rosary of labor miseries"? What else is it? Why is the image of a "rosary" very effective for unifying these memories?

(4) What kinds of contradictions (such as Gay Lib) does he describe in order to make the local lively and interesting?

(5) Is there anything in the essay to suggest that Flaherty is like an anthropologist describing a rare tribe to the world at large? Or is he more like an archaeologist? Consider his attention to the local's religion, language, and culinary customs. Does Flaherty want this effect? Does he want it to be noticed?

(6) Do Flaherty's obvious exaggerations make his story more or less believable? Do contradictions and inconsistencies seem more believable than consistencies?

(7) "It is all gone now." That's how Flaherty begins his wrap-up. How has he prepared the reader for his conclusion? How do you feel about the disappearance of Local 1268?

BRETT HAUSER: SUPERMARKET BOX BOY

STUDS TERKEL

He is seventeen. He had worked as a box boy at a supermarket in a middle-class suburb on the outskirts of Los Angeles. "People come to the counter and you put things in their bags for them. And carry things to their cars. It was a grind."

You have to be terribly subservient to people: "Ma'am, can I take your bag?" "Can I do this?" It was at a time when the grape strikers were passing out leaflets. They were very respectful. People'd come into the check stand, they'd say, "I just bought grapes for the first time because of those idiots outside." I had to put their grapes in the bag and thank them for coming and take them outside to the car. Being subservient made me very resentful.

It's one of a chain of supermarkets. They're huge complexes with bakeries in them and canned music over those loud-speakers—Muzak. So people would relax while they stopped. They played selections from *Hair*. They'd play "Guantana-mera," the Cuban Revolution song. They had *Soul on Ice,* the Cleaver book, on sale. They had everything dressed up and very nice. People wouldn't pay any attention to the music. They'd go shopping and hit their kids and talk about those idiots passing out anti-grape petitions.

Everything looks fresh and nice. You're not aware that in the back room it stinks and there's crates all over the place and the walls are messed up. There's graffiti and people are swearing and yelling at each other. You walk through the door, the music starts playing, and everything is pretty. You talk in hushed tones and are very respectful.

You wear a badge with your name on it. I once met some-one I knew years ago. I remembered his name and said, "Mr. Castle, how are you?" We talked about this and that. As he left, he said, "It was nice talking to you, Brett." I felt great, he remembered me. Then I looked down at my name plate. Oh shit. He didn't remember me at all, he just read the name plate. I wish I put "Irving" down on my name plate. If he'd have said, "Oh yes, Irving, how could I forget you . . . ?" I'd have been ready for him. There's nothing personal here.

You have to be very respectful to everyone—the customers, to the manager, to the checkers. There's a sign on the cash register that says: Smile at the customer. Say hello to the cus-tomer. It's assumed if you're a box boy, you're really there 'cause you want to be a manager some day. So you learn all the little things you have absolutely no interest in learning.

The big things there is to be an assistant manager and even-tually manager. The male checkers had dreams of being man-ager, too. It was like an internship. They enjoyed watching how the milk was packed. Each manager had his own domain. There was the ice cream manager, the grocery manager, the dairy case manager . . . They had a sign in the back: Be

good to your job and your job will be good to you. So you take
an overriding concern on how the ice cream is packed. You
just die if something falls off a shelf. I saw so much crap there
I just couldn't take. There was a black boy, an Oriental box
boy, and a kid who had a Texas drawl. They needed the job
to subsist. I guess I had the luxury to hate it and quit.

When I first started there, the manager said, "Cut your
hair. Come in a white shirt, black shoes, a tie. Be here on
time." You get there, but he isn't there. I just didn't know
what to do. The checker turns around and says, "You new?
What's your name?" "Brett." "I'm Peggy." And that's all they
say and they keep throwing this down to you. They'll say,
"Don't put it in that, put it in there." But they wouldn't
help you.

You had to keep your apron clean. You couldn't lean back
on the railings. You couldn't talk to the checkers. You couldn't
accept tips. Okay, I'm outside and I put it in the car. For a
lot of people, the natural reaction is to take out a quarter and
give it to me. I'd say, "I'm sorry, I can't." They'd get offended.
When you give someone a tip, you're sort of suave. You take a
quarter and you put it in their palm and you expect them to
say, "Oh, thanks a lot." When you say, "I'm sorry, I can't,"
they feel a little put down. They say, "No one will know."
And they put it in your pocket. You say, "I really can't." It
gets to a point where you have to do physical violence to a
person to avoid being tipped. It was not consistent with the
store's philosophy of being cordial. Accepting tips was a cordial thing and made the customer feel good. I just couldn't
understand the incongruity. One lady actually put it in my
pocket, got in the car, and drove away. I would have had to
throw the quarter at her or eaten it or something.

When it got slow, the checkers would talk about funny
things that happened. About Us and Them. Us being the people who worked there, Them being the stupid fools who didn't
know where anything was—just came through and messed
everything up and shopped. We serve them but we don't
like them. We know where everything is. We know what time
the market closes and they don't. We know what you do with
coupons and they don't. There was a camaraderie of sorts. It
wasn't healthy, though. It was a put-down of the others.

There was this one checker who was absolutely vicious. He

took great delight in making every little problem into a major crisis from which he had to emerge victorious. A customer would give him a coupon. He'd say, "You were supposed to give me that at the beginning." She'd say, "Oh, I'm sorry." He'd say, "Now I gotta open the cash register and go through the whole thing. Madam, I don't watch out for every customer. I can't manage your life." A put-down.

It never bothered me when I would put something in the bag wrong. In the general scheme of things, in the large questions of the universe, putting a can of dog food in the bag wrong is not of great consequence. For them it was.

There were a few checkers who were nice. There was one that was incredibly sad. She could be unpleasant at times, but she talked to everybody. She was one of the few people who genuinely wanted to talk to people. She was saying how she wanted to go to school and take courses so she could get teaching credit. Someone asked her, "Why don't you?" She said, "I have to work here. My hours are wrong. I'd have to get my hours changed." They said, "Why don't you?" She's worked there for years. She had seniority. She said, "Jim won't let me." Jim was the manager. He didn't give a damn. She wanted to go to school, to teach, but she can't because every day she's got to go back to the supermarket and load groceries. Yet she wasn't bitter. If she died a checker and never enriched her life, that was okay, because those were her hours.

She was extreme in her unpleasantness and her consideration. Once I dropped some grape juice and she was squawking like a bird. I came back and mopped it up. She kept saying to me, "Don't worry about it. It happens to all of us." She'd say to the customers, "If I had a dime for all the grape juice I dropped . . ."

Jim's the boss. A fish-type handshake. He was balding and in his forties. A lot of managers are these young, clean-shaven, neatly cropped people in their twenties. So Jim would say things like "groovy." You were supposed to get a ten-minute break every two hours. I lived for that break. You'd go outside, take your shoes off, and be human again. You had to request it. And when you took it, they'd make you feel guilty.

You'd go up and say, "Jim, can I have a break?" He'd say, "A break? You want a break? Make it a quick one, nine and a half minutes." Ha ha ha. One time I asked the assistant manager, Henry. He was even older than Jim. "Do you think I can have a break?" He'd say, "You got a break when you were hired." Ha ha ha. Even when they joked it was a put-down.

The guys who load the shelves are a step above the box boys. It's like upperclassmen at an officer candidate's school. They would make sure that you conformed to all the prescribed rules, because they were once box boys. They know what you're going through, your anxieties. But instead of making it easier for you, they'd make it harder. It's like a military institution.

I kept getting box boys who came up to me, "Has Jim talked to you about your hair? He's going to because it's getting too long. You better get it cut or grease it back or something." They took delight in it. They'd come to me before Jim had told me. Everybody was out putting everybody down . . .

From *Working*, 1972.

QUESTIONS

(1) Do you think Brett Hauser's first sentence in the selection was the first thing he said to Terkel? Is it a good opening?

(2) What is he saying about the customers and the grapes? How would a more formal, written essay have added details?

(3) How does Brett Hauser want you to feel about the supermarket based on the details given in paragraphs two and three? What does he want you to feel about him?

(4) Without necessarily meaning to, does Hauser make you feel that the unpleasant characteristics of his job are characteristic of all jobs?

(5) Why is the sentence, "I guess I had the luxury to hate it and quit," so important? Would the tone of the essay have been different if he didn't have that luxury? Would your reactions be different? How?

(6) Is the description of the tipping fiasco meant to be funny? How else could it be described?

(7) When Hauser divides the world into US and THEM with which group does he want the reader to identify? Can you identify with both?

(8) "Everybody was out putting everybody down. . . ." Why? What was there about the work, its frustrations and limitations, that encouraged the exercise of petty power?

(9) Would you like to work in the supermarket? Would you like to work with Brett Hauser?

BARBARA HERRICK: EXECUTIVE

STUDS TERKEL

She is thirty; single. Her title is script supervisor/producer at a large advertising agency; working out of its Los Angeles office. She is also a vice president. Her accounts are primarily in food and cosmetics. "There's a myth: a woman is expected to be a food writer because she is assumed to know those things and a man doesn't. However, some of the best copy on razors and Volkswagens has been written by women."

She has won several awards and considerable recognition for her commercials. "You have to be absolutely on target, dramatic and fast. You have to be aware of legal restrictions. The FTC gets tougher and tougher. You must understand budgetary matters: will it cost a million or can it be shot in a studio in one day?"

She came off a Kansas farm, one of four daughters. "During high school, I worked as a typist and was an extremely good one. I was compulsive about doing every tiny job very well." She graduated from the University of Missouri. According to Department of Labor statistics, she is in the upper one percent bracket of working women.

In her Beverly Hills apartment are paintings, sculpted

works, recordings (classic, folk, jazz, and rock), and many
books, most of them obviously well thumbed.

Men in my office doing similar work were being promoted,
given raises and titles. Since I had done the bulk of the work,
I made a stand and was promoted too. I needed the title, because clients figured that I'm just a face-man.

A face-man is a person who looks good, speaks well, and
presents the work. I look well, I speak well, and I'm pleasant
to have around after the business is over with—if they acknowledge me in business. We go to the lounge and have
drinks. I can drink with the men but remain a lady. (Laughs.)

That's sort of my tacit business responsibility, although this
has never been said to me directly. I know this is why I travel
alone for the company a great deal. They don't anticipate any
problems with my behavior. I equate it with being the good
nigger.

On first meeting, I'm frequently taken for the secretary, you
know, traveling with the boss. I'm here to keep somebody
happy. Then I'm introduced as the writer. One said to me
after the meeting was over and the drinking had started,
"When I first saw you, I figured you were a—you know. I never
knew you were the person *writing* this all the time." (Laughs.)
Is it a married woman working for extra money? Is it a lesbian? Is it some higher-up's mistress?

I'm probably one of the ten highest paid people in the
agency. It would cause tremendous hard feelings if, say, I
work with a man who's paid less. If a remark is made at a
bar—"You make so much money, you could buy and sell me"—
I toss it off, right? He's trying to find out. He can't equate me
as a rival. They wonder where to put me, they wonder what
my salary is.

Buy and sell me—yeah, there are a lot of phrases that show
the reversal of roles. What comes to mind is swearing at a
meeting. New clients are often very uptight. They feel they
can't make any innuendoes that might be suggestive. They
don't know how to treat me. They don't know whether to acknowledge me as a woman or as another neuter person who's
doing a job for them.

The first time, they don't look at me. At the first three
meetings of this one client, if I would ask a direction question,

they would answer and look at my boss or another man in the room. Even around the conference table. I don't attempt to be—the glasses, the bun, and totally asexual. That isn't the way I am. It's obvious that I'm a woman and enjoy being a woman. I'm not overly provocative either. It's the thin, good nigger line that I have to toe.

I've developed a sixth sense about this. If a client will say, "Are you married?" I will often say yes, because that's the easiest way to deal with him if he needs that category for me. If it's more acceptable to him to have a young, attractive married woman in a business position comparable to his, terrific. It doesn't bother me. It makes me safer. He'll never be challenged. He can say, "She'd be sensational. I'd love to get her. I could show her what a real man is, but she's married." It's a way out for him.

Or there's the mistress thing: well, she's sleeping with the boss. That's acceptable to them. Or she's a frustrated, compulsive castrator. That's a category. Or lesbian. If I had short hair, wore suits, and talked in a gruff voice, that would be more acceptable than I am. It's when I transcend their labels, they don't quite know what to do. If someone wants a quick label and says, "I'll bet you're a big women's libber, aren't you?" I say, "Yeah, yeah." They have to place me.

I travel a lot. That's what gets very funny. We had a meeting in Montreal. It was one of those bride's magazines, honeymoon-type resorts, with heart-shaped beds and the heated pool. I was there for three days with nine men. All day long we were enclosed in this conference room. The agency account man went with me. I was to talk about the new products, using slides and movies. There were about sixty men in the conference room. I had to leave in such a hurry, I still had my gaucho pants and boots on.

The presentation went on for an hour and a half. There was tittering and giggling for about forty minutes. Then you'd hear the shift in the audience. They got interested in what I was saying. Afterwards they had lunch sent up. Some of them never did talk to me. Others were interested in my life. They would say things like, "Have you read *The Sensuous Woman?*" (Laughs.) They didn't really want to know. If they were even more obvious, they probably would have said,

"Say, did you hear the one about the farmer's daughter?" I'd have replied, "Of course, I'm one myself."

The night before, there was a rehearsal. Afterwards the account man suggested we go back to the hotel, have a nightcap, and get to bed early. It was a 9:00 A.M. meeting. We were sitting at the bar and he said, "Of course, you'll be staying in my room." I said, "What? I have a room." He said, "I just assumed. You're here and I'm here and we're both grown up." I said, "You assumed? You never even asked me whether I wanted to." My feelings obviously meant nothing to him. Apparently it was what you *did* if you're out of town and the woman is anything but a harelip and you're ready to go. His assumption was incredible.

We used to joke about him in the office. We'd call him Mr. Straight, because he was Mr. Straight. Very short hair, never grew sideburns, never wore wide ties, never, never swore, never would pick up an innuendo, super-super-conservative. No one would know, you see?

Mr. Straight is a man who'd never invite me to have a drink after work. He would never invite me to lunch alone. Would never, never make an overture to me. It was simply the fact that we were out of town and who would know? That poor son of a bitch had no notion what he was doing to my ego. I didn't want to destroy his. We had to work together the next day and continue to work together.

The excuse I gave is one I use many times. "Once when I was much younger and innocent, I slept with an account man. The guy turned out to be a bastard. I got a big reputation and he made my life miserable because he had a loose mouth. And even though you're a terrifically nice guy and I'd like to sleep with you, I feel I can't. It's my policy. I'm older and wiser now. I don't do it. You have to understand that." It worked. I could never say to him, "You don't even understand how you insulted me."

It's the always-having-to-please conditioning. I don't want to make any enemies. Only of late, because I'm getting more secure and I'm valued by the agency, am I able to get mad at men and say, "Fuck off!" But still I have to keep egos unruffled, smooth things over . . . I still work with him and he never mentioned it again.

He'll occasionally touch my arm or catch my eye: We're really sympatico, aren't we baby? There may be twelve men and me sitting at a meeting and they can't call on one of the girls or the receptionist, he'd say, "Let's have some coffee, Barbara. Make mine black." I'm the waitress. I go do it because it's easier than to protest. If he'd known my salary is more than his I doubt that he'd have acted that way in Denver—or here.

Part of the resentment toward me and my salary is that I don't have a mortgage on a home in the Valley and three kids who have to go to private schools and a wife who spends at Saks, and you never know when you're going to lose your job in this business. Say, we're having a convivial drink among peers and we start grousing. I'm not allowed to grouse with the best of them. They say, "Oh, you? What do you need money for? You're a single woman. You've got the world by the balls." I hear that all the time.

If I'm being paid a lot of attention to, say by someone to whom I'm attracted, and we've done a job and we're in New York together for a week's stretch, we're in the same hotel, suppose I want to sleep with him? Why not? Here's my great double standard. You never hear it said about a man in my capacity—"He sleeps around." It would only be to his glory. It's expected, if he's there with a model, starlet, or secretary. In my case, I constantly worry about that. If I want to, I must be very careful. That's what I'm railing against.

This last shoot, it was an exasperating shot. It took hours. We were there all day. It was exhausting, frustrating. Between takes, the camera man, a darling man, would come back to where I was standing and put his arms around me. I didn't think anything of it. We're hardly fucking on the set. It was his way of relaxing. I heard a comment later that night from the director: "You ought to watch your behavior on the set with the camera man." I said, *"Me* watch it? Fuck that! Let *him* watch it." He was hired by me. I could fire him if I didn't like him. Why *me,* you see? *I* have to watch.

Clients. I get calls in my hotel room: "I want to discuss something about production today that didn't go right." I know what that means. I try to fend it off. I'm on this tightrope. I don't want to get into a drunken scene ever with a client and to literally shove him away. That's not going to do me any good. The only smart thing I can do is avoid that sort of scene. The way I avoid it is by suggesting an early morning breakfast meeting. I always have to make excuses: "I drank too much and my stomach is really upset, so I couldn't do it right now. We'll do it in the morning." Sometimes I'd like to say, "Fuck off, I know what you want."

"I've had a secretary for the last three years. I hesitate to use her . . . I won't ask her to do typing. It's hard for me to use her as I was used. She's bright and could be much more than a secretary. So I give her research assignments, things to look up, which might be fun for her. Rather than just say, 'Here, type this.'

"I'm an interesting figure to her. She says, 'When I think of Women's Lib I don't think of Germaine Greer or Kate Millett. I think of you.' She sees my life as a lot more glamorous than it really is. She admires the externals. She admires the apartment, the traveling. We shot two commercials just recently, one in Mexico, one in Nassau. Then I was in New York to edit them. That's three weeks. She takes care of all my travel details. She knows the company gave me an advance of well over a thousand dollars. I'm put up in fine hotels, travel first class. I can spend ninety dollars at a dinner for two or three. I suppose it is something—little Barbara from a Kansas farm, and Christ! look where I am. But I don't think of it, which is a funny thing."

It used to be the token black at a big agency was very safe because he always had to be there. Now I'm definitely the token woman. In the current economic climate, I'm one of the few writers at my salary level getting job offers. Unemployment is high right now among people who do what I do. Yet I get calls: "Will you come and write on feminine hygiene products?" Another, involving a food account: "We need you, we'll pay you thirty grand and a contract. Be the answer for Such-an-such Foods." I'm ideal because I'm young enough to have four or five solid years of experience behind me. I know how to handle myself or I wouldn't be where I am.

I'm very secure right now. But when someone says to me,

"You don't have to worry," he's wrong. In a profession where I absolutely cannot age, I cannot be doing this at thirty-eight. For the next years, until I get too old, my future's secure in a very insecure business. It's like a race horse or a show horse. Although I'm holding the job on talent and responsibility, I got here partly because I'm attractive and it's a big kick for a client to know that for three days in Montreal there's going to be this young brunette, who's very good, mind you. I don't know how they talk about me, but I'd guess: "She's very good, but to look at her you'd never know it. She's a knockout."

I have a fear of hanging on past my usefulness. I've seen desperate women out of jobs, who come around with their samples, which is the way all of us get jobs. A lot of women have been cut. Women who had soft jobs in an agency for years and are making maybe fifteen thousand. In the current slump, this person is cut and some bright young kid from a college, who'll work for seven grand a year, comes in and works late every night.

Talk about gaps. In a room with a twenty-two-year-old, there are areas in which I'm altogether lost. But not being a status-quo-type person, I've always thought ahead enough to keep pace with what's new. I certainly don't feel my usefulness as a writer is coming to an end. I'm talking strictly in terms of physical aging (Laughs.) It's such a young business, not just the consumer part. It's young in terms of appearances. The client expects agency people, especially on the creative end, to dress a certain way, to be very fashionable. I haven't seen many women in any executive capacity age gracefully.

The bellbottoms, the beads, beards, and sideburns, that's the easy, superficial way to feel part of the takeover culture. It's true also in terms of writing. What kind of music do you put behind the commercial? It's ridiculous to expect a sheltered forty-two-year-old to anticipate progressive rock. The danger of aging, beyond touch, out of reach with the younger market . . .

The part I hate—it's funny. (Pause.) Most people in the business are delighted to present their work and get praise for it—and the credit and the laughter and everything in the commercial. I always hate that part. Deep down, I feel demeaned. Don't question the adjectives, don't argue, if it's a cologne or a shampoo. I know, 'cause I buy 'em myself. I'm the

BARBARA HERRICK: EXECUTIVE

biggest sucker for buying an expensively packaged hoax thing. Face cream at eight dollars. And I sell and convince.

I used Erik Satie music for a cologne thing. The clients didn't know Satie from Roger Williams. I'm very good at what I do, dilettantism. I go into my act: we call it dog and pony time, show time, tap dance. We laugh about it. He says, "Oh, that's beautiful, exactly right. How much will it cost us?" I say, "The music will cost you three grand. Those two commercials you want to do in Mexico and Nassau, that's forty grand. There's no way I can bring it in for less." I'm this young woman, saying, "Give me forty thousand dollars of your money and I will go away to Mexico and Nassau and bring you back a commercial and you'll love it." It's blind faith.

Do I ever question what I'm selling? (A soft laugh.) All the time. I know a writer who quit a job equivalent to mine. She was making a lot of money, well thought of. She was working on a consumer finance account. It's blue collar and black. She made this big stand. I said to her, in private, "I agree with you, but why is this your test case? You've been selling a cosmetic for years that is nothing but mineral oil and women are paying eight dollars for it. You've been selling a cake mix that you know is so full of preservatives that it would kill every rat in the lab. Why all of a sudden . . . ?"

If you're in the business, you're in the business, the fucking business! You're a hustler. But because you're witty and glib . . . I've never pretended this is the best writing I can do. Every advertising writer has a novel in his drawer. Few of them ever do it.

I don't think what I do is necessary or that it performs a service. If it's a very fine product—and I've worked on some of those—I love it. It's when you get into that awful area of hope, cosmetics—you're just selling image and a hope. It's like the arthritis cure or cancer—quackery. You're saying to a lady, "Because this oil comes from the algae at the bottom of the sea, you're going to have a timeless face." It's a crock of shit! I know it's part of my job, I do it. If I made the big stand my friend made, I'd lose my job. Can't do it. I'm expected to write whatever assignment I'm given. It's whorish. I haven't written enough to know what kind of writer I am. I suspect, rather than a writer, I'm a good reader. I think I'd make a good editor. I have read so many short stories that I bet you I could turn out a better anthology than anybody's done yet, in certain categories. I remember, I appreciate, I have a feeling I could . . .

POSTSCRIPT: *Shortly afterward she was battling an ulcer.*

From *Working*, 1972.

QUESTIONS

(1) How does Terkel's introduction set the scene for Barbara Herrick's description of herself?

(2) Why does Barbara Herrick repeat the phrase "good nigger" in regard to herself on the job? How do you feel about her using that phrase?

(3) Is the subject of the selection Barbara Herrick's work? If yes, what specifically about her work? If no, what is the center of her statement?

(4) "Do I ever question what I'm selling?" Is it herself she's selling?

(5) At the end of the selection, how do you feel about advertising? Do you have any feelings about female executives? How do you feel about the person, Barbara Herrick?

(6) Is the *Postscript* surprising? What does it convey to you in addition to the simple medical fact? Of what is the fact a symbol?

ALEX HALEY AND THE ROOTS OF *ROOTS*

JIMMY BRESLIN

In August of 1964, Ken McCormick, the chief editor of Doubleday, the book publishers, took a writer named Alex Haley to
lunch at a place called Le Marmiton in Manhattan. One of the
great publishing customs is that nearly all business is conducted over leisurely, expensive luncheons, for which the publisher always pays. Haley at this time was a regular at such
luncheons, and he always ate powerfully before doing any
talking. If he did not do this, his stomach would get mad
at him.

McCormick brought along his secretary, Lisa Drew, 24.

To justify his free lunch on this day, Haley not only had an
idea for a book, but he had the title: "Before This Anger."
The civil unrest in America was increasing and nobody at the
table knew where it would lead. It was Haley's idea to take
another time, the South of the 1920s, 1930s, and 1940s when
people were able to get along because each knew his place, and
tell of it. In its own odd, unfair way the system worked, Haley
explained. He wanted to write of it through his family in
Henning, Tenn., who survived through decades when blacks
lived with the word "boy" because they knew of no other way.

The idea did not whisper of great success as McCormick
thought about it over coffee. The book would be in great contrast to the present, the 1960s, and perhaps readers wouldn't
be so interested in it. Still, McCormick felt it was a book which
should be done. One function of book publishing is to take a
piece of life at a particular time, pickle it and leave it as a
record for those who follow.

Then there was Haley. If he wanted to do the book, let him
do it. Probably the best way to encourage a writer is to tell
him to write what he wants. McCormick's interest in Haley
was for more than a single book. Haley had spent 20 years as
a cook in the Coast Guard. His style was developed writing
love letters home for people on his ship who were illiterate.

Haley wrote a story about one series of letters, written for the chief cook, and it was bought by the Reader's Digest. Anybody in the book business who saw the story did not forget it, nor did they forget the name of the author.

Now, at the end of the lunch, Alex came in for the score, the advance. McCormick mentioned a figure of around $7,500. Alex soared: Anything in four figures was a victory.

Alex went away and began working on his book. However, as the advance disappeared, Alex felt in need of many editorial consultations over lunches. One day, McCormick said to his secretary, Lisa Drew, "I'm tied up today. Why don't you take Alex to lunch? He's hungry, and you could find out how things are going with the book."

Lisa Drew went to lunch with Haley at the Chateau Madrid. Haley began talking of expanding on the book idea. At first, he was going back past the 1920s, all the way to a great-grandfather who was alive at the time of the Emancipation Proclamation. Then at another few luncheons, Haley told Lisa Drew that he was going back beyond his family in this country. "I'm going right to the beginning, to Africa."

When she got back to the office at 3 o'clock from one of them, she told McCormick, "If he can do what he's telling me, he's got the greatest book of all time."

He also had what most writers consider to be the No. 1 problem in world history: being broke. By 1967, three years after agreeing to do the book, Alex Haley was in Rome, N.Y., writing the autobiography of Malcolm X, and inventing a thing called the Playboy Interview. He also could be found on the stage at Manhattan College's spring lecture series, or at Penn State's winter lecture series or at any other place that would put up money to hear a writer speak.

These activities usually form the basis for the mysterious writer's block. The writer says the words are frozen in his brain and he cannot produce. What he actually means is that his check to the landlord failed to clear the hurdle and he has to be at Ohio Wesleyan tonight, for a two-hour talk, clearing $700, or he will be living in the streets, and not for research.

The year 1967 became 1970. Lisa Drew now was an editor at Doubleday. In the fall of that year she went to hear Alex speak at the Library of Congress. Instead of watching part of

Haley's life drip away on a stage in front of a bored audience, Lisa Drew became mesmerized by the lecture. It was the basic story of how Alex Haley had gathered material for this book he said he was writing. When Lisa came back to New York, she told everybody how powerful the material was. "The original advance went up," she says. "I think in the end we had $50,000 invested."

Haley in San Francisco now, calling Lisa and saying, "Baby, it's coming next week. A whole batch of copy." Next week came and went. Then Haley would put in another call and say, "I'm just retyping it now and sending it in." These are known as "confidence calls."

In October of 1973, 900 pages arrived in the mail at Doubleday. "After nine years I didn't believe it was on hand," Lisa Drew says. "It was too long, it was undisciplined and it was magnificent."

Lisa called in and asked when more pages could come. "Oh, you could have tons of them right now," Alex said. "But you see I'm writing in pieces, some early scenes and then some in the middle, and none of it would make any sense to you." Nobody writes a book that way. But writers lie this way when they've been too lazy to work.

One year later, in 1974, she finally received another 200 pages and in February of 1975, Haley called and set a deadline. "By June 30, this book will be finished." In May, Lisa Drew called and asked how realistic was the June date. "If we had it by then, it would be great because we could have the book out for the bicentennial," she said.

"Oh, that'll be great. Don't worry, you'll have it," Haley said.

On June 15, two weeks before the deadline, Alex Haley called Lisa Drew. "I'm going to make it right on time, don't worry," he said. When she suggested that he come to New York for a week of editing, Haley said, "Well, why don't you come down here?" He was in Jamaica.

On June 30, Lisa Drew arrived at Haley's house in Jamaica. She began to go over the manuscript. "You read it" Alex said. "I've got a little fixing to do." He began typing as quickly as he could. Lisa Drew spent four days going over the manuscript. And Alex Haley sat at the typewriter for incredibly long stretches.

Finally, Lisa Drew was finished with what she had: about 60 percent of the book. She walked up to Haley, whose fingers were flying at the typewriter.

"Have any more?" she said.

He handed her the 20 pages he had done overnight.

"That's fine, now where's the bulk of it?" she said.

"Well, it's coming," Alex Haley said.

She stopped him. "When are you really going to finish?"

"September," Alex Haley said.

When Lisa Drew left for New York, Haley passed out in bed. He got up and sent 100 pages to Doubleday in July, another 100 in August, and in September, October and November. In the first week of December the last 100 pages arrived.

Haley was brought to New York and he was given a couple of days to sit in the Doubleday offices and go over the edited manuscript. The production schedule was so tight that Lisa Drew made Haley swear he would only correct errors. He would add nothing new. She gave him the copy and went into her office. Haley disappeared with the manuscript. She could not locate him on the phone. Five days later, a package for Lisa Drew was left on the wrong floor at Doubleday. When she received it—Haley's manuscript—she found the last 187 pages had been rewritten.

"The production people were wonderful in this instance," she said. "They made the change."

It was good they did. For the last 187 pages are perhaps the most powerful part of this book, a book which started out as "Before This Anger" and drew a $7,500 advance and ended up as *Roots* and will bring Alex Haley, besides satisfaction, money in any neighborhood you care to mention. But start at $10 million.

Lisa Drew, who was a 24-year-old secretary when it started, was found over a drink last week.

"So now you're a big shot," she was told.

"No, I'm just older," she said. She is now 37.

From New York Daily News, 1977.

QUESTIONS

(1) Breslin says: "One function of book publishing is to take a piece of life at a particular time, pickle it and leave it as

a record for those who follow." Is that a function of or a reason for writing? Does he fulfill that function in this column?

(2) What kinds of acts of faith went into writing *Roots?*

(3) Is Breslin's definition of a writer's block a good one? What is your version of the writer's block?

(4) In what ways does Breslin use the techniques of the big book he is describing in his short essay? Does he reveal the roots of *Roots?*

MINNESOTA MARSHA

GAIL SHEEHY

She was a white girl saddled with an
illegitimate child. In Hell's Bedroom,
most girls are.
She had a goal—a business or a home
of her own someday. Most girls do.
She has been through five years and
six pimps and has gone exactly nowhere.
Most girls don't.
By the time I met her, it was too late to
change what Hell's Bedroom had done to
a nice girl like . . .
Minnesota Marsha

The long thin girl was wearing long thin earrings—ivory elephants dangling on gold chains—for good luck. We found her near dawn in the deserted canyon of Eighth Avenue. She was swaying gracefully by the curbstone like some exotic nightbloom that grows wild in cement and survives on city poisons. She has left five years of her life on these paving-stones. To show for it she has twenty-seven direct prostitution arrests, one grand larceny conviction and a vague memory of being picked up by the pross van roughly fifteen hundred times. Marsha is her day name. Sandy is her night name. Her real name is impenetrably Polish and she is white and of course she comes from Minneapolis. This night, for safety only, her companion is the plump, moist Valerie.

It is a silly question to ask a prostitute why she does it. The top salary for a teacher with a BA in New York City public schools is $13,950; for a registered staff nurse, $13,000; for a telephone operator, about $8,000. The absolute daily minimum a pimp expects a streetwalker to bring in is $200 a night. That comes to easily $70,000 a year. These are the highest-paid "professional" women in America.

Marsha answers the question without my asking: "Everyone in life has a goal they want to reach. Prostitutes too. This is the fastest way of getting money as a woman, by using your best years to sell what you can sell the easiest. You look at people that work jobs every day, like a waitress or a bellhop—they have to work nineteen or twenty *years* for what we can make in a year, maybe even in six months."

Six months?

Marsha tucks her lower lip behind her teeth, almost modestly. "I work twelve hours a day. When I was on top, before this crackdown on prostitution, if I lucked up I could make ten grand in a month."

But rare is the streetwalker who keeps any of her money. This leaves everyone, including policemen who have spent years riding the pross van, confounded. And so I ask again, as I have asked so many girls: How much of this money do you turn over to your pimp, and why?

"I give him *all* of it," Valerie breaks in with her half-lunatic eyes blazing. She is the former addict with only nine months in this game, and she wants to talk:

"I never had a man before. I worked independent. But I love it, I love it! Because he gives me en-ee-thing I want, a new outfit, silver jewelry. I've only got one wife-in-law, and I'm the first one of his girls she's ever gotten along with. We both have separate apartments on the East Side. He spends tonight with me, tomorrow with her and so on. That's why I know whatever we have together is mine, all *mine*."

To Valerie (as to most street girls), the pimp is still sacred, a superbeing created in her own desperate brain in whom she is investing all hopes, dreams and goals for the future. She wears his beatings proudly as symbols of affection. He is the father-substitute; he disciplines, he cares. She submits gladly to his sadistic lovemaking. The pimp as lover takes her money, tricks her, gives her raw sex but denies her an ounce of emotion, and drops her ten minutes later for another woman—exactly reversing the sadomasochistic process she must play with her own tricks. In this way she can reaffirm herself (at least every other night) as that adoring, devoted, sacrificial lamb—the "feminine" woman. Prostitutes are unbelievably romantic. There is one sentence they all utter with total conviction: "I couldn't stand to live and sleep with someone I didn't love—*I gotta love him!*"

"There goes my man in the green Eldorado." Valerie wriggles all over and points like a dog on the hunt. "See him parking at the end of the block? Probably cutting reefer."

What does her man do, I ask.

"He doesn't do *nothing*. But the way he does nothing is *beautiful.*"

Valerie is still new enough to labor under the standard fantasy of a prostitute's future with her pimp. "I want my daughter back. So my man and I will drive down and kidnap her from that welfare family . . . and then my man will have to get me a bigger apartment—it might cost $600—and then I'll drop her with a baby-sitter while I work days and my man will watch her at night. He'll save my money. Someday we'll get a business—"

"—A restaurant or a little boutique, right?" Marsha completes the fantasy for her friend. Valerie nods vigorously. "And if not a business, someday he'll get you a home, right?" Again the girl nods. The goals are always, pathetically, the same.

"I don't care how many girls you ask," Marsha turned to me to add, "wherever you ask them, Los Angeles or Eighth Avenue, not one girl has an explanation for her pimp. My goal was to take two or three grand and put it down in a business. But the main thing is, being a prostitute and having a record, you have a hard time getting credit."

In her five years on the street Marsha has run through six

pimps and watched hundreds of babies like Valerie turn old, bitter, and broke.

"Ain't nobody out there your friend," she says, letting down her words with the dull thud of unburdened experience. "The only really good friend you got, to tell you the truth, is your man. If he isn't your friend—"

Marsha turned, directing my eyes to the obvious. We looked down the long ugly blacktop desert that is Eighth Avenue at four in the morning.

"—you ain't got nobody."

The veteran doesn't cry anymore, she doesn't even kick much. But there are small, telling signs that most of the spirit and all of the illusions have gone out of her work. She no longer bothers to curl her hair. She has lost track of her little black cashbook, along with her ex-pimp; Marsha never tries to recover such things. Her losses are too painful to face.

And some nights when she is all played out, when not even her own man wants her, when the wheel of street fortune turns and jams and turns up new faces and keeps turning, she tries to escape into a restaurant and have a quiet supper. An innocent John stops by to ask the price. She breaks a chair over his head.

"If a girl were to come up to me today and say 'I want to be a prostitute,' I'd tell her, 'No matter how bad it is, go back home.'"

[The] observation that prostitutes might just be looking for the easy way out could apply to Valerie. Her father is a foreign trade expert in the Nixon Administration; he has had two wives in addition to this daughter who ran delinquent at the age of thirteen. But at least she had a father *there*.

Marsha's home life could have been worse, but not much. Over the days, as we talked, she parted with her memories in bursts and silences—the small hidden agonies would explode, followed by lakes in the conversation meant to cover despair. These colorless lakes were blanketed by expressions such as "this 'n' that" or "See, so." That was the only way Marsha could tell me how it was back home, by pretending to herself it wasn't that bad.

"We started with six kids in the family. We lived twenty or thirty miles outside Minneapolis, they call that Coon Rapids.

I was the youngest. Then my two closest sisters took me out drinkin' in Anoka County with a bunch of guys one night and they got killed. See, so.

". . . the rest of us kids stuck together after that. We didn't have much to do with our parents because my ma was an alcoholic and she had cancer of the breast and she had an operation on that. And then she had ulcers and they took a third of her stomach out. Then she had cancer of the female organs, they had to come out too. All this happened from the time I was ten to thirteen.

"Then ma got in the habit of using these drugs, see so.

". . . they must have been heavy barbiturates, the hospital gave them to her when she came home to dope her up. Got so she'd just have to have them. Us kids would throw them down the toilet. My dad got so he couldn't be around her. So he started goin' out with other women, this 'n' that.

". . . in the last three years, I'd say, my father has been making a rerun of my mother's life. He started the pills, the alcohol, and now he's in the same position—he's useless. Last time I was back home [she left New York in February of 1972 and tried to stick it out in Minneapolis for three months] they had him in the state hospital. He escaped from there and got lost and they found him in the International Airport Hotel. He'd eaten a lot of pills and drunk a lot of liquor so I guess he got in one of his depressed moods. 'Cause they found him trying to cut his wrists.

"We were glad when ma and daddy split up. Us girls and our mom moved to the city. Ma was getting welfare. How much I don't know. She'd take the welfare checks and cash them, and we wouldn't see her for two, three weeks. She'd be out on a drunk, this 'n' that.

". . . one morning I heard the fire engines. She'd fallen asleep on the couch with a cigarette. So there went everything we had. See, so."

And then Marsha would play quietly for a while with her white elephant earrings, like the little girl she never had the chance to be.

One evening we were touring around Hell's Bedroom together in the back of a cab. We'd decided Marsha should give me a hooker's guide to Times Square. She was alive, laughing, issuing commands to the cab driver the way only a prostitute can do; she was in control. All at once her mind leaped back to another car, another rejection. . . . She was in high school and her aunt had taken in the family after the fire. But Marsha's was always the "down-rated family" of all the Polish relatives. Her aunt kept calling Marsha and her sisters "a bunch of sluts" because they had some friends and laughs; her children didn't. One night the aunt threw them all out of the house. They went to their mother's room to appeal for help; where could they stay now? The mother was in bed at the time. Their only remaining possession was a raunchy old car parked in a lot behind the aunt's house. The mother coaxed her four daughters to go outside and sit in the car. She would be out in a few minutes.

"We waited and waited and waited," Marsha says, recalling that first night in the car, as if still groping for some rationale, some handle to the chaos that went by the name home life. "Ma never came out. So I went in to see for myself. She had gone back to sleep.

"Next day, to make it look good, she brought us some rolls and lunchmeat. We made our own sandwiches in the car. Ma said she was going to the Cities to find us all a place to stay. She kept telling us she couldn't find a good enough place, this 'n' that.

"Me and my sisters—Gerry, June and Marge—we all slept in the car behind my aunt's house for four months."

And then our cab passed the Raymona Hotel and Marsha had to get out and go back to work.

From *Hustling*, 1973.

QUESTIONS

(1) How does Sheehy, in the first paragraph, transform the cliché of the city as a jungle into an effective metaphor for the world she is writing about?

(2) How does the emphasis on "safety" at the end of the first paragraph alter your expectations about what Sheehy will say about prostitutes?

(3) How does Sheehy make you feel about Valerie? What words control your reactions?

(4) What words and/or details prepare you for Sheehy's statement that the pimp is "the father-substitute" before she says it? Why is this effective writing?

(5) Sheehy reveals how trapped in her own fantasies Valerie is. Can you make any assumptions about her customers' fantasies? Are they both destructive?

(6) If you interviewed the pimp in the green Eldorado, what do you think he might say about Valerie?

(7) What does Sheehy reveal about Marsha by having her interrupt Valerie to complete Valerie's expression of her dreams?

(8) What are all the implications of the statement, "Her losses are too painful to face"?

(9) Is "lakes in the conversation" a good image to use in connection with Marsha? Why?

(10) Why does Sheehy let Marsha tell her own story without interruption? Should she interpret it for us?

(11) Is Marsha's story of living in the car an effective illustration of the theme of parent-child relationships Sheehy is using in her presentation of the prostitutes? Is there an implicit contrast or connection (or both) with the green Eldorado?

(12) What kinds of feelings does Sheehy have for Marsha? For Valerie? What kinds of feelings does she want the reader to have?

NIXON'S NIGHT OUT

CHARLES COLSON

One night in early October 1971 I was working late with George Shultz, director of the Office of Management and Budget, preparing for delicate negotiations with union leaders over wage- and price-control policies. By 9:00 P.M. we had papers strewn all over Shultz's office.

We had just finished watching the President's television address to the nation on the economy, and I was expecting his call.

A few minutes after nine the phone rang. "Well, what did you think of it, Chuck?" he asked. "How did you like the point I made about public cooperation? Remember, that's what you were so concerned about." We rambled on.

About four minutes into the conversation, however, he asked, "Where is Eugene Ormandy tonight?"

"I don't know," I answered, wondering what the conductor of the Philadelphia Orchestra had to do with a speech on economics.

The President explained that Julie had been to the Kennedy Center a few days earlier for an Ormandy performance which she had highly recommended. "Find out if Ormandy is still at the center. I might want to go tonight," he said.

Simple enough, I thought. But through the White House operators I discovered that staff members who usually handled such details had left for the day. Shultz's secretary, Barbara Otis, began thumbing through newspapers. There were performances listed for the two other theaters in the Kennedy Center—the Opera House and the Eisenhower Theater—but none for the Concert Hall nor any mention of Eugene Ormandy.

I was becoming a trifle concerned; four or five minutes had passed, and the President would be getting restless. Recognizing my distress, Shultz had abandoned the complex papers that were spread out on his desk. All three of us, the director of the Office of Management and Budget, his secretary, and the

President's special counsel, were flipping through newspapers and weekly entertainment magazines.

White House operators, who had never failed us in reaching anyone, anywhere, anytime, were now frantically trying every conceivable number at the Kennedy Center: backstage phones, the manager's office, emergency numbers—all to no avail.

Six minutes had elapsed since the President's call. As I feared, he called again. He was very pleasant. "Just wondered if you have found out what is at the Kennedy Cener?"

"Not yet, sir. We're still searching."

He made a muttering noise, cleared his throat, and suggested I call him back when I had the information.

I was getting nowhere in Shultz's office and decided to return to my own. My resourceful secretary, Joan Hall, would surely be able to handle this.

Joan came up with a reasonable idea. She called Eugene Ormandy at his home in Philadelphia.

"Mr. Ormandy, this is the White House calling."

"Really."

"Yes, the President is trying to find out if you are at the Kennedy Center tonight."

Long pause. "No. I am here at home reading a book."

"Oh. Well, thank you. Sorry to have disturbed you."

Joan hung up a bit sheepishly. I have often wondered what thoughts went through Mr. Ormandy's mind that evening about the President, and how well we were managing the nation's affairs.

Previously, in handling special tasks for the President, I had remained cool. And never before had I been given such a simple request. But in those few moments after his second call—it was now about 9:25 P.M.—I began to panic. Ormandy wasn't at the Kennedy Center, but what if the President liked what *was* there? I had never had anything to do with arranging his travel.

Meanwhile Joan continued making calls to the social office, the newspapers, the military aide's office, and elsewhere, trying to find out what was playing at the Concert Hall. Harried, frustrated, I decided to send a message to the President through his valet, Manolo Sanchez.

"Manolo, this is Mr. Colson."

"Yes, sir. Do you want to speak to the President?"

'No, no. Has he . . . er . . . retired for the night?"

'No, Mr. Colson. He is walking around the Lincoln Room. He seems restless, sir."

"Manolo, please take him a note. Tell him that Mr. Ormandy—Yes, O-r-m-a-n-d-y—is not playing at the Kennedy Center."

I hoped that the note from Manolo would satisfy the President. After all, it was now 9:30 P.M., really too late to go anywhere. Maybe—I hoped he would just decide to read a good book. But no.

At 9:35 P.M. the President called again. "Well, Chuck, you found out that Ormandy wasn't at the Kennedy Center, eh?"

"Yes, sir."

"That's very good, Chuck, very good," he replied. There was a short pause. "Do you suppose, Chuck, you might find out what *is* playing there?"

I explained that none of the papers had been of any help.

"Have you thought about calling the Kennedy Center, or should I?" the President asked, deliberately measuring each word.

I told him that I had tried that, but the phones didn't answer, that I would keep trying and call him back.

He said, "That is very good. You do that," and hung up.

By now my tie was down and I was perspiring. My assistant, Dick Howard, was also in the office calling friends, seeking their help.

Then Joan signaled me. She had on the phone the head waitress from the Kennedy Center restaurant, La Grande Scène. The young lady, Raquel Ramirez, was Spanish and did not speak English very well. Would I talk with her? Yes, I sure would.

"Miss Ramirez, my name is Charles Colson . . . Colson . . . C-o-l-s-o-n. Yes, I am a special counsel to the President— the President of the United States, that is. . . . Yes, that's right. . . . Mr. Nixon."

I loosened my tie further.

"Now, Miss Ramirez, the President would like to go to the Concert Hall tonight. But we cannot seem to discover what is playing there. Would you be kind enough to walk over to the Concert Hall and find out what is going on?"

This is utterly ridiculous, I thought. She will think I'm a nut, that this is a practical joke.

"The President wants me to go over to the Concert Hall?" a small voice asked incredulously.

Carefully I went through it again. "I'll wait on the line until you come back," I said desperately.

La Grande Scène is on the fourth floor of the mammoth building at the far south end. Fortunately—the only break so far in the evening—the Concert Hall is also on the south end. It is a good ten-minute walk from one end of the center to the other.

For some reason that waitress believed me. I waited for what seemed like an eternity. Within a few minutes, she was back, explaining that the hall seemed to be filled with military officers in dress uniforms, and a military band was playing. I asked her for one other small favor: to go backstage, find someone who looked like he might be in authority, and tell him that the President might be coming and to make necessary arrangements.

With this clue, Joan reached the duty officer at the Pentagon and learned that this was a formal black-tie affair for senior officers, plus a performance by the four military bands. With a sigh of relief I called the President at 9:53 P.M. to tell him it was a military concert, private, by invitation only.

"These are the same bands you hear at the White House, sir. I don't think you are missing anything. These bands will come and play for you any time you like."

"Marvelous," he replied. "That is just what I feel like hearing tonight, but I'm not dressed. If it's black tie, I'll have to change."

"Do you really want to go to all that trouble—I mean, you must be tired," I suggested meekly. I should have known better. That was the surest way to guarantee that he would go.

"Have the car at the south entrance in five minutes, Chuck."

I sat for a long instant frozen in horror. How did I start this process by which the President could have a night on the town? There were Secret Service men to notify, and there was the problem of carrying that vital little black briefcase housing the nuclear-alert device. Doctors, the press, radio hookups—for the President to walk across the street involved assembling a small army.

Fortunately, my assistant had been an advance man for a year-and-a-half. He called W-16, the Secret Service control office in the White House basement. He would take care of getting the President to the Kennedy Center, Dick told me as he pushed me out the door. "You get down to the Concert Hall and let someone know that the President is coming."

Dashing out the door, I jumped into a White House limousine Joan had called. "Come on, step on it. The President is right behind us," I shouted to the driver, forgetting to give him directions. The driver looked startled, then suspicious. Finally, when I told him our destination, we shot out of the driveway.

As we sped down Virginia Avenue toward the Kennedy Center at seventy miles an hour, I could listen on the two-way radio to the frantic calls from W-16 summoning agents back to the White House, calling for the President's car and an accompanying Secret Service car. All but two agents had retired for the night, I later learned.

Suddenly a horrible thought occurred to me. What if the Concert Hall performance was already over?

My stomach began to tighten as I imagined the President arriving at the Kennedy Center only to find the crowd pouring out. We had been unable, except through the waitress at La Grande Scène, to let anyone know that the President even might be on his way. Would they believe her? As I thought about it, I became even more mortified. Why should they believe her? I wouldn't have.

When we arrived at the south entrance to the Kennedy Center, I was relieved to see one of the President's own Secret Service agents there with a radio plug in his ear. The professionals had taken over. Backstage were a collection of stagehands, a tall and very distinguished man standing in the shadows, and the conductor of the Marine Band. Cheerily I gave him the news: "The President is on his way to listen to your concert."

He turned pale. "It's too late. Tell him not to come. All four service bands are now playing together on the stage. It is a final medley. In six minutes the program will be over."

"The President will be here any moment. You'll have to play something. Play the medley over again," I said firmly.

Marines follow orders. The conductor took a full breath, stared at me for an instant, then turned and marched onto the stage. He began whispering into the ear of the Army conductor.

The Marine nodded his head up and down vehemently.

The Army musician shook his head stonily from side to side.

More whispers. The same thing all over again. One head bobbing up and down—the other shaking side to side.

Good God, I thought, this whole performance will wind up in a war between the Army and the Marines.

Suddenly there was another flurry of whispering. Then the Army conductor began nodding his head up and down. I sighed in relief.

As the pantomime was going on, I peered into the hall full of women in evening gowns and men in dark-blue dress uniforms trimmed with gold braid. I began to wonder what they would think when they heard the medley that was now being played repeated note for note.

The Marine conductor returned backstage with his colleagues from the Navy and Air Force, working out additional numbers that would extend the program another half hour. It was then I recognized the tall, distinguished man nearby. He was William McCormick Blair, Jr., director of the Kennedy Center, former Ambassador to Denmark, and a prominent Washington socialite. He, along with much of the Washington establishment, viewed us Nixon men as uncultured intruders at his center.

I introduced myself to Blair, who dilated his nostrils and said, "This is highly irregular, you know."

I explained that the President had a regular box at the Kennedy Center, and had the prerogative to use it at any time. In the future, I promised, some better communications would be arranged in the event the President again had a last-minute desire to attend a performance.

"I have had a very clear understanding with the White House that the President will always give us twenty-four hours' notice before he attends," he said testily.

I decided I didn't have time to stand there arguing. I was also afraid that if he made one more complaint, I might punch him in the nose.

Expecting the President at any moment, I sped back down the passageway to the double doors which led back into the main lobby. I was running and there was no point in slowing down. So I hit the two release handles at full speed.

Pow! The doors exploded open. Barely a foot away was a startled President and an agitated Secret Service man who had started for his gun. I had nearly knocked the President down!

"Well . . . Chuck!"

I noticed that the President was wearing a red smoking jacket with black lapels. I started to tell him he had forgotten to change, but quickly thought better of it. "Everything is in order," I said breathlessly. "You can go directly to your box."

"Where is the box?" the Secret Service agent asked.

"I'll lead the way," I said nonchalantly, not knowing the location but hoping that I could bluff it through.

Halfway down the long passageway leading to the back of the hall, the President turned and said, "Have you made arrangements for them to play the you-know-what, Chuck?" He didn't want to come right out and say it, but I knew he meant "Hail to the Chief."

According to protocol it had to be played when he entered the hall. Once more I sped backstage to find my new friend, the Marine conductor, grateful that the Secret Service agent would now have to find the entrance to the President's box.

The Marine band leader did not seem happy to see me. "Watch for the President. When he appears in his box, have the band play "Hail to the Chief," I told him.

The conductor looked startled. "The four bands are still on stage. They have never played 'Hail to the Chief' together, and I don't see how they could do it without rehearsing."

I must have looked on the verge of apoplexy because he raised his hand. "Wait a moment." Another consultation. More pantomime. Then he was back. "We'll have the Marine Band play it alone," he said.

Back down the long hallway I loped until I found the President's box. To my relief, the Secret Service agent was guarding the door. The President was standing alone in the small ante-room which is between the open entrance hall of the mezza-nine and his box. The scene is forever engraved in my con-sciousness. The President was staring at the wall, his arms hanging limply by his side in the most dejected posture I have ever witnessed. I imagined that he was either counting to ten or else repeating over and over to himself, "Colson must go. . . . Colson must go. . . ."

I went into the box, brought out General Haig, who was using it that evening, opened the door wide so the Marine conductor would get the signal, and ushered the President in. The Marine Band then struck up "Hail to the Chief," and the President began waving to the cheering crowd.

Slowly I returned to my waiting limousine. My legs were weak. In the car I advised the Secret Service command post by radio that the President was in his box and they should do whatever they normally do to take the President home after the performance.

At home, halfway through the second Scotch, it did occur to me that I should let someone other than the Secret Service know that the President was at the Kennedy Center. I called Ron Ziegler, the press secretary, and gave him the news.

"The President couldn't be there," he said stiffly, "Other-wise I would have been notified."

The next day H. R. Haldeman summoned me to his office and dressed me down for breaking every rule in the book. "You know, Chuck, this isn't funny. You could have put the President's life in jeopardy. The Secret Service wasn't pre-pared. It was a thoroughly stupid thing for you to do."

I agreed it certainly had been stupid, but I asked what I should do if it ever happened in the future.

"Just tell him he can't go, that's all. He rattles his cage all the time. You can't let him out." While I pondered the star-tling thought, the usually stern Haldeman softened. "The President enjoyed himself and it came out well. I guess that's what counts."

The next time the President called me, to my relief it had to do with the war in Vietnam, inflation, and negotiations with Russia.

From Born Again, 1976.

QUESTIONS

(1) In what ways does Colson's job in the White House sound like Brett Hauser's in the supermarket?

(2) Why is the first paragraph so important in the essay? How does it set up what follows?

(3) The basic technique of the essay is the simple statement of details given carefully, exactly, in strict chronological order. Does this logical presentation make clearer the insanity of what is being so logically described?

(4) To tell the story properly must the narrator be willing to deal harshly with himself? Does he? How do you feel about the way he presents himself?

(5) Does this funny story say anything important about power, self-respect, respect for others? How?

REPORT FROM ENGINE CO. 82

DENNIS SMITH

The day has begun to come alive. I have watched the mist around the street lights fade as the morning light appeared. It is now 7:00 A.M., and the kitchen is filled with men and empty coffee cups. Engine 85 has returned from the third alarm, and stories are being exchanged about fires. Billy Valenzio has relieved Knipps at housewatch, and Knipps and I sit at a table talking of the first day we walked into the quarters of Engine 82. He, Kelsey, and I were assigned together. Kelsey is sleeping, his eye bandaged. Knipps will drive him home when the tour is done. Tony Indio has been admitted into the hospital.

An alarm comes in, and the men of Engine 85 move out as
Valenzio hollers "Eighty-five only." Minutes pass, and the
bells ring again. Box 2743, the inevitable 2743—Charlotte and
170th Streets. Valenzio yells, in an attempt at early morning
humor, "Eighty-two and Thirty-one goes, you know where.
Chief goes too."

We reach the corner of Charlotte Street, and see an old man
lying at the base of the alarm box. His throat is cut, and he
lies in a small sea of his own plasma. We are too late to help
him for his head is thrown to one side, and I can see into the
hole in his neck. His eyes have rolled back under his open lids,
lost forever. Nothing could have helped him but the preven-
tion of the murder. McCartty comes over with a blanket, and
lays it gently over him, shielding him from the filth of Charlotte Street.

A passerby stands next to us, a middle-aged black with gray-
ing hair. His face is sullen, but distinguished and proud. "He
was a nice man," he says looking down at the blanketed body.

"Do you know him?" Lieutenant Welch asks. "Do you know
his name?"

"No," the man replies, "I don't know his name. They called
him 'the old Jew,' that's all. He owns the laundromat, and he
came here every morning with a bag of change for the machines. I guess they killed him for a bag of nickels and dimes."

Ten years ago the South Bronx was a mostly Jewish and
Irish neighborhood, but as they progressed economically in
the American system they moved from the tenements to better
buildings in the North Bronx, or to small ranch houses in the
suburbs of Long Island. As they moved out, blacks and Puerto
Ricans moved in. As blacks and Puerto Ricans moved in, the
less successful whites moved out to other tenements, but in
white neighborhoods. There are still bars in the neighborhood named "Shannon's," and "The Emerald Gem," but they
are frequented by men with black faces, and there are signs in
Spanish saying "Iglesia Chistiana de Dios," hanging obtru-
sively in front of stained-glass Stars of David on abandoned
synagogues. But, some merchants have lingered on, working
hard for a dollar-by-dollar survival. Like this old man whose
last act in life was to call the Fire Department, to pull the
alarm that would keep him alive.

There is a trail of blood from the laundromat to the alarm

box, a distance of ten steps. There are footprints in the trail, placed there by careless passersby, who pause momentarily on their way to work, ask a question or two, and continue their journeys.

The ambulance comes, and we place the body on an antiseptic, sheeted stretcher. McCartty folds the redstained blanket as he steps from the ambulance. It will have to go to the cleaners, or to a laundromat. The police have arrived, and are talking to Chief Niebrock. Our job is finished. From the back step of the apparatus I can see the old man's keys, hanging, still and forgotten, from the padlock on the door of his business place.

It is ten minutes to eight now, and the sun begins to break through threatening clouds. In another hour I will take a shower, change into clean clothes, and drive home for a day of sleep. Right now though, there is nothing to do but drink still more coffee, and wait for the men of the day tour to arrive for work.

Charlie McCartty, as usual, is the center of attention in the kitchen. Most of us are sitting wearily in chairs, trying to relax after a hectic night tour, but McCartty is pacing up and down the kitchen floor berating a probationary fireman for not cleaning the kitchen.

"Ninety percent of this job is professional work, fighting fires, and making inspections, and all that," he says, "but the other ten percent is pure bullshit."

The probie, Frank Parris, starts to grin as he collects the empty cups from the tables.

"The ten percent bullshit," Charlie continues, "is your responsibility, and that is to keep this kitchen clean, and make sure there is fresh coffee at all times. If ya do that right, then maybe we'll teach ya about the other ninety percent."

Parris is one of the most conscientious probies we have ever had in the big house, and knows, as well as all of us, that Charlie is just making noise. Parris wipes the tables with a sponge as Charlie continues to pace, and mutter.

"When I was a probie, I did everything I could to make the senior men happy, but none of you guys would know about that—that was in the days of leather lungs and wooden fire hydrants, when horses pulled the rigs. I even used to service the mares when they got restless. That's when a probie was a

probie." Charlie is a pleasant diversion, and he has got the
men laughing, and interested in his soliloquy. But, three sharp
rings on the department phone redirect everyone's attention.
"Eighty-two and Thirty-one, get out." Valenzio's voice
carries through the firehouse. "And the Chief," he adds. "1280
Kelly Street."

We can smell the smoke as the pumper leaves quarters. Up
Tiffany Street, and down 165th Street. As we turn into Kelly
the smoke has banked down to the street, making it difficult
to see even ten feet away. Valenzio pulls the pumper to the
first hydrant he sees. We will have to stretch around the apparatus, but at least we know we have a hydrant that works.
The building is occupied, and we will have to get water on
the fire first.

Engine 73 arrives and helps us with the stretch. Between
the lifts and banks of the smoke, we can see that the job is on
the top floor, five flights up. But, there is enough manpower
for the stretch now, so I drop the hose and head for the mask
bin. Valenzio has the pumper connected to the hydrant by the
time I have the mask donned, and Jerry Herbert has the aerial
ladder of the truck up, and placed by the top floor fire escape.
He is climbing up it as I enter the building.

The fifth floor is enveloped with smoke, and I can barely
see in front of me. Billy-o and McCartty are working on the
door of the burning apartment, but it is secured inside with
a police lock—a long steel bar, stretched from one side to the
other like the gate of Fort Apache. The smoke is brutal, and
Billy-o has a coughing fit between ax swings. Charlie pulls on
the halligan with all his strength, as Billy-o hammers with the
head of the ax. Finally, the door begins to move, and Charlie
and Billy-o work their tools, one complementing the other,
like a computed machine, until one side of the door is free.
Still coughing and choking, Charlie puts his shoulder to the
door, and it swings inward, and out of its brackets to the floor.

Charlie and Billy-o dive to the floor, for the fire lunges out
to the hall. Willy Boyle has the nozzle. I ask him if he wants
me to take it, since I have the mask, but he replies that he
thinks he can make it.

"Let's go," Lieutenant Welch says.

Boyle makes it about ten feet into the apartment, but it is
an old building, and the plaster falls freely from the ceiling

in large pieces. Boyle's helmet is thrown from his head by the
falling ceiling. Lieutenant Welch orders me up to take the
line. Boyle has to back out, because it is unsafe to operate in
an inferno like this without something protecting the head.

Herbert has entered the apartment from the front. He can
hear McCartty and Billy-o banging at the door. All but the
end room of the apartment is burning, and the smoke and the
fire are being drawn there by the open window. Jerry crawls
along the floor, realizing that the room could go up in a second. He hears a slight moan, coming from the far side of the
bed that stands in the middle of the room. The room is blind
dark with smoke, and Jerry crawls to the sound, patting his
hand before him as he goes. He reaches the other side of the
bed, and the fire begins to lap at the ceiling above him. The
smoke has taken everything from him, but he knows he can't
back out now.

His hand gropes searching before him, until at last he feels
the soft give of a woman's body. There is a child by her side.
Jerry picks the child up and hurries on his knees to the window. As he nears it, he sees Rittman enter, and he yells to him.
Rittman takes the child in his arms, and climbs out of the
apartment. Jerry knows that he is in trouble, for the fire is
coming at him fast. He grabs the woman under the arms, and
pulls her to the window, keeping his head as low as he can.
She is a slight woman, and he pulls her easily. As he lifts her
out to the fire escape he can hear the front door give way, and
at that moment the room lights up completely in fire.

I am swinging the nozzle back and forth across the ceiling.
The floor is cluttered with debris, furniture, fallen plaster,
and it is difficult moving forward.

"Keep pushing, Dennis. Keep pushing," Lieutenant Welch
says.

"Give me some more line," I yell to him through the mask,
and he yells back to Royce and Knipps. We reach the front
room, and as I lift my leg to get a better support, the floor
gives way and my leg goes down, caught between the smolder-
ing boards of the floor. Lieutenant Welch sees what has happened, and calls Royce up to the nozzle.

"Easy now," I say to Knipps as he helps me. "Just pull me
out, easy." The smoke is lifting as Royce gets the last room,
and I rip my face piece off to breathe freely. Lieutenant Welch

yells back to me, "Go down and take the mask off, and check for injuries."

I start to move out, but the way is blocked by the men of Ladder 31. They are kneeling in the middle of the hall. "It's a baby," one of them says. I go to a window to get some air. The mask is heavy on my shoulders, and I want to sleep. Breathe. It's a baby. Breathe deep, I can feel my stomach moving. I had to crawl over it. In the middle of the hall. Breathe. The air tastes good. We all had to crawl over it. My mouth is full of coffee and veal. The taste is horrible as my stomach empties, and I can feel the terror of a thousand children as I lean across the sill.

A few minutes pass until the hall is clear. I go down a few steps and take my mask off. I lay it on the stairs, and pull my pants down. I examine the top of my leg, but it's only bruised. I lift the heavy canister of air, the self-contained breathing apparatus, and carry it in my arms down the stairs.

Billy-o is sitting on the vestibule steps, waiting for the ambulance. The baby is wrapped in a borrowed bedspread, and lies like a little bundle in Billy-o's arms. A little package of dead life, never having had a chance to live.

I lay the mask on the floor, and sit below him on the bottom step. I look up, and he shakes his head. Mucus is hanging and drying beneath his nose, and his face is covered with grime and the dark spots of burnt paint chips. He feels, no he knows, that the baby could have been saved.

"How the hell can a fire get going like that before someone turns in an alarm?" He continues to shake his head in dejection. "And that police lock. What a mark of the poor when they have to barricade themselves in like that."

"What is it?" I ask him, looking toward his arms.

"It's a little girl about two years old. She never had a chance, but at least they got her mother and sister out."

"Did you give her mouth to mouth?" I ask.

"We couldn't. She was roasted so bad, the skin was burnt completely off her face. The poor little thing. She never had a chance."

I don't say anything further, nor does Billy. I look up at his eyes. They are almost fully closed, but I can see they are wet, and tearing. The corneas are red from heat and smoke, and light reflects from the watered surfaces, and they sparkle. I wish my wife, my mother, everyone who has ever asked me why I do what I do, could see the humanity, the sympathy, the sadness of these eyes, because in them is the reason I continue to be a firefighter.

From *Report from Engine Co. 82*, 1972.

QUESTIONS

(1) This selection begins: "The day has begun to come alive." Yet, for the fireman it will involve death. How does Smith make you feel about that paradox?

(2) Does the matter-of-fact tone in describing the murder victim—"I can see into the hole in his neck"—make the scene more vivid? What details in the description reveal the kind of world in which Smith works?

(3) What does the exchange between McCartty and Parris reveal about how the men feel toward each other, and their work, and themselves? Is there any comparison possible with Nixon and Colson? With Brett Hauser and the supermarket manager? Is the seriousness of the work reflected in the seriousness of the kidding?

(4) Do the details given make the fire seem like an unusual one or a routine one? Is there any such thing as "routine" in this job?

(5) Are the relationships among the men in the firehouse repeated when they are out on a job?

(6) How does the author convey to the reader the sense of chaos and confusion at the scene of the fire in very clear prose?

(7) Do the details of the death of the child have a different feeling from that of the death of the old man? Is that because the death of the old man was not the "responsibility" of the firefighters?

(8) What details in this selection make it clear how it feels to be a fireman in contrast to an impersonal essay describing what a fireman does?

THE ART OF SURGERY

RICHARD SELZER

Someone asked me why a surgeon would write. Why, when
the shelves are already too full? They sag under the dead-
weight of books. To add a single adverb is to risk exceeding
the strength of the boards. A surgeon should abstain. A surgeon, whose fingers are more at home in the steamy gulleys of
the body than they are tapping the dry keys of a typewriter.
A surgeon, who feels the slow slide of intestines against the
back of his hand and is no more alarmed than were a family
of snakes taking their comfort from such an indolent rubbing.
A surgeon, who palms the human heart as though it were
some captured bird.

Why should he write? Is it vanity that urges him? There is
glory enough in the knife. Is it for money? One can make too
much money. No. It is to search for some meaning in the
ritual of surgery, which is at once murderous, painful, healing, and full of love. It is a devilish hard thing to transmit—
to find, even. Perhaps if one were to cut out a heart, a lobe of
the liver, a single convolution of the brain, and paste it to a
page, it would speak with more eloquence than all the words
of Balzac. Such a piece would need no literary style, no mass
of erudition or history, but in its very shape and feel would
tell all the frailty and strength, the despair and nobility of
man. What? Publish a heart? A little piece of bone? Prepos-
terous. Still I fear that is what it may require to reveal the
truth that lies hidden in the body. Not all the undressings of
Rabelais, Chekhov, or even William Carlos Williams have
wrested it free, although God knows each one of those doctors made a heroic assault upon it.

I have come to believe that it is the flesh alone that counts.
The rest is that with which we distract ourselves when we are
not hungry or cold, in pain or ecstasy. In the recesses of the
body I search for the philosophers' stone. I know it is there,
hidden in the deepest, dampest cul-de-sac. It awaits discovery.
To find it would be like the harnessing of fire. It would illu-

---

minate the world. Such a quest is not without pain. Who can gaze on so much misery and feel no hurt? Emerson has written that the poet is the only true doctor. I believe him, for the poet, lacking the impediment of speech with which the rest of us are afflicted, gazes, records, diagnoses, and prophesies.

I invited a young diabetic woman to the operating room to amputate her leg. She could not see the great shaggy black ulcer upon her foot and ankle that threatened to encroach upon the rest of her body, for she was blind as well. There upon her foot was a Mississippi Delta brimming with corruption, sending its raw tributaries down between her toes. Gone were all the little web spaces that when fresh and whole are such a delight to loving men. She could not see her wound, but she could feel it. There is no pain like that of the bloodless limb turned rotten and festering. There is neither unguent nor anodyne to kill such a pain yet leave intact the body.

For over a year I trimmed away the putrid flesh, cleansed, anointed, and dressed the foot, staving off, delaying. Three times each week, in her darkness, she sat upon my table, rocking back and forth, holding her extended leg by the thigh, gripping it as though it were a rocket that must be steadied lest it explode and scatter her toes about the room. And I would cut away a bit here, a bit there, of the swollen blue leather that was her tissue.

At last we gave up, she and I. We could no longer run ahead of the gangrene. We had not the legs for it. There must be an amputation in order that she might live—and I as well. It was to heal us both that I must take up knife and saw, and cut it off. And when I could feel it drop from her body to the table, see the blessed *space* appear between her and that leg, I too would be well.

Now it is the day of the operation. I stand by while the anesthetist administers the drugs, watch as the tense familiar body relaxes into narcosis. I turn then to uncover the leg. There, upon her kneecap, she has drawn, blindly, upside down for me to see, a face; just a circle with two ears, two eyes, a nose, and a smiling upturned mouth. Under it she has printed SMILE, DOCTOR. Minutes later I listen to the sound of the saw, until a little crack at the end tells me it is done.

So. I have learned that man is not ugly, but that he is Beauty itself. There is no other his equal. Are we not all dying, none faster or more slowly than any other? I have become receptive to the possibilities of love (for it is love, this thing that happens in the operating room), and each day I wait, trembling in the busy air. Perhaps today it will come. Perhaps today I will find it, take part in it, this love that blooms in the stoniest desert.

All through literature the doctor is portrayed as a figure of fun. Shaw was splenetic about him; Molière delighted in pricking his pompous medicine men, and well they deserved it. The doctor is ripe for caricature. But I believe that the truly great writing about doctors has not yet been done. I think it must be done *by* a doctor, one who is through with the love affair with his technique, who recognizes that he has played Narcissus, raining kisses on a mirror, and who now, out of the impacted masses of his guilt, has expanded into self-doubt, and finally into the high state of wonderment. Perhaps he will be a nonbeliever who, after a lifetime of grand gestures and mighty deeds, comes upon the knowledge that he has done no more than meddle in the lives of his fellows, and that he has done at least as much harm as good. Yet he may continue to pretend, at least, that there is nothing to fear, that death will not come, so long as people ask it of him. Later, after his patients have left, he may closet himself in his darkened office, sweating and afraid.

A writing doctor would treat men and women with equal reverence. For what is the "liberation" of either sex to him who knows the diagrams, the inner geographies of each? I love the solid heft of men as much as I adore the heated capaciousness of women—women in whose penetralia is found the repository of existence. I would have them glory in that. Women are physics and chemistry. They are matter. It is their bodies that inform of the frailty of men. We have not their cellular, enzymatic wisdom. Man is albuminoid, proteinaceous, laked pearl; woman is yolky, ovoid, rich. Both are exuberant bloody growths. I would use the defects and deformities of each for my sacred purpose of writing, for I know that it is the marred and scarred and faulty that are subject to grace. I would seek the soul in the facts of animal economy and profligacy. Yes, it is the exact location of the soul that I am after.

The smell of it is in my nostrils. I have caught glimpses of it in the body diseased. If only I could tell it. Is there no mathematical equation that can guide me? So much pain and pus equals so much truth? It is elusive as the whippoorwill that one hears calling incessantly from out the night window, but which, nesting as it does low in the brush, no one sees. No one but the poet, for he sees what no one else can. He was born with the eye for it.

Once I thought I had it: Ten o'clock, one night; the end room off a long corridor in a college infirmary; my last patient of the day; degree of exhaustion suitable for the appearance of a vision, some manifestation. The patient is a young man recently returned from Guatemala, from the excavation of Mayan ruins. His left upper arm wears a gauze dressing which, when removed, reveals a clean punched-out hole the size of a dime. The tissues about the opening are swollen and tense. A thin brownish fluid lips the edge, and now and then a lazy drop of the overflow spills down the arm. An abscess, inadequately drained. I will enlarge the opening to allow better egress of the pus. Nurse, will you get me a scalpel and some . . .

What happens next is enough to lay Francis Drake avomit in his cabin. No explorer ever stared in wilder surmise than I into that crater from which there now emerges a narrow gray head whose sole distinguishing feature is a pair of black pincers. The head sits atop a longish flexible neck arching now this way, now that, testing the air. Alternately it folds back upon itself, then advances in new boldness. And all the while, with dreadful rhythmicity, the unspeakable pincers open and close. Abscess? Pus? Never. Here is the lair of a beast at whose malignant purpose I could but guess. A Mayan devil, I think, that would soon burst free to fly about the room, with horrid blanket-wings and iridescent scales, raking, pinching, injecting God knows what acid juice. And even now the irony does not escape me, the irony of my patient as excavator excavated.

With all the ritual deliberation of a high priest I advance a surgical clamp toward the hole. The surgeon's heart is become a bat hanging upside down from his rib cage. The rim achieved—now thrust—and the ratchets of the clamp close

upon the empty air. The devil has retracted. Evil mocking
laughter bangs back and forth in the brain. More stealth. Lying in wait. One must skulk. Minutes pass, perhaps an hour.
. . . A faint disturbance in the lake, and once again the thing
upraises, further and further, hovering. Acrouch, strung, the
surgeon is one with his instrument; there is no longer any
boundary between its metal and his flesh. They are joined in
a single perfect tool of extirpation. It is just for this that he
was born. Now—thrust—and clamp—and *yes*. Got him!

Transmitted to the fingers comes the wild thrashing of the
creature. Pinned and wriggling, he is mine. I hear the dry
brittle scream of the dragon, and a hatred seizes me, but such
a detestation as would make of Iago a drooling sucktit. It is
the demented hatred of the victor for the vanquished, the
warden for his prisoner. It is the hatred of fear. Within the
jaws of my hemostat is the whole of the evil of the world,
the dark concentrate itself, and I shall kill it. For mankind.
And, in so doing, will open the way into a thousand years of
perfect peace. Here is Surgeon as Savior indeed.

Tight grip now . . . steady, relentless pull. How it scrab-
bles to keep its tentacle-hold. With an abrupt moist plop the
extraction is complete. There, writhing in the teeth of the
clamp, is a dirty gray body, the size and shape of an English
walnut. He is hung everywhere with tiny black hooklets.
Quickly . . . into the specimen jar of saline . . . the lid
screwed tight. Crazily he swims round and round, wiping his
slimy head against the glass, then slowly sinks to the bottom,
the mass of hooks in frantic agonal wave.

"You are going to be all right," I say to my patient. "We
are *all* going to be all right from now on."

The next day I take the jar to the medical school. "That's
the larva of the warble fly," says a pathologist. "The fly usually bites a cow, and deposits its eggs beneath the skin. There,
the egg develops into the larval form which, when ready, bur-
rows its way to the outside through the hide, and falls to the
ground. In time it matures into a full-grown warble fly. This
one happened to bite a man. It was about to come out on its
own, and, of course, it would have died."

The words *imposter, sorehead, servant of Satan* spring to
my lips. But now he has been joined by other scientists. They

nod in agreement. I gaze from one gray eminence to another,
and know the mallet-blow of glory pulverized. I tried to save
the world, but it didn't work out.

No, it is not the surgeon who is God's darling. He is the
victim of vanity. It is the poet who heals with his words,
stanches the flow of blood, stills the rattling breath, applies
poultice to the scalded flesh.

Did you ask me why a surgeon writes? I think it is because
I wish to be a doctor.

From *Harper's Magazine*, 1975.

QUESTIONS

(1) How does the phrase in the opening paragraph, "the
steamy gulleys of the body," prove exactly the opposite of
what the sentence seems to be saying? Is it in itself an answer
to the opening question? How do all the details in the first
paragraph combine to answer the first question?

(2) Does the essay demonstrate just how "murderous, painful, healing, and full of love" the art of surgery is?

(3) The word "devilish" appears almost casually in the second paragraph. Having read the entire essay does the word
now seem casual? Why does he use it?

(4) Does the essay reveal "the truth that lies hidden in the
body"?

(5) What does Selzer mean when he says he agrees with Emerson "that the poet is the only true doctor"? What is the impediment of speech to which he refers?

(6) What details, what words reveal his feelings about the
blind, diabetic woman? About her ulcerated leg? About both?
What do the comparisons, the metaphors and similes, make
you feel?

(7) Do you believe him when he says: "It was to heal us both
that I must take up knife and saw, and cut it off"? Why?

(8) Is what the young woman wrote on her leg a good answer to the question why should a doctor write? How else could he share what he learned and felt? Was it worth sharing?

(9) How does Selzer connect religion and poetry with the pain and pus of surgery? Is he justified? Is that part of what he means when he says only a doctor in love with his technique can write about it?

(10) Would a "writing doctor" treat men and women with equal reverence? What, judging from this essay, would he bring to his treatment that a non-writing doctor might not?

(11) The incident with the student is a parable. How does Selzer make his parable sum up the religious awe and artistic devotion he thinks should characterize the surgeon's work?

(12) What specific words does Selzer use, right from the beginning and throughout the essay, to emphasize his approach to his work as if it were a sacred, a religious calling?

THE SENSE OF THE 70s

OF THE

RACE

Ghosts. That's what Maxine Hong Kingston learned to call the Caucasians among whom she and her parents lived. There were Ghost Teachers and the Druggist Ghost to threaten or disturb her. They were alien; they were mysterious; they were powerful. At least they were when she was a child, a Chinese child in California, growing up in two worlds. Now she is a woman, and the selection from her autobiography details some of her attempts to understand those ghosts of her childhood, especially the ones that continue to haunt her.

No American decade has, of course, been free of racial ghosts. This country began with the confrontation of white and red. Black was here before the pilgrims. The Civil War is the great symbol of America's racial divisions, divisions so deep that the country almost split apart. And each decade seems to add to the list of martyrs the victims of the national inability to learn from experience.

Yet here too the seventies were different. There were still confrontations and killings, and the division of urban and rural threatened to replace the older one of North and South. But the tone was different from the sixties. The sixties were militant and public; the seventies "laid-back" and inward. The turning inward affected the way people thought and wrote about race. The turning inward became the search for roots.

Alex Haley created a story, a book, a myth, a symbol. He set out to find his roots and in so doing he recounted the epic story of the black person's journey from Africa to America. Haley's account, presented here in his own condensation, is a remarkable document of the personal decade. He wanted to find his particular ancestors. He discovered on his quest that he belonged to a larger family than he ever imagined. Roger

Wilkins's brief essay describes the effect one version of Haley's work had in putting to rest some of America's racial ghosts.

Alice Walker is a poet and novelist. Arthur Ashe has won both the United States Open tennis championship and, in 1975, the Wimbledon title. They speak from different perspectives on black achievement in sports and in the arts. They both write, however, of the legacy of pain and sacrifice on which the black star draws.

Richard Rodriguez also knows about sacrifice. He knows about the sacrifices of a Chicano family to educate a son and the sacrifices that the son makes to get one kind of education. Only when it is almost over, when the ambition is almost realized, can they question what exactly has been sacrificed for whom, and whether it was worth it.

Stan Steiner allows Frank Tenorio, a Pueblo Indian from the San Felipe Pueblo in New Mexico, to speak for himself. But first he makes a connection with Watergate; and the whole question of ecology and pollution and power somehow seems different. Again, however, as in almost all of the literature of the seventies, it is the personal testimony that is wanted, the personal statement that is respected. Of course that makes the connection with Watergate doubly ironic.

The struggle for racial identity in the seventies seems very like the struggle for sexual identity. There is a sense of trying to get to a *person*-ality by getting through gender and color. The writers represented both here and in the "Male/Female" section of this book seem to want to define for themselves a sexual identity and a racial identity that will allow them to be more fully human.

Race. Sex. Volatile subjects in a placid pleasure-seeking decade. But growth and change were there, with and without confrontations. In both race and sex, men and women were looking for new definitions, new forms of identification. There had to be new understandings, a new pride in roots, a new joy in separateness before there could be any coming together, any melting in any pot.

Bill Bradley describes a basketball clinic held not far from the site of the first and second battles of Wounded Knee, nineteenth- and twentieth-century assaults on the American Indian by the American government. At the end of the clinic, Willis Reed, a black man, says to a red boy, ". . . you can be

the first Indian to play in the NBA." Maybe the new racial
identification will lead eventually to the reconciliation that
has eluded America for more than three hundred and sixty
years. But not until the old lies are done with, not until the
individual truths are faced, not until the ghosts are laid to
rest.

THE AFRICAN

ALEX HALEY

My Grandma Cynthia Murray Palmer lived in Henning, Tenn. (pop. 500), about 50 miles north of Memphis. Each summer as I grew up there, we would be visited by several women relatives who were mostly around Grandma's age, such as my Great Aunt Liz Murray who taught in Oklahoma, and Great Aunt Till Merriwether from Jackson, Tenn., or their considerably younger niece, Cousin Georgia Anderson from Kansas City, Kan., and some others. Always after the supper dishes had been washed, they would go out to take seats and talk in the rocking chairs on the front porch, and I would scrunch down, listening, behind Grandma's squeaky chair, with the dusk deepening into night and the lightning bugs flickering on and off above the now shadowy honeysuckles. Most often they talked about our family—the story had been passed down for generations—until the whistling blur of lights of the southbound Panama Limited train *whooshing* through Henning at 9:05 P.M. signaled our bedtime.

So much of their talking of people, places and events I didn't understand: For instance, what was an "Ol' Massa," an "Ol' Missus" or a "plantation"? But early I gathered that white folks had done lots of bad things to our folks, though I couldn't figure out why. I guessed that all that they talked about had happened a long time ago, as now or then Grandma or another, speaking of someone in the past, would excitedly thrust a finger toward me, exclaiming, "Wasn't big as *this* young 'un!" And it would astound me that anyone as old and grey-haired as they could relate to my age. But in time my head began both a recording and picturing of the more graphic scenes they would describe, just as I also visualized David killing Goliath with his slingshot, Old Pharaoh's army drowning, Noah and his ark, Jesus feeding that big multitude with nothing but five loaves and two fishes, and other wonders that I heard in my Sunday school lessons at our New Hope Methodist Church.

The furthest-back person Grandma and the others talked
of—always in tones of awe, I noticed—they would call "The
African." They said that some ship brought him to a place
that they pronounced " 'Naplis." They said that then some
"Mas' John Waller" bought him for his plantation in "Spot-
sylvania County, Va." This African kept on escaping, the
fourth time trying to kill the "hateful po' cracker" slave-
catcher, who gave him the punishment choice of castration or
of losing one foot. This African took a foot being chopped off
with an ax against a tree stump, they said, and he was about
to die. But his life was saved by "Mas' John's" brother—"Mas'
William Waller," a doctor, who was so furious about what
had happened that he bought the African for himself and
gave him the name "Toby."

Crippling about, working in "Mas' William's" house and
yard, the African in time met and mated with "the big house
cook named Bell," and there was born a girl named Kizzy. As
she grew up her African daddy often showed her different
kinds of things, telling her what they were in his native tongue.
Pointing at a banjo, for example, the African uttered, *"ko";*
or pointing at a river near the plantation, he would say,
"Kamby Bolong." Many of his strange words started with a
"k" sound, and the little, growing Kizzy learned gradually that
they identified different things.

When addressed by other slaves as "Toby," the master's
name for him, the African said angrily that his name was
"Kin-tay." And as he gradually learned English, he told young
Kizzy some things about himself—for instance, that he was not
far from his village, chopping wood to make himself a drum,
when four men had surprised, overwhelmed, and kidnapped
him.

So Kizzy's head held much about her African daddy when
at age 16 she was sold away onto a much smaller plantation in
North Carolina. Her new "Mas' Tom Lea" fathered her first
child, a boy she named George. And Kizzy told her boy all
about his African grandfather. George grew up to be such a
gamecock fighter that he was called "Chicken George," and
people would come from all over and "bet big money" on his
cockfights. He mated with Matilda, another of Lea's slaves;
they had seven children, and he told them the stories and
strange sounds of their African great-grandfather. And one of

those children, Tom, became a blacksmith who was bought away by a "Mas' Murray" for his tobacco plantation in Alamance County, N.C.

Tom mated there with Irene, a weaver on the plantation. She also bore seven children, and Tom now told them all about their African great-great-grandfather, the faithfully passed-down knowledge of his sounds and stories having become by now the family's prideful treasure.

The youngest of that second set of seven children was a girl, Cynthia, who became my maternal Grandma (which today I can only see as fated). Anyway, all of this is how I was growing up in Henning at Grandma's, listening from behind her rocking chair as she and the other visiting old women talked of that African (never then comprehended as *my* great-great-great-great-grandfather) who said his name was *"Kintay,"* and said *"ko"* for banjo, *"Kamby Bolong"* for river, and a jumble of other *"k"*-beginning sounds that Grandma privately muttered, most often while making beds or cooking, and who also said that near his village he was kidnaped while chopping wood to make himself a drum.

The story had become nearly as fixed in my head as in Grandma's by the time Dad and Mama moved me and my two younger brothers, George and Julius, away from Henning to be with them at the small black agricultural and mechanical college in Normal, Ala., where Dad taught.

To compress my next 25 years: When I was 17 Dad let me enlist as a mess boy in the U.S. Coast Guard. I became a ship's cook out in the South Pacific during World War II, and at night down by my bunk I began trying to write sea adventure stories, mailing them off to magazines and collecting rejection slips for eight years before some editors began purchasing and publishing occasional stories. By 1949 the Coast Guard had made me its first "journalist"; finally with 20 years' service, I retired at the age of 37, determined to make a full time career of writing. I wrote mostly magazine articles; my first book was "The Autobiography of Malcolm X."

Then one Saturday in 1965 I happened to be walking past the National Archives building in Washington. Across the interim years I had thought of Grandma's old stories—otherwise I can't think what diverted me up the Archives' steps. And when a main reading room desk attendant asked if he could help me, I wouldn't have dreamed of admitting to him some curiosity hanging on from boyhood about my slave forebears. I kind of bumbled that I was interested in census records of Alamance County, North Carolina, just after the Civil War.

The microfilm rolls were delivered, and I turned them through the machine with a building sense of intrigue, viewing in different census takers' penmanship an endless parade of names. After about a dozen microfilmed rolls, I was beginning to tire, when in utter astonishment I looked upon the names of Grandma's parents: Tom Murray, Irene Murray . . . older sisters of Grandma's as well—every one of them a name that I'd heard countless times on her front porch.

It wasn't that I hadn't believed Grandma. You just *didn't* not believe my Grandma. It was simply so uncanny actually seeing those names in print and in official U.S. Government records.

During the next several months I was back in Washington whenever possible, in the Archives, the Library of Congress, the Daughters of the American Revolution Library. (Whenever black attendants understood the idea of my search, documents I requested reached me with miraculous speed.) In one source or another during 1966 I was able to document at least the highlights of the cherished family story. I would have given anything to have told Grandma, but, sadly, in 1949 she had gone. So I went and told the only survivor of those Henning front-porch storytellers: Cousin Georgia Anderson, now in her 80s in Kansas City, Kan. Wrinkled, bent, not well herself, she was so overjoyed, repeating to me the old stories and sounds; they were like Henning echoes: "Yeah, boy, that African say his name was '*Kin-tay*'; he say the banjo was '*ko*,' and river '*Kamby-Bolong*,' an' he was off choppin' some wood to make his drum when they grabbed 'im!" Cousin Georgia grew so excited we had to stop her, calm her down, "You go 'head, boy! Your grandma an' all of 'em—they up there watching what you do!"

That week I flew to London on a magazine assignment. Since by now I was steeped in the old, in the past, scarcely a tour guide missed me—I was awed at so many historical places and treasures I'd heard of and read of. I came upon the Ro-

setta stone in the British Museum, marveling anew at how
Jean Champollion, the French archeologist, had miraculously
deciphered its ancient demotic and hieroglyphic texts . . .

The thrill of that just kept hanging around in my head. I
was on a jet returning to New York when a thought hit me.
Those strange, unknown-tongue sounds, always part of our
family's old story . . . they were obviously bits of our original African *"Kin-tay's"* native tongue. What specific tongue?
Could I somehow find out?

Back in New York, I began making visits to the United Nations Headquarters lobby; it wasn't hard to spot Africans. I'd
stop any I could, asking if my bits of phonetic sounds held
any meaning for them. A couple of dozen Africans quickly
looked at me, listened, and took off—understandably dubious
about some Tennesseean's accent alleging "African" sounds.

My research assistant, George Sims (we grew up together in
Henning), brought me some names of ranking scholars of African linguistics. One was particularly intriguing: a Belgian-
and English-educated Dr. Jan Vansina; he had spent his early
career living in West African villages, studying and tape-
recording countless oral histories that were narrated by certain very old African men; he had written a standard textbook,
"The Oral Tradition."

So I flew to the University of Wisconsin to see Dr. Vansina.
In his living room I told him every bit of the family story in
the fullest detail that I could remember it. Then, intensely,
he queried me about the story's relay across the generations,
about the gibberish of *"k"* sounds Grandma had fiercely muttered to herself while doing her housework, with my brothers
and me giggling beyond her hearing at what we had dubbed
"Grandma's noises."

Dr. Vansina, his manner very serious, finally said, "These
sounds your family has kept sound very probably of the tongue
called 'Mandinka.' "

I'd never heard of any "Mandinka." Grandma just told of
the African saying *"ko"* for banjo, or *"Kamby Bolong"* for a
Virginia river.

Among Mandinka stringed instruments, Dr. Vansina said,
one of the oldest was the *"kora."*

"Bolong," he said was clearly Mandinka for "river." Pre-
ceded by *"Kamby,"* it very likely meant "Gambia River."

Dr. Vansina telephoned an eminent Africanist colleague, Dr. Philip Curtin. He said that the phonetic *"Kin-tay"* was correctly spelled *"Kinte,"* a very old clan that had originated in Old Mali. The Kinte men traditionally were blacksmiths, and the women were potters and weavers.

I knew I must get to the Gambia River.

The first native Gambian I could locate in the U.S. was named Ebou Manga, then a junior attending Hamilton College in upstate Clinton, N.Y. He and I flew to Dakar, Senegal, then took a smaller plane to Yundum Airport, and rode a van to Gambia's capital, Bathurst. Ebou and his father assembled eight Gambia government officials. I told them Grandma's stories, every detail I could remember, as they listened intently, then reacted. " *'Kamby Bolong'* of course is Gambia River!" I heard. "But more clue is your forefather's saying his name was *'Kinte.'* " Then they told me something I would never even have fantasized—that in places in the back country lived very old men, commonly called *griots,* who could tell centuries of the histories of certain very old family clans. As for *Kintes,* they pointed out to me on a map some family villages, Kinte-Kundah, and Kinte-Kundah Janneh-Ya, for instance.

The Gambian officials said they would try to help me. I returned to New York dazed. It is embarrassing to me now, but despite Grandma's stories, I'd never been concerned much with Africa, and I had the routine images of African people living mostly in exotic jungles. But a compulsion now laid hold of me to learn all I could, and I began devouring books about Africa, especially about the slave trade. Then one Thursday's mail contained a letter from one of the Gambian officials, inviting me to return there.

Monday I was back in Bathurst. It galvanized me when the officials said that a *griot* had been located who told the *Kinte* clan history—his name was Kebba Kanga Fofana. To reach him, I discovered, required a modified safari: renting a launch to get upriver, two land vehicles to carry supplies by a roundabout land route, and employing finally 14 people, including three interpreters and four musicians, since a *griot* would not speak the revered clan histories without background music.

The boat Baddibu vibrated upriver, with me acutely tense: Were these Africans maybe viewing me as but another of the pith-helmets? After about two hours, we put in at James Island, for me to see the ruins of the once British-operated James Fort. Here two centuries of slave ships had loaded thousands of cargoes of Gambian tribespeople. The crumbling stones, the deeply oxidized swivel cannon, even some remnant links of chain seemed all but impossible to believe. Then we continued upriver to the left-bank village of Albreda, and there put ashore to continue on foot to Juffure, village of the *griot*. Once more we stopped, for me to see *toubob kolong*, "the white man's well," now almost filled in, in a swampy area with abundant, tall, saw-toothed grass. It was dug two centuries ago to "17 men's height deep" to insure survival drinking water for long-driven, famishing coffles of slaves.

Walking on, I kept wishing that Grandma could hear how her stories had led me to the *"Kamby Bolong."* (Our surviving storyteller Cousin Georgia died in a Kansas City hospital during this same morning, I would learn later.) Finally, Juffure village's playing children, sighting us, flashed an alert. The 70-odd people came rushing from their circular, thatch-roofed, mud-walled huts, with goats bounding up and about, and parrots squawking from up in the palms. I sensed him in advance somehow, the small man amid them, wearing a pillbox cap and an off-white robe—the *griot*. Then the interpreters went to him, as the villagers thronged around me.

And it hit me like a gale wind: every one of them, the whole crowd, was *jet black*. An enormous sense of guilt swept me—a sense of being some kind of hybrid . . . a sense of being impure among the pure. It was an awful sensation.

The old *griot* stepped away from my interpreters and the crowd quickly swarmed around him—all of them buzzing. An interpreter named A. B. C. Salla came to me; he whispered: "Why they stare at you so, they have never seen here a black American." And that hit me: I was symbolizing for them twenty-five millions of us they had never seen. What did they think of me—of us?

Then abruptly the old *griot* was briskly walking toward me. His eyes boring into mine, he spoke in Mandinka, as if instinctively I should understand—and A. B. C. Salla translated:

"Yes . . . we have been told by the forefathers . . . that many of us from this place are in exile . . . in that place called America . . . and in other places."

I suppose I physically wavered, and they thought it was the heat; rustling whispers went through the crowd, and a man brought me a low stool. Now the whispering hushed—the musicians had softly begun playing *kora* and *balafon,* and a canvas sling lawn seat was taken by the *griot,* Kebba Kanga Fofane, aged 75 "rains" (one rainy season each year). He seemed to gather himself into a physical rigidity, and he began speaking the *Kinte* clan's ancestral oral history; it came rolling from his mouth across the next hours . . . 17th- and 18th-century *Kinte* lineage details, predominantly what men took wives; the children they "begot," in the order of their births; those children's mates and children.

Events frequently were dated by some proximate singular physical occurrence. It was as if some ancient scroll were printed indelibly within the *griot's* brain. Each few sentences or so, he would pause for an interpreter's translation to me. I distill here the essence:

The *Kinte* clan began in Old Mali, the men generally blacksmiths ". . . who conquered fire," and the women potters and weavers. One large branch of the clan moved to Mauretania from where one son of the clan, Kairaba Kunta Kinte, a Moslem Marabout holy man, entered Gambia. He lived first in the village of Pakali N'Ding; he moved next to Jiffarong village; ". . . and then he came here, into our own village of Juffure."

In Juffure, Kairaba Kunta Kinte took his first wife, ". . . a Mandinka maiden, whose name was Sireng. By her, he begot two sons, whose names were Janneh and Saloum. Then he got a second wife, Yaisa. By her, he begot a son, Omoro."

The three sons became men in Juffure. Janneh and Saloum went off and founded a new village, Kinte-Kundah Janneh-Ya. "And then Omoro, the youngest son, when he had 30 rains, took as a wife a maiden, Binta Kebba.

"And by her, he begot four sons—Kunta, Lamin, Suwadu, and Madi . . ."

Sometimes, a "begotten," after his naming, would be accompanied by some later-occurring detail, perhaps as ". . . in time of big water (flood), he slew a water buffalo." Having named those four sons, now the *griot* stated such a detail.

"About the time the king's soldiers came, the eldest of these four sons, Kunta, when he had about 16 rains, went away from this village, to chop wood to make a drum . . . and he was never seen again . . ."

Goose-pimples the size of lemons seemed to pop all over me. In my knapsack were my cumulative notebooks, the first of them including how in my boyhood, my Grandma, Cousin Georgia and the others told of the African *"Kin-tay"* who always said he was kidnapped near his village—while chopping wood to make a drum . . .

I showed the interpreter, he showed and told the *griot,* who excitedly told the people; they grew very agitated. Abruptly then they formed a human ring, encircling me, dancing and chanting. Perhaps a dozen of the women carrying their infant babies rushed in toward me, thrusting the infants into my arms—conveying, I would later learn, "the laying on of hands . . . through this flesh which is us, we are you, and you are us." The men hurried me into their mosque, their Arabic praying later being translated outside: "Thanks be to Allah for returning the long lost from among us." Direct descendants of Kunta Kinte's blood brothers were hastened, some of them from nearby villages, for a family portrait to be taken with me, surrounded by actual ancestral sixth cousins. More symbolic acts filled the remaining day.

When they would let me leave, for some reason I wanted to go away over the African land. Dazed, silent in the bumping Land Rover, I heard the cutting staccato of talking drums. Then when we sighted the next village, its people came thronging to meet us. They were all—little naked ones to wizened elders—waving, beaming, amid a cacophony of crying out; and then my ears identified their words: *"Meester Kinte! Meester Kinte!"*

Let me tell you something: I am a man. But I remember the sob surging up from my feet, flinging up my hands before my face and bawling as I had not done since I was a baby . . . the jet-black Africans were jostling, staring . . . I didn't care, with the feelings surging. If you really knew the odyssey of us millions of black Americans, if you really knew how we came in the seeds of our forefathers, captured, driven, beaten, inspected, bought, branded, chained in foul ships, if you really knew, you needed weeping . . .

Back home, I knew that what I must write, really, was our

black saga, where any individual's past is the essence of the
millions'. Now flat broke, I went to some editors I knew, describing the Gambian miracle, and my desire to pursue the
research; Doubleday contracted to publish, and Reader's Digest to condense the projected book; then I had advances to
travel further.

What ship brought Kinte to Grandma's " 'Naplis" (Annapolis, Md., obviously)? The old *griot's* time reference to "king's
soldiers" sent me flying to London. Feverish searching at last
identified, in British Parliament records, "Colonel O'Hare's
Forces," dispatched in mid-1767 to protect the then British-
held James Fort whose ruins I'd visited. So Kunta Kinte was
down in some ship probably sailing later that summer from
the Gambia River to Annapolis.

Now I feel it was fated that I had taught myself to write in
the U.S. Coast Guard. For the sea dramas I had concentrated
on had given me years of experience searching among yellow-
ing old U.S. maritime records. So now in English 18th Century marine records I finally tracked ships reporting themselves in and out to the Commandant of the Gambia River's
James Fort. And then early one afternoon I found that a
Lord Ligonier under a Captain Thomas Davies had sailed on
the Sabbath of July 5, 1767. Her cargo: 3,265 elephants' teeth,
3,700 pounds of beeswax, 800 pounds of cotton, 32 ounces of
Gambian gold, and 140 slaves; her destination: "Annapolis."

That night I recrossed the Atlantic. In the Library of Congress the Lord Ligonier's arrival was one brief line in "Ship-
ping In The Port Of Annapolis—1748-1775." I located the author, Vaughan W. Brown, in his Baltimore brokerage office.
He drove to Historic Annapolis, the city's historical society,
and found me further documentation of her arrival on Sept.
29, 1767. (Exactly two centuries later, Sept. 29, 1967, standing,
staring seaward from an Annapolis pier, again I knew tears).
More help came in the Maryland Hall of Records. Archivist
Phebe Jacobsen found the Lord Ligonier's arriving customs
declaration listing, "98 Negroes"—so in her 86-day crossing, 42
Gambians had died, one among the survivors being 16-year-
old Kunta Kinte. Then the microfilmed Oct. 1, 1767, Maryland Gazette contained, on page two, an announcement to
prospective buyers from the ship's agents, Daniel of St. Thos.

Jenifer and John Ridout (the Governor's secretary): "from the River GAMBIA, in AFRICA . . . a cargo of choice, healthy SLAVES . . ."

"My Furthest-back Person—'The African,' "
from *The New York Times Magazine,* 1972.

QUESTIONS

(1) What kinds of suggestions of "roots" and home are given in the first paragraph? How does Haley make you feel that "roots" are important?

(2) In what ways does Haley strike a balance between his individual quest for his forebears and all black people redefining their African roots?

(3) How does Haley prepare the reader for the *griot,* the oral historian of the clan? Is Grandma a kind of *griot?*

(4) How does he suggest that his interest in his roots is a natural human impulse? Why is it also special for him?

(5) How many different "journeys" does Haley record in this essay? Is "journey" the central theme? Do all the references to journeys and travel give Kinte's "crippling about" a special urgency?

(6) Is the *griot's* narrative reminiscent of the Bible? Is the *griot's* function and style of narrative like that in any other culture or group you know?

(7) How do the references to "drums" relate to each other and help unify the essay?

(8) Does Haley imply that the past is there waiting to be recovered by anyone willing to make the effort? How does he connect past and present in this essay?

THE BLACK GHOSTS OF HISTORY

ROGER WILKINS

Something quite remarkable happened in this country last week. An estimated 130 million Americans shared an experience unlike any in our history as we sat night after night watching the television adaptation of Alex Haley's tale of his family's passage through more than 200 years of African and American history.

It is too early, and too presumptuous, for one man to fathom the impact of that event. It is sufficient for now to filter a few random reactions through one black person's consciousness.

Roots had an impact on everyone who watched, black or white. White reactions included Jimmy Breslin's cousin, over 70, whose distress increased with each scene until he tuned in disgust to *The Rockford File* for something wholesome; the bigoted New York cab driver who announced, "I'm against the nigger, but after watching *Roots* I can understand why he got that way"; the journalist who observed, "This may be the first time millions of whites ever really identified with blacks as human beings."

Though most in the huge audience were white, *Roots* was for me primarily a black experience. And a joyous one. The essence of the racial struggle in America has not been physical, or legal, or even spiritual. It has been existential, about truth and falsehood, reality and illusion. The ABC television series offered one black man's vision of historical reality—more or less shared by millions of his black countrymen—and spread it large before the American people. In that sense, *Roots* may have been the most significant civil rights event since the Selma-to-Montgomery march of 1965.

Since black people were injected into American society more than three centuries ago, the form of their oppression by whites at any particular time was viewed by most whites as the norm, and therefore defended on factual, moral and psychological grounds. They thus had to construct and defend a peculiar view of reality: Blacks are lazy and dumb and require the stern discipline of slavery to be made productive *or*, since all civil rights goals had been achieved in the 1960s, affirmative action was not only unnecessary but also unfair "reverse discrimination."

Blacks through history have struggled to free themselves and whites from such distortions and fantasies. One of their struggles has been to revise the white view of blacks and *Roots* helped to do this as surely as the Montgomery bus boycott. Just as Montgomery projected a vision of the ordinary Southern black as pious and determined, instead of stupid and indolent, so did *Roots* portray slaves as substantially more intelligent and effective than the bumbling Sambos who have been passed along in story, song and psyche.

Another struggle has been to revise the whites' views of themselves. Actions and judgments that whites have seen as benign, commonplace or defensible, have been seen by blacks as insensitive, unfair or cruel. Though it is unfair to pin on this generation of white Americans the sins of the slavers, it is altogether appropriate for them to be reminded that white people on this continent were once capable of treating gross cruelty as the natural order of things—just as many Americans now take the ravaged South Bronx or the bloated black unemployment rate as the natural order of things.

And although blacks were never entirely ensnared by white fantasies, the white vision of humanity has been so pervasive that it did indeed warp black peoples' visions of themselves and impair their ability to function as human beings. My parents, as typical college-educated Americans, did not know enough of Africa or of slavery to protect me from the overwhelming shame that I felt because of the misinformation that washed over this culture. Just as the revolution in black consciousness removed many of those shackles in the late sixties, the story of Kunta Kinte filled blacks at all levels with great pride and chased the shame.

Finally, there has been a vulgar view of history that Americans of all colors pass from generation to generation. *Roots* has been criticized for some historical inaccuracies, but they are as nothing when compared with the egregious misinformation about slavery, and about the blacks and whites who participated in it, that all generations have taken as knowl-

edge. *Roots* is substantially closer to historical and psychological truth and has provided a common pool of information to
all young Americans to carry forward.

When I came in last Saturday night and found my 12-year-
old son and a white classmate in front of the set and rooting
together for Chicken George to prevail over his mean master-
father, I knew something very good was happening in my
country.

From *The New York Times*, 1977.

QUESTIONS

(1) Is TV a kind of electronic *griot?* Should it be?

(2) Haley's book recounts his search, but reading a book is an
individual act. Does Wilkins explain why it was important to
recreate the story on TV were it could be experienced by millions simultaneously?

(3) With what examples does Wilkins make most convincing
his argument that *Roots* was good for America?

JUDITH JAMISON DANCES "CRY"

ALICE WALKER

I sit up ramrod straight against any disappointment, strain-
ing my eyes across the backs of people in front of me. Conscious, against my will, that they are white; waiting to watch
a black woman dance.

Suddenly, Jamison is on the stage. Her presence is startling.
The theater falls silent, anticipation its only breath.

There is only herself, dressed in white, with cropped hair;
but she fills the stage completely.

She is tall.

Across the footlights her skin is a chocolate velvet glow; her eyes, under enormous false eyelashes, are intense. A little hard. She acknowledges her audience only by her coolness, the composure of her body's flowing lines.

Her body arches, as if from sleep.

She begins to dance.

The music of Alice Coltrane moves across the theater like a fog. For a long moment it obscures direction.

Jamison searches through the music with her body. Her long arms stretch out, casual and controlled. The music is atonal, floating, and seems to drift into the corners of the stage. Jamison finds the music's fiber, wraps it first around her fingers, then her arms, like a shawl, and turning shows it to her audience.

They had not seen it, until revealed by her. They see it is a complex new treasure they had almost missed. They are grateful. The cool smile of a sorceress begins on Jamison's lips, but is not allowed to flower.

The audience continues to applaud, but Jamison forgets them. Moves away, like a woman moved by visions. Or by a nightmare.

She is on her knees, scrubbing the floor with a long white rag. A voice, too shallow somehow, sings "Been on a Train." The truth is deeper than the voice, and Jamison finds it: on her knees she becomes Anonymous Black Female Body. Anonymous in slave coffles, anonymous in canebrakes, anonymous in cotton rows. Anonymous in the ghetto tenements and other people's kitchens. The North Star of the Underground Railroad shines in Jamison's face. Sweat, like a silver dew, glistens in the hollow of her throat.

Pain becomes the muscles of her arms. Sadness the shortness of her hair.

She *has been* on a train. For she is Harriet Tubman, the "conductor" of the Underground Railroad, raising her machete against the killer swamps, and Sojourner Truth, in agony and indignation, baring her breasts in Town Hall. She is the grandmother of Langston Hughes, holding in her hands the bullet-riddled shawl of Sheridan Leary. The mother of Malcolm shut up, away. She is the mother of King, peering

from a window down a quiet Atlanta street. And the wife of
Medgar Evers, the moment she knew for sure she had heard a
shot, and moved to open her side door.

Pain, like the cry of a giant bird, fills the stage. Flows out
onto an audience sunk into Time.

Jamison dances.

The music becomes a rocking sound. Fast and complex: a
tapestry of Blues and Spirituals; underneath, the sustaining
drums of Africa. "The Voices of East Harlem" urge her to
leap out of, and into, herself.

"Right On, Be Free."

Bending her body and swaying to one side, and pushing
outward with clenched fists, the music is given form by her
torso. A supple, muscular stalk that strains in the struggle
that is the black woman's life. Her fibrous, loving gift.

Her full breasts are beautiful and rich; and when she whirls
beyond her chains, her cheekbones and neck and thighs and
knees are angular music.

She creates her own space, and fills it, dancing.

"To all black women everywhere—especially our mothers."
They too sit and watch: those who make up the anonymous
dead and those who will never die. Their names and the energy from their prayers are conjured up for celebration; a
long ribbon of light that Jamison claims with joy, and tucks
around her own head.

The music of a sobbing Midnight, but a Hallelujah day-
break.

Jamison's body is alive with sweat, but her movements are
effortless, as if the air itself aids them. She is of wind and fire.
A definite river. Cutting her own path strongly, but always
with grace.

She is in her own space, dancing.

Like a strong wind, or like a tornado, Jamison begins to
whirl. Between her slender fingers the "rag" she scrubbed

with becomes a snow-white shawl, then a turban. Rising from her knees, flinging off the sorrow but retaining the reverence, she has crowned herself.

She is a queen.

She is in her own space, dancing.

New York, the stage, the audience, begin to fade. Her dress, frothy and willful as the sea, is tamed by Jamison's long legs. She leaps through the air, and seems to hang there, like a powerful fountain of water, frozen in midair. Her face, regal and aloof, evokes an ecstasy.

She is the center of a world.

The applause is like thunder. "Brava" inadequate.
Jamison accepts a bouquet of roses the color of blood. "For all black women everywhere—especially our mothers." For this moment, she is all of us.

From Ms. Magazine, 1973.

QUESTIONS

(1) In what ways is the style of the essay appropriate to its subject, the description of a dancer? Does the form of the essay suggest movement?

(2) What are Alice Walker's feelings in the first two paragraphs? Why is "ramrod" an important word?

(3) Does Walker try to describe directly how Jamison dances, or to tell what it feels like to watch her?

(4) Does all of the audience feel what Alice Walker feels? Does Judith Jamison care? For whom is she dancing?

(5) How does Alice Walker connect the "famous" and the "anonymous"? Does the dance make the connection for her?

(6) Why does Walker stress the "color of blood"?

(7) Does Walker risk letting her style go too far? Does the risk add to her power?

(8) How many varied feelings—anger, pride, joy, pain—can you identify in this brief essay? Which words convey what feelings?

GOING HOME AGAIN: THE NEW AMERICAN SCHOLARSHIP BOY

RICHARD RODRIGUEZ

At each step, with every graduation from one level of education to the next, the refrain from bystanders was strangely the same: "Your parents must be so proud of you." I suppose that my parents were proud, although I suspect, too, that they felt more than pride alone as they watched me advance through my education. They seemed to know that my education was separating us from one another, making it difficult to resume familiar intimacies. Mixed with the instincts of parental pride, a certain hurt also communicated itself—too private ever to be adequately expressed in words, but real nonetheless.

The autobiographical facts pertinent to this essay are simply stated in two sentences, though they exist in somewhat awkward juxtaposition to each other. I am the son of Mexican-American parents, who speak a blend of Spanish and English, but who read neither language easily. I am about to receive a Ph.D. in English Renaissance literature. What sort of life—what tensions, feelings, conflicts—connects these two sentences? I look back and remember my life from the time I was seven or eight years old as one of constant movement away from a Spanish-speaking folk culture toward the world of the English-language classroom. As the years passed, I felt myself becom-

ing less like my parents and less comfortable with the assumption of visiting relatives that I was still the Spanish-speaking
child they remembered. By the time I began college, visits
home became suffused with silent embarrassment: there seemed
so little to share, however strong the ties of our affection. My
parents would tell me what happened in their lives or in the
lives of relatives; I would respond with news of my own. Polite questions would follow. Our conversations came to seem
more like interviews.

A few months ago, my dissertation nearly complete, I came
upon my father looking through my bookcase. He quietly fin-
gered the volumes of Milton's tracts and Augustine's theology
with that combination of reverence and distrust those who are
not literate sometimes show for the written word. Silently, I
watched him from the door of the room. However much he
would have insisted that he was "proud" of his son for being
able to master the texts, I knew, if pressed further, he would
have admitted to complicated feelings about my success. When
he looked across the room and suddenly saw me, his body
tightened slightly with surprise, then we both smiled.

For many years I kept my uneasiness about becoming a success in education to myself. I did so in part because I wanted
to avoid vague feelings that, if considered carefully, I would
have no way of dealing with; and in part because I felt that
no one else shared my reaction to the opportunity provided
by education. When I began to rehearse my story of cultural
dislocation publicly, however, I found many listeners willing
to admit to similar feelings from their own pasts. Equally impressive was the fact that many among those I spoke with
were *not* from nonwhite racial groups, which made me realize
that one can grow up to enter the culture of the academy and
find it a "foreign" culture for a variety of reasons, ranging
from economic status to religious heritage. But why, I next
wondered, was it that, though there were so many of us who
came from childhood cultures alien to the academy's, we
voiced our uneasiness to one another and to ourselves so in-
frequently? Why did it take *me* so long to acknowledge publicly the cultural costs I had paid to earn a Ph.D. in Renaissance English literature? Why, more precisely, am I writing
these words only now when my connection to my past barely
survives except as nostalgic memory?

Looking back, a person risks losing hold of the present while being confounded by the past. For the child who moves to an academic culture from a culture that dramatically lacks academic traditions, looking back can jeopardize the certainty he has about the desirability of this new academic culture. Richard Hoggart's description, in *The Uses of Literacy,* of the cultural pressures on such a student, whom Hoggart calls the "scholarship boy," helps make the point. The scholarship boy must give nearly unquestioning allegiance to academic culture, Hoggart argues, if he is to succeed at all, so different is the milieu of the classroom from the culture he leaves behind. For a time, the scholarship boy may try to balance his loyalty between his concretely experienced family life and the more abstract mental life of the classroom. In the end, though, he must choose between the two worlds: if he intends to succeed as a student, he must, literally and figuratively, separate himself from his family, with its gregarious life, and find a quiet place to be alone with his thoughts.

After a while, the kind of allegiance the young student might once have given his parents is transferred to the teacher, the new parent. Now without the support of the old ties and certainties of the family, he almost mechanically acquires the assumptions, practices, and style of the classroom milieu. For the loss he might otherwise feel, the scholarship boy substitutes an enormous enthusiasm for nearly everything having to do with school.

How readily I read my own past into the portrait of Hoggart's scholarship boy. Coming from a home in which mostly Spanish was spoken, for example, I had to decide to forget Spanish when I began my education. To succeed in the classroom, I needed psychologically to sever my ties with Spanish. Spanish represented an alternate culture as well as another language—and the basis of my deepest sense of relationship to my family. Although I recently taught myself to read Spanish, the language that I see on the printed page is not quite the language I heard in my youth. That other Spanish, the spoken Spanish of my family, I remember with nostalgia and guilt: guilt because I cannot explain to aunts and uncles why I do not answer their questions any longer in their own idiomatic language. Nor was I able to explain to teachers in graduate school, who regularly expected me to read and speak Spanish with ease, why my very ability to reach graduate school as a student of English literature in the first place required me to loosen my attachments to a language I spoke years earlier. Yet, having lost the ability to speak Spanish, I never forgot it so totally that I could not understand it. Hearing Spanish spoken on the street reminded me of the community I once felt a part of, and still cared deeply about. I never forgot Spanish so thoroughly, in other words, as to move outside the range of its nostalgic pull.

Such moments of guilt and nostalgia were, however, just that—momentary. They punctuated the history of my otherwise successful progress from *barrio* to classroom. Perhaps they even encouraged it. Whenever I felt my determination to succeed wavering, I tightened my hold on the conventions of academic life.

Spanish was one aspect of the problem, my parents another. They could raise deeper, more persistent doubts. They offered encouragement to my brothers and me in our work, but they also spoke, only half jokingly, about the way education was putting "big ideas" into our heads. When we would come home, for example, and challenge assumptions we earlier believed, they would be forced to defend their beliefs (which, given our new verbal skills, they did increasingly less well) or, more frequently, to submit to our logic with the disclaimer, "It's what we were taught in our time to believe. . . ." More important, after we began to leave home for college, they voiced regret about how "changed" we had become, how much further away from one another we had grown. They partly yearned for a return to the time before education assumed their children's primary loyalty. This yearning was renewed each time they saw their nieces and nephews (none of whom continued their education beyond high school, all of whom continued to speak fluent Spanish) living according to the conventions and assumptions of their parents' culture. If I was already troubled by the time I graduated from high school by that refrain of congratulations ("Your parents must be so proud. . . ."), I realize now how much more difficult and complicated was my progress into academic life for my parents, as they saw the cultural foundation of their family erode, than it was for me.

Yet my parents were willing to pay the price of alienation

and continued to encourage me to become a scholarship boy because they perceived, as others of the lower classes had before them, the relation between education and social mobility. Lacking the former themselves made them acutely aware of its necessity as prerequisite for the latter. They sent their children off to school in the hopes of their acquiring something "better" beyond education. Notice the assumption here that education is something of a tool or license—a means to an end, which has been the traditional way the lower or working classes have viewed the value of education in the past. That education might alter children in more basic ways than providing them with skills, certificates of proficiency, and even upward mobility, may come as a surprise for some, but the financial cost is usually tolerated.

Complicating my own status as a scholarship boy in the last ten years was the rise, in the mid-1960s, of what was then called "the Third World Student Movement." Racial minority groups, led chiefly by black intellectuals, began to press for greater access to higher education. The assumption behind their criticism, like the assumption of white working-class families, was that educated opportunity was useful for economic and social advancement. The racial minority leaders went one step further, however, and it was this step that was probably most revolutionary. Minority students came to the campus feeling that they were representative of larger groups of people—that, indeed, they were advancing the condition of entire societies by their matriculation. Actually, this assumption was not altogether new to me. Years before, educational success was something my parents urged me to strive for precisely because it would reflect favorably on *all* Mexican-Americans—specifically, my intellectual achievement would help deflate the stereotype of the "dumb Pancho." This early goal was only given greater currency by the rhetoric of the Third World spokesmen. But it was the fact that I felt myself suddenly much more a "public" Mexican-American, a representative of sorts, that was to prove so crucial for me during these years.

One college admissions officer assured me one day that he recognized my importance to his school precisely as deriving from the fact that, after graduation, I would surely be "going back to [my] community." More recently, teachers have urged me not to trouble over the fact that I am not "representative" of my culture, assuring me that I can serve as a "model" for those still in the *barrio* working toward academic careers. This is the line that I hear, too, when being interviewed for a faculty position. The interviewer almost invariably assumes that, because I am racially a Mexican-American, I can serve as a special counselor to minority students. The expectation is that I still retain the capacity for intimacy with "my people."

This new way of thinking about the possible uses of education is what has made the entrance of minority students into higher education so dramatic. When the minority group student was accepted into the academy, he came—in everyone's mind—as part of a "group." When I began college, I barely attracted attention except perhaps as a slightly exotic ("Are you from India?") brown-skinned student; by the time I graduated, my presence was annually noted by, among others, the college public relations office as "one of the fifty-two students with Spanish surnames enrolled this year." By having his presence announced to the campus in this way, the minority group student was unlike any other scholarship boy the campus had seen before. The minority group student now dramatized more publicly, if also in new ways, the issues of cultural dislocation that education forces, issues that are not solely racial in origin. When Richard Rodriguez *became* a Chicano, the dilemmas he earlier had as a scholarship boy were complicated but not decisively altered by the fact that he had assumed a group identity.

The assurance I heard that, somehow, I was being useful to my community by being a student was gratefully believed, because it gave me a way of dealing with the guilt and cynicism that each year came my way along with the scholarships, grants, and, lately, job offers from schools which a few years earlier would have refused me admission as a student. Each year, in fact, it became harder to believe that my success had anything to do with my intellectual performance, and harder to resist the conclusion that it was due to my minority group status. When I drove to the airport, on my way to London as a Fulbright Fellow last year, leaving behind cousins of my age who were already hopelessly burdened by financial insecurity and dead-end jobs, momentary guilt could be relieved by the thought that somehow my trip was beneficial to persons other

than myself. But, of course, if the thought was a way of dealing with the guilt, it was also the reason for the guilt. Sitting
in a university library, I would notice a janitor of my own
race and grow uneasy; I was, I knew, in a rough way a benefi-
ciary of his condition. Guilt was accompanied by cynicism.
The most dazzlingly talented minority students I know today
refuse to believe that their success is wholly based on their
own talent, or even that when they speak in a classroom anyone hears them as anything but *the* voice of their minority
group. It is scarcely surprising, then, though initially it probably seemed puzzling, that so many of the angriest voices on
the campus against the injustices of racism came from those
not visibly its primary victims.

It became necessary to believe the rhetoric about the value
of one's presence on campus simply as a way of living with
one's "success." Among ourselves, however, minority group
students often admitted to a shattering sense of loss—the feeling that, somehow, something was happening to us. Especially
from students who had not yet become accustomed, as by that
time I had, to the campus, I remember hearing confessions of
extreme discomfort and isolation. Our close associations, the
separate dining-room tables, and the special dormitories helped
to relieve some of the pain, but only some of it.

Significant here was the development of the ethnic studies
concept—black studies, Chicano studies, et cetera—and the related assumption held by minority group students in a number of departments that they could keep in touch with their
old cultures by making these cultures the subject of their
study. Here again one notices how different the minority student was from other comparable students: other scholarship
boys—poor Jews and the sons of various immigrant cultures—
came to the academy singly, much more inclined to accept the
courses and material they found. The ethnic studies concept
was an indication that, for a multitude of reasons, the new
racial minority group students were not willing to give up so
easily their ties with their old cultures.

The importance of these new ethnic studies was that they
introduced the academy to subject matter that generally deserved to be studied, and at the same time offered a staggering
critique of the academy's tendency toward parochialism. Most
minority group intellectuals never noted this tendency toward

academic parochialism. They more often saw the reason for, say, the absence of a course on black literature in an English department as a case of simple racism. That it might instead be an instance of the fact that academic culture can lose track of human societies and whole areas of human experience was rarely raised. Never asking such a question, the minority group students never seemed to wonder either if as teachers their own courses might suffer the same cultural limitations other seminars and classes suffered. Consequently, in a peculiar way the new minority group critics of higher education came to justify the academy's assumptions. The possibility that academic culture could encourage one to grow out of touch with cultures beyond its conceptual horizon was never seriously considered.

Too often in the last ten years one heard minority group students repeat the joke, never very funny in the first place, about the racial minority academic who ended up sounding more "white" than white academics. Behind the scorn for such a figure was the belief that the new generation of minority group students would be able to avoid having to make similar kinds of cultural concessions. The pressures that might have led to such conformity went unexamined.

For the last few years my annoyance at hearing such jokes was doubtless related to the fact that I was increasingly beginning to sense that I was the "bleached" academic the minority group students found so laughable. I suppose I had always sensed that my cultural allegiance was undergoing subtle alterations as I was being educated. Only when I finished my course work in graduate school and went off to England for my dissertation year did I grasp how far I had traveled from my cultural origins. My year in England was actually my first opportunity to write and reflect upon the kind of material that I would spend my life producing. It was my first chance, too, to be free simultaneously of the distractions of course-work and of the insecurities of trying to find my niche in academic life. Sitting in the reading room of the British Museum, I no longer doubted that I had joined academic society. Ironically, this feeling of having finally arrived allowed me to look back to the community whence I came. That I was geographically farther away from my home than I had ever been lent a metaphorical resonance to the cultural distance I suddenly felt.

But the feeling was not pleasing. The reward of feeling a part of the world of the British Museum was an odd one. Each morning I would arrive at the reading room and grow increasingly depressed by the silence and what the silence implied—that my life as a scholar would require self-absorption. Who, I wondered, would find my work helpful enough to want to read it? Was not my dissertation—whose title alone would puzzle my relatives—only my grandest exercise thus far in self-enclosure? The sight of the heads around me bent over their texts and papers, many so thoroughly engrossed that they wouldn't look up at the silent clock overhead for hours at a stretch, made me recall the remarkable noises of life in my family home. The tedious prose I was writing, a prose constantly qualified by footnotes, reminded me of the capacity for passionate statement those of the culture I was born into commanded—and which, could it be, I had now lost.

As I remembered it during those gray English afternoons, the past rushed forward to define more precisely my present condition. Remembering my youth, a time when I was not restricted to a chair but ran barefoot under a summer sun that tightened my skin with its white heat, made the fact that it was only my mind that "moved" each hour in the library painfully obvious.

I did need to figure out where I had lost touch with my past. I started to become alien to my family culture the day I became a scholarship boy. In the British Museum the realization seemed obvious. But later, returning to America, I returned to minority group students who were still speaking of their cultural ties to their past. How was I to tell them what I had learned about myself in England?

A short while ago, a group of enthusiastic Chicano undergraduates came to my office to ask me to teach a course to high school students in the *barrio* on the Chicano novel. This new literature, they assured me, has an important role to play in helping to shape the consciousness of a people currently without adequate representation in literature. Listening to them I was struck immediately with the cultural problems raised by their assumption. I told them that the novel is not capable of dealing with Chicano experience adequately, simply because most Chicanos are not literate, or are at least not yet comfortably so. This is not something Chicanos need to apologize for (though, I suppose, remembering my own childhood ambition to combat stereotypes of the Chicano as mental menial, it is not something easily admitted). Rather the genius and value of those Chicanos who do not read seem to me to be largely that their reliance on voice, the spoken word, has given them the capacity for intimate conversation that I, as someone who now relies heavily on the written word, can only envy. The second problem, I went on, is more in the nature of a technical one: the novel, in my opinion, is not a form capable of being true to the basic sense of communal life that typifies Chicano culture. What the novel as a literary form is best capable of representing is solitary existence set against a large social background. Chicano novelists, not coincidentally, nearly always fail to capture the breathtakingly rich family life of most Chicanos, and instead often describe only the individual Chicano in transit between Mexican and American cultures.

I said all of this to the Chicano students in my office, and could see that little of it made an impression. They seemed only frustrated by what they probably took to be a slick, academic justification for evading social responsibility. After a time, they left me, sitting alone.

There is a danger of being misunderstood here. I am not suggesting that an academic cannot reestablish ties of any kind with his old culture. Indeed, he can have an impact on the culture of his childhood. But as an academic, one exists by definition in a culture separate from one's nonacademic roots and, therefore, any future ties one has with those who remain "behind" are complicated by one's new cultural perspective.

Paradoxically, the distance separating the academic from his nonacademic past can make his past seem, if not closer, then clearer. It is possible for the academic to understand the culture from which he came "better" than those who still live within it. In my own experience, it has only been as I have come to appraise my past through categories and notions derived from the social sciences that I have been able to think of Chicano life in cultural terms at all. Characteristics I took for granted or noticed only in passing—the spontaneity, the passionate speech, the trust in concrete experience, the willingness to think communally rather than individually—these are all significant phenomena to me now as aspects of a total culture. (My parents have neither the time nor the inclination to think about their culture as a culture.) Able to conceptualize a sense of Chicano culture, I am now also more attracted to that culture than I was before. The temptation now is to try to preserve those traits of my old culture that have not yet, in effect, atrophied.

The racial self-consciousness of minority group students during the last few years evident in the ethnic costumes, the stylized gestures, and the idiomatic though often evasive devices for insisting on one's continuing membership in the community of the past, are also indications that the minority group student has gained a new appreciation of the culture of his origin precisely because of his earlier alienation from it. As a result, Chicano students sometimes become more Chicano than most Chicanos. I remember, for example, my father's surprise when, walking across my college campus one afternoon, we came upon two Chicano academics wearing serapes. He and my mother were also surprised—indeed offended—when they earlier heard student activists use the word "Chicano." For them the term was a private one, primarily descriptive of persons they knew. It suggested intimacy. Hearing the word shouted into a microphone by a stranger left them bewildered. What they could not understand was that the student activist finds it easier than they to use "Chicano" in a more public way, for his distance from their culture and his membership in academic culture permits a wider and more abstract view.

The Mexican-Americans who begin to call themselves Chicanos in this new way are actually forming a new version of what it means to be a Chicano. The culture that didn't see itself as a culture is suddenly prized and identified for being one. The price one pays for this new self-consciousness is the knowledge of just that—it is *new*—and this knowledge is not available to those who remain at home. So it is knowledge that separates as well as unites people. Wanting more desperately than ever to assert his ties with the newly visible culture, the minority group student is tempted to exploit those characteristics of that culture that might yet survive in him. But the self-consciousness never allows one to feel completely at ease with the old culture. Worse, the knowledge of the culture of the past often leaves one feeling strangely solitary. At home, I hear relatives speak and find myself analyzing too much of what they say. It is embarrassing being a cultural anthropologist in one's own family's kitchen. I keep feeling myself little more than a cultural voyeur. I often come away from family gatherings suspecting, in fact, that what conceptions of my culture I carry with me are no more than illusions. Because they were never there before, because no one back home shares them, I grow less and less to trust their reliability: too often they seem no more than mental bubbles floating before an academic's eye.

Many who have taught minority group students in the last decade testify to sensing characteristics of a childhood culture still very much alive in these students. Should the teacher make these students aware of these characteristics? Initially, most of us would probably answer negatively. Better to trust the unconscious survival of the past than the always problematical, sometimes even clownish, re-creations of it. But the cultural past cannot be assured of survival; perhaps many of its characteristics are lost simply because the student is never encouraged to look for them. Even those that do survive do so tenuously. As a teacher, one can only hope that the best qualities in his minority group students' cultural legacy aren't altogether snuffed out by academic education.

More easy to live with and distinguishable from self-conscious awareness of the past are the ways the past unconsciously survives—perhaps even yet survives in me. As it turns out, the issue becomes less acute with time. With each year, the chance that the student is unaware of his cultural legacy is diminished as the habit of academic reflectiveness grows stronger. Although the culture of the academy makes innocence about one's cultural past less likely, this same culture, and the conceptual tools it provides, increases the desire to want to write and speak about the past. The paradox persists.

Awaiting the scholarship boy who finally acknowledges the fact that his perceptions of reality have changed is the dilemma of action. The sentimental reaction to this knowledge entails merely a refusal to renew contact with one's nonacademic culture lest one contaminate it. The problem, however, with this sentimental solution is that it overlooks the way academic culture renders one capable of dealing with the transactions of mass society. Academic culture, with its habits of conceptualization and abstraction, allows those of us from other cultures to deal with each other in a mass society. In this sense academic culture does have a profound political impact. Although people intent upon social mobility think of education as a means to an end, education does become an end: its culture allows one to exist more easily in a society increasingly anonymous and impersonal. The truth is, the academic's distance from his own experience brings the capacity for communicating with bureaucracies and understanding one's position in society—a prerequisite for political action.

If the sentimental reaction to nonacademic culture is to fear changing it, the political response, typical especially of working-class and lately minority group leaders, is to see higher education solely in terms of its political and social possibilities. Its cultural consequences, in this view, are disregarded. At this time when we are so keenly aware of social and economic inequality, it might seem beside the point to warn those who are working to bring about equality that education alters culture as well as economic status. And yet, if there is one main criticism that I, as a minority group student, must make of minority group leaders in their past attacks on the "racism" of the academy, it is that they never distinguished between my right to higher education and the desirability of my actually entering the academy—which is another way of saying again that they never recognized that there were things I could lose by becoming a scholarship boy.

Certainly, the academy changes those from alien cultures more than it is changed by them. While minority groups had an impact on higher education, largely because of their advantage in coming as a group, within the last few years students such as myself, who finally ended up certified as academics, also ended up sounding very much like the academics we found when we came to the campus. I do not enjoy making such admissions. But perhaps now the time has come when questions about the cultural costs of education ought to be delayed no longer. Those of us who have been scholarship boys know in our bones that our education has exacted a large price in exchange for the large benefits it has conferred upon us. And what is sadder to consider, after we have paid that price, we go home and casually change the cultures that nurtured us. My parents today understand how they are "Chicanos" in a large and impersonal sense. The gains from such knowledge are clear. But so, too, are the reasons for regret.

From *The American Scholar*, 1974.

QUESTIONS

(1) Does Rodriguez succeed in making you feel the tension between the two "sentences" of autobiographical fact? Why do those two sentences come in the second paragraph? What is the relation of fact to feeling in this essay?

(2) Is this essay a reverse of Haley's? Is it comparable to "The African" in any way?

(3) Rodriguez writes, in the third paragraph, of the combination of "reverence and distrust" in his father. What kind of contradictory combinations exist in him? Are they the theme of his essay?

(4) Is it natural for him to identify with a boy in a book—the "scholarship boy"—rather than a real person? Does this reveal even more about himself than Rodriguez seems to realize?

(5) How often and in how many ways are "price" and "cost" used in this essay? What is being bought and sold?

(6) How does Rodriguez feel about being *a credit to his race?* How do some of the other people in the essay, including his parents, feel about that cliché? What are the problems in being an individual and, at the same time, a representative of something?

(7) Why, specifically, is it different and harder for a "racial scholarship boy" in contrast to an "economic scholarship boy"?

(8) What kind of temptations are there for Rodriguez to sell out? To whom? For what?

(9) What kinds of "families" or "communities" does Rodriguez live in?

(10) Is the entire essay evidence that "academic culture can lose track of human societies and whole areas of human experience . . ."? He is speaking about curricula, but is he also describing what happened to him when he acquired "academic culture"?

(11) How does Rodriguez convey his sense of the feeling of the two cultures between which he was divided? Did he have to become an "alien" to understand "alienation"?

(12) Is what he says about the novel as a literary form a description of his own situation, his own "solitary existence"?

(13) Is the sentence, "After a time, they left me, sitting alone . . . ," the climax of the essay? Does the tone change after this? Is everything after this sentence an attempt to reach those students who left?

(14) To whom is the end of the essay addressed?

(15) In the last paragraph Rodriguez describes the power of the academy to change those from alien cultures. Is this also symbolic of the process of Americanization of ethnic groups? For better or worse or both?

THE WHITE MAN'S SUICIDE

STAN STEINER

"Personal penance" was what he called it.

It was soon after he had been convicted of criminal conspiracy in the Watergate cover-up that John Ehrlichman, former domestic policy adviser to former President Richard Nixon, announced that rather than go to prison he would like to work with the Pueblos of New Mexico—to do "penance."

Life on Indian reservations "is no easy life," Ehrlichman's lawyer, Ira Lowe, had told Judge John Sirica. His client would, however, sacrifice the comforts of a prison cell to go into the "remote" mountains of northern New Mexico to "help" the poor Indians. "We have talked to the Pueblos and found out what their needs were," Lowe said. Ehrlichman could help them solve their land and water problems; he was a "land use lawyer," and he was "sympathetic" to Indians.

The director of the Northern Pueblo Council, Herman Agoyo, listened politely but with surprise to the unsolicited offer. He did not say no and Ehrlichman's lawyer took that to mean yes.

Governor Lucario Padilla of Santa Clara Pueblo, who was chairman of the council, replied that they did indeed have some water problems. "We could certainly use some plumbers in our struggle to establish our water rights." Though he thought perhaps Ehrlichman "would be more useful in providing community service in the form of ditch [digging] work, as spring is at hand."

That might be of more help to him than he could be of help to them, Governor Padilla said. "Being compassionate people, we would be pleased to assist in the rehabilitation of a felon, but we do question whether Mr. Ehrlichman's offer of legal assistance is all that appropriate," the governor said, "at this point in time."

And then the governors of the eight pueblos met and unanimously "denied Mr. John Ehrlichman's request."

"This trial just ended before Judge Sirica has focused at-

tention of the non-Indian community in this country on lack
of credibility insofar as political institutions are concerned.
We needed no Watergate to be made aware of the fact that
the government agencies are not above verbal duplicity,"
Governor Padilla said.

"One can only wonder what sort of assistance Ehrlichman
contemplates when he offers to help the Pueblo Indians of
New Mexico."

The pretense of penance was poorly timed. It came at an
uncharitable moment.

On the sun-baked plazas of the Pueblos there was already a
surfeit of government lawyers who the people wished would
go home. The State of New Mexico had launched another of
its endless court cases to destroy Pueblo self-government, this
time by denying their age-old water rights. And the federal
government had sent some uninvited lawyers to "defend" the
Pueblos. "The fox is protecting us against the other foxes,"
said Frank Tenorio, from the San Felipe Pueblo.

An eloquent and scholarly man, Tenorio was secretary of
the All-Indian Pueblo Council. His sense of justice was not,
however, recognized by the courts.

For thousands of years his Pueblo, like most of those in the
valley of the Rio Grande, had been building their homes and
farming their fields along the river. Now the newcomers in
the growing cities and agribusinesses of New Mexico needed,
and were determined to take away, the ancestral water rights
of the villagers. The state engineer, Steve Reynolds, had filed
suit claiming the water belonged to the state. Pojoaque,
Nambe, Tesuque, and San Ildefonso Pueblos had contested
this, in a landmark case known as *New Mexico* v. *Aamodt*.
The case was a "mess," Tenorio said.

If the water was taken, the people would "shrivel," Tenorio
said. "Water is the blood of the people." And the Pueblos
"were shocked by a statement by Vearle Payne, Chief Judge
of the U.S. District Court of New Mexico, that 'Pueblo Indians are not considered by Congress to have any reserved water
rights. . . .' This decision," said Tenorio, put the Pueblos
"firmly under the thumb of the states."

And so the Pueblos wished to fire the government lawyers
and hire their own. Their right to hire their own lawyers was
denied them by Judge Payne, a ruling later overturned by a

higher court. Still, they feared "the government was getting ready to 'throw' the case."

In the spring of 1976 the United States Supreme Court ruled that the State of New Mexico did indeed have jurisdiction over the Indians' water rights, reversing one hundred years of moral promises and legal decisions.

One day that autumn, the Pueblo leader journeyed north to Shiprock to ask for the aid of the Navajos, the traditional enemies of the Pueblos. The old enemies were no longer enemies, Tenorio said, for now they had common enemies, who wished to take away the water of all the Indian people.

This is what he said:

> My name is Frank Tenorio. I am a Pueblo Indian from San Felipe Pueblo in New Mexico. I have been involved in the fight to save our people's water for many years. Against us we have arrayed the forces of federal, state, and local governments, as well as private interests of powerful corporations and individuals. In our fight we stand alone against the combined interests of the most powerful country the world has ever known.
>
> In a way I might be termed a hematologist. This is a medical doctor who concerns himself with problems of the blood. For water is the blood of the Pueblo people.
>
> There has been a lot said about the sacredness of our land, which is our body and the value of our culture, which is our soul; but if the blood of the people stops its life-giving flow, or becomes polluted, all else will die and many thousands of years of our communal existence will come to an end.
>
> Surely the Great Spirit did not intend for us to shrivel up and die and our bones to be scattered, only to be remembered in anthropology textbooks.
>
> If a Pueblo who died twenty thousand years ago should return to live with his relatives today, he would be perfectly at home. We have kept our relationship with nature and now we as a people see that we are one of the few custodians of this kind of knowledge left. Maybe this kind of knowledge is what the world will need to survive.
>
> Our old enemies, the Anglos and the Spanish, have now settled among us. They will not give back to us what they have stolen, but we have survived. We have survived the Spanish, the Anglos, and the technological revolution. But now we face our greatest enemies. They do not go by the name of Coronado, or Cortez, or Custer, but by the name of the Army Corps of Engineers, San Juan–Chama Diversion Project, Salt River Project, and so forth.
>
> In facing these new adversaries who threaten our existence, I know now how my Pueblo brothers who have passed on felt when they stood on the rooftops of their pueblos and saw for the first

time these people with white skins, with shining armor, shooting fire out of sticks and logs, which were killing their people and destroying their homes.

We learned their powers and we survived them. We will also learn the ways of all our adversaries who hide behind such initials as BIA [Bureau of Indian Affairs] or BLM [Bureau of Land Management], and we will survive them, too.

Basic to our problem is the conflict of interest in the federal government regarding Indian affairs. The Department of the Interior is charged with the protection and preservation of natural resources for the public good. It is also charged with the protection and development of Indian lands. . . . When there is a conflict between public interest and Indian interest, the Indian loses.

Our present situation is analogous to a farmer who has his chickens and his foxes in the same coop and who is charged both with feeding the foxes and keeping the chickens alive. We all know the results to be expected from this kind of setup.

Our water, our sacred water, is a good example of what is happening to us.

It must be remembered that with the ever-expanding and wasteful urbanization of Indian country, we Indian people of the Southwest find ourselves with the last good land and the last good water left. As the white man wastes his resources, he casts a covetous eye on what we have preserved for our own needs. We have not wasted our resources.

There is something suicidal in the non-Indian's belief in ever-expanding development and his belief in his ability to be able to continually reform nature through technology. The Southwest, in terms of water supply, can only support a limited number of people; that is a fact of life. The fact is that the Great Spirit put only so much water on this earth, and that is a fact the white man refuses to confront.

We Pueblo Indians are rapidly approaching an Armageddon—a final, decisive battle between our right to survive and the prolongation of the white man's suicide.

Our first line of defense has been and should be the Winters Doctrine. This doctrine was enunciated by the Supreme Court in 1908. It states that land reserved for the Indians by law or treaty—that is, Indian reservations—is entitled to use water rising or flowing on this land, to develop it now and in the future, whether or not Indians are now using the water. This doctrine is in direct conflict with the prior-appropriation laws used in most states.

The law is on our side, but might is not.

As you recall, the Supreme Court in the early 1800s ruled that the Cherokee tribe could not be removed from their ancestral homes in Georgia. President Andrew Jackson said, "The Supreme Court has made its decision; now let them enforce it." The Cherokees were removed. History seems to be repeating itself with the Pueblo Indians today.

People in power have always stolen from Indian People. But I must hand it to the present United States government; never has any government gone to so much expense and into so much detail in order to steal something from somebody. I guess that is the American Way.

The fact is that our water is being taken and our whole way of life is threatened.

We Indian people do not always understand the laws, largely because they are numerous, complex, and ever-changing. But we do understand fairness. Fairness is the right to exist as a people. . . . Fairness is living up to one's solemn agreements and contracts. . . . And fairness is having enough water to raise one's corn and feed one's family. . . .

My people back home do not fully understand what is happening to them. We grow up believing that people will do the right thing, if they know what the right thing is. This is our belief in America. It is up to this nation as a whole to prove us right or wrong.

From *The Vanishing White Man*, 1976.

QUESTIONS

(1) What does the opening anecdote of John Ehrlichman's offer reveal about continuing attitudes toward Indians?

(2) Does Steiner provide enough background for Frank Tenorio's statement? Do the "facts" prepare the reader for the emotion of the statement?

(3) How does Tenorio's statement about "law" versus "might" reflect back upon the use of Watergate as an introduction?

(4) Is Tenorio's argument effective? If yes, why? If no, why?

(5) How does Tenorio's speech mingle elements of ancient Indian style and modern American idiom? Is the mixture a good one for his purposes?

(6) Is Tenorio's statement that the Pueblo Indians have kept their relationship with nature for 20,000 years a powerful part of his argument?

(7) Is his evocation of the advent of the Spaniards in their armor with their firearms effective? What relationship does he

imply exists between the Spaniards and the present government?

(8) Is Tenorio speaking only for the Pueblo Indians? Is his speech more general than that? What are the stakes he is arguing for?

THE WOMAN WARRIOR

MAXINE HONG KINGSTON

Long ago in China, knot-makers tied string into buttons and frogs, and rope into bell pulls. There was one knot so complicated that it blinded the knot-maker. Finally an emperor outlawed this cruel knot, and the nobles could not order it anymore. If I had lived in China, I would have been an outlaw knot-maker.

Maybe that's why my mother cut my tongue. She pushed my tongue up and sliced the frenum. Or maybe she snipped it with a pair of nail scissors. I don't remember her doing it, only her telling me about it, but all during childhood I felt sorry for the baby whose mother waited with scissors or knife in hand for it to cry—and then, when its mouth was wide open like a baby bird's, cut. The Chinese say "a ready tongue is an evil."

I used to curl up my tongue in front of the mirror and tauten my frenum into a white line, itself as thin as a razor blade. I saw no scars in my mouth. I thought perhaps I had had two frena, and she had cut one. I made other children open their mouths so I could compare theirs to mine. I saw perfect pink membranes stretching into precise edges that looked easy enough to cut. Sometimes I felt very proud that my mother committed such a powerful act upon me. At other times I was terrified—the first thing my mother did when she saw me was to cut my tongue.

"Why did you do that to me, Mother?"

"I told you."

"Tell me again."

"I cut it so that you would not be tongue-tied. Your tongue would be able to move in any language. You'll be able to speak languages that are completely different from one another. You'll be able to pronounce anything. Your frenum looked too tight to do those things, so I cut it."

"But isn't 'a ready tongue an evil'?"

"Things are different in this ghost country."

"Did it hurt me? Did I cry and bleed?"

"I don't remember. Probably."

She didn't cut the other children's. When I asked cousins and other Chinese children whether their mothers had cut their tongues loose, they said, "What?"

"Why didn't you cut my brothers' and sisters' tongues?"

"They didn't need it."

"Why not? Were theirs longer than mine?"

"Why don't you quit blabbering and get to work?"

If my mother was not lying she should have cut more, scraped away the rest of the frenum skin, because I have a terrible time talking. Or she should not have cut at all, tampering with my speech. When I went to kindergarten and had to speak English for the first time, I became silent. A dumbness—a shame—still cracks my voice in two, even when I want to say "hello" casually, or ask an easy question in front of the check-out counter, or ask directions of a bus driver. I stand frozen, or I hold up the line with the complete, grammatical sentence that comes squeaking out at impossible length. "What did you say?" says the cab driver, or "Speak up," so I have to perform again, only weaker the second time. A telephone call makes my throat bleed and takes up that day's courage. It spoils my day with self-disgust when I hear my broken voice come skittering out into the open. It makes people wince to hear it. I'm getting better, though. Recently I asked the postman for special-issue stamps; I've waited since childhood for postmen to give me some of their own accord. I am making progress, a little every day.

My silence was thickest—total—during the three years that I covered my school paintings with black paint. I painted layers of black over houses and flowers and suns, and when I drew on the blackboard, I put a layer of chalk on top. I was making a stage curtain, and it was the moment before the curtain parted or rose. The teachers called my parents to school, and I saw they had been saving my pictures, curling and cracking, all alike and black. The teachers pointed to the pictures and looked serious, talked seriously too, but my parents did not understand English. ("The parents and teachers of criminals were executed," said my father.) My parents took the pictures home. I spread them out (so black and full of possibilities) and pretended the curtains were swinging open, flying up, one after another, sunlight underneath, mighty operas.

During the first silent year I spoke to no one at school, did not ask before going to the lavatory, and flunked kindergarten. My sister also said nothing for three years, silent in the playground and silent at lunch. There were other quiet Chinese girls not of our family, but most of them got over it sooner than we did. I enjoyed the silence. At first it did not occur to me I was supposed to talk or to pass kindergarten. I talked at home and to one or two of the Chinese kids in class. I made motions and even made some jokes. I drank out of a toy saucer when the water spilled out of the cup, and everybody laughed, pointing at me, so I did it some more. I didn't know that Americans don't drink out of saucers.

I liked the Negro students (Black Ghosts) best because they laughed the loudest and talked to me as if I were a daring talker too. One of the Negro girls had her mother coil braids over her ears Shanghai-style like mine; we were Shanghai twins except that she was covered with black like my paintings. Two Negro kids enrolled in Chinese school, and the teachers gave them Chinese names. Some Negro kids walked me to school and home, protecting me from the Japanese kids, who hit me and chased me and stuck gum in my ears. The Japanese kids were noisy and tough. They appeared one day in kindergarten, released from concentration camp, which was a tic-tac-toe mark, like barbed wire, on the map.

It was when I found out I had to talk that school became a misery, that the silence became a misery. I did not speak and felt bad each time that I did not speak. I read aloud in first grade, though, and heard the barest whisper with little squeaks come out of my throat. "Louder," said the teacher, who scared the voice away again. The other Chinese girls did not talk either, so I knew the silence had to do with being a Chinese girl.

Reading out loud was easier than speaking because we did not have to make up what to say, but I stopped often, and the teacher would think I'd gone quiet again. I could not understand "I." The Chinese "I" has seven strokes, intricacies. How could the American "I," assuredly wearing a hat like the Chinese, have only three strokes, the middle so straight? Was it out of politeness that this writer left off strokes the way a Chinese has to write her own name small and crooked? No, it was not politeness; "I" is a capital and "you" is lower-case. I stared at that middle line and waited so long for its black center to resolve into tight strokes and dots that I forgot to pronounce it. The other troublesome word was "here," no strong consonant to hang on to, and so flat, when "here" is two mountainous ideographs. The teacher, who had already told me every day how to read "I" and "here," put me in the low corner under the stairs again, where the noisy boys usually sat.

When my second grade class did a play, the whole class went to the auditorium except the Chinese girls. The teacher, lovely and Hawaiian, should have understood about us, but instead left us behind in the classroom. Our voices were too soft or nonexistent, and our parents never signed the permission slips anyway. They never signed anything unnecessary. We opened the door a crack and peeked out, but closed it again quickly. One of us (not me) won every spelling bee, though.

I remember telling the Hawaiian teacher, "We Chinese can't sing 'land where our fathers died.'" She argued with me about politics, while I meant because of curses. But how can I have that memory when I couldn't talk? My mother says that we, like the ghosts, have no memories.

After American school, we picked up our cigar boxes, in which we had arranged books, brushes, and an inkbox neatly, and went to Chinese school, from 5:00 to 7:30 P.M. There we chanted together, voices rising and falling, loud and soft, some boys shouting, everybody reading together, reciting together and not alone with one voice. When we had a memorization test, the teacher let each of us come to his desk and say the lesson to him privately, while the rest of the class practiced copying or tracing. Most of the teachers were men. The boys who were so well behaved in the American school played tricks on them and talked back to them. The girls were not mute. They screamed and yelled during recess, when there were no rules; they had fist-fights. Nobody was afraid of children hurting themselves or of children hurting school property. The glass doors to the red and green balconies with the gold joy symbols were left wide open so that we could run out and climb the fire escapes. We played capture-the-flag in the auditorium, where Sun Yat-sen and Chiang Kai-shek's pictures hung at the back of the stage, the Chinese flag on their left and the American flag on their right. We climbed the teak ceremonial chairs and made flying leaps off the stage. One flag headquarters was behind the glass door and the other on stage right. Our feet drummed on the hollow stage. During recess the teachers locked themselves up in their office with the shelves of books, copybooks, inks from China. They drank tea and warmed their hands at a stove. There was no play supervision. At recess we had the school to ourselves, and also we could roam as far as we could go—downtown, Chinatown stores, home—as long as we returned before the bell rang.

At exactly 7:30 the teacher again picked up the brass bell that sat on his desk and swung it over our heads, while we charged down the stairs, our cheering magnified in the stairwell. Nobody had to line up.

Not all of the children who were silent at American school found voice at Chinese school. One new teacher said each of us had to get up and recite in front of the class, who was to listen. My sister and I had memorized the lesson perfectly. We said it to each other at home, one chanting, one listening. The teacher called on my sister to recite first. It was the first time a teacher had called on the second-born to go first. My sister was scared. She glanced at me and looked away; I looked down at my desk. I hoped that she could do it because if she could, then I would have to. She opened her mouth and a voice came out that wasn't a whisper, but it wasn't a proper voice either. I hoped that she would not cry, fear breaking up her voice like twigs underfoot. She sounded as if she were trying to sing though weeping and strangling. She did not pause or stop to end the embarrassment. She kept going until she said the last word, and then she sat down. When it was my turn, the same voice came out, a crippled animal running on broken legs. You could hear splinters in my voice, bones rubbing jagged against one another. I was loud, though. I was glad I didn't whisper. There was one little girl who whispered.

You can't entrust your voice to the Chinese, either; they want to capture your voice for their own use. They want to fix up your tongue to speak for them. "How much less can you sell it for?" we have to say. Talk the Sales Ghosts down. Make them take a loss.

We were working at the laundry when a delivery boy came from the Rexall drugstore around the corner. He had a pale blue box of pills, but nobody was sick. Reading the label we saw that it belonged to another Chinese family, Crazy Mary's family. "Not ours," said my father. He pointed out the name to the Delivery Ghost, who took the pills back. My mother muttered for an hour, and then her anger boiled over. "That ghost! That dead ghost! How dare he come to the wrong house?" She could not concentrate on her marking and pressing. "A mistake! Huh!" I was getting angry myself. She fumed. She made her press crash and hiss. "Revenge. We've got to avenge this wrong on our future, on our health, and on our lives. Nobody's going to sicken my children and get away with it." We brothers and sisters did not look at one another. She would do something awful, something embarrassing. She'd already been hinting that during the next eclipse we slam pot lids together to scare the frog from swallowing the moon. (The word for "eclipse" is *frog-swallowing-the-moon*.) When we had not banged lids at the last eclipse and the shadow kept receding anyway, she'd said, "The villagers must be banging and clanging very loudly back home in China."

("On the other side of the world, they aren't having an eclipse, Mama. That's just a shadow the earth makes when it comes between the moon and the sun."

"You're always believing what those Ghost Teachers tell you. Look at the size of the jaws!")

"Aha!" she yelled. "You! The biggest." She was pointing at me. "You go to the drugstore."

"What do you want me to buy, Mother?" I said.

"Buy nothing. Don't bring one cent. Go and make them stop the curse."

"I don't want to go. I don't know how to do that. There are no such things as curses. They'll think I'm crazy."

"If you don't go, I'm holding you responsible for bringing a plague on this family."

"What am I supposed to do when I get there?" I said, sullen, trapped. "Do I say, 'Your delivery boy made a wrong delivery'?"

"They know he made a wrong delivery. I want you to make them rectify their crime."

I felt sick already. She'd make me swing stinky censers around the counter, at the druggist, at the customers. Throw dog blood on the druggist. I couldn't stand her plans.

"You get reparation candy," she said. "You say, 'You have tainted my house with sick medicine and must remove the curse with sweetness.' He'll understand."

"He didn't do it on purpose. And no, he won't, Mother. They don't understand stuff like that. I won't be able to say it right. He'll call us beggars."

"You just translate." She searched me to make sure I wasn't hiding any money. I was sneaky and bad enough to buy the candy and come back pretending it was a free gift.

"Mymotherseztagimmesomecandy," I said to the druggist. Be cute and small. No one hurts the cute and small.

"What? Speak up. Speak English," he said, big in his white druggist coat.

"Tatatagimme somecandy."

The druggist leaned way over the counter and frowned. "Some free candy," I said. "Sample candy."

"We don't give sample candy, young lady," he said.

"My mother said you have to give us candy. She said that is the way the Chinese do it."

"What?"

"That is the way the Chinese do it."

"Do what?"

"Do things." I felt the weight and immensity of things impossible to explain to the druggist.

"Can I give you some money?" he asked.

"No, we want candy."

He reached into a jar and gave me a handful of lollipops. He gave us candy all year round, year after year, every time we went into the drugstore. When different druggists or clerks waited on us, they also gave us candy. They had talked us over. They gave us Halloween candy in December, Christmas candy around Valentine's day, candy hearts at Easter, and Easter eggs at Halloween. "See?" said our mother. "They understand. You kids just aren't very brave." But I knew they did not understand. They thought we were beggars without a home who lived in back of the laundry. They felt sorry for us. I did not eat their candy. I did not go inside the drugstore or walk past it unless my parents forced me to. Whenever we had a prescription filled, the druggist put candy in the medicine bag. This is what Chinese druggists normally do, except they give raisins. My mother thought she taught the Druggist Ghosts a lesson in good manners (which is the same word as "traditions").

My mouth went permanently crooked with effort, turned down on the left side and straight on the right. How strange that the emigrant villagers are shouters, hollering face to face. My father asks, "Why is it I can hear Chinese from blocks away? Is it that I understand the language? Or is it they talk loud?" They turn the radio up full blast to hear the operas, which do not seem to hurt their ears. And they yell over the singers that wail over the drums, everybody talking at once, big arm gestures, spit flying. You can see the disgust on American faces looking at women like that. It isn't just the loudness. It is the way Chinese sounds, chingchong ugly, to American ears, not beautiful like Japanese sayonara words with the consonants and vowels as regular as Italian. We make guttural peasant noise and have Ton Duc Thang names you can't remember. And the Chinese can't hear Americans at all; the language is too soft and western music unhearable. I've watched a Chinese audience laugh, visit, talk-story, and holler during a piano recital, as if the musician could not hear them. A Chinese-American, somebody's son, was playing Chopin, which has no punctuation, no cymbals, no gongs. Chinese piano music is five black keys. Normal Chinese women's voices are strong and bossy. We American-Chinese girls had to whisper to make ourselves American-feminine. Apparently we whispered even more softly than the Americans. Once a year the teachers referred my sister and me to speech therapy, but our voices would straighten out, unpredictably normal, for the therapists. Some of us gave up, shook our heads, and said nothing, not one word. Some of us could not even shake our heads. At times shaking my head no is more self-assertion than I can manage. Most of us eventually found some voice, however faltering. We invented an American-feminine speaking personality.

From *The Woman Warrior*, 1975.

QUESTIONS

(1) Is this essay a discussion of speech or of silence, or both? Explain.

(2) Are the author's two reactions to what her mother did understandable? How do you feel about her mother's motive?

(3) Is the "flash-forward" from the kindergarten to the present effective? What does it accomplish? How does she keep the time shift clear?

(4) Twice Kingston compares Japanese and Chinese. What might be one Caucasian reaction? Could that be related to her idea of "ghosts"?

(5) How does she show that "the silence had to do with being a Chinese girl"?

(6) The subject of the selection is "communication" in one form or another. How many examples of non-communication are there in it?

(7) "My mouth went permanently crooked with effort. . . ." Are there any other permanent effects of her experiences?

(8) How well does the dialogue in the scene with the druggist convey the feelings of all those involved? What feelings can you sort out from the dialogue? Why is the dialogue especially effective at this point in the selection?

SEND YOUR CHILDREN TO THE LIBRARIES

ARTHUR ASHE

Since my sophomore year at University of California, Los Angeles, I have become convinced that we blacks spend too much time on the playing fields and too little time in the libraries.

Please don't think of this attitude as being pretentious just because I am a black, single, professional athlete.

I don't have children, but I can make observations. I strongly believe the black culture expends too much time, energy and effort raising, praising and teasing our black children as to the dubious glories of professional sport.

All children need models to emulate—parents, relatives or friends. But when the child starts school, the influence of the parent is shared by teachers and classmates, by the lure of books, movies, ministers and newspapers, but most of all by television.

Which televised events have the greatest number of viewers?—Sports—The Olympics, Super Bowl, Masters, World Series, pro basketball playoffs, Forest Hills. ABC-TV even has sports on Monday night prime time from April to December.

So your child gets a massive dose of O. J. Simpson, Kareem Abdul-Jabbar, Muhammad Ali, Reggie Jackson, Dr. J. and Lee Elder and other pro athletes. And it is only natural that your child will dream of being a pro athlete himself.

But consider these facts: For the major professional sports of hockey, football, basketball, baseball, golf, tennis and boxing, there are roughly only 3,170 major league positions available (attributing 200 positions to golf, 200 to tennis and 100 to boxing). And the annual turnover is small.

We blacks are a subculture of about 28 million. Of the 13½ million men, 5 to 6 million are under 20 years of age, so your son has less than one chance in 1,000 of becoming a pro. Less than one in a thousand. Would you bet your son's future on something with odds of 999 to 1 against you? I wouldn't.

Unless a child is exceptionally gifted, you should know by the time he enters high school whether he has a future as an athlete. But what is more important is what happens if he doesn't graduate or doesn't land a college scholarship and doesn't have a viable alternative job career. Our high school dropout rate is several times the national average, which contributes to our unemployment rate of roughly twice the national average.

And how do you fight the figures in the newspapers every day. Ali has earned more than $30 million boxing, O. J. just signed for $2½ million, Dr. J. for almost $3 million, Reggie Jackson for $2.8 million, Nate Archibald for $400,000 a year. All that money, recognition, attention, free cars, girls, jobs in the offseason—no wonder there is Pop Warner football, Little League baseball, National Junior Tennis League tennis, hockey practice at 5 A.M. and pickup basketball games in any center city at any hour.

There must be some way to assure that the 999 who try but don't make it to pro sports don't wind up on the street corners or in the unemployment lines. Unfortunately, our most widely recognized role models are athletes and entertainers—"runnin'" and "jumpin'" and "singin'" and "dancin.'" While we are 60 percent of the National Basketball Association, we are less than 4 percent of the doctors and lawyers. While we are about 35 percent of major league baseball we are less than 2 percent of the engineers. While we are about 40 percent of the National Football League, we are less than 11 percent of construction workers such as carpenters and bricklayers.

Our greatest heroes of the century have been athletes—Jack Johnson, Joe Louis and Muhammad Ali. Racial and economic discrimination forced us to channel our energies into athletics and entertainment. These were the ways out of the ghetto, the ways to get that Cadillac, those alligator shoes, that cashmere sport coat.

Somehow, parents must instill a desire for learning alongside the desire to be Walt Frazier. Why not start by sending black professional athletes into high schools to explain the facts of life.

I have often addressed high school audiences and my message is always the same. For every hour you spend on the athletic field, spend two in the library. Even if you make it as a pro athlete, your career will be over by the time you are 35. So you will need that diploma.

Have these pro athletes explain what happens if you break a leg, get a sore arm, have one bad year or don't make the cut for five or six tournaments. Explain to them the star system, wherein for every O. J. earning millions there are six or seven others making $15,000 or $20,000 or $30,000 a year.

But don't just have Walt Frazier or O. J. or Abdul-Jabbar address your class. Invite a benchwarmer or a guy who didn't make it. Ask him if he sleeps every night. Ask him whether he was graduated. Ask him what he would do if he became disabled tomorrow. Ask him where his old high school athletic buddies are.

We have been on the same roads—sports and entertainment—too long. We need to pull over, fill up at the library and speed away to Congress and the Supreme Court, the unions and the business world. We need more Barbara Jordans, Andrew Youngs, union card-holders, Nikki Giovannis and Earl Graveses. Don't worry: we will still be able to sing and dance and run and jump better than anybody else.

I'll never forget how proud my grandmother was when I graduated from U.C.L.A. in 1966. Never mind the Davis Cup in 1968, 1969 and 1970. Never mind the Wimbledon title, Forest Hills, etc. To this day, she still doesn't know what those names mean.

What mattered to her was that of her more than 30 children and grandchildren, I was the first to be graduated from college, and a famous college at that. Somehow, that made up for all those floors she scrubbed all those years.

From *The New York Times*, 1977.

QUESTIONS

(1) Ashe's statistics are convincing. Are they convincing enough to overcome the impact of a repeated television image? Does the TV image influence the child long before he can get to the library?

(2) Ashe's statement about his grandmother is similar to Alice Walker's description of Judith Jamison. The connection is unintentional. Is it effective?

(3) Why is "Don't worry: we will still be able to sing and dance and run and jump better than anybody else" such a good sentence? Why does it appear where it does? How does one sentence like this affect the entire essay?

LIFE ON THE RUN

BILL BRADLEY

The season ended in Boston against the Celtics with DeBusschere on the sidelines suffering from torn stomach muscles. Now, it is a day in June at 6:15 A.M. As I pull up to Newark Airport, the sun appears as a red ball, rising from behind the two distant towers of Manhattan's World Trade Center. The rest of the sky is dark. I am early for the flight.

Phil Jackson has asked Willis Reed and me to join him in staging a basketball clinic at the Oglala Sioux Indian reservation in Pine Ridge, South Dakota. One year ago on the reservation twelve Sioux warriors, members of the American Indian Movement, forcibly occupied the Sacred Heart Catholic Church at Wounded Knee for two and a half weeks, much to the chagrin of 300 federal law enforcement officers summoned to the scene. The tension still runs high according to Mike-Her-Many-Horses, a friend of Phil's from college. Some of Mike's relatives died at the first Wounded Knee Massacre in 1890.

Ten minutes before the scheduled flight departure a green Oldsmobile stops in front of the United Airlines terminal. Willis Reed steps out. He takes his fishing tackle boxes and his camping clothes from the car (he is going hunting in Montana after the clinic), checks in ("OK, Mr. Reed, glad to have you flying with us to Denver"), and walks to the gate. ("Isn't that Willis Reed? Hey, Willis, how's the leg?") He limps noticeably. We settle into the row with extra leg room at the front of the DC-10's first class section.

After we are in the air for forty-five minutes, Willis and I begin to talk about his leg and his future, both of which at the moment are uncertain. "I went to see Dr. O'Donohue four days ago," he says. "He said that what I was feelin' in the play-offs against Boston was a, what'ya call it, a Baker's cyst or maybe a spur deep inside the back of my knee. If I wanted to play he said that I'd have to have another operation."

"When were you last healthy?" I ask.

"I felt pretty good in the final L.A. series in 1973, like, you know, the best since 1971, when I started havin' the tendon trouble in my left knee. With legs like this . . ." he looks at his knees. "No athlete can play unless he's healthy. You want to do it but you can't; it's not severe pain but just enough to prevent you from getting into good shape."

"You going to have the operation?" I ask.

Willis's big left hand moves across the side of his face, covering and then exposing first his nose and mouth and then his cheek. His fingers meet under his chin, where they pause momentarily. His face looks wrinkled as he looks up and says, "I don't know. I don't know. You got to be up for an operation—emotionally up just like for a game. I'm not now. I've had a severely strained shoulder, bone chips removed in my ankle, an operation in my left knee for tendonitis, and an operation in my right knee for a torn cartilage. The pain the first four or five days after an operation is horrible. You just lay there and can't move. You call for the nurse to give you a shot to numb the pain; you sleep an hour and then it's the same thing. On my left knee they put the cast on too soon and the leg didn't have anyplace to go. It swelled up like a balloon. The pain was a monster. With the right knee I had a 103° temperature for three days. I don't know. I don't know if I want to go through all that again, particularly when, if I played after it, I might get a permanent injury. Medicine can't help me now. I guess I need somethin' more. But I got two years on my contract."

"Will the Garden honor your contract if you quit?"

"It depends on whether they say I have to get the operation. They said they thought I was OK. I say, 'hey, I did too, but you see what O'Donohue says.'" He starts fidgeting with the medal that hangs around his neck. "I had planned to retire in two years. I'd have enough money, then, to get by on;

no big numbers, but enough to be my own man. I don't want
to quit now, but with the knee, the operation, and the money
being doubtful, I don't know. I got to decide in a week."

We switch to Frontier Airlines in Denver. When we arrive
in Rapid City the sun is shining brightly; the horizon wide
open. There are few trees; just grass and space. It is startling
at first. Mike-Her-Many-Horses greets us at the airport. He
wears his straight black hair in a ponytail. His shoulders are
broad and his hips narrow. He smiles easily. After a brief TV
interview at the studio in "Rapid" we drive 50 miles to the
reservation in Mike's pickup truck. Mike says that he is so
used to the rolling open hills that he can't leave them. One
summer he worked in Glacier National Park in Montana but
left after three weeks because "the mountains and trees gave
me the feeling I was closed in." We drive slowly through a
town called Scenic on the edge of the reservation; then past
the Long Horn Saloon, the Badlands Jail, and a gas station.
"Since the reservation is dry," Mike says, "here's where people
go to let off steam. There is no law and in that saloon there
are lots of shootings and stabbings."

"You carry a gun on you?" Willis asks.

"No, I keep one in the back of the pickup."

The reservation land is 4,353 square miles of dirt buttes
and "cheet" grass; mostly badlands, which means *bad land*.
Originally the Sioux treaties with the U.S. government had
guaranteed the Sioux the fertile Black Hills, then a holy
ground, but when gold was discovered in them, the treaties
were abrogated and thousands of fortune hunters occupied
and settled the area with the help of the U.S. Army. Later
when there was a large immigration from Northern Europe to
the West—Phil Jackson's ancestors were in this group—the reservation shrank further until it has become land of great
acreage but of little productive value for a people who have
never escaped their nomadic past.

We pass a fenced-off field of about 200 acres. The man who
leased the Indian land from the Bureau of Indian Affairs for
$1 an acre has put up a sign which warns Indians—no tres-
passing, no hunting, no firewood. Mike says there are some
deer and antelope in the hills and catfish in the White River,
which runs through the land. We pass a house that belongs to
an Indian jockey, who lives well on the reservation with his

racing winnings. Windmills stand behind houses, whining in the wind and providing energy to pump water. At intervals along the desolate two-lane highway, cars lie abandoned and rusting in the fields as if they were the successors of the dinosaurs that died in the area; as if the Indians drove them to death taking out their fury on the white man's machines.

Driving to Pine Ridge, the reservation's main town (pop. 1,000), we stop at Wounded Knee. The Sacred Heart Church, or what's left of it, sits on a small hill overlooking a little valley through which runs the Wounded Knee Creek. One year earlier hundreds of U.S. marshals with automatic weapons lined the hills and banks of the creek. On the charred foundation of the church are scribbled "AIM Wounded Knee 1890– 1973" and "Fuck you Dick ———," the last name is rubbed out. Behind the church is the graveyard, where some of Mike's relatives lie buried. The old souvenir shop and museum have collapsed, and along the road is a monument and sign commemorating the events of 1890, when on the morning of December 28, the U.S. Seventh Cavalry surrounded an encampment of Oglala Sioux and with the help of Hotchkiss guns killed 194 men, women and children. It was the last recorded skirmish between the U.S. Army and the American Indian. We get out of the car and walk to the sign. Willis limps like a wounded buffalo, each step painful. I wonder how he will get through his demonstration this evening. The wind whips through the "cheet" grass and jack pines, providing an eerie background hum. Willis, Mike, and Phil stand silhouetted against the sky reading the inscription on the sign: "Unrest on the reservation was due to a reduction in beef rations by the U.S. Congress and to the ghost-dancing of Chief Kicking Bear and Sitting Bull, who said that by wearing the ghost shirt and doing the ghost dances of Wovoka, the Piaute mystic, the warriors would become immune to the white man's bullets; could openly defy the soldiers and white settlers; *and could bring back the days of the old buffalo herds.*"

"Those days ain't never comin' back," says Willis.

We slowly move back to the car and then on to Pine Ridge. About thirty Indian kids await us in the gym. During my demonstration they are silent and still; quite different from the nervous fidgeting of inner-city kids. They ask me only two questions:

"If a ball player don't get hurt or nothin', how long can he play?"

"What happens if you punched a referee in the mouth?"

Finally, Willis Reed comes on the court, positions himself at the low post, and begins to explain pivot play. "You take the ball with both hands, turn, and shoot. Always keep the ball high. Now if he plays you to the right, you fake and go left. If he plays you to the left, go right. Or, you can turn all the way around like this, and show him the ball and drive. After you drive once you've got him set up for the drop dribble. Face him, fake a drive, take one bounce away from the basket, turn, and shoot. You'll have him flat-footed."

Willis doesn't move much, and when one of the kids asks him if he will play next year, he says yes and he expects the Knicks to be in contention for the title. In closing, Willis gives the group a little lecture about hard work, responsibility, and the need to set goals. He says practice and study go hand in hand with a clean life. He speaks with the assurance of a man whose life has been built upon moral certainties. He says never to get down when you lose because there is always another game. He is glistening with sweat; though he is still standing in one spot, his tee shirt is wet. The kids are enraptured. "There isn't much these days that hasn't been done," he says. "There's been a man on the moon and somebody has already run a mile in 3:55. But you have a chance for a real first: One of you can be the first Indian to play in the NBA."

From *Life on the Run*, 1976.

QUESTIONS

(1) How many "scenes" does Bradley present? How does he make you see them?

(2) What do you think of Bill Bradley by the end of the selection? Of Willis Reed?

(3) How do concrete details make the essay clear and convincing? Give specifics.

(4) Why does Reed go through with the demonstration even though he is in pain? "He speaks with the assurance of a man

whose life has been built upon moral certainties." Why is that statement convincing? Would it be less effective earlier in the essay?

(5) How would you describe the tone of this selection?

(6) What words and images are repeated as if this very factual narrative were a short story or a poem?

(7) What are some of the larger implications of that last sentence, for the boy, for America?

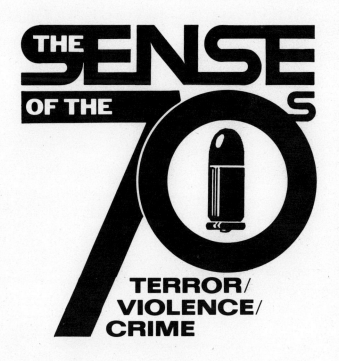

THE SENSE
OF THE
70s

TERROR/
VIOLENCE/
CRIME

Arthur Bremer set out to kill Richard Nixon, changed his mind, and shot Governor George Wallace instead. Like Nixon, Bremer didn't trust history and so he kept his own record. He wanted his diary to be found and published so that he would at last be known and recognized. That diary is one of the artifacts of the age of exposure, a glimpse into the mad mind of an assassin, a view of the pitiful and terrifying person seething behind the smile and the sunglasses.

The United Press International story from Texas also deals with killing. This, however, is more religious than political. It is the story of a ritual slaying, a strange version of the Abraham and Isaac story, in which a father sacrifices his son in the name of what he believes to be sacred.

Guns appear throughout this section. Because ours is a technological age, there are strong connections between the psychology of violence and the technology of terror. Larry Woiwode's essay is a documentation of some of those connections. One definition of madness is that a momentary fantasy becomes a permanent state of mind. Woiwode's essay is a frighteningly sane exposition of the reality and the fantasy of the gun in the American psyche.

Tom Wicker also writes about guns. A columnist for *The New York Times* who had written on the need for prison reform, on September 10, 1971, he was summoned from a sophisticated Washington lunch to serve as a mediator in the Attica prison uprising. He was plunged into a personal and social hell and was forced to confront some truths about himself and his society, truths usually kept hidden, locked away like the inmates behind the prison walls. He writes about himself in the third person as "Wicker" partly because he is different from the man he is describing. The man who lived through the experience at Attica is not the same man who approached its forbidding walls on a warm September afternoon. Inside those walls, he saw the human face of what he had thought of as a social problem.

Gail Sheehy saw another face of violence. She was a reporter covering the civil war in Northern Ireland. An American, of comfortable middle-class background, talented, sure of herself, she suddenly saw the meaning of political violence. She describes how that vision shattered her world. She may never have read Herman Melville's poem from the American civil war, "Shiloh, A Requiem," but she would always understand its line: "What like a bullet can undeceive!"

Terrorism is the name given to political violence. Kenny Moore, a marathon runner on the U.S. Olympic track team in 1972, describes what it was like when the brutal world invaded the Olympic village and automatic weapons challenged the hammers and javelins of the athletes. The story of the raid on Entebbe is a good companion piece to that of the Munich massacre. Philip Ross describes the remarkable teamwork that achieved a victory for anti-terrorism.

Most Americans, however, are not afraid of political terrorism. Not the assassin with the automatic rifle, but the mugger with the knife is the figure of our nightmares. That mugger is the faceless stranger who plunges into our lives, bullying, threatening, hurting. James Willwerth, a young reporter, puts a face on that mugger. He befriended "Jones" in order to present him to us. Willwerth has great difficulty suspending his moral and legal judgments—a real dilemma for the journalist who wants to show what actually happens—but he does let Jones present himself in his own terms. This allows the reader to see "the criminal" in a new and different way.

Jones the mugger says he does not attack women and worries about his own mother when he hears of women being attacked. The sentiment is perhaps only sentimental, but any code of ethics is probably better than none at all. Susan Brownmiller considers the relations between the sexes stripped of sentiments and codes. Brownmiller set out to understand the nature and history of rape. She studied the authorities on the psychology of sex and of violence and read the history of brutality practiced on women. Her conclusions, presented in the opening of her book which is reprinted here, are startling.

Terror. Violence. Crime. The danger is that we will make political slogans of the words and forget that they stand for things that human beings do to other human beings.

GUNS

LARRY WOIWODE

Once in the middle of a Wisconsin winter I shot a deer, my only one, while my wife and daughter watched. It had been hit by a delivery truck along a country road a few miles from where we lived and one of its rear legs was torn off at the hock; a shattered shin and hoof lay steaming in the red-beaded snow. The driver of the truck and I stood and watched as it tried to leap a fence, kicked a while at the top wire it was entangled in, flailing the area with fresh ropes of blood, and then went hobbling across a pasture toward a wooded hill. Placid cows followed it with a curious awe. "Do you have a rifle with you?" the driver asked. "No, not with me. At home." He looked once more at the deer, then got in his truck and drove off.

I went back to our Jeep where my wife and daughter were waiting, pale and withdrawn, and told them what I was about to do, and suggested that they'd better stay at home. No, they wanted to be with me, they said; they wanted to watch. My daughter was three and a half at the time. I got my rifle, a .22, a foolishly puny weapon to use on a deer but the only one I had, and we came back and saw that the deer was lying in some low brush near the base of the hill; no need to trail its blatant spoor. When I got about a hundred yards off, marveling at how it could have made it so far in its condition through snow that came over my boot tops, the deer tried to push itself up with its front legs, then collapsed. I aimed at the center of its skull, thinking, *This will be the quickest,* and heard the bullet ricochet off and go singing through the woods.

The deer was on its feet, shaking its head as though stung, and I fired again at the same spot, quickly, and apparently missed. It was now moving at its fastest hobble up the hill, broadside to me, and I took my time to sight a heart shot. Before the report even registered in my mind, the deer went down in an explosion of snow and lay struggling there, spouting blood from its stump and a chest wound. I was shaking by now. Deer are color-blind as far as science can say, and as I went toward its quieting body to deliver the coup de grace, I realized I was being seen in black and white, and then the deer's eye seemed to home in on me, and I was struck with the understanding that I was its vision of approaching death. And then I seemed to enter its realm through its eye and saw the countryside and myself in shades of white and gray. *But I see the deer in color,* I thought.

A few yards away, I aimed at its head once more, and there was the crack of a shot, the next-to-last round left in the magazine. The deer's head came up, and I could see its eye clearly now, dark, placid, filled with an appeal, it seemed, and then felt the surge of black and white surround and subsume me again. The second shot, or one of them, had pierced its neck; a gray-blue tongue hung out over its jaw; urine was trickling from below its tail; a doe. I held the rifle barrel inches from its forehead, conscious of my wife's and daughter's eyes on me from behind, and as I fired off the final and fatal shot, felt myself drawn by them back into my multicolored, many-faceted world again.

I don't remember my first gun, the heritage is so ingrained in me, but know I've used a variety of them to kill birds, reptiles, mammals, amphibians, plant life, insects (bees and butterflies with a shotgun), fish that came too close to shore—never a human being, I'm quick to interject, although the accumulated carnage I've put away with bullets since boyhood is probably enough to add up to a couple of cows, not counting the deer; and have fired, at other targets living and fairly inert, an old ten gauge with double hammers that left a welt on my shoulder that lasted a week, a Mauser, a twelve-gauge sawed-off shotgun, an M-16, at least a dozen variations on the .22—pump, bolt action, level action, target pistols, special scopes and sights and stocks—a .410 over-and-under, a zip gun that blew up and scattered shrapnel that's still imbedded in my arm, an Italian carbine, a Luger, and, among others, a fancily engraved, single-trigger, double-barreled twenty gauge at snowballs thrown from behind my shoulder out over a bluff; and on that same bluff on the first day of this year, after some wine and prodding, I found myself at the jittering rim of stutters from a paratrooper's lightweight machine gun with a collapsible, geometrically reinforced metal stock, watched the spout of its trajectory of tangible tracers go off across the night toward the already-set sun, and realized that this was perhaps the hundredth weapon I'd had performing in my hands.

I was raised in North Dakota, near the edge of the West, during the turbulence and then the aftermath of the Second World War, which our country ended in such an unequivocal way there was a sense of vindication about our long-standing fetish for guns, not to say pride in it, too. "Bang! Bang! You're dead," returns to me from that time without the least speck of friction or reflection. When we weren't playing War, or Cowboys and Indians, or Cops and Robbers, we were reading War Comics (from which you could order for less than a dollar little cardboard chests of plastic weaponry and soldiers to stage your own debacles), or Westerns, or listening to *The Lone Ranger* and *Richard Diamond, Private Detective,* and other radio shows—all of which openly glorified guns, and the more powerful the better.

My fantasies, when I was frustrated, angry, or depressed, were rife with firearms of the most lethal sort, flying shot, endless rounds of shattering ammunition; the enemy bodies blown away and left in bloody tableaux. And any gun was an engineered instrument—much more far-ranging and accurate than bows and arrows or slingshots—that detached you from your destructiveness or crime or sometimes even from being a source of death.

I've only owned three firearms in my life as an adult. Two I brought back to the shops within a week after I'd bought them, realizing I was trying to reach out in some archaic way, and the limits to my maturity and imagination that that implied, plus the bother to my daughter of their powing sounds; and the third, the .22, after trembling over it a few years and using it to shoot holes in the floor to enact a between-the-legs suicide, I gave away. To my younger brother. Who was initiated into the buck-fever fraternity in the forests of northern Wisconsin when he was an adolescent by a seasoned local who said to him, "If you see anything moving out there tomorrow, boy, *shoot* it. You can check out later what it is. Nobody gives a shit up here." And on a hunting trip years later, an acquaintance from the village my brother lived in then, a lawyer, was shot in the head with a deer rifle, but somehow survived. And even went back to practicing law. It was thought to be an accident at first, what with all the bullets embroidering the air that day, and then rumor had it that another member of the party hunting on adjoining land, an old friend of the lawyer's, had found out a week before the season that the lawyer had been having his wife for a while. The two men were polite enough to one another in the village after that, my brother said, but not such good friends, of course. Just balanced, justice-balanced males.

For months and seasons after I'd shot the crippled doe, every time we passed the field in our Jeep, my daughter would say, "Here's where Daddy shooted the deer." In exactly that manner, using the tone and detachment of a storyteller or tourist guide. And I'd glance into the rearview mirror and see her in her car seat, studying the hill with troubled and sympathetic eyes. One day I stopped. "Does it bother you so much that I shot it?" I asked. There was no answer, and then I saw that she was nodding her head, her gaze still fixed on the hill.

"Well, if I wouldn't have, it could have suffered a long time. You saw how badly hurt it was. It couldn't have lived that way. I didn't like doing it, either, but it was best for the deer. When I told the game warden about it, he even thanked me and said, 'Leave it for the foxes and crows.' They have to eat, too, you know, and maybe the deer made the winter easier for them." And I thought, Oh, what a self-justifying fool and ass and pig you are. Why didn't you leave her at home? Why didn't you go to the farmer whose land the deer was on, which would have been as quick or quicker than going back for the .22—a man who would have had a deer rifle, or at least a shotgun with rifled slugs, and would have put the deer away with dispatch in one shot and might have even salvaged the hide and venison? And who could say it wouldn't have lived, the way some animals do after tearing or chewing off a limb caught in a trap? Who was to presume it wouldn't have preferred to die a slow death in the brush, looking out over the pasture, as the crimson stain widening in the snow drew away and dimmed its colorless world until all went black? Why not admit that I was a common back-country American and, like most men of my mold, had used an arsenal of firearms to kill and was as excited about putting away a deer as moved by compassion for its suffering? Then again, given my daughter's understanding and the person I am, perhaps she sensed this, and more.

I once choked a chicken to death. It was my only barefaced, not to say barehanded, confrontation with death and the killer in me and happened on my grandparents' farm. I couldn't have been more than nine or ten and no firearms were included or necessary. I was on my knees and the chicken fluttered its outstretched wings with the last of the outraged protest. I gripped, beyond release, above its swollen crop, its beak gaping, translucent eyelids sliding up and down. An old molting specimen. A hen, most likely; a worse loss, because of eggs, than a capon or cock. My grandfather, who was widely traveled and world-wise, in his eighties then, and had just started using a cane from earlier times, came tapping at that moment around the corner of the chicken coop and saw what I was doing and started gagging at the hideousness of it, did a quick assisted spin away and never again, hours later nor for the rest of his life, for that matter, ever mentioned the homicidal incident to me. Keeping his silence, he seemed to understand; and yet whenever I'm invaded by the incident, the point of it seems to be his turning away from me.

My wife once said she felt I wanted to kill her. A common enough feeling among long-married couples, I'm sure, and not restricted to either sex (I know, for instance, that there were times when she wanted to kill me), but perhaps with firsthand experience infusing the feeling, it became too much to endure. I now live in New York City, where the clock keeps moving toward my suitcase, alone, and she and my daughter in the Midwest. The city has changed in the seven years since the three of us lived here together. There are more frivolous and not-so-frivolous wares—silk kerchiefs, necklaces and rings, roach clips, rolling papers, socks, a display of Florida coral across a convertible top, books of every kind—being sold in the streets than anybody can remember seeing in recent years. People openly saying that soon it will be like the thirties once were, with us *all* in the streets selling our apples, or whatever, or engaged in a tacit and friendly sort of gangsterism to survive. Outside my window, a spindly deciduous species has a sign strung on supporting posts on either side of it, in careful handlettering, that reads, THIS TREE GIVES OXYGEN. GIVE IT LOVE. More dogs in the streets and parks than they'd remembered, and more canine offal sending up its open-ended odor; at least half the population giving up cigarette smoking, at last, for good, they say, and many actually are. The mazed feeling of most everywhere now of being in the midst of a slowly forging and forgiving reciprocity. An air of bravura about most everybody in maintaining one's best face, with a few changes of costumish clothing to reflect it, perhaps, no matter what might yet evolve. A unisex barbershop or boutique on nearly every other block, it seems.

Sometimes I think this is where I really belong. Then a man is gunned down in a neighborhood bar I used to drop into and the next day a mob leader assassinated, supposedly by members of his own mob. *Perhaps this is where I'm most at home,* I equivocate again and have an image of myself in a Stetson traveling down a crosstown street at a fast-paced and pigeon-toed shamble toward the setting sun (setting this far east, but not over my wife and daughter yet), my eyes cast down and shoulders forward, hands deep in my empty Levi's pockets, a suspect closet-faggot-cowboy occasionally whistled at by queens.

I won't (and can't) refute my heritage, but I doubt that I'll use a firearm again, or, if I do, only in the direst sort of emergency. Which I say to protect my flanks. The bloody, gunfilled fantasies seldom return now, and when they do they're reversed: I'm the one being shot, or shot at, or think I am.

From *Esquire Magazine,* 1975.

QUESTIONS

(1) What difference does it make that Woiwode delays until the second sentence the fact that the deer he killed was hurt?

(2) List the adjectives in the first two paragraphs. Which are especially effective?

(3) The first three paragraphs are like a brief documentary movie. How does Woiwode use colors to establish the mood of that movie?

(4) What kinds of specific feelings does Woiwode imply he had in the catalogue of guns that he lists? Are any of those

feelings connected with feelings he had when he killed the deer?

(5) What connections does Woiwode make between his country's consciousness and his private fantasies with regard to guns? Could the same connections be made now? Is TV the same as, or different from, his comic books in its attention to guns?

(6) What point(s) does he make in using his brother and his brother's experiences with the members of the "buck-fever fraternity"?

(7) Does he mean "embroidering" in the description of the Wisconsin hunt to be an ironic undercutting of "males"?

(8) Why didn't he leave his daughter at home? What did he want her to see? What did he want her to think of him?

(9) Why does he relate the incident of strangling the chicken? To what is he confessing? How is this anecdote from his own childhood related to his thoughts about his daughter?

(10) At the end of the essay, Woiwode's fantasy world has changed completely. How do the details of the changes in his life in the two paragraphs before the last one prepare the reader for this change?

TEXAS FATHER PLACED ON PROBATION IN KILLING OF SON WHO USED DRUGS

UNITED PRESS INTERNATIONAL

ORE CITY, Tex., Jan. 17 (UPI)—Forrest Grigg was a father worried about his 20-year-old son's involvement with drugs.

"I tried everything," said the 51-year-old former professional football player. "I thought we'd get him straight, and then he'd start again. He'd get a job, then quit and spend the money on this stuff. He kept maintaining he was all right."

On the night of Oct. 31, Mr. Grigg could not stand the strain any longer. He walked into his son's bedroom, folded the hands of the sleeping youth across his chest and shot him in the temple.

Mr. Grigg's one-day murder trial was held last week in this small northeast Texas town. After the jury deadlocked 9 to 3 in favor of acquittal, Mr. Grigg changed his plea to guilty to voluntary manslaughter. District Judge Virgil Mulanaux gave the father a five-year probated sentence for killing Mike Grigg.

"Yes, I did it for him," Mr. Grigg said yesterday. "I didn't care what the sentence was. It didn't enter my mind. There wasn't any question about me killing him.

"I would say I'd probably be condemned for doing it," he continued, "but I had two different men come up to me after the trial and say they came awful close to doing that themselves. Course I guess I was the only one crazy enough to have done it."

He paused, then said, "I'll tell you, this old world is sure different than it was."

For years, there had been few signs of father-son animosity.

"He was my pride and joy, and we did all sorts of things together—until all this happened three years ago," Mr. Grigg said. "But he changed, he changed completely."

Mr. Grigg, who played professional football in the 1940s and 1950s for Buffalo, the Chicago Bears and the Cleveland Browns, said that his easy-going, likable son was fine until he became involved with drugs. His sports activities ceased, and in his senior year he was expelled from the 230-student Ore City High School because his hair was too long. He finished school by correspondence.

The relationship between father and son worsened after he left school. Mr. Grigg said he knew his son used drugs and was not trying to rehabilitate himself.

Mr. Grigg said that Mike was not an addict and, to his knowledge, used only Valium and marijuana.

"But my estimation is any drugs are dangerous," Mr. Grigg said. "He was using pills, marijuana, cheap wine. He was not on the needle. But you mix any one of those with alcohol and it gives you more kick. He got to where he had no ambition or attention for anything."

From The New York Times, 1977.

QUESTIONS

(1) The reporter has used dialogue—actually direct quotations from Mr. Grigg—for most of the story. Why is that so effective?

(2) Like a good short story, each detail suggests a great deal and by the end a complete world has been created. How many more details of this world can you supply from the evidence provided in the brief news story?

(3) Would the story be more effective if more details were given?

JONES: PORTRAIT OF A MUGGER

JAMES WILLWERTH

1. "I hit the streets each day about twelve and I walk around."
. . . Jones . . . was telling me about a typical day's work during this period.

"This day I was wearing jeans and cut-off sneakers and a dark knit. It was early in November and starting to get cool. The dude I worked with then was the best crime partner I ever had. He's doin' five-to-ten for robbery now."

Jones was living at home. From that sanctuary, he moved into the larger city as a hunter might.

"We walked up First Avenue and stood in front of a supermarket. This dude came out. He had given the woman a check, and she had given him a lot of bills. You can watch people through the glass and see this.

"He lived about a block away, and we followed him into his building. It was quick; he had the bags in his arms, and I put the knife right above his heart. He said he was a working man and all that bullshit and then we took the roll; it was big, but it was only ones, like maybe thirty-five dollars. We went back to the projects to let things cool off in case he called the cops."

If the police were called, the victim would be put in a patrol car and driven around the neighborhood. The police would take a description of Jones and his accomplice. But most likely, the man would walk to his apartment and open the door with his passkey before he called the police. By the time they arrived, Jones would be blocks away.

"Then we saw this dude coming out of the building across from us. It was later in the afternoon by now, and he was between the doors. He had let the first door lock behind him, and we came in through the other way—he couldn't go in or out. I had the knife out, but I didn't even touch him. He kept on saying, 'Just take it—don't hurt me . . .' "

The man, middle-aged and wise, survived. He had the sense not to frighten or anger his assailant; so he endured fear and humiliation and theft—but not violence or death.

"He might have been around forty. Sometimes you don't remember the faces, just the things they say. He had about fifty dollars and change. We left the change. We went into another part of the projects and let things cool off again.

"We caught the next dude, who was thirty-nine or forty, the same way. He was the kind you had to show you wasn't playing. I pulled the knife and I said, 'Look, we just want your money.' He said, 'What? what?' So I hit him with the handle of the knife. That didn't faze him. I put the knife up against here"—Jones pokes his finger into my stomach—"and wow, he almost had a heart attack! He goes, 'Ah! Ahhhhh-hhhhh!' and wow, I was feelin' bad. Then he says something about how you can't leave your house any more, you get robbed, you know? My man says to check his belt. So far we had about thirty-five dollars. I pulled the belt out and it had two hundred-dollar bills behind a zipper."

As the man says, you can't leave your house any more.

"Then we saw this white dude. If you see a white dude

down here, something's strange; this one had come to get
dope. We said, 'Hey, man, why don't you come over here?
We'd like to talk to you.' He had about seventy dollars. He
said he would come back for us, and there's a lot of racketeers
around that area, so we decided to cool it for a few days. We
split up the cash and I laid up with my share. We had wanted
to put together some money and cop a lot of dope. This wasn't
enough, but I figured we should stay off the streets for a while
anyway."

Not bad. Half of $337 for a day's work. Yet *not* enough. It
would not sustain Jones very long, for as always the Law of
Easy Money was at work. Anything above the price of a day's
habit would be spent blindingly fast.

2. "This was in the daytime. We were downtown, and the guy
I was with had a lot of heart. We saw a dude coming out of a
store with a bag in his arms; he was dressed nice. We followed
him to his building and got in the elevator with him; he
pressed nine, so we pressed seven. Then we ran up the two
flights of stairs, and got there as he got out. The elevator door
had closed behind him.

"The dude was strong, and he knew what was happening.
He dropped the bag and started to fight. We both went for
him. I grabbed his shirt collar—you can lead a dude around
that way—but my nails broke and I lost my grip. My man got
scared now; he stabbed him with his K-55."

The K-55 is a smaller version of the .007. Both knives are
favorite muggers' tools. The K-55 has a long metal handle,
and a locking blade that is at most three or four inches long.
The .007, which Jones has, is more expensive, with a hefty
wooden handle and a longer blade. Neither is spring-action; a
practiced thumb and forefinger action forces the blade out of
the handle. A powerful wrist snap and a click! complete the
movement. With practice the knife opens as fast as any switch-
blade.

"It was a quick thing, and that did it."

Jones's accomplice has "heart." It means that he is capable
of sudden, reckless violence. Jones does not approve of this;
one part of him does not. He grinds his teeth at the memory.

"He was against the wall holding himself. He was stabbed
now, and he was screaming and we took his money—one hun-

dred and fifty dollars—and split. I was scared! We ran down nine flights of stairs. I knew if I got busted, the courts would hang me."

Jones's face is tight, tense. He looks at me, and the tension reaches across the space between us. Several seconds pass before he says anything.

"I dreamed about this for three days. It was the horror of the thing; I was part of it. My man had trouble pulling the blade out of the dude. He had to pull hard, and the blood ran all down him."

Jones sits forward. "I don't know if I want to talk about it." Silence. He puts his hand under his chin, and says nothing for seconds. Then he starts again.

"The dream went almost the way it happened. It would start to happen, and I would wake up; I would go back to sleep and see him being stabbed. Moms and Pops thought I was crazy—I was punching the wall in my sleep. They asked what I was doing—I told them it was nothing. I had been down with stabbings as a kid; but then I knew the dude. He had done something to abuse me."

Jones is lost in his grim memory.

"When you don't know the person you are doing the harm to, taking his money is enough. This dude hadn't done shit to me and now he was being stabbed and I was part of it. There are dudes out there I wouldn't mind killing, but it's a bitch to stab someone you don't know.

"We ran to a park. When we stopped, I asked my man why he did it. He said he didn't know why. I didn't want to show I was afraid, so I dropped it."

3. "It isn't so safe in the streets. The cops are out; everybody is uptight. Buildings are better."

The man in the hallway might have been thirty-five years old. He was Chinese; but his face was hardly inscrutable; it showed pain and fright and humiliation. He had managed to shut the street door in time to keep one of his assailants out of the hallway. But the other was upon him. He flailed and pushed and moved as fast as he could.

"I hit him in the face a couple of times. Then I hit him again. I felt the blow crush something, something went squish. I looked at my hand and it was okay—so it had to be him."

In the darkness the man moaned and became silent. Jones let him fall. He turned to let his partner into the building. No one had heard the fight.

"It was kinda funny. He had been up against the wall and he was goin' uhhhhh, uhhhhhhh . . . and he didn't have any place to go. When I let go, he just dropped. I let my man in. We was in a hurry—we took the dude's money and ran, it was about twenty dollars. There was cops all over that night."

"Did the man die?" I ask, sick at the thought.

"I don't know. I never read the newspapers afterward—I don't want to feel sorry about what happened. Some dudes are different. They want everybody to know about it. Not me."

4. A neon-colored night. Jones and I walk down Houston Street, past the mute wilderness of an empty park. "I've got to get some fresh air," he'd said. "Sometimes when I've been sleeping and smoking, I get to thinking and my nerves start bothering me. I've got a lot of things on my mind."

We are talking now about women and old people—as victims. Jones is opposed to the idea.

"An old man can have a weak heart and die from the shock of the beating—that can be Murder One. It's premeditated because they say you planned the mugging. Mugging by itself is a robbery and assault charge, which is easier to beat."

This is a recurring bit of ambivalence. Jones will not mug women or old men he considers helpless. It is not just a matter of ethics; pragmatism is involved. A murder charge means a lot of prison time. And women tend to scream; you have to silence them, fast. More prison time.

A middle-aged woman hurries by, clutching her purse tightly. Jones pauses to watch her.

"Now that's a *shame*. She's alone, and she's afraid of being mugged. I see women like that, and I think of Moms. If a dude hurt her, that would bring me out in the streets like a wild man! I would *really* hurt someone. If someone hits Pops, he can take it. A woman is a different thing."

It's nice to have ideals, I am thinking. Then I ask: "Who *does* hit women?"

"Dudes afraid to face men."

He drifts for a moment as the middle-aged woman disappears.

"If a woman starts screaming, somebody, even a punk, will want to help her. Then you got two people to deal with. A woman like this can make you want to hurt her, which is a drag. I think about my mother. If someone took her off, it would hurt me; she can't really get down with a dude and win."

"If you saw a woman being mugged, would you help her?"

Jones says nothing. We pass a patrol car idling outside an all-night coffee shop. Then he nods.

"Yeah. If the woman was getting hurt, I would help her. Dudes who get down with women have no heart. I would definitely get into it."

5. Jones spreads clear polish on his thumbnail with a tiny brush to toughen the sharpened surface. We are talking about mugging techniques.

"I'm into drops now. You lay outside a bank, or a check-cashing place; you know the dudes have cash. You can be even more selective if you want. Today, like, I watched faces going in and out of this bank. Tomorrow I'll go back again. If I see those faces again, I'll know they aren't going to the bank for themselves. So I'll pick a face and follow it to its store. As a rule, stores make one drop a day. They usually make those drops between two and three o'clock. I'll time this dude for a few days. Say he's pretty close to between two and two-thirty. I make it my business to be there."

He turns to his other thumb, dipping the brush into the small jar again.

"You have to remember the faces you've taken off. You see a dude twice, you give him a rest; because if your face becomes familiar, it's trouble. I don't walk much in the areas where I work."

"You'll mug a man twice?"

"Oh yeah. He'll be slick for a while after the first time. But he'll drop his guard again. It ain't *his* money. He isn't going to risk his life for it."

Jones is into the talk now. His hands loop and dive in the space in front of him.

"It's not worth it to fuck with people on the street. The regular dude, he's like you and me. He's working, he's got a wife and kids. He don't carry much money—and he might fight. The dude with the drop, he's got more money, and he's got insurance."

"Do you still hit people randomly?"

"Yeah, sometimes. I prefer drops, but you have to plan for them. If you need money right away, you resort to the old street thing."

"How do you spot the right person to mug?"

"You walk behind a dude. If he keeps looking around, if he's leery, you know something is up. If he's got no money, he's got nothing to worry about, right? You walk beside him, and if he's looking over his shoulder—if he's got eyes in the back of his head—you've got your man."

"What's the most you've gotten?"

"One time me and my man saw this fat dude, and I just had this feeling, you know? We followed him into this build-ing and *wow,* he had cash everywhere! In his pockets, in his belt, in his shoes, in a case he was carrying . . . we got a thousand dollars. Sometimes a good drop is worth that much, too."

I am thinking. When Jones works regularly, he says he makes more than a hundred dollars a day. Perhaps several thousand dollars a month, perhaps $20,000 a year. It is tax free. A $1,200 paycheck has about $900 left after the govern-ment gets its bite. So he has the equivalent of a $25,000 job.

Let's assume Jones is bragging—that he makes only half that amount. Thus he is making ten thousand tax-free dollars a year. He may be short on social security and medical plans, but at ten thousand after taxes he is doing better than most of New York City's office workers, delivery men, factory peo-ple, cops, and firemen. Not to mention free-lance writers. And he pays no rent.

Twenty thousand—if he was not exaggerating—means he does as well as the middle-level executives of Madison Avenue and Wall Street. He could drink in Sardi's after the theater, shop on Fifth Avenue, attend Lincoln Center concerts, and consult *The New York Times* restaurant guide for three-star French restaurants.

Yet Jones is constantly broke. He takes money from his women, borrows from his parents, and hits me up practically every time we get together (and always pays me back). He dresses well and uses expensive drugs—but they can't possibly

account for all the money he spends. Yet beyond the drugs
and clothes, he lives like a welfare recipient. *Why?* There
never seems to be a satisfactory answer.

One reason may be the blackly ironic economics of the
ghetto. Goods and services cost more. Groceries in a bodega
cost as much as gourmet foods on the fashionable Upper East
Side; small stores must have a high margin to survive. Even
supermarkets, as congressional studies have shown, are higher.
Public transportation is usually poorer, and gypsy cabs cost
plenty. Rent is cheap, but the tenants often must put money
into the apartments to make them livable. Cheap furniture
and household items are sold at exorbitant prices through
deceptive time payment plans. The furniture wears out before the payments are finished.

But economics is not the answer, even the largest part of it.
The problem is lifestyle.

"A thousand-dollar rip-off means you can relax for a while,
right?"

"Oh no! I go through it in three or four days. I buy clothes,
I go out, I get high. I get shoes, or a knit, or slacks—I get a lot
of things I don't need. You just live while the money's there;
that's the rule of the street. That's one thing dope did—it
made me live for the day. When I've got money, I don't sleep
for three or four days—you're just *buying* something all the
time. If you've got the money that easy and that fast, it doesn't
have any value."

Jones and money are like a lion and its latest kill. The meat
is eaten now—day-old flesh is for jackals. Let the future take
care of itself.

Jones doesn't entirely believe this, of course. He feels
trapped by street life—somehow heroin disrupted his life in
more than chemical ways. He sees cars and nice apartments
and legitimate money around him, and he tells himself he
should save his resources and buy things that last. But at
night, when he is alone and thinking about his life, he sees
two images. One reaches out, gently saying work and save, become stable.

The other shrieks that nothing matters: get it *now.* And he
knows that this vision—and he hates himself for knowing it—
has more strength than its cautious, thoughtful twin.

"You have a car and cash in the bank," he says to me in

gloomy moments. "You *have* things. And I have a yellow sheet
and a hole in my arm. Wow, what *happened?*"

From Jones: Portrait of a Mugger, 1974.

QUESTIONS

(1) A quality of street crime, of a mugging, is its suddenness.
To the victim it seems to come from nowhere and to be over
in seconds that last forever. How does Willwerth convey this
sense of suddenness?

(2) What effect does the alternation of the reporter's comments and the mugger's statements have?

(3) Is there any implication that Jones's job requires skill,
knowledge, and dedication? Does that matter?

(4) What feelings do you have about Jones from his description of the mugging in section two? What details make this
description so chilling?

(5) What makes the first sentence of section three ironic?

(6) How does the discussion of "ideals" in section four contribute to a more complex picture of Jones than that evoked
by simply labelling him a "mugger"? Does it make any fundamental change in a reader's attitude?

(7) The theme of section five is "lifestyle." How many kinds
of lifestyles does it deal with?

(8) Does mugging dictate a lifestyle? Does a lifestyle dictate
mugging?

BLOODY SUNDAY

GAIL SHEEHY

Without warning, in the middle of my thirties, I had a breakdown of nerve. It never occurred to me that while winging
along in my happiest and most productive stage, all of a sudden simply staying afloat would require a massive exertion of
will. Or of some power greater than will.

I was talking to a young boy in Northern Ireland where I
was on assignment for a magazine when a bullet blew his face
off. That was how fast it all changed. We were standing side
by side in the sun, relaxed and triumphant after a civil rights
march by the Catholics of Derry. We had been met by soldiers
at the barricade; we had vomited tear gas and dragged those
dented by rubber bullets back to safety. Now we were surveying the crowd from a balcony.

"How do the paratroopers fire those gas canisters so far?" I
asked.

"See them jammin' their rifle butts against the ground?"
the boy was saying when the steel slug tore into his mouth
and ripped up the bridge of his nose and left of his face nothing but ground bone meal.

"My God," I said dumbly, "they're real bullets." I tried to
think how to put his face back together again. Up to that moment in my life I thought everything could be mended.

Below the balcony, British tanks began to plow into the
crowd. Paratroopers jackknifed out of the tanks with high-
velocity rifles. They sprayed us with steel.

The boy without a face fell on top of me. An older man,
walloped on the back of the neck with a rifle butt, stumbled
up the stairs and collapsed upon us. More dazed bodies pressed
in until we were like a human caterpillar, inching on our
bellies up the steps of the exposed outdoor staircase.

"Can't we get into somebody's house!" I shouted. We
crawled up eight floors but all the doors to the flats were
bolted. Someone would have to crawl out on the balcony in
open fire to bang on the nearest door. Another boy howled

from below: "Jesus, I'm hit!" His voice propelled me across the balcony, trembling but still insulated by some soft-walled childhood sac that I thought provided for my own indestructibility. A moment later, a bullet passed a few feet in front of my nose. I hurled myself against the nearest door and we were all taken in.

The closets of the flat were already filled with mothers and their clinging children. For nearly an hour the bullets kept coming. From the window I saw three boys rise from behind a barricade to make a run for it. They were cut down like dummies in a shooting gallery. So was the priest who followed them, waving a white handkerchief, and the old man who bent to say a prayer over them. A wounded man we had dragged upstairs asked if anyone had seen his younger brother. "Shot dead," was the report.

Something like this had happened to my own brother in Vietnam. But the funeral took place in the bland Connecticut countryside, and I was a few years younger. So neatly had the honor guard tricornered the victim's flag, it looked like a souvenir sofa pillow. People had patted my hands and said, "We know how you must feel." It made me think of the strangers who were always confiding in me that they were scheduled for surgery or "taking it easy" after a heart attack. All I had for their pain were the same words: "I know how you must feel." I had known nothing of the sort.

After the surprise massacre, I was one among trapped thousands cringing in the paper-walled bungalows of the Catholic ghetto. All exits from the city were sealed. Waiting was the only occupation. Waiting for the British army to perform a house-to-house search.

"What will you do if the soldiers come in here firing?" I asked the old woman who was harboring me.

"Lie on me stomach!" she said.

Another woman was using the telephone to confirm the names of the dead. Once upon a time I was a Protestant of strong faith; I tried to pray. But that silly game of childhood kept running through my mind . . . *if you had one wish in the whole world* . . . I decided to call my love. He would say the magic words to make the danger go away.

"Hi! How are you?" His voice was absurdly breezy; he was in bed in New York.

"I'm alive."

"Good, how's the story coming?"

"I almost wasn't alive. Thirteen people were murdered here today."

"Hold on. CBS News is talking about Londonderry right now—"

"It's called Bloody Sunday."

"Can you speak up?"

"It's not over. A mother of fourteen children was just run down by a tank."

"Now look, you don't have to get in the front lines. You're doing a story on Irish women, remember that. Just stick with the women and stay out of trouble. Okay, honey?"

From the moment I hung up on that nonconversation, my head went numb. My scalp shrank. Some dark switch was thrown, and a series of weights began to roll across my brain like steel balls. I had squandered my one wish to be saved. The world was negligent. Thirteen could perish, or thirteen thousand, I could perish, and tomorrow it would all be beside the point.

As I joined the people lying on their stomachs, a powerful idea took hold: *No one is with me. No one can keep me safe. There is no one who won't ever leave me alone.*

I had a headache for a year.

When I flew home from Ireland, I couldn't write the story, could not confront the fact of my own mortality. In the end, I dragged out some words and made the deadline but at an ugly price. My short temper lengthened into diatribes against the people closest to me, driving away the only sources of support who might have helped me fight my demons. I broke off with the man who had been sharing my life for four years, fired my secretary, lost my housekeeper, and found myself alone with my daughter Maura, marking time.

As spring came, I hardly knew myself. The rootlessness that had been such a joy in my early thirties, allowing me to burst the ropes of old roles, to be reckless and selfish and focused on stretching my newfound dream, to roam the world on assignments and then to stay up all night typing on caffeine and nicotine—all at once that didn't work anymore.

Some intruder shook me by the psyche and shouted: *Take stock! Half your life has been spent. What about the part of*

you that wants a home and talks about a second child? Before
I could answer, the intruder pointed to something else I had
postponed: *What about the side of you that wants to contribute to the world? Words, books, demonstrations, donations—is
this enough? You have been a performer, not a full participant. And now you are 35.*

To be confronted for the first time with the arithmetic of
life was, quite simply, terrifying.

From Passages, 1976.

QUESTIONS

(1) In what ways is "Without warning" a good introductory
phrase for this selection? Is "without warning" an essential
element for the victim of violence?

(2) How does the balance of the first half and second half of
the first sentence of the second paragraph make you *feel* her
thesis?

(3) Why is "dented" in the second paragraph a good word?
How does it relate to the rest of the selection? Is Sheehy one
of the "dented"?

(4) How specifically does Sheehy make you see what she saw,
feel what she felt?

(5) This selection is the opening of a book about "passages,"
changes in one's life. What sentences indicate Sheehy's passages, her changes from child-adult to adult-adult?

(6) What is she implying in the description of her brother's
funeral? Is upper-middle class America ("bland Connecticut")
insulated from violent and sudden death?

(7) When she called her lover, was she really calling her father? Or God? What did she want?

(8) What kinds of numbers does Sheehy use to illustrate "the
arithmetic of life"?

THERE HAVE BEEN SHOOTINGS IN THE NIGHT

KENNY MOORE

I was torpid, just out of bed, ready to jog on a humid, glaring day. The Olympic Village gate was locked. A guard, dressed in silly turquoise, said, "There have been shootings in the night. You cannot leave."

I started back to my room. On the way I met my teammate, hammer thrower George Frenn, whose parents were born in Lebanon. He told me Arab terrorists had broken into the Israeli quarters, shot two people and taken others hostage. George was seething. "I hate lunatics," he said.

I lived in an apartment on the fifth floor of the U.S. building with Frank Shorter, Steve Savage, Jon Anderson and Dave Wottle, all middle- or long-distance runners. Frank was on our terrace, staring at police lines, ambulances and newsmen assembled under cover near the Israeli dorm, 150 yards away.

"I haven't felt this way since Kennedy was killed," he said. "Imagine those poor guys over there. Every five minutes a psycho with a machine gun says, 'Let's kill 'em now,' and someone else says, 'No, let's wait a while.' How long could you stand that?"

We took turns on the terrace, plucking seeds from a fennel plant there and grinding them into our palms. Below, people played chess or Ping-Pong. The trading of Olympic pins continued. Athletes sunbathed by the reflecting pool. It seemed inappropriate, but what was one supposed to do? The scratchy, singsong notes of European police sirens sounded incessantly. Rumors leaped and died. There were 26 hostages. There were seven. The terrorists were killing a man every two hours. They were on the verge of surrender.

At 3:30 P.M. I phoned a friend in the press village.

"Have you heard?" he asked. "The Games are stopped."

"Stopped? You mean postponed or canceled?"

"Postponed for now. But they say it may be impossible to start them again."

I went back to the room, where my wife Bobbie was waiting, and I wept. I experienced level after level of grief: for my
own event, the marathon, those years of preparation now useless; for the dead and doomed Israelis; and for the violated
sanctuary of the Games.

In Mexico and here the village had been a refuge, admittedly imperfect, from a larger, seedier world in which individuals and governments refused to adhere to any humane code.
For two weeks every four years we direct our kind of fanati-
cism into the essentially absurd activities of running and
swimming and being beautiful on a balance beam. Yet even
in the rage of competition we keep from hurting each other,
and thereby demonstrate the meaning of civilization. I shook
and cried as that illusion, the strongest of my life, was shattered.

In the evening Bobbie and I walked around. We met Ron
Hill, the British marathoner. Ron was agitated. "Why should
this stop the Games? It's all political, isn't it? Let the police
seal the thing off. The rest of the town isn't affected. I want
that marathon to stay on Saturday."

"They're talking about a one-day postponement," I said.
"Surely one day shouldn't matter."

"It does to me," he said.

Tom Dooley, one of our walkers, responded, "All political?
Those people are just politically dead?"

Hailu Ebba, the Ethiopian, 1,500-meter runner, said, "I
have led a calm life. I can't believe those people are in that
building and could get killed. They could shut this whole
place down. Running is not that important."

At 10 P.M. Bobbie and I decided to spend the night away
from the village. On our way to the front gate, the only one
where exit or entry was permitted, we met John Carlos. John,
often strident, now was muted, thoughtful. He shook his head.
"People were upset over what I did in 1968," he said, "but I
just expressed my feelings. I didn't hurt anybody. Now what
are they going to say? Can they tell the difference?"

At the gate, the guards were now admitting no one, nor permitting anyone to leave. Hoover Wright, one of our assistant
coaches, and his wife were also trying to get out. We looked at
each other in confusion. Someone who knew him shouted
from the crowd: "Hoover, there's going to be shooting! There's
going to be shooting!"

We turned to check other exits and met Lee Evans, who said it was impossible. We went back, through the rising furor, to the room.

After a few minutes Dave Wottle came in from, to our amazement, a run. "I went out the back gate," he said. He had covered a three-mile loop and returned to the rear of the village, where he found his way barred by ropes. He jumped the ropes and then the fence. "I heard some guards yelling 'halt!' but I just waved without looking. After 50 yards I came to another group of guards. One recognized me. He said, 'It's Wottle,' and they laughed." When Dave looked back, he saw five guards returning guns to their holsters. "If I had known they were so jumpy, I'd have walked around out there all night."

Then it seemed over. Anderson and Savage, who had been kept outside the main gate for an hour, came in and told how helicopters had taken terrorists and hostages to an airport. The late news said the Israelis had been rescued. We went to bed, shaken by the prolonged anxiety but relieved.

We awoke to the final horror. The first newspapers said, "Sixteen Dead."

I walked to the memorial service. Russian soccer players were practicing on a field beside the stadium. Concession stands were open, smelling of sauerkraut. The program was long-winded in four languages. The crowd applauded when Brundage said the Games would go on.

"The Games *should* go on," said Tom Dooley, "and they will. But for the wrong reasons. The Germans don't want any hitches in their organization. There are the financial considerations. Those people who applauded just want to see who will win the 5,000 and the hell with the rest."

"What are the right reasons?" I asked.

"Just one. To stay together. Who wins or loses now is ridiculously unimportant, considered against these men's deaths. But we have to stay together."

"Can we go to future Olympics, knowing this might happen again?"

He was quiet for a moment. "I don't know. Maybe Olympians will have to be like the early Christians now. We'll have to conduct our events in catacombs, in quiet forests."

From *The Best of Sports Illustrated*, 1973.

QUESTIONS

(1) A basic contrast in the essay is between the "ordinary" world of the athletes and the "nightmare" of the terrorists. How is this contrast established?

(2) In what way(s) is the following sentence the theme of the essay: "It seemed inappropriate, but what was one supposed to do?"

(3) What provokes Moore's weeping? Does it seem appropriate?

(4) Is "the rage of competition" without "hurting each other" the "meaning of civilization"?

(5) Does Moore's shattered illusion have anything in common with Gail Sheehy's shattered illusions?

(6) What does he gain by letting the athletes state their own positions in direct quotations?

(7) How does Moore feel about Dave Wottle's actions? Does he convey to the reader a sense of his own complicated responses?

(8) What are all the possible meanings of the sentence: "We awoke to the final horror"?

(9) What were the right reasons and the wrong reasons for continuing the games? For stopping them?

(10) What does Moore make you feel about the memorial services? How?

THE GREAT ISRAELI RESCUE

PHILIP ROSS

At 11 P.M. on July 3, 105 tired and frightened people were settling down for their sixth night of imprisonment in the transit lounge of an old air terminal building in east central Africa. Four of them were playing bridge at a table in the rear under overhead neon lights. Most of the others were trying unsuccessfully to sleep on bug-ridden mattresses that had been laid out on the wooden floor. The whirring fans did little to relieve the stench from the diarrhea epidemic that had weakened them all.

Just outside the building, a German man and woman in their twenties sat relaxing at a small round table with two of their eight Arab friends. Their Kalashnikov submachine guns lay casually on the ground. Over the entrance to the building they guarded was a sign that read, WELCOME TO UGANDA.

It had been a terrifying week for the hostages inside. In Tel Aviv the previous Sunday, they had happily boarded an Air France flight, headed for vacations in Europe and North America. But during a stopover in Athens en route to Paris, the two German terrorists and two of the Arabs had boarded the plane. Brandishing pistols and hand grenades shortly after takeoff, they had ordered the pilot to fly first to Benghazi, Libya, for refueling, then on to Entebbe Airport in Uganda.

The hijackers could not have received a more gracious welcome. Six other pro-Palestinian Arabs greeted them as they disembarked. Ugandan soldiers showered them with fresh weapons and backup support. And President Idi Amin, a man who had once announced plans to erect a memorial to Adolf Hitler in Uganda's capital city, Kampala, arrived in his field marshal's uniform to denounce Israel.

On Tuesday, the terrorists had made their demands. They wanted the release of 53 imprisoned terrorists, 40 held in Israel, the others in France, West Germany, Switzerland, and Kenya. Unless their Thursday deadline was met, they warned, they would kill the hostages and blow up the Air France plane.

That same day, the terrorists had separated from the others the 59 Israeli passengers and those with dual nationalities or Jewish-sounding names. As one of the Arabs shouted, "Israelis to the right!" and with the German man and woman looking on, many of the older Jews began to weep. Their memories went back 35 years to the Nazi guards who met their trains at the concentration camps. The Jews they told to step to the right had been taken directly to the gas chambers.

A day after the separation at Entebbe, the terrorists had released 47 of the non-Jewish passengers. On Thursday, after Israel agreed to negotiate and the deadline was extended to Sunday, 100 more were let go. The Air France crew of eight men and four women were told they could leave. They decided to stay with the Jews.

In the two days that followed, Nachum Dahan, a 26-year-old welder whom the terrorists suspected of being an Israeli soldier, was severely beaten. Akiva Laxer, a lanky 30-year-old attorney who was in Munich in 1972 when the eleven Israeli athletes were massacred, and who had been on his way to the Montreal Olympics to attend a memorial service for them, was pistol-whipped for picking up some pillows without asking permission. The others had been left alone to wait and to listen to the fair-haired, baby-faced German man reassure them that everything would be all right, that they had nothing to fear.

Of all the hostages, only thirteen-year-old Benny Davidson had expressed any hope that Israel's army could part the waters and deliver them from bondage. For the others on this evening of July 3—thirteen hours before their captors' deadline—Israel's acquiescence to the demands for the release of the imprisoned terrorists was the only way out.

There was no way they could escape. Even if they could overpower their guards, there were still the 20 unfriendly Ugandan soldiers on the roof and the 50 or so others stationed elsewhere around the airport. The hostages were prisoners not only of their captors, but also of a state.

The possibility of a military intervention seemed equally remote. They were 2,200 miles from home. Their army had never before operated away from the Middle East.

Until earlier that day, Israel's government had reluctantly reached the same conclusion. From the moment the plane had been hijacked, Prime Minister Yitzhak Rabin's shaky government had been considering military options. But each of the plans that Chief of Staff Mordechai Gur presented seemed too risky. Too many hostages might be killed. A government that previously had been perceived as weak and indecisive would undoubtedly be brought down by a people who were still recovering from the trauma of the Yom Kippur war three years earlier.

The small group of cabinet members Rabin had picked to help him handle the crisis—Defense Minister Shimon Peres, Transportation Minister Gad Yaakobi, Foreign Minister Yigal Allon, Justice Minister Chaim Zadok, and Minister Without Portfolio Israel Galili—had tried to be helpful. One suggested that they kidnap Idi Amin. Another wanted former Defense Minister Moshe Dayan to fly to Uganda to negotiate with its president. Both proposals were rejected.

A more direct approach didn't pan out either. Baruch Bar-Lev, a retired colonel who now sold stereo equipment in Tel Aviv, had once headed an Israeli military mission to Uganda. Shortly after the hijacking, Bar-Lev called his old friend Amin. He told him that this was a golden opportunity to change his image as a cruel man. He reminded Amin of his dead mother. He warned him that God would punish anyone who permitted something to happen to the "children of the Bible."

Amin at first agreed to have Bar-Lev come to Uganda and discuss the matter further. Then, inexplicably, he changed his mind and called off the trip.

As the week wore on, relatives of the hostages stormed Rabin's office in Tel Aviv, demanding that he turn the 40 terrorists in Israeli prisons over to the hijackers. On Thursday, with no workable military plan on the horizon, the full 22-man cabinet had unanimously voted to negotiate.

Now, two days later, there was a plan. It had been run through successfully the night before at a full-scale model of Entebbe that had been hastily built on an army base, possibly in the Sinai. There were still dozens of possible hitches, but it just might work.

Like many of the ministers who gathered in the Tel Aviv

cabinet room at two on this afternoon of July 3, Gideon
Hausner had his doubts. Still, as Lieutenant General Gur laid
out the details, the 61-year-old chief prosecutor at the Adolf
Eichmann trial reassured himself that "if our chief of staff tells
us the army can do it, we should trust him. They have proven
themselves before. They are not adventurers."

So precarious was the timing of the mission that at 3 P.M.
the cabinet members were told the planes had just left but
could be recalled if there was a negative vote. They deliber-
ated for another half hour. The vote to proceed was unanimous. The meeting ended with a prayer.

The details of the raid continue to be a tightly guarded secret. Military spokesmen will neither confirm nor deny reports. Commandos who took part in the raid have been kept
away from the public and all reporters. Hostages were de-
briefed after the mission and told not to discuss any military
operations they may have seen. Still, many of the facts have
either emerged or can be inferred.

At three o'clock on the afternoon of July 3, two or three
Hercules C-130 troop and vehicle transport planes took off
from an air base in southern Israel, probably near Sharm el-
Sheikh, deep in southern Sinai. They were accompanied by a
Boeing 707 that carried 23 doctors who would set up a field
hospital at Nairobi Airport in Kenya to care for the 25 or 30
casualties that were expected. The Israelis would later say
they "imposed" themselves on the Kenyans, but all information suggests that the Kenyans, who bear no love for Idi
Amin, approved the Israeli landing in advance.

A second 707 apparently was also in the squadron, carrying
top army and air-force officers and a backup communications
system.

As the planes headed south over the Red Sea, probably accompanied part of the way by Israeli Phantom and Mirage
fighter jets and perhaps flying high so that they would appear
to be commercial passenger planes if they were picked up on
radar, they carried between 100 and and 200 paratroopers,
soldiers from the crack Golani brigade, other infantry units,
communications and maintenance specialists, and 10 other
doctors who could go right to work at Entebbe.

The C-130s also carried jeeps, light-weight armored personnel carriers, command cars, and a Peugeot 404 mini-truck with its top and rear panels removed.

There has been considerable speculation about the intelligence reports the Israeli raiders carried with them. The most dramatic, which is completely unconfirmed, is that three black African agents working for Mossad, Israel's CIA, had penetrated Entebbe days before and sent back vital information.

What is known to be fact is that until Uganda broke off relations with Israel four years ago, Israeli civilian and military advisers had been all over Entebbe. An Israeli construction firm, Sollel-Boneh, designed and built the airport ten years ago, so there were detailed blueprints. Also available were updated aerial reconnaissance photographs and information provided by the non-Jewish passengers who had been released earlier in the week and by the Nairobi staff of El Al, Israel's commercial airline.

As the Israeli planes continued through several storm systems on a rough eight-hour trip over Ethiopia and Kenya, their occupants knew where the Ugandan soldiers at Entebbe were stationed, and that there were far fewer of them than the 500 to 1,000 that had originally been believed. They knew about the terrorists' habits. They knew security was lax. And they also knew that the old passenger building that held the hostages was not, despite the terrorists' warning, booby-trapped.

Still, the critical element in the whole mission was surprise. The strike force had to land at Entebbe undetected, make its way quickly to the old terminal building, and overcome the terrorists before they could react. The dress rehearsal the night before had taken 55 minutes. Now, when it counted, seconds would mean lives.

There have been several versions of how the Israelis achieved their surprise, which Lieutenant General Gur would later say involved "a certain amount of tricks."

According to one account, the first Hercules radioed the control tower at Entebbe to announce itself as an Air France flight bringing in the terrorists for an exchange, and the second C-130 identified itself as an East African Airways flight that was due in at about that time.

This is highly improbable. If the first Hercules said it was bringing in prisoners, the entire airport would have been alerted, along with Idi Amin. All indications are that the control tower was taken by surprise, and that Amin first heard about the raid after it was over, in a phone call from Baruch Bar-Lev.

Another report said just the opposite. This one had the planes coming in secretly over Lake Victoria to touch down with their lights off and engines cut at the end of a runway that was some distance from the control tower. The plausibility of this explanation is underlined by the summary execution of Entebbe's three air-traffic controllers a day after the Israeli mission.

Some said the planes dropped flares and set off diversionary explosions to cause confusion. Others argue that if there were explosions, they were set off by a team of Israeli commandos who had traveled 35 miles from the Kenyan border earlier in the day to guide the planes in and cut the airfield's communication links and radar system.

None of these accounts is known to be true. All that can safely be said is that with the 707 command plane apparently circling the airport, the C-130s touched down shortly after 11 P.M.—midnight, Ugandan time—came to a quick halt, and opened their huge rear hatches. What came out of them is at the heart of a guessing game.

According to *The New York Times,* the first vehicle to roll down the ramp was a black Mercedes sedan bearing Idi Amin's license-plate number and a heavyset Israeli commando disguised in blackface. Behind it came two Land-Rovers manned by paratroopers dressed as Palestinian boydguards. The whole ruse, according to this account, was designed to create the minute or so of confusion that was necessary for the commandos to reach the hostages before the terrorists could kill them.

The *Times* report said this plan worked. The first contingent of Ugandan soldiers that the motorcade encountered threw up their hands in salute, and the Israelis were on their way.

Confronted with this account, an Israeli military spokesman laughed. "Maybe we landed by boat from Lake Victoria," he said, "and crawled onto the airfield wearing crocodile suits."

Despite the Israeli joke, there were indications that some James Bond scheme had in fact been carried out. Several of the hostages seemed to hedge when asked if all the soldiers had been in military uniform. "I really don't remember," one of them said uneasily, "but what difference would it make if I told you that not all of them were?"

What the Israelis themselves confirm is that three units poured out of the Hercules in the jeeps and other vehicles. The first, armed with bazookas, mortars, hand grenades, and machine guns, headed directly toward the hostages. The second spread out to gain control of the rest of the airport. The third tried unsuccessfully to get the airfield's fuel pumps working.

The operation commander was Brigadier General Dan Shomron, a 39-year-old hero of the six-day war. The first unit, led by 30-year-old Lieutenant Colonel Yehonatan Netanyahu, a handsome young soldier-poet who made the dean's list during the one year he attended Harvard, drove toward the old terminal building, shooting the only two Ugandan soldiers who stood in the way. They arrived at their destination in less than a minute.

The terrorists, sitting at the table outside the building, were taken completely by surprise. The German woman—still not definitively identified—who had reminded many of the hostages of an SS guard as she barked out orders, was shot with one of the Arabs as they tried to snap in their ammunition clips. The second Arab ran a few feet, stumbled, and was gunned down as he tried to get off a shot. The German man—identified as Wilfried Böse, although several hostages would later say he bore no resemblance to the photograph they saw in the papers—ducked into the building and was killed just after he fired his machine gun.

While most of Netanyahu's unit attacked the building from the front, several commandos swarmed in from the side, raced to the second floor, and killed two Arabs who were hiding in a toilet, another not far away, and several Ugandan soldiers who had opened fire from the roof. The three remaining Arab terrorists apparently slipped out the rear of the building and escaped.

The hostages themselves saw none of this. In fact, not one
of them made a connection between the first, isolated shots
and the arrival of Israeli soldiers. They hadn't heard the
planes land. The terrorists sitting outside seemed so relaxed.
And Amin's statement when he visited them earlier in the evening that negotiations were proceeding caused many of the
hostages to conclude that an exchange might be imminent.

"Those dumb Ugandans," a man who had been playing
bridge in the rear of the room mumbled at the first, distant
sound of gunfire, "one of them must have pulled his trigger
by mistake."

Like most of the others, Gabriela Rubenstein had been
lying on a mattress, half asleep. "My god," the 29-year-old
Sabra thought. "This is the end. The Ugandans have decided
to kill us."

Her husband, Avri, who was looking for a place farther
from the bathrooms to move their mattress, reacted differently. "That crazy Amin," he thought, "he's changed his mind
and decided to free us."

Perhaps half a minute passed in silence. Then the shooting
began again, but this time it was all around them, shattering
the front windows of the building and causing panic as the
room began to fill with dust and smoke.

Gabriela and about twenty others crawled along the floor
to a hallway in the rear that separated the two bathrooms.
When they got there, they found three young Ugandans who
had been cleaning the bathrooms when the firing began. Now,
the two women and a man had thrown their hands in the air
as if to surrender, and were running hysterically in and out
of the hallway. Gabriela and the others forced them to the
floor. Then she began to cry. Avri was still in the main room,
directly in the line of fire. She wanted to be holding him when
they died.

Michal Warshavsky, a pretty, almond-eyed student who was
fifteen but liked telling people she was older, also thought her
life was over. But as she lay next to Gabriela, she was glad she
had been traveling alone to visit her uncle in Paris. If she had
been with her mother, she thought, she would have fallen
apart. Now she had to be brave. She could hear several people
screaming, and for some reason it calmed her down.

Hadassah David, a Rumanian immigrant who, with her husband, Yitzhak, had survived Auschwitz, was one of those screaming in the hallway. "My husband is out there," she yelled toward the main room. "He's not going to make it. He's not going to make it."

Sarah and Uzi Davidson had been taking their sons to California to visit relatives. Now her younger boy, Benny, who had said the soldiers would come, was lying in the hallway crying, "Mommy, I don't want to die."

In the main room Claude and Emma Rosenkowitz dropped to the floor and threw their bodies over their ten-year-old son and five-year-old daughter. When the children began to cry, Emma pleaded with them to set an example for the five other young children in the room. Now, as the bullets thumped into the pillars and light-green and rust-colored walls around them, the Rosenkowitz children were still.

Hadassah David's husband, Yitzhak, was putting out one of the small fires that had started when Jean-Jacques Maimoni was gunned down near the front door. For days Maimoni, a nineteen-year-old Moroccan immigrant, had been cheering up the others. Once, he had set up a "bar," taken orders for alcoholic and soft drinks, and then served the coffee and tea that were actually available.

When David noticed him now, Maimoni was trying to crawl away from the entrance. David reached out for him, but the youth had stopped moving. (He was dead, shot by Israeli commandos who mistook him for one of the Arabs.) Before he could withdraw his outstretched arm, David felt a sharp pain in his shoulder. He became unconscious as a pool of blood formed around him.

Lying on the floor nearby and covering his head, Akiva Laxer, who had been going to the memorial service in Montreal, now felt someone jabbing him every few seconds and asking. "Are you alive?"

There was no need for Jocelyne Monier to have been here in the first place. She was French and Christian. But when the terrorists had begun freeing the non-Jews, she had chosen to remain behind with her Jewish boyfriend. Others had begged to be let go. Neither she nor her boyfriend would do so.

Jocelyne had been sleeping because she had been given a

sedative for acute diarrhea. When she awoke now, it was because of a burning sensation in her thigh. She looked down to see blood pouring from her leg.

Dr. Yitzhak Hirsch and his wife, Lila, both of whom had also survived Auschwitz, were friends of the Davids. As the shooting continued, they heard Hadassah David shouting for her husband from the rear hallway, but here in the main room, they couldn't spot him. "If I am to die now," Lila Hirsch thought, "please let it be quick."

Dr. Hirsch saw the German terrorist race through the front door into the room and aim his submachine gun at the hostages lying on the floor. The German hesitated, then turned around to face the airfield. A volley of shots rang out and he slumped to the floor.

Two days before, after the Jews had been separated from the others, Yitzhak David had rolled up his shirt sleeve and pointed out his concentration-camp number to the German. "Your parents killed my parents because they were Jewish," he said, "and now you are ready to kill me for the same reason." The German seemed almost apologetic. "I am not a Nazi," he said. "I am an idealist."

Dr. Hirsch would never know whether it was this conversation that had caused the German to pause now and not shoot the hostages.

From the first shots, perhaps ten or fifteen minutes had passed. Some of the hostages thought it was a shorter time, others longer. None of them had stopped to check his or her watch.

Whatever the time span, the hostages who lay in the main room or in the hallway continued to believe that Idi Amin was either killing or saving them. What changed their minds were the first words they heard, shouted from a bullhorn just outside the building.

"*Anachnu Yisraelim!*"

"We are Israelis!"

It took a few seconds for it to register with most of the hostages. It didn't seem possible.

To Akiva Laxer, who is an Orthodox Jew, the first paratrooper to jump through the open window seemed like the angel of deliverance. Lila Hirsch thought of the American soldiers who had liberated the concentration camps.

When two or three other soldiers entered, Josef Hadad, a Moroccan immigrant who had started this trip to find work in Europe because he was tired of paying high taxes and serving 60 days of reserve duty in the Israeli army each year, began shouting, "These are our men! These are our men!"

The Air France crew, who lay stretched out in one corner of the room with several French Jews, understood what was happening only after someone translated for them.

The soldiers began running among the hostages, looking for terrorists and shouting for everyone to lie down. Emma Rosenkowitz almost managed a smile. No one could have been lying any flatter.

Suddenly, Emma remembered the three Ugandans in the bathroom. "Don't shoot them," she screamed. "They're not soldiers and they have no weapons." The commandos left them alone.

Two or three minutes passed before the soldiers told them all to get up and prepare to go. The firing had stopped outside, but as most of the hostages stood up, it began again with new intensity. The Ugandans had opened fire from the control tower, and just outside the building, Lieutenant Colonel Netanyahu fell, killed by a shot in the back.

Inside, everyone hit the floor again. Michal Warshavsky turned to the French steward beside her. "In your whole life," the fifteen-year-old whispered, "you will never see soldiers like this."

Emma Rosenkowitz also felt a surge of joy, but it was short-lived. She began to think about Maalot, the Israeli village where terrorists had taken over a school building two years before. The army had gone in shooting. Twenty children had been killed.

Avri and Gabriela Rubenstein had found each other by this time and were lying together. "Did you ever think we'd be rescued this way?" Avri asked. "Not in my wildest dreams," she said.

Dr. Hirsch was too busy to think. He saw someone bleeding badly nearby, and took some bandages from his overnight bag. Throwing them to the soldier nearest the body, he got his first look at the wounded man's face. It was his friend, Yitzhak David.

All week long, 52-year-old Pasco Cohen had been boosting his fellow hostage's morale. "You are lucky to be with me," he said. "I'm a specialist at getting out of dangerous places. I survived the Holocaust. I've taken part in all of Israel's wars. I've faced death many times."

Now Cohen disobeyed the soldiers' warning. He got to his feet and began looking around for his thirteen-year-old son. He had only taken a few steps when a shot rang out. An Israeli soldier outside had mistaken him, like Maimoni, for a terrorist. Cohen lurched forward.

Four or five minutes later, the shooting stopped and one of the soldiers told them to get up again. "There is a plane outside," he said. "We will take you home now."

Most of the hostages were only partially dressed. Those who could grabbed pants, dresses, and shoes. One young woman started to leave wearing only a bra and panties. A soldier took off his shirt and threw it around her.

Yosef Hadad's wife, Lisette, reached for her slacks. There were two bullet holes in them.

A man of about 30 was leaning over his mother's body and screaming that she had died of a heart attack. When Claude Rosenkowitz walked over to urge him to leave, he saw the bullet wound in Ida Borowicz's chest.

Jocelyne Monier and her boyfriend began crawling over shattered glass, blood still streaming from Jocelyne's leg. A soldier kneeled down and lifted her up on his back.

Dr. Hirsch took his first good look at the inert form of Yitzhak David. He was sure his friend was dead, and asked someone for a blanket. As he began to cover David, Hirsch saw him stir. Quickly, he lifted him onto his shoulders and began walking to the entrance. When he got outside, David had regained consciousness and was able to make it on his own.

Akiva Laxer grabbed Pasco Cohen's two children and led them and their dazed mother past their father, who was being lifted onto a stretcher.

Ilan Har-Tuv, a Jerusalem economist, took a last look back before leaving. His 75-year-old mother, Dora Bloch, had been taken to a Kampala hospital the day before with a throat ailment. She would not be making this trip. She would not be in New York the following week for her other son's wedding. A day after the raid, the old woman was reportedly dragged from her hospital bed and strangled.

As they ran from the building and into the darkness, the hostages passed the bullet-ridden bodies of Jean-Jacques Maimoni and the German terrorist. A few glanced down. Most didn't.

Outside, the night was cool and clear. As he ran, Avri Rubenstein turned for a last look at the building that had been his prison for six days. There was a fire burning on the second floor.

Nearly half the hostages raced to the Peugeot mini-truck and the command car which were waiting, their lights off and engines running, about 30 yards away. Without panic, they piled on top of each other until there was no more room. The front windshield of the command car was collapsible. A soldier helped Dr. Hirsch lay Yitzhak David across it.

The others ran, parents carrying children, young leading old, soldiers bearing stretchers, and others turning around to fire at the control tower. In the distance, they could see explosions coming from the eleven MIG's that another Israeli unit was destroying.

One Hercules C-130 had taxied to within 300 yards, its rear door beckoning the hostages home. As they reached it and ran gasping up the ramp, several stumbled and fell. Others stopped to pick them up.

Then they were in—the living, the wounded, and the two who were already dead. For perhaps ten minutes, the dozen or so soldiers aboard did repeated head counts as the hostages lay huddled on the floor. The dazed French captain, Michel Bacos, kept asking for his copilot, the one with the mustache. The copilot was sitting directly in front of him.

The rear hatch slammed shut and the plane began to move. The night before, the dry run had taken 55 minutes. The actual raid had taken 53.

Inside the plane, stretchers were hung from pillars along the ribbed sides, and doctors were already working on the most seriously wounded. The earplugs which were distributed helped seal off the roar of the engines and the cries of pain.

As the Hercules and the Boeing command plane headed for Nairobi to refuel and drop off the wounded, they left behind a second Hercules, which would wait half an hour for a commando unit to mop up, fingerprint the seven dead terrorists, and evacuate their wounded and the dead Lieutenant Colonel Netanyahu. An estimated twenty Ugandan soldiers lay dead as well, their bodies strewn around the airport.

On the short hop to Kenya, the hostages got their first look at the Israeli soldiers. They looked so young now without their battle gear, almost like children. One of the soldiers suggested that everyone sing. He started by himself, but quickly stopped when no one followed.

Yitzhak David and Pasco Cohen were taken off in Nairobi. David would recover and return to Israel in four days. The thirteen-year-old son Cohen had been looking for would say Kaddish three days later at his father's grave.

On the seven-hour trip to Israel, Claude and Emma Rosenkowitz hummed softly to their children. Sarah Davidson put her head on her older son's shoulder and for the first time this week, she cried.

Michal Warshavsky had begun to think of the stories she would have for her girl friends in Jerusalem.

Yosef Hadad told his wife that he no longer cared about the high taxes or reserve duty. Their home was in Israel.

Akiva Laxer passed out water and, with several others, silently prayed.

Shortly after the plane had left Kenya, cabinet member Gideon Hausner received a call at his Jerusalem home. "It was successful beyond all expectation," he was told.

As the plane crossed the Red Sea and took them home, there was silence on board. The sun had begun to rise. It was July 4, and at Tel Aviv's Ben-Gurion Airport, huge crowds had already begun to celebrate.

From New York Magazine, 1976.

QUESTIONS

(1) Why does Ross begin on the night of the rescue instead of at "the beginning"?

(2) Does the mention of the 1972 Munich Olympics suggest a long chain of terrorist acts? Does this stretch back to the Nazis and the concentration camps? Is part of the power of this article the suggestion that the terrorist chain of "triumphs" was broken?

(3) Why does Ross specify that Gideon Hausner was the chief prosecutor at the Adolf Eichman trial?

(4) Is there any special symbolism in the flight of the rescue planes over the Red Sea?

(5) How do Ross's admissions of doubts and uncertainties and the presentation of alternative explanations strengthen his narrative?

(6) How does Ross achieve a detailed and coherent account of the crowded chaos of the rescue?

(7) Why is the detail that the German terrorist aimed his submachine gun at the hostages but did not fire important? Do you believe it?

(8) What does Ross accomplish by his cutting back and forth between the present in Entebbe and the Nazi past?

(9) Why is the story written in the form of many short paragraphs? How is the form related to the content?

(10) Is the juxtaposition of the Red Sea and July 4th in the last paragraph deliberate? What kind of suggestions does it make?

ATTICA

TOM WICKER

September 8, 1971

The police car moved quickly through Attica village, past a
sign announcing a population of 2975 and one of those municipal directories that listed nine churches and, among other organizations, an historical society, a garden club, Grange 1058,
a rod-and-gun club, and a rodeo association. But the town did
not seem much of a place in its isolation, and Wicker was surprised to learn later that it boasted—in addition to the prison,
its major employer—a Westinghouse plant, lumber mills, a
box factory, two banks, and two weekly newspapers. From
Route 98, [State Trooper John] Anna turned on Main Street,
crossed Tonawonda Creek in the middle of town and made a
right turn on Exchange Street, up a hill. A few hundred feet
further on, Anna braked the car for a roadblock.

"I'm taking Mr. Wicker in to meet with the commissioner,"
Anna said to the man in uniform who bent over to peer into
the car; the uniform appeared to be that of a county sheriff's
department. The man who wore it was carrying a rifle and
had a heavy pistol in a holster at his hip; a long billy club
hung from his belt, as did a heavy flashlight. There were three
other deputies manning the roadblock. Each carried the same
weapons, except that one had a shotgun instead of a rifle.
There were a lot of weapons in that roadblock, Wicker
thought, and no way to know how many more in the police
car parked at the side of the road.

It was his first glimpse of the profuse weaponry available to
the law officers on duty during the Attica uprising. But
Wicker did not then understand that so many guns must
sooner or later become a force in themselves, an imperative
acting upon the men who supposedly control them. If the
weapons are in hand, the question of those who have them
ultimately becomes, "Why not use them?" The more weapons,
the more insistent the question; and the burden of explaining

why *not* to use them falls on those who have no guns. But those who have no guns have little credence with those who do.

Anna displayed his credentials and they were through the roadblock in seconds. To the left in a parklike setting of trees and lawn there was a substantial Georgian mansion—the home of the Attica Correctional Facility's superintendent Vincent Mancusi, and the most imposing dwelling in Attica village. Just beyond this house rose the prison wall—massive, sand-colored, ugly, frightening in the darkening afternoon. The first sight of Attica's walls often overwhelms visitors; and for men who are going to be locked within those walls, the impact can be much worse, as one has recalled:

> In 1969, they moved 44 of us to Attica from Sing Sing. . . . We were shackled, chained, handcuffed, the whole thing. . . . I first saw Attica from a distance as we came down from Batavia . . . and I can still remember the thought that went through my mind: "Oh my God, this is a concentration camp!" . . . I knew that at last I was going to the big house.

No American institution, in fact, is so forbidding as the prison. This may be because so few Americans know anything more about prisons than what they may have gleaned from old Cagney and Bogart movies. As men abhor the unknown, they shun the prison. It is, they tell themselves, none of *their* business, no concern of the ordinary citizen, who need never go there. As for the others, no one *had* to commit the crime that put him or her in that dark place. To the extent the prison is thought of at all by the law-abiding citizen, it is likely to evoke vaguely shocking impressions of rape and violence, unspeakable acts. Where a prison must unavoidably be seen, good men and women are apt to hasten past as if it were a cemetery—which in some ways it is. More often, the prison is hidden from the general view.

Wherever it may be located, the great walls rise, typically, like those of an ancient, turreted fortress. Like a fortress, too, the prison is designed as much to keep outsiders out as to keep inmates in. The American fortress prison conceals, in fact, a classically closed society. No one not a part of its harsh life can really know what goes on behind the walls. No one within, not the most alert warden, not the best-informed inmate with his avid ear to the grapevine, can know with exactitude every-

thing that happens in its shadowed society. The great world
goes about its business, but the prison is a dark pocket of mystery and silence—"the black flower of civilized society," Hawthorne called it.

In New York state, in particular, comfortable society had
by 1971 made certain that the black flower flourished mostly
out of sight—hence mostly out of mind of the comfortable.
Attica isolated in Wyoming County far to the northwest,
Dannemora on the Canadian border, Great Meadow, Green
Haven, Wallkill, Auburn, Clinton, with their idyllic names—
all were well-hidden from the great population centers where
crime flourished. When criminals were banished from society
in New York state, most were as effectively removed from
their communities and families and jobs—if any—as if they
had been swallowed by the sea; which meant that law-abiding
or at least unapprehended citizens did not have to gaze upon
these human warehouses and thus be aware of the repressed or
warped or mistreated or hopeless or malignant humanity
within.

But the hiding of the prisons had other pernicious consequences. Families and friends had difficulty visiting during
the limited hours when it was permitted; the round trip bus
fare from New York City to Batavia (nine hours each way)
was $33.35, and the round trip taxi fare from Batavia to the
prison was $12.00. Medical and legal and social work agencies,
abundant in the cities, could not easily extend their services
to the far corners of the state. Small, prison-based communities like Attica, far from the clash and clangor of urban life,
came to have exclusive jurisdiction over the city's offenders.
Since in contemporary times those offenders were more and
more often black or Spanish-speaking, the prison-based villages, white and rural, had less and less understanding or sympathy for their charges.

Tom Wicker had realized little of any of this on the late
afternoon when he first saw the walls of Attica. He had no
more real knowledge, if perhaps a deeper abstract concern,
than any other American who never had been "sent up."
Twenty years earlier, he had been the information director—
or publicity man—for the State Board of Public Welfare in
North Carolina, and each month had had to visit the state
prison in Raleigh—begun in 1869, its main building com-

pleted in 1883—to "close" the Board's professional magazine at
the prison print shop. But he remembered little more of that
experience than the niggling fear he had felt while being led
through the prison yard and while going about his business
with the inmate printers. As a reporter and columnist in
Washington, he had followed the emergence of the fear of
crime as a major political issue. In studying it, he had become
intellectually convinced that prisons were, in bureaucratic jar-
gon, "counter-productive"—that they were, as Ramsey Clark
had called them in a book to which Wicker had contributed
an admiring foreword, "factories of crime."

From such conviction had sprung his articles on Martin
Sostre and prisoners' rights; from a general engagement with
the disadvantaged and maltreated, he had leaped to instinctive
sympathy for George Jackson and to the realization that
prison-wise blacks were not going to believe the strange official story of his death—as indeed few had believed it. But none
of that came to any real experience of prisons or prisoners,
and Wicker was painfully aware of his ignorance as John
Anna drove slowly across the paved parking area in front of
the massive wall, before which an olive drab helicopter waited
ominously.

The wall seemed to stretch for miles. At the midpoint of
the paved area it turned outward at a slight angle and came
to a point; but the point was blunted by a six-sided turret rising higher than the walls and topped by an incongruous cu-
pola. The official entrance to the prison was through this
turret, and above the door—sharply arched, rather like that of
a Gothic church—prominent letters announced "Attica Correctional Facility." Anna hurried Wicker into the turret and
explained the visitor to an unimpressed guard in gray-blue
prison uniform. When he had signed them in, they went out
the other side of the turret and into an open area between the
mighty wall and the main prison buildings.

Ordinarily, Wicker judged, this would have been a quiet
and almost parklike area, save for the wall looming above it;
green lawn stretched away on either side of a concrete walk.
That afternoon, the area was full of activity. State troopers
and sheriff's officers were there in force, some lounging about,
some in formations, some eating at stands that had been
hastily erected. The atmosphere was tense, military; many of

the men wore heavy, polished boots; some were in crash or battle helmets. Wicker was self-conscious in his casual clothes, as if he had appeared without socks for a formal dinner. Again, he was struck by the overwhelming presence of weapons. Every officer seemed to have a pistol at his side, a heavy club; many carried rifles and shotguns; some had tear-gas launchers; others had gas masks swinging at their belts. There were military-looking trucks, stacks of boxes, extended fire hoses, commanding men moving about, shouted orders—every sign, Wicker thought, of an army preparing to move out. Faces grim and unsmiling peered at him, but no one spoke to him.

Perhaps 50 yards beyond the turret, the walkway led to the main lobby of the administration building. It was crowded with men, noisy with their talk, which echoed from the hard institutional walls, the concrete floor. Anna paused, looking around.

"I'm supposed to turn you over to Captain Williams," he told Wicker, who had read in *The Times* about Captain Henry F. Williams of Troop A, New York State Police. Captain Williams, who had been put in tactical command of all police forces at Attica, looked to Wicker like a man who would be quite willing to issue an order to attack—not that he was military in appearance. His short-sleeved white shirt was stretched tight across a sizeable paunch, he was wearing dark glasses, and—unlike most of the men in the lobby—was carrying no visible weapons. But to Tom Wicker, Captain Williams looked like a tough man indeed—there was a lot of muscle in that paunch and under the jowls a bull neck that appeared unyielding. His hair was cropped into an unfashionable crew-cut and his narrow black knit tie had an air about it of woe to the hippies.

"Glad to have you here," Williams said, shaking hands. "Sure hope you can help us out."

"I'll try, Captain. What do you want me to do?"

"Well the other observers are meeting upstairs with the commissioner. You might as well go right on up."

"How's it looking?"

Williams shook his head, unsmiling. "Something's got to give. We can't wait much longer." He did not say why, but designated a trooper to show Wicker the way.

"I sure wish you all the luck in the world," John Anna said

shaking hands. "You fellows sure are going to need it in there."

"What do you really think?" Wicker said, out of Captain Williams' hearing. "Can we do anything?"

"I sure hope so," Anna said. "I sure hope you can just get those boys out of there alive."

As he watched Anna walk away, Wicker suddenly realized he had thought almost not at all about the hostages. For the first time, as he watched Anna hurrying back toward the prison entrance, Wicker began to realize the possibilities of what he had been so precipitately pulled into. Men might die here. The summons from Arthur Eve had caught him unprepared and he had rushed off to Attica almost without thinking, dashing to the airport while drowsy with wine, without a suitcase or a toothbrush or a clean shirt, on the vague assumption that he would return to Washington that night or at the latest the next morning.

On the flight to Buffalo, while studying *The Times'* account of the inmates' rebellion, if he had had any coherent notion of what he was expected to do at Attica, it was that he and a few other persons trusted by the inmates would give a sort of guarantee by their presence—a good-faith endorsement—to whatever agreement was to be reached by inmate and prison negotiators. With no better sense of his mission than that, he had caught the first plane, in part because of his reporter's instinct to go where the action was, more because of a certain faint pride at having been asked for help by men who had so few to whom they could turn.

Now, in the military preparations all about him, in the clicking and gleaming of the omnipresent weapons, in Captain Williams's laconic *something's got to give,* John Anna's gravity, above all from the overwhelming sense of the great walls closing about him, isolating him from the ordinary world and its accepted restraints, Wicker sensed that he might have gone beyond his depth. Here amid the guns, within the secretive walls, there was not likely to be the orderly and due process to which he was accustomed, upon which his calling so heavily relied. The threat of violence was all about him, in the very atmosphere of Attica. Lives—even his own—might depend upon something he did or said or failed to do.

He looked with foreboding at the grim faces around him, at

the military bustle. He did not know what to do or even where to start, and he sensed that he probably had no real business being there at all. For most of his life he had followed the advice of Heyst's father in *Victory*—"Look on, and make no sound." He had lived by the reporter's peculiar standard, the ethic of the press box rather than of the participant. At Attica, he might no longer be able to play his easy, familiar role of privileged onlooker.

But he followed his guide up the stairs with a curious kind of resolution. It was high time, he thought, that he held himself to a line. What was a life if it was never put to challenge, not just by foolhardy choice but as a logical and perhaps inevitable consequence of the way a person had lived and believed? However little he might actually belong there, his life and work had brought him to Attica, almost as if to demand of him that he validate the work by committing the life. As for *how* he met the challenge, that seemed for the moment less important than that he should recognize and accept it.

Besides, he thought irrelevantly, with sudden bravado, as if the wine had returned to his brain, he had had a good, long run for it; he had come a long way before they laid a glove on him.

From *Attica: A Time to Die,* 1975.

QUESTIONS

(1) Tom Wicker talks about himself throughout in the third person—"Wicker was surprised"—how effective is this?

(2) In how many ways is the simple statement, "Wicker was surprised," the theme of the selection?

(3) Does he suggest that policemen and criminals are alike in an addiction to violence?

(4) How does Wicker make the reader see and understand "hidden" things, things kept out of sight?

(5) Why should a prison be of any concern to an ordinary law-abiding citizen? Should all prison sentences be for life?

(6) Are old Cagney and Bogart movies good places to learn about prisons?

(7) Does Wicker indicate that the town is in any way the captive of the prison?

(8) Is the distinction between "law-abiding" and "unapprehended" citizens a good one?

(9) One theme of the selection is the education of Tom Wicker. How does he integrate details learned later with his story of seeing the prison and entering it for the first time? Is this a good way to convey essential information to the reader?

(10) Is the admission that he was "painfully aware of his ignorance" a first step in learning? How does he show that it is necessary to have some knowledge of a subject before you even know you are ignorant?

(11) Why do Captain Williams's statements, "Something's got to give. We can't wait much longer," sound so ominous?

(12) Is there a special "ethic of the press box" that is different from the ethic of participation?

(13) Does Wicker imply that the police are ready to invade the prison as if it were a foreign country? How is that connected with everything else he says about the prison in American society?

(14) How do you feel about "Wicker," the person you have met in this selection? What kind of person does he seem to be?

NOTE

On Monday morning, September 13, 1971, law enforcement officers stormed the yard and cell block where the rebellious prisoners had gathered and the hostages were held. In the attack, which lasted eight minutes, two hostages were seriously

injured by the inmates. Ten hostages and twenty-nine inmates were killed by the guns of the state troopers and correc-
tion officers.

AN ASSASSIN'S DIARY

ARTHUR BREMER

I'm back to writting. May 4, 1972 Thursday. 10 days have
passed since my last entry. And even then I was a week behind
in writting things down. Had to get away from it for a while.
Needed some fresh air & exercise.

When I came back up untill my last entry, I morned my
failures & stayed indoors—back to the exact same existence I
had as befor the trip. Everything was the SAME except 1 had
less money. Much less.

I had to get away from my thoughts for a while. I went to
the zoo, the lake front, saw *Clockwork Orange* & thought
about getting Wallace all thru the picture—fantasing my self
as the Alek on the screen come to real life—but without "my
brothers" & without any "in and out." Just "a little of the old
ultra violence."

I've decided Wallace will have the honor of—what would
you call it?

Like a novelist who knows not how his book will end—I
have written this journal—what a shocking surprise that my
inner character shall steal the climax and destroy the author
and save the anti-hero from assasination!!

It may sound exciting & fascinating to readers 100 years from
now—as the Booth conspricy seems to us today; but to this
man it seems only another failure. And I stopped tolerating
failure weeks ago.

As I said befor, I Am A Hamlet.

It seems I would of done better for myself to kill the old
G-man Hoover. In death, he lays with Presidents. Who the

hell ever got buried in 'Bama for being great? He certainly won't be buryed with the snobs in Washington.

SHIT! I won't even rate a TV enteroption in Russia or Europe when the news breaks—they never heard of Wallace. If something big in Nam flares up I'll end up at the bottom of the 1st page in America. The editors will say—"Wallace dead? Who cares." He won't get more than 3 minutes on network TV news. I don't expect anybody to get a big thobbing erection from the news. You know, a storm in some country we never heard of kills 10,000 people—big deal—pass the beer and what's on T.V. tonight.

I hope my death makes more sense than my life.

Still feel—& have for a while—a general weakness in my heart.

The whole country's going liberal. I can see it in McGovern. You know, my biggest failure may well be when I kill Wallace. I hope everyone screams & hollers & everything!! I hope the rally goes mad!!!

May the 16th is primary date in that beautiful state across Lake Michigan—Michigan. Wallace is believed to be strong there. He'll have a rally in Detroit. I'm sure of it, once this week's primaries are over.

I wish I could give it to the Nixonites who crossed over and made Wally-boy look strong with over 300,000 votes in Indiana. A recurring fantasy of mind is to kill 50 or so cops & dicks in unmarked cars in this little community. I hate those unmarked cars & I can spot 'um anywhere.

I passed some time in Milwaukee's misdemenor courts—would like to see a falony trail but I have to spend all next week in Michigan on business.

When I heard that ½ of the states votes were in the Detroit area, I decided right then to go to Kalamazoo & meet him there.

A short drive from Jackson. I stayed at a hotel overlooking the Kalamazoo National Guard Armory where he'ld talk. Watched it carefully. Wanted everything perfect. Paper said 10% chance of rain Sat., today, afternoon. I'm checked out of my room & sitting in my car now & writing & its raining like a son-of-a-bitch. Will this spoil everything?

Was *very* warm yesterday. This morning I could smell rain in the air. He'ld talk at a $25 plate dinner. Then at the

Armory, capacity 2,300. Then leave for Maryland tonight for 2 days of campaning. They have a primary the 16th too.

He drew 4–6,000 in 1968 at a near by city Park. Read the paper in the beautiful mall area of town. Listened to rock music, in a park. A small ineffective protest is planned today.

Wanted to be the 1st in line. Thought I saw people standing in front of the place at 9 this morning. They moved on. Rain is letting up slowly now. It's about 1:30. He isn't in Warren yet. But I'll soon be on the front steps of the Kalamazoo Armory to welcome him. Got a sign from campaing headquarters here. To shield the go for the gun.

Is there any thing else to say?

My cry upon firing will be, "A penny for your thoughts."

From *An Assassins Diary*, 1972.

QUESTIONS

(1) How did you feel when you read this selection? What characteristics of the person and/or his world seemed most significant to you?

(2) If you had seen this diary before the shooting would you have believed that its author would have gone through with it?

(3) If you had come upon the diary by accident, would you have gone to the police with it? Would you have done anything?

(4) From the evidence in this selection from Arthur Bremer's diary, how would you describe his motive or motives?

THE MASS PSYCHOLOGY OF RAPE

SUSAN BROWNMILLER

Krafft-Ebing, who pioneered in the study of sexual disorders, had little to say about rape. His famous *Psychopathia Sexualis* gives amazingly short shrift to the act and its doers. He had it on good authority, he informed his readers, that most rapists were degenerate, imbecilic men. Having made that sweeping generalization, Krafft-Ebing washed his hands of the whole affair and turned with relish to the frotteurs and fetishists of normal intelligence who tickled his fancy.

Sigmund Freud, whose major works followed Krafft-Ebing's by twenty to forty years, was also struck dumb by the subject of rape. We can search his writings in vain for a quotable quote, an analysis, a perception. The father of psychoanalysis, who invented the concept of the primacy of the penis, was never motivated, as far as we know, to explore the real-life deployment of the penis as weapon. What the master ignored, the disciples tended to ignore as well. Alfred Adler does not mention rape, despite his full awareness of the historic power struggle between men and women. Jung refers to rape only in the most obscure manner, a glancing reference in some of his mythological interpretations. Helene Deutsch and Karen Horney, each from a differing perspective, grasped at the female fear of rape, and at the feminine fantasy, but as women who did not dare to presume, they turned a blind eye to the male and female reality.

And the great socialist theoreticians Marx and Engels and their many confreres and disciples who developed the theory of class oppression and put words like "exploitation" into the everyday vocabulary, they, too, were strangely silent about rape, unable to fit it into their economic constructs. Among them only August Bebel tried to grasp at its historic importance, its role in the very formulation of class, private property and the means of production. In *Woman Under Socialism* Bebel used his imagination to speculate briefly about the prehistoric tribal fights for land, cattle and labor power within an acceptable Marxist analysis: "There arose the need of labor power to cultivate the ground. The more numerous these powers, all the greater was the wealth in products and herds. These struggles led first to the rape of women, later to the enslaving of conquered men. The women became laborers and objects of pleasure for the conqueror; their males became slaves." He didn't get it quite right, making the rape of women secondary to man's search for labor, but it was a flash of revelation and one that Engels did not achieve in his *Origin of the Family*. But Bebel was more at ease researching the wages and conditions of working-women in German factories, and that is where his energies went.

It was the half-crazed genius Wilhelm Reich, consumed with rage in equal parts toward Hitler, Marx and Freud, who briefly entertained the vision of a "masculine ideology of rape." The phrase hangs there in the opening chapter of *The Sexual Revolution,* begging for further interpretation. But it was not forthcoming. The anguished mind was in too great a state of disarray. A political analysis of rape would have required more treachery toward his own immutable gender than even Wilhelm Reich could muster.

And so it remained for the latter-day feminists, free at last from the strictures that forbade us to look at male sexuality, to discover the truth and meaning in our own victimization. Critical to our study is the recognition that rape has a history, and that through the tools of historical analysis we may learn what we need to know about our current condition.

No zoologist as far as I know, has ever observed that animals rape in their natural habitat, the wild. Sex in the animal world, including those species that are our closest relations, the primates, is more properly called "mating," and it is cyclical activity set off by biologic signals the female puts out. Mating is initiated and "controlled," it would seem, by the female estrous cycle. When the female of the species periodically goes into heat, giving off obvious physical signs, she is ready and eager for copulation and the male becomes interested. At other times there is simply no interest, and no mating.

Jane Goodall, studying her wild chimpanzees at the Gombe Stream reserve, noted that the chimps, male and female, were "very promiscuous, but this does not mean that every female

will accept every male that courts her." She recorded her observations of one female in heat, who showed the telltale pink
swelling of her genital area, who nevertheless displayed an
aversion to one particular male who pursued her. "Though
he once shook her out of the tree in which she had sought
refuge, we never saw him actually 'rape' her," Goodall wrote,
adding, however, "Nonetheless, quite often he managed to
get his way through dogged persistence." Another student of
animal behavior, Leonard Williams, has stated categorically,
"The male monkey cannot in fact mate with the female without her invitation and willingness to cooperate. In monkey
society there is no such thing as rape, prostitution, or even
passive consent."

Zoologists for the most part have been reticent on the subject of rape. It has not been, for them, an important scientific question. But we do know that human beings are different. Copulation in our species can occur 365 days of the
year; it is not controlled by the female estrous cycle. We females of the human species do not "go pink." The call of
estrus and the telltale signs, both visual and olfactory, are absent from our mating procedures, lost perhaps in the evolutionary shuffle. In their place, as a mark of our civilization,
we have evolved a complex system of psychological signs and
urges, and a complex structure of pleasure. Our call to sex
occurs in the head, and the act is not necessarily linked, as it
is with animals, to Mother Nature's pattern of procreation.
Without a biologically determined mating season, a human
male can evince sexual interest in a human female at any time
he pleases, and his psychologic urge is not dependent in the
slightest on her biologic readiness or receptivity. What it all
boils down to is that the human male can rape.

Man's structural capacity to rape and woman's corresponding structural vulnerability are as basic to the physiology of
both our sexes as the primal act of sex itself. Had it not been
for this accident of biology, an accommodation requiring the
locking together of two separate parts, penis into vagina, there
would be neither copulation nor rape as we know it. Anatomi-
cally one might want to improve on the design of nature, but
such speculation appears to my mind as unrealistic. The human sex act accomplishes its historic purpose of generation of
the species and it also affords some intimacy and pleasure. I

have no basic quarrel with the procedure. But, nevertheless, we cannot work around the fact that in terms of human anatomy the possibility of forcible intercourse incontrovertibly exists. This single factor may have been sufficient to have caused the creation of a male ideology of rape. When men discovered that they could rape, they proceeded to do it. Later, much later, under certain circumstances they even came to consider rape a crime.

In the violent landscape inhabited by primitive woman and man, some woman somewhere had a prescient vision of her right to her own physical integrity, and in my mind's eye I can picture her fighting like hell to preserve it. After a thunderbolt of recognition that this particular incarnation of hairy, two-legged hominid was not the Homo sapiens with whom she would like to freely join parts, it might have been she, and not some man, who picked up the first stone and hurled it. How surprised he must have been, and what an unexpected battle must have taken place. Fleet of foot and spirited, she would have kicked, bitten, pushed and run, *but she could not retaliate in kind.*

The dim perception that had entered prehistoric woman's consciousness must have had an equal but opposite reaction in the mind of her male assailant. For if the first rape was an unexpected battle founded on the first woman's refusal, the second rape was indubitably planned. Indeed, one of the earliest forms of male bonding must have been the gang rape of one woman by a band of marauding men. This accomplished, rape became not only a male prerogative, but man's basic weapon of force against woman, the principal agent of his will and her fear. His forcible entry into her body, despite her physical protestations and struggle, became the vehicle of his victorious conquest over her being, the ultimate test of his superior strength, the triumph of his manhood.

Man's discovery that his genitalia could serve as a weapon to generate fear must rank as one of the most important discoveries of prehistoric times, along with the use of fire and the first crude stone axe. From prehistoric times to the present, I believe, rape has played a critical function. It is nothing more or less than a conscious process of intimidation by which *all men* keep *all women* in a state of fear.

From *Against Our Will*, 1975.

QUESTIONS

(1) Is the fact that Krafft-Ebing had "little to say about rape" in itself a significant fact for Brownmiller's thesis? Is Freud's silence on the topic equally significant?

(2) Is the phrase "the penis as weapon" a good one? Would it fit in any other selections in this section?

(3) What conclusion does Brownmiller want you to have come to by the end of the third paragraph?

(4) What are the implications of the sentence beginning: "But Bebel was more at ease . . ."?

(5) How does Brownmiller want the reader to feel about Bebel? About Wilhelm Reich?

(6) How do you react to Jane Goodall's distinction between never raping but often getting his way "through dogged persistence"? Is this a distinction without a difference? How might Sally Kempton react?

(7) Is, "What it all boils down to is that the human male can rape," what it all boils down to?

(8) Is it accurate to say that other primates *can't* rape, or that, in contrast with humans, they *don't* rape?

(9) Why is the clause, *"but she could not retaliate in kind"* italicized?

(10) Is the statement of her thesis clear and forceful? Is the use of imaginative examples effective?

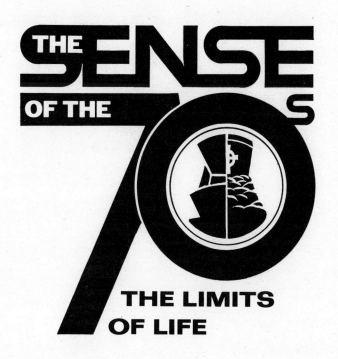

THE SENSE OF THE 70's

OF THE

70s

THE LIMITS OF LIFE

It seems fitting to begin a section on the limits of life with the celebration of a birth. Donald Sutherland's essay is such a celebration of a different kind of birth, of birth directly into a human community rather than a mechanical receptacle.

After the celebration of that joyous few hours, however, the section turns dark, and the other limit of life dominates. Daniel Callahan's careful essay will please militants on neither side of the abortion question. In it he coins a term, *conceptus,* "that which has been conceived," to avoid the emotional entanglements of foetus or child, thing or person. He does not, however, use the term to avoid any of the problems that made the language so emotional in the first place. This essay is part of the conclusion of a long book written before the Supreme Court decision on the legal status of abortion. Callahan's thesis is that legalization is only a necessary first step in dealing with abortion. If a person is legally free to do something then that person still faces the moral and psychological burden of a choice. To pretend that the question of abortion is settled simply because it is legal is to trivialize the profound human mystery of the creation of life and to take a harrowing step toward state regulated morality.

Alive is a study of survival at extreme biological and psychological limits. On October 12, 1972, a Uruguayan plane carrying forty passengers and a crew of five crashed in a remote area of the snow-covered Andes. Most of the passengers were young men, members of an amateur rugby team flying to Chile for a match, along with some relatives and friends. Twenty-seven of those on board survived the crash. Sixteen of those survived the incredible ordeal of ten weeks of isolation on the desolate mountain peak in the wreckage of the plane. Piers Paul Read describes one of the things the young people had to do in order to survive before two of them were able to make their way down from the mountain to summon help.

Paige Mitchell in her book *Act of Love* details a death in a family on the Atlantic coast of New Jersey. On June 17, 1973, a Sunday, Father's Day, George Zygmanik had a motorcycle accident. He was twenty-six, married, and the father of a four-year-old son. The accident left him completely paralyzed from the neck down. He begged his younger brother Lester not to let him live in that state. Lester promised.

The excerpt printed here follows Lester Zygmanik through the day and night of June 20, 1973 as he moved from the hospital to the family farm and back to the hospital. Mitchell counterpoints Lester's isolated struggle with his promise and his immersion in a family: Sonia Zygmanik, his widowed mother; Jeannie, George's wife; Barbara Petruska, a friend from high school—it was on her motorcycle that George was riding when he had the accident—Victor Kazma, Jeannie's father. On June 20, 1973, Lester kept his promise.

Some people may not be able to read Richard Selzer's "The Corpse." With a surgeon's intimate knowledge he tells a truth usually kept hidden. Thus the essay is an important document in the age of exposure. But, for some, in detailing exactly what is done to a human body to prepare for its civilized disposal, Selzer will have gone too far. He says that he is telling a truth already known, but not admitted. Perhaps T. S. Eliot was right: "Humankind cannot bear very much reality." In any case, no revelations of the decade, no secrets from high places or from behind locked doors, are more chilling than these.

The Savage God is a study of suicide, and, in it, Alvarez incorporates a rare document: the detailed account of an attempted suicide, a statement of the actions and feelings of someone who tried to kick the habit of living. The details are clear, authentic, and compelling because Alvarez is a careful writer and because the attempt he is describing was his own.

"The Long Habit" to which Lewis Thomas refers is the habit of living. Doctor Thomas is a physician and scientist with a poet's eye and a philosopher's mind. His book, *The Lives of a Cell* is a classic of the seventies, a book which will outlive the decade because it changes permanently our understanding of ourselves.

Birth and death are not exactly new topics, but in the seventies they were re-understood. Abortion became legal in America. Karen Ann Quinlan became a national symbol for the problem of anyone's "last rights." Gary Gilmore's last words, "Let's get it over with," still echo, still haunt. Who? how? why? how much? The questions of control won't go away. Control of one's own life and death, control of another's; what exactly are the limits? If history is the record of changes in human possibility, then the history of the seventies will include its changes in what were the physical and the moral boundaries of life itself.

CHILDBIRTH IS NOT FOR MOTHERS ONLY

DONALD SUTHERLAND

It was the most incredible, wonderful, terrifically joyful, sexual, sensual, loving time of our lives. It was so intensely personal that it's hard to believe we didn't discover it all by ourselves. But it is as common as dying, or making love, or being born. It's what the hospitals categorize as "normal childbirth," and it was extraordinary for us because we did it together. Because we planned and studied to overcome the established obstructions that would prevent us from doing it together, all three of us. Because, despite the assurances that babies are crying just to breathe—to make their lungs work—it has to be a sad, uncomfortable journey, and we wanted to try and make it as good as it could be.

We chose Robert A. Bradley's "Husband-Coached Childbirth" method because it seemed to insure our mutual participation more than any other. We took classes together for three months; we exercised together every day. We found a doctor, a hospital, and a truly dedicated nursing staff that eagerly supported both Bradley and ourselves. They assured us certain freedoms; there would be no medication, no shaving of the pubic hair, no legs in stirrups, no tied-down wrists, no premature breaking of the bag of waters. We would be able to conduct privately, in a darkened room, the first stage of labor; work together with the staff in a quiet delivery room during the second stage; and while Francine was still on the delivery table, I would be able to place our newborn child on her breast for the first feeding. And then, when everybody was dressed, all three of us would go home.

The final obstacle was work. Filming "The Day of the Locust" with John Schlesinger would extend through Francine's term, so this clause was agreed to and placed in my contract: "On or about the first of February, the actor will be unable to present himself for reasons of family."

Working on the premise that most discomfort is created by tension, Francine totally relaxed through each contraction, breathing from her diaphragm. I monitored this and the tension in her body, telling her each 10 or 15 seconds, the elapsed time of the contraction. As they intensified, we darkened the room; she lay on her side in a sleeping position while I stood in front of her and rubbed the tension out of her back. Working this way, we did not deal with the overall time of labor; we dealt only with each individual contraction as it came along.

. . . .

Transition. Francine's cervix was dilated more than nine centimeters. The bag of waters burst, and we started to push. It was 8:30. Francine would clear her lungs, take a breath, push for about a minute—head down, knees up, squatting on her back. Then, between contractions, she would sleep. In the delivery room, I cooled her face with crushed ice; she pushed again; we watched in the overhead mirror as the head began to crown. Then she was crying and said, "On my stomach. . . ." I turned and saw the baby. . . .

The baby was born at 9:51. And the only pitfall of working together was laughing, which, when it occurred during the contraction, caused Francine her only discomfort throughout the birth. As she put it, "Quite literally, it only hurt when I laughed."

He was a boy. And we couldn't stop saying how beautiful he was, and counting his fingers and toes. When the blood stopped pumping through his umbilical cord, the cord was cut, and I put him on Francine's breast; he heard the voice which he had been hearing for the past few months and started to suck, not milk but antibodies and vitamins to protect him from this change of state.

The nurses took him to the nursery because hospital regulations insist that a pediatrician check him out before he leaves. We drank a glass of orange juice in the delivery room; we went down the hall, looked at him through the glass and waited.

When he was ready, we left for home, and stopped for some gas on the way. The attendant, looking through the window he was wiping, said, "That's a cute little baby. How old is he?" And we said, "Four hours," and started to laugh and cry at the same time.

From *Ms. Magazine*, 1974.

QUESTIONS

(1) Are all significant experiences "common" and "unique" or "normal" and "extraordinary" in the way Sutherland describes?

(2) Where does the "tension" of which Sutherland speaks come from?

(3) Being there is new and important for the father. How does this father help the reader "to be there"?

(4) How would you have reacted if you were the attendant in the gas station?

(5) Is Sutherland *urging* anything? Is he trying to convince you of anything? If so, does he succeed?

ABORTION DECISIONS: PERSONAL MORALITY

DANIEL CALLAHAN

The strength of pluralistic societies lies in the personal freedom they afford individuals. One is free to choose among religious, philosophical, ideological and political creeds; or one can create one's own highly personal, idiosyncratic moral code and view of the universe. Increasingly, the individual is free to ignore the morals, manners and mores of society. The only limitations are upon those actions which seem to present clear and present dangers to the common good, and even there the range of prohibited actions is diminishing as more and more choices are left to personal and private decisions. I have contended that, apart from some regulatory laws, abortion decisions should be left, finally, up to the women themselves. Whatever one may think of the morality of abortion, it cannot be established that it poses a clear and present danger to the common good. Thus society does not have the right decisively to interpose itself between a woman and the abortion she wants. It can only intervene where it can be shown that some of its own interests are at stake *qua* society. Regulatory laws of a minimal kind therefore seem in order, since in a variety of ways already mentioned society will be effected by the number, kind and quality of legal abortions. In short, with a few important stipulations, what I have been urging is tantamount to saying that abortion decisions should be private decisions. It is to accept, in principle, the contention of those who believe that, in a free, pluralistic society, the woman should be allowed to make her own moral choice on abortion and be allowed to implement that choice.

But pluralistic societies also lay a few traps for the unwary. It is not a large psychological step from saying that individuals should be left free to make up their own minds on some crucial moral issues (of which abortion is one) to an adoption of the view that one personal decision is as good as another, that any decision is a good one as long as it is honest or sincere, that a free decision equals a correct decision. However short the psychological step, the logical gap is very large. As absence of cant, hypocrisy and coercion may prepare the way for good personal decisions. But that is only to clean the room, and something must then be put in it. The hazard is that, once cleaned, it will be filled with capriciousness, sentimentality, a thinly disguised conformity to the reigning moral taste, or strongly felt but inadequately analyzed moral opinions. This is a particular danger in affluent pluralistic societies, heavily dominated by popular tastes, communication media and the absence of shared values. Philosophically, the view that all values are equally good and all private moral choices on a par is all but dead; but it still has a strong life at the popular level, where there is a tendency to act as if, once personal freedom is legally and socially achieved, moral questions cease to exist.

A considerable quantity of literature exists in the field of

ethics concerned with such problems as subjective and objective values, the meaning and use of ethical principles and
moral rules, the role of intentionality. That literature need
not be reviewed here. But it is directly to the point to observe
that a particular failing of the abortion-on-request literature
is that it persistently scants the moral problem of how a
woman, if granted the desired legal freedom to make her own
decision about abortion, should go about making that decision. Up to a point, this deficiency is understandable. The immediate tactical problem has been to get the laws changed or
repealed; that has been the burden of the public struggle,
which has concentrated on statutes and legislators rather than
on the moral contents and problems of personal decision-
making. It is reasonable and legitimate to say that a woman
should be left free to make the decision in the light of her
own personal values; that is, I believe, the best legal solution.
But it leaves totally untouched the question of how, once
freedom is achieved, she ought to go about the personal business of forming a coherent, rational, sensitive moral perspective and opinion on abortion. After freedom, what then? Society may have no right to demand that a woman give it good
reasons why she should have an abortion before permitting
it. But this does not entail that the woman should not, as a
morally responsible person, have good reasons to justify her
desires or acts in her own eyes.

This is only to say that a solution of the legal problem is
not the same as a solution to the moral problem. That the
moral struggle is transferred from the public to the private
sphere should not be taken to mean that the moral problem
has been solved; only its public aspect, under a permissive
law or a repeal of all laws, has been dealt with. The personal
problem will remain.

Some women will be part of a religious group or ethical tradition which they freely choose and which can offer them
something, possibly very much, in the way of helpful moral
insight consistent with that tradition. The obvious course in
that instance is for them to turn to their tradition to see what
it has to offer them on the particular problem of abortion.
But what of those who have no tradition to repair to or those
who find their tradition wanting on this problem? One way or
another, they will have to find some way of developing a set

of ethical principles and moral rules to help them act responsibly, to justify their own conduct in their own eyes. To press
the problem to a finer point, what ought they to think about
as they try to work out their own views on abortion?

Only a few suggestions will be made here, taking the form
of arguing for an ethic of personal responsibility which tries,
in the process of decision-making, to make itself aware of a
number of things. The biological evidence should be considered, just as the problem of methodology must be considered; the philosophical assumptions implicit in different uses
of the word "human" need to be considered; a philosophical
theory of biological analysis is required; the social consequences of different kinds of analyses and different meaning
of the word "human" should be thought through; consistency
of meaning and use should be sought to avoid *ad hoc* and ar-
bitrary solutions.

It is my own conviction that the "developmental school"
offers the most helpful and illuminating approach to the
problem of the beginning of human life, avoiding, on the one
hand, a too narrow genetic criterion of human life and, on
the other, a too broad and socially dangerous social definition
of the "human." Yet the kinds of problems which appear in
any attempt to decide upon the beginning of life suggest that
no one position can be either proved or disproved from biological evidence alone. It becomes a question of trying to do
justice to the evidence while, at the same time, realizing that
how the evidence is approached and used will be a function
of one's way of looking at reality, one's moral policy, the values and rights one believes need balancing, and the type of
questions one thinks need to be asked. At the very least, however, the genetic evidence for the uniqueness of zygotes and
embryos (a uniqueness of a different kind than that of the
uniqueness of sperm and ova), their potentiality for development into a human person, their early development of human
characteristics, their genetic and organic distinctness from the
organism of the mother, appear to rule out a treatment even
of zygotes, much less the more developed stages of the conceptus, as mere pieces of "tissue," of no human significance or
value. The "tissue" theory of the significance of the conceptus
can only be made plausible by a systematic disregard of the
biological evidence. Moreover, though one may conclude that

a conceptus is only potential human life, in the process of continually actualizing its potential through growth and development, a respect for the sanctity of life, with its bias in favor even of undeveloped life, is enough to make the taking of such life a moral problem. There is a choice to be made and it is a moral choice. In the near future, it is likely that some kind of simple, safe abortifacient drug will be developed, which either prevents implantation or destroys the conceptus before it can develop. It will be tempting then to think that the moral dilemma has vanished, but I do not believe it will have.

It is possible to imagine a huge number of situations where a woman could, in good and sensitive conscience, choose abortion as a moral solution to her personal or social difficulties. But, at the very least, the bounds or morality are overstepped when, either through a systematic intellectual negligence or a willful choosing of that moral solution most personally convenient, personal choice is deliberately made easy and problem-free. Yet it seems to me that a pressure in that direction is a growing part of the ethos of technological societies; it is easily possible to find people to reassure us that we need have no scruples about the way we act, whether the issue is war, the suppression of rebellion and revolution, discrimination against minorities or the use of technological advances. Pluralism makes possible the achieving of freer, more subtle moral thinking; but it is a possibility constantly endangered by cultural pressures which would simplify or dissolve moral doubts and anguish.

The question of abortion "indications" returns at the level of personal choice. I have contended that the advent of permissive laws should not mean a cessation of efforts to explore the problem of "indications." When a woman asks herself, as she ought, whether her reasons for wanting an abortion are sound reasons—which presumes abortion is a serious enough moral issue to warrant the need to provide oneself with good reasons for choosing it—she will be asking herself about justifiable indications. Thus, transposed from the legal to the personal level, the kinds of concerns adumbrated in the earlier chapters on indications remain fully pertinent. It was argued in those chapters that, with the possible exception of exceedingly rare instances of a direct threat to the physical life of the mother, one cannot speak of general categories of abortion indications as *necessitating* an abortion. In a number of circumstances, abortion may be a wise and justifiable solution to a distressed pregnancy. But when the language of necessity is used, the implication is that no other conceivable alternative is available. It may be granted, willingly enough, that some set of practical circumstances in some (possibly very many) concrete cases may indicate that abortion is the only feasible option open. But these cases cannot readily be determined in advance, and, for that reason, it is necessary to say that no formal indication as such (e.g., a psychiatric indication) entails a necessary, predetermined choice in favor of abortion.

The word "indication" remains the best word, suggesting that a number of given circumstances will bring the possibility or desirability of abortion to the fore. But to escalate the concept of an indication into that of a required procedure is to go too far. Abortion is *one* way to solve the problem of an unwanted or hazardous pregnancy (physically, psychologically, economically or socially), but it is rarely the only way, at least in affluent societies (I would be considerably less certain about making the same statement about poor societies). Even in the most extreme cases—rape, incest, psychosis, for instance—alternatives will usually be available and different choices, open. It is not necessarily the end of every woman's chance for a happy, meaningful life to bear an illegitimate child. It is not necessarily the automatic destruction of a family to have a seriously defective child born into it. It is not necessarily the ruination of every family living in overcrowded housing to have still another child. It is not inevitable that every immature woman would become even more so if she bore a child or another child. It is not inevitable that a gravely handicapped child can hope for nothing from life. It is not inevitable that every unwanted child is doomed to misery. It is not written in the essence of things, as a fixed law of human nature, that a woman cannot come to accept, love and be a good mother to a child who was initially unwanted. Nor is it a fixed law that she could not come to cherish a grossly deformed child. Naturally, these are only generalizations. The point is only that human beings are as a rule flexible, capable of doing more than they sometimes think they can, able to surmount serious dangers and challenges, able to grow and mature, able to transform inauspicious beginnings into satisfactory conclusions. Everything in life, even in procreative and family life, is not fixed in advance; the future is never wholly unalterable.

Yet the problem of personal question-asking must be pushed a step farther. The way the questions are answered will be very much determined by a woman's way of looking at herself and at life. A woman who has decided, as a personal moral policy, that nothing should be allowed to stand in the way of her own happiness, goals and self-interest will have no trouble solving the moral problem. For her, an unwanted pregnancy will, by definition, be a pregnancy to be terminated. But only by a Pickwickian use of words could this form of reasoning be called moral. It would preclude any need to consult the opinion of others, any need to examine the validity of one's own viewpoint, any need to, for instance, ask when human life begins, any need to interrogate oneself in any way, intellectually or morally; will and desire would be king.

Assuming, however, that most women would seek a broader ethical horizon than that of their exclusively personal self-interest, what might they think about when faced with an abortion decision? A respect for the sanctity of human life should, I believe, incline them toward a general and strong bias against abortion. Abortion is an act of killing, the violent, direct destruction of potential human life, already in the process of development. That fact should not be disguised, or glossed over by euphemism and circumlocution. It is not the destruction of a human person—for at no stage of its development does the conceptus fulfill the definition of a person, which implies a developed capacity for reasoning, willing, desiring and relating to others—but it is the destruction of an important and valuable form of human life. Its value and its potentiality are not dependent upon the attitude of the woman toward it; it grows by its own biological dynamism and has a genetic and morphological potential distinct from that of the woman. It has its own distinctive and individual future. If contraception and abortion are both seen as forms of birth limitation, they are distinctly different acts; the former precludes the possibility of a conceptus being formed, while the latter stops a conceptus already in existence from developing. The bias implied by the principle of the sanctity of human life is toward the protection of all forms of human life, espe-

cially, in ordinary circumstances, the protection of the right
to life. That right should be accorded even to doubtful life;
its existence should not be wholly dependent upon the personal self-interest of the woman.

Yet she has her own rights as well, and her own set of responsibilities to those around her; that is why she may have
to choose abortion. In extreme situations of overpopulation,
she may also have a responsibility for the survival of the species or of a people. In many circumstances, then, a decision in
favor of abortion—one which overrides the right to life of that
potential human being she carries within—can be a responsible moral decision, worthy neither of the condemnation of
others nor of self-condemnation. But the bias of the principle
of the sanctity of life is against a routine, unthinking employment of abortion; it bends over backwards not to take life and
gives the benefit of the doubt to life. It does not seek to diminish the range of responsibility toward life—potential or
actual—but to extend it. It does not seek the narrowest definition of life, but the widest and the richest. It is mindful of individual possibility, on the one hand, and of a destructive human tendency, on the other, to exclude from the category of
"the human" or deny rights to those beings whose existence is
or could prove burdensome to others.

The language used to describe abortion will have an important bearing on the sensitivities and imagination of those
women who must make abortion decisions. Abortion can be
talked about in the language of medical technology and technique—as, say, "a therapeutic procedure involving the emptying of the uterine contents." That language is neutral, clinical, unemotional. Or abortion can be talked about in the
emotive language of relieving woman from suffering, or meeting the need for freedom among women, or saving a nation
from a devastating overpopulation. Both kinds of language
have their place, for abortion has more than one result and
meaning and abortion can legitimately be talked about in
more than one way. What is objectionable is a conscious manipulation of language to incite an irrational emotional response, to allay doubts or to mislead the imagination. Particularly misleading is one commonly employed mixture of
rhetorical modes by advocates of abortion on request. That is
the use of a detached, clinical language to describe the actual

operation itself combined with an emotive rhetoric to evoke the personal and social goods which an abortion can bring about. Thus, when every effort is made to suggest that emotion and feeling are perfectly appropriate to describe the social and personal goals of abortion, but that a clinical language only is appropriate when the actual technique and medical objective of an abortion is described, then the moral imagination is being misled.

Any human act can be described in impersonal, technological language, just as any act can be described in emotive language. What is wanted is an equity in the language. It is fair enough and to the point to say that in many circumstances abortion will save a woman's health or her family. It only becomes misleading when the act itself, as distinguished from its therapeutic goal, is talked about in an entirely different way. For, abortion is not just an "emptying of the uterine contents." It is also an act of killing; there will be no abortion unless the conceptus is killed (or its further existence made impossible, which amounts to the same thing). If it is appropriate to evoke the imagination and elicit sympathy for those women in a distressed pregnancy who could be helped by abortion, it is no less appropriate to evoke the imagination about what actually occurs in an abortion "procedure."

Imagination should also come into play at another point. It is often argued by proponents of abortion that there is no need for a woman ever to take any chances in a distressed pregnancy, particularly in the instance of an otherwise healthy woman who, if she has an abortion on one occasion, could simply get pregnant again on another, more auspicious occasion. This might be termed the "replacement theory" of abortion indications: since fetus "x" can be replaced by fetus "y," then there is no reason why a woman should have any scruples about such a replacement. This way of conceiving the choices effectively dissolves them; it becomes important only to know whether a woman can get pregnant again when she wants to. But this strategy can be employed only at the price of convincing oneself that there is no difference whatever among embryos or fetuses, that they all have exactly the same potentiality. But even the sketchiest knowledge of the genetic uniqueness of each conceptus (save in the instance of monozygotic twins), and thus the different genetic potentialities of each, should raise doubts on that point. Yet, having said that, I would not want to deny that the possibility of a further pregnancy could have an important bearing on the moral reasoning of a woman whose present pregnancy was threatening. If, out of a sense of responsibility toward her present children or her present life situation, a woman decided that an abortion was the wisest, most moral course, then the possibility that she could become pregnant later, when these responsibilities would be less pressing, would be a pertinent consideration.

The goal of these remarks is to keep alive in the consciences of women who have an abortion choice a moral tension; and it is to hope that they will be willing to bear the pain and the uncertainty of having to make a moral choice. It is the automatic, unthinking and unimaginative personal solution of abortion questions which women themselves should be extremely wary of, either for or against an abortion. A woman can, with little trouble, find both people and books to reassure her that there is no problem about abortion at all; or people and books to convince her that she would be a moral monster if she chose abortion. A woman can choose in advance the views she will listen to and thus have her predispositions confirmed. Yet a willingness to keep alive a moral tension, and to be wary of precipitous solutions, presupposes two things. First, that the woman herself wants to do what is right, realizing that what is right may not always be that which is most convenient, most easy or most immediately apt to solve a pressing problem. It is simply not the case that what one wants to do, or would like to do, or is predisposed to do is necessarily the right thing to do. A willingness seriously to entertain that moral perception—which, of course, does not in itself imply a decision for or against an abortion—is one sign of moral seriousness.

Second, moral seriousness presupposes one is concerned with the protection and furthering of life. This means that, out of respect for human life, one bends over backwards not to eliminate human life, not to desensitize oneself to the meaning and value of potential life, not to seek definitions of the "human" which serve one's self-interest only. A desire to respect human life in all of its forms means, therefore, that one voluntarily imposes upon oneself a pressure against the taking of life; that one demands of oneself serious reasons for doing so, even in the case of a very early embryo; that one use not only the mind but also the imagination when a decision is being made; that one seeks not to evade the moral issues but to face them; that one searches out the alternatives and conscientiously entertains them before turning to abortion. A bias in favor of the sanctity of human life in all of its forms would include a bias against abortion on the part of women; it would be the last rather than the first choice when unwanted pregnancies occurred. It would be an act to be avoided if at all possible.

A bias of this kind, voluntarily imposed by a woman upon herself, would not trap her; for it is also part of a respect for the dignity of life to leave the way open for an abortion when other reasonable choices are not available. For she also has duties toward herself, her family and her society. There can be good reasons for taking the life even of a very late fetus; once that also is seen and seen as a counterpoise in particular cases to the general bias against the taking of potential life, the way is open to choose abortion. The bias of the moral policy implies the need for moral rules which seek to preserve life. But, as a policy which leaves room for choice—rather than entailing a fixed set of rules—it is open to flexible interpretation when the circumstances point to the wisdom of taking exception to the normal ordering of the rules in particular cases. Yet, in that case, one is not genuinely taking exception to the rules. More accurately, one would be deciding that, for the preservation or furtherance of other values or rights—species-rights, person-rights—a choice in favor of abortion would be serving the sanctity of life. That there would be, in that case, conflict between rights, with one set of rights set aside (reluctantly) to serve another set, goes without saying. A subversion of the principle occurs when it is made out that there is no conflict and thus nothing to decide.

From Abortion: Law, Choice, Morality, 1970.

QUESTIONS

(1) This selection comes from the end of a long book on abortion. Does the tone indicate that it is meant as the conclusion of a detailed study?

(2) How would you describe the tone of the essay? Is it appropriate to the subject?

(3) What does Callahan mean when he says that on the popular level "there is a tendency to act as if, once personal freedom is legally and socially achieved, moral questions cease to exist"? Do you agree?

(4) Is "After freedom, what then?" a good sentence? Why?

(5) Is the theme of this essay "A solution of the legal problem is not the same as a solution to the moral problem"? If yes, does he develop it well? If no, what do you think is the theme?

(6) Are the questions in the fifth paragraph a useful way to introduce the points he wants to make? Do you have to know the answers before you can ask such questions?

(7) Is the essay itself a good example of the difference between *necessity* (it must be so) and *responsibility* (considering all the factors involved I have decided to . . .)?

(8) In arguing for uncertainty, is he convincing?

(9) Is this essay likely to satisfy proponents or opponents of abortion on demand? In either case, why?

(10) Callahan describes "technological" and "emotive" language. How would you describe his language?

(11) Is his emphasis on imagination proper?

(12) Are his discussions of and recommendations for "moral seriousness" convincing?

(13) How would you paraphrase his conclusion?

(14) Do you agree with his conclusion?

ALIVE

PIERS PAUL READ

Their food supplies were running out. The daily ration of a scrap of chocolate, a capful of wine, and a teaspoonful of jam or canned fish—eaten slowly to make it last—was more torture than sustenance for these healthy, athletic boys; yet the strong shared it with the weak, the healthy with the injured. It was clear to them all that they could not survive much longer. It was not so much that they were consumed with ravenous hunger as that they felt themselves grow weaker each day, and no knowledge of medicine or nutrition was required to predict how it would end.

Their minds turned to other sources of food. It seemed impossible that there should be nothing whatsoever growing in the Andes, for even the meanest form of plant life might provide some nutrition. In the immediate vicinity of the plane there was only snow. The nearest soil was a hundred feet beneath them. The only ground exposed to sun and air was barren mountain rock on which they found nothing but brittle lichens. They scraped some of it off and mixed it into a paste with melted snow, but the taste was bitter and disgusting, and as food it was worthless. Except for lichens there was nothing. Some thought of the cushions, but even these were not stuffed with straw. Nylon and foam rubber would not help them.

For some days several of the boys had realized that if they were to survive they would have to eat the bodies of those who had died in the crash. It was a ghastly prospect. The corpses lay around the plane in the snow, preserved by the intense cold in the state in which they had died. While the thought of cutting flesh from those who had been their friends was deeply repugnant to them all, a lucid appreciation of their predicament led them to consider it.

Gradually the discussion spread as these boys cautiously mentioned it to their friends or to those they thought would be sympathetic. Finally, Canessa brought it out into the open.

He argued forcefully that they were not going to be rescued; that they would have to escape themselves, but that nothing could be done without food; and that the only food was human flesh. He used his knowledge of medicine to describe, in his penetrating, high-pitched voice, how their bodies were using up their reserves. "Every time you move," he said, "you use up part of your own body. Soon we shall be so weak that we won't have the strength even to cut the meat that is lying there before our eyes."

Canessa did not argue just from expediency. He insisted that they had a moral duty to stay alive by any means at their disposal, and because Canessa was earnest about his religious belief, great weight was given to what he said by the more pious among the survivors.

"It is meat," he said. "That's all it is. The souls have left their bodies and are in heaven with God. All that is left here are the carcasses, which are no more human beings than the dead flesh of the cattle we eat at home."

Others joined the discussion. "Didn't you see," said Fito Strauch, "how much energy we needed just to climb a few hundred feet up the mountain? Think how much more we'll need to climb to the top and then down the other side. It can't be done on a sip of wine and a scrap of chocolate."

The truth of what he said was incontestable.

A meeting was called inside the Fairchild, and for the first time all twenty-seven survivors discussed the issue which faced them—whether or not they should eat the bodies of the dead to survive. Canessa, Zerbino, Fernández, and Fito Strauch repeated the arguments they had used before. If they did not they would die. It was their moral obligation to live, for their own sake and for the sake of their families. God wanted them to live, and He had given them the means to do so in the dead bodies of their friends. If God had not wished them to live, they would have been killed in the accident; it would be wrong now to reject this gift of life because they were too squeamish.

"But what have we done," asked Marcelo, "that God now asks us to eat the bodies of our dead friends?"

There was a moment's hesitation. Then Zerbino turned to his captain [Marcelo Pérez was captain of the rugby team] and said, "But what do you think *they* would have thought?"

Marcelo did not answer.

"I know," Zerbino went on, "that if my dead body could help you to stay alive, then I'd certainly want you to use it. In fact, if I do die and you don't eat me, then I'll come back from wherever I am and give you a good kick in the ass."

This argument allayed many doubts, for however reluctant each boy might be to eat the flesh of a friend, all of them agreed with Zerbino. There and then they made a pact that if any more of them were to die, their bodies were to be used as food.

Marcelo still shrank from a decision. He and his diminishing party of optimists held onto the hope of rescue, but few of the others any longer shared their faith. Indeed, a few of the younger boys went over to the pessimists—or the realists, as they considered themselves—with some resentment against Marcelo Pérez and Pancho Delgado. They felt they had been deceived. The rescue they had been promised had not come.

The latter were not without support, however. Coche Inciarte and Numa Turcatti, both strong, tough boys with an inner gentleness, told their companions that while they did not think it would be wrong, they knew that they themselves could not do it. Liliana Methol agreed with them. Her manner was calm as always but, like the others, she grappled with the emotions the issue aroused. Her instinct to survive was strong, her longing for her children was acute, but the thought of eating human flesh horrified her. She did not think it wrong; she could distinguish between sin and physical revulsion, and a social taboo was not a law of God. "But," she said, "as long as there is a chance of rescue, as long as there is *something* left to eat, even if it is only a morsel of chocolate, then I can't do it."

Javier Methol agreed with his wife but would not deter others from doing what they felt must be done. No one suggested that God might want them to choose to die. They all believed that virtue lay in survival and that eating their dead friends would in no way endanger their souls, but it was one thing to decide and another to act.

Their discussions had continued most of the day, and by midafternoon they knew that they must act now or not at all, yet they sat inside the plane in total silence. At last a group of four—Canessa, Maspons, Zerbino, and Fito Strauch—rose and

went out into the snow. Few followed them. No one wished
to know who was going to cut the meat or from which body
it was to be taken.

Most of the bodies were covered by snow, but the buttocks
of one protruded a few yards from the plane. With no exchange of words Canessa knelt, bared the skin, and cut into
the flesh with a piece of broken glass. It was frozen hard and
difficult to cut, but he persisted until he had cut away twenty
slivers the size of matchsticks. He then stood up, went back
to the plane, and placed them on the roof.

Inside there was silence. The boys cowered in the Fairchild.
Canessa told them that the meat was there on the roof, drying
in the sun, and that those who wished to do so should come
out and eat it. No one came, and again Canessa took it upon
himself to prove his resolution. He prayed to God to help him
do what he knew to be right and then took a piece of meat in
his hand. He hesitated. Even with his mind so firmly made up,
the horror of the act paralyzed him. His hand would neither
rise to his mouth nor fall to his side while the revulsion which
possessed him struggled with his stubborn will. The will prevailed. The hand rose and pushed the meat into his mouth.
He swallowed it.

He felt triumphant. His conscience had overcome a primitive, irrational taboo. He was going to survive.

Later that evening, small groups of boys came out of the
plane to follow his example. Zerbino took a strip and swallowed it as Canessa had done, but it stuck in his throat. He
scooped a handful of snow into his mouth and managed to
wash it down. Fito Strauch followed his example, then Maspons and Vizintín and others.

Meanwhile Gustavo Nicolich, the tall, curly-haired boy,
only twenty years old, who had done so much to keep up the
morale of his young friends, wrote to his *novia* in Montevideo.

Most dear Rosina:
　I am writing to you from inside the plane (our *petit hotel* for
the moment). It is sunset and has started to be rather cold and
windy which it usually does at this hour of the evening. Today
the weather was wonderful—a beautiful sun and very hot. It reminded me of the days on the beach with you—the big difference
being that then we would be going to have lunch at your place at

midday whereas now I'm stuck outside the plane without any food at all.

Today, on top of everything else, it was rather depressing and a lot of the others began to get discouraged (today is the tenth day we have been here), but luckily this gloom did not spread to me because I get incredible strength just by thinking that I'm going to see you again. Another of the things leading to the general depression is that in a while the food will run out: we have only got two cans of seafood (small), one bottle of white wine, and a little cherry brandy left, which for twenty- six men (well, there are also boys who want to be men) is nothing.

One thing which will seem incredible to you—it seems unbelievable to me—is that today we started to cut up the dead in order to eat them. There is nothing else to do. I prayed to God from the bottom of my heart that this day would never come, but it has and we have to face it with courage and faith. Faith, because I came to the conclusion that the bodies are there because God put them there and, since the only thing that matters is the soul, I don't have to feel great remorse; and if the day came and I could save someone with my body, I would gladly do it.

I don't know how you, Mama, Papa, or the children can be feeling, you don't know how sad it makes me to think that you are suffering, and I constantly ask God to reassure you and give us courage because that is the only way of getting out of this. I think that soon there will be a happy ending for everyone.

You'll get a shock when you see me. I am dirty, with a beard, and a little thinner, with a big gash on my head, another one on my chest which has healed now, and one very small cut which I got today working in the cabin of the plane, besides various small cuts in the legs and on the shoulder; but in spite of it all, I'm all right.

From *Alive,* 1974.

QUESTIONS

(1) Is Read's approach to the material a good one? Does he deliberately "underwrite" this very emotional description?

(2) Does the sense of community Read describes in the first paragraph have any effect on the subsequent events he describes? How would the last acts in the selection appear if the boys had been brutal and selfish in the opening?

(3) Does Read allow Canessa's arguments to work directly on the reader? How are you affected by them?

(4) "Greater love hath no man than this, that a man lay down his life for his friends" (John 15:13) is the epigraph of the book. How does Read suggest that it applies in this scene?

(5) How does Read convey the sense that "it was one thing to decide and another to act"? Does he make you feel the conflict between the intellectual decision and the instinctive reaction?

(6) Why does Read quote Gustavo Nicolich's letter directly? Why do you think Nicolich delays the statement about eating the dead until the third paragraph?

(7) From the evidence of the letter do you think Read did a good job of re-creating the events and the feelings leading up to the use of the corpses for food?

NOTE

These are the full names of those mentioned in the text. Those marked with an asterisk did not survive the ordeal. Roberto Canessa (a medical student who had completed two years of an eight year course); Adolfo "Fito" Strauch; Gustavo Zerbino; Daniel Fernández; *Marcelo Pérez (the captain of the rugby team); *Pancho Delgado; Jose Luis "Coche" Inciarte; *Numa Turcatti; *Liliana Methol; Javier Methol (her husband); *Daniel Maspons; Antonio Visintín; *Gustavo Nicolich.

ACT OF LOVE

PAIGE MITCHELL

*I gave it a lot of thought. You don't know how much thinkin'
I did on it. I had to do somethin' I knew would definitely put
him away. And the only thing I knew that would definitely do
that would be a gun. And the gun I used—I had to think about
usin' that particular gun. See, I have other guns in this house.
I have twelve-gauge shotguns with big lead pellets which would
be my preference, really. Those are the ones you'd use if you
were going to shoot a deer. I wanted to make sure this was done
fast and quick. I knew, I felt . . . I'd have one chance to do
this. I gave it a lot of thought. You understand? I wanted to
make sure he would definitely die.*

Lester Zygmanik

June 20, 1973

On that Wednesday morning, June 20, three days after his
brother's motorcycle accident, the sky threatened rain. It
seemed fitting.

Outside the hospital, thunder rolled when they came to take
George. Then Lester watched his brother grow smaller as
they carried the stretcher down the corridor. Finally, George
disappeared behind elevator doors, and all that was left was
the flickering light that stopped at surgery.

After that, a summer rain began on the window, and the
clock moved slowly. Jeannie wept. Victor kept saying, "It's in
God's hands."

Lester left the hospital. He took Jeannie's car. He drove
around aimlessly, feeling helpless and frightened. Traffic enveloped him. Horns honked, brutal, impersonal. He drove
erratically, assailed by waves of fatigue and disorder. Once,
he heard grotesque laughter. Once, he found himself on the
rainy highway, propelled by a wish to flee.

He returned around noon. He was told his brother had been taken to recovery. In the corridor, the surgeon's voice echoed: "Your brother will never use his arms or legs again." The surgeon's face blurred. "We may never be able to remove the tracheotomy."

The hallway grew cavernous. He was overwhelmed by intolerable pain. Then an eerie silence encompassed him, and he felt nothing.

He took the elevator downstairs. In the cafeteria, he talked to Victor, but he couldn't feel the muscles of his mouth. The counter was crowded. Sitting nearby was the doctor who had come in the morning to take George to surgery. The doctor was still wearing his green cap.

The doctor frowned. "If you want to know what your brother will be like, go over to the East Orange Veterans' Hospital. There are men there, deteriorating. . . ."

He felt something shatter, like breaking glass. Fear assaulted his body. He found it difficult to breathe.

The doctor pushed at his cap. "I saw cases like your brother in service. These people dry up. They turn to skin and bone. They get terrible bedsores. Somebody has to be with them twenty-four hours a day."

He tried to protect himself from a roaring darkness.

The doctor shook his head. "I'd rather be dead than like your brother."

Then the doctor was gone, and, behind him, Victor said, "It's in God's hands."

He turned on Victor, cursing.

On October 30, under the Prosecutor's questioning, Juanita Johnson would say, "It was sometime after eleven P.M. I was working the night shift with Mr. Blannett. I saw the defendant come into the room. I said, 'Good evening.' He didn't answer me. He went past me. He went over to his brother's bed and he stood there. Then we heard this loud noise."

It stopped raining in the afternoon. The air turned warm. He paced the parking lot, sweating. After a while, he lost the boundaries of his body. Once, he found himself at the ocean, running.

It was late afternoon before they let him see his brother.

With his mother, he stood beside his brother's bed. His
brother slept, swollen, distorted by pain. He turned away,
trembling. In his head, the doctors' voices condemned his
brother to a wasteland. He closed his eyes. He willed himself
into the glassy silence where he felt nothing, heard nothing
beyond his brother's demand: "I want you to promise to kill
me. I want you to swear to God."

He went down to the lobby and asked Victor to drive him
home.

Victor stayed with him. Victor kept saying, "Give God a
chance."

He couldn't sit still. He kept moving around the kitchen,
back and forth, feeling dizzy, as if his legs might collapse.
Finally, he shouted, "Do you think God's gonna help my
brother?"

He began to make telephone calls, but he found hearing
difficult—and, after a while, he couldn't remember whom he
was talking to, or what he was saying, only that he was
shouting.

After sundown, his mother and Jeannie came back—and
Victor said, "I'm tired. I have to go home."

He followed Victor out to the car, saying, "Please—go
with me."

Long after Victor's taillights vanished, he stood in the
darkness, crying. Then the air turned still, and the fog enclosed him in a silent world where nothing existed beyond
his brother's need.

He moved automatically.

At half past nine, he crossed the land, heading toward the
woods. Once, he stopped because he thought he heard somebody call him, but there was only darkness, so he moved on.
Then the dogs heard him coming and began to bark.

When he reached the clearing, he chose his spot, far from
the house and the women. It took a few minutes to anchor the
shotgun. Then he marked the barrel, twelve inches from the
tip. The beagles fell quiet. Harsh and shrill, the handsaw
struck metal. He had chosen his weapon, a smooth-bore shotgun, the one he used to shoot rabbits. Sawed off, it would kill
a man.

The air was damp. Pale shafts of moonlight pierced the

fog. He worked patiently, steadily. Once, he stopped because he thought he heard somebody crying, but there was nothing. Then the gun barrel shuddered and broke. Severed, twelve inches of cylinder lay at his feet. The dogs set up a howl. He couldn't remember whether or not he had fed them.

He left the gun in the car. When he entered the kitchen, the women were sitting there. "The dogs need water," he said. His mother rose, weeping. It took him a moment to remember why Jeannie was staring at him.

Last night, his brother had said to her: "I want you to promise not to interfere. I want you to swear to God."

From a long way off, he seemed to hear the church bell ringing.

On October 30, Katherine Kealy, a registered nurse with gentle brown eyes, would testify for the Prosecution. In a soft, breathless voice, she would say, "I saw Lester in the hall. I was on my way to Room 322. He was outside of Room 321, Intensive Care. There was no conversation. I was in the next room when I heard a loud noise. I checked to see what happened. At first, I didn't realize—because Lester was still there. Then, looking at the patient, I realized he had been shot."

His mother filled the dog pail. Then the screen door slammed and he heard her climb the cellar stairs. He took a seat at the table, waiting for something, he didn't know what. Then he remembered his mother would probably find the pieces of the sawed-off gun.

He picked up a newspaper. Then his mother came back. Jeannie got a flashlight and, together, they left. A long time went by. Finally, the women returned and Jeannie began to shriek, "What are you going to do?" Over and over, "What are those pieces? What are you going to do?"

Jeannie went upstairs to check the guns. When she came back, she said again. "Where's the gun? What are you going to do?"

Finally, he shouted. "You know what I'm going to do!"

He found himself outside. He seemed to be floating. It was difficult to remember where he had hidden the gun. When he came back to the kitchen, his mother was waiting to take the gun. Relieved, he watched her put the gun on the bureau. Then she lay down on the bed and closed her eyes. He was tired. He wanted to lie down and close his eyes.

Barbara Petruska came in. Then the telephone began to ring. His head began to clang with jarring sounds. On the phone, his own voice disappeared. All he could hear was Jeannie saying, "He's got a gun. I don't know what he's going to do."

When Barbara Petruska touched his shoulder, he pushed her across the room, shouting, "If my father was alive, he'd kill all of you!"

After that, the kitchen turned quiet.

He said, "Where's a candle?" His voice was calm.

"In the garage," Jeannie said. "What are you going to do?"

He found the candle.

At the kitchen table, Jeannie and Barbara watched him empty the shotgun shell into the ashtray. Then he lit the candle and melted wax into the shell, adding some of the pellets. He was aware the women were shouting, but no sounds penetrated. He was aware his mother was lying on the bed with her eyes closed.

He went upstairs and put on a jacket.

When he came back to the kitchen, he concealed the shotgun under his coat, turned his back to the women, and asked, "Does it show?"

Somebody said, "I can see it."

He switched the shotgun to the other side. "Can you see it now?"

Somebody said, "No."

He turned around. He stood a moment, waiting for something, he didn't know what. Then he said to Jeannie, "I want you to go to the hospital with me. Please, come to the hospital with me?"

On October 30, twenty-five-year-old Robert Blannett, a graduate nurse who wore a Fu Manchu mustache, would draw a diagram of Intensive Care for the jury. He would sketch a desk, six beds, six patients. Near the window, the bed which had been occupied by George Zygmanik would be marked with an X. Then Blannett would testify, "After he shot his brother, he shook his head."

It was a twenty-mile drive.

Beyond his windshield, fog created ghostly shadows. Then the illusion of his father's presence was dispelled by darkness—and he understood he was alone.

The road was deserted. Once, he slowed because he thought he heard a police siren. Then night enveloped him—and the world contained only the two of them, him and his brother.

The parking lot was desolate, empty. It was raining again, a light, drizzling rain. He had the feeling he was somewhere else, watching himself. He began to see images and strange, blinding lights.

Then he found himself in the elevator, no longer able to recall why he had come. So he decided he was simply taking an elevator. Then the elevator stopped, and he heard his brother say: "You're the man now."

He walked slowly down the corridor. He remembered that the neurosurgeon had said, "Your brother has a head, he has eyes, ears, and a mouth—he's not better off dead." Then the doctors had disappeared. Everybody had disappeared. Last night, he had given his promise.

He found himself standing in front of Room 321, waiting for something. But nobody came. His choice became clear. He could run. Or he could do what his brother had asked him to do.

The room was dark. At the far end, his brother was suspended in air. There was a light on his brother. He crossed the room. "Are you in pain?" he said.

His brother nodded. His brother opened his eyes and closed them again. Behind his brother's bed was a window. Reflected in the glass was a desk. Two people were at the desk. He wondered why they weren't looking at him. He wondered why they weren't crying.

He loaded the shotgun. "I'm here to end your pain," he said. "Is that all right with you?"

His brother nodded. His brother's eyelids flickered.

"Close your eyes, George," he said, "I'm going to kill you." Then he raised the shotgun to his brother's temple.

He felt no pressure from the trigger, heard no explosion, felt nothing. In the silence afterward, he listened to the air in the tracheotomy still being pumped into his brother's throat.

He pulled the tracheotomy.

He laid his hand on his brother's chest and said, "I love you, George. God gless you, George."

Slowly, he turned and walked out.

From Act of Love, 1976.

QUESTIONS

(1) Is the form of the selection—the quick succession of brief paragraphs—appropriate to the content? Does the style help to establish the "facts" of the case, separate from any moral or legal judgment of the action?

(2) Does Mitchell make you feel what Lester Zygmanik felt? How does she use the doctors on one hand and Victor Kazma, his brother's father-in-law, on the other to show you the pressures on him?

(3) Are the "flashforwards" to testimony at Lester's murder trial effective? Is the style of the italicized material the same as or different from the main narrative?

(4) George demanded Lester's promise before the operation that he would kill him if he were left paralyzed. Does Mitchell make you feel that Lester was "alone" with that promise even though there were people around? How?

(5) The brothers were both close to their father before he died. How does Mitchell make you feel Lester's longing for his father's guidance in her description?

(6) Why does Mitchell explain in such detail the preparations Lester Zygmanik made? How does it affect the reader?

(7) How does Mitchell manipulate past, present, and future to convey Lester's state of mind? Does she succeed in conveying that state of mind?

(8) Why does Lester ask his brother's wife Jeannie to come with him? Why doesn't she?

NOTE

On November 5, 1973, Lester Mark Zygmanik was found not guilty of the murder of his brother, "by reason of insanity."

THE CORPSE

RICHARD SELZER

Shall I tell you once more how it happens? Even though you know, don't you?

You were born with the horror stamped upon you, like a fingerprint. All these years you have lived you have known. I but remind your memory, confirm the fear that has always been prime. Yet the facts have a force of their insolent own.

Wine is best made in a cellar, on a stone floor. Crush grapes in a barrel such that each grape is burst. When the barrel is three-quarters full, cover it with a fine-mesh cloth, and wait. In three days, an ear placed low over the mash will detect a faint crackling, which murmur, in two more days, rises to a continuous giggle. Only the rendering of fat, or a forest fire far away, makes such a sound. It is the buzz of fermentation! Remove the cloth and examine closely. The eye is startled by a bubble on the surface. Was it there and had it gone unnoticed? Or is it newly come?

But soon enough more beads gather in little colonies, winking and lining up at the brim. Stagnant fluid forms. It begins to turn. Slow currents carry bits of stem and grape meat on voyages of an inch or so. The pace quickens. The level rises. On the sixth day, the barrel is almost full. The teem must be poked down with a stick. The air of the cellar is dizzy with fruit flies and droplets of smell. On the seventh day, the fluid is racked into the second barrel for aging. It is wine.

Thus is the fruit of the earth taken, its flesh torn. Thus is it given over to standing, toward rot. It is the principle of corruption, the death of what is, the birth of what is to be.

You are wine.

> SHE: Is he dead, then?
> HE: I am sorry.
> SHE: Oh, God.
> HE: I should like to ask . . . because of the circumstances of your husband's death, it would be very helpful . . . to do . . . an autopsy.
> SHE: Autopsy? No, no, not that. I don't want him cut up.

Better to have agreed, madam. We use the trocar on all, autopsied or merely embalmed. You have not heard of the suction trocar? Permit me to introduce you to the instrument.

A hollow steel rod some two feet in length, one end, the tip, sharp, pointed; to the other end there attaches rubber tubing, which tubing leads to the sink; near this end the handle, sculpted, the better to grip with; just inside the tip, holes, a circle of them, each opening large enough to admit the little finger or to let a raisin pass. This is the trocar.

A man stands by the table upon which you lie. He opens the faucet in the sink, steps forward, raises the trocar. It is a ritual spear, a gleaming emblem. Two inches to the left and two inches above your navel is the place of entry. (Feel it on yourself.) The technician raises this thing and aims for the spot. He must be strong, and his cheeks shake with the thrust. He grunts.

Wound most horrible! It is a goring.

The head of the trocar disappears beneath the skin. Deeper and deeper until the body wall is penetrated. Another thrust, and he turns the head north. First achieved is the stomach, whose stringy contents, food just eaten, are sucked into the holes. A three-inch glass connector interrupts the rubber tubing. Here one is spectator as the yield rushes by. Can you identify particular foods? Beets are easy, and licorice. The rest is merely . . . grey.

Look how the poker rides—high and swift and lubricious. Several passes, and then the trocar is drawn expertly back until the snout is barely hidden beneath the skin. The man takes aim again, this time for the point of the chin, he says. Then he dives through the mass of the liver, across the leaf of the diaphragm, and into the right chambers of the heart. Black blood fills the tubing. Thrust and pull, thrust and pull, thunking against the spine, the staves of the ribs, shivering the timbers, the brute bucking as it rides the magnificent forearm of the Licensed Embalmer in high rodeo.

The heart is empty. The technician turns the tool downward, into the abdomen once more. Now are the intestines pierced, coil upon coil, collapsing their gas and their juice to the sink. It is brown in the glass connector. Thunk, thunk, the rod smites the pelvis from within. The dark and muffled work is done: the scrotum is skewered, the testicles mashed, ablaze with their billion whiptail jots. All, all into the sink—and then to the sewer. This is the ultimate suck.

The technician disconnects the tubing from the sink, joins the tubing to a pump. He fires the motor; preservative fluid boils up, streams into the trocar, thence to thorax and abdomen.

The trocar is doubly clever.

> HE: Urea combines with the phenol to make plastic. We, in effect, plasticize the body.
> SHE: I do not want him plastic.
> HE: It's only a word.
> SHE: Jesus, words.
> HE: There is the problem of the mouth.
> SHE: Jesus, problems.
> HE: It is all words, all problems. Trust me; I see. I . . . am . . . a physician. I really know, don't you see?
> SHE: All right, then. The mouth. Tell me.

Our technician forces the mouth shut, holds it there, assessing. Buckteeth are a problem, he says. Sometimes you have to yank them to get the mouth closed. He removes his hand, and the mandible drops again. Now he takes a large flat needle. It is S-shaped, for ease of grasping. A length of white string hangs through the eye of this needle. He draws back the bottom lip with thumb and forefinger. He passes the needle into the lower gum. Needle and string are pulled through and out, and the lip allowed to rest. Next, the upper lip is held away, and the needle is passed up into the groove at the crest of the upper gum, thence to the left nostril, through the nasal septum into the right nostril, finally plunging back into that groove and once again to the mouth. This stitchery will not be seen. Pledgets of cotton are inserted to fill out a sag here, a droop there, lest the absence of teeth or turgor be noticed.

What? No penny enslotted here for Charon? No bite of honey cake for mad Cerberus?

No. Only cotton.

About this invented fullness the jaws are drawn to as the string is tied. One square knot is followed by two grannies. Prevents slippage, Death's tailor says. Gone is all toothy defiance. In its place, there is only the stuffed pout of anything filled too much. Now the plastic caps are inserted beneath the eyelids—pop, pop. And here—hold still—we are ready for cosmetics.

The case is opened importantly. It is of alligator hide, imitation of this. Within are shelves for the jars, slots for the brushes, as many as the vanity Death's whore requires. The technician selects three jars. Red, yellow, blue; daubs a bit of each on the palette; mixes, turns, and wipes—until the color of your skin is matched. More blue for Negroes, says he; less yellow and more blue for them. He has said something unarguable—and is now quiet. Many a sidelong glance later, he is ready. He steps to the head of the table and applies the paint, massages the color into the skin of face and hands. This is what shows, he says. And one must do, but not overdo, he says. At last our fellow approves. How lovely the morning, pockless glow! It is a wholesome look—a touch of evening blue in the hollows of the lids. Oh, yes, art is truly bottled sunshine.

Who, but a moment ago, was huffing rider of the belly is now artist, configuring Death, shaping it. He has rebuilt a ravaged chin, replaced an absent nose, he says. Give him enough plaster and a bit of paint and he can make a man, he says. I wait for him to lean over and blow into these nostrils. He can make anything except life, he says.

Thus combed and shaved (lemon-scented Colgate is nice) and powdered, the corpse gleams, a marquis upon ruched velvet, banked with fierce forced blossoms.

SHE: Embalming belittles death.

HE: On the contrary, art dignifies. It is the last passion. For both fellows, don't you know?

SHE: But there must be some other way. As for myself, mind you, I prefer to be of use. I have made arrangements that my body be given to a medical school for dissection. I carry this little card that so states. In case of accident.

HE: A gesture in the grand style. You join a gallant band. So many are concerned with the appearance of the flesh, leaving ill-considered its significance. Well . . . its usefulness.

Forty-feet long, four wide, and seven deep is THE TANK. It is set into the ground at the very bottom of the medical school. If Anatomy be the firstborn of Medicine, then the tank is its sunken womb. Here at the very center of stench it lies; here is the bite of embalming fluid sharpest. Tears overwhelm the eyes. The tank demands weeping of this kind. It is lidded, covered by domed metal, handle at apex, like a casserole of chow mein.

Let me remove this lid. Behold! How beautiful they are, the bodies. With what grace and pomp each waits his turn. Above the fluid, a center rod, like a closet rod, suspends them in a perfect row; forty soldiers standing in the bath, snug as pharaohs, only heads showing, all facing, obediently, the same way.

Come, walk the length of the tank. We review these warriors who, by their bearing, salute us. Arteries have been pumped full of fluid. It helps the flesh to sink, lest feet float to the top in embarrassing disarray. Thus weighted, the bodies swim readily to erect posture. Upon each head, worn with a certain nonchalance, are the tongs, the headdress of this terrible tribe. The hooks of the tongs are inserted one into each ear, then sunk home by pulling on the handle. Each set of tongs is then hung from the center rod by a pulley. In this way the bodies can be skimmed back and forth during the process of selection, or to make room for another.

We end skin overcoats on a rack.

A slow current catches the brine and your body sways ever so slightly, keeping time. This movement stirs the slick about your shoulders. Iridescent colors appear, and little chunks of melt, shaken off in annoyance, it seems, bob up and down.

Does some flame far below, at the center of the earth, thus bring this tank to lazy boil? Or is it the heat from hell? Look. A dead fly floats, one wing raised in permanent effort at extrication. A fly? Well, of course. There is food here.

It is wine.

> SHE: I want nothing done. Let him be put in the ground as he is.
> HE: You are distraught. Perspective. What you need is perspective. Listen. Outside the rain is falling, soft as hair. (A pause.) No toilette, then?

Dead, the body is somehow more solid, more massive. The shrink of dying is past. It is as though only moments before a wind had kept it aloft, and now, settled, it is only what it is— a mass, declaring itself, an ugly emphasis. Almost at once the skin changes color, from pink-highlighted yellow to grey-tinted blue. The eyes are open and lackluster; something, a bright dust, had been blown away, leaving the globes smoky. And there is an absolute limpness. Hours later, the neck and limbs are drawn up into a semiflexion, in the attitude of one who has just received a blow to the solar plexus.

One has.

Even the skin is in rigor, is covered with goose bumps. Semen is forced from the penis by the contraction of muscle. The sphincters relax, and the air is poisonous with loosed sewage. Colder and colder grows the flesh, as the last bit of warmth disperses. Now you are meat, meat at room temperature.

Examine once more the eyes. How dull the cornea, this globe bereft of tension. Notice how the eyeball pits at the pressure of my fingernail. Whereas the front of your body is now drained of color, the back, upon which you rest, is found to be deeply violet. Even here, even now, gravity works upon the blood. In twenty-four hours, your untended body resumes its flaccidity, resigned to this everlasting posture.

You stay thus.

You do not die all at once. Some tissues live on for minutes, even hours, giving still their little cellular shrieks, molecular echoes of the agony of the whole corpus. Here and there a spray of nerves dances on. True, the heart stops; the blood no longer courses; the electricity of the brain sputters, then shuts down. Death is now *pronounceable*. But there are outposts where clusters of cells yet shine, besieged, little lights blinking in the advancing darkness. Doomed soldiers, they battle on. Until Death has secured the premises all to itself.

The silence, the darkness, is not for long. That which was for a moment dead leaps most sumptuously to life. There is a busyness gathering. It grows fierce.

There is to be a feast. The rich table has been set. The board groans. The guests have already arrived, numberless bacteria that had, in life, dwelt in saprophytic harmony with their host. Their turn now! Charged, they press against the membrane barriers, break through the new softness, sweep across plains of tissue, devouring, belching gas—a gas that puffs eyelids, cheeks, abdomen into bladders of murderous vapor. The slimmest man takes on the bloat of corpulence. Your swollen belly bursts with a ripping sound, followed by a long mean hiss.

And they are at large! Blisters appear upon the skin, enlarge, coalesce, blast, leaving brownish puddles in the declivities. You are becoming gravy. Arriving for the banquet late, of course, and all the more ravenous for it, are the twin sisters Calliphora and raucous Lucilia, the omnipresent greenbottle flies, their costumes metallic sequins. Their thousands of eggs are laid upon the meat, and soon the mass is wavy with the humped creamy backs of maggots nosing, crowding, hungrily absorbed. Grey sprays of fungus sprout in the resulting marinade, and there lacks only a mushroom growing from the nose.

At last—at last the bones appear, clean and white and dry. Reek and mangle abate; diminuendo the buzz and crawl. All, all is eaten. All is done. Hard endlessness is here even as the revelers abandon the skeleton.

You are alone, yet again.

> HE: Come, come, we are running out of time. How, at last, would you dispose of your husband? You must make a decision.
> SHE: Why must I?
> HE: Because you are the owner of the body. It is your possession.
> SHE: Oh, cremation, dammit. I'm sick of this business.
> HE: Brava! Man is pompous in the grave, splendid in ashes.
> SHE: A smaller package to mail.
> HE: You are doing the right thing, I assure you. The physiognomy does not endure in the grave. There is no identity. Cremation is tidy. I can see that you abhor the slough of putrefaction. Who wouldn't?

To the prettiness again. . . .

The good fellow slides you into the oven, and ignites the

fire. If you are burned in your casket, an exhaust fan sucks away the wood ash, until there is only your body. He observes through a peephole at the back of the oven. Now he turns off the exhaust, and lets the flames attack the body. Three hours later, at two thousand degrees Fahrenheit, it is done. The oven is turned off, is let cool overnight. The next day a rear door is opened, and the ashes are examined. Intact pieces of bone are pulverized with a mallet. With a little broom the residue is whisked into an urn. The operator is fastidious, down to smallest bits of dust.

The modern urn is no garnished ossuary, but a tin can indistinguishable from that which holds coffee by the pound. It is unadorned. Pry open the lid and see the expensive white doily, of the best embossed paper, creased like a priest's napkin. Unfold it, and gaze upon the contents. Shocking! They are not ashes but chunks of bone, and recognizable as such. Some as big as your thumbnail, chalky, charred. A tin of cinders. Coals and calx—with the odor of smoke and the semen-smell of cooked bone.

> SHE: How do I know that it is my husband's ashes that you give me? That they are not his but some other's—an old woman's, a dog's?
> HE: A vile and baseless suspicion. Now, in the matter of the cremains . . .
> SHE: The what?
> HE: Your husband's cremains.
> SHE: His ashes?
> HE: Yes. Many bereaved find it a soothing term, less harsh than . . . you know. . . .

But you are right to question.

Who knows the fate of his bones? His ashes? To what purpose tamp them into sad sepulchral pitchers? I have seen the cremation of two, even three, together. Later, the ashes were shoveled into cans in equal amounts, and labeled. Why not? Great religions have flourished on more spurious assumptions. The idea is not new. Were not the ashes of Achilles mingled with those of his lover Patroclus? Ah, you say, it is one thing to burn lovers, then fondly stir their ashes together; quite another to have one's urn-fellows selected at random.

Yet are not all our greatest intimacies merest chance?

He: Have you considered the disposition of the ashes?

She: The toilet?

He: I am afraid, madam, that we have reached an impasse. You prefer neither cremation nor embalming. You are repelled alike by anatomical dissection, and the moist relentment of putrefaction. Why don't you admit that you are ashamed of death? You think it is a disgrace to be dead.

She: That's it. Yes. A disgrace. That's it exactly.

He: Exactly, yes.

She: If you know everything, then what is your choice? For yourself?

He: That is not the point.

Ah, but it is the point. Listen. On the banks of the Hudson, midway between Manhattan and Montreal, squats the lizard town of Troy. In the back room of Moriarity's Saloon, the November meeting of the Druids of Eld is taking place. Harry Bascomb rises to deliver the invocation:

"From insomnia, as from bad dreams; from lack of love; from waiting so long you forget why; from enlargement of the prostate; from running out of coal; from constipation; from a sniveling son, and a daughter who flunks Deportment; from the pox and from the gout; from a grave full of worms—in Moriarity's, in the woes of day, and the throes of night—O Lord, deliver us."

This is followed by the ineffably sad sound of men trying to laugh together.

"The subject for tonight is what to do with your mortal remains. You first, Georgie."

Georgie assumes a leprechaun stoop and a high Irish voice. "I want me heart cut out and placed in a little silver box," he says, "with napkins and red candle wax all around. The rest ye can cast on terra damnata, and piss on it."

"You're next, Doc. Surely you've learned from the dying whispers of your fellow men?"

"Nothing. Nothing."

"What? A physician? Sawbones? Nothing? We can endure your hideous facts."

The doctor shivers despite the warmth of the saloon, and hugs his chest with his arms. He is fresh from debate with next of kin, weary, weary. There is a stain on his vest more terrible than the Ancient Mariner's eye.

"I want," he begins, "to be buried—unembalmed and un-boxed—at the foot of a tree. Soon I melt and seep into the ground, to be drawn up by the roots. Straight to the top, strung in the crown, answering the air. There would be the singing of birds, the applause of wings."

"Fed to a tree? All right, then. But a cow would do the tree more good."

Then all sing:

> O what shall be done with our dead, old boys?
> We'll run out of ground very soon.
>
> O what shall we do with our dead, old boys?
> It seems a shame to waste them.

Then all drink their wine.
Wine?

From *Esquire Magazine*, 1975.

QUESTIONS

(1) What does Selzer accomplish with the questions in the opening paragraph? Can you hear a special tone of voice in the questions? Could you describe it?

(2) Why are "horror," "fingerprint," and "insolent" good words in the second paragraph?

(3) Why does Selzer put the description of the making of wine at the beginning of the essay? Is it an unnecessary digression?

(4) Is there a contrast between the tone of the prose and the actions of the technician? What does Selzer feel in this description? What does he want you to feel? What are the most startling words he uses?

(5) Is it possible to "paraphrase" this essay? If not, why?

(6) What do you think is the theme of this essay?

(7) Why do you think Selzer wrote this essay in the style(s) in which he did?

(8) What is the effect of the closing question on the reader?

SUICIDE

A. ALVAREZ

After all this, I have to admit that I am a failed suicide. It is a dismal confession to make, since nothing, really, would seem to be easier than to take your own life. Seneca, the final authority on the subject, pointed out disdainfully that the exits are everywhere: each precipice and river, each branch of each tree, every vein in your body will set you free. But in the event, this isn't so. No one is promiscuous in his way of dying. A man who has decided to hang himself will never jump in front of a train. And the more sophisticated and painless the method, the greater the chance of failure. I can vouch, at least, for that. I built up to the act carefully and for a long time, with a kind of blank pertinacity. It was the one constant focus of my life, making everything else irrelevant, a diversion. Each sporadic burst of work, each minor success and disappointment, each moment of calm and relaxation, seemed merely a temporary halt on my steady descent through layer after layer of depression, like an elevator stopping for a moment on the way down to the basement. At no point was there any question of getting off or of changing the direction of the journey. Yet, despite all that, I never quite made it.

I see now that I had been incubating this death far longer than I recognized at the time. When I was a child, both my parents had half-heartedly put their heads in the gas oven. Or so they claimed. It seemed to me then a rather splendid gesture, though shrouded in mystery, a little area of veiled intensity, revealed only by hints and unexplained, swiftly suppressed outbursts. It was something hidden, attractive and not for the children, like sex. But it was also something that undoubtedly did happen to grownups. However hysterical or comic the behavior involved—and to a child it seemed more ludicrous than tragic to place your head in the greasy gas oven, like the Sunday roast joint—suicide was a fact, a subject that couldn't be denied; it was something, however awful, that people did. When my own time came, I did not have to discover it for myself.

Maybe that is why, when I grew up and things went particularly badly, I used to say to myself, over and over, like some latter-day Mariana in the moated grange, "I wish I were dead." It was an echo from the past, joining me to my tempestuous childhood. I muttered it unthinkingly, as automatically as a Catholic priest tells his rosary. It was my special magic ritual for warding off devils, a verbal nervous tic. Dwight Macdonald once said that when you don't know what to do with your hands you light a cigarette, and when you don't know what to do with your mind you read *Time* magazine. My equivalent was this one sentence repeated until it seemingly lost all meaning: "Iwishiweredead . . . Iwishiweredead . . . Iwishiweredead. . . ." Then one day I understood what I was saying. I was walking along the edge of Hampstead Heath, after some standard domestic squabble, and suddenly I heard the phrase as though for the first time. I stood still to attend to the words. I repeated them slowly, listening. And realized that I meant it. It seemed so obvious, an answer I had known for years and never allowed myself to acknowledge. I couldn't understand how I could have been so obtuse for so long.

After that, there was only one way out, although it took a long time—many months, in fact—to get there. We moved to America—wife, child, *au pair* girl, myself, and trunk-upon-trunk-load of luggage. I had a term's appointment at a New England university and had rented a great professorial mansion in a respectably dead suburb, ten miles from the campus, two from the nearest shop. The house was Germanic, gloomy and far too expensive. For my wife, who didn't drive, it was also as lonely as Siberia. The neighbors were mostly twice her age, the university mostly ignored us, the action was nil. There wasn't even a television set in the house. So I rented one and she sat disconsolately in front of it for two months. Then she gave up, packed her bags, and took the child back to England. I didn't even blame her. But I stayed on in a daze of misery. The last slide down the ice slope had begun and there was no way of stopping it.

My wife was not to blame. The hostility and despair that poor girl provoked in me—and I in her—came from some pure, infantile source, as any disinterested outsider could have told me. I even recognized this for myself in my clear moments. I was using her as an excuse for troubles that had their roots deep in the past. But mere intellectual recognition did no good, and anyway, my clear moments were few. My life felt so cluttered and obstructed that I could hardly breathe. I inhabited a closed, concentrated world, airless and without exits. I doubt if any of this was noticeable socially: I was simply more tense, more nervous than usual, and I drank more. But underneath I was going a bit mad. I had entered the closed world of suicide, and my life was being lived for me by forces I couldn't control.

When the Christmas break came at the university, I decided to spend the fortnight in London. Maybe, I told myself, things would be easier, at least I would see the child. So I loaded myself up with presents and climbed on a jet, dead drunk. I passed out as soon as I reached my seat and woke to a brilliant sunrise. There were dark islands below—the Hebrides, I suppose—and the eastern sea was on fire. From that altitude, the world looked calm and vivid and possible. But by the time we landed at Prestwick the clouds were down like the black cap on a hanging judge. We waited and waited hopelessly on the runway, the rain drumming on the fuselage, until the soaking fog lifted at London Airport.

When I finally got home, hours late, no one was there. The fires were blazing, the clocks were ticking, the telephone was still. I wandered around the empty house touching things, frightened, expectant. Fifteen minutes later, there was a noise at the front door and my child plunged shouting up the stairs into my arms. Over his shoulder I could see my wife standing tentatively in the hall. She, too, looked scared.

"We thought you were lost," she said. "We went down to the terminal and you didn't come."

"I got a lift straight from the airport. I phoned but you must have left. I'm sorry."

Chilly and uncertain, she presented her cheek to be kissed. I obliged, holding my son in my arms. There was still a week until Christmas.

We didn't stand a chance. Within hours we were at each other again, and that night I started drinking. Mostly, I'm a social drinker. Like everyone else, I've been drunk in my time but it's not really my style; I value my control too highly. This time, however, I went at the bottle with a pure need, as though parched. I drank before I got out of bed, almost before my eyes were open. I continued steadily throughout the morning until, by lunchtime, I had half a bottle of whiskey inside me and was beginnnig to feel human. Not drunk: that first half-bottle simply brought me to that point of calm where I usually began. Which is not particularly calm. Around lunchtime a friend—also depressed, also drinking—joined me at the pub and we boozed until closing time. Back home, with our wives, we kept at it steadily through the afternoon and evening, late into the night. The important thing was not to stop. In this way, I got through a bottle of whiskey a day, and a good deal of wine and beer. Yet it had little effect. Toward evening, when the child was in bed, I suppose I was a little tipsy, but the drinking was merely part of a more jagged frenzy which possessed us all. We kept the hi-fi booming pop, we danced, we had trials of strength: one-arm push-ups, handstands, somersaults; we balanced pint pots of beer on our foreheads, and tried to lie down and stand up again without spilling them. Anything not to stop, think, feel. The tension was so great that without the booze, we would have splintered into sharp fragments.

On Christmas Eve, the other couple went off on a skiing holiday. My wife and I were left staring at each other. Silently and meticulously, we decorated the Christmas tree and piled the presents, waiting. There was nothing left to say.

Late that afternoon I had sneaked off and phoned the psychotherapist whom I had been seeing, on and off, before I left for the States.

"I'm feeling pretty bad," I said. "Could I possibly see you?"

There was a pause. "It's rather difficult," he said at last. "Are you really desperate, or could you wait till Boxing Day?"

Poor bastard, I thought, he's got his Christmas, too. Let it go. "I can wait."

"Are you sure?" He sounded relieved. "You could come round at six-thirty, if it's urgent."

That was the child's bedtime; I wanted to be there. "It's all right," I said, "I'll phone later. Happy Christmas." What did it matter? I went back downstairs.

All my life I have hated Christmas: the unnecessary presents and obligatory cheerfulness, the grinding expense, the anticlimax. It is a day to be negotiated with infinite care, like a minefield. So I fortified myself with a stiff shot of whiskey before I got up. It combined with my child's excitement to put a glow of hope on the day. The boy sat among the gaudy wrapping paper, ribbons and bows, positively crowing with delight. At three years old, Christmas can still be a pleasure. Maybe, I began to feel, this thing could be survived. After all, hadn't I flown all the way from the States to pull my marriage from the fire? Or had I? Perhaps I knew it was unsavable and didn't want it to be otherwise. Perhaps I was merely seeking a plausible excuse for doing myself in. Perhaps that was why, even before all the presents were unwrapped, I had started it all up again: silent rages (not in front of the child), muted recriminations, withdrawals. The marriage was just one aspect of a whole life I had decided, months before, to have done with.

I remember little of what happened later. There was the usual family turkey for the child and my parents-in-law In the evening we went out to a smart, subdued dinner party, and on from there, I think, to something wilder. But I'm not sure. I recall only two trivial but vivid scenes. The first is very late at night. We are back home with another couple whom I know only slightly. He is small, dapper, cheerful, an unsuccessful poet turned successful journalist. His wife is faceless now, but him I still see sometimes on television, reporting expertly from the more elegant foreign capitals. I remember him sitting at our old piano, playing 1930s dance tunes; his wife stands behind him, singing the words; I lean on the piano, humming tunelessly; my wife is stretched, glowering, on the sofa. We are all very drunk.

Later still, I remember standing at the front door, joking with them as they negotiate the icy steps. As they go through the gate, they turn and wave. "Happy Christmas," we call to each other. I close the door and turn back to my wife.

After that, I remember nothing at all until I woke up in the hospital and saw my wife's face swimming vaguely toward me through a yellowish fog. She was crying. But that was three days later, three days of oblivion, a hole in my head.

It happened ten years ago now, and only gradually have I been able to piece together the facts from hints and snippets, recalled reluctantly and with apologies. Nobody wants to remind an attempted suicide of his folly, or to be reminded of

it. Tact and taste forbid. Or is it the failure itself which is
embarrassing? Certainly, a successful suicide inspires no deli-
cacy at all; everybody is in on the act at once with his own exclusive inside story. In my own case, my knowledge of what
happened is partial and second-hand; the only accurate details
are in the gloomy shorthand of the medical reports. Not that
it matters, since none of it now means much to me personally.
It is as though it had all happened to another person in another world.

It seems that when the poet-journalist left with his wife,
we had one final, terrible quarrel, more bitter than anything
we had managed before, and savage enough to be heard
through his sleep by whoever it was who was staying the night
in the guest room above. At the end of it, my wife marched
out. When she had returned prematurely from the States, our
own house was still leased to temporary tenants. So she had
rented a dingy flat in a florid but battered Victorian mansion
nearby. Since she still had the key to the place, she went to
spend the night there. In my sodden despair, I suppose her
departure seemed like the final nail. More likely, it was the
unequivocal excuse I had been waiting for. I went upstairs to
the bathroom and swallowed forty-five sleeping pills.

I had been collecting the things for months obsessionally,
like Green Stamps, from doctors on both sides of the Atlantic.
This was an almost legitimate activity, since in all that time I
rarely got more than two consecutive hours of sleep a night.
But I had always made sure of having more than I needed.
Weeks before I left America, I had stopped taking the things
and begun hoarding them in preparation for the time I knew
was coming. When it finally arrived, a box was waiting stuffed
with pills of all colors, like jellybeans. I gobbled the lot.

The following morning the guest brought me a cup of tea.
The bedroom curtains were drawn, so he could not see me
properly in the gloom. He heard me breathing in an odd way
but thought it was probably a hangover. So he left me alone.
My wife got back at noon, took one look and called the ambulance. When they got me to hospital I was, the report says,
"deeply unconscious, slightly cyanosed, vomit in mouth, pulse
rapid, poor volume." I looked up "cyanosis" in the dictionary:
"A morbid condition in which the surface of the body becomes blue because of insufficient aeration of the blood." Ap-

parently I had vomited in my coma and swallowed the stuff; it was now blocking my right lung, turning my face blue. As they say, a morbid condition. When they pumped the barbiturates out of my stomach, I vomited again, much more heavily, and again the muck went down to my lungs, blocking them badly. At that point I became—that word again—"deeply cyanosed"; I turned Tory-blue. They tried to suck the stuff out, and gave me oxygen and an injection, but neither had much effect. I suppose it was about this time that they told my wife there wasn't much hope. This was all she ever told me of the whole incident; it was a source of great bitterness to her. Since my lungs were still blocked, they performed a bronchoscopy. This time they sucked out a "large amount of mucus." They stuck an air pipe down my throat and I began to breathe more normally. The crisis, for the moment, was over.

This was on Boxing Day, December 26. I was still unconscious the next day and most of the day after that, though all the time less and less deeply. Since my lungs remained obstructed, they continued to give me air through a pipe; they fed me intravenously through a drip tube. The shallower my coma, the more restless I became. On the evening of the second day the airway was removed. During the afternoon of the third day, December 28, I came to. I felt them pull a tube from my arm. In a fog I saw my wife smiling hesitantly, and in tears. It was all very vague. I slept.

I spent most of the next day weeping quietly and seeing everything double. Two women doctors gently cross-questioned me. Two chunky physiotherapists, with beautiful, blooming, double complexions, put me through exercises—it seems my lungs were still in a bad state. I got two trays of uneatable food at a time and tried, on and off and unsuccessfully, to do two crossword puzzles. The ward was thronged with elderly twins.

At some point the police came, since in those days suicide was still a criminal offense. They sat heavily but rather sympathetically by my bed and asked me questions they clearly didn't want me to answer. When I tried to explain, they shushed me politely. "It was an accident, wasn't it, sir?" Dimly, I agreed. They went away.

I woke during the night and heard someone cry out weakly. A nurse bustled down the aisle in the obscure light. From the other side of the ward came more weak moaning. It was taken up faintly from somewhere else in the dimness. None of it was desperate with the pain and sharpness you hear after operations or accidents. Instead, the note was enervated, wan, beyond feeling. And then I understood why, even to my double vision, the patients had all seemed so old: I was in a terminal ward. All around me, old men were trying feebly not to die; I was thirty-one years old, and despite everything, still alive. When I stirred in bed I felt, for the first time, a rubber sheet beneath me. I must have peed myself, like a small child, while I was unconscious. My whole world was shamed.

The following morning my double vision had gone. The ward was filthy yellow and seemed foggy in the corners. I tottered to the lavatory; it, too, was filthy and evil-smelling. I tottered back to bed, rested a little and then phoned my wife. Since the pills and the booze hadn't killed me, nothing would. I told her I was coming home. I wasn't dead, so I wasn't going to die. There was no point in staying.

The doctors didn't see it that way. I was scarcely off the danger list; my lungs were in a bad state; I had a temperature; I could relapse at any time; it was dangerous; it was stupid; they would not be responsible. I lay there dumbly, as weak as a newborn infant, and let the arguments flow over me. Finally I signed a sheaf of forms acknowledging that I left against advice and absolving them from responsibility. A friend drove me home.

From *The Savage God*, 1970.

QUESTIONS

(1) Why is "incubating this death" a good phrase? Consider also, "a respectably dead suburb." Is this literal or figurative?

(2) In how many ways does Alvarez describe the survival of the child inside the man? Is this part of his theme? Does he imply that this was an element in his suicide attempt? In all suicide attempts?

(3) What does he mean by "the closed world of the suicide"? How is that related to the "freedom" of which he speaks in the first paragraph?

(4) How does he use the missed connection at the airport as part of his story? Does it border on the symbolic?

(5) Is his story a Christmas story? Is Christmas another "closed world" for him?

(6) Is the actual presentation of the suicide attempt effective? Why? Does he write about it as if "it had all happened to another person in another world"?

(7) Is there a connection between being a new person and being an "infant" again? What does he imply in this comparison?

THE LONG HABIT

LEWIS THOMAS

We continue to share with our remotest ancestors the most tangled and evasive attitudes about death, despite the great distance we have come in understanding some of the profound aspects of biology. We have as much distaste for talking about personal death as for thinking about it; it is an indelicacy, like talking in mixed company about venereal disease or abortion in the old days. Death on a grand scale does not bother us in the same special way: we can sit around a dinner table and discuss war, involving 60 million volatilized human deaths, as though we were talking about bad weather; we can watch abrupt bloody death every day, in color, on films and television, without blinking back a tear. It is when the numbers of dead are very small, and very close, that we begin to think in scurrying circles. At the very center of the problem is the naked cold deadness of one's own self, the only reality in nature of which we can have absolute certainty, and it is unmentionable, unthinkable. We may be even less willing to face the issue at first hand than our predecessors because of a secret new hope that maybe it will go away. We like to think, hiding the thought, that with all the marvelous ways in which we seem now to lead nature around by the nose, perhaps we can avoid the central problem if we just become, next year, say, a bit smarter.

"The long habit of living," said Thomas Browne, "indisposeth us to dying." These days, the habit has become an addiction: we are hooked on living; the tenacity of its grip on us, and ours on it, grows in intensity. We cannot think of giving it up, even when living loses its zest—even when we have lost the zest for zest.

We have come a long way in our technologic capacity to put death off, and it is imaginable that we might learn to stall it for even longer periods, perhaps matching the life-spans of the Abkhasian Russians, who are said to go on, springily, for a century and a half. If we can rid ourselves of some of our chronic, degenerative diseases, and cancer, strokes, and coronaries, we might go on and on. It sounds attractive and reasonable, but it is no certainty. If we became free of disease, we would make a much better run of it for the last decade or so, but might still terminate on about the same schedule as now. We may be like the genetically different lines of mice, or like Hayflick's different tissue-culture lines, programmed to die after a predetermined number of days, clocked by their genomes. If this is the way it is, some of us will continue to wear out and come unhinged in the sixth decade, and some much later, depending on genetic timetables.

If we ever do achieve freedom from most of today's diseases, or even complete freedom from disease, we will perhaps terminate by drying out and blowing away on a light breeze, but we will still die.

Most of my friends do not like this way of looking at it. They prefer to take it for granted that we only die because we get sick, with one lethal ailment or another, and if we did not have our diseases we might go on indefinitely. Even biologists choose to think this about themselves, despite the evidences of the absolute inevitability of death that surround their professional lives. Everything dies, all around, trees, plankton, lichens, mice, whales, flies, mitochondria. In the simplest creatures it is sometimes difficult to see it as death, since the strands of replicating DNA they leave behind are more conspicuously the living parts of themselves than with us (not that it is fundamentally any different, but it seems so). Flies do not develop a ward round of diseases that carry them off, one by one. They simply age, and die, like flies.

We hanker to go on, even in the face of plain evidence that long, long lives are not necessarily pleasurable in the kind of society we have arranged thus far. We will be lucky if we can postpone the search for new technologies for a while, until we have discovered some satisfactory things to do with the extra time. Something will surely have to be found to take the place of sitting on the porch re-examining one's watch.

Perhaps we would not be so anxious to prolong life if we did not detest so much the sickness of withdrawal. It is astonishing how little information we have about this universal process, with all the other dazzling advances in biology. It is almost as though we wanted not to know about it. Even if we could imagine the act of death in isolation, without any preliminary stage of being struck down by disease, we would be fearful of it.

There are signs that medicine may be taking a new interest in the process, partly from curiosity, partly from an embarrassed realization that we have not been handling this aspect of disease with as much skill as physicians once displayed, back in the days before they became convinced that disease was their solitary and sometimes defeatable enemy. It used to be the hardest and most important of all the services of a good doctor to be on hand at the time of death and to provide comfort, usually in the home. Now it is done in hospitals, in secrecy (one of the reasons for the increased fear of death these days may be that so many people are totally unfamiliar with it; they never actually see it happen in real life). Some of our technology permits us to deny its existence, and we maintain flickers of life for long stretches in one community of cells or another, as though we were keeping a flag flying. Death is not a sudden-all-at-once affair; cells go down in sequence, one by one. You can, if you like, recover great numbers of them many hours after the lights have gone out, and grow them out in cultures. It takes hours, even days, before the irreversible word finally gets around to all the provinces.

We may be about to rediscover that dying is not such a bad

thing to do after all. Sir William Osler took this view: he disapproved of people who spoke of the agony of death, maintaining that there was no such thing.

In a nineteenth-century memoir on an expedition in Africa, there is a story by David Livingston about his own experience of near-death. He was caught by a lion, crushed across the chest in the animal's great jaws, and saved in the instant by a lucky shot from a friend. Later, he remembered the episode in clear detail. He was so amazed by the extraordinary sense of peace, calm, and total painlessness associated with being killed that he constructed a theory that all creatures are provided with a protective physiologic mechanism, switched on at the verge of death, carrying them through in a haze of tranquillity.

I have seen agony in death only once, in a patient with rabies; he remained acutely aware of every stage in the process of his own disintegration over a twenty-four-hour period, right up to his final moment. It was as though, in the special neuropathology of rabies, the switch had been prevented from turning.

We will be having new opportunities to learn more about the physiology of death at first hand, from the increasing numbers of cardiac patients who have been through the whole process and then back again. Judging from what has been found out thus far, from the first generation of people resuscitated from cardiac standstill (already termed the Lazarus syndrome), Osler seems to have been right. Those who remember parts or all of their episodes do not recall any fear, or anguish. Several people who remained conscious throughout, while appearing to have been quite dead, could only describe a remarkable sensation of detachment. One man underwent coronary occlusion with cessation of the heart and dropped for all practical purposes dead, in front of a hospital; within a few minutes his heart had been restarted by electrodes and he breathed his way back into life. According to his account, the strangest thing was that there were so many people around him, moving so urgently, handling his body with such excitement, while all his awareness was of quietude.

In a recent study of the reaction to dying in patients with obstructive disease of the lungs, it was concluded that the process was considerably more shattering for the professional observers than the observed. Most of the patients appeared to be preparing themselves with equanimity for death, as though intuitively familiar with the business. One elderly woman reported that the only painful and distressing part of the process was in being interrupted; on several occasions she was provided with conventional therapeutic measures to maintain oxygenation or restore fluids and electrolytes, and each time she found the experience of coming back harrowing; she deeply resented the interference with her dying.

I find myself surprised by the thought that dying is an all-right thing to do, but perhaps it should not surprise. It is, after all, the most ancient and fundamental of biologic functions, with its mechanisms worked out with the same attention to detail, the same provision for the advantage of the organism, the same abundance of genetic information for guidance through the stages, that we have long since become accustomed to finding in all the crucial acts of living.

Very well. But even so, if the transformation is a coordinated, integrated physiologic process in its initial, local stages, there is still that permanent vanishing of consciousness to be accounted for. Are we to be stuck forever with this problem? Where on earth does it go? Is it simply stopped dead in its tracks, lost in humus, wasted? Considering the tendency of nature to find uses for complex and intricate mechanisms, this seems to me unnatural. I prefer to think of it as somehow separated off at the filaments of its attachment, and then drawn like an easy breath back into the membrane of its origin, a fresh memory for a biospherical nervous system, but I have no data on the matter.

This is for another science, another day. It may turn out, as some scientists suggest, that we are forever precluded from investigating consciousness by a sort of indeterminacy principle that stipulates that the very act of looking will make it twitch and blur out of sight. If this is true, we will never learn. I envy some of my friends who are convinced about telepathy; oddly enough, it is my European scientist acquaintances who believe it most freely and take it most lightly. All their aunts have received Communications, and there they sit, with proof of the motility of consciousness at their fingertips, and the making of a new science. It is discouraging to have had the wrong aunts, and never the ghost of a message.

From *The Lives of a Cell*, 1972.

QUESTIONS

(1) Are Thomas's comparisons and contrasts in the first paragraph effective? Are they connected in any way with the comparisons and contrasts in the last paragraph?

(2) Why is the ironic use of a cliché—"they die like flies"—powerful in this context?

(3) List some of the scientific terms used in the essay. Then list some of the homely words like "hanker." What is the effect? Why does Thomas mix his vocabulary this way?

(4) Thomas talks about "quietude" and "tranquility." Does his style reflect the point he is making?

(5) Why is it necessary for him to tell of having seen "agony in death"? What does that do for the credibility of his essay?

(6) What kinds of contrasts and connections does he make in the essay between the body and the mind? Between psychology and biology?

(7) Is "the long habit" psychological, or biological, or both?

(8) Is the "ghost" of the last sentence an echo of "our remotest ancestors" in the first? What does that demonstrate about unity in an essay?

THE SENSE OF THE 70s

A SENSE OF
THE FUTURE

The Future, will it be 1984 or 2001? Or neither—merely a predictable, recognizable extension of the present? Prophecy is a hazardous business, "without honor" as the Bible reminds us, but a fascinating, necessary and finally honorable enterprise.

The prophets gathered in this section offer their own unique perspective on the future. George Steiner's "A Future Literacy" reminds us that we must achieve a much greater degree of mathematical and scientific literacy in the future if we wish to thrive and prosper. Andrew Kopkind focuses on future sexuality, suggesting that androgyny will produce the maximum freedom of expression for the individual—once liberated from the "jailhouse of gender."

Considering both the scientific focus of Steiner and the tangential genetic concern of Kopkind, Arthur Lubow explores the perils and possibilities of DNA research. Possibilities and perils of an entirely different order are examined by Norman Macrae, the deputy editor of *The Economist,* in his essay "America's Third Century." Macrae argues that America can and should continue to be the leading nation of the world in the century ahead, but to do so it must overcome internal impulses toward stagnation.

Taking a more radical view of the future George Leonard sugests, through the metaphor of "The Ultimate Athlete," that America needs a new mythic revitalization. He argues that the new perspective will come through an increased awareness and control of the body and an appreciation of life as "a game of games . . . a dance."

These essays make it clear that one thing will be certain. We will continue to operate under the ancient Chinese curse: "May you live in interesting times."

A FUTURE LITERACY

GEORGE STEINER

Changes of idiom between generations are a normal part of social history. Previously, however, such changes and the verbal provocations of young against old have been variants on an evolutionary continuum. What is occurring now is new: it is an attempt at a total break. The mumble of the dropout, the silence of the teen-ager in the enemy house of his parents, are meant to destroy. Cordelia's asceticism, her refusal of the mendacities of speech, proves murderous. So does that of the autistic child, when it stamps on language, pulverizing it to gibberish or maniacal silence. We empty of their humanity those to whom we deny speech. We make them naked and absurd. There is a terrible, literal image in "stone-deafness," in the opaque babble or speechlessness of the "stoned." Break off speech to others, and the Medusa turns inward. Hence something of the hurt and despair of the present conflict between generations. Deliberate violence is being done to those primary ties of identity and social cohesion produced by a common language.

But are there no other literacies conceivable, "literacies" not of the letter?

I am writing in a study in a college of one of the great American universities. The walls are throbbing gently to the beat of music coming from one near and several more distant amplifiers. The walls quiver to the ear or to the touch roughly eighteen hours a day, sometimes twenty-four. The beat is literally unending. It matters little whether it is that of pop, folk, or rock. What counts is the all-pervasive pulsation, morning to night and into night, made indiscriminate by the cool burn of electronic timbre. A large segment of mankind, between the ages of thirteen and, say, twenty-five, now lives immersed in this constant throb. The hammering of rock or of pop creates an enveloping space. Activities such as reading, writing, private communication, learning, previously framed with silence, now take place in a field of strident vibrato. This means that the essentially linguistic nature of these pursuits is adulterated; they are vestigial modes of the old "logic."

Yet we are unquestionably dealing with a literacy, with codes of recognition so widespread and dynamic that they constitute a "meta-culture." Popular musics have their semantics, their theory of genres, their intricate play-offs of esoteric against canonic types. Folk and pop, "trad music" and rock, count their several histories and corpus of legend. They show their relics. They number their old masters and rebels, their betrayers and high priests. Precisely as in classical literacy, so there are in the world of jazz or of rock'n'roll degrees of initiation ranging from the vague empathies of the tyro (Latin on sundials) to the acid erudition of the scholiast. At the same time there is an age factor which makes the culture of pop more like modern mathematics and physics than the humanities. In their execution of and response to popular music, the young have a tension-span, a suppleness of appropriation denied to the old. Part of the reason may be a straightforward organic degeneracy: the delicate receptors of the inner ear harden and grow opaque during one's twenties.

In short, the vocabularies, the contextual behavior-patterns of pop and rock, constitute a genuine *lingua franca,* a "universal dialect" of youth. Everywhere a sound-culture seems to be driving back the old authority of verbal order.

If music is one of the principal "languages outside the word," mathematics is another. Any argument on a postclassic culture and on future literacy will have to address itself, decisively, to the role of the mathematical and natural sciences. Theirs may very soon be the central sphere. Statistics can be shallow or ambiguous in interpretation. But those which tabulate the growth of the sciences do, in plain fact, map a new world. More than 90 percent of all scientists known to human record are now living. The number of papers which may be regarded as relevant to an advance in chemistry, physics, and the biological sciences—that is, the recent, active literature in these three fields alone—is estimated as being in excess of three and a quarter million. The critical indices in the sciences—investment, publication, number of men trained, percentage of the gross national product directly implicated in research and development—are doubling every seven to ten years. Between now and 1990, according to a recent projection, the number of monographs published in mathematics, physics, chemistry, and biology will, if aligned on an imaginary shelf, stretch to the moon.

Less tangibly, but more significantly, it has been estimated that some 75 percent of the most talented individuals in the developed nations, of the men and women whose measurable intelligence comes near the top of the curve in the community, now work in the sciences. Politics and the humanities thus seem to draw on a quarter of the optimal mental resources in our societies, and recruit largely from below the line of excellence. It is almost a platitude to insist that no previous period in history offers any parallel to the current exponential growth in the rate, multiplicity, and effects of scientific-technological advance. It is equally obvious that even the present fantastic pace (interleaved, as it may be, by phases of disillusion or regrouping in certain highly developed nations) will at least double by the early 1980s. This phenomenology brings with it wholly unprecedented demands on information absorption and rational application. We stand less on that shore of the unbounded which awed Newton than amid tidal movements for which there is not even a theoretic model.

One can identify half a dozen areas of maximal pressure, points at which pure science and technological realization will alter basic structures of both private and social life.

There is the galaxy of biomedical "engineering." Spare-part surgery, the use of chemical agencies against the degeneration of aging tissues, preselection of the sex of the embryo, the manipulation of genetic factors toward ethical or strategic ends— each of these literally prepares a new typology of man. So does the direct chemical or electrochemical control of behavior. By implanting electrodes in the brain, by giving personality-control drugs, the therapist will be able to program alterations of consciousness; he will touch on the electrochemistry of motive to determine the deed. Memory transfer through biochemical transplant, for which controversial claims are now being made, would alter the essential relations of ego and time. Unquestionably, our current inroads on the human cortex dwarf all previous images of exploration.

The revolutions of awareness that will result from full-scale computerization and electronic data processing can only be crudely guessed at. At some point in 1969, the information-handling capacity of computers—that is, the number of units of information which can be received and stored—surpassed that of the 3.5 billion brains belonging to the human race. By 1975, computers will be leading by a fifty-to-one ratio. By whatever criterion used, size of memory, cost, speed and accuracy of calculation, computers are now increasing a thousandfold every fifteen years. In advanced societies, the electronic data bank is becoming the pivot of military, economic, sociological, and archival procedures. Though a computer is a tool, its powers are such that they go far beyond the model of governed, easily limited instrumentality. Analogue and digital computerization are transforming the relations of density, of authority, between the human intellect and available knowledge, between personal choice and projected possibility. Connected to telephone lines or to more sophisticated arteries of transmission, multipurpose computers will become a routine presence in all offices and most homes. It is probable that this electronic cortex will simultaneously reduce the singularity of the individual and immensely enlarge his referential and operational scope. Inevitably, the mathematical issues of electronic storage and information-retrieval are becoming the focus of the study of mind.

Another main area is that of large-scale ecological modification. There is a good deal of millenarian naïveté and recoil from adult politics in the current passion for the environment. Nevertheless, the potentialities are formidable. Control of weather, locally at least, is now conceivable, as is the economic exploitation of the continental shelves and of the deeper parts of the sea. Man's setting or "collective skin" is becoming malleable on a scale previously unimaginable. Beyond these fields lies space exploration. Momentary boredom with the smooth histrionics of the thing ought not to blur two crucial eventualities: the establishment of habitable bases outside a polluted, overcrowded, or war-torn earth, and, remote as it now seems, the perception of signals from other systems of intelligence or information. Fontenelle's inspired speculations of 1686 *Sur la pluralité des mondes* are now a statistical commonplace.

We cannot hope to measure the sum and consequence of these developments. Yet all but the last-mentioned are in definite sight. That not one of these exploding horizons should even have appeared in T. S. Eliot's *Notes Toward the Definition of Culture* indicates the pace of mutation since 1948 when that book appeared. Our ethics, our central habits of consciousness, the immediate and environmental membrane we inhabit, our relations to age and to remembrance, to the children whom we may select and program, are being transformed. As in the twilit times of Ovid's fables of mutant being, we are in metamorphosis. To be ignorant of these scientific and technological phenomena, to be indifferent to their effects on our mental and physical experience, *is to opt out of reason.* A view of postclassic civilization must, increasingly, imply a vision of the sciences, of the language-worlds of mathematical and symbolic notation. Theirs is the commanding energy: in material fact, in the "forward dreams" which define us. Today, our dialectics are binary.

But the motives for trying to incorporate science into the field of common reference, of imaginative reflex, are better than utilitarian. And this is so even if we take "utilitarian," as we must, to include our very survival as a species. The true motives ought to be those of delight, of intellectual energy, of moral venture. To have some personal *rapport* with the sciences is, very probably, to be in contact with that which has the most force of life and comeliness in our reduced condition.

At seminal levels of metaphor, of myth, of laughter, where the arts and the worn scaffolding of philosophic systems fail us, science is active. Touch on even its more abstruse regions and a deep elegance, a quickness and merriment of the spirit come through. Consider the Banach-Tarski theorem whereby the sun and a pea may be so divided into a finite number of disjointed parts that every single part of one is congruent to a unique part of the other. The undoubted result is that the sun may be fitted into one's vest pocket, and that the component parts of the pea will fill the entire universe solidly, no vacant space remaining either in the interior of the pea or in the universe. What surrealist fantasy yields a more precise wonder? Or take the Penrose theorem in cosmology which tells us that under extreme conditions of gravitational collapse a critical stage is reached whereby no communication with the outside world is possible. Light cannot escape the gravitational field. A "black hole" develops representing the locale of a body of near-zero volume and near-infinite density. Or, even more remarkable, the "collapse-event" may open "into" a new universe hitherto unapprehended. Here spin the *soleils noirs* of Nerval and romantic trance. But the marvelous wit is that of fact. Very recent observations of at least two bodies, a companion to the star Aur and the supergiant star Her 89, suggest that Penrose's model of a "hole in space" is true. "Constantly, I seek a poetry of facts," writes Hugh Mac-Diarmid:

> Even as
> The profound kinship of all living substance
> Is made clear by the chemical route.
> Without some chemistry one is bound to remain
> Forever a dumbfounded savage
> In the face of vital reactions.
> The beautiful relations
> Shown only by biochemistry
> Replace a stupefied sense of wonder
> With something more wonderful
> Because natural and understandable.

That "poetry of facts" and realization of the miraculous delicacies of perception in contemporary science already inform literature at those nervepoints where it is both disciplined and under the stress of the future. It is no accident that Musil was trained as an engineer, that Ernst Jünger and Nabokov should be serious entomologists, that Broch and Canetti are writers schooled in the exact and mathematical sciences. The special, deepening presence of Valéry in one's feelings about the afterlife of culture is inseparable from his own alertness to the alternative poetics, to the "other metaphysics" of mathematical and scientific pursuit. The instigations of Queneau and of Borges, which are among the most bracing in modern letters, have algebra and astronomy at their back. And there is a more spacious, central instance. Proust's only successor is Joseph Needham. By that I mean something entirely concrete. *A La Recherche du temps perdu* and *Science and Civilization in China* represent two uncannily sustained, controlled flights of the re-creative intellect. They exhibit what Coleridge termed "esemplastic powers," that many-branched coherence of design which builds a great house of language for memory and conjecture to inhabit. The

China of Needham's passionate recomposing—so inwardly
shaped before he went in search of its material truth—is a
place as intricate, as lit by dreams, as the way to Combray.
Needham's account, in an "interim" essay, of the misreadings
and final discovery of the true hexagonal symmetry of the
snow crystal has the same exact savor of manifold revealing
as the Narrator's sightings of the steeple at Martinville. Both
works are a long danse of the mind.

It is often objected that the layman cannot share in the life
of the sciences. He is "bound to remain forever a dumbfounded savage" before a world whose primary idiom he cannot grasp. Though good scientists themselves rarely say this,
it is obviously true. But only to a degree. Modern science is
centrally mathematical; the development of rigorous mathematical formalization marks the evolution of a given discipline, such as biology, to full scientific maturity. Having no
mathematics, or very little, the "common reader" is excluded.
If he tries to penetrate the meaning of a scientific argument,
he will probably get it muddled, or misconstrue metaphor to
signify the actual process True again, but of a truth that is
halfway to indolence. Even a modest mathematical culture
will allow some approach to what is going on. The notion that
one can exercise a rational literacy in the latter part of the
twentieth century without a knowledge of calculus, without
some preliminary access to topology of algebraic analysis, will
soon seem a bizarre archaicism. These styles and speech-forms
from the grammar of number are already indispensable to
many branches of modern logic, philosophy, linguistics, and
psychology. They are the language of feeling where it is, today, most adventurous. As electronic data-processing and cod-
ing pervade more and more of the economics and social order
of our lives, the mathematical illiterate will find himself cut
off. A new hierarchy of menial service and stunted opportunity may develop among those whose resources continue to be
purely verbal. There may be "word-helots."

Of course, the mathematical literacy of the amateur must
remain modest. Usually he will apprehend only a part of the
scientific innovation, catching a momentary, uncertain glimpse
of a continuum, making an approximate image for himself.
But is this not, in fact, the way in which we view a good deal
of modern art? Is it not precisely through intervals of selective

appropriation, via pictorial analogies which are often naïve in the extreme, that the nonmusician assimilates the complex, ultimately technical realities of music?

The history of science, moreover, permits of a less demanding access, yet one that leads to the center. A modest mathematical culture is almost sufficient to enable one to follow the development of celestial mechanics and of the theory of motion until Newton and Laplace. It takes no more than reasonable effort to understand, at least along major lines, the scruple, the elegance of hypothesis and experiment which characterize the modulations of the concept of entropy from Carnot to Helmholtz. The genesis of Darwinism and the subsequent re-examinations which lead from orthodox evolutionary doctrine to modern molecular biology are one of the "very rich hours" of the human intellect. Yet much of the material, and many of its philosophical implications, are accessible to the layman. This is so, to a lesser degree, of some part of the debate between Einstein, Bohr, Wolfgang Pauli, and Max Born—from each of whom we have letters of matchless honesty and personal commitment—on the issue of anarchic indeterminacy or subjective interference in quantum physics. Here are topics as crowded with felt life as any in the humanities.

The absence of the history of science and technology from the school syllabus is a scandal. It is an absurdity to speak of the Renaissance without knowledge of its cosmology, of the mathematical dreams which underwrote its theories of art and music. To read seventeenth- and eighteenth-century literature or philosophy without an accompanying awareness of the unfolding genius of physics, astronomy, and algebraic analysis during this period is to read only at the surface. A model of neo-classicism which omits Linnaeus is hollow. What can be said responsibly of romantic historicism, of the new mappings of time after Hegel, which fails to include a study of Buffon, Cuvier, and Lamarck? It is not only that he humanities have been arrogant in their assertions of centrality; it is that they have often been silly. We need no poet more urgently than Lucretius.

Where culture itself is so utterly fragmented, there is no need to speak of the sciences as separate. What does make them so different from the present state of the humanities is their collectivity and inner calendar. Overwhelmingly, today, science is a collective enterprise in which the talent of the individual is a function of the group. But, as we have seen, more and more of current radical art and anti-art aspires to the same plurality. The deep divergence between the humanistic and scientific sensibilities is one of temporality. Very nearly by definition, the scientist knows that tomorrow will be in advance of today. A twentieth-century schoolboy can manipulate mathematical and experiential concepts inaccessible to a Galileo or a Gauss. For a scientist the curve of time is positive. Inevitably, the humanist looks back. The essential repertoire of his consciousness, the props of his daily life as a scholar or critic, are from the past. A natural bent of feeling will lead him to believe, perhaps silently, that the achievements of the past are more radiant than those of his own age. The proposition that "Shakespeare is the greatest, most complete writer" mankind will ever produce is a logical and almost a grammatical outrage. But it carries conviction. And even if a Rembrandt or a Mozart may, in future, be equaled (itself a gross, indistinct notion), they cannot be surpassed. There is a profound logic of sequent energy in the arts, but not in additive progress in the sense of the sciences. No errors are corrected or theorems disproved. Because it carries the past within it, language, unlike mathematics, draws backward. This is the meaning of Eurydice. Because the realness of his inward being lies at his back, the man of words, the singer, will turn to the place of necessary shadows. For the scientist, time and the light lie before.

Here, if anywhere, lies the division of the "two cultures" or, rather, of the two orientations. Anyone who has lived among scientists will know how intensely this polarity influences lifestyle. Their evenings point to tomorrow, *e santo è l'avvenir.*

From *The Atlantic Monthly,* 1971.

QUESTIONS
(1) In his opening paragraph, George Steiner states that although children have always rebelled against parents in word as well as in deed, the language gap today is of a special character. What is that character?

(2) According to Steiner, pop music is a "literacy" of its own. How does he develop this idea?

(3) What are the implications Steiner wishes to draw from his statistics about the growth of science?

(4) What does the author refer to when he says, "we are in metamorphosis"?

(5) What is Steiner's purpose in mentioning the scientific interest of many of the most highly regarded of contemporary writers?

(6) What is the point of comparison between Marcel Proust's *Remembrance of Things Past* and Joseph Needham's *Science and Civilization in China*.

(7) The conclusion suggests that the scientist inevitably looks ahead, the humanist looks back. Does this fact suggest that the two modes of knowledge are irreconcilable?

(8) For whom was this essay originally written, people of a scientific or a humanistic bent?

AMERICA'S THIRD CENTURY

NORMAN MACRAE

RECESSIONAL FOR THE SECOND GREAT EMPIRE?

The two hundred years since the United States won their fortuitous victory in their Revolutionary War have been the two centuries of the world's material advance. It is probable that three centuries of material advance will be all that is needed.

For the first 10,000 years of man's existence as a producing animal—from about 8000 BC when commercial agricultural cultivation probably began, down to about 1776—people did not grow much richer. By 2076 people sensibly may not want to grow much richer, but for quite a few years yet most people most definitely will.

And this a main reason for worry at America's 200th birthday. There is a danger that the Americans, with all their power for dynamism and good, may be about to desert what should be their manifest and now rather easy destiny of leading the rest of us towards a decent world society and an abundant cheap lunch. If they do, the leadership of the world may be yielded from American to less sophisticated hands, at a perilous moment.

During research for this survey the fears listed here seemed to me to be (a) obvious, (b) avertible, (c) not recognised by nine-tenths of the Americans to whom I spoke. Indeed, the largest cohorts of very intelligent Americans are looking for their favourite fears in precisely the opposite directions.

This sets a problem about the order in which the arguments in this survey should be set down. It is a pity to begin by clodhopping on corns. The survey's main arguments are that:

(1) The two great empires that have ruled the first two centuries of industrial advance—the British in 1776–1876, and the American in 1876–1976—have handled the task of world leadership surprisingly well. But the Americans on the eve of 1976 are showing the same symptoms of a drift from dynamism as the British did at the end of their century in 1876.

(2) World leadership is therefore liable to pass into new hands quite early in the century 1976–2076. During this century the world will face some extraordinary opportunities, and also some bizarre dangers.

(3) The opportunities will probably include an ability to put material living standards in the twenty-first century more or less wherever men want them. I explain later why I think that the remarkable upturn in around 1776 in all of this survey's charts will continue (indeed, probably accelerate) for a while, and why I share the Hudson Institute's guess that mankind could transform its present annual gross world product (gwp) of around \$5½ trillion made by 4 billion people to,

some time within the lifetime of kids already adolescent, a "satiating" gwp of between $100 trillion and $350 trillion for a world population of between 10 billion and 30 billion people. Somewhere in that range (perhaps between about twice and five times today's average American income per head for everybody) men may stop growing much richer because they will no longer want to grow much richer.

(4) During these next few years, however, the bizarre dangers will include the destructive (because quite small groups of fanatics and terrorists and even individual criminals will very soon have the capability of destroying the planet) and, for example, the biophysical (because the present orthodox method of creating a human being—namely, by copulation between two individuals giving no thought to what the product will be—may quite soon change). Sex is already 99.99 percent for fun, and technology is bound to home in on the pre-planned twice-in-a-lifetime occasion when it will be for reproduction. Our children will probably "progressively" be able to order their babies with the shape and strength and level of intelligence that they choose, as well as alter existing human beings so as to insert artificial intelligence, retune brains, change personality, modify moods, control behaviour. And lots of even more horrid things like that. The pace and sophistication with which some of these things are not done will hang on the world's leading nations, whom other peoples will most wish to emulate or will most fear to fall behind. It will be very desirable to retain strong and calm American influence in this period, rather than to yield all of world leadership to (at best) the inexperienced Japanese.

(5) America's contribution in its third century will depend largely on how its three main institutions evolve in or out of pace with the changing times. These three main institutions are, in reverse order of importance: its business corporations; its government; and its mechanisms for living together (what takes over from church, family, pioneer spirit, small-town togetherness, the probably-failed experiment of suburbia—during a century when the third and greatest transport revolution, that of telecommunications, should gradually allow an increasing number of breadwinners to live in whatever communities they wish to form and to telecommute daily into their New York offices from homes in Tahiti or the Alps).

This summary has set a lot of angels dancing on the point of a pin. It may seem clumsy to try to pick out the pattern of the dance by first brooding on what may happen to American business during these next few years. But I think that the influence of this might be decisive for the lifetime of my children, just as what happened to British and then American business in the years immediately after 1776 and 1876 largely shaped the two centuries 1776–1876 and 1876–1976.

At one stage of my journey through America in 1975, this thought made me rather glum.

AMERICA JOINS THE FABIAN SOCIETY

The first century of material advance after 1776, based on the invention of steam power and the transport revolution of the railways, was led by Great Britain. During this period it was widely understood that God was an Englishman because the most efficient businessmen temporarily were.

The British century ended in around 1876 as it became apparent that the most efficient businessmen now weren't. The second century of material advance from 1876–1976, based on the invention of manufacturers' assembly line techniques and the transport revolution of the internal combustion engine, was therefore led by the United States. There were societal, psychological and technological reasons why America was ready in 1876 to take over industrial leadership from old Britain. Awkwardly, these same reasons can be cited in 1975 to suggest that old America may be about to give up that leadership to somebody else.

The chief reason why 1876 ushered in America's century was that entrepreneurs' verve was by then most likely to sprout in that nation so largely self-selected from families enterprising enough to have migrated across the wide ocean, and yet new enough not yet to have created the aristocratic or jealous or intellectual institutions which castigate moneymaking as *infra dig* or unfair. The surge into the Henry Ford revolution should have been as organisable in the Britain of 1876 as in the America. What was missing in Britain by that moralising Gladstone's and that do-gooding Disraeli's day was the incentive provided by any accordance of social standing to business panache.

Remember how easy the surge after 1876 was—just as, for different reasons, see below, I am going to maintain that a much bigger surge after 1976 is also going to be. Our grandfathers lived in a time when any bankworthy member of the middle class anywhere with a good entrepreneurial idea could expect to be profiting from it (and to have set course to change the world?) within a few months. The Ford Motor Company was founded in mid-June, 1903, with a cash capital equal to today's price of a small suburban house and only 125 employees; it sold its first cars to customers that October, and made a profit from then on. Yet between 1876–1910—while America was rearing Rockefeller, Morgan, Harriman, Carnegie, Frick and Ford to seize this new age of opportunity—what single name of a new and domestically-based British entrepreneur springs easily to mind?

The main reason for Britain's entrepreneurial decay around 1876 was that a century's experience as top dog had by then become debilitating. The British upper class was strengthening its gut feeling that new sorts of commerce were surely rather vulgar, while the British business-decision-making class had itself become bureaucratic and protectionist rather than enterpreneurial. As each new technological development appeared in the late 19th century there were interests in Britain (entrenched among employers as well as in craft unions) who had prospered from the development which it would replace, so they united to wish that the new idea would please go away. America gained also because its industrial revolution was from the start based on technology geared to the market, as Edison and the half-million other American patentees of 1870–1900 sought dynamically to devise conveniences for the many instead of to dredge up ideas fascinating to the few. By contrast the British industrial revolution had even originally been based on more leisurely and gentlemanly science, as scholars like Newton and Watt looked at an apple or a kettle and then thought of a most ingenious wheeze.

America's entrepreneurial verve instead of Britain's businesses' bureaucracy, America's output-oriented technology instead of Britain's scientific curiosity whether the moon was made of green cheese, America's bloody-clawed capitalism instead of Britain's good corporate citizenship whose attempt at paternalism was bound to fall down a class and generation gap. In 1876 those were young America's strengths, while these were old Britain's senescent disease.

And today? The Briton travelling through America in 1975 at first has the eerie feeling that he has gone back to when grandfather knew H. G. Wells. The entrepreneurial fervour of the industrial age seems to be dying in the west. I think . . . that this first impression is too gloomy, but it will be good neighbourliness first to rub America's birthday nose into the warning signs.

Treason of the clerks

The bad news for the world's teeming masses this bicentennial is that in America the whole concept of thrustful business is in danger of becoming unloved. The intellectuals have joined in the sneering against it, making it fashionable to believe that stagnation is not only wise but clever. This is exactly how it was when Britain's post-1876 decline began. It is strange that peoples do not see that not learning from history is bunk.

Through most of history, businessmen have been told by the upper classes of society that they are pushful upstarts. Since businessmen want most to rise in society, this has naturally often discouraged them from starting to push up. As even de Tocqueville said in the patchy book which many Americans regard as their national legitimation, the church in the late middle ages provided the first hope of a dynamic challenge to the old stagnant feudalism—as the clergy opened its ranks to all classes, to the poor and the rich, to the villein and the lord, to every uppity Becket. But by the time societies were rich enough for top churchmen to have a nice life, provided nobody disturbed them, the church comfortably joined itself to the rest of the establishment in deprecating restless change, although it still good-naturedly said it was in favour of succour of the poor.

The breakthrough towards continuing material advance therefore waited on the emergence of another part of the upper class which was ready to reassure the lively that panache was respectable. This new class came in England in the 17th century when King Charles II favoured intellectuals interested in the scientific method, perhaps because he sought male company among an establishment different from that which had lost his father his head. After a century's slow germination, intellectuals in ferment played a major part in awakening Britain in the first seven-eighths of its 1776–1876 century—agricultural innovators against the squires, freetraders against the mercantilism of governments, and doctors who favoured a chemical feast against opponents of some advances like chloroform. Then, just after the mid-19th-century, this new British ginger group followed the old church into favouring a decent gentlemanly stagnation.

By around 1876 a British intellectual could have a pleasant life in contemplation, and his most natural resentment (like the resentment of the squire, the parson and the bureaucrat) came to be against vulgar people who were restlessly and commercially pushful. After about 1876 a "progressive intellectual" in British public life no longer meant a person who believed in progress and change; no longer a person who was eager to rout down to the roots of every way of doing things, so as to cut and graft wherever an improvement in production or effectiveness or competitiveness or individual liberty could be secured. A "progressive intellectual" meant a paternalist, who did not like change very much but was eager to pass on in welfare benefits a larger part of the easy growth in national income which his own anti-growth attitudes now made it slightly more difficult to attain.

And that is exactly what has happened in America in these years just before 1976. The United States has joined the Fabian Society of about 1903. Many of the new Democrat members of Congress, including some presidential aspirants, would find that Fabian Society their most natural home, militant middle-class feminism and all, but plus the old American disease. When upper-class Americans impose snob values on emotional populists, they often think that they have gotten religion—and catch the lynching spirit.

It would be impertinent for a foreigner to object to America's creeping ethic of anti-dynamism if it had merely sprung from American selfishness. When you have a gnp per head over $7,000 a year, you naturally begin to regard growing much richer as a bit of a bore—although American Christians and humanists should be reminding zero-growth Americans that, by discontinuing their own industrial dynamism which has helped so much to drive world technology up through the bud, they could cruelly reduce the forward prospects of the 2 billion angry people on incomes under $200 a year with whom we share this rather small planet. But the real horror today is that America is not going slowly stagnationist out of selfishness. On campuses across the continent, a peculiarly innumerate anti-growth cult is being taught to a generation of idealistic kids as if it was high moral philosophy, or even a religion.

Industrophobia

This is a familiar fault in that otherwise lovely, brave continent. Remember G. K. Chesterton?

> There is nothing the matter with Americans except their ideals. The real American is all right; it is the ideal American who is all wrong.

Idealist Americans should ponder the delay they caused to the trans-Alaska oil pipeline, without humbug.

There can be no real pretence this delay was motivated by any environmentalists' thoughtful belief that the 15 square miles covered by this pipeline would spoil the view of the other 599,985 square miles of Alaskan wilderness which are hardly looked at by anybody anyway (the few adventurous tourists who do travel through this wilderness will certainly detour deliberately to what will be the pipeline's slightly contrasting and therefore mildly interesting sight). There can also be no pretence that, at least after its initial redesign, the pipeline will be unfair to local wildlife; for them it will be an occasionally-useful shelter from the Arctic wind. Instead, the delay stemmed from a desire to be nasty to oil companies, plus aristocratic resentment that poorer people growing richer can become more uncouth. The delay could have been justified if it had been used to make the pipeline's building less of a drunkards' gold rush, less expensive, more integrated with the community. But, of course, the costs and urgency created by the delay made each of these factors worse.

It was an unforeseen misfortune that this spasm of industrophobia should have come at a time when the delay to oil pipements has certainly cut America's employment, has certainly aggravated the oil crisis for the energy-short destitute countries, has necessitated shabby compromises in American foreign policy. In order to make more symmetrical an Alaskan view for practically nobody, the unemployment of black teenagers in New York City has been pushed up the last few percentage points towards 40 percent, a few tens of thousands more brown men have starved to death in Bangladesh, and several hundred thousand Israeli families have been put in greater danger. It would be vindictive to hammer home these truths to the hangdog, but there still aren't any hangdogs. It was eerie during my trip across the campuses of the continent to hear so many supposedly left-wing young Americans who still thought they were expressing an entirely new and progressive philosophy as they mouthed the same prejudices as Trollope's 19th-century Tory squires: attacking any further expansion of industry and commerce as impossibly vulgar, because ecologically unfair to their pheasants and wild ducks. Some of their emotions were rather nicely expressed. The upper class has always had the ability to sound persuasive while being fatuous, to dress gamekeepers' selfishness in pretty witty phrases. At this fin de siècle that mood is infecting the Americans, the upper class of the world. It needs to be turned back.

From *The Economist,* 1975.

QUESTIONS

(1) The word "recessional" signifies a stately, dignified withdrawal. In what sense is the author suggesting that America is engaged in such a withdrawal?

(2) The author lists five major points that move from the past to the future. Are they logically related or are they connected to each other in some other way?

(3) In his fifth point the author characterizes America's three major institutions. What are these three?

(4) What do you think is meant by the reference to "the probably failed experiment of suburbia"?

(5) What were the factors that checked the growth of the English economy in the latter half of the nineteenth century?

(6) How are these factors paralleled in recent developments in America?

(7) Who was de Tocqueville? What was the Fabian Society? Consult an encyclopedia in looking for the answers.

(8) What is the author suggesting in using the term "industrophobia"? Who are the industrophobes?

ANDROGYNY

ANDREW KOPKIND

You see them in shopping malls and Manhattan boutiques, in locker rooms and ladies' lounges, in school rooms, factories, kitchens, bedrooms, on television and in the movies. They wear pants suits and leisure suits, jeans and caftans, blow-dry haircuts, herbal perfumes; they are rock singers who twirl their hips, coeds who dig the Alaskan pipeline, a football tackle who crochets, a Brownie in the Little League, a President-elect who broadcasts love and compassion and weeps at the news of his election. They practice the many ways of androgyny, but they rarely recognize its profound novelty. They are—we are—skirting the edge of a revolution in sexual consciousness so radical that it could make the disruptions of the last decade seem like tantrums in a sandbox.

Androgyny—literally, man-woman—is as old as prehistoric myth and as new as next fall's fashions. It is as banal as unisex hairdos and as basic as human equality, as pop as David Bowie and as cultivated as Virginia Woolf. It stretches from Bloomsbury to Bloomingdale's. Its expressions are the many mixtures of manners, styles and values assigned by custom—or law—to only one or the other sex: dominance, breadwinning, decisiveness to males; dependence, child rearing, tenderness to females. Convention calls it a sin, or a joke, to reassign those

roles; both comedy and religion contain plenty of cautionary
tales on the subject. But androgyny implies not a mere exchange or reversal of the roles, but liberation from them, the
removal of the stereotypes of sex, an escape from the jailhouse
of gender.

"Behavior should have no gender," Stanford psychologist
Sandra Bem insists. What people do for a living, what they
wear, how they express themselves or how they confront the
everyday world has nothing to do with their sex types. That,
at least, is the androgynous ideal. If true androgynes evolve
from this heavily stereotyped society, they will be tender and
dominant, dependent and decisive, ambitious and nurturing
according to their human temperament, not their gender.

But for most people, the reality of manners and morals in
our sex-polarized civilization is so far from that ideal plane
that it is hard to see how it will be reached, what is pushing us
there—and why it should be an ideal in the first place.

Simply to sense the androgynous current that runs beneath
the surface of ordinary events is difficult enough. The heads
that bob up seem only tenuously connected: Mick Jagger,
Patti Smith, Twyla Tharp, Lauren Hutton, Cary Grant; tuxedoed women in *Vogue;* families that share a hair dryer in
TV commercials; middle-aged couples in matching acrylic
leisure/pants suits; father minding the kids while mothers go
to the office. They all partake of an androgynous sensibility
that was almost unknown a generation ago. Some people *look*
androgynous: they incorporate masculine and feminine body
characteristics and mannerisms in a hybrid whole. Others *behave* androgynously: they work, play or act in ways not completely "appropriate" to their gender. And still others *feel* androgynous: their emotions do not correspond to the list of
acceptable passions assigned to their sex.

There is no uniform scale yet in use that measures the
development of an androgynous personality (although Sandra
Bem is working on the problem: she believes healthy sexual
adjustment should be plotted against androgynous perfection, not masculine/feminine polarity). Nor is there a way to
chart the movement toward androgyny in the society at large.
But almost everyone has impressions that something peculiar
is happening to sex roles. By and large, role changing is still
a joke or a sin. But one morning, not too far in the future, the

critical mass of Americans may wake up and realize that androgyny is on its way—and all hell will break loose.

The trend began decades ago, but between the death of Victoria and the dawn of Aquarius androgyny was confined to
hothouse environments of intellectuals, actors, musicians and
other freaks. It hardly moved out of Bloomsbury, Greenwich
Village or the Hollywood Hills.

Then the marshaled forces of the sexual revolution in the
late 1960s propelled androgyny out of its bohemian closets
and into Middle American family rooms. The bottom line of
feminism and gay liberation has been the obliteration of socially defined roles. Women no longer have to look, act or feel
the way men's fantasies dictate. Homosexuals can be free of
the emotional straitjackets tailored by heterosexual demands.
In back of those battlelines, others removed from the struggles
have the opportunity—and the impetus—to summon up those
parts of themselves that were always restrained by propriety.

In the beginning the muse of androgyny created denim, un-
styled and impersonal, then washed, crushed, crimped and
flared—but preeminently the unisex texture. Soon men and
women were sharing work boots, hiking boots, Frye boots,
clogs, Adidas sneakers, Earth Shoes; jogging suits, snowmo-
bile suits, jumpsuits, silk shirts, beads and bracelets, pendants
and necklaces, turquoise rings, perfumes.

"Men's scents used to be a joke," Annette Green of New
York's Fragrance Foundation reports. "Hai Karate advertised
with grunts. And then Aramis came along and it took the
male perfume market seriously." And no wonder. American
men last year spent $208 million on cologne, an increase of
18 percent over the previous year. According to *Beauty Fashion* magazine, "the sound barrier of masculinity has been
smashed and the blue-collar worker does not consider it 'fag-
gish' to use the heavier colognes."

The androgynous sensibility invaded high fashion: Gern-
reich and Courreges added a dimension of spacey, sexy masculinity to feminine frills. Cardin began tailoring men's
clothes to emphasize sleek figures and forms. Men and women
could now wear their new suits with the same style of turtleneck sweater—and a piece of jewelry if they chose. The Marl-
boro dude became the Winston androgyne, showing off his

gold good-luck charm hanging deep in his cleavage, his blow-dry hair immobile in strong wind or calm.

The imported flotsam and jetsam of the Third World made its way from hippie head shops and college-town bazaars to fashionable unisex boutiques. Most of it was well-suited for androgynous wear: who knew whether maharajas or maharanis wore a particular style of shirt or piece of jewelry; who cared whether a camel driver or his wife fancied sheepskin jackets. At home any sex could play the import game.

Better than the Third World as a spring of unisex styles was Outer Space. If sex-typed fashions could be altered on the road from Morocco, they were ready-to-wear from Krypton. Androgyny is a prevailing theme in futurist and other-worldly literature: men and women in sci-fi movies set centuries ahead in time are often identically clothed, ornamented—and conveniently bald, whether because of evolution or advanced barbering. Space is the great sex leveler. Technology and convenience, at least, demand that Soviet male and female cosmonauts wear unisex clothing, perform the same tasks and treat each other as equals. It might somehow be awkward for a cosmonaut man to hold the space hatch open for a cosmonaut woman on their way down the stairs to a new planet.

Space and science fiction allow a different kind of escape from mundane sex roles. Two of the most androgynous rock stars—David Bowie and Elton John—have futurist personae: Bowie has been, on different occasions, Ziggy Stardust (a man from Mars) and the Man Who Fell to Earth. John plays as Captain Fantastic and sings in "Rocket Man," one of his early hits, "I'm not the man they think I am at home/Oh! no, no, no/I'm a rocket man." And the most twisted androgynous fantasy of all is Alice Cooper, who transcends sex roles altogether with the force of corruption and mockery.

The politics of pure androgyny has always had significant historical support, while under social attack. Philosophers and psychologists have maintained that each human has "masculine" and "feminine" characteristics, but society channels individuals into that category in which behavior matches sexual appearance. The other half—the unused complement of traits—is then lost, forgotten or repressed, often with dire results for the person's psyche or soul.

Aristophanes, Plato's character in *The Symposium,* formulated the famous allegory of three original sexes—male, female and hermaphrodite—split into halves by Zeus; each half has spent the succeeding aeons searching for its mate to regain completion (as homosexual man, lesbian female and heterosexual). Hinduism, Buddhism and Zoroastrianism all contain visions of Creation that postulate androgynous beings cleaved into single, incomplete sexes. Freud and Jung saw evidence of continuing conflict between masculine and feminine instincts, or unconscious memories in the individual. Contemporary psychotherapists often encourage patients to awaken their submerged "other" selves to achieve healthy wholeness. In therapy, if not in life, men are supposed to cry and solicit affection, women are helped to express anger and assert their independence. D. H. Lawrence—by turns an egregious male chauvinist and prophet of androgyny—saw in "The Rainbow" the evolution of a feminine principle that would renew the world spoiled by men. Proust, Artaud, Cocteau, Apollinaire—there is a hidden literary history of androgyny that only now can be understood in a social context.

But the doctors—of the church, of philosophy, of medicine and literature—have not always been helpful. They customarily confuse androgynous behavior with sexual preference or with gender identity. Their confusion has become common fallacy, so that many people mistake androgyny for bisexuality or homosexuality or neuter sexuality—or with hermaphroditism or transsexuality. It is none of the above. Androgyny is the principle that *unties* gender and sexual orientation from human activity. Androgynous people can be male or female, heterosexual or homosexual. They can be as sexually hot as Jagger or Dietrich or as cool as Bowie or Audrey Hepburn. They move toward an existence in which those aspects of sexuality do not confine their behavior.

As for sexual preference, Sandra Bem argues that it is utterly irrelevant "to anything other than the individual's own love or pleasure," and should be ignored as a social fact, no more or less interesting than the color of one's eyes or the length of fingernails. Roles of emotion or behavior based on sex, she continues, are not only absurd but destructive of human health and happiness; to be poured into a masculine or feminine mold makes both men and women unable to cope with the complexities of life.

In a series of devilishly clever experiments, in which subjects chose simple tasks or performed certain actions, Bem saw that the most highly "polarized" men and women neither enjoyed themselves nor performed effectively. In one test, in which subjects were supposed to interact with a tiny kitten, the "super-feminine" women could not deal with the nurturing task, while the more androgynous women handled the situation best. Bem and her colleagues have a long way to go to flesh out their pioneering studies. But they seem to have discovered that traditional sex roles constrict both men and women and impair their power to fulfill themselves in work and play.

But if orientation and roles are irrelevant and absurd, gender clearly is not. "Even if people were all to become psychologically androgynous, the world would continue to consist of two sexes, male and female would continue to be one of the first and most basic dichotomies that young children would learn and no one would grow up ignorant of or even indifferent to his or her gender," Bem writes. The point is that even gender has limited relevance: it does not demand inevitable roles. Women can be comfortable with their female bodies, but they do not have to bear or raise children—unless they want to. Men can be secure in their masculine physiques, but they do not have to chase girls, play basketball, father families or join the career rat race—unless it pleases them to do so. Such decisions can be left to individual personality and inclination.

Finally, it does not really matter whether traits of temperament are inherited or acquired, or even if they are in some ways attached to gender. Perhaps there are evolved "feminine" or "masculine" qualities—or perhaps they are arbitrarily assigned, like "masculine" and "feminine" rhymes, or "male" and "female" plugs and sockets. Not to worry: one follows or ignores the logic of one's instincts or wishes—not what social convention determines them to require. "Androgyny," Columbia Professor Carolyn Heilbrun writes, "seeks to liberate the individual from the confines of the appropriate."

Definitions are necessary and distinctions are required precisely because androgyny is so ill-considered in our culture. We cannot describe it in our "dead language," as Adrienne

Rich says scornfully, because our concepts and the words that signify them are tied to sex-role stereotypes. An aboriginal Eskimo who never left the North Pole could describe a world without snow only in terms of snow. We sexual aborigines can describe a world without sex roles only in terms of sex roles.

Alexandra Kaplan and Joan Bean, whose compilation of recent research papers on androgyny (*Beyond Sex-Role Stereotypes*) marks the beginning of a new approach to sexual psychology, contend that androgynous people have always existed, but until now they have been "invisible" to social scientists—and almost everyone else except the odd poet or the chroniclers of the bizarre. So there is no readily available vocabulary to describe the "hybrid" androgynous qualities that are being born: the trait between dominance and dependence, synthesizing tender and competitive, or combining assertive and nurturing.

If a man steps out of his assigned roles he is denigrated as a "sissy." If a woman oversteps hers, she is chastised as "mannish." More than most men, who have the power to set the language as well as the rules of social games, women and homosexuals have always known the perils of exceeding propriety. Even after a decade of women's liberation, females who dress, behave or work in previously "masculine" territory are conspicuous, isolated and subtly or blatantly condemned (often with patronizing praise). In the same way, gay men who inhabit the "feminine" category of man-loving are pushed into grotesque expressions of all the other qualities in that sex role: they are called "queens" and they act out that assigned part with mincing manners, campy styles and drag. If society says that a woman in a "man's job" is mannish, she will act that way; if it says gays are "sissies," they will ultimately act out their own parodies.

Not only homosexuals are deformed by such typecasting. Men of whatever sexual orientation who exhibit tenderness or shyness, or who easily express their feelings, are usually treated with contempt or condescension. One of the saddest examples of the genre was Adlai Stevenson, whose sensitive, slightly vulnerable wit was widely deprecated in Washington as evidence of his lack of guts, vigor, clout—in short, "balls." Lyndon Johnson despised him for it: "Why, he has to sit down to pee," Johnson once said of Stevenson. So much for the popularity of androgynous qualities.

Senator Muskie's well-known outburst of emotion in New Hampshire during his 1972 presidential primary campaign probably cost him the Democratic nomination. And this year, Jimmy Carter's lack of "decisiveness," his rhetoric of "compassion" and his soft-spoken manners surely diminished his popularity in those constituencies least responsive to those slightly androgynous qualities. Not for nothing did Carter slip in the polls as his personality became more familiar. Americans expect their presidents to be high up on the index of masculinity (self-reliant, defends own beliefs, independent, assertive, strong personality, competitive, individualistic, etc.) and nowhere near the items on the femininity list (yielding, shy, gullible, soft-spoken, compassionate, childlike, eager to soothe hurt feelings, etc.).

Early in the primaries a particularly astute though unliberated aunt of a friend of mine saw Carter on television and decided some "presidential" dimension of masculinity was missing. *"Faigele!"* she pronounced in her Bronx Yiddish idiom— "Fairy!"—and walked away from the TV. Her idiom had no other word for what she saw.

Carter is hardly a sexual ideologue's vision of an androgyne, nor did Muskie or Stevenson come close to that idea. Beneath their thinnish skins beat macho hearts. But it's obvious that, more than many political leaders, they moved slightly centerward from the polar masculine stereotype. Kennedy spoke of vigor and strength, Carter conveyed compassion and love. No matter how real or disingenuous either candidate's rhetoric may have been, the identity they projected was strikingly different. One writer on sexual topics recently mused that Carter's victory was an important sign of a changing national consciousness, and that perhaps an androgyne could someday be president of the United States.

The President is presumably no *faigele,* despite Aunt Frieda's suspicions, nor are most of the men who are beginning to acquire androgynous manners. But a sex-stereotyped society can imagine no other category for androgynous men except a sexual one. Similarly, most of the women who wear "man's style" clothes, sport unisex tastes and invade masculine precincts of work or study are not lesbians. Yet custom gives androgynous women pejorative labels and locks them in a sexual role. Even an acquisition of high fashion does not always help: the classiest models are called "Vogue dykes," an epithet that manages to combine the joke and the sin of androgyny. The most glaring irony of all is that in a more androgynous world it would not be necessary, or even intelligent, to make any distinctions or disclaimers of sexual orientation in relation to behavior.

But in the sex-typed world there is clearly a connection between homosexual and feminist *culture* and androgynous *styles.* Gays in large measure make up the androgynous vanguard; feminists are both theoreticians and practitioners of androgyny. Sexual outcasts (it makes no difference whether self or society does the casting) are able to invent new roles because they are not allowed to maintain the old ones. Self-reliant, assertive women have to develop their own feminist culture: the dominant society will not let them back into the world of wallflowers and housewives on their own terms. Gay men who have been consigned to the "sissy" world of emotional self-consciousness cannot travel back to the land of passionless masculinity and cold rationality. But their new makeshift culture contains the available models for later androgynous styles.

The preeminent example of an androgynous community in the early years of the century, way before the recent liberation movements were born, was the Bloomsbury set, the informal but internally cohesive group of English writers, critics, artists and floating intellectuals who hung on in a slightly unfashionable section of London during and after the First World War. At its center was Virginia Woolf, her husband Leonard, sister Vanessa Bell and brother-in-law Clive Bell, the biographer Lytton Strachey, the economist John Maynard Keynes and the critic Roger Fry. On the periphery, but very much revered, was the novelist E. M. Forster.

The artistic and intellectual output of Bloomsbury was prodigious. But, most of all, it was a unique model of a civilized community based on equality. The members recognized the basis of their civilization: "The equality of the sexes, the outer manifestation of the equality of the masculine and feminine impulses, are essential to civilization," Carolyn Heilbrun writes of Bloomsbury in her trenchant study *Toward a Recognition of Androgyny*. Virginia Woolf was convinced that she and her world were approaching androgyny, although she feared that the ideal would explode as it neared reality; perfection and completion could not exist in imperfect, fragmented surroundings. She saw a signal of androgyny in a single, silent falling leaf, "pointing to a force in things which one has overlooked."

Many of the Bloomsbury setters were homosexual or bisexual, and the byways of "inappropriate" sexuality were always very much in their hearts and minds. There were famous romantic triangles and quadrangles, scandalous ruptures of ceremony, hilarious practical jokes. Lytton Strachey appeared before the tribunal trying him for conscientious objection to military service wearing earrings, shoulder-length hair, an outlandish robe, and carrying an air pillow, which he blew up before the judges. He said it was necessary for his hemorrhoids. When asked what action he would take if a German soldier attempted to rape his sister, he replied impishly, "I should try to interpose my body." The Bloomsbury biographer, David Gadd, calls Strachey's response "a memorable reply whose monstrous ambiguity was fully appreciated by Lytton's three sisters," who were in the courtroom. But despite the famous japes, a premium was placed on the conquest of the vices of the old social order: jealousy, competitiveness, vindictiveness. Because of the sexual orientation of many in the group, its self-proclaimed androgyny has always been confused with the preferences of the members. But the truth of the situation was the other way around: the members' extraordinary sexual orientation gave them both perspective and motivation to explore innovative, androgynous relationships.

Bloomsbury gives historic context and some intellectual nuances to the new androgyny, but not much more. When you look for androgyny today you are apt to find it in much less transcendantal places. Former Los Angeles Ram Rosey Greer crochets his own pretty things and sings a pop song, "It's All Right to Cry," but he owes little of his sensibility to Lytton Strachey. It is seen in fleeting glimpses: Minnesota Viking Fran Tarkenton sending a touchdown pass to teammate Sammy White, and the two of them celebrating the event by holding hands as they walk back down the field—not in the old back-slapping jock gesture but in a manner that two schoolgirls would have used.

On the screen it is the androgynous Fred Astaire in *That's Entertainment, II,* soft-shoeing alongside the heavily masculine Gene Kelly—still charming and still macho after all these years. Or Garbo, Dietrich or Katherine Hepburn, in almost any of their old roles—but especially opposite leading men with an androgynous bent: Grant, for example, not Gable.

In fact, there's so much androgynous manhood around that some new Hollywood stars are making a buck on the backlash. Sylvester Stallone, writer and hero of *Rocky,* told *The New York Times'* Judy Klemesrud, "I don't think that even Women's Lib wants all men to become limp-wristed librarians. I don't know what's happening to men these days. There's a trend toward a sleek, subdued sophistication and a lack of participation in sports. In discos, men and women look almost alike, and if you were a little bleary-eyed, you'd get them mixed up. I think it's wrong. . . . There doesn't seem to be enough real men to go around."

Bloomsbury had indicated that in its origins androgyny would flower in the upper registers of social class and intellect, and that it would be carried along on a politically progressive, countercultural movement. Those connections still hold. Androgyny in the seventies has been limited to the educated middle class and the radical counterculture. You look for androgynous styles in *Vogue* and Bloomingdale's, not *McCall's* and Penney's. Economic status and social registry somehow give people the security to discard the anchors of sex roles.

Androgyny in the twentieth century may have begun in England, but it is hardly surprising that it is blooming in America. There are both particular and general forces contributing to its forward motion. The economic necessity for women to work—and its social acceptance—has made the old roles of housewifery, and the emotions that go with them, absurd and often dysfunctional. Simply to break through conventional feminine roles is to move towards an androgynous synthesis.

But beyond that, the constellation of brand-new needs, demands and desires in "postindustrial" America has brought across-the-board changes in consciousness. For instance, the

transformation of the nature of work from farm and factory
to "services" has propelled many young men out of traditional
"masculine" work roles and the emotional haberdashery
suited to those jobs. Their new roles often let them share family roles formerly consigned to women. The men do not automatically become androgynous, but they are not so securely
tied to the masculine pole any more.

Along the leading edge of change, the vectors point toward
equality—in the political economy as well as the political culture. If the coming issue in government is redistribution of
wealth, the issue in human relationships is the redistribution
of power. It is equality not for its own sake, not because it is
self-evident or endowed by the Creator, but because the next
stages of social evolution cannot function well without it. The
sage political economist Robert Heilbroner wrote recently
that the gross inequalities of American capitalism will destroy
it. In the same way, gross inequalities in communities and
families will destroy them. Alexandra Kaplan and Joan Bean
see androgyny growing as the structure of the acquisitive society weakens. "A society that supports androgyny would probably not be based on capitalistic consumerism, which is a
direct outgrowth of the competitive, achievement-oriented
values of the male model. Flexibility in sex-role norms seems
to be more related to a social-welfare economy," they say.

Gloria Steinem noted recently that hard and fast distinctions between the sexes always accompany stages of imperial
expansion in a society—those times when men think it necessary to keep women semislaves, in order to bear and rear offspring for the expanding nation. As we near a no-growth,
resource-short, shrinking political economy in America, she
continues, the polarized patriarchy will begin to break up.

In time, evolutionary changes may follow the economic
ones. If women are less necessary as sexual objects and men as
sexual subjects, their physical characteristics could be transformed. Gone would be the classic Rubenesque female, two-
thirds breasts and hips; gone too the stallionoid male, the
walking phallic symbol. There need be no dimunition of
sexual activity or pleasure. In fact, psychologists find that
sexual fulfillment is increased as partners move toward an androgynous center. One writer told me, "Men and women who
keep to the myth of their sex type stay separated even when

they're together. They are afraid of each other, always aware of the differences. They may extol those differences, but the important ones aren't in their sex attributes but in their humanity. Androgyny doesn't mean a race of sexless androids, but a wider variety of sexual possibilities than exists now."

The convulsions that will accompany the collapse of the old sexual culture will make most recent political events seem puny by comparison. In fact, they may have already begun. A great deal of nonsense will be loosed upon the world, as freed men and women scramble for new standards of behavior and anchors of being. People will mistake transient excesses for final accountings, bemoan the leveling of differences, extol the former virtues. Those with vested interests in polarized roles will predict the direst consequences of androgyny. They will not only be men. Or women. Renee Richards, the transsexual, sees only calamity arising as the familiar signposts fall.

"If someone can be sex-tied," she sighs, "there's so much less anxiety. I mean, I'd rather have pink rooms for girls and blue for boys. How can you tell who's who in a yellow room?"

From *New Times Magazine*, 1977.

QUESTIONS

(1) What is the "jailhouse of gender" referred to in the second paragraph of the essay?

(2) How do clothing fashions exhibit the "androgynous sensibility"?

(3) What is the relation of the popularity of science fiction to androgyny?

(4) How does the author distinguish the androgynous person from the usual categories of people as homosexual, heterosexual or bisexual?

(5) What are the qualities of President Carter that the author identifies as androgynous?

PLAYING GOD WITH DNA

ARTHUR LUBOW

It would be so much simpler if they would just say there's no risk. No danger of infection, no way a man-made microbe can crawl out of a lab and start an epidemic, no chance that manufacturing new organisms will derail the locomotive of evolution. So you ask hopefully: "Is there any risk?" And instead of an answer, you get an analogy.

"There is a possibility that a band of monkeys could type out the Preamble to the Constitution," says a Harvard Medical School professor. "But it is such a small probability that we don't even have numbers to express it." The monkey analogy is a good one. It appeals not to your knowledge of the simian mentality, but to your common sense. Who knows? Maybe if you put a dozen monkeys in Independence Hall, they would feel inspired. But you give the professor the benefit of the doubt; and he hopes you will be equally generous about his work with recombinant DNA. When he splices together two cells to create a new living organism, he is confident that nothing sinister will happen. Since you're watching over his shoulder, he wants you to be confident too.

An amateur celebrity, the researcher is nervous: he blinks like a bat in the light. He is accustomed to obscurity. Thousands of whitecoated scientists work quietly in their laboratories, writing articles with polysyllabic titles for arcane journals—and most of us could not care less. "I am not much interested," said a former secretary of defense, "in why potatoes turn brown when they are fried." But every once in a while a paper marked with chicken scratchings explodes with the power of a thousand suns. We look at the mushroom cloud over Hiroshima, and suddenly we want to know everything. A scientific question has become a political problem, and the man with a pencil or test tube is suddenly a public personage. The recondite paths of nuclear physics led to the perilous crossings of atomic power. And now molecular biology, the

most exciting frontier of modern science, has brought us to a
similarly troubling vista.

For the first time, the scientific establishment has announced that there are some nonhuman experiments that
should be prohibited. For the first time, a community—Cambridge, Massachusetts, the home of Harvard and MIT—has
declared that it will not permit certain scientific work to proceed within its borders. "People want to know what the hell
they're doing in these laboratories," says the mayor of Cambridge. "And since they're spending United States tax dollars,
we have a right to know." A scientist warns in *The New York
Times Magazine* that recombinant DNA work may "endanger
the future of mankind." Scientists have formed two camps,
each savaging the other's intelligence and integrity.

The controversy is flaring on the front lines of science:
molecular biology. Since the 1950s, molecular biologists have
scooped up the lion's share of Nobel prizes in medicine and
physiology. Buckets of federal money have irrigated the field.
Compared to its sisters, chemistry and physics, biology is still
an infant, but in the last two decades it has grown faster than
the hyperpituitary boy in a Wonder Bread commercial. Scientists now have a fair understanding of the genetic process in
primitive creatures such as bacteria, but they have never had
a way to examine the setup in animals similar to man. They
now have a way. It is called recombinant DNA.

"It is a revolution," says James Watson, who won a Nobel
prize for his work on the structure of DNA. "It is *the* way to
go. I would say that everyone who is seriously interested in
the detailed structure of the gene is now using this technology." Just as splitting the atom accelerated the progress of
physics, so recombinant DNA can speed the growth of modern
biology. Researchers say their work may even disclose a cure
for cancer. But theoretical risks accompany potential benefits,
and the threat of recombinant DNA has been compared to the
danger of nuclear radiation. Not since the congressional investigations of atomic energy in the fifties has science sparked
such a heated political discussion. Scientists all over the world
are watching the Cambridge saga. They know that the threat
extends beyond Harvard and MIT. There is a domino effect.
Already the United States Senate, the New York State Attorney General and the cities of San Diego, Princeton, New

Haven and Bloomington, Indiana, are pondering the public
health dangers.

Not only molecular biologists are worried. The mayor of
Cambridge is turning his sights on other laboratories. The
NIH (National Institutes of Health), which drafted guidelines
for work with recombinant DNA, is considering similar restrictions on all experimenters with animal cells. A chink in
the form of a question mark has cracked the scientific mega-
structure. There hasn't been such a fateful biological question
since the Sphinx posed the riddle on the road to Thebes. But
among all these scientists there is no Oedipus, and the question lingers unanswered in the air.

Is there any risk?

For the crucial questions about recombinant DNA, we have
very few answers. The scientific technique, though, is disarm-
ingly simple to understand. The genetic code for every form
of life is contained in a giant molecule called DNA. The
DNA molecule or a close relative is found in all cells, from
amoebas to zebras. Of course every cell is full of molecules, but
DNA is the king of the roost. It decides which proteins a cell
will synthesize. By manufacturing the proper proteins, a cell
can perform its individual function—producing insulin, trans-
mitting nerve impulses, growing a blond hair. It is the DNA
that decides whether a cell will be part of a man or a mushroom.

In molecular terms, sexual reproduction is merely a min-
gling of DNA. Each parent contributes half a DNA set to
form a new cell. Obviously, the new cell is a recombination of
the parents' DNA; but the word "recombinant" is reserved for
something far less common—the recombination of DNA from
different species.

The mouse who falls in love with an elephant is a likely
subject for a droll fable. Everyone knows that animals from
different species can't mate. In some cases, closely related
species are able to have a go at it, but often the offspring are
sterile: for every nectarine, there is a mule. But in biological
laboratories, modern Dr. Frankensteins have found a way to
create brand-new forms of life. Perhaps it's a sign of the times
that the new creatures are not ten-foot monsters with spokes
through their necks, but colorless cells invisible to the naked

eye. The DNA of mice and elephants can now be joined—inside bacteria.

The DNA molecule in bacteria usually takes the form of a chromosome ring. However, many types of bacteria have snippets of DNA left over, which appear as smaller rings in the cell. These rings are called plasmids. When bacteria reproduce asexually, both the chromosome and the plasmids duplicate themselves, the cell divides, and *voilà!* Two cells. With some bacteria, this happens every 20 minutes.

A modest bit of merchandise, the plasmid, but it boasts two very useful features. It can often move from one cell into another. And it can be split in specific places by substances called restriction enzymes. For the recombinant DNA maestro, these properties make it worth considerably more than its weight in gold.

Using restriction enzymes as chemical cutters, a scientist can split the plasmid DNA and the DNA of some other organism—say, a mouse. He can then take a piece of the mouse DNA and insert it into the plasmid, seal the plasmid up with other enzymes, and put it back into the bacterium. When the bacterium divides, so does the plasmid, including the mouse DNA portion. In a day, the scientist can have millions of pieces of the mouse DNA he wants to examine.

But every silver lining has its cloud. Bacteria are wonderful reproduction machines, making limitless quantities of identical mouse, cat, fruit fly or other kinds of DNA to order. They are so useful because, even after you perform recombinant surgery on them, they are still free-living organisms. As it happens, the particular bacteria that scientists use for this transaction, *E. coli,* live quite happily in a wide range of locales, including the place they're named for, the human colon or bowel. If swallowed accidentally, they might take up residence in the human body. And so they pose—a risk.

In one dire vision, conjured up by critics of recombinant DNA research, some *E. coli* bacteria carrying foreign genes escape from the laboratory and perform untold mischief in the human body. To honor Michael Crichton, in whose novel, *The Andromeda Strain,* bacteria from the upper atmosphere wreak bloodcurdling havoc on earth, we shall call this the Andromeda-strain scenario. In another more mystical vision, the introduction of new forms of life upsets the master plan of evolution. Of special concern is the mongrelization of higher life forms with primitive organisms like bacteria. We shall call this the evolutionary-disaster scenario.

Our heads filled with nightmares, we run to the scientists for some answers. To our chagrin, we discover a Catch-22: the riddles posed by recombinant DNA technology can be solved only by experimenting with the technology. There are too many unknowns to give a flat answer. On the Andromeda-strain scenario, Charles Thomas of Harvard Medical School is skeptical: "The idea that one could paste together two segments of DNA so that that act would simultaneously confer a selective advantage on that organism and have it be dangerous is something I can't buy." Across the river at Harvard College, Mark Ptashne offers an extended metaphor: "If you tell somebody from Mars you're going to put a Ford motor on a lawn mower, he asks, 'Can it be dangerous?' You say it may be. He says, 'It may destroy the world.' You say that is very unlikely, but you can't prove it won't. It's not scientific talk. It's science-fiction talk. Every time you make a mutant of *E. coli,* you can't be sure what will happen, but all attempts to make the strain virulent have failed."

Talk about evolutionary disaster is even less concrete. "I don't think we are doing something which has never happened before," says James Watson. "But it's impossible to say. It's not a meaningful question." Unlike Watson, David Hogness of Stanford, a leading researcher in the field, does not dismiss the question. He argues that recombinations *are* part of evolution. He challenges the notion that, in nature, genetic material does not leapfrog across species barriers. He thinks there are natural mechanisms by which animal DNA can enter a bacterial chromosome: "People started in this field with the assumption that we were doing something new that had never been known in the world, but I no longer think that is true." Another pioneer in recombinant DNA work, Paul Berg of Stanford, is more forthright: "There isn't a single person that I know of who can document the existence of a barrier."

And so, in the absence of facts, the debate turns to personalities, to my word against yours, to imaginative scenarios. The debating platform moves from the musty pages of medical journals to the strobe-lit hearing rooms of politicians. And in the commotion, in the clouds of smoke above hypothetical fires, an uncrackable nut of a question remains unanswered.

Is there any risk?

Around Harvard Square, Cambridge Mayor Alfred E. Vellucci is known as the man who wanted to convert Harvard Yard into a parking lot. Just the thought of an ax touching one of those majestic elms is enough to choke the throat of any crimson-blooded alumnus. Few men besides the fun-loving mayor recall the birth of this legend. "In 1957, student cars were everywhere, and the people of Cambridge had no place to park their cars," Vellucci recounts in his thick Boston accent. "I wrote to Harvard and MIT and got no answer. I wrote again. No answer. So I proposed to the city council that we cut down the trees in Harvard Yard, pave it and turn it into a parking lot. You should have seen how fast they moved! They got their cars off the street immediately."

After the parking affair, Harvard appointed a special representative for community relations, but the relations are still not so good. "Oh, you know," Vellucci says, "like a couple of lovers—off again, on again." The mayor and Harvard are fighting these days over the construction of a medium-containment laboratory to be used, among other purposes, for work with recombinant DNA. The building would be nearly completed had Vellucci not read a June article in the Boston *Phoenix,* a local weekly. In the article, entitled "Biohazards at Harvard," professor of biology Ruth Hubbard was quoted as saying that the risks of recombinant DNA are "worse than radiation danger."

Vellucci read the article on the Monday morning it appeared. While he was discussing it with his aides, a secretary announced that George Wald and Ruth Hubbard were outside. "They came in and they talked to me about the thing and it was dangerous," Vellucci recalls. "So I said to them, 'If I call a special meeting of the city council to discuss this matter, will you come?' And they said, 'Yes.'"

Dr. Wald remembers it a little differently. A white-haired man with a theatrical personal style (as someone remarked, "When you talk to George, you always imagine there are 5,000 people standing behind you"), Wald won a Novel prize in 1967 for his work on the visual pigments of the eye. More recently he has been celebrated for his speeches on behalf of the antiwar movement and other left-liberal causes. He and his wife, Ruth Hubbard, are both biology professors at Harvard. Wald says that even before their talk Vellucci had decided to call a meeting. But the Walds were instrumental. They gave the mayor what he needed—"people with credentials." Vellucci explains: "If I'm gonna take a stand against this goddamn thing, I need some people on *my* side. And since they said they would come, I was fortified, I was ready for a meeting, and that is the reason why we then flung the challenge at Harvard and MIT to send *their* scientists over here because I knew *I* had scientists on *my* side!" He pounds the table for emphasis.

As it turned out, there were two meetings, because so many people wished to speak. The meetings were staged before over-flow crowds on hot summer nights, made even hotter by the glare of television lights. In addition to the Walds, Jon King, an associate professor of biology at MIT, appeared as a major spokesman against the work. On what Vellucci likes to call "the Harvard team" there were several Nobel laureates and other distinguished scientists. To open the first meeting, a contingent from the Cambridge public high school sang "This Land Is Your Land." Who's in charge here: citizens or scien-tists? The point was clear.

"It's about time the scientists began to throw all their god-damned shit right out on the table so that we can discuss it," Vellucci growls. In his office hang framed portraits of past mayors, palpable presences admonishing him to safeguard the health of Cambridge citizens. "Who the hell do the scientists think that *they* are that they can take federal tax dollars that are coming out of our tax returns and do research work that we then cannot come in and question?"

In his cranberry doubleknit jacket and black pants, with his yellow-striped blue shirt struggling to contain a beer belly, right down to his crooked teeth and overstuffed pockets, Al Vellucci is the incarnation of middle-American frustration at these *scientists,* these technocrats, these smartass Harvard egg-heads who think they've got the world by a string and wind up dropping it in a puddle of mud. And who winds up in the puddle? Not the eggheads. No, it's always Al Vellucci and the ordinary working people who are left alone to wipe them-selves off. "They say, y'know, it's all right to dip apples into red dye, to dip candy into red dye, and don't worry about it, it doesn't affect you at all. And then you have the United States Department of Drugs come out and tell you, no, don't eat any more apples dipped into red dye, y'see, don't eat any more candy that's been dipped into red dye. And everybody's saying, don't take the pill because we're gonna tell you why the pill is no good for ya—y'know, these are all *scientists* who did all this work." Al Vellucci isn't buying any of it.

After the second meeting last July, the Cambridge city council voted a three-month ban on all medium-containment recombiant DNA work. The council later extended the moratorium through mid-December, to provide time for a council-appointed study group to prepare a review and recommendations. The council is closely split on the issue, and no one is predicting its final verdict, but Vellucci has already decided how he will vote. "I have learned enough about recombinant DNA molecules in the past few weeks to take on all the Nobel prize winners in the city of Cambridge," he says. "Regardless of what the review board says, I'm opposed to this work. If they say they're against it, fine, they're against it. If they say 'We're in favor of this thing with safeguards,' it is my intention to call up Dr. Wald, Dr. Hubbard and Dr. King and invite them into this office and have them sit down and go over the whole review with me. I have an obligation to a whole lot of lay people in this city who do not understand this whole goddamn thing. And so I don't want to take a chance."

The controversy over recombinant DNA has a particular poignancy for Paul Berg, because he was the first person to raise the question of risk. Six years ago, in his Stanford laboratory, Berg discovered a way to construct synthetic tails for DNA molecules. By adding these "sticky ends," he planned to insert a given DNA fragment into *E. coli* bacteria. The DNA he wanted to examine, SV 40, has been carefully studied by geneticists because it is able to incorporate itself into the chromosomes of the host cell. It also causes cancer in mice. With his newfound technique, Berg hoped to clone segments of SV 40—to multiply it by using *E. coli* as the host. He never thought of a possible danger: by transforming a cancer virus, he might be manufacturing a mutant with maligant powers.

In the summer of 1971, one of Berg's graduate students was

attending a summer program at Cold Spring Harbor laboratory in New York, and she described Berg's experiment to an
audience of biologists. The reaction was one of shock. "Several people called me up and pleaded with me not to do it,"
Berg recalls. "I went to talk to a number of scientists, and they
all said not to do it—the unknowns were too great and the
risks too significant. I could never convince myself or anyone
else that I could reduce the risk to zero. So we turned that
experiment off."

Two years later, at a summer conference of biochemists held
in New Hampshire, Herbert Boyer of the University of San
Francisco described his experiments with plasmids and restriction enzymes. Because natural substances—restriction enzymes—created the "sticky ends" that Berg had laboriously
manufactured with synthetic tails, Boyer and others could
now easily concoct hybrid plasmids, recombining the DNA of
bacteria and other organisms. "It was obvious to everyone in
the room that now you could do these things, that you didn't
need anything fancy—all you needed were the restriction enzymes," says Berg. The conference authorized a letter, published in the journal *Science,* warning that since new organisms "with biological activity of unpredictable nature"
could be created, "prudence suggests the potential hazard be
seriously considered."

Because Berg had grappled with these issues two years
earlier, the National Academy of Sciences, to which the public
letter had been addressed, asked him to form a committee.
And so in the spring of 1974, a committee of a dozen leading
molecular biologists met at MIT and drafted a second public
letter. If there is anything in this world that reproduces faster
than bacteria it is committees, so, naturally enough, one of the
MIT committee's recommendations was the formation of a
committee by the director of the NIH to develop guidelines
for researchers of "potentially hazardous recombinant DNA
molecules." The scientists also called for an international conference to discuss the problem; the conference was held in
February 1975 at the Asilomar center in California. In anticipation of the conference, the MIT group asked researchers
to refrain voluntarily from two types of experiments: the introduction of toxin-formation or antibiotic-resistance genes
into bacteria that do not naturally contain such genes, and the

addition of tumor virus or other animal DNA into bacteria or viruses—since such hybrid organisms might "possibly increase the incidence of cancer or other diseases."

By the time of the Asilomar conference, some scientists were beginning to have second thoughts. They feared that dramatizing the risks had been a mistake. Joshua Lederberg, a Nobel laureate and one of the giants of molecular genetics, pointed out that the MIT letter implied that scientists could not be trusted to police themselves. James Watson had another worry. "The scientists were a bunch of jackasses for raising the question of danger when they could not quantitate it," he says now. "I became very worried about the whole thing because in setting regulations I couldn't decide whether it was more dangerous to put yeast DNA or drosophila DNA or human DNA into *E. coli,* and I couldn't distinguish the difference. I just found the whole Asilomar thing irrational."

What was created at Asilomar was a graded-risk system of regulation. Some work would be banned outright for now—roughly, the sort of experiments described in the Berg moratorium letter—and other experiments could be conducted only under specified conditions. The threat was that organisms posing unknown dangers could escape from the lab; the procedures thrashed out at Asilomar would confine experiments believed to be potentially hazardous to more carefully controlled laboratories. Two sorts of containment procedures would be used. The first, physical containment, assigned experiments to workplaces with increasing safety provisions, ascending from P1 to P4. A second system of biological containment required for certain experiments the use of deliberately weakened *E. coli* which, even if they escaped, would be unable to survive outside a pampered laboratory environment. With some modifications, these regulations were adopted by the NIH (and later by the National Science Foundation). Although it has no police powers, the NIH provides funds for most of this research and it therefore wields a formidable carrot.

That is how the matter rests today. The NIH guidelines are in use. Most scientists are reconciled to them; a smaller group think they are needlessly strict but grudgingly follow them. However, there is a third group of scientists unhappy with the regulations, and although relatively small in number, they speak in a loud voice. For they think the guidelines are irresponsibly lax, and if experiments proceed, the public health and even the future of the planet are threatened.

In drafting guidelines, the scientists at Asilomar and NIH worried mainly about the threat of an epidemic—the Andromeda-strain scenario. But even with the recommended precautions, some critics fear the experiments are habardous. Because no one understands the intricacies of cell genetics, no one can say with assurance that an apparently innocuous combination of genes will not produce a virulent strain of *E. coli.* The pathogens needn't be as flamboyant as the fictional Andromeda strain, which congealed the blood into paste. "What worries me," says Jon King of MIT, "are the organisms where you won't identify the symptoms. If you're making a really virulent agent, you'd catch it. We're talking about things that would affect you in very mild ways."

To pose a hazard once it escaped, an organism must do three things: survive outside the laboratory; beat out enough competitors in the already existing jungle of microorganisms to establish an ecological niche; and produce some dangerous effect, since the great majority of bacteria are harmless. Most scientists believe the odds against the accidental creation of such an organism are inexpressibly great, but Jon King is unconvinced. "Especially in a technological society that is filled with new chemicals, there is a very good chance that there are new niches that can be exploited," he says. "We do not understand why some microorganisms make you sick. These people are saying they can't possibly make a pathogenic organism, but they can't even tell the difference between existing pathogenic and nonpathogenic organisms. It's an argument you make because you want to refute the possibility of danger without exploring it."

Andromeda scenarists object vehemently to the use of *E. coli,* bacteria that live happily in our gut. "A few years of research would have led to an organism other than *E. coli,*" says Erwin Chargaff, a retired Columbia professor who worked on nucleic acid composition in the 1940s. "This is really incredible. It's beyond imagination. Because *coli* is a symbiont of all of us, it is part of us, more than any other organism.

Now the argument is we know more about *E. coli* than any other organism. But I think such clever people could learn in five or ten years enough about other organisms."

Experimenters with recombinant DNA stress that they are using a strain of *E. coli* that is not known to survive outside the laboratory. For research that seems especially hazardous, an even weaker variety of *E. coli* is required. "I recognize that *E. coli* represents a risk—we pointed it out in the first letter we wrote—but the insistence that we abandon this research until we find another organism is unrealistic," says Paul Berg. "We may never find another organism. We have an incredible background of information on *coli*. It would be necessary to find an organism that you can predict will be safe when you find it." James Darnell of Rockefeller University argues that because so much is known about it, the laboratory strain of *E. coli* "is not the most dangerous but perhaps the safest organism to use." "I would definitely feed recombinant DNA to my 16-year-old daughter if it were not considered idiosyncratic," says Charles Thomas of Harvard Medical School. "It goes without saying I'd drink it myself."

But disease is not the only concern. Even if no Andromeda-type germ is produced, Robert Sinsheimer fears, recombinant DNA work jeopardizes life on this planet. Sinsheimer, chairman of the Caltech biology department, is the leading spokesman for the prophets of evolutionary disaster, the second scenario. This Southern Californian, tan beneath his white tennis shirt, speaks with the fervor of a repented sinner, animated by the same passions that drove former Communists like Whittaker Chambers to lead the red-baiting crusades of the fifties. Only six years ago Sinsheimer was predicting that man could "rise above his nature to chart his destiny," and that in genetic engineering lay "the potential for worlds yet undreamt." He has had second thoughts.

Sinsheimer is now the most eminent opponent of the guidelines. He fears that even if no virulent recombinant is produced, merely the exchange of DNA among organisms that normally honor barriers as rigid as South African apartheid can have dire evolutionary consequences. In the evolution that Darwin described, new combinations of genes are constantly formed by reproduction within a species. Occasionally, a novel combination or a spontaneous mutation provides a natural advantage to an organism, and that organism is better equipped to survive. It lives longer, it reproduces more often and its genes have a greater likelihood of persisting. Over a time scale of aeons, more organisms with these genes survive, and the species gradually evolves in a particular direction.

Sinsheimer argues that an especially rigid barrier divides the genetic material of lower forms lacking a defined nucleus, such as bacteria, and higher forms such as animals and plants. This taboo is now being broken by man. "Genetic recombination among species has not been allowed in nature," he says. "I'm willing to concede it may happen occasionally, but there's no evidence for it and I have no idea of how to estimate the rate. You are changing in a short period of time the biological equilibrium that has been evolving over a very long period of time. The consequences are unpredictable. If these organisms do reproduce and find a suitable niche, there's no way we can get them back. We can't even find them. And how do we know what will evolve after they're out?"

To a scientist, the intuitiveness of Sinsheimer's argument makes it seem almost mystical. "I think Sinsheimer has allowed his imagination to crawl away with him," says Nobel laureate David Baltimore of MIT. Sinsheimer's argument evokes a passionate response for two reasons. First, he is an eminent scientist, and he can't be brushed off with talk of professional jealousy or pitiable ignorance. Second, he talks of unknowables and unquantifiables, so his opponents find themselves shadow-boxing with phantoms.

"One of the tragedies is that Bob Sinsheimer refuses to be specific and articulate his concerns," Paul Berg complains. "What is this barrier? What is the evidence that there is this barrier, and what would happen if it were breached? What he talks about is that it is unnatural. When they wanted to start immunizing people, that was also said to be unnatural. For one guy, no matter how eminent he is, to go up and say 'I fear,' and then to expect the whole world to stop—I don't care how eminent he is, it's not going to happen."

Still, Sinsheimer is undaunted. "The burden of proof belongs on the other side," he says. "I've thought about the problem of genetic engineering longer than most people and I'm not as sanguine as I would have been ten years ago." He favors phasing out the use of *E. coli* in recombinant DNA work "as fast as possible" and the confinement of all experiments "transferring DNA between species that do not normally exchange genetic material" to P4 (top security) facilities. He believes the NIH guidelines are too soft. "I don't think it's smart," he says. "I don't think it's sensible. We've got only one biosphere. The graded-risk concept doesn't make sense when you have only one thing to lose, as in the biosphere. I think the potential exists for some kind of biological catastrophe through the introduction of new kinds of organisms. You've got to be more careful. You can't just go blasting ahead when so much is unknown in an area of potential catastrophe."

Slow down. That's what the critics say, and they think they're being quite reasonable. "What kind of disaster could happen from going slow?" asks Jon King. An aide to Mayor Vellucci says he is puzzled: "I don't quite understand what the enormous urgency to plough ahead is based on." If the research poses a serious risk, why not proceed under the tightest P4 conditions, until the light of knowledge wipes away these shadows of doubt? Why the rush?

But asking scientists to slow down is like asking hawks to walk. It goes against their nature. "Chargaff's thing to slow down—this is a perfectly normal response for someone who hasn't *moved* for the past 30 years," says James Watson, his watery blue eyes gleaming, his hair wiring off his head as if electrically charged. Chargaff isn't the only loud-mouthed tortoise on Watson's list. "Ruth Wald hasn't had a good idea in ten years," Watson says. "She hates molecular biologists because she isn't one. . . . I'm sure [they] would like science to slow down. If it slowed down, [they] could be part of it."

In science, the slow of foot drop out of the race. Already European researchers working without guidelines have performed experiments that Americans are itching to try. "Essentially our work is crawling," moans Paul Berg. "This thing is slowed down now. I can't do the experiments I could do. We're not doing one-tenth of what could be done." David Hogness says if King and Sinsheimer had their way and assigned his research to P4 conditions, "I wouldn't do it. I wouldn't do experiments under Mars-shot conditions. It would be a serious question whether I would continue the research."

The most irritating thing about this controversy is it takes up so much time. Matthew Meselson of Harvard informs a reporter at 10 A.M. that this is his fifth call from the press that morning; as they speak, his secretary takes call number six. David Baltimore of MIT says, "At this point, 30 percent of my time is being taken up by talking on this issue." It is not just the hours subtracted, it is the diffusion of energy, the distraction from single-minded effort. To be a first-rank scientist, you must think science all the time. When you come home at night, you can't bring your test tubes with you, yet your mind lags behind in the laboratory. As James Watson puts it, "It's a world of total domination—you have to be manic."

From *New Times Magazine*, 1977.

QUESTIONS

(1) In your own words define DNA.

(2) To what, according to the author, does the word "recombinant" refer, in connection with DNA?

(3) What are the two features of the plasmid that make it so valuable in the recombinant process?

(4) The author divides the dangers of DNA research into two, "the Andromeda-strain scenario" and "the evolutionary-disaster scenario." Explain each of these.

(5) What system of regulation has been worked out in order to control the dangers of DNA research?

(6) What is the probability of accidental creation of new forms of life?

(7) What is the argument against DNA that invokes the "evolutionary disaster syndrome" as charted by Professor Robert Sinsheimer?

(8) Look at the last sentence of the essay. What possible double meaning might the author intend?

THE ULTIMATE ATHLETE

GEORGE LEONARD

Looking backward beyond "history" and forward beyond "the year 2000," we realize that this entire period actually constitutes only one brief segment of the larger human journey. In my book *The Transformation*, I outlined the earlier transformations (from primitive hunting and gathering band to tribal village, from tribal village to civilized state) that led to the current period, detailed the characteristics of the Epoch of Civilization, and argued that a major Transformation into something quite different was already under way. Since the publication of that book, in 1972, it has become increasingly apparent that the current major mode of social organization no longer works. Time-honored principles of economics, agriculture, education, and social control are revealed in the light of present realities as faulty. Individual alienation increases at an alarming rate. The entire social structure, with all its mighty physical works, now appears to us as somehow fragile and vulnerable.

Clearly, some great change is under way. We might have seen it earlier had we not been seduced by technological futurism. "The year 2000," which turns out to have been merely a strategy for justifying "the same, only more so," has kept us from seeing the present, where a transformation is already occurring. We should have known it all along. Existence is not fixed. Even the mightiest social organism eventually evolves into something else. This evolution means the death of old forms, but it does not necessarily mean the catastrophic death of individual human beings. Still, the odds on a relatively peaceful transformation seem rather long at this moment. We face the possibility of physical catastrophe along with the breakdown of old forms in the absence of new. We face the possibility of variations on the theme of a police state as social leaders react to the rise of anarchic tendencies. But we also face the possibility—it would be both cowardly and illogical simply to dismiss it—of a less dreadful change, in which our enormous untapped potential would be used to the full: long odds, enormous difficulties, miracles!

Some sort of transformation is inevitable. The present social machinery can probably be glued together and heated up a few more times, at least in nations as wealthy as the United States. But each passing year brings us closer to the realization that our present way of doing and being cannot last much longer. If the shift to a new mode of existence is to take place voluntarily, intelligently, and noncatastrophically, much work needs to be done. Our energy-economic system must be converted from exponential growth to something approaching a steady state, a process which itself will require great amounts of energy. The resulting economic dislocation must be dealt with courageously and equitably, with a sense of sacrifice on the part of the more affluent. Even more important, we must learn to appreciate new kinds of wealth in states of being, and new kinds of energy in the varieties of bodily flows described earlier. These matters, make no mistake about it, are by no means ethereal. Changes in the nature of what is satisfying and rewarding to human individuals must go along with necessary and significant reforms in politics, health care, defense and foreign policy, law, justice, and individual rights.

Just how such reforms are to be carried out is not the province of this book. For them to occur at all, however, we need to have some positive vision of a new life, some sense of hope that will make the tremendous effort and the inevitable heartbreaks seem worthwhile. Perhaps more than anything else, we need new myths to guide us. We need mythic beings to provide us models of behavior, to give us maps and clues and a steady compass with which we can orient ourselves during our evolutionary journey. America's old mythic heroes—Paul Bunyan, the Westering pioneer and cowboy, Horatio Alger and the World War II defender of Mom and Apple Pie—have done their jobs, but are worse than useless under present circumstances. And we have become rather quickly disenchanted with the heroes of the technological myth—Hal the Computer, the emotionless astronaut, the disembodied think-tank expert.

Perhaps, then, it is not inappropriate that we look to the field of sports, physical education, and the body for our transforming myth. Since the turn of the century we have seen many signs of rapid human evolution, foreshadowings of transformation, as one supposedly unsurpassable physical limitation after another has been surpassed. There are few more satisfying confirmations of human potentiality than those found in the records of the modern Olympics, from 1896 to the present, and it sometimes seems that the sports section is the only part of the daily paper that contains good news.

Even more significant is the central cultural role that sports play, a role, as previously noted, that anthropologists are only now fully realizing. Myths and games, in fact, are very closely allied both in their social function and in the way they provide this function. In entering a mythic ritual, a tribal youth actually *becomes* a jaguar or an eagle. Thus transfigured in the closed and meaningful system of the ritual, he gains the central meaning in what otherwise might be a meaningless life. Such mythic commitment is no luxury; it is necessary for a society's very survival. In the same way, the boy playing stickball who says, "I'm Hank Aaron. Who're you?" has made a certain mythic commitment, has found meaning, structure, a model, and a measure of hope in the midst of anomie. And in such sports as aikido, even middle-aged men and women can leave awkward lives behind for a while and aspire to becoming a new kind of samurai, dedicated to the uses of balance and power for reconciliation and transcendence. It is important to bear in mind that mythic commitment, whether "religious" or "athletic," provides not just cognitive meaning but a way of walking, sitting, standing, and relating to the world. It is this guidance in *being*, rather than merely *doing*, that is almost totally lacking in our current academic education.

Some critics, noting the aggressive, territorial, warlike nature of many of our conventional games, would somehow simply eliminate these games and de-emphasize all sports. There is a foolish vanity in this criticism; for the structure provided by sports is especially crucial in a time when every other structure seems uncertain. The way of being, the lifestyle, gained from a mythic commitment to football, for example, may have certain dangers in these times, but it is probably less dangerous than no way of being at all. Rather than simply attacking conventional games, we might better work for reform and change of emphasis in certain attitudes within these games. We also might help create new games—we need new games just as we need new myths.

And we need a mythic sports figure to be our model and guide on the journey that now speeds us toward inconceivable destinations.

If the Ultimate Athlete is defined as whoever best serves as model and guide on our present evolutionary journey, it becomes relatively easy to see that many of our well-known sports figures cannot fulfill this role. Mark Spitz, for example, certainly provided a model in the matter of surpassing physical limitations when he won an unprecedented seven gold medals in the 1972 Olympics, breaking seven world records in the process. But he has not shown us the sensitivity, awareness, and largeness of being that we obviously need at this time. Perhaps it was his obsessive and single-minded training regimen that limited him. In any case, though I could be wrong, I cannot see Spitz as one who joins body, mind, and spirit in a balanced and centered manner.

In the same way, many of our top athletic performers suffer the unfortunate consequences of overspecialization and exploitation. By the time they near the end of their careers (and I am thinking here of Mantle, Mays, Aaron, Unitas), a slight note of bitterness has crept into their voices; their eyes reveal a certain habitual melancholy; there are faint lines of suspicion and even resentment around their mouths. Yes, sports have been good to me, each of them tells us. I wouldn't have had it any other way. And yet there is something left unsaid, an undertone of yearning and regret. Those towering drives, those impossible yet inevitable catches, those delicious episodes of speed and balance and flow—where are they now? It is as if they wait in the film library to be replayed on some more significant occasion. We have been used and rewarded and now we are being retired, these great performers seem to say to us. But there must be a better way of understanding what we have done, beyond figures in record books and relics in the Hall of Fame—*something else.*

I for one would like to pour out my gratitude to Mantle, Mays, Aaron, Unitas, Spitz, and many others for the great moments they have given us. I believe those moments inform us about the nature of human life and give hints of human destinations. When we consider the mythic quality of sports and the gamelike nature of human existence, their feats begin to take on the significance they deserve. I also appreciate the long years of strenous effort that build foundations for transcendence, even when that effort becomes unbalanced. I offer absolutely no commiseration, though, for the travail of a hard training schedule. In the words of Shivas Irons, "You are a lucky man if you can find a strong beautiful discipline, one that takes you beyond yourself." Discipline, freely chosen, fully experienced, may indeed turn out to have been one of those essential transformational elements that have been neglected and even denigrated by our present culture.

In spite of all that our great athletic performers have given us, however, it would be stretching things to call any one of them the Ultimate Athlete. Other names come to mind—Charles Lindbergh, Jacques-Yves Cousteau, Roger Bannister, Sir Edmund Hillary—names of people whose feats and lives have taken them beyond the rather narrow confines of the sports establishment. I've taken no pains to conceal that Lindbergh has a special appeal for me. His Atlantic crossing, as *Time* magazine noted on the occasion of his death in 1974, was "one of those pristinely pure but magnificently eloquent gestures that awaken people everywhere to life's boundless potential." And the boldness of his thought, his sense of Cosmos and his later efforts to save the planetary environment join to lift Lindbergh above the level of temporary fame. But then I think of flaws, of mistakes of judgment during his middle years, of a certain rigidity of thought. And that is precisely the trouble with naming any one individual, even provisionally, the Ultimate Athlete.

We had better avoid unnecessary limitations. By looking only at this culture, we miss athletic wonders that have already occurred and close our minds to those still to come. Indian yogis regularly perform feats of bodily control that our science considered impossible—until confirmed by the very science that doubted them. The *lung gom* walkers of Tibet stride day and night for thousands of miles at a steady pace of about seven miles an hour to confirm their mastery of the inner life. Some Tibetan monks, practicing the discipline of *tumo*, can produce intense bodily heat. Sitting nude on an ice-covered lake, they demonstrate the state of their art by wrapping themselves in sheets dipped into water through a hole cut in the ice, drying one sheet after another during the course of a single night.

Scores of reliable witnesses have testified to demonstrations by Morihei Uyeshiba, in which he seemed to go beyond the limitations of known physical law. On one occasion, completely surrounded by men with knives, Uyeshiba reputedly disappeared and reappeared at the same instant, looking down at his attackers from the top of a flight of stairs. Uyeshiba refused to repeat this feat, saying that the effort involved might take several months from his life; and I very much doubt that such episodes can ever be confirmed. But it's impossible not to be impressed by the number and quality of the eyewitness reports on Uyeshiba's seemingly supernatural athleticism. Jeremy Ets-Hokin, a San Francisco businessman and civic leader who holds black belts in judo and karate, told me of a remarkable demonstration he happened to see in Tokyo in 1962. Challenged to prove his powers, Uyeshiba, a small, spare man who was then seventy-eight years old, invited four of the toughest judokas from Kotokan, the Establishment *dojo* of judo, to attack him. A large group of distinguished Japanese witnesses gathered at the edge of the mat. Uyeshiba seated himself, cross-legged, in the center and was blindfolded. He meditated for some two minutes, after which the judokas, described by Ets-Hokin as "real bruisers, big beefy sons of bitches," attacked one after another, at full force, from behind. Uyeshiba threw his attackers easily. They landed on their backs, looking bewildered.

It was not long after this that my teacher, Robert Nadeau, became a student of Uyeshiba. "After I'd been there six months," he told me, "*O-sensei* [the honorary term, Teacher of Teachers] motioned for me to attack him. With all my years of training in the martial arts, I wanted to show him what I had, so I really came in hard. But when I got close to him, it was like I'd entered a cloud. And in the cloud there's a giant spring that's throwing me out of the cloud. I find myself flying through the air and I come down with a hard, judo-type slap-fall. Lying there, I look around for *O-sensei,* but he isn't to be seen. Finally, I turn all the way around, the one place I wouldn't have expected him to be, and there he is, standing calmly."

The films of Uyeshiba in action seem to corroborate his legendary powers. In one film, taken by an American student with an 8mm. movie camera, two attackers are converging on Uyeshiba with great speed. Uyeshiba is seen at one point in the film as facing the converging attacks and seemingly trapped. In the next frame, he is seen as having moved forward a couple of feet, and he is facing back in the opposite direction. While Uyeshiba appears to shift from one position to another in a fraction of a second (or in no time at all!) the oncoming movement of the attackers proceeds sequentially, a fraction of a step at a time, until the two collide and are pinned by the Master.

Whether or not Uyeshiba's feats can be scientifically validated, the fact remains that those who were best acquainted with the Master are convinced that he was operating "in another dimension," especially in his last years. Again and again he seems to have "just disappeared," or to have created "a warp in time and space." Such terms as these recur repeatedly in descriptions of Uyeshiba's work, and may serve to remind us of possibilities that lie beyond the rather rigid strictures of this culture.

Since the time of Newton, the West has operated, insofar as has been possible, within a well-defined, easily measured set of dimensions—space, time, energy, mass, momentum, acceleration—and has made great technological progress. We might also say that the startling gains in athletic prowess over the past seventy-five years are largely the result of improved technology in training methods, equipment, nutrition. But behind each improvement that can be attributed to "technology," there lies a powerful human intentionality, the purpose of which is evolution, transcendence, transformation. It is significant that race horses, in spite of the most intensive scientific breeding, have posted a proportionate increase in speed which is only a fraction of that shown by human runners during the same period.

Ultimately, human intentionality is the most powerful evolutionary force on this planet. It will use any tool that comes to hand in order to achieve its purpose, and when that tool

outlives its usefulness, it will reach for another. Using New-
tonian dimensions of reality and an instrumental technology,
human intentionality has erected an impressive man-made
environment and has made notable improvements in communications, transportation, agriculture, and disease control.
But there are now signs of a slowdown in the rate of progress
available from present modes of technology and definitions of
reality. In addition, we are seeing the many unhappy side effects that develop when technology is carried beyond human
limits. The end of our present technological thrust does not
mean the end of our evolutionary journey but a redefinition
of "progress" and a shift to new means of furthering the in-
exorable process toward which life always tends. It is important that we not mistake the tool for the force behind it.

Our present technology is only a tool. It did not create our
recent progress; intentionality did. In the same way, we must
avoid confusing any one set of dimensions of reality for reality
itself. Reality always involves an interplay between the observer and the observed. When our powers of observation expand, so shall our reality.

To further its evolutionary purposes, human intentionality
will someday use tools that do not now exist and will operate
in dimensions that confound our present-day science. It may
well be that we shall first become aware of these changes in
the field of sports and the human body. We may now be seeing
a leveling-off in the spectacular increase in athletic performance, especially in track events, as if improvements possible
through current technology have just about run their course.
Some sports experts are now speculating that future improvements will involve mental or psychological rather than physical factors. The "nonphysical" factors have, of course, always
had a key role in athletic greatness. But we have also seen how
other factors, which seem mystical or even magical to us, can
exist in even the most conventional sports setting. When the
"mental" aspects of sports are given more attention and when
the "mystical" aspects are allowed to rise from the underground to full awareness, then it is possible that new sports
breakthroughs will become commonplace. The question is not
whether a three-and-a-half-minute mile will be run (I believe
it most certainly will) but *what* events will be held.

By thinking of the Ultimate Athlete in terms of sports and

tracks and records as they now exist we would be limiting ourselves. Human evolution will continue, *must* continue. The Olympic Games that lie beyond the perceptual wall labeled "the year 2000" may well include events and modes of observation that are extremely hard for us to imagine. Perhaps there will be a prize for the athlete who best integrates body, mind, and spirit. Perhaps there will be psychic events honoring the athlete who best controls astral projection or who best demonstrates psychokinesis. The athlete who waits beyond our timid expectations possesses the power to precipitate heaven into earth and bring to us, through body, mind, and spirit, the ingredients of our next evolutionary step.

Our present-day athletes inspire us and turn our thoughts to human evolution. But to avoid being limited, the Ultimate Athlete, our model and guide, must remain mythic. Being mythic, the Ultimate Athlete must present an ideal that is universal. If the ideal is universal, it may have even more meaning for the average person than for the renowned performer who already is locked into an existing sports specialty. Look again at the ideal that has emerged from these pages. The Ultimate Athlete is:

—one who joins body, mind, and spirit in the dance of existence;
—one who explores both inner and outer being;
—one who surpasses limitations and crosses boundaries in the process of personal and social transformation;
—one who plays the larger game, the Game of Games, with full awareness, aware of life and death and willing to accept the pain and joy that awareness brings;
—one who, finally, best serves as model and guide on our evolutionary journey.

This ideal, which must remain tentative and open-ended, does not exclude anyone because of physical disabilities. In fact, the overweight, sedentary, middle-aged man or woman becomes a hero just by making a first laborious, agonizing circuit of the track. Six months or a year later, many pounds lighter, eyes glowing, that person may provide a model of the potential that exists in every one of us. To go a step further: if that same person, recognizably transformed in body, mind, and spirit, takes this experience as the impetus for further explorations and boundary crossings and the heightening of awareness, then he or she must be said to have embodied the ultimate athletic ideal.

There is a woman I know who fits this description. For almost a year now we have run on the same track, and I have seen her undergo a metamorphosis. We have never spoken, but when we pass (she is running at a good clip nowadays) our eyes meet and we smile. I am sentimental about running and sometimes moved to tears by great races. No world class runner, however, has inspired me as has this woman whose name I do not know and whose accomplishment will appear in no book of records. If she has achieved so much from so little, then what is not possible?

The chinning bar still stands there in the spring sunlight. The boys and girls still sit on a grassy bank waiting for their names to be called. The man with a crew cut looks down at his clipboard and speaks. Once more the fat boy rises, walks to the chinning bar, reaches up to touch the smooth metal, then walks away, his head bobbing from side to side as his classmates watch in silence.

The scene begins to fade. The fat boy vanishes. The instructor, the chinning bar, the boys and girls waver and dissolve. I can hold them in place no longer. The fat boy, whose name is Babcock, is gone. He has played his part in our little drama. We can let him go now. But there is another Babcock we have not yet dealt with, a creature of flesh and blood who will not so lightly leave our world.

Who is this creature we have let slip away from us? He is just another fat boy, an inevitable casualty of most present-day physical-educational programs. He is also the culmination of a remarkable evolutionary journey, the repository of the experience of eons, the representation of order beyond the power of itself to fully comprehend. He is a creature of more than 10-billion twinkling neurons, capable of conspicuous errors and nearly infinite creative connections. But more than all this, he is one of our children, like us—vulnerable and proud, a child of our race who feels hope and shame and love, who might someday become involved in the creation of life. He is a fat boy, born in the image of God; but he is walking away from us, one more of life's possibilities lost.

Surely, this is not the end of the story. There must be some way to bring him back, for he has more than the usual limitations to surpass and thus may someday inform us with more than the usual authority about transformation. Surely, there are physical activities that will return to him the bodily joy he was born with. Surely, there are games for him that will allow him to experience the mythic intensity of play. Surely, there are ways for him to sense the flow of energy in and around his body, and to perceive the larger body that joins all existence in the universal dance.

Babcock has appeared to us as a symbol of limitations, a victim of our system. But he is not alone. Whenever we settle for the pitifully low definitions of human functioning that now prevail we share his predicament. When we realize how greatly he may surpass himself, we renounce those definitions that limit us and our race. Babcock is actually a symbol of unsuspected potential, and we might eventually profit more by how we respond to our Babcocks than our O. J. Simpsons. The ultimate athletic ideal may be high, but, by its very nature, it is never quite out of anyone's reach. *In potentia,* in the interplay of ideal actuality, Babcock is the Ultimate Athlete, and so are you and I.

The answer has been here with us all along, too close, too much a part of us to notice: not "mere flesh" but central metaphor of human existence, my body and yours (body of the Ultimate Athlete), holding the ocean, encompassing the stars, offering direct access to the Cosmos itself. For we have seen that body *is* spirit, that its every cell re-enacts the dance of love and death, that in the relationship of these cells we may trace the anatomy of all relationship. There is no single Ultimate Athlete; there are millions waiting to be born. Running, falling, flying, diving—each of us may get in shape or even set new records. But the body of the Ultimate Athlete— fat or thin, short or tall—summons us beyond these things toward the rebirth of the self, and, in time, the unfolding of a new world.

From *The Ultimate Athlete,* 1974.

QUESTIONS

(1) What is the "great change" the author alludes to in the second paragraph?

(2) In the third paragraph the author sketches an outline of world transformation. What, in his view, is the most critical element in this transformation?

(3) What is the basis of the author's argument that we must look to the body, to physical education for our "transforming myth"?

(4) How would you express the difference the author notes between "being" and "doing"?

(5) What conclusion is the author led to after describing the extraordinary feats of Morihei Uyeshiba?

(6) What is the author referring to in his phrase "the Game of Games"?

(7) What does the story of Babcock represent about our society?

(8) What, finally, is the ultimate athlete?